Lecture Notes in Computer Science 3816

Commenced Publication in 1973
Founding and Former Series Editors:
Gerhard Goos, Juris Hartmanis, and Jan van Leeuwen

Editorial Board

David Hutchison
  Lancaster University, UK
Takeo Kanade
  Carnegie Mellon University, Pittsburgh, PA, USA
Josef Kittler
  University of Surrey, Guildford, UK
Jon M. Kleinberg
  Cornell University, Ithaca, NY, USA
Friedemann Mattern
  ETH Zurich, Switzerland
John C. Mitchell
  Stanford University, CA, USA
Moni Naor
  Weizmann Institute of Science, Rehovot, Israel
Oscar Nierstrasz
  University of Bern, Switzerland
C. Pandu Rangan
  Indian Institute of Technology, Madras, India
Bernhard Steffen
  University of Dortmund, Germany
Madhu Sudan
  Massachusetts Institute of Technology, MA, USA
Demetri Terzopoulos
  New York University, NY, USA
Doug Tygar
  University of California, Berkeley, CA, USA
Moshe Y. Vardi
  Rice University, Houston, TX, USA
Gerhard Weikum
  Max-Planck Institute of Computer Science, Saarbruecken, Germany

Goutam Chakraborty (Ed.)

Distributed Computing and Internet Technology

Second International Conference, ICDCIT 2005
Bhubaneswar, India, December 22-24, 2005
Proceedings

Volume Editor

Goutam Chakraborty
Iwate Prefectural University
Department of Software and Information Science, Intelligent Informatics Lab.
Iwate 020-0193, Japan
E-mail: goutam@soft.iwate-pu.ac.jp

Library of Congress Control Number: 2005937591

CR Subject Classification (1998): D.1.3, C.2.4, D.2, F.2, H.3, H.4, D.4.6, K.6.5

ISSN   0302-9743
ISBN-10   3-540-30999-3 Springer Berlin Heidelberg New York
ISBN-13   978-3-540-30999-4 Springer Berlin Heidelberg New York

This work is subject to copyright. All rights are reserved, whether the whole or part of the material is concerned, specifically the rights of translation, reprinting, re-use of illustrations, recitation, broadcasting, reproduction on microfilms or in any other way, and storage in data banks. Duplication of this publication or parts thereof is permitted only under the provisions of the German Copyright Law of September 9, 1965, in its current version, and permission for use must always be obtained from Springer. Violations are liable to prosecution under the German Copyright Law.

Springer is a part of Springer Science+Business Media

springer.com

© Springer-Verlag Berlin Heidelberg 2005
Printed in Germany

Typesetting: Camera-ready by author, data conversion by Scientific Publishing Services, Chennai, India
Printed on acid-free paper   SPIN: 11604655   06/3142   5 4 3 2 1 0

Program Chair's Message

Distributed computing and Internet technology are two key areas of research which have set the agenda for numerous initiatives for the development of innovative tools and techniques leading to a convergence of communication and computing. Many conferences around the globe promote new evolving research ideas in these areas. The International Conference on Distributed Computing and Internet Technology, ICDCIT in short, is one of these, but with a special characteristic. ICDCIT focuses on important cutting-edge research in the area and aims to offer the participants a concise program and a proceedings with excellent papers.

This is the second year of the conference, and we already enjoy a much greater support from the research community. For this year's conference, 426 papers were received from all continents, spread over 27 countries, close to a 100% increase in volume of submissions compared to ICDCIT 2004. I would like to thank everyone who submitted their works to ICDCIT 2005.

The conference and these proceedings are divided into five tracks, namely:

- Distributed Computing (DC) track
- Internet Technology (IT) track
- System Security (SS) track
- Software Engineering (SE) track
- Data Mining (DM) track

The five track chairs, Arunabha Sen of Arizona State University, USA (DC track), Mukesh Mohania of IBM India Research Lab., India (DM track), Sanjay K. Madria of University of Missouri-Rolla, USA (IT track), Indrajit Ray of Colorado State University, USA (SS track), and Gopal Gupta of University of Texas at Dallas, USA (SE track) took the leading role to select an excellent set of papers in their respective tracks. The track chairs received the necessary support from 103 members of the Program Committee and a number of additional reviewers in reviewing a large number of submissions. The review work is time-consuming, difficult, voluntary, takes up free time, and requires honest attention. My special thanks to all reviewers for their help.

In spite of the sincere efforts of all, it was still a difficult task to make the acceptance decisions. Many of the submissions were of very good quality, and we had to work very hard to select only 59 papers out of 426 submissions. Most of the accepted papers were reviewed by three reviewers.

The papers are divided into two categories, long and short. Several factors, other than the quality, were considered to categorize long and short papers. One of the main considerations was how much length is required to express the novelty of the work. We finally have 16 long and 9 short papers in the DC track, 5 long and 3 short papers in the DM track, 6 long and 3 short papers in the IT track, 7 long in the SE track, and 6 long and 4 short papers in the SS track.

The opening ceremony and pre-conference tutorials on various related topics were held on December 21. The technical program started on December 22 and continued for three days. The program was arranged in single track so as to enable participants to attend sessions of different tracks. Papers from the DM, IT, SE, and SS tracks were divided into two sessions, whereas DC track sessions were held on the first two days of the conference.

The program also included two plenary talks. The first talk was delivered by S. S. Iyengar from Louisiana State University, USA. The second talk was delivered by He Jifeng from the International Institute for Software Technology (IIST) Macau. Prof. Iyenger's talk on "The Distributed Sensor Networks — An Emerging Technology" was focused on new ideas about the use of distributed systems for emerging technology, while Prof. Jifeng's talk on "Linking Theories of Concurrency by Retraction" dealt with semantics of concurrency.

All the conference committee members contributed towards the success of ICDCIT 2005. And it was a pleasant experience for me to work with them. The one name that sticks out is R. K. Ghosh, Steering Committee Chair. He really steered the group with his past experience as Program Chair of ICDCIT 2004. Then of course the five track chairs, Arunabha Sen, Mukesh Mohania, Sanjay Madria, Indrajit Ray, and Gopal Gupta, were the five pillars on which the conference stood. In addition to time-to-time advice, Vijay Kumar, General Chair, and Hrushikesha Mohanty, Steering Committee member, helped in many other ways at difficult times. Pabitra Mitra (Publicity Chair), M. M. Gore (Tutorial Chair), Madhabananda Das (Scholarship Chair), Jyotiranjan Hota (Finance Chair) did an excellent job to fulfil their responsibilities. Finally my special thanks to A. Samanta (Advisory Committee Member and Chancellor KIIT) for his support and encouragement and P. K. Mishra (Organizing Chair) for taking care of all local arrangements. For the publishing process at Springer, I would like to thank Alfred Hofmann, Executive Editor, and Ms. Anna Kramer for their constant help and cooperation. And without the financial support from KIIT, we could not possibly imagine taking this project.

Last, but not least, thanks to all the authors whose scholarly submissions allowed us to offer an excelled technical program, and the attendees for lively interactions. Enjoy the proceedings — I am sure you will find plenty of interesting material.

December 2004   Goutam Chakraborty

General Chair's Message

We witness the evolution of a fully connected information space as a result of recent advances in communication technology, networking and distributed computing. The information space has significantly narrowed the virtual separation among these areas, which we used to perceive as quite orthogonal as a result of our lack of understanding. The complementary nature of areas such as software engineering, networking and system security, database systems, data mining, etc., are highly visible to researchers and practitioners, and a good research contribution now derives equal share from a number of these areas. Conferences, journals, and other publication avenues recognize the significance of this unified space and create their submission structure accordingly.

The International Conference on Distributed Computing and Internet Technology (ICDCIT) has clearly recognized the complementary nature of these areas and has built a platform to honor the contributions of national and international researchers. ICDCIT 2005 stood on the foundation of ICDCIT 2004 and took the conference series several steps further. It presented itself as a highly competitive international computer science event. The submissions to the conference were categorized broadly into five tracks to provide a suitable platform to researchers, practitioners, and students. These tracks are identified as: (a) Distributed Computing, (b) Internet Technology, (c) System Security, (d) Data Mining, and (e) Software Engineering.

I am very happy to recognize the contributions of the Steering Committee members, conference officers, student volunteers, and other secretarial staff members. I thank them for their hard work. It was mainly due to their effort that ICDCIT 2005 received a large number of submissions from many countries, including India.

I thank the Kalinga Institute of Industrial Technology, Bhubaneswar, for creating the necessary environment for ICDCIT 2005. My special thanks go to Chancellor A. Samanta and Pro-chancellor P. K. Misra for their support and the momentum they generated for the forward march. I also thank Springer for publishing the ICDCIT proceedings in their LNCS series.

December 2004   Vijay Kumar

Conference Organization

Advisory Committee

Steering Chair: Ratan K. Ghosh, Indian Institute of Technology Kanpur, India

General Chair: Vijay Kumar, University of Missouri-Kansas City, USA

Advisors:
    A. Samanta, KIIT, Bhubaneswar, India
    Chris George, UNU/IIST, Macau, China
    Gautam Barua, IIT Guwahati, India
    Hrushikesha Mohanty, University of Hyderabad, India
    Krithi Ramamritham, IIT Bombay, India
    Pradeep Khosla, CMU, USA
    P. K. Mishra, KIIT, Bhubaneswar, India
    R. K. Shyamasundar, TIFR, India
    R. K. Ghosh, IIT Kanpur, India

Program Committee

Program Chair: Goutam Chakraborty, Iwate Prefectural University, Japan

Editorial Committee:
    Ratan K. Ghosh, Indian Institute of Technology Kanpur, India
    Vijay Kumar, University of Missouri-Kansas City, USA
    Hrushikesha Mohanty, University of Hyderabad, India

Track Chairs:
    Distributed Computing: Arunabha Sen, Arizona State University, USA
    Internet Technology: Sanjay K. Madria, University of Missouri-Rolla, USA
    Systems Security: Indrajit Ray, Colorado State University, USA
    Software Engineering: Gopal Gupta, University of Texas at Dallas, USA
    Data Mining: Mukesh Mohania, IBM India Research Lab., India

Tutorial Chair: M. M. Gore, NIT, Allahabad, India

Scholarship Chair: Madhabananda Das, KIIT, Bhubaneswar, India

Publicity Chair: Pabitra Mitra, IIT Kanpur, India

Organizing Chair: P. K. Mishra, KIIT, Bhubaneswar, India

Finance Chair: Jyotiranjan Hota, KIIT, Bhubaneswar, India

Program Committee Members

Distributed Computing Track

Ajay Datta, Univ. of Nevada, Las Vegas, USA
Albert Burger, Heriot-Watt University, UK
Anup Kumar, Univ. of Louisville, USA
Aniruddha Gokhale, Vanderbilt University, USA
Anwitaman Datta, École Polytechnique Fédérale de Lausanne (EPFL), Switzerland
Ambuj Mahanty, IIM, Kolkata, India
Bhabani Sinha, ISI, Kolkata, India
Bharat B. Bhargava, Purdue University, USA
B. S. Panda, IIT Delhi, India
Bhed Bahadur Bista, Iwate Prefectural University, Japan
David Wei, Fordham University, USA
Debasish Chakraborty, Tohoku University, Japan
D. Saha, IIM, Kolkata, India
D. Janki Ram, IIT Madras, India
Gautam Das, Univ. of Texas, Arlington, USA
G. Sajith, IIT Guwahati, India
Glenn Mansfield, Cyber Solutions Inc., Japan
K. Gopinath, IISc Bangalore, India
Krithi Ramamritham, IIT Mumbai, India
Mainak Chaudhuri, IIT Kanpur, India
Matthieu Latapy, Univ. of Paris 7, France
M. M. Gore, MNNIT, Allahabad, India
Mohammed Atiquzzaman, Univ. of Oklahoma, USA
Nabanita Das, ISI, Kolkata, India
Partha Dasgupta, Arizona State University, USA
Prem Uppuluri, Univ. of Missouri-Kansas City, USA
Raj Kannan, Lousiana State University, USA
Ravi Prakash, Univ of Texas, Dallas, USA
R. C. Hanshdah, IISc Bangalore, India
S. K. Aggarwal, IIT Kanpur, India
Somprakash Bandyopadhyay, IIM Kolkata, India
Subir Bandhyopadhyay, University of Windsor, Canada
Suman Bannerjee, University of Wisconsin, Madison, USA
Supratim Biswas, IIT Mumbai, India
Vipin Chaudhary, Wayne State University, USA
Yoshikuni Onozato, Gunma University, Japan

Internet Technology Track

> Anirban Mandal, Univ. of Tokyo, Japan
> Antonio Badia, Univ. of Louisville, USA
> Debajyoti Mukhopadhyay, Techno India, Kolkata, India
> Gajanan Chinchwadkar, Sybase Inc., USA
> Gi-Chul Yang, Mokpo National University, South Korea
> Gruenwald Le, University of Oklahoma, USA
> Kajal Claypool, Univ. of Massachusetts, Lowell, USA
> Kalpdrum Passi, Laurentian University, Canada
> Leszek Lilien, Purdue University, USA
> N. L. Sarda, IIT Bombay, India
> S. K. Gupta, IIT Delhi, India
> Shiyong Lu, Wayne State University, USA
> Sourav Bhowmick, NTU, Singapore
> Takahiro Hara, Osaka University, Japan
> Tan Kian Lee, NUS, Singapore
> Wee Keong Ng, NTU, Singapore

System Security Track

> Aditya Bagchi, ISI Kolkata, India
> Brajendra Panda, University of Arkansas, USA
> Csilla Farkas, University of South Carolina, USA
> Duminda Wijesekera, George Mason University, USA
> Ehud Gudes, Ben Gurion University, Israel
> Elena Ferrari, Università degli Studi dell'Insubria, Italy
> Indrakshi Ray, Colorado State University, USA
> Martin Olivier, Univ. of Pretoria, South Africa
> Nasir Memon, Polytechnic University, USA
> R. K. Shyamsundar, TIFR, India
> Rajni Goel, Howard University, USA
> Ravi Mukkamala, Old Dominion University, USA
> Sabrina De Capitani di Vimercati, Univ. of Milan, Italy
> Sibabrata Ray, University of Alabama, USA
> Sukumar Nandi, IIT Guwahati, India
> Vijay Atluri, Rutgers University, USA
> Vijay Varadharajan, Macquarie University, Australia

Software Engineering Track

Abhik Roychoudhury, National University of Singapore, Singapore
Bernhard K. Aichernig, UNU/IIST, Macau, China
Adolfo Villafiorita, Istituto Ricerca Scientifica e Tecnologica, Italy
Bikram Sengupta, IBM India Research Lab., India
Biplav Srivastava, IBM India Research Lab., India
Dang Van Hung, UNU/IIST, Macau
H. Mohanty, Univ. of Hyderabad, India
Hai-Feng Guo, Univ. of Nebraska, USA
Joao Cangussu, Univ. of Texas at Dallas, USA
Paddy Krishnan, Bond University, Australia
Sagar Naik, University of Waterloo, Canada
Sukhamay Kundu, Louisiana State University, USA
Suresh Manandhar, York University, UK
Zhiming Liu, United Nations University, Macau, China

Data Mining Track

Anirban Mondal, Univ. of Tokyo, Japan
Asaf Adi, IBM Haifa Labs., Israel
Deendayal Dinakarpandian, Univ. of Missouri-Kansas City, USA
Indranil Bose, The Univ. of Hong Kong, Hong Kong, China
Janez Brank, Jozef Stefan Institute, Ljubljana, Slovenia
Jean-Gabriel Ganascia, Univ. Pierre et Marie Curie, France
Jorge Bernardino, Univ. of Coimbra, Portugal
Krishna Kummamuru, IBM India Research Lab., India
Ladjel Bellatreche, ENSMA, France
Michael Schrefl, Institut für Wirtschaftsinformatik, Austria
Ng Wee Keong, NTU, Singapore
Rajeev Gupta, IBM India Research Lab., India
Pabitra Mitra, IIT Kanpur, India
Shalab Goel, Hyperion, USA
Torben Bach Pedersen, Auburg University, Denmark
Vladimir Estivill-Castro, Griffith University, Australia
Werner Winiwarter, Univ. of Vienna, Austria
Y. Yao, Univ. of Regina, Canada
Yue-Shi Lee, Ming Chuan University, Taiwan

List of Referees

Asaf Adi
S. K. Aggarwal
Bernhard K. Aichernig
Mohammed Atiquzzaman
Vijay Atluri
Antonio Badia
Aditya Bagchi
Ajay Bansal
Ladjel Bellatreche
Jorge Bernardino
Bharat B. Bhargava
Bhed Bahadur Bista
Indranil Bose
Albert Burger
Venkatesan Balakrishnan
Suman Bannerjee
Somprakash Bandyopadhyay
Subir Bandhyopadhyay
Kalyan Basu
Sourav Bhowmick
Supratim Biswas
Shane Bracher
Joao Cangussu
Kaojia Cao
Debasish Chakraborty
Vipin Chaudhary
Mainak Chaudhuri
Xin Chen
Gajanan Chinchwadkar
Krishna Prasad Chitrapura
Lawrence Chung
Kajal Claypool
Gautam Das
Nabanita Das
Nibedita Das
Partha Dasgupta
Anwitaman Datta
Ajay Datta
Deendayal Dinakarpandian
Jing Dong
Alpana Dubey
Vladimir Estivill-Castro
Csilla Farkas

Leonidas Fegaras
Elena Ferrari
Colin Fidge
Gavin Finnie
Jean-Gabriel Ganascia
Ankit Goel
Rajni Goel
Shalab Goel
Aniruddha Gokhale
M. Goller
K. Gopinath
M. M. Gore
Ehud Gudes
Hai-Feng Guo
Rajeev Gupta
S. K. Gupta
R. C. Hanshdah
Takahiro Hara
Dang Van Hung
Morihiro Hayashida
D. Janki Ram
Sachindra Joshi
Janez Brank Jozef
Raj Kannan
R. Kaushik
Ng Wee Keong
Srividya Kona
Paddy Krishnan
Krishna Kummamuru
Anup Kumar
Rajeev Kumar
Sukhamay Kundu
Matthieu Latapy
Gruenwald Le
Tan Kian Lee
Yue-Shi Lee
David Levine
Xiaoshan Li
Xiaoshan Li
Leszek Lilien
Miao Liu
Zhiming Liu
Xiaojian Liu

Rohit M. Lotlikar
Lunjin Lu
Shiyong Lu
Ambuj Mahanty
Monika Maidl
Ajay Mallya
Suresh Manandhar
Glenn Mansfield
Setsuro Matsuda
Nasir Memon
Sun Meng
H. Mohanty
Anirban Mandal
Pabitra Mitra
Debajyoti Mukhopadhyay
Krishnendu Mukhopadhyaya
Ravi Mukkamala
Sudheendra Murty
Sagar Naik
Wee Keong Ng
Sukumar Nandi
Martin Olivier
Yoshikuni Onozato
B. S. Panda
Brajendra Panda
Kalpdrum Passi
Torben Bach Pedersen
Ravi Prakash
Krithi Ramamritham
Bhaskaran Raman
Indrakshi Ray
Sibabrata Ray
Marco Roveri
Abhik Roychoudhury

D. Saha
Diptikalyan Saha
G. Sajith
N. L. Sarda
Michael Schrefl
Bikram Sengupta
R. K. Shyamsundar
Y. N. Singh
Bhabani Sinha
Luke Simon
Sumit W Sorde
Biplav Srivastava
Phil Stocks
Vivy Suhendra
Angelo Susi
Roberto Tiella
Udaya Kiran Tupakula
Prem Uppuluri
Vijay Varadharajan
Ranga Raju Vatsavai
Adolfo Villafiorita
Sabrina De Capitani di Vimercati
Qian Wang
David Wei
Duminda Wijesekera
Werner Winiwarter
Matthew Wright
Y. Yao
Gi-Chul Yang
Gabriele Zacco
Naijun Zhan
Wei Zhang
Xiangpeng Zhang
Ling Zhou

Table of Contents

Plenary Talk I

The Distributed Sensor Networks – An Emerging Technology
   S.S. Iyengar 1

Distributed Computing

Distributed Computing Track Chair's Message
   Arunabha Sen 2

Network Protcols

Efficient Binding Lifetime Determination Schemes in HMIPv6
   Sun Ok Yang, SungSuk Kim, Chong-Sun Hwang 3

A Fast Search and Advanced Marking Scheme for Network IP Traceback Model
   Jia Hou, Moon Ho Lee 15

Design and Performance Evaluation of Token-Based MAC Protocols in WDM Burst Switched Ring Networks
   Li-Mei Peng, Young-Chul Kim, Kyoung-Min Yoo, Kyeong-Eun Han, Young-Chon Kim 21

Routing in Mobile Ad Hoc Network

Self-stabilizing Energy-Aware Routing Algorithm in Wireless Sensor Network with Limited Mobility
   Smruti Padhy, Diganta Goswami 27

Position Based Gradient Routing in Mobile Ad Hoc Networks
   Anand Praksh Ruhil, D.K. Lobiyal, Ivan Stojmenovic 39

Distributed Clustering Algorithm for Finding Virtual Backbone in Ad Hoc Networks
   B. Paul, S.V. Rao 50

Merging Clustering Algorithms in Mobile Ad Hoc Networks
Orhan Dagdeviren, Kayhan Erciyes, Deniz Cokuslu 56

Performance Study and Implementation of Self Organized Routing Algorithm for Mobile Ad Hoc Network Using GloMoSim
K. Murugan, S. Shanmugavel 62

Communication and Coverage in Wireless Networks

Self-stabilizing Deterministic TDMA for Sensor Networks
Mahesh Arumugam, Sandeep S. Kulkarni 69

Effect of Mobility on Communication Performance in Overloaded One-Dimensional Cellular Networks
Michihiro Inoue, Noriaki Yoshiura, Yoshikuni Onozato 82

Distributed Time Slot Assignment in Wireless Ad Hoc Networks for STDMA
Subhasis Bhattacharjee, Nabanita Das 93

Efficient Algorithm for Placing Base Stations by Avoiding Forbidden Zone
Sasanka Roy, Debabrata Bardhan, Sandip Das 105

Secured Communication in Distributed Systems

Secure Two-Party Context Free Language Recognition
Anshuman Singh, Siddharth Barman, K.K. Shukla 117

Autonomous Agent Based Distributed Fault-Tolerant Intrusion Detection System
Jaydip Sen, Indranil Sengupta 125

Cleaning an Arbitrary Regular Network with Mobile Agents
Paola Flocchini, Amiya Nayak, Arno Schulz 132

Query and Transaction Processing

Multi-attribute Hashing of Wireless Data for Content-Based Queries
Yon Dohn Chung, Ji Yeon Lee 143

A Tool for Automated Resource Consumption Profiling of Distributed Transactions
B. Nagaprabhanjan, Varsha Apte 154

An Efficient Algorithm for Removing Useless Logged Messages in
SBML Protocols
  JinHo Ahn 166

Theory of Distributed Systems

Divide and Concur: Employing Chandra and Toueg's Consensus
Algorithm in a Multi-level Setting
  *Rahul Agarwal, Mahender Bisht, S.N. Maheshwari,
  Sanjiva Prasad* 172

Distributed Multiple Hypothesis Testing in Sensor Networks Under
Bandwidth Constraint
  Chandrashekhar Thejaswi PS, Ranjeet Kumar Patro 184

A Scalable Multi-level Distributed System-Level Diagnosis
  Paritosh Chandrapal, Padam Kumar 192

Analysis of Interval-Based Global State Detection
  Punit Chandra, Ajay D. Kshemkalyani 203

Grid Computing

A Two-Phase Scheduling Algorithm for Efficient Collective
Communications of MPICH-G2
  Junghee Lee, Dongsoo Han 217

Towards an Agent-Based Framework for Monitoring and Tuning
Application Performance in Grid Environment
  Sarbani Roy, Nandini Mukherjee 229

GDP: A Paradigm for Intertask Communication in Grid Computing
Through Distributed Pipes
  *D. Janakiram, M. Venkateswara Reddy, A. Vijay Srinivas,
  M.A. Maluk Mohamed, S. Santosh Kumar* 235

Internet Technology

Internet Technology Track Chair's Message
  Sanjay K. Madria 242

Internet Search and Query

Rewriting Queries Using View for RDF/RDFS-Based Relational Data Integration
Huajun Chen 243

An Effective Searching Method Using the Example-Based Query
Kil Hong Joo, Jaeho Lee 255

On Communicating with Agents on the Network
Rajat Shuvro Roy, M. Sohel Rahman 267

E-Commerce

Applying Fuzzy Logic to Recommend Consumer Electronics
Yukun Cao, Yunfeng Li, Xiaofeng Liao 278

Generic XML Schema Definition (XSD) to GUI Translator
V. Radha, S. Ramakrishna, N. Pradeep Kumar 290

Off-Line Micro-payment System for Content Sharing in P2P Networks
Xiaoling Dai, John Grundy 297

Browsing and Analysis of Web Elements

FlexiRank: An Algorithm Offering Flexibility and Accuracy for Ranking the Web Pages
Debajyoti Mukhopadhyay, Pradipta Biswas 308

Adaptable Web Browsing of Images in Mobile Computing Environment: Experiments and Observations
Atul Kumar, Anjali Bhargava, Bharat Bhargava, Sanjay Madria 314

An Incremental Document Clustering Algorithm Based on a Hierarchical Agglomerative Approach
Kil Hong Joo, SooJung Lee 321

Systems Security

System Security Track Chair's Message
Indrajit Ray 333

Theory of Secured Systems

A Game Based Model of Security for Key Predistribution Schemes in Wireless Sensor Network
Debapriyay Mukhopadhyay, Suman Roy 334

E-mail Worm Detection Using the Analysis of Behavior
Tao Jiang, Wonil Kim, Kyungsuk Lhee, Manpyo Hong 348

Verifiably Encrypted Signature Scheme Without Random Oracles
M. Choudary Gorantla, Ashutosh Saxena 357

Intrusion Detection and Ad Hoc Network Security

An Improved Intrusion Detection Technique for Mobile Adhoc Networks
S. Prasanna, V. Vetriselvi 364

User Revocation in Secure Adhoc Networks
Bezawada Bruhadeshwar, Sandeep S. Kulkarni 377

A Hybrid Method to Intrusion Detection Systems Using HMM
C.V. Raman, Atul Negi 389

Secured Systems Techniques

Enhanced Network Traffic Anomaly Detector
Suresh Reddy, Sukumar Nandi 397

Statistically Secure Extension of Anti-collusion Code Fingerprinting
Jae-Min Seol, Seong-Whan Kim 404

An Improvement of Auto-Correlation Based Video Watermarking Scheme Using Perceptual Masking for Motion
Hyun-Seong Sung, Seong-Whan Kim 410

Validation of Policy Integration Using Alloy
Manachai Toahchoodee, Indrakshi Ray 420

Plenary Talk II

Linking Theories of Concurrency by Retraction
He Jifeng 432

Software Engineering

Software Architecture

Software Engineering Track Chair's Message
  Gopal Gupta 433

Software Architecture

Integrating Architecture Description Languages: A Semantics-Based Approach
  Qian Wang 434

Automated Runtime Validation of Software Architecture Design
  Zhijiang Dong, Yujian Fu, Yue Fu, Xudong He 446

Software Optimization and Reliability

Analyzing Loop Paths for Execution Time Estimation
  Abhik Roychoudhury, Tulika Mitra, Hemendra Singh Negi 458

A Technique for Early Software Reliability Prediction
  Rakesh Tripathi, Rajib Mall 470

Formal Methods

Executable Requirements Specifications Using Triggered Message Sequence Charts
  Bikram Sengupta, Rance Cleaveland 482

Efficient Symmetry Reduction for an Actor-Based Model
  M.M. Jaghoori, M. Sirjani, M.R. Mousavi, A. Movaghar 494

Validated Code Generation for Activity Diagrams
  A.K. Bhattacharjee, R.K. Shyamasundar 508

Data Mining

Data Mining Track Chair's Message
  Mukesh Mohania 522

Data Clustering Techniques

An Approach to Find Embedded Clusters Using Density Based Techniques
  S. Roy, D.K. Bhattacharyya 523

Using Sub-sequence Information with kNN for Classification of Sequential Data
  *N. Pradeep Kumar, M. Venkateswara Rao, P. Radha Krishna,
  Raju S. Bapi* 536

Distance-Based Outliers in Sequences
  Girish Keshav Palshikar 547

Capturing Market Intelligence from Customer Feedback E-mails Using Self-enhancing Bolztmann Machine-Based Network of Knowledge Maps
  N. Pradeep Kumar, Tapati Bandopadhyay 553

Multidimensional Data Mining

Algorithm for Fuzzy Clustering of Mixed Data with Numeric and Categorical Attributes
  Amir Ahmad, Lipika Dey 561

Dissemination of Multidimensional Data Using Broadcast Clusters
  Ilias Michalarias, Hans-J. Lenz 573

Multidimensional Frequent Pattern Mining Using Association Rule Based Constraints
  S. Vijayalakshmi, S. Suresh Raja 585

A Classification Based Approach for Root Unknown Phylogenetic Networks Under Constrained Recombination
  M.A.H. Zahid, Ankush Mittal, R.C. Joshi 592

Author Index 605

The Distributed Sensor Networks – An Emerging Technology

S.S. Iyengar

Louisiana State University, USA

Abstract. Distributed Sensor networks have a wide range of real-time applications in aerospace, automation, defense, medical imaging, robotics, and weather prediction. Over the past several years, scientists, engineers, and researchers in a multitude of disciplines have been clamoring for more detailed information without much success. This new evolving technology can provide solutions to a variety of these technology related problems. Professor Iyengar in this talk will give an overview of these impact areas based on his experience in working with various industries like Oak ridge National Lab, Jet Propulsion Lab, and Naval Research Lab. His talk is also based on his experiences of working with scientists from Raytheon, Boeing during the last few years.

Distributed Computing Track Chair's Message

Arunabha Sen

Arizona State University, USA

Abstract. The Distributed Computing track of ICDCIT 2005 received 181 papers. Based on the review by the members of the Program Committee, 16 full and 9 short papers were selected for inclusion in the proceedings of the conference. The accepted papers cover a wide range of topics in Distributed Computing. Design of MAC protocol, network architecture and routing protocol for Wireless Ad-Hoc Networks seem to attract the attention of many researchers. 5 of the 16 accepted full papers fall in this area. The other popular areas include, Network Security, Sensor Networks, Fault Detection and Recovery and Grid Computing. Each of these areas will have at least 3 papers in the proceedings. The Distributed Computing track will also have papers in the areas of Cellular Networks, Peer-to-Peer Networks, Optical Networks, Information Retrieval, QoS and Mobile IP. We have put together a program that covers many important areas of Distributed Computing. We hope you will find the papers in this track informative, interesting and useful.

Efficient Binding Lifetime Determination Schemes in HMIPv6*

Sun Ok Yang[1], SungSuk Kim[2], and Chong-Sun Hwang[1]

[1] Dept. of Computer Science & Engineering, Korea University, Seoul, S. Korea
{soyang, hwang}@korea.ac.kr
[2] Corresponding author. Dept. of E-Businees, SeoKyeong University, Seoul, S. Korea
sskim03@skuniv.ac.kr

Abstract. Mobile IP represents a global solution, providing mobility management for a wide variety of radio technologies, devices and applications. Significant research results relating to extensions for MIPv6 have been reported over the last several years. However practical and common issues exist within the technology, in particular, the specification of Binding Update Lifetime has a substantial impact on the system performance. In this paper, binding lifetime determination schemes are devised to obtain high energy-efficiency mobile nodes in HMIPv6. Some people may stay within some area for a long time and thus the related information can be very useful in decreasing the frequency of binding update messages. That is, if each user maintains a profile locally based on moving history; this can be very useful in fixing the lifetime in terms of current location. In addition, the resident time is occasionally affected by the daily arrival time as well as the subnet. Thus, we expand the scheme to consider the time region of arrival time per each subnet. We study the performance improvement of our schemes through extensive simulations.

1 Introduction

Mobile IP [1] represents a global mobility solution, providing mobility management for a wide variety of radio technologies, devices and applications. It allows a *Mobile Node (MN)* to change location without requiring restart of any applications or termination of any ongoing communication. Significant research resulting in various extensions for Mobile IPv6 (MIPv6) has been reported over the last several years. This work deals with a number of aspects: Fast Handovers for MIPv6 [2], QoS Guarantees with MIPv6 [3], Cellular IP [4] and Mobile IP with Paging [5]. However there are practical and common issues, of which much less attention is paid. This problem related to the specification of the Binding Update Lifetime [1]. Hierarchical Mobile IPv6 (HMIPv6) [6], differentiating the local mobility from global mobility is more appropriate to the Internet. It has been developed by the IETF with new functionality for improving the performance of MIPv6 in terms of handoff delay. In HMIPv6 (see Fig. 1), a Binding is

---

* This research was supported by University IT Research Center Project.

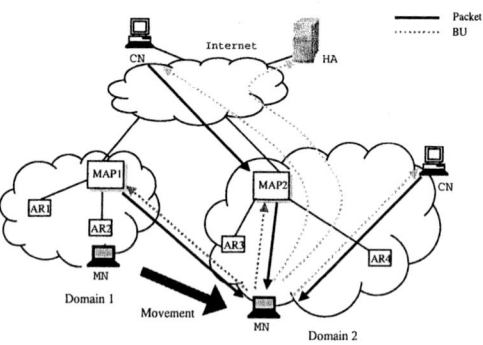

Fig. 1. Hierarchical Mobile IPv6

the association of the home address of a MN with an *on Link Care-of-Address (LCoA)* or a *Regional Care-of-Address (RCoA)*, for that mobile node, along with the remaining lifetime for that association. A lifetime is specified whenever a MN transmits a *Binding Update (BU) Message* to the *Mobility Anchor Point (MAP)*, its *Home Agent (HA)* and relevant *Correspondent Nodes (CNs)*. This lifetime is identified where specifications of a lifetime impact system performance. If the lifetime is set too short, HA quickly detects that the MN is disconnected from the network, but resulting in a large number of BU messages over the wireless link. This is one of the main reasons of HA processing overload and deterioration of MN energy efficiency and wireless bandwidth utilization. The reverse, when a long lifetime BU message is received, HA and CNs keep it in a binding cache until the lifetime expires. If a MN disconnects from the network, the problem occurs since HA cannot know this situation until the lifetime is refreshed. In addition, the binding record will eventually occupy more space in both data structures, *Binding Cache* and *Binding Update List*, of the MNs [1]. Therefore, an approach for determining proper binding lifetime is needed in the context of HMIPv6 networks.

In our previous work [7], a *Profile-Based Strategy (PBS)* in MIPv6 was proposed to determine the BU lifetime dynamically. Based on that work, binding lifetime determination schemes is presented in order to provide energy-efficiency of MN in HMIPv6. If information containing each MN's mobility pattern is available, this is helpful in predicting future movement behavior. A MN gathers related information whenever it leaves a subnet and periodically computes the lifetime values for all visited subnets, maintaining them in its profile. When a MN migrates any subnet, and there is a record for the subnet in the profile, an adaptive lifetime is applied to the BU lifetime. In addition, another regularity pattern can be found in the daily arrival time as well as the visited subnet. Thus, an expanded scheme is proposed considering the time region of arrival for each subnet. Simulation work is performed to present the efficiency of the proposed ideas over MIPv6 and HMIPv6.

The paper is organized as follows. The binding management and schemes for dynamically setting the lifetime are presented in Section 2. The schemes are compared with that in MIPv6 and HMIPv6 with regard to the number of BU messages in Section 3. Finally, the conclusions and further work are discussed in Section 4.

2 Dynamic Lifetime Determination

In this section, the proposed schemes, which reduce the number of BU messages from MNs, are described. To do so, a new type of BU message is first introduced in HMIPv6 and then the algorithms to determine BU lifetime will be proposed using local profile information.

Binding Management. As previously mentioned, a binding for a MN is the triplet that contains the home address, LCoA or RCoA, and the binding lifetime. With HMIPv6, every node has a *Binding Cache*, which is used to hold the bindings for other nodes. If a node receives a BU, it will add this binding to its *Binding Cache*. In addition, every MN has a *Binding Update List*, used to store information regarding each BU transmitted by this MN, for which the lifetime has not expired. A binding entry is removed from either the *Binding Cache* or *Binding Update List*, whenever its lifetime has expired.

Considering that some kinds of people (such as office worker, housewife, shopkeeper) have comparatively regular movement patterns in some subnets, i.e., they will not move out of their subnet for a predictable period of time. In contrast, others (such as taxi driver, salesman) move around completely irregular. That is, past movements for such users cannot be used to accurately predict current movements within the subnet. If information regarding each MN's past movements is maintained locally and is available, the proper BU lifetime can be provided whenever the MN enters a subnet. In this paper, three kinds of BU messages are used according to the lifetime.

(1) BU_α has a default lifetime (LT_α), which is the same value as one used in existing MIPv6 [1]. After switching to a new MAP, MN may transmit BU_α to its previous MAP, asking it to redirect all incoming packets to its new CoA.
(2) BU_β has a adaptive lifetime (LT_β), which is computed based on local profile. A MN has to transmit it to the MAP, its HA and CNs.
(3) BU_0 contains a zero lifetime value (LT_0). When a MN migrates a subnet in another domain before the BU_β has expired, it will be used to notify both HA and external CNs that the cached data regarding the BU_β has become stale and the data requires removal.

Both BU_α and BU_0 are originally used in MIPv6 but the BU_β is newly devised in this paper. Of course, if the MN does not move out of the subnet, although LT_β expires, BU_α will be used hereafter.

Resident Time Based Scheme (RT). When a MN leaves a subnet, information (*moving log*) regarding the visit, is recorded. The log contains an ordered

```
// Whenever a MN moves out a subnet.
// Count_b : Threshold of Count
If ( MN has visited subnet m ){
    t_n = DT_n - AT_n
    If ( t_n > p * LT_a ){
        Record moving log
        Count_m = Count_m + 1
        Sum_m = Sum_m + t_n  }
}

//Periodic calculation
Mean_m = Sum_m / Count_m
For ( all moving logs for subnet m ){
    Calculate Var_m   //equation (1)
    Determine mobility type  }
If ( Count_m < Count_b ) LT = LT_a
Else{ If (Mean_m <= p * LT_a or mobility type C )
        LT = LT_a
    Else{ LT_β = Mean_m *V
        LT = LT_β  }
}
```

Fig. 2. Resident Time Based Scheme

pair (l, AT, DT), which represents the subnet identifier, *Arrival Time (AT)* and *Departure Time (DT)*, respectively. The average resident time and the frequency of logs in each subnet are considered when the adaptive lifetime (LT_β) is calculated. This scheme is named the *resident time based scheme (RT)*. When a MN moves to another m, it adds current visit information to a moving log. The average resident time for all visited subnets is periodically calculated, and the scheme is described in Fig. 2. At first, the resident time (t_n) for n^{th} visit to subnet m is computed by simply subtracting AT from the DT.

In Fig. 2, a comparison of t_n and $\rho * DLT$ is used to exclude the moving log where the resident time is small (that is, the case where a MN recently passed by the subnet, for a moment while moving to specific destination). It is assumed that t_n is compared with ρ (≥ 1) times as long as DLT. Sum_m and $Count_m$ represent total resident time and total visit number to subnet m respectively. During the calculation, if the number of visits to subnet m is fewer than the constant value ($count_b$), the BU_α will be used since poor (or no) regularity is found in subnet m. The variance rate, as well as the average resident time, in this case is considered. To begin with, the movement patterns for all subnets in the profile are divided into *mobility types A, B*, and *C* to present the degree of accuracy of the profile. To quantify the difference, the variance is calculated for all subnets as Eq. (1):

$$Var_m = \frac{1}{n}\sum_{i=1}^{n}(t_i - Mean_m)^2 \qquad (1)$$

If Var_m is smaller than the constant δ_1, subnet m is classified as *mobility type A* (the most reliable subnet). If Var_m is larger than constant δ_1 and smaller than constant δ_2, the subnet is classified as *mobility type B*. Otherwise; the subnet belongs to *mobility type C*. The lifetime value for the next BU is calculated by multiplying the mean resident time by the difference constant, V, according to

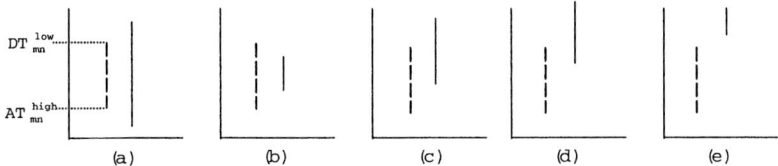

Fig. 3. Various Cases of Visiting Time

mobility type. Namely, the constant value in *mobility type A* (V_A) is larger than that in *mobility type B* (V_B). The calculated value, LT_β, will be used as the lifetime for BU_β when the MN visits subnet m, after creating the profile. If a MN migrates to a subnet within another domain before LT_β has expired, the previous MAP has to transmit a BU_0 to both HA and external CNs.

Time Region Based Scheme (TR). The resident time for some subnets often depends on the arrival time. In this way, another scheme is devised, a *Time Region based scheme (TR)* by expanding the *RT*. This scheme also considers the time region of the arrival time to enhance the accuracy of the profile. During periodic calculations, the mean resident time per (*subnet ID, time region*) pair, must be considered, not simply the subnet. To do so, a scheme to determine the time regions from moving logs is required. Five different cases are considered, as shown in Fig. 3. The following information is also maintained in the profile per time region:

- AT_{mn}^{high} the highest (or latest) arrival time
- DT_{mn}^{low} the lowest (or earliest) departure time
- $Count_{mn}$ the number of visits included in the nth time region
- $TotalCount_{mn}$ the total number of visits considered in the nth time region

Where subscriptions n and m mean n^{th} time region to subnet m. Since the time region is considered, as well as the visiting subnet, each time region maintains its visiting number ($TotalCount_{mn}$, $Count_{mn}$) separately.

In the figure, the vertical dotted line represents the time interval ($Interval_{mn}$ = DT_{mn}^{low} - AT_{mn}^{high}) that one time region calculated. The solid line presents the current visiting time. In the case of Fig. 3-(e), it is natural to exclude a new visit from the time region. Visit in Fig. 3-(a) or (b) requires to verification of the MN resides too long or too short in the subnet. If the resident time is longer than $\frac{3}{2} \times Interval_{mn}$ or shorter than $\frac{1}{2} \times Interval_{mn}$, the difference between both grows too long and thus, the current visiting log cannot provide reliable information. That is, the log is completely excluded; if the log is not too long, the log is also used in periodic calculations. In addition it must be considered not only the length of resident time but also the time that a MN has arrived must be considered. Fig. 3-(c) and (d) initially appear to be similar cases. However, if both are considered, the time region does not provide useful information. Thus, the following process is required for an accurate determination.

> middle = $Interval_{mn}/2$
> if (middle ≥ arrival time of current visit)
>   the current log include into the nth time region
> else the current log is excluded

Then, if the current log is included into n^{th} time region of subnet m, $Count_{mn}$ and $TotalCount_{mn}$ all increase by 1. Otherwise, only $TotalCount_{mn}$ increases by 1 (Fig. 3-(a) and (b)), since this variable will be used to determine the accuracy of the profile. If the arrival time in the current visit is earlier than AT_{mn}^{high}, it is enough to be considered contrary to the cases shown in Fig. 3-(c), (d), and (e). The moving log excluded from the above algorithm will be used to form another time region, except the regions described in Fig. 3-(a) and (b). After time regions are determined using this method, mostly the algorithm to determine mobility type is similar to the RT with one exception. In the RT, only Var_m is considered per visited subnet. However, both comparisons between ratio Countmn and TotalCountmn and Var_m are required to evaluate the usefulness of the information regarding the time region. That is, if Var_m is smaller than δ_1 and $\frac{Count_{mn}}{TotalCount_{mn}}$ is larger than γ_1, the time region to subnet m is regarded as *mobility type A*. If Var_m is greater than δ_2 or $\frac{Count_{mn}}{TotalCount_{mn}}$ is smaller than γ_2, it is considered that without regularity (*mobility type C*). In the other cases, the average resident time is adjusted as *mobility type B*.

Disconnection. In the proposed schemes, the scheme of most important is disconnection. If a MN cannot connect to its CN or HA due to various reasons, some packets may be lost. This is because the CNs assume that the MN is alive and is now transmitting packets until the lifetime expires. This situation creates two cases. The first case, disconnection occurs when a MN is moving. The MN transmits new BUs to both HA and CNs after forming a new CoA. That is, it is the establishment of new connectivity. In the second case, disconnection occurs when a MN stays. If the MN is now communicating, it simply transmits BUs as in HMIPv6. The probability of disconnection, however, is very small except for a voluntary power-off, because of the advance of mobile communication technology. This means that the probability of loss of packets resulting from disconnection is extremely small. Therefore this problem is not investigated in this paper.

3 Performance Analysis

In order to examine the performance of the two proposed schemes, the RT and TR, an experimental evaluation is achieved. In the experiments, the main interest focuses on energy-efficiency in terms of the bandwidth usage, thus the schemes are both compared to HMIPv6.

3.1 Simulation Models

The simulation model for the schemes is depicted in Fig. 4. Each MN collects log data in the form (l, AT_n, DT_n), whenever it leaves a visited subnet. It is

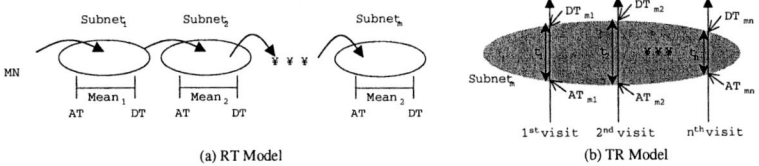

Fig. 4. Simulation Models

assumed that the resident time at any subnet follows a Gamma distribution [8] with shape parameter α. As is generally known, a Gamma distribution is selected because it can be shaped to represent many distributions, as well as measure data that cannot be characterized by a particular distribution.

The Eq. (2), (3), and (4) describe the density function for resident time, the mean of resident time at a visited subnet and the variance of resident time, respectively. In the equations, t is the resident time at each visited subnet. It is important to note, however, that the resident time follows an exponential distribution where parameter $\alpha = 1$, $\lambda = 1/E(t)$ in a Gamma distribution. The results are shown as the amount of bandwidth allocated by BU messages.

$$f(t) = \frac{\lambda^{\alpha}}{\Gamma(\alpha)}(\lambda t)^{\alpha-1} l^{-\lambda t}, t \geq 0 \quad (2)$$

$$E(t) = \frac{\alpha}{\lambda} \quad (3)$$

$$V(t) = \frac{\alpha}{\lambda^2} \quad (4)$$

All parameters set as constant in the previous section are presented in Table 1 where ρ and $Count_b$ are used to check whether to consider the current movement log or not, and δ_1, δ_2, γ_1 and γ_1 to determine mobility type of the subnet. The values are selected from various experiment settings however they will not affect the overall performance seriously. V_A and V_B mean the weight value for the calculated lifetime of *mobility type* A and B, respectively. The disconnection rate (ζ) is set at 0.001 but does not affect overall performance since both schemes and HMIPv6 treat disconnection in the same manner. It is also assumed that the energy cost to compute and maintain profile is negligible considering the communication cost. Issue relating to the degree of accuracy of the profile is beyond the scope of this paper and thus, is not developed further.

3.2 The Results

In following (5), (6) and (7), BW_{MIPv6}, BW_{HMIPv6} and $BW_{proposal}$ are the amounts of the allocated bandwidth for BUs in MIPv6, HMIPv6 and the proposed schemes, respectively. $Size_{BU}$ is defined as the size of a BU (68bytes = IPv6 header (40bytes) + Binding Update Extension Header (28bytes)) [9]. f_{HA} is denoted as the BU emission frequency from the MN to its HA and f_{CN} is the average BU emission frequency from the MN to its CNs. When a MN migrates, κ represents the intra-domain moving rate. The domain-crossing rate is

Table 1. Parameter Settings

parameter	value	meaning
ρ	2	
$Count_b$	10	threshold of Count
δ_1	10	constant value to determine mobility type A
δ_2	50	constant value to determine mobility type C
γ_1	0.8	constant value of $\frac{Count_{mn}}{TotalCount_{mn}}$ for mobility type A
γ_2	0.6	constant value of $\frac{Count_{mn}}{TotalCount_{mn}}$ for mobility type C
κ	0.3	intra-domain moving rate
V_A	1.0	V value for mobility type A
V_B	0.8	V value for mobility type B
ζ	0.001	disconnection rate

1-κ, meaning the number of crossing domains divided by the total number of crossing subnets. The MN transmits M consecutive BUs to its external CNs, and transmits another BU to its HA, receiving a BA from HA. In (5) [9], $\#CN$ is the number of CNs that are not on the home network. When a MN, using MIPv6, migrates along subnets, it transmits a BU to each CN and to its HA equal to f_{CN} and f_{HA}. In (6) [9], $\#CN$ is the number of external CNs of MN. When it is migrating within a foreign domain, the BU is also transmitted to both external CNs and the HA at a refreshment frequency (f_{REF}). Even though MN does not cross out of a domain, it should transmit messages periodically if it is based on MIPv6 or HMIPv6. If the profile information proposed in this paper can be used, the refreshment frequency may be reduced to f_{RT_REF}, although the MAP should transmit an additional BU, f_{ADD}, to its external CNs and HA (7). In case of inter-domain movement, the total levels of bandwidth allocated to BUs are equal among the three schemes.

$$BW_{MIPv6} = Size_{BU} \times \{\kappa \times (f_{CN} \times (\#CN+1) + f_{HA}) + (1-\kappa) \times (M \times \#CN + 2)\} \quad (5)$$

$$BW_{HMIPv6} = Size_{BU} \times \{\kappa \times f_{REF} \times (\#CN+1) + (1-\kappa) \times (M \times \#CN + 2)\} \quad (6)$$

$$BW_{proposal} = Size_{BU} \times \{\kappa \times f_{RT\_REF} \times (\#CN+1) + (1-\kappa) \times (M \times \#CN + 2) + f_{ADD}\} \quad (7)$$

$$f_{ADD} = \begin{cases} \#CN+1 & \text{if visiting subnet is in the profile} \\ 0 & \text{otherwise} \end{cases}$$

Figure 5 represents the comparison among the *RT*, MIPv6, and HMIPv6 in a Gamma distribution where the mean resident time varies from 7 to 100 minutes and the variance is set to 0.01, 1, 25 and 100. In this case, resident time less than 7 minutes is not considered since a MN will do exactly the same. It is assumed that a MN migrates as *mobility type A* in 5% of the all subnets recorded in the profile, *mobility type B* in another 15% of the subnets, and *mobility type*

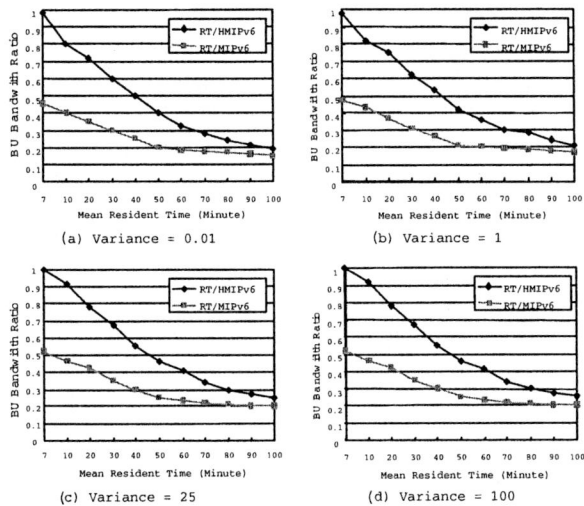

Fig. 5. Gamma Distribution

C in the remaining 80%. As mentioned in Section III.C. The subnets recorded as *mobility type A* provide more reliable information for their subsequent visits than those with *mobility type B* or C. During local movement within a foreign domain, BU bandwidth depends on $\#CN$, f_{CN}, f_{HA}, f_{REF} and f_{RT-REF}. Since the behaviors of the BU bandwidth ratio are almost identical when $\#CN$ is 2 or 10, Fig. 5 presents the results where $\#CN=2$. In the figure, the Y-axis value is a relative value comparing the schemes. That is, if the value is smaller than 1.0, the RT saves more bandwidth than the other scheme. At first, it is known that variance has little influence on overall performance. The reason is as follows: Users have irregular movement patterns and variance is one of the factors that affect irregularity. Thus, the profile is used to capture reliable information unaffected by the factors, i.e., variance. In Fig. 6, experiments are made when the parameter is set at $\alpha=1$, $\lambda = 1/E(t)$ in a Gamma distribution and resident time follows an exponential distribution.

From the Fig. 5 and 6, both the ratio of RT to MIPv6 and the ratio of RT to HMIPv6 decrease as mean resident time increases. For example, in the case where mean resident time $=100$ in Fig. 5-(a), only 20% of messages are

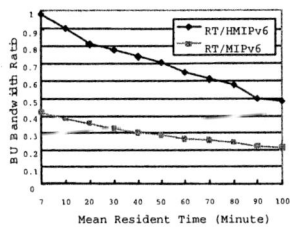

Fig. 6. Exponential Distribution

required, compared with MIPv6 and HMIPv6. The other figures show similar results. This indicates that bandwidth usage in the RT is the most efficient than the others and HMIPv6 provides better usage than MIPv6. The reason is that in the case of MIPv6, BUs are transmitted to its HA and CNs when the MN is roaming locally but HMIPv6 just forces transmission of the BUs refresh to MAP periodically. The RT only transmits the BUs to its MAP similar to HMIPv6, and moreover, refresh time is also lengthened if a long resident time is computed for the current location from the profile.There may be differences between the computed lifetime and real resident time. In spite of this, the level of reduced bandwidth is substantial, in subnets where MNs are determined as consisting mainly of *mobility type A* or *B*. In particular, when a MN does not migrate across domains frequently, most of the signaling load is generated by the refreshing BUs. The central improvements proposed in this paper, are achieved by decreasing the number of periodic refreshing BUs.

If a MN leaves the current subnet before the lifetime expires, the MAP should transmit BU_0 to delete the binding cache in it's HA and external CNs. Therefore, additional f_{ADD} messages require delivery. This may represent a problem when a MN does not follow the previous movement pattern, especially when the current resident time is much shorter than the determined lifetime. However, if the current resident time is longer than 7 minutes for a subnet, the maximum 75-80% of BU messages can be reduced, fully counteracting the negative effect due to the additional messages. Another point to note here is that the mean resident time can be much longer than 100 minutes in reality, although the time is set from 7 to 100 minutes in the experiments. Some kinds of users - for example, office workers, clerks, housewives and so on - stay very long in a domain, and therefore will only transmit a small number of messages. If the user moves out, the default mechanism in HMIPv6 will be used and thus there is little additional overhead. Thus, the energy efficiency of the proposed schemes can improve over the results presented in this paper. If an algorithm is devised, to extract useful and reliable information from a profile, the efficiency is greatly improved. However, this is beyond the scope of this paper, and therefore does not require detailed discussion.

The second experiments are to examine the effects on the time region of the arrival time (see Fig. 7). The ratio of TR to RT is investigated in a Gamma distribution where the variance is set at 0.01, 1, 25 and 100. In the experiments, only the subnets where good regularity is obtained from the profile, were considered. It is assumed that 40% of all the subnets recorded as *mobility type A* or *B* in their profile have only one time region, another 40% subnets have two time regions, and the remaining have three or more time regions. From the figure, it is shown that variance represents an important role in performance, unlike previous results. When variance is set 0.01 and 1, the TR displays an improved bandwidth usage than the RT. However, as it is set to high value (i.e., 25 and 100), the RT is superior over the TR. The reason can be found from the profile information. If there are two or more time regions in a subnet m, each mean resident time is different, among them,Var_m also has a high value in the RT,

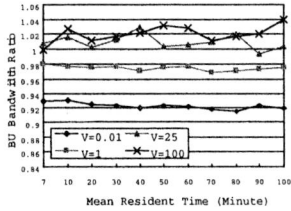

Fig. 7. The Comparison of TR and RT in Gamma Distribution

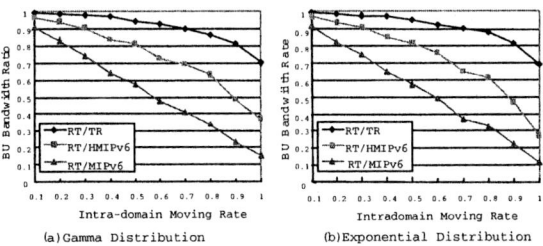

Fig. 8. The Comparison of BU bandwidth with various intra-domain moving ratio

determining the subnet as *mobility type B* or *C*. However, the TR can diminish Var_m by grouping the logs into time regions. This indicates that if some regularity for both subnet and arrival time is obtained, the computed lifetime can provide more correct reliability.

Figure 8 represents the effect of the intra-domain moving rate (κ). If κ is set to a high value, the probability is high that the MN may reside within an intra-domain, not migrating out to another domain. In this case, if the current subnet is recorded as type A or B, it indicates that the MN will rarely leave the current location before new lifetime expires. Naturally, HMIPv6 and the proposed schemes demonstrate improved bandwidth usage over MIPv6 due to the same reason. In addition, the RT can also reduce the number of BUs lower than HMIPv6. However, as κ increases, the volume of the bandwidth in the TR increases at a faster rate than that in the RT. The reason is that information in the profile down to the details applies to the TR within a MAP domain. In other words, the number of BUs transmitted to the HA and CNs becomes larger than that of the RT when the MN is moving within a MAP. However, it's HA and CNs maintain a more accurate binding cache in the TR than that the RT.

4 Conclusion

In this paper, binding lifetime determination schemes (TR and RT) for periodic binding update messages in HMIPv6, are proposed. The overhead incurred by frequent BUs is reduced, by capturing some regularity in movement patterns of each MN. That is, from the MN's arrival time as well as the resident time in visited subnets, the proper lifetime is computed and applied dynamically. The main contributions in this paper are allowing limited wireless bandwidth to be utilized effectively, and greatly improving the energy efficiency in the MN, by reducing the number of BUs. However, the accuracy of the profile is required for more in depth analysis, to ascertain the effects of each parameter through data mining schemes, since the proposed schemes are based on local profiles.

References

1. B. Johnson, C. Perkins and J. Arkko, Mobility Support in IPv6, RFC 3775, IETF, 2004.
2. Rajeev Koodli, "Fast Handovers for Mobile IPv6", IETF Internet Draft, draft-ietf-mobileip-fast-mipv6-08.txt, 2003.
3. Hemant Chaskar, "Requirements of a QoS Solution for Mobile IPv6", IETF Internet Draft, draft-ietf-mobileip-qos-requirements-04.txt, 2003.
4. Campbell, J. Gomez, C-Y. Wan, Z. Turanyi, and A. Valko, "Cellular IP", IETF Internet Draft, 1999.
5. C. Castelluccia, "Extending Mobile IP with Adaptive Individual Paging: A Performance Analysis," *INRIA*, 1999.
6. H. Soliman, C. Castellucia, K. E. Malki and L. Bellier, "Hierarchical MIPv6 mobility management (HMIPv6)", IETF Internet Draft, draft-ietf-mobileip-hmipv6-08.txt, 2003.
7. S. Yang, U. Song, J. Gil and C. Hwang, "A Profile-Based Dynamic Binding Update Strategies in Mobile IPv6", In Proc. Internationa Conference on Wireless Networks, 2002, pp. 238-244.
8. Y. B. Lin, W. R. Lai and R. J. Chen, "Performance Analysis for Dual Band PCS Networks", *IEEE Journal on Transactions on Computers*, Vol. 49, No.2, 2000, pp 148-159.
9. C. Castelluccia, "HMIPv6: A Hierarchical Mobile IPv6 Proposal," *ACM SIGMOBILE Mobile Computing and Communication Review (MC2R)*, Vol.4, No.2, Jan. 2000, pp 48-59.

A Fast Search and Advanced Marking Scheme for Network IP Traceback Model

Jia Hou[1,2] and Moon Ho Lee[2]

[1] School of Electronics & Information Engineering, Soochow University,
Suzhou 215006, China
houjiastock@hotmail.com
[2] Institute of Information & Communication, Chonbuk National University,
Chonju 561-756, Korea
moonho@chonbuk.ac.kr

Abstract. Defending against distributed denial-of-service (DDoS) attack is one of the hardest security problems on the internet today. In this paper, we investigate a fast search algorithm for IP trace back, which is similar to the Viterbi algorithm and it has simple implementation. The approach is capable of tracking back attacks as quickly as possible. Our research can feature low network and router overhead, and support incremental deployment.

1 Introduction

Denial-of-service (DoS) attacks pose an increasing threat to today's internet [1]. A serious problem to fight these DoS attacks is that attackers use incorrect or spoofed IP addresses in the attack packets and hence disguise the real origin of the attacks. Due to the stateless nature of the internet, it is difficult problem to determine the source of these spoofed IP packets, which is called the IP traceback problem. One solution is to let routers probabilistically mark the packets with partial path information during packet forwarding [2]. The victim then reconstructs the complete paths after receiving a modest number of packets that contain the marking. We refer to this type of approach as the IP marking approach. This approach has a low overhead for routers and the networks. It can support incremental deployment.

In this paper, we address the problem of identifying the source of the attack, and present a fast search algorithm with advanced marking scheme to solve the IP traceback problem. The results of our proposal have the same low router and network overhead as that of FMS proposed in [2], yet our approach is efficiently and accurately to obtain the reconstruction of attacking path under DDoS.

In particular, our approach can reconstruct the attacking path within seconds with a low false positive rate. Further, the proposed fast search algorithm is implemented similarly as that of the Viterbi algorithm [3]. It can efficiently compare with the reference distance and decide the correct path by a high probability. This prevents a compromised router from forging other uncompromised routers markings.

2 Fast Search and Advanced Marking Scheme for IP Traceback

We refer to the packets used in DDoS attacks as the attack packets. We call a *router false positive* if it is in the reconstructed attack path but not in the real attack graph.

Similarly, we call a *router false negative* if it is in the true attack graph but not in the reconstructed attack path. And we call a solution to the IP trace back problem robust if it has very low rate of router false positives and router false negatives. At first, we propose a router map from victim by using set partition, as shown in Fig.1. It divides the routers and IP addresses to several levels according to the reference distances. Next, after comparing with the differences from the routers and IP addresses, we use the IP marking scheme to encode the information for tracing. The basic idea of the IP marking approach is that the routers can record the differences of the IP addresses and probabilistically write some encoding of partial path information into the packets [2]. The IP marking scheme reserves two static fields of the size of IP addresses, "start" and "end", and a static distance field in each packet. Each router of the network should update these fields. By using this IP marking scheme, any packet written by the attacker will describe a difference from the authenticated packet. Normally, the difference is greater than that of the conventional case without attacking.

Definition 1: Each router marks the packet with a probability q. When the router decides to mark the packet, it will write its own IP address into the start field and put zero into the distance field. Otherwise, we should indicate its previous routers have marked this packet if the distance field was already zero. Finally, it always should increment the distance field, if the router didn't mark the packet. Thus, the distance field in the packet indicates the number of routers, and such information that the packet has traversed from the router which marked the packet to the victim.

In general, the distances describe the differences of the two IP addresses, and the IP addresses have implied several levels or local information, which was applied to set partition mapping, as shown in Fig.1. Obviously, this hidden levels or local information can be applied to IP marking scheme for reducing the time of trace back.

For example, there are two IP addresses. One is 210.117.184.25, and the other is 210.117.186.35, thus we can write the information of distance as $210.117.184.25 - 210.117.186.35 = 0.0.2.10$. Clearly, there are 4-levels on the IP representation. And based on "0.0.2.0" and "0.0.0.10", the distances on different levels record the path of direct way to original IP source and the local information of IP addresses. Therefore, comparing with the distance on higher level is a fast way to find shortest attacking path and its location.

Definition 2: The victim can use the edges marked in the attack packets to reconstruct the attack graph. For each attack path with distance d, the expected number of packets needed to reconstruct the path is bounded by

$$Np = \frac{In(d)}{\Pr(x)} = \frac{In(d)}{q(1-q)^{d-1}}, \quad (1)$$

where $In(d)$ is the number of packets indicates with d, and $\Pr(x)$ denotes the write probability of the distance d at router x. $\Pr(x)$ can be computed by using

$$\Pr(x) = \Pr(d=0)\Pr(d \neq 0) = q(1-q)^{d-1}. \quad (2)$$

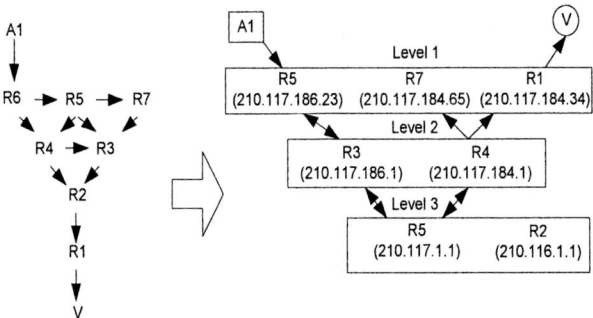

Fig. 1. Set partition map of the fast search algorithm

According to the Viterbi algorithm [3], we should the difference of the distances on each level and then decide the reconstructed path for next step. Thus, the pair-wise probability of choosing a correct path based on a reference path is given as

$$Pe(d) = \begin{cases} \sum_{k=(d+1)/2}^{d} \binom{d}{k} q^k (1-q)^{d-k}, d = odd; \\ \sum_{k=(d/2)+1}^{d} \binom{d}{k} q^k (1-q)^{d-k} \\ + \frac{1}{2}\binom{d}{d/2}[q(1-q)]^{d/2}, d = even. \end{cases} \quad (3)$$

Marking Scheme: The router always can increase the distance field which it decides not to mark the packet. The XOR of two neighboring routers encode the edge between the two routers of the upstream router map. The edge field of the marking will contain the XOR result of two neighboring routers, expect for samples from routers one hop way from the victim. Since $a \oplus b \oplus a = b$, we can start from markings of the routers by one hop away from the victim, and then hop-by-hop, decode the previous routers, as shown in Fig.2. The reason to use two independent hash functions is to distinguish the order of the two routers in the XOR results. For the proposed fast search algorithm, XOR operations also present the difference between two IP addresses. Thus, calculating the XOR operations on higher levels will be helpful to find the up-level locations or IP information on the correct path.

For example, the attacker uses the path "210.117.184.23, 210.117.186.45, 210.118.184.35" to attack the IP "210.118.184.44". Based on the calculations for higher level, we can first get "0.118.0.0" and "0.117.0.0", and second, we can decide the next level "0.117.186.0" and "0.117.184.0". Finally, the attacker IP "210.117.184.23" can be found. Unlike the conventional reconstruction, the calculation of "210.118.184.35" is skipped in the proposed set partition search algorithm, therefore, the speed of searching is increased.

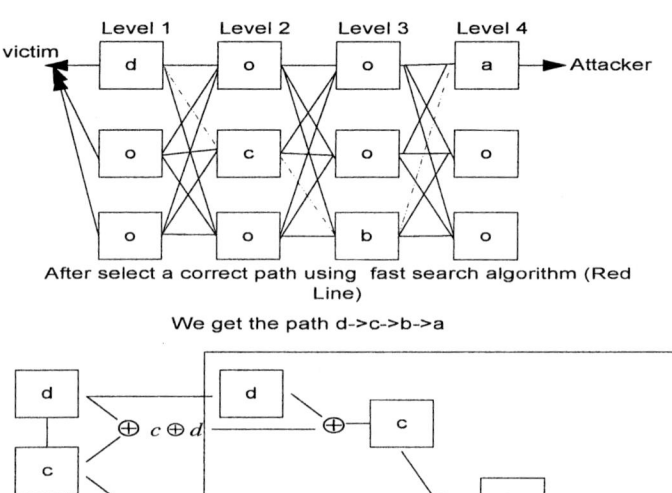

Fig. 2. Set partition map of the fast search algorithm

Marking and Reconstruction

Marking procedure at router R_i: For each packet P, let u be a random number from $[0,1)$. If $u \leq q$ then $P.\text{distance} \leftarrow 0$ and $P.\text{edge} \leftarrow h(R_i)$ (Hash function). Else, if ($P.\text{distance} = 0$) then $P.\text{edge} \leftarrow P.\text{edge} \oplus h'(R_i)$, and $P.\text{distance} \leftarrow P.\text{distance} + 1$.

Reconstruction procedure at victim v: Let S_d (The set of routers at distance d to the victim in the reconstructed attack graph) be empty for $0 \leq d \leq \max(d)$. For each child R of v in G_m (Upstream router map), if $h(R) \in \Psi_0$ then insert R into S_0.

    For $d := 0$ to $\max(d) - 1$,
        For each y in S_d and each x in Ψ_{d+1}
            $z = x \oplus h'(y)$.
        For each child u of y in G_m
            If $h(u) = z$ then insert u into S_{d+1}
        Output S_d for $0 \leq d \leq \max(d)$.

The victim repeats the steps until it reaches the maximal distance marked in the packets, denotes as $\max(d)$. The proposed searching exploits the Viterbi algorithm to find the maximum distance from the attacker with less computation complexity.

Analysis: Assume a DDoS attack, and let $|M_d|$ denote the number of routers in the attack graph at distance d from the victim. Let t_y denote the in-degree of element y in the S_{d-1} (the number of y's children) in G_m, and recall that $|\Psi_d|$ is the number of unique edge segments received by the victim with de distance field marked as d. With 11 bits hash value, the expected number of false positives among y's children in G_m is

$$Fp = t_y \cdot |\Psi_d|/2^{11}, \tag{4}$$

if we assume that has functions are good random, we have

$$E(\Psi_d) = (1 - (1 - 1/2^{11})^{|M_d|}) \cdot 2^{11}. \tag{5}$$

Numerical Results: For example, in the conventional scheme [4], we have $t_y = 32$, and $|M_d| = 64$. But in the proposed case, the t_y and $|M_d|$ can reduce about

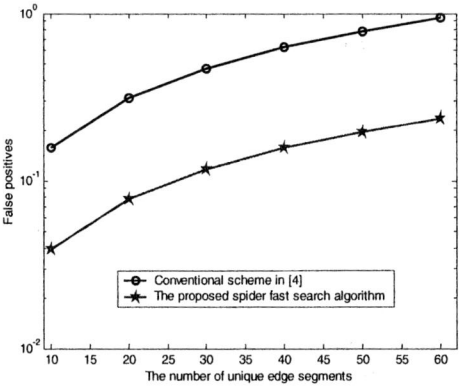

Fig. 3. False positive of the proposed fast search algorithm

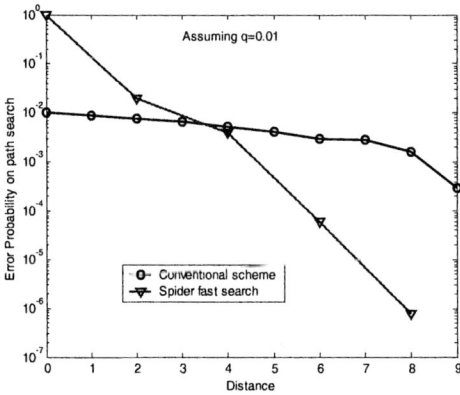

Fig. 4. Error probability on the path search

1/4 of conventional one. The false positive of the proposed fast search algorithm is shown in Fig.3. Further, the error probability on path search of the proposed algorithm can be improved following the increasing of the distance. The computation complexity of the proposed scheme is much lower than the fragmet marking scheme (FMS), $O(\sum_{d}|s_d|\cdot|\Psi_{d+1}|)$ instead of $O(\sum_{d}|s_d|\cdot|\Psi_{d+1}|^8)$. Also, given the same marking probability q, this scheme needs 1/8 of the packets in FMS for the reconstruction.

3 Conclusion

We present a fast search algorithm with advanced IP marking scheme. It allows the victim to trace back the approximate origin of spoofed IP packets. Our technique has very low network and router overhead, and it can support incremental deployment.

Acknowledgement

This work was supported by Chonbuk National University (Post-Doc.), and ITRC supervised by IITA, Korea.

References

1. J. Howard: An Analysis of Security Incidents on The Internet. Ph.D Thesis, Carnegie Mellon University, (1998)
2. S. Savage, D. Wetherll, A. Karlin, and T. Anderson: Practical Network Support for IP Traceback. Proc. 2000 ACM SIGCOMM, Vol.1, USA, (2000), 415–438
3. G.D. Forney. Jr.: The Viterbi Algorithm. IEEE Proceedings, Vol.61, no.3, (1973) 268-278
4. D.X. Song, and A. Perrig: Advanced and Authenticated Marking Scheme for IP Trace Back. Proc. IEEE INFORCOM, Vol.2, USA, (2001) 878-889

Design and Performance Evaluation of Token-Based MAC Protocols in WDM Burst Switched Ring Networks

Li-Mei Peng, Young-Chul Kim, Kyoung-Min Yoo,
Kyeong-Eun Han, and Young-Chon Kim[*]

Department of Computer Engineering, Chonbuk National University,
Jeonju 561-756, Korea
Tel: +82-63-270-2413, Fax: +82-63-270-2394
{mini0729, yckim}@chonbuk.ac.kr

Abstract. Token-based MAC(Medium Access Control) Protocols are proposed for WDM Burst-Switched Ring Network which consists of nodes using TT-TR(Tunable Transmitter-Tunable Receiver). The node architectures with TT-TR may make an efficient use of network resources, even though traffic pattern such as IP traffic with high self-similarity are dynamically changed, and can also support good expandability. However, MAC protocols suitable for TT-TR node architecture must be designed with consideration for various factors in order to use the limited resources of network efficiently. A variety of Token-based MAC protocols are suggested to increase the performance while reducing the processing overhead at each node. The performance of the MAC protocols are evaluated and compared in terms of average packet delay, channel utilization and burst loss rate through OPNET simulation. Finally, we provide insight into the design of MAC protocols by investigating the effect of various parameters.

1 Introduction

Optical burst switching(OBS) [1]-[2] is a promising method that can transport data over a Wavelength Division Multiplexing(WDM) network. It combines the best of circuit switching and packet switching paradigms, but has better bandwidth utilization than OPS and faster switching time than OCS. In OBS, the transmission of each burst is preceded by the transmission of a burst control packet(BCP), which occurs on a separate channel. Therefore, O/E/O conversions are only required on control channels.

Previous researchers proposed node architectures with FT-TR(Fixed Transmitter-Tunable Receiver) [3] or TT-FR(Tunable Transmitter-Fixed Receiver) [5]. In [3], nodes can transmit without worrying about channel collisions since no other node can transmit with the same wavelength. However, there's a waste of bandwidth because bursts that maybe discarded are transmitted. In [5], receivers would be more leisurely and it's a waste of receiver resource as a node can only transmit one burst each time.

To overcome the drawbacks of FT-TR and TT-FR, we proposed the node architecture based on TT-TR (Tunable Transmitter-Tunable Receiver), which is scalable and flexible as all nodes can use all channels. However, these are at the expense of higher

---

[*] Correspondance author.

resource contention opportunity. To minimize the drawbacks and use the TT-TR architecture optimally, appropriate medium access control (MAC) protocols are required. With such purpose, we elaborate on MAC protocols based on multi-token.

The rest of this paper is organized as follows. Section 2 presents architectures of the OBS ring network and the OBS node. Section 3 describes the proposed MAC protocols. The performance evaluation of our MAC protocols and the effect of various burst sizes on our MAC protocols are investigated by simulation in section 4. Finally, Section 5 provides some concluding remarks.

2   OBS Ring Network and TT-TR Node Architecture

We design a unidirectional ring network consisting of N OBS nodes as shown in Figure 1. Each node acts as a source node(insert and send bursts), as an intermediate node(pass through bursts) and as a destination node(receive bursts).

Figure 2 shows the TT-TR based node architecture. Each node can access all wavelengths and has two kinds of FIFO queue: transmission queue and Token queue. Transmission queues consist of N VOQ(Virtual Output Queue). Bursts arriving at each node are firstly buffered to their VOQ according to their destination. As nodes may own multi-token simultaneously, Token queue is also needed to serve Tokens in their arrival order and each Token corresponds to each wavelength. Each fiber supports $W+1$ channels, one control channel and W data channels. Correspondingly, W Tokens are used for the W data channels. Nodes can access the i-th wavelength if and only if it captures the i-th Token. Except BCP format in the general OBS network, another control format called Token is involved to imply the current available wavelength. Both of them are transmitted through the control channel.

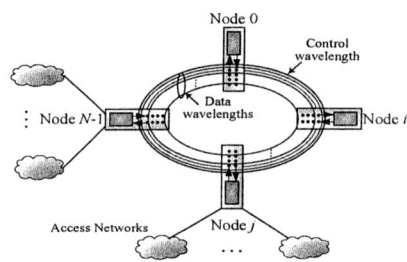
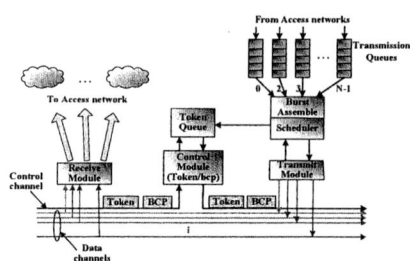

Fig. 1. OBS ring network   **Fig. 2.** Node architecture based on TT-TR

3   Design of Medium Access Control(MAC) Protocol

Several variants occur when calculating offset time. Xu et al.[3] investigated MAC protocols using JET(Just Enough Time) and ODD(Only Destination Delay) schemes. We propose MAC protocols based on JET scheme in this paper.

As the accessibility of each wavelength is limited by Token, the token release time or token rotation time(TRT) is crucial to our protocols. Therefore, CA(Collision

Avoidance) and IR(Immediately Release) protocols are proposed, differentiated by the token release time. Both of them consist of two algorithms described as follows.

3.1 CA Based MAC Protocol

In CA based protocol, Tokens are released after completing each burst transmission.

3.1.1 CA/T_RR(Token_Only with Round_Robin)

CA/T_RR protocol uses multiple Tokens and serves transmission queues in a Round Robin manner. At the transmitter side, if node i captures an available Token, it firstly checks whether the transmission queue j selected by RR is eligible. If yes, node i gets a packet out, generates and sends BCP; then transmits the burst after offset time; finally it releases the Token. If no, node i releases Token to the downstream node directly. At the receiver side, node j receives and reads BCP; then tunes to wavelength i to receive the coming burst. However, the collision may occur when other bursts arrive at node j through other wavelengths simultaneously.

3.1.2 CA/PARC (Previous Avoidance of Receiver Collision)

CA/PARC protocol is used to reduce receiver collision previously in the source node. Each node maintains a CIT(Channel Information Table) recording the reservation information of each wavelength. If node intends to send a burst selected by RR, firstly checks its destination; then determines if there exist bursts reserved on other wavelengths forwarding for the same destination via CIT. If such bursts exist and the current reserved burst overlaps with them in time, reservation fails and releases Token directly. If such bursts don't exist or exist but not overlap with the current burst, resource reservation for burst succeeds and node processes the burst transmission. Nevertheless, CA/PARC protocol isn't completely 'receiver collision free', because the current node doesn't know the reservation information in other nodes, but it reduces the burst loss to some significant extent compared to CA/T_RR protocol.

3.2 IR Based MAC protocol

In CA protocol, Tokens are released after completing burst transmission, so it is predicted to present poor resource utilization. Therefore, IR protocol is proposed to guarantee the resource utilization and reuse. In IR protocol, tokens are released immediately after completing BCP transmission, i.e., offset time earlier than bursts.

3.2.1 IR/T_RR

The processing is similar to that of CA/T_RR protocol, except for the difference in token release time. As Tokens are released immediately after BCP and earlier than bursts, wavelength contention is likely to occur when bursts from upstream node overlap with the bursts being transmitted in the current node. Figure 3 and Figure 4 shows such contention for wavelength. When Token i arrives at Node j after BCP1, Node j starts to reserve resources for Burst2 on Wi. After offset1 time, Burst1 will pass Node j through Wi, meanwhile, Node j intends to send Burst2 through the same Wi after offset2 time. As shown in Figure 8, Burst1 and Burst2 will content for Wi leading to burst loss. To avoid this, each node reads the reservation information in CIT before sending a burst. If the outgoing burst overlaps with the cutting-through burst, reservation fails and the node releases Token directly; otherwise, reservation succeeds, the node generates and sends BCP; adds the reservation information to its own CIT and updates it; then release Token; finally, it transmits the burst.

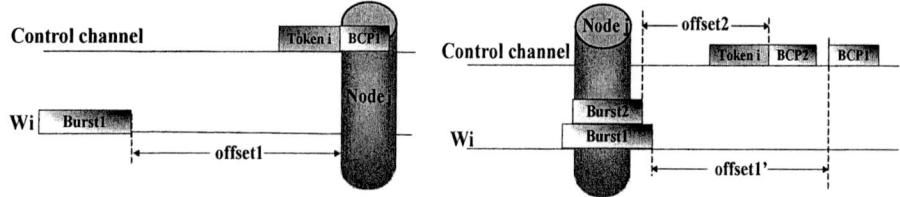

Fig. 3. Before token arrives   **Fig. 4.** After token arrives

3.2.2 IR/PARC

IR/PARC protocol is used to reduce the receiver collision in IR/T_RR protocol. The process is also similar to CA/PARC protocol, except that each node should read the CIT twice before transmitting a burst to reduce both the wavelength contention and the receiver collision. Node firstly reads reservation information of the current data channel in CIT to avoid the wavelength contention in a source node; then reads the reservation information of all data channels to reduce receiver collision in destination.

4 Simulation and Results

We simulated an OBS ring network with 12 nodes and each node is separated by 5km. The number of wavelengths per fiber is set to 5 and each runs at 1Gbps. The average burst size is 10^5 bits(100μs). Packets are generated by exponential distribution.

Figure 5 shows the average packet delay versus offered load. The performance for CA is much higher than that of IR. Due to the long token rotate time(TRT) in CA, packets are buffered and wait Tokens for a long time. The performance of the PARC scheme is higher than T_RR scheme for both CA and IR protocol. This is because the delay in CIT for avoiding wavelength contention and receiver collision. Figure 6 shows the channel utilization. IR/PARC protocol exhibits the best performance, followed by IR/T_RR, CA/PARC and CA/T_RR. In IR, packets have more opportunities to be transmitted, thus it presents a better performance. The performance for CA protocol is limited to less than 50% and increases slightly due to the long average TRT. As offered load increases packets are generated faster than Tokens rotate, meaning that network traffic intensity is saturated. After the saturated point, even if many more packets are generated, they're buffered to wait for Tokens. As a result, the number of transmitted packets increases slightly when offered load continuously increases, leading to a slight increase in channel utilization. Figure 7 shows the Burst loss rate. The behavior for CA is unexpectedly higher than that of IR firstly and than becomes lower. Even with the light offered load, the TRT for CA protocol is large enough to saturate network traffic. Thus, once node j transmits a burst, it waits a long time to use the same wavelength again. During this long period, node j only uses the rest 3 data channels in fact, increasing the traffic intensity for the 3 channels as well as the collision and burst loss probability.

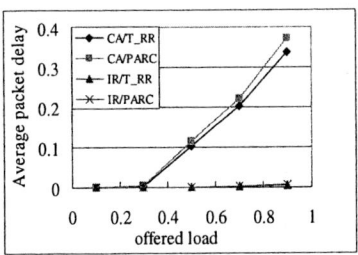

Fig. 5. Average packet delay

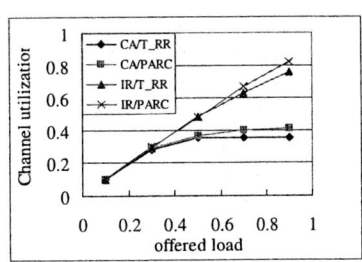

Fig. 6. Channel utilization

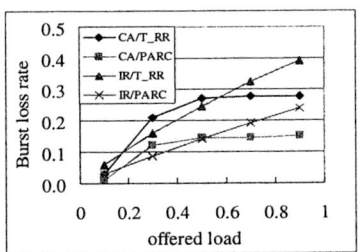

Fig. 7. Burst loss rate

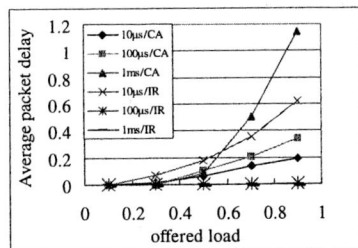

Fig. 8. Average packet delay

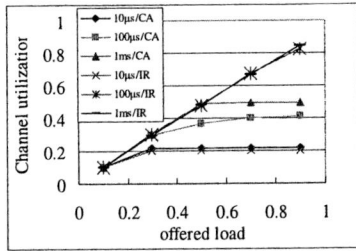

Fig. 9. Channel utilization

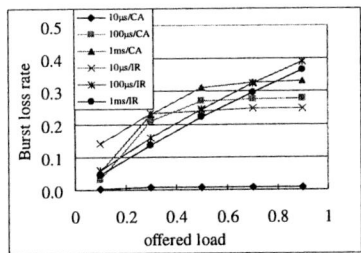

Fig. 10. Burst loss rate

Finally, we investigate the effect of various burst sizes ranging from 10^4 bits(10μs) to 10^6 bits(1ms). The average packet delay increases with the packet size for CA and the behavior reverses for IR(Figure 8). Specifically, because the average TRT for CA protocol increases dynamically when increases burst size, bursts would be queued to wait an even longer time for Tokens. Figure 9 and Figure 10 present the channel utilization and the burst loss rate. Channel utilization performs better for larger bursts in both CA and IR protocol. However, it's at the cost of longer packet delay and higher burst loss rate shown in Figure 8 and Figure 10. The behavior indicates that the burst loss rate performance is affected by both the burst size or traffic intensity.

5 Conclusion

In this paper, multi-token based MAC protocols were proposed for OBS ring network with TT-TR node architecture. We designed CA and IR protocols to use the limited resource in TT_TR architecture efficiently. Each of them includes two variants called T_RR scheme and PARC scheme. Performances of the four protocols are evaluated by OPNET simulation. IR protocol performs better than CA protocol for both T_RR and PARC, and PARC seems to be better than T_RR. In addition, the variety of burst sizes was evaluated by simulation and was proved to influence our MAC protocols. IR protocol prefers larger bursts while the performance for CA will be seriously delayed in the case of a large burst. As a result, it is important to determine an appropriate burst size for a network. Otherwise, the performance may suffer from delays, inefficiency, or undesirable burst loss.

Acknowledgments

This work was supported in part by the Korea Science and Engineering Foundation (KOSEF) through OIRC project and IITA.

References

1. C. Qiao, M. Yoo, "Optical burst switching (OBS) - a new paradigm for an Optical Internet," J. High Speed Network (JHSN), vol. 8, no. 1, pp. 69-84, 1999
2. Y. Chen, C. Qiao, X. Yu, "Optical burst switching: A new area in optical networking research", IEEE Network, 18(3), pp. 16-23, May/June 2004
3. Lisong Xu et al., "A simulation Study of Optical Burst Switching Access Protocols for WDM Ring Network", Computer Networks, 41(2), Jan. 2003
4. B. C. Kim, You-Ze Cho, Dong Mongomery., "An Efficient Optical Technique for Multi-Hop", IEICE TRANS. COMMUN., vol. E87-B, no. 6, Jun. 2004
5. Y. Arakawa, N. Yamanaka, I. Sasase, "Performance of Optical Burst Switched WDM Ring network with TTFR System", The first IFIP Optical Networks & Technologies Conference 2004 (OpNeTec2004), Pisa, Italy, pp. 95-102, October, 2004
6. I. Baldine, G. N. Rouskas, H. G. Perros, D. Stevenson., "Jumpstart: A just-in-time Signaling Architecture for WDM Burst-switched Networks", IEEE Communication, 40(2):82-89, Feb. 2002
7. L. Xu, H. G. Perros, G. N. Rouskas, "Techniques for optical packet switching and optical burst switching", IEEE Communication, 39(1):136-142, Jan. 2001.

Self-stabilizing Energy-Aware Routing Algorithm in Wireless Sensor Network with Limited Mobility

Smruti Padhy and Diganta Goswami

Indian Institute of Technology, Guwahati,
North Guwahati - 781039, India

Abstract. Application of sensor networks in different fields is an interesting area to work with and has already drawn widespread attention. Since sensors have limited supply of on-board energy, efficient management of network is a compulsion in extending life of the sensor. At the same time, frequent damage to sensors and link failure occur because of the adverse environment in which they are deployed. A sensor network has to tolerate and recover from these failures themselves with no external help. In this respect, we have designed a self-stabilizing energy-aware routing protocol in a sensor network. Our protocol ensures the sensor network, starting from an arbitrary state, eventually set up reliable communication in network with minimum energy consumption and in a finite number of steps.

1 Introduction

Explosive growth in research in miniaturization and low-power design has been observed in the last few years leading to large-scale highly distributed systems of wireless unattended sensors. One of the major problems with sensors in such situations are that they are energy-constrained and their batteries can not be recharged. Therefore, designing energy-aware algorithms becomes an important factor for extending the lifetime of sensors. On the other hand, in such sensor network applications, both sensors and sensor network infrastructure are prone to various kinds of failures. Despite these, a sensor network should ensure a certain level of reliability and must function correctly to achieve its mission. In this respect, we design a routing protocol which is energy-aware and tolerant to transient node/link failure by using a technique called self-stabilization [1]. Being self-stabilizing guarantees that the system will converge to the intended behavior in finite time regardless of the system starting state (initial state of the sensor nodes and the initial messages on the link) without the help of any external agents. Some basic concepts and overview of the technique *self-stabilization* are given in in [2], [3], [4] and [5] and a survey on wireless sensor networks and existing routing protocols for sensor networks can be found in [6].

Only a small number of self-stabilizing routing protocols for the wireless sensor network has been proposed till date. One such protocol is based on directed diffusion method [7] [8]. A request for data from an initiator node is broadcast in the network, and the positive answers from the sensors are forwarded back to the initiator (following a Shortest-Path-Tree (SPT) construction rooted at the initiator). The sensor nodes, starting from an arbitrary state and following this protocol, establish reliable communication in the network in a finite number of steps. A self-stabilizing routing protocol called Logical Grid Routing Protocol (LGRP) which was used in the project *A line in the Sand* was proposed by Arora et al. in [9]. LGRP uses the localization or neighborhood detection service to determine a set of reliable nearby neighbors called as the logical neighbors. The root node periodically transmits beacons in order to construct and maintain a routing tree. The logical neighbors of the root receive these beacons and set the root to be their parent. These one-hop neighbors of the root then start propagating their own beacons. Upon receiving a beacon from a logical neighbor, a node selects it as its parent if it is a closer to the root. In case a node does not receive any beacons from any such neighbors, a node selects a neighbor which is farther from the root as its parent. LGRP is self-stabilizing and can tolerate node fail-stops. But neither of these two works take into account the energy-awareness.

2 System Model

In the system architecture, which is taken from [10], sensor nodes are grouped into clusters controlled by a single command node. Sensors are only capable of radio-based short-haul communication and are responsible for probing the environment to detect a target/event. Every cluster has a gateway node that manages sensors in the cluster. Here the gateway nodes are assumed to have a mobilizer and thus have the capability to move. We also assume that the sensor nodes are stationary and all the sensor nodes are located within the communication range of the gateway in a cluster. Clustering the sensor network is performed by the command node. The command node will inform each gateway node of the ID and location of sensors allocated to the cluster. Sensors receive commands from and send readings to the gateway node which processes these readings.

Gateway nodes are assumed to be less-energy constrained than the sensors and interface the command node with the sensor network via long-haul communication link. The gateway node sends to the command node reports generated through fusion of sensor readings. The command node performs system-level fusion of collected reports for an overall situation awareness. The sensor is assumed to be capable of operating in an active mode or a low-power stand-by mode. It is also assumed that a sensor can act as a relay to forward data from another sensor. The on-board clocks of both the sensors and gateways are assumed to be synchronized, e.g. via the use of GPS.

Sensor networks are subject to a wide variety of faults and unreliability. Inexpensive hardware, limited resources and extreme environment conditions all contribute to causing these fault. Here we assume that when the system is in operation, any number of communication links or sensor nodes may fail for some time and then may again come up after some time.

3 The Proposed Protocol

In the following subsections we give the description of the protocol and the data structures used and then present the algorithm.

3.1 Protocol Description

The gateway node of a cluster receives command from the command node to send the data. The sensing-enabled node is in the direct transmission range of the gateway. So, the gateway directly sends a REQUEST message to the sensing-enabled node to sense the environment and send the data. The node senses the environment and sends the DATA to its neighbor in the path specified by the gateway to relay it further to reach the gateway in specified time. So, a communication path is set up from sensing-enabled node to the gateway for the data. This is the correct behavior of our system when the gateway is not moving.

Now, if the gateway moves to a new position within its own cluster, the path from the sensing-enabled node to the newly positioned gateway is divided into two sub-paths. The first sub-path (named as sub-path 1) constitutes the path from sensing-enabled node to one hop neighbor of the old position of the gateway, (call it as *prev_one_hop_neigh*). The second sub-path (named as sub-path 2) constitutes the path from *prev_one_hop_neigh* to the newly positioned gateway. When the gateway moves to a new position it sends an UPDATE message to *prev_one_hop_neighs*. All the data which are in its path to old position of the gateway are then forwarded to new positioned gateway. When all such data reaches the gateway, fresh paths are set up for the same request. So, a communication path is established between sensing enabled node and the new position gateway. This is the correct behavior when the gateway has made some movements.

Suppose at some point of time, the gateway doesn't receive the data in a specified time and the gateway is stationary. Then the gateway knows either some sensors have failed in the path or there is some communication link failure. To get the data, the gateway node try to establish communication with the sensor by again sending a REQUEST message to the sensor. At the same time the gateway constructs a subset from the neighbors of the sensor on the basis of available energy. The sensors having more available energy are selected in the subset. The gateway sends an ENQUIRY message to this subset to enquire about the status of the originating data. Two situations may arise – link failure and node failure.

If there is a link failure in the path from the sensing-enabled node to the gateway, the sensing-enabled node will send the DATA to the subset of its neighbor in response to their ENQUIRY message. The neighbors forward this DATA to the gateway in the path specified by the gateway. The gateway will get more than one copy of DATA. It accepts the DATA which reaches first. The sensor piggybacks its updated energy-level into DATA message as it forwards the message. The gateway updates the energy-level of each sensor in its local memory and updates its routing table. It finds the least cost path to the sensor for future use.

If a sensing-enabled node fails, then the subset of neighbors of the failed node will not able to contact the sensor. On timeout, a neighbor which wants to take the role of the failed sensor sends a message to the gateway with a *role-bit* set. The gateway then selects a neighbor to the failed sensor in the least cost path and sends a REQUEST message to it to sense and send the DATA.

Suppose at some point of time, the gateway moves to a new position within the cluster and the gateway doesn't receive some data in its new position. Then there are two possibilities : there may be node/link failures in sub-path 1 or in sub-path 2.

- node/link failure in sub-path 1: If the data has not reached at previous one hop neighbors, then there is node/link failure in sub-path 1. After a specified timeout, gateway sends fresh request with fresh path to sensing-enabled nodes and its subset of its neighbors as in stationary case.
- node/link failure in sub-path 2: If there is node/link failure in sub-path 2 and data has reached *prev_one_hop_neigh*, then it is forwarded to new positioned gateway through alternative paths specified by the gateway in response to the ENQUIRY message to *prev_one_hop_neighs* and subset of its neighbors.

In both the above situations, the communication path is set up and the system is brought back to normal operation.

When the gateway moves along the boundary, it is forced to come inside the cluster to its previous position inside the cluster. During this transition, the data is stored in the input buffer of the previous one hop neighbors till the gateway reaches its previous position. Then, the data is forwarded towards the gateway. Again, the system behaves correctly.

For gateway to set up the least cost path between the gateway and sensors, we first assume that the gateway and sensors are connected by bi-directional wireless links with a cost associated with each direction. Each link may have a different cost for each direction due to different energy levels of the nodes at each end. The cost of a path between two nodes is defined as the sum of the costs of the links traversed. The routing algorithm can find the shortest-path from the gateway to the sensor and then using the transpose property. To account for energy conservation, delay optimization and other performance metrics, we use the cost function for a link as defined in [10].

3.2 Data Structures and Functions Used

Each sensor node has a unique local ID, LID_v, and knows only its direct neighbors, so it can distinguish among its adjacent wireless links. Each sensor node maintains several variables of different types. The underlying layer of topological maintenance protocol computes the variables N_v (the set of neighbors of v) and *current_time* (the current time). S_v denotes a subset of N_v. The gateway node selects S_v depending on the energy available at each of the sensors. Other variables are listed below:

- *inp_buf*: Each node contains a local memory to store the request messages.
- *sensed*: It is set to *true* by the sensing unit whenever new data is collected.
- *SU*: the sensing unit data structure which contains the complete collected data, and it has the following fields: *attr* (name of the attribute), *value*

(value of the attribute detected by the sensing unit) and *other* (other fields depending on the type of the sensor which enhance the description of the sensed fact or phenomena). The sensing unit sets the Boolean variable *sensed* to *true* whenever new data is collected and stores in the data structure *SU*. Later on, the algorithm processes the data and sets the variable *sensed* back to *false*.
- *wait_msg*: It is set to *true* when a neighbor waits for a data from data originating sensor.

The gateway node has three variables:

- *thru_nbr*: Sets to *true* when a message is forwarded through neighbors due to link failure.
- *role_nbr*: Sets to *true* when a neighbor takes up a role.
- *once_send*: Sets to *true* when gateway node sends message to a node for the first time.
- *mobilized*: The location finding system sets it to *true* when the gateway moves to a new position. It is set to *false* when the gateway is not moving.

The following types of messages (fields are shown along with) are used by our protocol:

- DATA: *src_id, relay_id, dest_id, attr, value, time, expire, path, role-bit*.
- REQUEST: *org_id, relay_id, attr, value, time, expire, path*.
- ENQUIRY: *org_id, relay_id, attr, value, time, expire, path, mobile-bit*.
- UPDATE: *id, new_position, forward_bit*.

The roles of each of the fields are indicated below.

- *src_id*: sender's local id.
- *org_id*: sensor id where the data is originating.
- *relay_id*: relay sensor's local id.
- *dest_id*: destination sensor local id.
- *attr*: name of the attribute.
- *value*: value of the attribute.
- *time*: time when the data was sent.
- *expire*: interval for which the data is valid.
- *path*: path of the data.
- *role-bit*: It is set to 1 when a neighbor wants to take up the role of a failed sensor.
- *mobile_bit*: It is set to 1 when the gateway moves to a new position and enquires to its previous one hop neighbors about the data which is not received.
- *id*: sensor's local id.
- *new_position*: new position of the gateway.
- *forward_bit*: It is set to 1 when the gateway has moved to a new position and the previous one hop neighbors need to forward the data destined for new positioned gateway. It is set to 0 when the gateway in new position receives data destined for it.

The algorithm uses the following functions:

data_expiry(msg): checks for data msg expiry, return true if expired.
request_expiry(): checks for the validity of a request message in the input buffer. If it has expired, then returns true.
exist(msg): checks whether the REQUEST msg exists in the input buffer. If exists, then returns true.
wait(): The sensor has to wait for specified time for the gateway to come its previous position.

3.3 Self-stabilizing Energy-Aware Routing Algorithm(SSEA)

The energy-aware self-stabilizing algorithm for sensor network is presented below.

Predicates
$On\_limit \equiv \forall i(Th \leq energy_i \leq Max\_value)$
$wrong\_time \equiv inp\_buf[i].time > current\_time$
$wrong\_neigh \equiv \neg(inp\_buf[i].dest\_id \in N_{relay\_id})$
$move\_limit \equiv (0 \leq move \leq max\_mov)$

The algorithm executed by a gateway node

[0.01] $\neg On\_limit \longrightarrow$ remove the entry of sensor from the routing table.
[0.02] $On\_limit \land \neg mov\_limit \longrightarrow$ Gateway is forced to stay within the cluster by moving to its previous position.
[0.1] On receive command from the command node $\longrightarrow$
    send REQUEST(msg) to sensor, say, v
    once_send=true; thru_nbr = false; role_nbr = false
[0.2] rcv DATA(msg) from sensor $v \longrightarrow$ if $\neg(data\_expiry(msg))$ then
    Do the processing according to the mission
[0.3] $timeout_1 \land \neg$ rcv DATA (msg) $\land$(thru_nbr== *false*) $\land$ (role_nbr== *false*)$\land$(mobilized ==*false*) $\longrightarrow$ Construct the subset of neighbors S_v
    send REQUEST(msg) to $v \land \forall \in S_v$ send ENQUIRY (msg) to u
[0.4] rcv DATA(msg) from u$\in S_v$ with role_bit not set to 1 $\land$ (mobilized == *false*)$\longrightarrow$ update the energy level of sensors in the path in its routing table
    find the least-cost path and the neighbor of v in that path
    thru_nbr= true
[0.5] rcv DATA(msg) from u$\in S_v$ with role_bit set to 1 $\land timeout_2 \land$(mobilized ==*false*) $\longrightarrow$ update the nodes energy level
    find the least-cost path
    if thru_nbr then DISCARD msg
    else the role of v is assigned to its neighbor in the least cost path
    role_nbr = true
[0.6] once_send $\land$ thru_nbr $\land$(mobilized ==*false*) $\longrightarrow$ send ENQUIRY(msg) to u
[0.7] once_send $\land$ role_nbr$\land$(mobilized ==*false*) $\longrightarrow$ send REQUEST(msg) to u

[0.8] (When the gateway moves to a new position within the cluster)
$\wedge$(mobilized $==true$) $\longrightarrow$ send UPDATE(new_position, path) to prev_one_hop sensors of the gateway.
[0.9] rcv DATA(msg) from prev_one_hop $\wedge$(mobilized $==true$)$\longrightarrow$ check for data_expiry() and process data as per mission.
[0.10] $timeout_3 \wedge \neg$rcv DATA(msg) from v $\wedge$(mobilized $==true$) $\longrightarrow$ send ENQUIRY(msg) to (prev_one_hop $\cup$ subset of its neighbors)
[0.11] $timeout_4 \wedge \neg$rcv DATA(msg) from prev_one_hop$\wedge$(mobilized $==true$) $\longrightarrow$ send ENQUIRY(msg) to subset of v
  send REQUEST(msg) to v with fresh path to new_positioned gateway
[0.12]once_send $\wedge$(thru_nbr $\vee$ role_nbr)$\wedge$(mobilized $==true$) $\longrightarrow$ send REQUEST(msg) to v with fresh path
[0.13]$timeout_5 \wedge$(mobilized $==true$) $\longrightarrow$ set mobilized = false
  send REQUEST(msg) with fresh path to sensors whose data are not received when the gateway moved to a new position.
  send UPDATE(forward_bit=0) TO prev_one_hop

Each of the sensor nodes execute the following code
[1.01] $\neg On\_limit \longrightarrow$ Switch yourself off
[1.02] On_limit $\wedge$ wrong_time $\longrightarrow$ delete inp_buf[i]
[1.03] On_limit $\wedge$ wrong_neigh $\longrightarrow$ delete inp_buf[i]
[1.1] rcv REQUEST(msg) from Gateway $\longrightarrow$
if(($msg.org\_id == LID_v$) $\wedge$ ($msg.dest\_id \epsilon N_{relay\_id}$) $\wedge$ ($msg.time < current\_time$) $\wedge$ ($msg.time + msg.expire > current\_time$)) then
  when(sensed$==true$) send DATA(msg) to nbr in the path
  if exist(msg) then update the path and time field in inp_buf[i]
  else add to inp_buf the msg
  sensed=$false$
  else DISCARD msg
[1.2] rcv DATA(msg) from nbr $\longrightarrow$
  if (msg.relay_id $== LID_v$)$\wedge \neg$ data_expiry()then
    if(msg.dest_id==gateway_id)$\wedge$(msg.dest_id $\notin N_{relay\_id}$)
    add the DATA to inp_buf
      if(forward_bit==1) send DATA (msg) to nbr in the path specified by new_positioned gateway else wait()
    if(msg.dest_id $\in N_{relay\_id}$) send DATA(msg) to msg.dest_id in the path
       if (wait_msg) then wait_msg=false else DISCARD msg
[1.3] $timeout_3 \wedge sensed \longrightarrow$ if ($\neg$request_expiry())
       send DATA to nbr in the path specified previously.
       sensed=false
       else DISCARD msg
[1.4] rcv ENQUIRY(msg) from Gateway with mobile_bit set to 0 $\longrightarrow$
  if((msg.org_id $\in N_{relay\_id}$) $\wedge$ (msg.relay_id $== LID_v$)$\wedge$ (msg.time $< current\_time$) $\wedge$ (msg.time+msg.expire $> current\_time$)) then
    send REQUEST(msg) to msg.org_id

wait_msg=true
else DISCARD msg

[1.5] wait_msg ∧ $timeout_4$ ⟶ role_bit=1
when(sensed=$true$) send DATA(msg) to nbr in the path

[1.6] rcv REQUEST(msg) from nbr ⟶ if ((msg.org_id==LID_v)∧ (msg.time < current_time) ∧ (msg.time + msg.expire> current_time)) then
send DATA(msg) to nbr
send DATA(msg) to nbr in the previous path

[1.7] rcv UPDATE(new_position) from the gateway ⟶
if(msg.id== LID_v)
if(any data in inp_buf to be forwarded to the gateway)
send DATA(msg) to nbr in the path towards
new_positioned gateway
set forward_bit=1

[1.8] rcv UPDATE(forward_bit=0) from the gateway ⟶
if(msg.id == LID_v) then set forward_bit=0

[1.9] rcv ENQUIRY(msg) from the Gateway with mobile_bit set to 1 ⟶
if((msg.org_id== LID_v)∧(msg.relay_id ∈ N_{org_id})∧ (msg.time < current_time) ∧ (msg.time+msg.expire > current_time)) then
if exist(DATA) then send DATA in the path specified to msg.relay_id
else if(msg.relay_id == LID_v)∧ (msg.relay_id ∈ N_{org_id})∧ (msg.time < current_time) ∧ (msg.time+msg.expire > current_time)) then
send ENQUIRY(msg) to org_id else DISCARD msg

[1.10] rcv ENQUIRY(msg) from nbr ⟶ if ((msg.org_id == LID_v) ∧ (msg.time < current_time) ∧ (msg.time+msg.expire > current_time)) then if exist(DATA)
send DATA(msg) to msg.relay_id in the specified path.

4 Proof of Correctness

We define the state predicate $L = L_1 \wedge L_2 \wedge L_3 \wedge L_4 \wedge L_5$ as the invariant for all legitimate states, where
L_1=On_limit
L_2=On_limit ∧¬wrong_time
L_3=On_limit ∧¬wrong_neigh
L_4=On_limit ∧ mov_limit
L_5=A communication path is eventually set from the source node to the Gateway

To prove *self-stabilization*, in Theorem 1 we show that starting from an arbitrary configuration, every computation of SSEA reaches a state in which L holds within a finite amount of time.

Property 1. Starting from any state, in any execution of SSEA, the guard 1.01 is enabled at most once and 0.01 is enabled at most the number of sensors in the cluster.

Proof. When the sensor's energy is below the threshold level, it will not be able to transmit data. If it remains turn on, then other sensors may continue to send data to it for relaying, thereby spending extra energy. Thus, such sensor should be switched off. Once it is switched off, it will never be alive again. So, guard[1.01] is enabled at most once. If any sensor in the relay path gets switched off, then alternate paths are selected between the sensing-enabled node and the gateway. If any sensing-enabled node runs out of energy, then the task of that node is assigned to another sensor (guard[0.5] is enabled and executed). So, the system remains in the legitimate state. When sensor's energy becomes below the threshold level, the gateway will remove the entry of that particular sensor from the routing table. Thus, the guard[0.01] is enabled at most the number of sensors in the cluster. The moment at which the number of sensors in the cluster falls below a certain number, the underlying layer's topological maintenance protocol will do re-organization so that the system will have optimal number of sensors. Thus, the system again goes to legitimate state.

Lemma 1. *The item On_limit is a closed attractor for the predicate L and is an invariant for all legitimate states.*

Proof. It follows directly from property 1.

Property 2. Starting from any state, in any execution of the SSEA, the guard 1.02 is enabled as many times as number of spurious message in the input buffer.

Proof. When the sensor's energy is above the threshold, it is alive and can send and receive messages. If there is any message in the input buffer with wrong time stamp (i.e, inp_buf[i].time > current_time), then the sensor executes the guard[1.02] and deletes the message from the input buffer. So, the guard[1.02] is executed as many times as number of messages with wrong time stamp.

Whenever a REQUEST/ENQUIRY message is received from the gateway (guard[1.1], [1.4], [1.9]) or a REQUEST message is received from a neighbor (guard[1.6]) or an ENQUIRY message from a neighbor (guard[1.10]), the timestamp of the message is checked. If message time is greater than the current time, the message is corrupted and it is discarded. In this case, the guards [1.1], [1.4], [1.6], [1.9] and [1.10] takes care of any wrong timestamp and the guard[1.02] is not enabled.

Lemma 2. *The item $\{\forall\ i,\ On\_limit \wedge \neg wrong\_time\}$ is a closed attractor for predicate L and an invariant for all legitimate state.*

Proof. It follows directly from property 2.

Property 3. Starting from any state, as long as there is no node/link crashes in the immediate neighborhood of a sensor, in any execution of the SSEA, the guard[1.03] is enabled at most the number of corrupt) messages (i.e, with wrong neighbor) in the input buffer. If c crashes have occurred in the immediate neighborhood, then the guard[1.03] is enabled at most once.

Proof. No crash: In any execution of SSEA, with On_limit true, no messages with wrong time stamp, and the gateway is not moving and there is no crash, each sensor checks its input buffer for any message with wrong neighbor. If there is any such message, guard[1.03] is enabled. The guard is eventually executed and the corrupt message is deleted from the input buffer. Thus, the guard[1.03] is enabled at most the number of messages with wrong neighbor in the input buffer. So, the gateway can send a REQUEST to sensor without fail by rightly specifying the path to the sensor. If the gateway moves to a new position with no crash in the immediate neighborhood of a sensor, then the previous one hop to the gateway successfully forwards the data to the new positioned gateway. Here, the guard[1.03] is not enabled.

c crashes: When a REQUEST message is received from the gateway, it is checked for any wrongly specified neighbor to sensing-enabled node. If there is any such specification, the message is discarded. Otherwise, the data is sent to the gateway node through the path specified by the gateway and the REQUEST is stored for valid period in the input buffer (guard[1.1]). The sensing-enabled node sends the data at regular interval towards the gateway in the path specified by the gateway in response to a valid REQUEST guard[1.3]. If c crashes occur in the immediate neighborhood of the sensing-enabled node with gateway in its original position and the gateway has specified a crashed node/link in the path, then the guard[1.03] is enabled and the REQUEST message is deleted from the input buffer. Then guards [0.3], [0.4], [0.5] may get enabled. The data is sent in different path and the task of the sensing enabled node is assigned to another.

When a data is received from a neighbor to further forward it, it is checked for wrong neighbor. If it found to have wrong neighbor, discard the message (guard[1.2] is enabled and executed). Otherwise, data is successfully forwarded to its neighbor as specified in the path. Similarly, when an ENQUIRY message is received with mobilized equals to false, it is checked whether sensing-enabled node is in the neighborhood of it. If not, then the message is discarded (guard[1.4]).

If c crashes occur in the immediate neighborhood of the sensing enabled node with gateway moving to a new position, then wrong neighbor is checked at previous one hop neighbor sensor. If there is any such neighbor, the message is discarded and the data is sent through alternate path from the previous one hop neighbor to new positioned gateway (guards[1.9] and [1.10] may get enabled). If there are crashes between sensing-enabled node and the old position of the gateway, the message with wrong neighbor is discarded and fresh route is set up (guard[0.11] may get enabled). In all these situations, the guard[1.03] is not enabled.

So, the guard [1.03] is enabled at most once when the sensor is sending data to a previous valid request and the immediate neighbor in the path crashes. In rest situations, guards [1.2], [1.4], [1.6], [1.9], [1.10] and [1.10] take care of any crash in the path.

Lemma 3. *The item* $\{On\_limit \wedge \neg\ wrong\_neigh\}$ *is a closed attractor for predicate L and an invariant for all legitimate state.*

Proof. It follows directly from property 3.

Property 4. Starting from any state, as long as the gateway makes movement within the cluster, in any execution of the SSEA, the guard[0.02] is not enabled. If the gateway makes movement c times along the boundary, then the guard [0.02] is enabled c times.

Proof. Gateway's movement within the cluster: When the gateway moves within the cluster, the gateway's movement is within the limit, i.e, move_limit is true. So, the guard[0.02] is not enabled. The location finding system of the gateway detects its movement. Then, the gateway sends its new position in the UPDATE message to previous one hop sensors to forward the data which are in its path towards the old positioned gateway(guard[0.8] is enabled and executed). When the data, which were in the path, reaches previous one hop sensors, they are forwarded to new positioned gateway (guard[1.2] gets enabled and executed). So, the gateway is able to receive all its data within a finite time in its new position. So, the system remains in the legitimate state.

Gateway's movement along the boundary: When the gateway makes any movement along the boundary of the cluster, then guard[0.02] is enabled. The guard is eventually executed and the gateway is forced to move to its previous position. If the gateway moves c times along the boundary of the cluster, it is forced to move to its previous position until it reaches a position within the cluster. So, the guard[0.02] is enabled c times. After the guard[0.02] is executed c times, the gateway is within the cluster. If there is any data in the input buffer of the previous one hop neighbor sensors of the previous position of the gateway, it remains there for some specified time period till the gateway reaches its previous position. After that time period, the data is sent to the gateway (guard [1.2] is enabled and executed). So the system goes to legitimate state.

Lemma 4. *The item On_limit $\wedge$ move_limit is a closed attractor for predicate L and an invariant for all legitimate states.*

Proof. It follows directly from property 4.

Theorem 1. *Starting from any arbitrary state, every computation of SSEA reaches a state in which L holds within a constant amount of time. In other words, starting from arbitrary state, a communication path is eventually set up between sensors and the gateway in a cluster in a finite amount time.*

Proof. It follows directly from lemma 1, lemma 2, lemma 3 and lemma 4.

5 Conclusion

In this paper, we have incorporated fault-tolerance to energy-aware routing for wireless sensor networks by the use of a technique called self-stabilization. A gateway node acts as a cluster-based centralized network manager that sets routes for sensor data and monitors latency throughout the cluster. The gateway tracks energy usage at every sensor node and changes in the mission and the environment. The gateway configures the sensors and the network to operate efficiently in order to extend the life of the network. Here, we have assumed that all sensors are stationary and the gateways are mobile. If any node/link failure occurs, the gateway selects another least cost path which is energy efficient. No initialization of the system is required. Our self-stabilizing protocol guarantees that starting from an arbitrary state and in fine number of steps, reliable communication is built in the network based on energy-awareness.

References

1. E. Dijkstra, "Self-stabilizing systems in spite of distributed control," *Communications of the ACM*, vol. 17, no. 11, 1974.
2. M. Flatebo, A. Datta, and S. Ghosh, "Self-stabilization in distributed systems," *In Readings in Distributed Computing Systems,IEEE Computer Press*, 1994.
3. J. Brzezinksi and M. Szychowiak, "Self-stabilization in distributed system: A short survey," *Foundations of Computing and Decision Sciences*, vol. 25, no. 1, 2000.
4. S. Dolev, *Self-Stabilization*. MIT Press, March 2000.
5. M. Gouda and N. Multari, "Self-stabilizing communication protocols," *IEEE Transaction on Computers*, vol. 40, no. 4, pp. 448–458, 1991.
6. I. Akyildiz, W. Su, Y. Sankarasubramaniam, and E. Cayirci, "Wireless sensor networks: A survey," *Computer Networks*, vol. 38, pp. 393–422, March 2002.
7. D. Bein and A. Datta, "A self-stabilizing directed diffusion protocols for sensor networks," *in IEEE Proceedings of the 2004 International Conference on Parallel Processing Workshops(ICPPW04)*, 2004.
8. C. Intanagonwiwat, R. Govidan, and D. Estrin, "Directed diffusion: A scalable and robust communication paradigm for sensor networks," *in Proceedings of the 6th Annual ACM/IEEE International Conference on Mobile Computing and Networking(MobiCom00)*, August 2000.
9. A. Arora, P. Dutta, and et al, "A line in the sand," *Computer Networks*, vol. 46, pp. 605–634, December 2004.
10. M. Younis, M. Youssef, and K. Arisha, "Energy-aware management for cluster-based sensor networks," *Computer Networks*, vol. 43, 2003.

Position Based Gradient Routing in Mobile Ad Hoc Networks

Anand Praksh Ruhil[1,*], D.K. Lobiyal[2], and Ivan Stojmenovic[3]

[1] National Dairy Research Institute, Karnal (Hariyana), India
anandpruhil@yahoo.com
[2] School of Computer and Systems Sciences,
Jawaharlal Nehru University, New Delhi – 110067, India
dkl@mail.jnu.ac.in
[3] SITE, Iniversity of Ottawa, Ottawa, Ont K1N6N5, Canada
www.site.uottawa.ca/~ivan

Abstract. This paper presents a gradient routing algorithm a modified approach of DIR (compass routing) method to suit for mobile ad hoc network. It is a direction based localized algorithm where each node makes forwarding decisions solely based on the position of itself, its neighbors and destination. Source node selects a neighbor node to forward a message which is closest (having minimum gradient i.e. angle) towards the direction of destination. This algorithm makes use of the position information of nodes to improve the performance of routing protocols in mobile ad hoc network. The performance of gradient algorithms is compared with other directional routing algorithms LAR and DREAM in mobile environment using proactive approach. The experimental results show that gradient algorithm have higher success rate and lower flooding rate compared to LAR and DREAM

1 Introduction

Ad hoc network is a collection of self-organized nodes equipped with the facility of wireless communication to receive and transmit the message. There is no fixed infrastructure to route a message from source to destination. Therefore each node also works as a router, and cooperates in forwarding a message to the next hop for multi hop routing in ad hoc network. Ad hoc networks can be divided into two classes static and mobile. In static ad hoc network the nodes remain static after becoming the part of network. In mobile ad hoc network (MANET), nodes can move in any direction, the topology of network changes dynamically with frequent linkages formation and breakage. This makes multi-hop routing in ad hoc network a most challenging task.

A number of routing protocols have been proposed recently to achieve efficient routing in mobile ad hoc network. These protocols are placed into two categories - topology based protocols and position based protocols. The former uses information about the links in the network to forward a message and the latter uses information about the position of hosts in the network. A survey of position based routing algorithms is presented in [1-3].

In position based routing, the strategies for selection of next hop by a source node to forward packets towards the destination can be categorized as progress based,

---

[*] Corresponding author.

distance based and direction based forwarding [4]. In distance based strategies a packet is forwarded to a neighbor that has minimum distance towards destination. In progress-based strategy a message is forwarded to a neighbor that has best progress towards destination. In direction based strategy a message is forwarded to a neighbor that is closest to the direction of destination i.e. having minimum angle between the lines from source to node and line from source to destination. A variant of direction based forwarding strategy is restricted directional flooding. In this approach a message is forwarded to all neighbors in a zone (restricted area) in the direction of destination. For example location aided routing (LAR) [5] and Distance routing effect algorithm for mobility (DREAM) [6].

In this paper we present a direction based routing using the position of nodes to improve the efficiency of routing protocols in mobile ad hoc network. This is a modified algorithm of the compass routing method [7]. Originally compass routing method was proposed to deliver a message in a geometric network based on the direction of destination. Later, Stojmenovic and Lin [4] referred this method as DIR and evaluated the performance with LAR, geographic distance routing (GEDIR) and many other methods in static network. Here we modify DIR method to make it suitable for mobile ad hoc network and named the new modified method as Gradient algorithm since as such DIR method is not able to handle the complexity of mobile network. The performance of gradient algorithm is evaluated in mobile environment on parameters - success rate, average minimum hop counts and flooding ratio with other highly publicized directional algorithms LAR (scheme 1) and DREAM. The experimental results show that Gradient algorithm has outperformed LAR and DREAM on all the performance parameters considered in this paper.

Mobility is introduced using random walk mobility model. Location updates are performed using proactive approach. We have designed and implemented our own code in VC++ for simulation and tested the performance of algorithms in a network of 200 nodes.

2 Related Work

With the advent of low cost GPS equipments a number of position based methods have been published in the literature in last few years. This paper discusses only the direction based localized algorithm where each node makes forwarding decisions solely based on the position of itself, its neighbors and destination. Kranakis, Singh and Urrutia [7] proposed compass routing method for Geometric Networks. This method requires the position information of destination, source and direction of the edges incident with source. The edge having closest slope to the line segment connecting the source and destination is selected as next hop. This process is repeated until the message is delivered to the destination. This method is not loop free inherently. Authors of paper [7] did not compare this method with any other protocols. Later, paper [4] referred this method as DIR and evaluated the performance with GEDIR, shortest path (SP), LAR, 2 hops GEDIR, flooding GEDIR and many other methods in static network and concluded that DIR and GEDIR are better than LAR.

Ko and Vaidya, [5] presented two schemes of location-aided routing (LAR) and Basagni, Chlamtac, Syrotiuk, and Woodward [7] presented a distance routing effect algorithm for mobility (DREAM) that floods the message in limited range called as request zone in the direction of destination to find a path from source to destination. The authors of paper [5] compared the performance of LAR schemes with flooding algorithm and shown the superiority of their algorithm over flooding. In DREAM [4] the authors have compared their algorithm with dynamic source routing (DSR) [8] on the parameters as percentage of messages delivered and average end-to-end delay. Through the simulation under favorable conditions authors reported that more than 80% of data messages have been delivered to their destination without resorting to a recovery routine.

3 Gradient Routing

3.1 Motivation

The motivation for modifying the DIR (compass) method is to make it suitable to handle the complexity of mobility. DIR method is simple and easy to understand since it does not require complex mathematical calculations. Moreover DIR method has performed better than LAR in static ad hoc network as shown in paper [4]. Therefore authors decided to improve DIR method for mobile ad hoc network and compared its performance with existing direction based protocols namely LAR and DREAM.

3.2 DIR Method

It is assumed that each node knows its own position and also the position of other nodes exactly in the network. Suppose source S needs to send a message to destination. S computes the angle of all its neighbors with the line joining S and D. Based on the minimum angle (i.e. slope) S selects a neighbor (say X) to forward a message. The node X will further forward the message to its neighbor which has the minimum angle with line joining X and D. This process continues until the message is delivered to D or dropped due to non availability of path. For example consider the figure 1 given below, source (S) selects its neighbor B as next hop since B has minimum slope with line segment $\overline{SD}$. Node B similarly will select its next hop to deliver a message to D until message is delivered to D or dropped due to non availability of path. This algorithm is inherently not loop free.

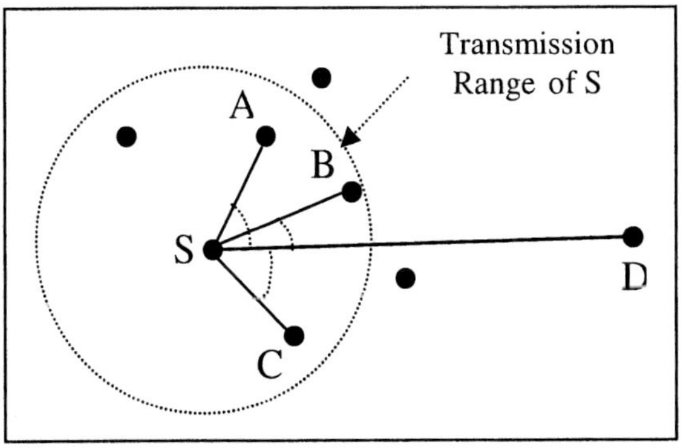

Fig. 1. Selection of next hop in DIR Method

3.3 Position Information

We assume that each node knows its current position precisely (error free) through a GPS device or based in the strength of signals received or by some other method. Each node maintains a location table containing the last known position information, time of updating the last known position and mobility speed of all other nodes in the network. The position information is updated independent of routing task. Position information is transmitted to one hop neighbors and in the entire network at regular interval. Location update scheme is described in detail in later section.

3.4 Expected Zone

In mobile environment it is difficult to locate a particular node exactly at any point of time since the nodes are in moving state. Therefore we can only try to estimate the probable location of a mobile node in an area (known as expected zone) drawn around the last known position of the node where the probability of finding a moving node is highest. The size of expected zone depends on moving speed and time elapsed since the last known position of the node. Consider a node S needs to send a message to node D at time t_c. Assume that node S knows the last position information of D updated at time t_ℓ (where $t_c > t_\ell$) and D is moving at an average speed v. S can expect the new location of D in a region defined by $R=v*(t_c - t_\ell)$ centered at location of D at time t_ℓ. This region is known as expected zone (as shown in figure 2 given below) since the probability of node D being in this region is very high. The shape of an expected zone may be a circle (figure 2(A)), a rectangle (figure 2(B)) or any other shape.

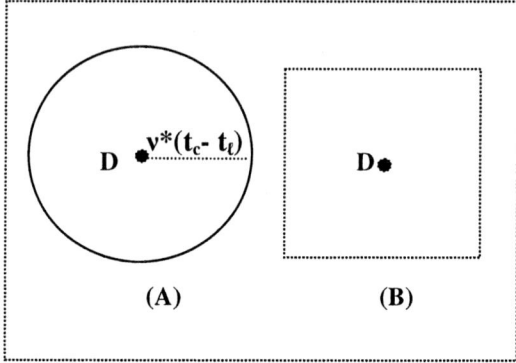

Fig. 2. Expected Zone

3.5 Request Zone

Source node S defines a request zone explicitly or implicitly to increase the probability of delivering a message to destination D. Source S forwards a message only to nodes those belong to the request zone. An explicitly defined request zone draws a specific area around the expected zone including source node. Nodes lying inside the specified area are members of the request zone. The request zone defined implicitly does not draw any such specific area rather the membership of nodes to the request zone is decided based on some particular criteria. Request zone includes the nodes that are the best choices for any probable location of destination D within the expected zone to forward a message. The shape of a request zone defined explicitly may be an angular one by drawing tangents from source on the circular expected zone as shown in figure 3(A). The shape of a request zone may also be a rectangle drawn from source at one end of diagonal and expected zone at other end of the diagonal as shown in figure 3(B) or any other shape.

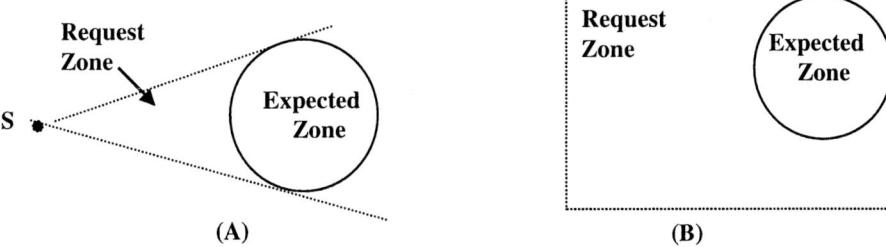

Fig. 3. Request Zone

3.6 Gradient Routing

Gradient routing is a modified and improved version of DIR method to make it suitable for mobile ad hoc network. A source node select next hops which are closer to destination (any possible position inside the expected zone) based on minimum angle (i.e. slope or gradient) with the line segment joining source and destination. Since gradient (i.e. slope or angle) plays significant role at each step in selection of next hop and delivering a message to destination therefore, it is named as gradient routing. Message is forwarded to only those neighbors which are best choices for a possible position of destination in the expected zone. The membership of request zone is determined implicitly. Gradient routing algorithm is described as follows:

Consider a source S initiates a routing process to send a message to destination D at time tc. S will look up the location table to know the last position information of D. Assume that position information of D was updated at time tl (where tc > t_ℓ) and D is moving at an average speed v. S can expect the new location of D in a circular region (known as expected zone) defined by the radius R=v*(tc- t_ℓ) centered at location of at time t_ℓ.

Since D can be located any where inside the expected zone therefore we have to cover the entire zone to reach D. To cover entire expected zone we propose to select certain equally spaced points on the boundary of an expected zone as probable destinations as shown in figure 4 given below. Further assume that destination may be any where inside the circle including the positions marked on boundary of the circle as probable destinations. S marks a node among its neighbors as next hop for each probable destination using DIR as basic algorithms for forwarding the message. To avoid the loop formation an additional condition on the selection of next hop is laid down that the angle between next hop and $\overline{SD}$ must be less than right angle. No specific request zone is drawn here to determine next hop. The marked nodes further mark their neighbor nodes as next hop to deliver a message to D. This process is repeated until massage is delivered to D or dropped due to non-availability of path. Once the message is reached inside the expected zone, message is flooded inside the expected zone to deliver the message to D since it is difficult to locate the exact position of D.

For example in the figure 4, S draw an expected zone around D and selects 16 (arbitrarily) equally spaced points as probable destinations on the boundary of expected zone. For each probable destination say U and U' (or any other point on the boundary), S determines A and B as next hops respectively (using DIR as basic algorithm) to deliver a message to D for any position of D inside the expected zone.

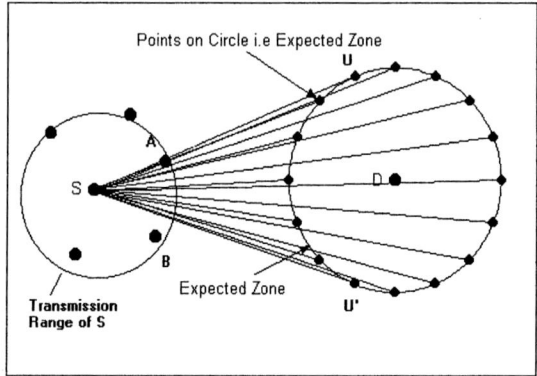

Fig. 4. Gradient Routing

3.7 Advantages

Gradient routing algorithm has the following advantages:

- Gradient routing is robust. Message can be delivered to destination through more than one route independent of each other. Failure of one route will not disconnect the source and destination since multiple routes exists.
- Gradient routing is adaptive to sleeping period operation due to existence of multiple routes. Failure of one route will not affect routing task.
- It is adaptive to mobility since at every step the source and intermediate nodes selects next hop based on the latest information available about the destination.
- It is loop free since message is forwarded to nodes lying towards destination.
- It is distributive and localized algorithm.
- This algorithm is suitable for routing as well as geocasting. Delivery of message is independent of location update tasks.
- This method is scalable in terms of number of nodes in the network.

4 Experimentation

We have simulated the protocols by implementing algorithms in VC++. We have considered a network of 200 nodes and assume that each node has equal transmission range R and the links are congestion free. The nodes are spread in the area L x W where L=640 units and W=480 units. Simulation was carried out by varying average degree K of the network (i.e. the average number of neighbors of a node in the network) as 5, 6, 7, 8, 9, 10, 11 and 15. Transmission range (R) is set as a function of K, number of nodes N and the network area using relation:

$$R = \sqrt{\frac{K*L*W}{\pi(N-1)}} \quad (1)$$

For each value K, 1000 pairs of source and destination are selected in one experiment. The experiment is repeated 10 times. Average values of success rate, minimum hop counts, and flooding ratio were calculated from the data generated through experiments.

Mobility is introduced using random walk model using proactive routing approach. Each node is moving at a speed of x units per clock tick with zero pause time in a random direction, where x is selected randomly for each node in interval [0, 2]. Random direction is selected between 0 to 2p for each clock tick independent of speed. A moving node is reflected back from the network boundary wall if it hits the wall. The first pair of source and destination is selected to transmit a data message after 25 clock ticks of the simulation. Thereafter pairs of source and destination are selected to transmit data messages with time difference between two pairs being exponentially distributed with the mean of 2 clock ticks. The size of expected zone is determined based on the speed and the time difference from the last known position independently at each node. The massage is flooded inside the expected zone once it reaches inside the expected zone.

4.1 Location Update Scheme

In this location update scheme each moving node sends a location update message at regular time interval (containing new position information, and current speed of the node). There are two types of location update messages i.e. short duration location update message and a long duration update message. Short duration messages are transmitted to one-hop neighbors at every 10 clock units whereas long duration messages are transmitted in the entire network at every 70 clock units. Since the network may be partitioned therefore long duration message may not reach to all nodes.

The source node transmits the message to its neighbor according to algorithm used if the time gap is smaller than a threshold value timeOut, otherwise source node drops the message and starts recovery procedure to deliver the message. Value of timeOut is computed by the formula:

$$timeOut = \left\lceil \frac{\sqrt{(L*W*P)/\pi}}{speed} \right\rceil \quad (2)$$

where, P is taken 20% area of the network that an expected zone (circle) can cover. This condition was necessary to restrict the size of expected zone since in some case it was found that the expected zone was large enough to cover the entire network. Since LAR is applied in proactive environment (instead of originally described as reactive one), therefore it is called as LAR-P.

5 Results and Discussion

The performance of Gradient routing algorithm is compared with two popular location based directional routing protocols namely LAR (Scheme 1) and DREAM on the following parameters:

5.1 Percentage of Successful Deliveries (Success Rate)

A message delivery is treated as successful if source and destination are found connected. Success rate is computed as the sum of the number of messages delivered successfully to destination divided by the total number of message sent.

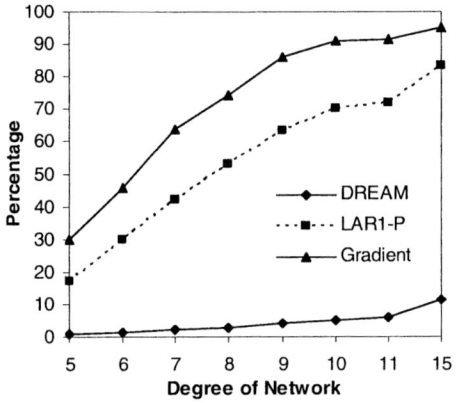

Fig. 5. Success Rate

Figure 5 (given above) show the success rate of protocols. Gradient routing has significantly higher success rate than LAR-P and DREAM. Success rate is extremely low in DREAM (less than 6% for K≤11) since for many cases expected zone is not formed or its size is very small and accordingly the size of request zone reduced. Source node is not able to find next hop (most of time) inside the request zone being small in size. The size of expected zone is determined by the radius $R = v*(t_c - t_\ell)$ where v is the mobility speed of destination. Mobility speed of each node is selected randomly in interval [0 2]. In case speed is zero (or very small number) then R becomes zero and consequently size of expected zone also becomes zero. Through the experiment we found that when size of expected zone is zero or very small then DREAM frequently fails to find next hop to forward the message inside the request zone. In this situation Gradient routing is able to find path and therefore it has maximum success rate.

5.2 Average Minimum Hop Counts

It is the sum of hop counts (taking the minimum hop counts in case of more than one successful deliveries for a given pair of source and destination) of all successful deliveries divided by total number of such deliveries. Average minimum hop counts plays an important role in measuring the performance of algorithms particularly when links are assumed to be congestion free. It signifies that in how many minimum hops an algorithm delivers a message from source to destination.

The results of average minimum hop counts are shown in figure 6 (given below). Gradient and LAR-P have almost similar hop counts while Gradient has significantly higher success rate than LAR-P. DREAM has minimum hop counts since its success rate is also very low.

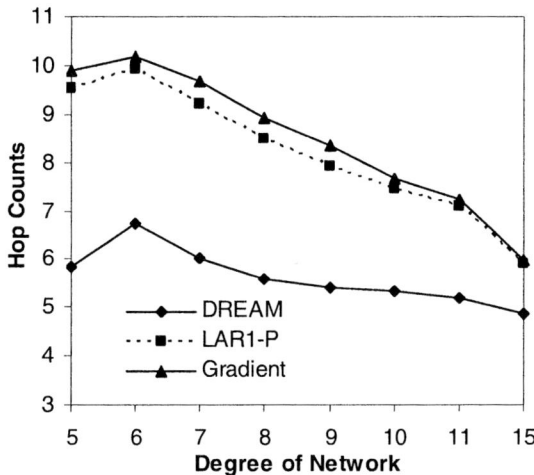

Fig. 6. Average minimum hop counts

5.3 Flooding Ratio

Flooding ratio of an algorithm exhibits the average load on the network during message delivery. It is computed as the percentage of marked nodes outside the expected zone from the total nodes outside the expected zone for forwarding the message. All message deliveries (successful and unsuccessful) have been considered for computing the flooding ratio. Each algorithm behaves in the same way inside the expected zone since flooding is applied inside the expected zone. Thus only the nodes marked outside the expected zone make difference in flooding a message in the network. Therefore only such nodes have been considered for computing flooding ratio.

Figure 7 (given below) shows the results for flooding. From this figure it is observed that LAR-P has maximum flooding ratio (approximately 19% at K=15). Gradient has significantly low flooding ratio (approximately 9% at K=15) in comparison to LAR- P. DREAM has lowest flooding ratio and its success rate was also low. It is also observed that flooding ratio increases rapidly with the value of K especially in LAR-P while in Gradient routing flooding ratio remains approximately same. The reason is that LAR-P does blind flooding in request zone and Gradient routing method selects only suitable neighbors which are best choice to forward the message to probable destination.

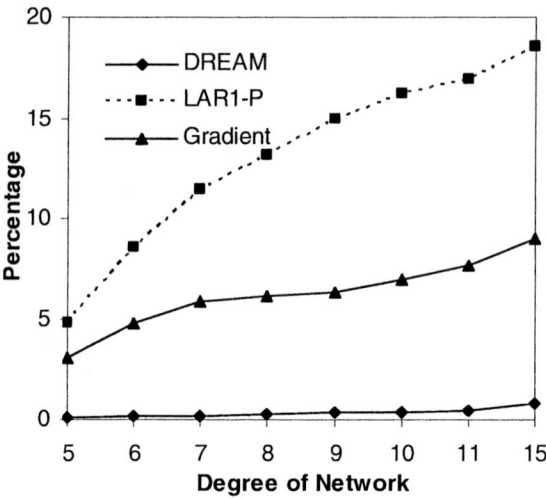

Fig. 7. Flooding Ratio

6 Conclusion

In this paper, we presented Gradient routing method (a modified version of DIR algorithm). This method is adaptive to mobile network and is inherently loop free. The performance of Gradient method is evaluated on the parameters - success rate, average minimum hop counts and flooding ratio. Its performance is compared with other directional routing protocols namely LAR and DREAM. The simulation results show that Gradient method has outperformed LAR and DREAM on all parameters. Gradient routing method maintains high success rate at low flooding rate and hop counts as degree of network increases. Therefore this method is also suitable for dense network.

References

1. Mauve M., Widmer J., and Hartenstein H.: A survey on Position-Based Routing in Mobile Ad Hoc Networks, IEEE Network (2001), 30-39.
2. Giordano S., Stojmenovic I., and Blazevic L.: Position based routing algorithms for ad hoc networks A taxonomy, (2001) http://www.site.uottawa.ca/~ivan/wireless.html
3. Stojmenovic I., Ruhil A.P., and Lobiyal D.K.: Voronoi diagram and convex hull based geocasting and routing in wireless networks, Proc. of Eighth IEEE ISCC, Antalya, Turkey, (2003) 51-56
4. Stojmenovic I. and Lin X.: Loop-Free Hybrid Single-Path/Flooding Routing Algorithms with Guaranteed Delivery for Wireless Networks, IEEE Transactions on Parallel and Distributed Systems, Vol. 12, No. 10, (2001) 1023-1032.
5. Ko Y.B. and Vaidya N.H.: Location-aided routing (LAR) in mobile ad hoc networks, MOBICOM, (1998) 66-75; Wireless Networks, Vol. 6, No. 4, (2000) 307-321.

6. Basagni S., Chlamtac I., Syrotiuk V.R., and Woodward B.A.: A distance routing effect algorithm for mobility (DREAM), Proceedings MOBICOM, (1998) 76-84.
7. Kranakis E., Singh H., and Urrutia J.: Compass Routing on Geometric Networks", Proceedings 11th Canadian Conference on Computational Geometry, Vancouver, (1999)
8. Johnson D. and Maltz D. A.: The Dynamic Source Routing in Ad-Hoc Wireless Networks (DSR), IETF, MANET working group, Internet draft, 21st February 2002. http://www.ietf.org/internet-drafts/draft-ietf-manet-dsr-07.txt

Distributed Clustering Algorithm for Finding Virtual Backbone in Ad Hoc Networks

B. Paul and S.V. Rao

Department of Computer Science & Engineering,
Indian Institute of Technology, Guwahati,
Guwahati - 781039, Assam, India
{bpaul, svrao}@iitg.ernet.in

Abstract. An important objective in designing a protocol is to save scarce resources like energy and bandwidth, and avoid the broadcast storm problem [1]. One way of addressing these problems is by forming a small virtual backbone. In this paper, we present a distributed clustering algorithm for forming a small backbone in ad-hoc network, based on connected dominating set. The time and message complexity of the algorithm is in $O(n)$.

1 Introduction

In ad hoc networks, the broadcast storm problem [1] is a bottleneck in the applications where the broadcasting is one of the major requirement. Recent research shows that this problem can be addressed efficiently by constructing a small backbone, since it is an efficient approach for routing in which message redundancy, contention, and collision can be reduced. But, unfortunately finding a smallest backbone is a NP-complete problem [2]. So, several researchers proposed various approximate algorithms for computing backbone.

One class of algorithms are based on connected dominating sets (CDS). Guha and Khuller [3], presented two centralized algorithms. The distributed version of these algorithms are proposed in [4]. A localized distributed algorithm is proposed in [5] by using two hop neighbors information. A distributed algorithm for forming a CDS with an approximation ratio of $O(\log \Delta)$ is presented in [6]. Alzoubi et al. proposed many algorithms [7, 8] for CDS construction. Spanning tree-based CDS algorithms are proposed in [7, 9, 10]. In [11], rule-k is proposed to decrease the size of the CDS generated in [5]. The Span [12] chooses a node in each region as a coordinator and connects them with other node.

Another class of algorithms are based on clustering using independent dominating sets. Baker and Ephremides [13] proposed linked cluster algorithm Gerla and Tsai [14] presented two distributed algorithm based on lowest ID and highest degree Improved version of these algorithms are proposed in [15]. Some algorithms are based on clustering using dominating sets. In [16], a distributed greedy algorithm is proposed for dominating sets.

In this paper we propose a distributed clustering algorithm for constructing a small connected dominating set. The rest of the paper is organized as follows: next section describes the proposed distributed algorithm for constructing a

CDS. The section 3, presents our simulation results. And finally we conclude in fourth and final section.

2 Proposed Distributed Algorithm

We assume that every node knows its 1-hop neighbors. This can be easily gathered by broadcasting HELLO packet by each node. This 1-hop information contains node ID and its cluster head. The cluster head information is gathered during cluster formation. Before discussing the algorithm we explain the variables maintained at each node. Each node maintains its unique identification, cluster head, and parent respectively in the variables *id*, *ClusterHead*, and *parent*. The variable *ClusterHead* can be used as a cluster ID. Moreover, each node maintains list of its children and list of backbone nodes in its vicinity respectively in *child* list, and *internal* list. The nodes in the *internal* list need not be from the same cluster. To distinguish nodes from other cluster, we store cluster head ID along with node ID. These nodes are sorted by *ClusterHead* and *id*.

Our algorithm works in two phases, in first phase clusters are formed and in second phase these clusters are connected to form a backbone. Formation of clusters starts with the identification of cluster heads. We explain the cluster formation phase using color code WHITE, GRAY, and BLACK. After first phase of the algorithm, cluster heads are marked BLACK and all other nodes are marked GRAY. Each node initially mark itself WHITE and acts according to the following algorithm.

1. Each node having lowest ID among its neighbors marks itself BLACK (cluster head) by setting *ClusterHead* to its own ID and broadcasts CHEAD message.
2. WHITE nodes receiving first CHEAD message marks itself GRAY, sets its *parent* and *ClusterHead* to sender ID, sends JOIN message to sender, and broadcasts DOMINATEE message.
3. WHITE node receiving first DOMINATEE message marks itself GRAY, sets *parent* to sender ID, *ClusterHead* to cluster head (which is received in DOMINATEE message), sends JOIN message to sender and broadcast the DOMINATEE message.
4. When any non-WHITE node receives the DOMINATEE message, it updates the sender information by noting senders cluster head in its 1-hop information.
5. Upon receiving first JOIN message, each node adds sender ID in *child* list and broadcast the DOMINATOR message. Note this DOMINATOR message is required for its neighbors to know that it has become an non-leaf node.
6. Subsequently, each node receiving the JOIN message, adds sender ID in *child* list.
7. Upon receiving the DOMINATOR message, each node adds the sender ID and cluster head (which is received in the DOMINATOR message), in its *internal* list.

Each cluster is a rooted spanning tree with cluster head as the root and all the non-leaf nodes form a connected dominating set. The next step is to connect these rooted spanning trees to form a single connected dominating set. We use *ClusterHead* value as a priority to initiate connection to join with other clusters. Lower the cluster head ID, higher the priority. Each node also maintains *connected* list to keep connection information. That is, which nodes in its cluster is connected to which node in other clusters. The variables *FromNode* and *ToNode* maintains node ID's of a node from its cluster and a node in other cluster. Their status, leaf/ non-leaf, is respectively stored in *FromStatus* and *ToStatus*. Cluster ID of *ToNode* is maintained in *ToClusterHead*. We maintain *connected* list by sorted order of *ToClusterHead*. Each node's *connected* list is initialized to null. Cluster are joined together as per the following algorithm.

1. Any node x having lower *ClusterHead* among its neighbor nodes of neighbor clusters, sends a REQUEST message to its cluster head through its parent, if x's cluster is not already connected by any node in its cluster.
2. Each node receiving REQUEST message forwards to its parent.
3. Upon receiving the REQUEST message, the cluster head node y adds this connection entry to *connected* list and sends PERMITTED message to its children, if y's cluster is not connected.
4. Every node receiving PERMITTED message checks its *connected* list, adds or modifies the connection entry and sends the PERMITTED message to its children.
5. When requested node receives the PERMITTED message, it acts like a connector between two clusters and sends the CONNECT message to node in other cluster. If more than one neighbor nodes are from other cluster, it sends to the node having lowest ID.
6. Upon receiving the CONNECT message, nodes adds or modifies the connection entry in its *connected* list and forwards the CONNECT message to its cluster head.
7. When cluster head receives the CONNECT message, it adds or modifies the connection entry and send the UPDATE message to its children.
8. Upon receiving the UPDATE message, each node adds or modifies the connection entry and forwards the UPDATE message to its children.

After the above steps, our algorithm forms a connected backbone in which all the non-leaf nodes of all clusters and connector nodes form a CDS.

2.1 Improvement

In previous algorithm, any node can become a connector. If both the connectors are leaf nodes in their respective cluster spanning trees, then increase in the size of the backbone is at least two. This is because, connector nodes are part of the backbone. If the connector nodes are non-leaf nodes, there is no increase in the size of the backbone, since non-leaf nodes are already part of the backbone. Therefore, we can reduce the size of the backbone if we can restrict connector nodes to non-leaf nodes. This can be achieved by modifying the first four steps of the previous algorithm, by giving priority to non-leaf node to become a connector. These modification are discussed below.

1. All leaf nodes having lower *ClusterHead* among its neighbor nodes of other clusters, send a REQUEST message to its cluster head, if the other cluster is not connected by any node in its cluster.
2. All non-leaf nodes send REQUEST2 message to its cluster head, if the other cluster is not connected. If connected, then sends a REQUEST2 message, if one of the following conditions is satisfied:
    - if the *FromNode* is leaf in its *connected* list, it checks for *ToNode* is leaf or non-leaf. If it is leaf, then send REQUEST2 message. And if it is non-leaf then it will check in its internal list whether it can establish a connection with any non-leaf node of other cluster. If it can, then sends REQUEST2 message.
    - if the *FromNode* is non-leaf and the *ToNode* is leaf then it checks whether the new connection can be made with the help of any non-leaf node in other cluster. Note, any node can check in its *internal* list, whether any non-leaf node in other cluster exists or not.

   Also note that while making the new connection, each node prefers to make the connection with an non-leaf node in the other cluster. For that each node uses their sorted *internal* list to search for neighbor non-leaf node in the other cluster.
3. The cluster head node acts according to the following way:
    - Upon receiving the first REQUEST message, the cluster head adds the connection entry to *connected* list and sends PERMITTED message to its *child* list, if no such entry exists for the that cluster in its *connected* list. Every node receiving PERMITTED message checks its *connected* list, adds the connection entry and sends the PERMITTED message to its *child* list.
    - Upon receiving the REQUEST2 message, the cluster head checks its *connected* list if any connection already exists or not. If not, it adds the respective connection entry in the *connected* list and sends the PERMITTED message to its *child* list. If already exists, then sends the PERMITTED message to its *child* list, if one of the following conditions is satisfied:
        * if the *FromNode* is leaf in its *connected* list, it checks for *ToNode* is leaf or non-leaf. If it is leaf, then it modifies its *connected* list and sends PERMITTED message. And if it is non-leaf and the *ToNode*, in new connection request, is also non-leaf node then it modifies its *connected* list and sends PERMITTED message.
        * if the *FromNode* is non-leaf and the *ToNode* is leaf and the *ToNode*, in new connection request, is non-leaf node then it modifies *connected* list and sends PERMITTED message.

      Every node receiving PERMITTED message checks its *connected* list, adds or modifies the connection entry, and sends the PERMITTED message to its *child* list.

Every node receiving the PERMITTED message updates its *connected* list and sends to its children. The remaining part of the previous algorithm is same. All the non-leaf nodes and connectors form a smaller CDS than the previous algorithm.

3 Simulation

In this section, we compare the size of the CDSs computed by our algorithms with existing methods using the *ds* custom simulator [17]. Random ad hoc network is generated with N hosts distributed evenly in a 50×50 square units. Transmission range R of each node is 10 units. In order to observe the impact of network density, simulations are conducted for the average vertex degree of 6, 18, and 30. For each value of d, we run our algorithms 250 times for different values of N. We have considered the connected undirected graph for each simulation. We have compare our algorithms with Span [12], Rule k [11], STCDS 1 [7], and STCDS 2 [9]. The results are reported in the figure 1. Our second algorithm gives smaller dominating set in large and dense graphs. Note that tree based approaches [7, 9, 10] gives smaller dominating set in comparison with cluster based approaches but the overhead and the complexity of those are much higher.

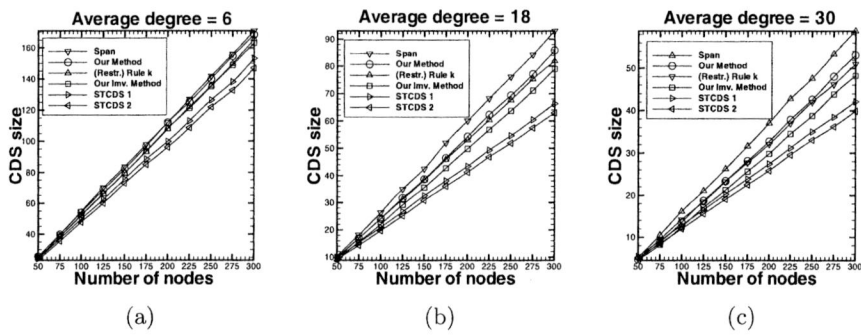

Fig. 1. Simulation results

4 Conclusion

In this paper, we have presented a distributed algorithm for forming small backbone in wireless ad hoc network based on clustering concepts. The size of the constructed backbone is further minimized by distributed algorithm. These algorithms are implemented and simulation results shows that our approach forms a small backbone in wireless ad hoc networks.

References

1. Ni, S., Tseng, Y., Cheng, Y., Sheu, J.: The broadcast storm problem in a mobile ad hoc network. In: Proc. MOBICOMM'99. (1999) 151–162
2. Clark, B.N., Colbourn, C.J., Johnson, D.S.: Unit disk graphs. Discrete Mathematics. **86** (1990) 165–177
3. Guha, S., Khuller, S.: Approximation algorithms for connected dominating sets. Algorithmica **20** (1998) 374–387

4. Bharghavan, V., Das, B.: Routing in adhoc networks using minimum connected dominating sets. In: IEEE International Conference on Communications (ICC'97). Volume 1., Montreal, Canada (1997) 376 – 380
5. Wu, J., Li, H.: On calculating connected dominating sets for efficient routing in adhoc wireless networks. In: Proc. of the 3rd Int'l Workshop on discrete algorithms and methods for mobile computing and communications. (1999) 7–14
6. Dubhashi, D., Mei, A., Panconesi, A., Radhakrishnan, J., Srinivasan, A.: Fast distributed algorithms for (weakly) connected dominating sets and linear-size skeletons. In: Proc. ACM-SIAM Symposium on Discrete Algorithms (SODA). (2003) 717–724
7. Alzoubi, K.M., Wan, P.J., Frieder, O.: Distributed heuristics for connected dominating set in wireless adhoc networks. IEEE ComSoc / KICS Journal of communications and networks **4** (2002) 22–29
8. Alzoubi, K.M., Wan, P.J., Frieder, O.: Message-optimal connected dominating sets in mobile adhoc networks. In: The Third ACM Int'l Symposium on mobile adhoc networking and computing. (2002) 157–164
9. Alzoubi, K.M., Wan, P.J., Frieder, O.: New distributed algorithm for connected dominating set in wireless adhoc networks. In: Proceedings of the 35th Annual Hawaii International Conference on System Sciences. (2002) 3849 – 3855
10. Wan, P.J., Alzoubi, K.M., Frieder, O.: Distributed construction of connected dominating set in wireless adhoc networks. In: Twenty-First Annual Joint Conference of the IEEE Computer and Communications Societies. (2002) 1597 – 1604
11. Dai, F., Wu, J.: An extended localised algorithm for connected dominating set formation in ad-hoc wireless networks. IEEE Transactions on Parallel and distributed systems **15** (2004)
12. Chen, B., Jamieson, K., Balakrishnan, H., Morris, R.: Span: an energy-efiicient coordination algorithm for topology maintenance in ad hoc wireless networks. ACM Wireless Netrworks J. **8** (2002) 481–494
13. Baker, D.J., Ephremides, A.: The architectural organization of a mobile radio network via a distributed algorithm. IEEE Transaction on Communications **29** (1981) 1694–1701
14. Gerla, M., Tsai, J.T.C.: Multicuster, mobile, multimedia radio network. ACM-Baltzer Journal of wireless networks **1** (1995) 255–265
15. Lin, C.R., Gerla, M.: Adaptive clustering for mobile wireless networks. IEEE Journal on Selected Areas in Communications **15** (1997) 1265–1275
16. Liang, B., Haas, Z.J.: Virtual backbone generation and maintenance in ad hoc network mobility management. In: Nineteenth Annual Joint Conference of the IEEE Computer and Communications Societies. (2000) 1293–1302
17. Dai, F.: Dominating set simulation program. http://www.cse.fau.edu/ fdai/adhoc (2001)

Merging Clustering Algorithms in Mobile Ad Hoc Networks

Orhan Dagdeviren, Kayhan Erciyes, and Deniz Cokuslu

Izmir Institute of Technology,
Computer Eng. Dept., Urla, Izmir 35340, Turkey
{orhandagdeviren, kayhanerciyes, denizcokuslu}@iyte.edu.tr

Abstract. Clustering is a widely used approach to ease implementation of various problems such as routing and resource management in mobile ad hoc networks (MANET)s. We first look at minimum spanning tree(MST) based algorithms and then propose a new algorithm for clustering in MANETs. The algorithm we propose merges clusters to form higher level clusters by increasing their levels. We show the operation of the algorithm and analyze its time and message complexities.

1 Introduction

MANETs do not have any fixed infrastructure and consist of wireless mobile nodes that perform various data communication tasks. MANETs have potential applications in rescue operations, mobile conferences, battlefield communications etc. Conserving energy is an important issue for MANETs as the nodes are powered by batteries only. Clustering has become an important approach to manage MANETs. In large, dynamic ad hoc networks, it is very hard to construct an efficient network topology. By clustering the entire network, one can decrease the size of the problem into small sized clusters. Clustering has many advantages in mobile networks. Clustering makes the routing process easier, also, by clustering the network, one can build a virtual backbone which makes multicasting faster. However, the overhead of cluster formation and maintenance is not trivial. In a typical clustering scheme, the MANET is firstly partitioned into a number of clusters by a suitable distributed algorithm. A Cluster Head (CH) is then allocated for each cluster which will perform various task on behalf of the members of the cluster. The performance metrics of a clustering algorithm are the number of clusters, the count of the nodes in a cluster and the count of the *neighbor nodes* which are the adjacent nodes between the formed clusters [1].

In this study, we search various graph theoretic algorithms for clustering in MANETs and propose a new algorithm. Constructing *Minimum Spanning Trees* is an important approach where part of a tree or a tree of a forest designates a cluster. Related work in this area is reviewed in Section 2, we describe and illustrate the operation of our algorithm in Section 3 and the final section provides the conclusions drawn.

2 Background: Clustering Using a Minimum Spanning Tree

An undirected graph is defined as $G = (V, E)$, where V is a finite nonempty set and $E \subseteq V \times V$. The V is a set of nodes v and the E is a set of edges e. A graph G is connected if there is a path between any distinct e. A graph $G_S = (V_S, E_S)$ is a spanning subgraph of $G = (V, E)$ if $V_S = V$. A spanning tree of a graph is an undirected connected acyclic spanning subgraph. Intuitively, a spanning tree for a graph is a subgraph that has the minimum number of edges for maintaining connectivity [3]. The idea is to group branches of a spanning tree into clusters of an approximate target size [4]. The resulting clusters can overlap and nodes in the same cluster may not be directly connected [2]. Gallagher, Humblet, Spira's Distributed Algorithm [5] and Srivastava, Ghosh's k-tree core Algorithm [6] are two algorithms which construct distributed minimum spanning trees in MANETs.

Gallagher, Humblet and Spira's Distributed Algorithm: Gallagher, Humblet and Spira [5] proposed a distributed algorithm which determines a minimum-weight spanning tree for an undirected graph that has distinct finite weights for every edge. Aim of the algorithm is to combine small fragments into larger fragments with outgoing edges. A fragment of an MST is a subtree of the MST. An outgoing edge is an edge of a fragment if there is a node connected to the edge in the fragment and one node connected that is not in the fragment. Combination rules of fragments are related with levels. A fragment with a single node has the level L = 0. Suppose two fragments F at level L and F' at level L';

- If L < L', then fragment F is immediately absorbed as part of fragment F. The expanded fragment is at level L'.
- Else if L = L' and fragments F and F' have the same minimum-weight outgoing edge, then the fragments combine immediately into a new fragment at level L+1
- Else fragment F waits until fragment F' reaches a high enough level for combination.

Under the above rules the combining edge is then called the core of the new fragment. The two essential properties of MSTs for the algorithm are:

- *Property* 1: Given a fragment of an MST, let e be a minimum weight outgoing edge of the fragment. Then joining e and its adjacent non-fragment node to the fragment yields another fragment of an MST.
- *Property* 2: If all the edges of a connected graph have different weights, then the MST is unique.

The upper bound for the number of messages exchanged during the execution of the algorithm is $5N\log_2 N + 2E$, where N is the number of nodes and E is the number of edges in the graph. A message contains at most one edge weight and $\log_2 8N$ bits. A worst case time for this algorithm is $O(N\log N)$ [5].

3   Our Algorithm

We propose a distributed algorithm which finds clusters in a mobile ad hoc network. We assume that each node has distinct *node_id*. Moreover, each node knows its *cluster_leader_id*, *cluster_id* and *cluster_level*. *Cluster_id* is identified by the maximum *node_id* of the node in a cluster. *cluster_level* is identified by the number of the nodes in a cluster. *Cluster_leader_id* is identified by the *node_id* of the leader node in a cluster. *Cluster_ leader_id* is equal to the *cluster_id*. We assume that each node initially knows the cluster information of adjacent nodes. The local algorithm consists of sending messages over adjoining links, waiting for incoming messages and processing messages. The finite state machine of the algorithm is shown in Fig. 1.

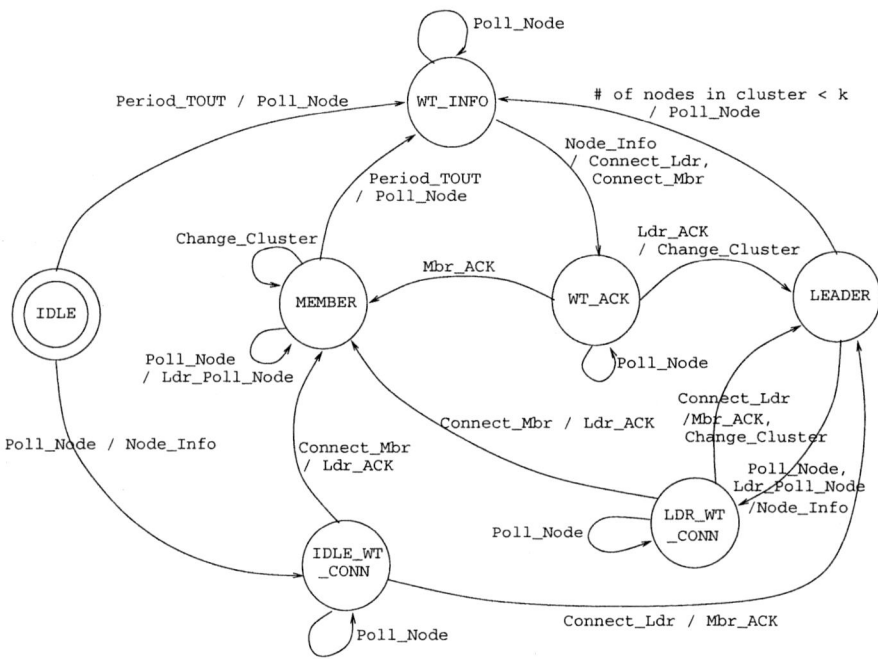

Fig. 1. Finite State Machine of the Algorithm

The algorithm requires the following sequence of messages. Firstly a node sends a *Poll_Node* message to a destination node. Destination node sends a *Node_Info* message back to originator node. Originator node then sends a *Connect_Ldr* or *Connect_Mbr* message to destination node to state it is the current leader or not. Destination node sends a *Ldr_ACK* or *Mbr_ACK* message to originator node. *Ldr_ACK* message shows that the originator node will become the new leader. *Mbr_ACK* message shows that the originator node will become the member of the new cluster.

Messages can be transmitted independently in both directions on an edge and arrive after an unpredictable but finite delay, without error and in sequence. Message types are *Poll_Node*, *Ldr_Poll_Node*, *Node_Info*, *Ldr_ACK*, *Mbr_ACK*, *Connect_Mbr*, *Connect_Ldr* and *Change_Cluster* as described below.

A cluster member node will send *Ldr_Poll_Node* message to the cluster leader node if the cluster member node receives a *Poll_Node* message from a node which is not in the same cluster. A node will multicast a *Change_Cluster* to all cluster member nodes to update their *cluster_id* and *cluster_level*. *Period_TOUT* message can be regarded as an internal message. *Period_TOUT* occurs for every node in the network to start clustering operation periodically. Every node in the network performs the same local algorithm. Each node can be either in *IDLE*, *WT_INFO*, *WT_ACK*, *MEMBER*, *LEADER*, *LDR_WT_CONN* or *IDLE_WT_CONN* states described below.

Initially all the nodes are in *IDLE* state before *Period_TOUT* occurs. A node in *WT_INFO* state waits for *Node_Info* message. A node in *WT_ACK* state waits for a Mbr_ACK or *Ldr_ACK*. A node in *LDR_WT_CONN* state waits for *Connect_Mbr* or *Connect_Ldr* message. A node in *IDLE_WT_CONN* state waits for *Connect_Mbr* or *Connect_Ldr* message. After the clustering operation is completed the nodes are either in *MEMBER* or *LEADER* state.

Timeouts can occur during communication. If a timeout occurs at a node either in *IDLE*, *WT_INFO*, *WT_ACK* or *IDLE_WT_CONN* states, it returns back to *IDLE* state, a node in *LDR_WT_CONN* state returns back to *LEADER* state, a node either in *LEADER* or *MEMBER* states doesn't change its state.

3.1 An Example Operation

Assume the mobile network in Fig. 2. Initially all the clusters are in *IDLE* state. *Period_TOUT* occurs in Node 1, Node 3, Node 4 , Node 9 and Node 12. Node 1 sends a *Poll_Node* message to Node 7 and sets its state to *WT_INFO*. Node 7 receives the *Poll_Node* message and sends *Node_Info* message to Node 1. Node 7 sets its state to *IDLE_WT_CONN*. Node 1 receives the *Node_Info* message and sends a *Connect_Ldr* message to Node 7 since the *node_id* of Node 7 is greater than node 1. Node 1 sets its state to *WT_ACK*. Node 7 receives the *Connect_Ldr* message and sends a *Mbr_ACK* message to Node 1. Node 1 receives the message and sets its state to *MEMBER*. Node 7 sends *Change_Cluster* message to Node 1 indicating that new cluster is formed between and Node 1 and Node 7. Node 8 and Node 9, Node 2 and Node 4 , Node 11 and Node 5, Node 3 and Node 6 are connected same as Node 1 and Node 2 to form clusters with level 2.

After clusters with level 2 are formed, Node 10 in *IDLE* state sends a *Poll_Node* message to Node 7. Node 10 sets its state to *WT_INFO*. Node 7 in *LEADER* state receives *Poll_Node* message and sends a *Node_Info* message to Node 10. Node 7 sets its state to *LDR_WT_CONN*. Node 10 in *WT_INFO_STATE* receives *NODE_INFO* message from Node 7 and sends a *Connect_Mbr* message to Node 7. Node 10 sets its state to *WT_ACK*. Node 7 receives *Connect_Mbr* and sends *Ldr_ACK* message to Node 10. Node 7 sets its state to *MEMBER*. Node 10 in *WT_ACK* state receives *Ldr_ACK* message and multicasts *Change_Cluster* mes-

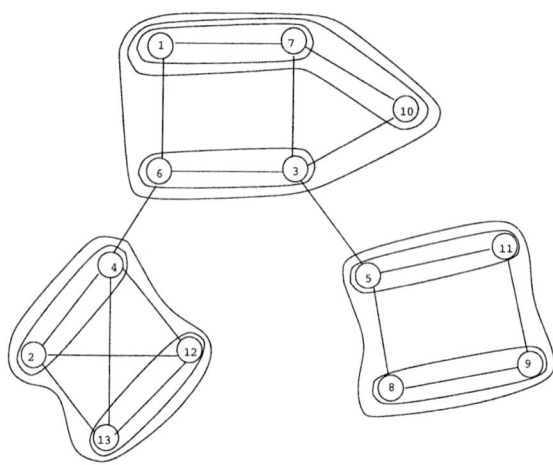

Fig. 2. Clusters obtained using our algorithm

sage to Node 1 and Node 7 to update new cluster information. Node 10 sets its state to *LEADER*. At the same time Node 13 in *LEADER* state sends a *Poll_Node* message to Node 4. 12, 13 and 2, 4 forms a new cluster as shown before. Beside this 5, 11 and 8, 9 are connected to form new clusters.

Table 1. Cluster Formation

Iteration	A	B	C
1	1 7 10 6 3	2 13	5 9
2	1-7 10 6-3	2-4 13-12	5-11 9-8
3	1-7-10 6-3	2-4-13-12	5-11-9-8
4	1-7-10-6-3	No Change	No Change

Node 6 in *LEADER* state sends a *Poll_Node* message to Node 1. Node 6 changes its state to *WT_INFO*. Node 1 in *MEMBER* state receives the *Poll_Node* message and sends a *Ldr_Poll_Node* message to Node 10. Node 10 in *LEADER* state receives the *Ldr_Poll_Node* message and sends a *Node_Info* message to Node 6. Node 10 sets its state to *LDR_WT_CONN* state. Node 6 in *WT_INFO* state receives the *NODE_INFO* and sends a *Connect_Ldr* message. Node 6 sets its state to *WT_ACK*. The cluster formation scheme is continued as shown in finite state machine in Fig. 1. Lastly the clusters in Fig. 2 are summarized in Tab. 1.

3.2 Analysis

Theorem 1. *Time complexity of the clustering algorithm has a lower bound of $\Omega(\log n)$ and upperbound of $O(n)$.*

Proof. Assume that we have n nodes in the mobile network. Best case occurs when each node can merge with each other exactly to double member count at each iteration such that Level 1 clusters are connected to form Level 2 clusters. Level 2 clusters are connected to form Level 4 clusters and so on. The clustering operation continues until the to Cluster Level becomes m. The lower bound is $\Omega(log N)$. Worst case occurs when a cluster is connected to a Level 1 cluster at each iteration. Level 1 cluster is connected to a Level 1 cluster to form a Level 2 cluster, Level 2 cluster is connected to a Level 1 cluster to form a Level 3 cluster and so on. The clustering operation continues until the Cluster Level becomes n. The upper bound is therefore $O(n)$.

Theorem 2. *Message complexity of our algorithm is $O(n)$.*

Proof. Assume that we have n nodes in our network. For every merge operations of two clusters 5 messages (*Poll_Node, Node_Info, Connect_Ldr/Connect_Mbr, Leader_ACK/Member_ACK, Change_Cluster*) are required. Total number of messages in this case is $5n$ which means message complexity has an upper bound of $O(n)$.

4 Conclusions

We proposed a new algorithm for clustering in MANETs and illustrated its operation. We showed the implementation of the algorithm and analyzed its time and message complexity. Our algorithm has a similar but more simplified structure than Gallagher's Algorithm [5]. The algorithm has a lower complexity and also we aim at forming clusters whereas the latter tries to find an MST. We are in the process of implementing the algorithm proposed in a simulated environment. We are planning to experiment various total order multicast and distributed mutual exclusion algorithms in such an environment where message ordering and synchronization are provided by the cluster heads on behalf of the ordinary nodes of the MANET.

References

1. Nocetti, F., B. et al, Connectivity based k-Hop clustering in wireless networks, Telecommunication Systems, (22)1-4,(2003), 205-220.
2. Chen , Y. P., Liestman, A. L., Liu, J., Clustering algorithms for ad hoc wireless networks, in Ad Hoc and Sensor Networks ed. Pan, Y. ,Xiao, Y., Nova Science Publishers, 2004.
3. Grimaldi, R. P., Discrete and Combinatorial Mathematics, An Applied Introduction, Addison Wesley Longman, Inc., 1999.
4. Banerjee, S., Khuller, S., A clustering scheme for hierarchical routing in wireless networks, CS-TR-4103, Univ. of Maryland, College Park, February 2000.
5. Gallagher, R. G., Humblet, P. A., Spira, P. M., A distributed algorithm for minimum-weight spanning trees, ACM Trans. on Programming Languages and Systems, (5)1, (1983), 66-77.
6. Srivastava, S., Ghosh, R., A cluster based routing using a k-tree core backbone for mobile ad hoc networks, Proceedings DIALM, (2002), 14-23.

Performance Study and Implementation of Self Organized Routing Algorithm for Mobile Ad Hoc Network Using GloMoSim

K. Murugan[1] and S. Shanmugavel[2]

[1] Ramanujan Computing Centre, Anna University,
Chennai, India
murugan@annauniv.edu
[2] Telematics Lab, Department of Electronics and Communication Engg,
Anna University, Chennai, India
ssvel@annainiv.edu

Abstract. Reducing power consumption and increasing battery life of nodes in an ad hoc network requires an integrated power control and routing strategy. To maximize the lifetime of mobile networks, the power consumption rate of each node must be evenly distributed. This objective alone cannot be satisfied by the use of routing algorithms proposed in previous work. In this paper a new route selection mechanism for MANET routing protocol, called as Self Organizing Routing (SOR). Self Organized Routing (SOR) algorithm is devised to enable high-energy nodes to participate in routing of data packets using a virtual backbone. Hence the lifetime and stability of the network is increased as nodes having high energy are involved in routing of packets. Based on the simulation results obtained using GloMoSim (simulator), it is observed that SOR algorithm increase the lifetime of mobile ad hoc networks and validate the environment suitable for the various techniques.

1 Introduction

The Mobile Ad hoc networks (MANETs) are instantly deployable without any wired base station or fixed infrastructure. A node communicates directly with the nodes within radio range and indirectly with all others using a dynamically determined multi-hop route. A key to designing efficient routing protocols for such networks lies in keeping the routing overhead and delay minimal. Ad hoc routing protocols can be broadly classified as table driven routing protocols and source initiated on-demand routing protocols. Table driven schemes are more expensive in terms of energy consumption as compared to the on-demand schemes because of the large routing overhead incurred in the former. Hence, the on-demand approach is a good base for designing minimum energy routing protocols. In an ad hoc network, many routing protocols, including DSR [1], HER [2], and EBTDR [2] operate on-demand. These protocols use source routing and each node maintains a cache of all routes that it has previously discovered or overheard in other packets. The source node chooses route for each packet it wishes to send using routes from its route cache. This use of caching can substantially reduce the overhead of routing protocol.

In this paper, work is focused on design and implementation of Self Organized Routing (SOR) algorithm in the existing DSR protocol. Self Organized Routing (SOR) algorithm is devised to enable high-energy nodes to participate in routing of data packets using a virtual backbone. Hence the lifetime and stability of the network is increased as nodes having high energy are involved in routing of packets. In addition to our work, the performance of the SOR algorithm is compared with the three existing version of MANET routing protocol, namely DSR, HER and EBTDR. In the EBTDR and HER algorithm, selection of routes should be based on the remaining battery level of the node. These algorithms are designed and implemented using Global Mobile Simulator (GloMoSim), a scalable simulation environment for network simulation.

The rest of the paper is organized as follows. Section 2 of this paper gives an overview of the basic operation of the DSR, EBTDR and HER protocol. In Section 3, explain the description of Self Organized Routing (SOR) algorithm. Section 4 presents the details of the simulator tools and environments. In Section 5, present the Simulation results and analysis. Finally, section 6 presents our conclusions.

2 MANET Routing Protocols

In this section, three different MANET routing protocols, namely, DSR, EBTDR and HER are discussed.

2.1 Dynamic Source Routing Protocol

This section provides an overview of the Dynamic Source Routing protocol (DSR) [1] as an example ad hoc network routing protocol. The operation of DSR is based on *source routing*, where in the source determines the complete sequence of hops to be used as the route for that packet to reach the destination.DSR divides the routing problem in two parts, *Route Discovery* and *Route Maintenance*, both of which operate *entirely* on-demand. In Route Discovery, a node actively searches through the network to find a route to an intended destination node. While using a route to send packets to the destination, Route Maintenance is the process by which the sending node determines if the route has broken. A node that has a packet to send to some destination searches its *route cache* for a route to that destination. If no cached route is found, the sending node initiates Route Discovery.

2.2 Energy Based Time Delay Routing (EBTDR) Algorithm

The EBTDR algorithm is based on the DSR protocol. The Route Discovery in the DSR protocol is modified so as to select the most energy efficient route by the destination node. Generally in an on-demand routing algorithm, when a source needs to know the route to a destination, it broadcasts a *RREQ* packet. The neighboring nodes on receiving the first-arrived *RREQ* packet relay this packet immediately to their neighbors. In the EBTDR algorithm, each node on receiving a request packet holds the packet for a period of time, which is inversely proportional to its current energy level [2]. After this delay period, the node forwards the request packet. This simple delay mechanism is motivated by the fact that the destination accepts only the first request packet and discards other duplicate requests. With this delay mechanism [2], request packets from nodes with lower energy levels are transmitted after a larger delay, whereas the request packets from nodes with higher energy levels are transmitted with a smaller delay.

2.3 Highest Energy Routing Algorithm

In this section, another new MANET routing protocols, Highest Energy Routing (HER) is described. In HER [3], an energy field in the RREQ packet is included, where the intermediate nodes insert their current energy level while forwarding the RREQ packet. The information on the remaining energy levels of intermediate nodes reaches the destination node. Thus this algorithm makes energy information of the various paths traversed available to the destination node. The destination node selects the route with the highest lifetime from a set of available routes.

3 Self Organized Routing (SOR) Algorithm

A Self Organized Routing algorithm is devised to enable high-energy nodes to participate in routing of data packets using a virtual backbone thereby minimizing the effects of broadcasting route request packets in the network. This protocol enable source nodes to unicast route request packet to reliable nodes thereby making the channel free for transmission of other nodes.

3.1 Initialization of Network

The network is said to be self organized as the nodes with higher energy participate more in transmission of packets in preference to the nodes weak in their energy levels. Nodes having higher energy are termed as root nodes. Root nodes broadcast hello packets containing the information of the destination reachable through them. The leaf nodes (nodes having weak energy profile) make entry of the presence of the root node in their cache and also the destination that could be reached through the root node. The broadcast by the root nodes takes place every 10 seconds and the latest information heard is entered in the hello packet (to be sent by the root node). A node entering a different partition learns of different routes to destinations in shorter intervals. If a root node receives a hello packet, then an entry of the initiator of the hello packet is made in the root cache. Thus a virtual backbone can be formed between the root nodes.

3.2 Route Discovery

DSR protocol performs the route discovery by flooding the network with the route request packets, but the SOR unicasts the route request packet only to the root nodes and maintains a timer for the route reply to come. If no entry in the root cache is found or the timer has expired, the source node floods the network with the route request packets like DSR. Thus the destination which receives the packet reply the route request packet to the source and drop all other route requests obtained from the same source like as in DSR. This variation in route discovery enables formation of stable routes with the high-energy nodes for transmission of packets. The routes so formed are less prone to link breakages and even if link breakages do occur due to mobility then by the use of salvaging, intermediate nodes obtain alternate route to the destination. As the root nodes broadcasts the destinations reachable in the hello packets, the surrounding nodes gets to update their cache of the latest information about its neighbors and obtain routes quickly.

3.3 Route Maintenance

In DSR, the route maintenance is done by the use of route errors packets that are piggy backed to the source. In SOR, in addition to the route maintenance of DSR, the root nodes periodical broadcast of the hello packet updates the cache in the surroundings of the root node. Through Update Route Caching (URC) mechanism, which is also one of the cache validation techniques [5], the link breakage information, is broadcasted in turn by the nodes that receive the route error packets.

4 Simulation Environments and Methodology

The routing protocols are implemented and simulated within the GloMoSim library [3][4]. We simulated a network of mobile nodes placed randomly within a 1000 x 1000 meter area. Each node has a radio propagation range of 250 meters and channel capacity of 2 Mb/s was chosen for each node. We used the IEEE 802.11 Distributed Coordination function (DCF) as the Medium Access Control (MAC) Protocol. Each simulation was executed for 900 seconds. Multiple runs with different seed values were conducted for each scenario and the collected data was averaged over those runs.

4.1 Performance Metrics

The following metrics are used in comparing the protocol performance.

Throughput: Measured as the ratio of the number of data packets delivered to the destination and the number of data packets sent by the sender.

End-to-End delay: It is the time between the reception of the last and first packet / total number of packets reaching the application layer.

Control Overhead: Measured as the total number of control packets transmitted during the simulation period.

Cache Hit ratio: Measured as the total no of hits at particular node to the total request.

Route Error Ratio: Measured as the ratio of the number of route errors registered due to link breakages because of mobility and energy drain to total number of data packets sent.

5 Simulation Results and Analysis

In this section, the performance results of various algorithms with respect to control overhead, throughput, end-to-end delay and average energy left are presented. Given below are the effects of our algorithm on the various parameters.

5.1 Performance Variation with Respect to Scatter and Nodal Density

Figure 1 shows the variation of proposed SOR with other routing protocols namely DSR, HER and EBTDR. The throughput of the proposed SOR is higher and tends to unity at all levels of nodes density. From figure 2, it can be seen that the efficient route maintenance in SOR, the number of route errors is less compared with other protocols. The pro-active nature of SOR also tends to find an alternate path to the destination while forwarding packets. From Figure 3 it can be inferred that there is marginal difference in the hit percentage when compared to DSR and HER The higher refresh rate in SOR causes removal of stale information in the route cache there by leading to lower hit percentage with negligible bad replies.

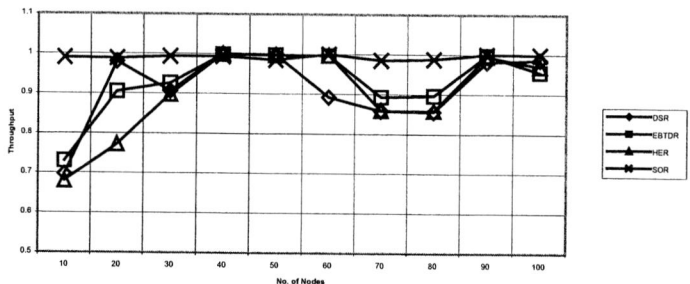

Fig. 1. No. of Nodes Vs Throughput

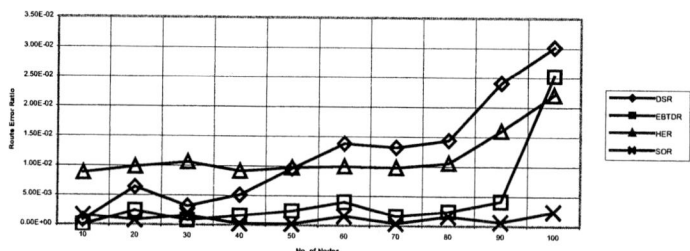

Fig. 2. No. of Nodes Vs Route Error Ratio

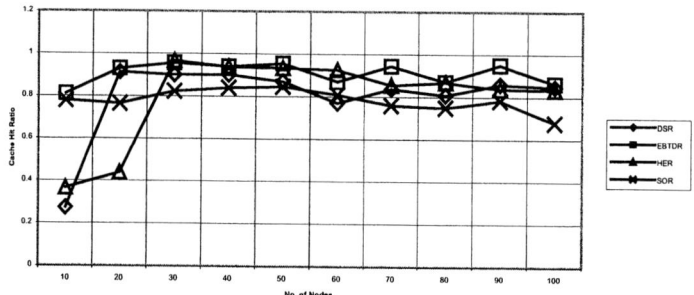

Fig. 3. No. of Nodes Vs Cache hit Ratio

5.2 Performance Variation with Respect to Traffic Load

From figure 4, as the load on the network increases, the hit percentage is maintained at a value greater than 60% on comparison to other routing protocols where the hit percentage drops below 50%. The statistics can conclude the efficient performance of the routing protocol SOR when compared to others. As the Error packets being generated in DSR, HER and EBTDR amount in 1000's the error packets in case of SOR are below 500 as shown in Figure 5. From figure 6, it is be seen that, the values for energy remaining in the nodes are stable at higher traffic loads and this stability is due to reduced propagation of errors and frequent updation of cache. The throughput of SOR has not dropped below 80% and is consistent at that value for higher loads in the traffic.

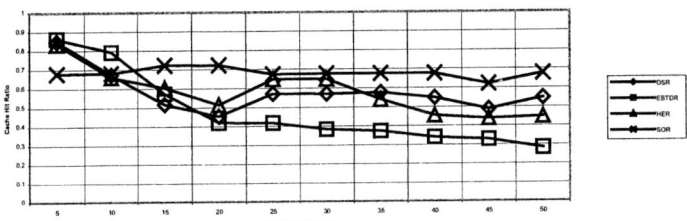

Fig. 4. Source Destination Pair Vs Cache Hit Ratio

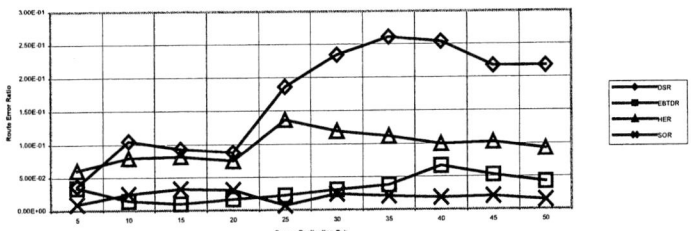

Fig. 5. Source Destination Pair Vs Route Error Ratio

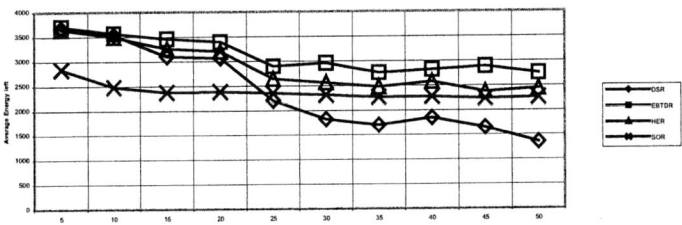

Fig. 6. Source Destination Pair Vs Average Energy left

5.3 Performance Variation with Respect to Speed

Link breakages in the case of mobile ad hoc networks are due to mobility and power constraint in nodes. From figures 7 and 8, it is seen that SOR has lower hit percentage and less number of route error packets generated with higher throughput performance. This is due to the periodic refreshing of the route caching in every ten seconds.

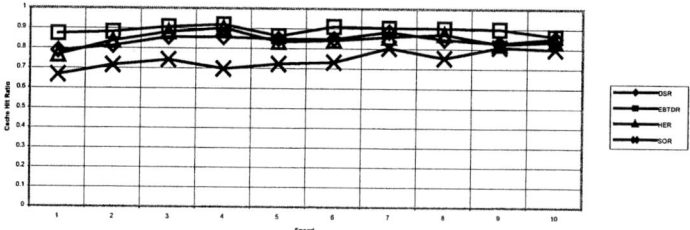

Fig. 7. Speed Vs Cache Hit Ratio

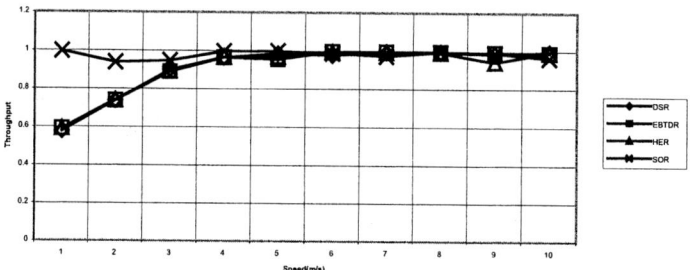

Fig. 8. Speed Vs Throughput

6 Conclusions

In SOR, the route established to forward data packet is stable compared to other protocols. The throughput of the proposed SOR is higher and tends to unity at all levels of nodes density. As the efficient route maintenance incorporated in SOR, the number of route errors is less compared to other protocols. Though the formation of reliable route is ascertained in the SOR, it is at the cost of power being consumed to broadcast the hello packet frequently. But the rate of power consumption with increase in the nodes density is less compared to other protocol. SOR has the hit percentage above 65% and is comparatively good in its throughput. Hence, SOR is a routing protocol that can be applied to congested environments and with higher nodal density.

References

1. Josh Broch, David B. Johnson, and David A. Maltz.: The Dynamic Source Routing Protocol for Mobile Ad Hoc Networks: Internet-Draft, draft-ietf-manet-dsr-03.txt, (1999).
2. K.Murugan, C.Sapthagiri Saravanan, S.Saravanan, J.Venkatakrishnan, S.Shanmugavel.: Delay and Energy Metric Based Routing Algorithms for Improving Efficiency for Mobile Ad Hoc Networks: Proceedings of 3rd Asian Mobile Computing Conference (AMOC 2004).
3. Glomosim user Manual http://pcl.cs.ucla.edu/projects/glomosim
4. Richard A.Meyer and Rajive Bagrodia, PARSEC User Manual Release 1.1, http://pcl.cs.ucla.edu. (1999)
5. K.Murugan, P.Sivasankar, Balaji and S.Shanmugavel: Implementation and Performance Study of Route Caching Mechanisms in DSR and HER Routing Algorithms for MANET: accepted to publish in ISAP05, Springer-Verlag, Lecturer Notes in computer Science (LNCS), 2005.

Self-stabilizing Deterministic TDMA for Sensor Networks[*]

Mahesh Arumugam and Sandeep S. Kulkarni

Software Engineering and Network Systems Laboratory,
Department of Computer Science and Engineering,
Michigan State University, East Lansing MI 48824
{arumugam, sandeep}@cse.msu.edu
http://www.cse.msu.edu/~{arumugam, sandeep}

Abstract. An algorithm for time division multiple access (TDMA) is found to be applicable in converting existing distributed algorithms into a model that is consistent with sensor networks. Such a TDMA service needs to be self-stabilizing so that in the event of corruption of assigned slots and clock drift, it recovers to states from where TDMA slots are consistent. Previous self-stabilizing solutions for TDMA are either randomized or assume that the topology is known upfront and cannot change. Thus, the question of feasibility of self-stabilizing deterministic TDMA algorithm where topology is unknown remains open.

In this paper, we present a self-stabilizing, deterministic algorithm for TDMA in networks where a sensor is aware of only its neighbors. This is the first such algorithm that achieves these properties. Moreover, this is the first algorithm that demonstrates the feasibility of stabilization-preserving, deterministic transformation of a shared memory distributed program on an arbitrary topology into a program that is consistent with the sensor network model.

1 Introduction

The ability to write programs in an abstract model and then transform them into a concrete model is crucial in distributed computing. This ability permits one to write abstract programs where several low level issues such as communication and race conditions among different processes can be ignored. Also, it is possible to thoroughly verify the abstract program using techniques such as model checking and/or theorem proving. Now, if we want to utilize the verification of the abstract program to deduce the verification of the concrete program then the transformation must preserve those properties.

For this reason, the problem of transformation from abstract programs to concrete programs has been studied in the literature [1, 2, 3, 4]. These transformations have also focused on preserving the *self-stabilization* [5, 6] property of the

---

[*] This work was partially sponsored by NSF CAREER CCR-0092724, DARPA Grant OSURS01-C-1901, ONR Grant N00014-01-1-0744, NSF Equipment Grant EIA-0130724, and a grant from Michigan State University.

original program. Self-stabilization refers to the ability of a system to recover from an arbitrary state to a state from where the computation proceeds in accordance with its specification. Since such a system recovers to legitimate states in-spite of unexpected (transient) faults, it is highly desirable for distributed computing.

Unfortunately, the results from [1,2,3,4] cannot be applied to deriving concrete programs for a sensor network, as the underlying model of computation in sensor networks is *write all with collision* (WAC) model [7]. In this model, the communication is (local) broadcast in nature and, hence, when a sensor executes an *action*, it can update the state of all its neighbors at once. However, if two neighbors of a sensor try to execute their actions simultaneously then a collision occurs and none of the actions are successful.

To redress this deficiency, recently approaches [7,8] have been proposed for transforming programs written in abstract models into WAC model. The transformation proposed in [7] takes any time division multiple access (TDMA) algorithm in WAC model (e.g., [9,10,11,12]) as input. If the algorithm in [9], which is self-stabilizing, deterministic and designed for grid based topologies, is used with [7] then the transformed program in WAC model is self-stabilizing and deterministically correct for grid based topologies. And, if the algorithms in [10,11,12], which are randomized, are used with [7] then the transformed program in WAC model is probabilistically correct. (Note that TDMA algorithm such as those in [13] cannot be used with [7], as the algorithm is not correct under WAC model. Rather, in [13], the authors assume that when two writes collide the result is an OR operation between them.) Likewise, since the transformation in [8] is randomized, it generates programs in WAC model that are probabilistically correct. Thus, if a self-stabilizing deterministic TDMA algorithm in WAC model were available then it would enable us to provide deterministic guarantees about the transformed program in WAC model. To the best of our knowledge, we are not aware of such algorithm for arbitrary networks.

With this motivation, in this paper, we propose a self-stabilizing deterministic TDMA algorithm. This algorithm can be used to transform existing self-stabilizing abstract programs into deterministically self-stabilizing programs in WAC model. This feature is useful as there is a large class of self-stabilizing programs in the literature (e.g., [5,6,14]) and there is a significant need for self-stabilization in sensor networks, where the environment is difficult to capture and, hence, ability to recover from unexpected transient faults is crucial.

Organization of the Paper. In Section 2, we precisely define the problem statement and the computational models. In Section 3, we present our self-stabilizing TDMA algorithm in shared-memory model. Subsequently, we transform this algorithm into WAC model in Section 4 and add stabilization in Section 5. Finally, in Section 6, we make the concluding remarks.

2 Preliminaries

Problem Statement. TDMA is the problem of assigning time slots to each sensor. Two sensors j and k can transmit in the same time slot if j does not interfere with the communication of k and k does not interfere with the communication of j. In other words, j and k can transmit in the same slot if the communication distance between j and k is greater than 2. Towards this end, we model the sensor network as a graph $G = (V, E)$, where V is the set of all sensors and E is the communication topology. Specifically, if sensors j and k can communicate with each other then the edge $(j, k) \in E$. The function $distance_G(j, k)$ denotes the distance between j and k in G. Thus, the problem statement of TDMA is shown in Figure 1.

Problem statement: TDMA
Given a communication graph $G=(V, E)$; assign time slots to V such that the following condition is satisfied:
  If $j, k \in V$ are allowed to transmit at the same time, then $distance_G(j, k) > 2$

Fig. 1. Problem statement of TDMA

Models of Computation. Programs are specified in terms of guarded commands; each guarded command is of the form, $g \longrightarrow st$, where g is a predicate over program variables, and st updates program variables. An action $g \longrightarrow st$ is enabled when g evaluates to true and to execute that action, st is executed.

A computation consists of a sequence $s_0, s_1, \ldots$, where s_{j+1} is obtained from s_j by executing actions in the program. A computation model limits the variables that an action can read and write. We split the actions into a set of processes. Each action is associated with one of the processes. We now describe how we model the restrictions imposed by the shared-memory and the WAC models.

Shared-memory model. In this model, in one atomic step, a sensor can read its state as well as the state of its neighbors (and update its private variables) and write its own variables using its own variables.

Write all with collision (WAC) model. In this model, each sensor consists of write actions (to be precise, write-all actions). Specifically, in one atomic action, a sensor can update its own state and the state of all its neighbors. However, if two or more sensors simultaneously try to update the state of a sensor, say k, then the state of k remains unchanged. Thus, this model captures the fact that a message sent by a sensor is broadcast. But, if multiple messages are sent to a sensor simultaneously then, due to collision, it receives none.

Assumptions. We assume that there is a base station that is responsible for token circulation. Such a base station can be readily found in sensor network applications, where it is responsible for exfiltrating the data to the outside world (e.g., in the extreme scaling project [15], the network is split into multiple sections and each section has at least one base station for data-gathering and network management). Next, we assume that each sensor knows the ID of the sensors that it can communicate with. This assumption is reasonable since the sensors collaborate among their neighbors when an event occurs. We assume that the maximum degree of the graph does not exceed a certain threshold, say,

d. This can be ensured by having the deployment follow a certain geometric distribution or using a predetermined topology. Finally, we assume that time synchronization can be achieved during token circulation. Whenever a sensor receives the token, it may synchronize its clock with respect to its parent. Also, we can integrate the algorithms proposed in literature (e.g., [16]).

3 Self-stabilizing TDMA in Shared-Memory Model

In this section, we present our algorithm in shared-memory model. In this algorithm, we split the system architecture into 3 layers: (1) token circulation layer, (2) TDMA layer, and (3) application layer. The token circulation layer circulates a token in such a way that every sensor is visited at least once in every circulation. In this paper, we do not present a new algorithm for token circulation. Rather, we only identify the constraints that this layer should satisfy. Specifically, this layer should recover from token losses and presence of multiple tokens. In other words, we require that this layer be self-stabilizing. We note that graph traversal algorithms such as [17, 18, 19, 20] satisfy these constraints. Hence, any of these algorithms can be used. The TDMA layer is responsible for assigning time slots to all the sensors. And, finally, the application layer is where the actual sensor network application resides. All application message communication goes through the TDMA layer. Now, we explain the TDMA layer in detail.

3.1 TDMA Layer

The TDMA layer uses a distance 2 coloring algorithm for determining the initial slots of the sensors. Hence, we present our algorithm in two parts: (1) distance 2 coloring and (2) TDMA slot assignment.

Distance 2 Coloring. Given a communication graph $G = (V, E)$ for a sensor network, we compute E' such that two distinct sensors x and y in V are connected if the distance between them in G is at most 2. To obtain distance 2 coloring, we require that $(\forall (i,j) \in E' :: color.i \neq color.j)$, where $color.i$ is the color assigned to sensor i. Thus, the problem statement is defined in Figure 2.

Problem statement: Distance 2 coloring
Given a communication graph $G=(V,E)$; assign colors to V such that the following condition is satisfied: $(\forall (i,j) \in E' :: color.i \neq color.j)$
where, $E' = \{(x,y) | (x \neq y) \land ((x,y) \in E \lor (\exists z \in V :: (x,z) \in E \land (z,y) \in E))\}$

Fig. 2. Problem statement of distance 2 coloring

In our algorithm, each sensor maintains two public variables: $color$, the color of the sensor and $nbrClr$, a vector consisting of $\langle id, c \rangle$ elements, where id is a neighbor of the sensor and c is the color assigned to corresponding sensor. Initially, $nbrClr$ variable contains entries for all distance 1 neighbors of the sensor, where the colors are undefined. A sensor can choose its color from K, the set of colors. To obtain a distance 2 coloring, $d^2 + 1$ colors are sufficient, where d is the maximum degree in the graph (cf. Lemma 3.1). Hence, K contains $d^2 + 1$ colors.

Whenever a sensor (say, j) receives the token from the token circulation layer, first, j reads $nbrClr$ of all its neighbors and updates its private variable $dist2Clr.j$. The variable $dist2Clr.j$ is a vector similar to $nbrClr.j$ and contains the colors assigned to the sensors at distance 2 of j. Next, j computes $used.j$ which contains the colors used in its distance 2 neighborhood. If $color.j \in used.j$, j chooses a color from $K - used.j$. Otherwise, j keeps its current color. Once j chooses its color, it waits until all its distance 1 neighbors have copied $color.j$. Towards this end, sensor l will update $nbrClr.l$ with $\langle j, color.j \rangle$ if j is a neighbor of l and $color.j$ has changed. Once all the neighbors of j have updated $nbrClr$ with $color.j$, j forwards the token. Thus, the algorithm for distance 2 coloring is shown in Figure 3. (For simplicity of presentation, in Figure 3, we represent action A3, where j forwards the token after all its neighbors have updated their $nbrClr$ values with $color.j$, separately. Whenever j receives the token, we require that action A3 is executed only after action A2 is executed at least once.)

```
sensor j
const
    N.j                              // neighbors of j
    K                                // set of colors
var
    public color.j                   // color of j
    public nbrClr.j                  // colors used by neighbors of j
    private dist2Clr.j               // colors used at distance 2 of j
    private used.j                   // colors used within distance 2 of j
begin
A1: (l ∈ N.j) ∧ (⟨l, c⟩ ∈ nbrClr.j) ∧ (color.l ≠ c)                    ⟶
    nbrClr.j := nbrClr.j − {⟨l, c⟩} ∪ {⟨l, color.l⟩}
A2: token(j)                                                            ⟶
    dist2Clr.j := {⟨id, c⟩|∃k ∈ N.j : (⟨id, c⟩ ∈ nbrClr.k) ∧ (id ≠ j)}
    used.j := {c|⟨id, c⟩ ∈ nbrClr.j ∨ ⟨id, c⟩ ∈ dist2Clr.j}
    if(color.j ∈ used.j)    color.j := minimum color in K − used.j
A3: token(j) ∧ (∀l ∈ N.j : (⟨j, c⟩ ∈ nbrClr.l ∧ color.j = c))           ⟶
    forward token
end
```

Fig. 3. Algorithm for distance 2 coloring in shared-memory model

Lemma 3.1. *If d is the maximum degree of a graph then $d^2 + 1$ colors are sufficient for distance 2 coloring. (cf. [21] for proofs of the theorems.)* □

Corollary 3.2. *For any sensor j, $used.j$ contains at most d^2 colors.* □

Theorem 3.3. *The above algorithm satisfies the problem specification of distance 2 coloring.* □

Theorem 3.4. Starting from arbitrary initial states, the above algorithm recovers to states from where distance 2 coloring is achieved. □

TDMA Slot Assignment. In our algorithm, *color.j* determines the initial TDMA slot of j. And, future slots are computed using the knowledge about the period between successive TDMA slots. Since the maximum number of colors used in any distance 2 neighborhood is $d^2 + 1$ (cf. Lemma 3.1), the period between successive TDMA slots, $P = d^2 + 1$, suffices. Once the TDMA slots are determined, the sensor forwards the token in its TDMA slot. And, the sensor can start transmitting application messages in its TDMA slots.

We note that identifying an optimal assignment is not possible as the problem of distance 2 coloring is NP-complete even in an offline setup [22]. In [23,24], approximation algorithms for offline distance 2 coloring in specific graphs (e.g., planar) are proposed. However, in this paper, we consider the problem of distributed distance 2 coloring where each sensor is only aware of its local neighborhood. In this case, given a sensor with degree d, the slots assigned to this sensor and its neighbors must be disjoint. Hence, at least $d + 1$ colors are required. Thus, the number of colors used in our algorithm is within d times the optimal.

Theorem 3.5. The above algorithm ensures collision-free communication. □

Since the distance 2 coloring algorithm is self-stabilizing (cf. Theorem 3.4), once the initial TDMA slots are recovered starting from arbitrary initial states, the sensors can determine the future TDMA slots.

Theorem 3.6. Starting from arbitrary initial states, the above algorithm recovers to states from where collision-free communication is restored. □

4 TDMA Algorithm in WAC Model

In this section, we transform the algorithm in Section 3 into WAC model that achieves token circulation and distance 2 coloring upon appropriate initialization. (The issue of self-stabilization is handled in Section 5.) In shared-memory model, in each action, a sensor reads the state of its neighbors as well as writes its own state. However, in WAC model, there is no equivalent of a read action. Hence, the action by which sensor j reads the state of sensor k in shared-memory model is simulated by requiring k to write the appropriate value at j. Since simultaneous write actions by two or more sensors may result in a collision, we allow sensors to execute in such a way that simultaneous executions do not result in collisions.

Observe that if collision-freedom is provided then the actions of a program in shared-memory model can be trivially executed in WAC model. Our algorithm in this section uses this feature and ensures that collision-freedom is guaranteed. In this algorithm, in the initial state, (a) sensors do not communicate and (b) *nbrClr* and *dist2Clr* variables contain entries such that the colors are undefined.

Distance 2 Coloring. Whenever a sensor (say, j) receives the token, j computes *used.j* which contains the colors used in its distance 2 neighborhood. If nbrClr.j (or dist2Clr.j) contains ⟨l, undefined⟩, l did not receive the token yet and, hence, color.l is not assigned. Therefore, j ignores such neighbors. Afterwards, j chooses a color such that color.j ∉ used.j. Subsequently, j reports its color to its neighbors within distance 2 using the primitive report_distance_2_nbrs (discussed later in this section) and forwards the token. Thus, the action by which k reads its neighbors (in shared memory model) is modeled as a write action where j reports its color using the primitive report_distance_2_nbrs. Figure 4 shows the transformed algorithm in WAC model.

```
sensor j
const    N.j, K
var      color.j, nbrClr.j, dist2Clr.j, used.j
begin
token(j)  ⟶   used.j := {c|⟨id, c⟩ ∈ nbrClr.j ∨ ⟨id, c⟩ ∈ dist2Clr.j}
               color.j := minimum color in K − used.j
               execute report_distance_2_nbrs
               forward token
end
```

Fig. 4. Algorithm for distance 2 coloring in WAC model

Note that the order in which the token is circulated is determined by the token circulation algorithm used in Section 3, which is correct under the shared-memory model (e.g., [17, 18, 19, 20]). Since token circulation is the only activity in the initial state, it is straightforward to ensure collision-freedom. Specifically, to achieve collision-freedom, if j forwards the token to k in the algorithm used in Section 3, we require that the program variables corresponding to the token are updated at j and k without collision in WAC model. This can be achieved using the primitive report_distance_2_nbrs. Hence, the effect of executing the actions in WAC model will be one that is permitted in shared-memory model.

Theorem 4.1. *The above algorithm satisfies the problem specification of distance 2 coloring.* □

TDMA Slot Assignment. Similar to the discussion in Section 3, the color of the sensor determines the initial TDMA slot. Subsequent slots can be computed using the knowledge about the TDMA period. If d is the maximum degree of the communication graph G, the TDMA period, $P = d^2 + 1$ suffices.

However, unlike the algorithm in Section 3 in shared-memory model, sensors do not start transmitting messages immediately as the TDMA message communication may interfere with the token circulation or the primitive report_distance_2_nbrs. Once the TDMA slots are determined, a sensor forwards the token in its TDMA slot. Hence, the token circulation does not collide with other TDMA slots. Next, a sensor waits until all the sensors in its distance 2 neighborhood have determined their TDMA slots before transmitting messages in its TDMA slots. A sensor learns this information when the sensors in its distance 2 neighborhood report their colors using the primitive report_distance_2_nbrs.

Thus, when a sensor starts transmitting application messages, all sensors in its distance 2 neighborhood have determined their TDMA slots and, hence, does not interfere with other TDMA slots and the primitive *report_distance_2_nbrs*.

Theorem 4.2. The above algorithm ensures collision-free communication. □

Implementation of *report_distance_2_nbrs*. Whenever a sensor (say, j) decides its color, this primitive reports the color to its distance 2 neighborhood. It updates the *nbrClr* value of its distance 1 neighbors and *dist2Clr* value of its distance 2 neighbors. Towards this end, j sends a broadcast message with its color and a schedule for its distance 1 neighbors. The sensors at distance 1 of j update their *nbrClr* values. Based on the schedule in the report message, each of the neighbors broadcast their *nbrClr* vectors. Specifically, if a distance 1 neighbor (say, l) of j is already colored, the schedule requires l to broadcast *nbrClr.l* in its TDMA slot. Otherwise, the schedule specifies the slot that l should use such that it does not interfere with the slots already assigned to j's distance 2 neighborhood. If there exists a sensor k such that $distance_G(l, k) \leq 2$, then k will not transmit in its TDMA slots, as l is not yet colored. (Recall that a sensor transmits application messages only if all its distance 2 neighbors have determined their TDMA slots.) Now, a sensor (say, m) updates *dist2Clr.m* with $\langle j, color.j \rangle$ iff $(m \neq j) \wedge (j \notin N.m)$. Thus, this schedule guarantees collision-free update of *color.j* at sensors within distance 2 of j. Furthermore, this primitive requires at most $d+1$ update messages.

5 Adding Stabilization in WAC Model

In Section 4, if the sensors are assigned correct slots then validating the slots is straightforward. Towards this end, we can use a simple diffusing computation to allow sensors to report their colors to distance 2 neighborhood and ensure that the slots are consistent. For simplicity of presentation, we assume that token circulation is used for revalidating TDMA slots. Now, in the absence of faults, the token circulates successfully and, hence, slots are revalidated. However, in the presence of faults, the token may be lost due to a variety of reasons, such as, (1) TDMA slots are not collision-free, (2) *nbrClr* values are corrupted, and/or (3) token is corrupted. Or, due to transient faults, there may be several tokens.

To obtain self-stabilization, we use the *convergence-stair* approach proposed in [25]. First, we ensure that if the system contains multiple tokens then it recovers to states where there is at most one token. Then, we ensure that the system recovers to states where there is a unique token (cf. Figure 5).

Step 1: Dealing with Multiple Tokens. In this step, we ensure that any token either returns to the base station within a predetermined time or it is lost. Towards this end, we ensure that a sensor forwards the token as soon as possible. To achieve this, whenever a sensor, say j, receives the token, j updates its color at its neighbors in its TDMA slot. (This can be achieved within P slots, where P is the TDMA period.) Furthermore, in the subsequent slots, (a) the neighbors relay this information to distance 2 neighbors of j and (b) j forwards the token.

(Both of these can be achieved within P slots.) If the TDMA slots are valid then any token will return in $2*P*|E_t|$ slots to the base station, where $|E_t|$ is number of edges traversed by the token. Otherwise, it may be lost.

- when new token circulation begins
- set a timer T_1 until which the token must return
- set TokensReceived := 0
- upon completing token circulation
- set TokensReceived := 1
- // do not recirculate until T_1 expires

- upon expiration of timer T_1
- // no sensor other than base station has the token
- if TokensReceived = 1
- start a new token circulation
  else
    wait until distance 3 neighborhood has stopped
    send *recovery token*

(a) Actions at the base station

- upon receiving a token
- verify *nbrClr* and *dist2Clr* variables
- forward token as soon as possible (see description)
- set a timer T_2 for return of the token

upon expiration of timer T_2
// suspend communication until new token arrives
set *nbrClr* and *dist2Clr* to undefined
upon receiving *recovery token*
recompute *nbrClr*, *dist2Clr*, *color*
wait until distance 3 neighborhood has stopped
forward *recovery token*

(b) Actions at the sensors

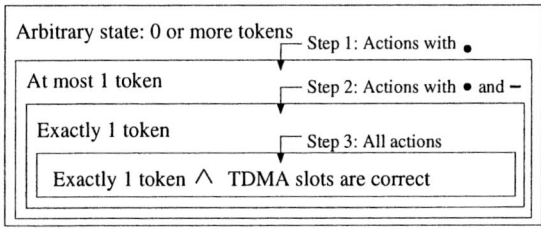

(c) Convergence to legitimate states

Fig. 5. Adding stabilization

In order to revalidate the slots, the base station initiates a token circulation once every *token circulation period*, P_{tc} slots. This value is chosen such that it is at least equal to the time taken for token circulation (i.e., $P_{tc} \geq 2*P*|E_t|$). Thus, when the base station (i.e., r) initiates a token circulation, it expects to receive the token back within P_{tc}. Towards this end, the base station sets a timeout for P_{tc} whenever it forwards the token. Now, if the base station sends a token at time t and it does not send additional token(s) before time $t + P_{tc}$ then all tokens at time t will return to the base station before time $t+P_{tc}$ or they will be lost. Hence, when the timeout expires, there is no token in the network. If the base station does not receive any token before the timeout expires, it concludes that the token is lost. Similarly, whenever a sensor (say, $j \neq r$) forwards the token, it expects to receive the token in the subsequent round within P_{tc}. Otherwise, it sets the color values in $nbrClr.j$ and $dist2Clr.j$ to undefined. And, stops transmitting until it recomputes $color.j$ and the sensors in its distance 2 neighborhood report their colors. Therefore, at most one token resides in the network at any instant.

Lemma 5.1. For any configuration, if the base station initiates a token circulation at time t and does not circulate additional tokens before time $t + P_{tc}$ then no sensor other than the base station may have a token at time $t + P_{tc}$. □

Steps 2 and 3: Recovery from Lost Token. Now, if the token is lost, the base station initiates a recovery by sending a *recovery token*. Before it sends the *recovery token*, it waits until the sensors in its distance 3 neighborhood have stopped transmitting. This is to ensure that the primitive *report_distance_2_nbrs* can update the distance 2 neighbors of the base station successfully. Let T_{rt} be the time required for sensors in the distance 3 neighborhood of the base station to stop transmitting. The value of T_{rt} should be chosen such that the sensors within distance 3 of the base station can detect the loss of the token within this interval. Although, the actual value of T_{rt} depends on the token circulation algorithm, it is bounded by P_{tc}. After T_{rt} amount of time, the base station reports its color to the sensors within distance 2 of it. As mentioned in Section 4, the primitive *report_distance_2_nbrs* ensures collision-free update since the sensors within distance 2 have stopped. Then, it forwards the *recovery token*.

When a sensor (say, j) receives the *recovery token*, it waits until the sensors in the distance 3 neighborhood of j have stopped. Then, j follows the algorithm in Section 4 to compute its color and report it to its distance 2 neighborhood.

Lemma 5.2. Whenever a sensor (say, j) forwards the *recovery token*, sensors within distance 2 of j are updated with $color.j$ without collision. □

The pseudo-code and illustration for stabilization are shown Figure 5. Once a sensor recomputes its color, it can determine its TDMA slots (cf. Section 4).

Theorem 5.3. With the above modification, starting from arbitrary initial states, the TDMA algorithm in WAC model recovers to states from where collision-free communication is restored. □

Time Complexity for Recovery. Suppose $T_{rt} = P_{tc}$, i.e., the base station waits for one token circulation before forwarding the *recovery token*. Now, when the base station forwards the *recovery token*, all the sensors in the network would have stopped transmitting. Further, whenever a sensor receives the token, it can report its color without waiting for additional time. To compute the time for recovery, observe that it takes (a) at most one token circulation time (i.e., P_{tc}) for the base station to detect token loss, (b) one token circulation for the sensors to stop and wait for recovery, and (c) at most one token circulation for the network to resume normal operation. Thus, the time required for the network to self-stabilize is at most $2 * P_{tc}+$ time taken for resuming normal operation. Since the time taken for resuming normal operation is bounded by P_{tc}, the time required for recovery is bounded by $3 * P_{tc}$. We expect that depending on the token circulation algorithm, the recovery time can be reduced. However, the issue of optimizing the recovery time is outside the scope of this paper.

Optimizations for Token Circulation and Recovery. Whenever the token is lost, it is possible that the slots are still collision-free. This could happen if the token is lost due to message corruption or synchronization errors. To deal with this problem, the base station can choose to initiate recovery only if it misses the token for a threshold number of consecutive attempts.

Additionally, to ensure that the token is not lost due to message corruption, whenever a sensor (say, j) forwards the token, it expects its successor (say, $k \in N.j$) to forward the token within a certain interval. If j fails to receive such *implicit acknowledgment* from k, j retransmits the token (in its TDMA slots) a threshold number of times. If a sensor receives duplicate tokens, it ignores such messages. Thus, the reliability of token circulation can be improved.

Optimizations for Controlled Topology Changes. Whenever a sensor is removed or fails, the slots assigned to other sensors are still collision-free and, hence, normal operation of the network is not interrupted. However, the slots assigned to the removed/failed sensors are wasted. We refer the reader to [21] on how the sensors can reclaim these slots.

Suppose a sensor (say, q) is added such that the maximum degree assumption is not violated. Towards this end, we require that whenever a sensor forwards the token, it includes its color and the colors assigned to its distance 1 neighbors. Before q starts transmitting application messages, we require q to learn the colors assigned to its distance 2 neighborhood. One way to achieve this is by listening to token circulation of its distance 1 neighbors. Once q learns the colors assigned to sensors within distance 2, it can choose its color. Thus, q can determine the TDMA slots. Now, when q sends a message, its neighbors learn q's presence and include it in subsequent token circulations. If two or more sensors are added simultaneously then these new sensors may choose conflicting colors and, hence, collisions may occur. Since our algorithm is self-stabilizing, the network self-stabilizes to states where the colors assigned to all sensors are collision-free. Thus, new sensors can be added to the network. However, if adding new sensors violates the assumption about the maximum degree of the communication graph, slots may not be assigned to the sensors and/or collisions may occur.

6 Conclusion

In this paper, we presented a self-stabilizing deterministic TDMA algorithm for sensor networks. Such algorithm suffice in transforming existing programs in shared memory model into WAC model. This is useful since many of the problems in sensor networks (e.g., routing, data diffusion, synchronization, leader election) have been extensively studied in distributed computing. Thus, this algorithm helps in quickly prototyping a sensor network application.

To our knowledge, this is the first algorithm that demonstrates the feasibility of deterministic transformation of shared memory distributed programs into a program in WAC model while preserving the property of self-stabilization on an arbitrary topology (where maximum degree of a node is known). By contrast, previous algorithms [9, 10, 11, 12] are limited to certain topologies (e.g., grid) or generate programs that are probabilistically correct.

There are several possible future directions for this work. One future direction is to develop a TDMA algorithm that (in addition to being deterministic and self-stabilizing) provides concurrency during recovery. Another future direction is to quantify the efficiency of the transformed program in WAC model using the TDMA algorithm proposed in this paper.

References

1. M. Gouda and F. Haddix. The alternator. *Workshop on Self-Stabilizing Systems*, 1999.
2. G. Antonoiu and P. K. Srimani. Mutual exclusion between neighboring nodes in an arbitrary system graph tree that stabilizies using read/write atomicity. *Euro-par'99 Parallel Processing*, 1999.
3. M. Nesterenko and A. Arora. Self-stabilization preserving atomicity refinements. *Journal of Parallel and Distributed Computing*, 62(5):766–791, 2002.
4. K. Ioannidou. Transformations of self-stabilizing algorithms. *Conference on Distributed Computing*, 2002.
5. E. W. Dijkstra. Self-stabilizing systems in spite of distributed control. *Communications of the ACM*, 1974.
6. S. Dolev. *Self-Stabilization*. The MIT Press, 2000.
7. S. S. Kulkarni and M. Arumugam. Transformations for write-all-with-collision model. *Computer Communications (Elsevier)*, 2005, to appear.
8. T. Herman. Models of self-stabilization and sensor networks. *In Proceedings of the International Workshop on Distributed Computing (IWDC)*, 2003.
9. S. S. Kulkarni and M. Arumugam. SS-TDMA: A self-stabilizing MAC for sensor networks. In *Sensor Network Operations*. IEEE Press, 2005, to appear.
10. T. Herman and S. Tixeuil. A distributed TDMA slot assignment algorithm for wireless sensor networks. *Algorithmic Aspects of Wireless Sensor Networks*, 2004.
11. C. Busch, M. M-Ismail, F. Sivrikaya, and B. Yener. Contention-free MAC protocols for wireless sensor networks. *18th Conference on Distributed Computing*, 2004.
12. V. Claesson, H. Lönn, and N. Suri. Efficient TDMA synchronization for distributed embedded systems. *IEEE Symposium on Reliable Distributed Systems*, 2001.
13. M. Ringwald and K. Römer. BitMAC: A deterministic, collision-free, and robust MAC protcol for sensor networks. *European Workshop on Sensor Networks*, 2005.
14. T. Herman. A comprehensive bibliography on self-stabilization - a working paper. http://www.cs.uiowa.edu/ftp/selfstab/bibiography.
15. A. Arora et al. ExScal: Elements of an extreme scale wireless sensor network. *International Conference on Embedded and Real-Time Computing Systems and Applications (RTCSA)*, 2005.
16. T. Herman. NestArch: Prototype time synchronization service. http://www.ai.mit.edu/people/sombrero/nestwiki/index/ComponentTimeSync, 2003.
17. C. Johnen, G. Alari, J. Beauquier, and A. K. Datta. Self-stabilizing depth-first token passing on rooted networks. *Workshop on Distributed Algorithms*, 1997.
18. F. Petit and V. Villain. Color optimal self-stabilizing depth-first token circulation. *Symposium on Parallel Architectures, Algorithms, and Networks*, 1997.

19. A. K. Datta, C. Johnen, F. Petit, and V. Villain. Self-stabilizing depth-first token circulation in arbitrary rooted networks. *Distributed Computing*, 13:207–218, 2000.
20. F. Petit. Fast self-stabilizing depth-first token circulation. *In Proceedings of the Workshop on Self-Stabilizing Systems, Springer*, LNCS:2194:200–215, 2001.
21. M. Arumugam and S. S. Kulkarni. Self-stabilizing deterministic TDMA for sensor networks. Technical Report MSU-CSE-05-19, Michigan State University, 2005.
22. E. L. Lloyd and S. Ramanathan. On the complexity of distance-2 coloring. *International Conference on Computing and Information*, 1992.
23. S. Ramanathan and E. L. Lloyd. Scheduling algorithms for multihop radio networks. *IEEE/ACM Transactions on Networking*, 1(2):166–177, April 1993.
24. S. O. Krumke, M. V. Marathe, and S. S. Ravi. Models and approximation algorithms for channel assignment in radio networks. *Wireless networks*, 2001.
25. M. G. Gouda and N. J. Multari. Stabilizing communication protocols. *IEEE Transactions on Computers*, 40(4):448–458, 1991.

Effect of Mobility on Communication Performance in Overloaded One-Dimensional Cellular Networks

Michihiro Inoue[1], Noriaki Yoshiura[2], and Yoshikuni Onozato[1]

[1] Department of Computer Science, Gunma University,
1-5-1 Tenjin-cho, Kiryu City, Gunma Prefecture, Japan
{inoue, onozato}@nztl.cs.gunma-u.ac.jp
[2] Computer Center, Gunma University,
1-5-1 Tenjin-cho, Kiryu City, Gunma Prefecture, Japan
yoshiura@lab.cc.gunma-u.ac.jp

Abstract. In this paper, we investigate the communication performance of one-dimensional cellular networks from the viewpoint of the mobile node's speed with the simulation method assuming various types of speed distributions. Simulation results are measured as blocking probabilities of both new and handoff calls and call completion probability. We can observe the phenomenon that blocking probabilities of both new and handoff calls are not related to the mobile node's speed distribution, but the call completion probability concerns with that under overloaded situation when the blocking probabilities are not small.

1 Introduction

In voice communication through the cellular networks, the speed of mobile nodes has influences on the communication performances. Because the mobile nodes with high speed have to make a successful handoff processes through its communication. Mobility of the mobile nodes in cellular networks is an important factor to execute location registration, reference, paging and so on. It is indispensable to understand accurately about the mobility of mobile nodes to utilize the radio resources efficiently and design the mobile communication networks appropriately.

In real mobile cellular communication systems, generally we can find that each mobile node moves with different speeds in the systems and its range of each speed will be different as time passes by. Therefore, we could suppose that the speed distribution of mobile nodes will not follow a constant speed. Many research papers related to mobile communication field have been done with the assumption that all mobile node move with constant speed.

Many researchers have studied the communication performances in the cellular networks considering the mobility of the mobile user. In Reference [4], the authors supposed that the mobile speed is constant and investigated the features of mobile communication traffic in the cellular networks by proposing the analytical approximation method and simulation method, especially in order to obtain the probability of handover between two cells and the mean holding time of a call in one cell. In References [1,2], the authors supposed the ring-shaped cellular networks and used the change of mobile user density to represent the investigated the time dependencies of the mobile communication traffic and executed the simulation. Moreover, some researches have assumed the probability of the mobile speed follows

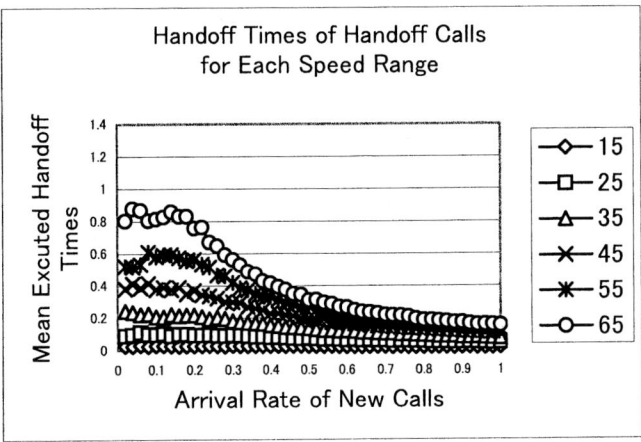

Fig. 4. Handoff times of handoff calls for each speed range in the case that the mobile node's speed is the uniform distribution

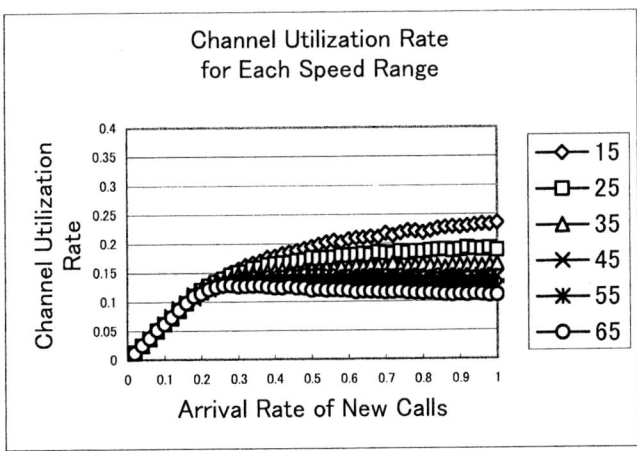

Fig. 5. Channel utilization rate for each speed range in the case that the mobile node's speed is the uniform distribution

about 0.2, the graphs of the call completion probabilities for high speed range have a steep slope, the one for middle speed range have a middle slope and the one for low speed range goes down slightly. This is because of the number of handoff times for each speed range. Since the number of handoff times for low speed mobile nodes is fewer than the number of handoff times for high speed mobile nodes, the high speed mobile nodes need to succeed the more handoff executed through their communication, as shown in Fig.4.

In Fig.5, the graphs of the channel utilization rates among different speed ranges have the same shape until the arrival rate of new calls takes about 0.2. After the arrival rate of new calls takes over about 0.2, the graphs of those rates among different speed ranges have different shapes. The graph for low speed range has higher rate than the graph for higher speed range.

3.2 Truncated Exponential Distribution

In the case that the mobile node's speed follows the truncated exponential distribution, the graphs of call completion probabilities, mean expected handoff times of handoff calls, and channel utilization rate are shown in Figs.6, 7, and 8, respectively.

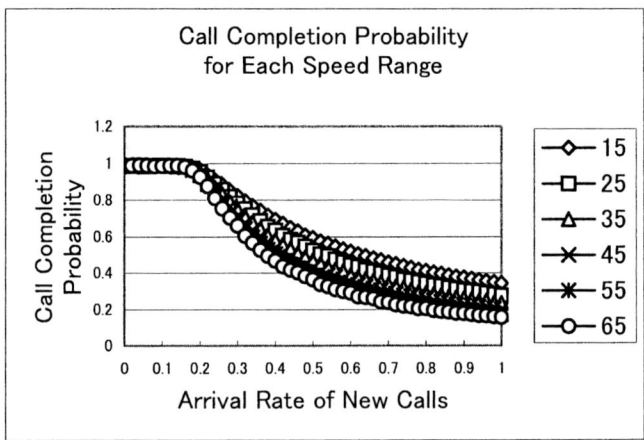

Fig. 6. Call completion probability for each speed range in the case that the mobile node's speed is the truncated exponential distribution

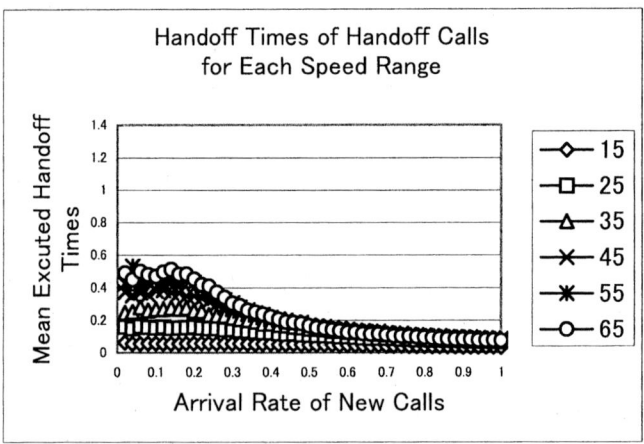

Fig. 7. Handoff times of handoff calls for each speed range in the case that the mobile node's speed is the truncated exponential distribution

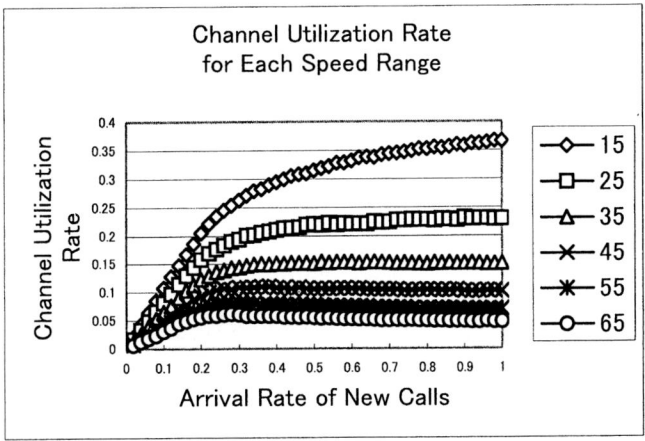

Fig. 8. Channel utilization rate for each speed range in the case that the mobile node's speed is the truncated exponential distribution

3.3 Reverse Truncated Exponential Distribution

In the case that the mobile node's speed follows the reveres truncated exponential distribution, the graphs of the call completion probabilities, mean executed handoff times of handoff calls, and channel utilization rate are shown in Figs.9, 10, and 11, respectively.

3.4 Comparison

Blocking probabilities of each arrival new or handoff calls for each speed range take almost the same value respectively, until the arrival rate of new calls takes about 0.2.

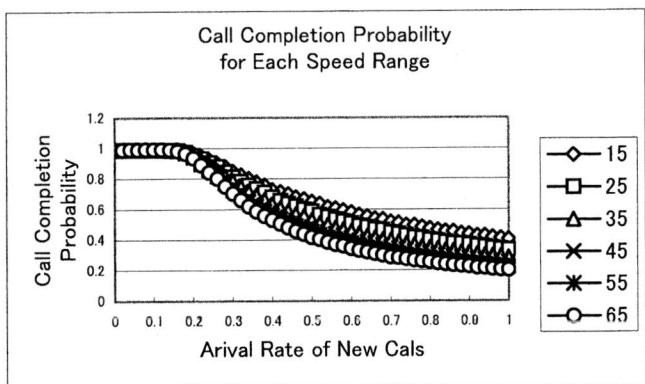

Fig. 9. Call completion probability for each speed range in the case that the mobile node's speed is the reverse truncated exponential distribution

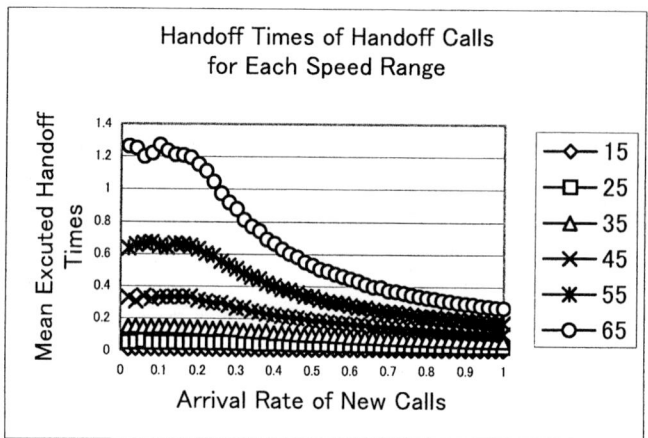

Fig. 10. Handoff times of handoff calls for each speed range in the case that the mobile node's speed is the reverse truncated exponential distribution.

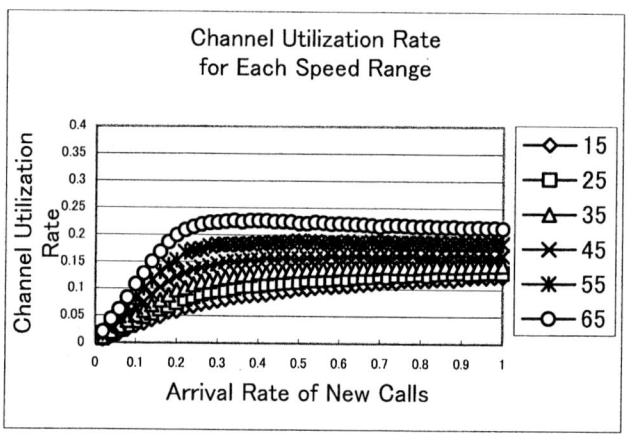

Fig. 11. Channel utilization rate for each speed range in the case that the mobile node's speed is the reverse truncated exponential distribution

The graphs of the call completion probability for each speed range will have same shape because enough channels are left for both new and handoff calls. After the arrival rate of new calls exceeds about 0.2, the demand of new and handoff call exceed the available channels. From the graphs of the channel utilization rates among different speed ranges, we can suppose that the blocking probability will begin to increase when the total channel utilization rate exceeds about 0.9 because the total of channel utilization rate of all speed ranges is about 0.9 in each speed distribution.

Channel utilization rate of each speed range will differ according to the speed distributions. Since the number of mobile nodes for each speed range will be different among three speed distributions, the number of new and handoff calls will also be different.

Call completion probability of each speed range will have different value because the number of handoff times will be changed by the mobile node's speed.

We also have investigated the call completion probability applied ordinal channel allocation systems to our simulation model. In ordinal channel allocation systems, new calls can use the rest of all channels without the reserved some channels for handoff calls. Handoff calls can use all channels in the cell including reserved channels. New calls will be restricted using the channels. Therefore the blocking probability of handoff calls will be improved compared to the systems without channel allocation systems. Especially, there are some differences of the call completion probability among the different speed ranges. The call completion probability for high-speed range will have higher probability than that for lower speed range. Therefore, in the heavy traffic situation, the fairness of the service provided from the cellular systems will not keep among the users with different mobile speed.

4 Conclusion

We have investigated the communication performances among the different speed distributions. Assuming the same mean call holding time for various speeds, we can find higher call completion probabilities, higher channel utilization rate for the lower speed of mobile node, in the overloaded traffic situation. Because once the call occupies the channel, the channel can be used until the call will have been completed.

In the future, we will propose a new channel allocation method to provide the same call completion probability among all users with different mobile speed by allocating the available reserved channels according to the demand of each mobile node with each speed range.

References

1. H.Ohtsuka., M.Sengoku., Y.Yamaguchi., T.Abe.: Basic study on mobile flows and telephone traffic. IEICE, Tech.Rep. CAS, No.249. (1987-3) 81-88
2. G.Montenegro., M.Sengoku., Y.Yamaguchi., T.Abe.: Time-dependent analysis of mobile communication traffic in a rig-shaped service area with nonuniform vehicle distribution. IEEE Transactions on Vehicular Technology, Vol.41. (1992) 243-254
3. S.Thipchaksurat., K.Kawanishi., U.Yamamoto., Y.Onozato.: Impact of Mobility on Blocking in One-dimensional Cellular Networks with New Call Channel Limiting Scheme. Proceedings of IEEE Global Telecommunications Conference (IEEE, Globecome2002). (2002-12)
4. P.V.Orlik., S.S.Rappaport.: A Model for Teletraffic Performance and Channel Holding Time Characterization in Weireless Cellular Communication with General Session and Dwell Time Distributions. IEEE Journal on Selected Areas in Communications, Vol.16, No5. (1998) 788-803

5. C.Bettstetter.: Mobility Modeling in Wireless Networks. ACM Mobile Computing and Communications Review, Vol.5, Number3. (2001-7) 55-67
6. C.Bettstetter., H.Hartenstein., X.Perez-costa.: Stochastic Properties of the Random Waypoint Mobility Model. Wireless Networks. (2004-10) 555-567
7. J.Yoon., M.Liu.: Random Waypoint Considered Harmful. The Conference on Computer Communications, Twenty-Second Annual Joint Conference of the IEEE Computer and Communications Societies (IEEE INFOCOM2003). (30 March - 3 April, 2003)

Distributed Time Slot Assignment in Wireless Ad Hoc Networks for STDMA

Subhasis Bhattacharjee and Nabanita Das

Advanced Computing and Microelectronics Unit,
Indian Statistical Institute,
203, B T Road, Kolkata 700108, India
{subhasisb_t, ndas}@isical.ac.in

Abstract. In this paper, a distributed technique is proposed to assign time slots to the nodes of an ad hoc network for Spatial Time Division Media Access (STDMA) to facilitate collision-free communication. An upper bound is established on the length of the time cycle assuming a constant bound on the degree of each node. The proposed algorithm is augmented to adapt with incremental changes in the topology.

1 Introduction

Since wireless ad hoc networks require no backbone infrastructure they can be flexibly and quickly deployed for many applications such as automated battlefield, search and rescue, and disaster relief. A communication session is achieved either through a single-hop radio transmission when the communicating nodes are within one another's transmission range, or by relaying through some intermediate nodes. As the nodes in ad hoc networks are free to move arbitrarily, the network topology may change frequently and unpredictably. Also resources like bandwidth and battery power are limited in many applications. Another major concern in ad hoc networks is that all nodes of the network use the same frequency channel for radio transmission. This along with the absence of central control makes the task of controlling the access to physical medium the most challenging issue. Poor control leads to collision among packets when two or more nodes with overlapped transmission region transmit simultaneously, whereas a very strict control leads to low throughput. The IEEE 802.11 MAC protocol provides some guidelines for accessing the physical medium based on CSMA/CA (*Carrier Sense Multiple Access with Collision Avoidance*) mechanism. This simple protocol is very effective when the medium is not heavily loaded. However, the protocol suffers form collision in transmitting control packets due to the fact that more than one node may sense the medium free and may decide to transmit simultaneously.

STDMA (spatial time division media access) [1] is a reasonable technique for managing wireless media access that substantially reduces collisions and improves fairness. Unlike TDMA, STDMA allows more than one node to transmit in the same time slot if their transmission regions are non-overlapping. Moreover,

STDMA allows ad hoc devices to conserve power by switching off the transceiver during those time slots where no message is expected. The challenges for implementing STDMA in ad hoc networks are that the time slot assignment algorithm should be distributed, scalable and adaptable to topology changes.

The problem of assigning TDMA time slots can be directly mapped to the standard problem of graph coloring [2]. There the coloring constraint is to ensure that no two nodes within the interfering distance may have the same color. However, in [3], it has been shown that this simple reduction of TDMA time slot assignment problem actually does not consider some additional opportunities of time division, and hence even a solution to minimum coloring does not necessarily produce the best result for TDMA. In that sense, the problem of optimum TDMA time slot assignment is harder than optimizing the number of colors. Many such problems are NP-complete and the approximation algorithms proposed so far are mostly not distributed [4]-[6].

Several Time Division Multiple Access (TDMA) based MAC protocols for ad hoc networks have been proposed in [7]-[9]. In STDMA time slot assignment [10]-[12], the length of the time cycle, i.e., the number of slots per cycle plays an important role. Earlier works on STDMA, in general keeps the length quite large, so that one slot is ensured per node. However, it may cause a large number of free unutilized slots per cycle, making inefficient use of channel. Also a node may have to wait for a long time before getting its turn.

In this paper, a distributed STDMA slot assignment technique is developed assuming that each node has a unique ID. An upper bound M on the number of neighbors within 2-hop distance of any node is established for an ad hoc network with a constant bound Δ on node degree. It dictates a limited number of slots $O(\Delta)$ (compared to $O(\Delta^6)$ [3]) in every cycle to ensure collision-free communication. Also, the scheme is augmented to rearrange the slots to adapt with limited perturbations in network topology. Besides collision free communication, the STDMA technique determines a transmission schedule for the nodes and hence enable the nodes to remain in the sleep mode in idle slots, saving energy significantly.

The rest of this paper is organized as follows. Section 2 describes the proposed model of the network. Section 3 derives the upper bound on the length of the time cycle. Proposed algorithm for STDMA is developed in section 4. Section 5 describes the rearrangement of STDMA scheduling when topology changes. Section 6 presents the concluding remarks.

2 Network Model

In this paper it is assumed that the system initializes with a set V of n ad hoc devices $\{v_1, v_2, \cdots, v_n\}$, deployed over a two dimensional region. All devices have equal transmission range r. The network is represented by a topology graph $G(V, E)$, an edge $(v_i, v_j) \in E$ if and only if the Euclidean distance of v_i and v_j is $\leq r$. In this paper it is assumed that $G(V, E)$ is always connected. Fig.1(a) shows a typical topology graph $G(V, E)$ with 15 nodes.

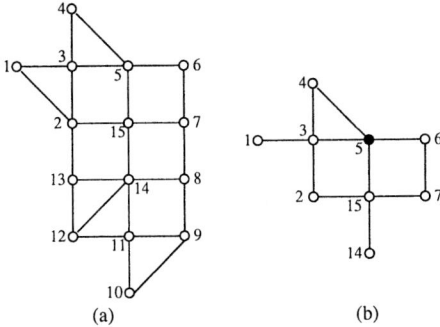

Fig. 1. (a) Topology graph (b) 2-hop Partial Graph as seen by node 5

2.1 Definitions and Assumptions

Definition 1. *For a given topology graph $G(V, E)$, for two nodes $v_i, v_j \in V$ the hop-distance $d(v_i, v_j)$ is the length of the shortest path between the two nodes in $G(V, E)$. v_i and v_j are said to be h-hop away if $d(v_i, v_j) = h$.*

Definition 2. *The h-hop neighbors of v_i in $G(V, E)$, $N^h(v_i)$ is the set of nodes $V' \subset V$, $V' = \{v_{i1}, \cdots, v_{ik}\}$ such that $d(v_i, v_{ij}) \leq h$ for $1 \leq j \leq k$.*

Definition 3. *The h-hop partial graph of v_i, $PG^h(v_i)$ is a subgraph $G'(V', E')$ of G induced by the node set $V' = N^h(v_i) \cup \{v_i\}$ but deleting the edges between any two h-hop away nodes of v_i.*

Example 1. For the topology graph $G(V, E)$ shown in Fig.1(a), the 2-hop partial graph of node 5, $PG^2(5)$ is shown in Fig.1(b).

The underlying assumptions of the model considered here are:

- Each device is identified by unique ID.
- Each device repeats the same time cycle divided into a fixed number of slots.
- Each device may start time cycles arbitrarily, but the slot boundaries are synchronized.
- The node degree is bounded by a constant Δ.

The time is slotted with each slot of a fixed time interval τ units. Each slot contains a short header H of τ_h units ($\tau_h \ll \tau$). The header is generally used for control purposes and T, the rest of the slot of duration ($\tau - \tau_h$) is used for message transmission. Fig.2 shows the time cycles at two different nodes v_i and v_j with different cycle boundaries.

2.2 Time Cycle Structure

For the given network model, an upper bound is established on the cardinality of $N^2(v_i)$, $\forall v_i \in V$, based on the node-degree bound Δ. This in turn limits the maximum number of slots required in a time cycle for STDMA.

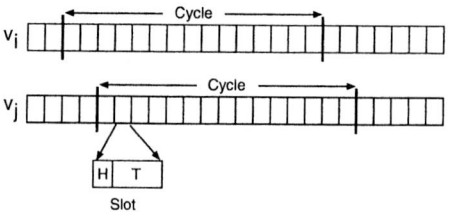

Fig. 2. The slots and cycles

Lemma 1. *Given a topology graph $G(V, E)$, any two nodes v_i and v_j of V can transmit during the same time slot without any collision only if $d(v_i, v_j) \geq 3$.*

Proof. Let the nodes v_i and v_j transmits during the same time slot. If $d(v_i, v_j) = 1$, both v_i and v_j will detect collision.

If $d(v_i, v_j) = 2$, there exists at least one node v_k, where $v_k \in N^1(v_i) \cap N^1(v_j)$. So, v_k will detect a collision.

If $d(v_i, v_j) \geq 3$, any path between these two nodes will contain at least two intermediate nodes, say, v_{ki} and v_{kj} such that $d(v_i, v_{ki}) = d(v_j, v_{kj}) = 1$. If v_i and v_j transmit during the same time slot, v_{ki} can receive the packet from v_i and v_{kj} can receive the packet from v_j without any collision. If there exists more than two intermediate nodes, then also it will be true. This proves that v_i and v_j can transmit simultaneously only if $d(v_i, v_j) \geq 3$. ∎

Lemma 2. *For any topology graph $G(V, E)$, $|N^2(v_i)| = min\{(19\Delta - 18), (\Delta^2 + 1)\}$, where Δ is the upper bound on the degree of any node $v_i \in V$, $\Delta \geq 2$.*

Proof. Let a node v_c be placed at $C(0,0)$ as shown in Fig. 3(a). Consider two circles A and B with radius r and $2r$, respectively, centered at C, r is the range of each node. Consider a chord PP' of B of length r perpendicular to x-axis such that x-axis bisects the line PP'. Hence, the co-ordinates of P and P' are $(\frac{\sqrt{15}}{2}r, \frac{r}{2})$ and $(\frac{\sqrt{15}}{2}r, -\frac{r}{2})$ respectively. Two circles E and F each with radius r are drawn centered at P and P' respectively. E and F intersect each other

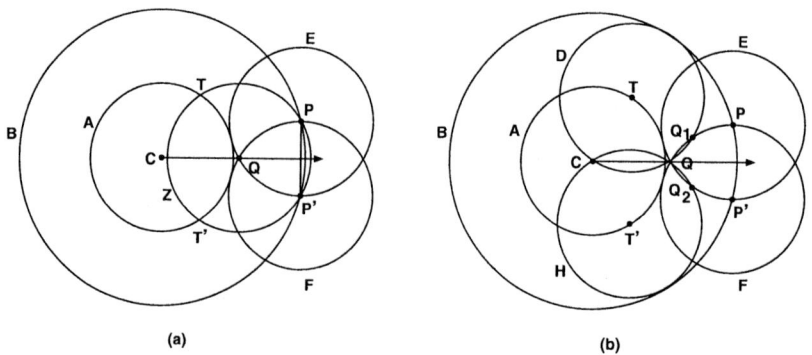

Fig. 3. Diagram for finding region boundaries in Lemma 1

on the x-axis at $Q = (\frac{\sqrt{15}-\sqrt{3}}{2}r, 0)$ inside the circle B. Consider the circle Z of radius r centered at Q intersecting the circle A at two points T and T' with coordinates $(\frac{\sqrt{15}-\sqrt{3}}{4}r, \sqrt{\frac{\sqrt{45}-1}{8}}r)$ and $(\frac{\sqrt{15}-\sqrt{3}}{2}r, -\sqrt{\frac{\sqrt{45}-1}{8}}r)$, respectively, as shown in Fig. 3(a).

Another circle D of radius r is drawn centered at T. It intersects the circle F at two points Q and $Q_1(\frac{\sqrt{15}+\sqrt{3}}{4}r, \frac{\sqrt{3\sqrt{5}-1-\sqrt{2}}}{2\sqrt{2}}r)$ as shown in Fig. 3(b). Similarly, the circle H of radius r centered at T' intersects the circle E at two points Q and $Q_2(\frac{\sqrt{15}+\sqrt{3}}{4}r, -\frac{\sqrt{3\sqrt{5}-1-\sqrt{2}}}{2\sqrt{2}}r)$ as shown in Fig. 3(b). The angle α subtended by ray $\overrightarrow{CQ_1}$ with the x-axis equals $\tan^{-1}\frac{\sqrt{2}(\sqrt{\sqrt{45}-1}-\sqrt{2})}{\sqrt{15}+\sqrt{3}} \approx 13.82°$.

Knowing the points Q, Q_1 and the angle α, the annular area between the circles B and A is partitioned into a set of regions as shown in Fig. 4. Two circles C_I and C_O of radius CQ and CQ_1 are drawn centered at C. Taking a point G on the circle A, the line segment $\overrightarrow{CG}$ is drawn that intersects the circles C_I, C_O and B at points K, L and M respectively. Consecutively, 26 rays are drawn $CG_1, \cdots, CG_{26}$ on both sides of CG_0, each making an angle α with the previous one as shown in Fig. 4. Using the points of intersection of the rays with the circles A, C_I, C_O and B, we mark 13 regions of E type and 13 regions of I type as shown in Fig. 4. Let these regions be denoted as E_i and I_i, $0 \leq i \leq 12$. Finally there will be a residual area R making an angle β of approximately $0.8204°$ (less than $1°$) as shown in Fig. 4. These E and I regions together with R cover all the regions where the 2-hop away nodes of v_c may lie. Let $n(x)$ denotes the number of nodes in a region x.

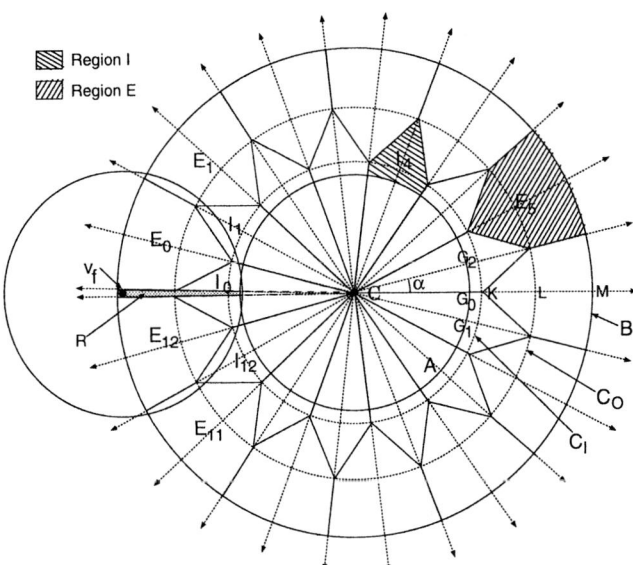

Fig. 4. The regions E and I to partition the annular region between circles A and B

Based upon the construction of E and I regions, following two observations can be made:
(a) all nodes in any E_i, or I_i region are connected to each other, and
(b) a node in I_i is connected to all nodes in the neighboring regions I_{i-1} and I_{i+1}, $\forall i = 0, \cdots, 12$ ($I_{-1} \equiv I_{12}$ and $I_{13} \equiv I_0$). It implies that $\sum_{i=0}^{12} n(I_i) < 6(\Delta - 1)$ as degree of any node is bounded by Δ, assuming that each node in I regions are connected to at least one node in $N^1(v_c)$.

Let v_f be one of the farthest 2-hop away node of v_c. Without loss of generality, let us assume that v_f is placed anywhere in the residual region R, as shown in Fig. 4. Then node v_f remains connected to all nodes within the regions E_0, E_{12} and R. It implies that $n(E_0) + n(E_{12}) + n(R) < (\Delta - 1)$. So, $\sum_{i=0}^{12} n(E_i) < 12(\Delta - 1)$.

Hence, at most $18(\Delta - 1)$ nodes can exist as 2-hop away neighbors of v_c assuming that each one is connected to v_c via at least one 1-hop neighbor within circle A. Therefore, $|N^2(v_c)| = (19\Delta - 18)$. It will be true for any node. However, for any network with a node-degree bound Δ, $|N^2(v_i)| \leq (\Delta^2 + 1)$. Hence it is evident that $|N^2(v_i)| = min\{(19\Delta - 18), (\Delta^2 + 1)\}$, for any $v_i \in V$, $\Delta \geq 2$. ∎

Theorem 1. *For a topology graph with a node degree bound $\Delta \geq 2$, $min\{(19\Delta - 18), (\Delta^2 + 1)\}$ slots are sufficient in a cycle to assign at least one slot to each node for collision-free transmission.*

Proof. Follows directly from Lemmata 1 and 2. ∎

In this paper it has been assumed that the time cycle includes $M = min\{(19\Delta - 18), (\Delta^2 + 1)\}$ slots.

3 Proposed Solution

The proposed methodology consists of two phases described below.

3.1 Initialization

As a set of ad hoc devices wake up they try to discover their neighbors during a predefined time t_d. Any node v_i may transmit a HELLO message with a small probability p, during the slot-header H of a time slot and listens during the remaining portion T of the slot. In the HELLO message, node v_i sends the ID's of all its 1-hop neighbors it has already discovered. Each node v_i repeatedly switches between the roles of sender and receiver randomly during this phase and gather knowledge about its 2-hop partial graph $PG^2(v_i)$.

Procedure Initialization(v_i, t_d) **begin**
$N^1(v_i) = \phi$
for slot=1 to t_d
   if $rand(0,1) < p$ **then** transmit HELLO message in header
   else wait to receive message
     if HELLO msg received from v_j, $N^1(v_i) = N^1(v_i) \cup \{v_j\}$; update $PG^2(v_i)$
end

3.2 TDMA Slot Assignment

Each node starts slot assignment after completing the initialization procedure.

Definition 4. *The slot assignment vector S_i of a node v_i is a vector of length M where, $S_i(j) = ID(v_k)$ if node $v_k \in (N^2(v_i) \cup \{v_i\})$ uses slot j for transmission, otherwise $S_i(j) = \phi$, $1 \leq j \leq M$.*

Example 2. Let us consider the node 5 of the network shown in Fig.1(a). Its 2-hop neighbor set is $N^2(5) = \{1, 2, 3, 4, 6, 7, 14, 15\}$. Assuming $M = 16$, a possible slot assignment vector S_5 is shown in Fig. 5. It indicates that, node 15 transmits during the time slot 2 and so on.

Definition 5. *The offset vector F_i^s with respect to a time slot s at a node v_i is a vector of length at most $(\Delta + 1)$ where each element of F_i^s is a tuple of the form (node, offset) computed from S_i and $N^1(v_i)$ as follows: $\forall v_j \in (N^1(v_i) \cup \{v_i\})$, if $\exists k$, such that $S_i(k) = v_j$ then $(v_j, k - s) \in F_i^s$.*

Example 3. Fig.5 shows F_5^9, the offset vector at node 5 with respect to current time slot 9. The F_5^9 contains 5 elements, one for each neighbor of 5. The element $(15, -7)$ in F_5^9 denotes that node 15 transmits on a slot which precedes 7 slots from the current slot 9 in node 5.

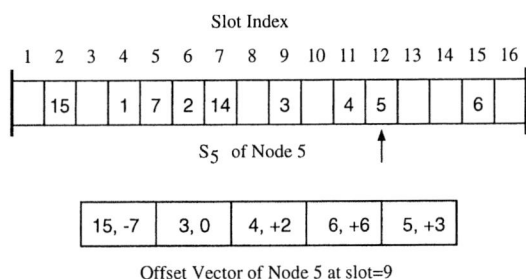

Fig. 5. The slot assignment vector and offset vector at node 5

Definition 6. *A slot assignment is consistent at node v_i if the slot selected by node v_i (i.e., $slot(v_i)$) is not used by any node $v_i \in N^2(v_i)$. The slot assignment of topology G is consistent if the slot assignment is consistent at every node in G.*

During this phase, each node v_i can assign a slot if and only if all $\{v_j : v_j \in N^2(v_i)$ and $ID(v_j) > ID(v_i)\}$ have already selected their slots. After a node selects its slot it broadcasts its offset vector and a Forward-Schedule message (FSM) asking a subset of its 1-hop neighbors in ascending order of their ID's to broadcast their offset vectors in successive slots, to inform the 2-hop neighbors who are yet to select their slots. The details of the procedure is given below.

Lemma 3. *A node sends at most $(\Delta + 2)$ messages each of length $O(\Delta)$ during slot assignment.*

Proof. The ASSIGNING operation is performed at any node only once, so at most one Forward-Schedule message is generated by any node. Each Forward-Schedule message contains an ordered set of at most Δ nodes who need to forward their *offset vector*s. Thus any node sends its *offset vector* at most $(\Delta+1)$ times; once just after its own slot assignment and at most Δ times after slot assignment of each of its neighbors. Again, both the *offset vector* and Forward-Schedule message contains $O(\Delta)$ elements. So, each node sends at most $(\Delta+2)$ messages of length $O(\Delta)$. ∎

Procedure Slot-Assignment(v_i) **begin**
$assigned = false$; $ready = false$;
$hN = \{v_j : v_j \in N^2(v_i) \text{ and } ID(v_j) > ID(v_i)\}$ // List of higher neighbors of v_i
do in each slot s
   if $assigned = false$ and $hN = \phi$ **then**
      do ASSIGNING - select free slot, update S_i, F_i^s, FSM
      send *offset vector* and Forward-Schedule message
      $assigned = true$
   else
    if scheduled to FORWARD at s
      do FORWARDING - send *offset vector* F_i^s
    else
      do WAITING - listen for incoming message
      if received *offset vector* message from v_j
         update S_i and hN
      if received Forward-Schedule message
         schedule to send *offset vector* message if required
until S_i contains an entry for each $v_j \in N^2(v_i)$
$ready = true$;
end

---

4 Dynamic Topology

The proposed time-slot assignment algorithm allocates slots to individual nodes and ensures collision-free communication assuming that the topology is static. However, as the nodes in ad hoc networks are mobile, it is obvious that the topology may change due to the mobility and/or failure of nodes. These changes in topology may happen due to the following reasons: (a) a new node is switched on, (b) a node is switched off, or (c) a node moves from one location to other. Case (c) can be considered as a combination of cases (a) and (b). Obviously, if a node switches off, its neighbors just make that slot free, keeping the remaining assignments unaltered. But if there is an addition of a new node slot assignments may have to be rearranged in the 2-hop neighborhood of the new node to avoid collision. The proposed algorithm is augmented to adapt with changes in topology provided there is no more additions within the 2-hop neighborhood of a new node until the system stabilizes. Some collisions may occur during the transition period. However, after some message exchanges among the 2-hop neighbors of the new node, finally the slots are rearranged, if necessary, and makes all communications conflict-free again.

4.1 A Node Is Switched On

Let the new node be v_{new}. It proceeds in the following way:

(1) sends a NEW message during header of each slot for its first cycle, and listens during the rest of the slots.
(2) on receiving *offset vector* from its 1-hop neighbors, v_{new} updates S_{new} and PG^2_{new}.
(3) if v_{new} does not detect any collision, it selects a free time slot, else, it waits for the colliding nodes to reassign their slots, and finally selects its own slot.
(4) intimates all its 2-hop neighbors, and the system starts normal operation.

Receiving a NEW message, the static neighbors of v_{new} send *offset vector* to v_{new} and send HOLD message to their 1-hop neighbors, requesting them to withhold normal data transfer and not to entertain any new node further. Once the slot assignment of v_{new} is over all the neighbors return back to normal operations.

The situation becomes complicated when collision is detected at v_{new} while receiving the *offset vector* from any neighbor. One such case is shown in Fig. 6. Let us assume that nodes 8 and 10 were not 2-hop neighbors of each other in the initial topology graph shown in Fig. 6(a). They use same time slot for transmission. Now the node v_{new} appears and the nodes 8 and 10 becomes 2-hop neighbors of each other through v_{new} as shown in Fig. 6(b). Now, the slots of 8 and 10 become inconsistent.

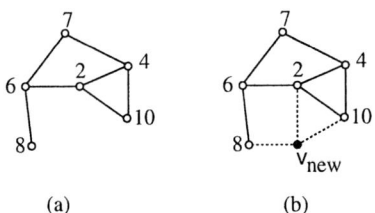

Fig. 6. Collision occurs at new node v_{new}

The new node v_{new} on detecting some collisions modifies the subsequent NEW messages by adding the offset of the slots where it has detected collisions. This allows the set of colliding nodes to identify themselves. Each colliding node $v_i \in N^1(v_{new})$ proceeds in the following way:

(1) sends INCONSISTENT message to all nodes in $N^2(v_i)$. The slot assignment of all nodes in $N^2(v_i)$ should remain unaltered until slot reassignment of v_i is over.

(2) broadcasts a SEARCH message with the ID of v_i and the ID of v_{new}
(3) wait for sufficient time to listen all incoming SEARCH messages
(4) collect the ID's of all colliding nodes from SEARCH messages, arrange in descending order, and reassign slot in its appropriate turn
(5) sends CONSISTENT message to all nodes in $N^2(v_i)$

The details of the procedures followed at the new node v_{new} and at any node $v_i \in N^1(v_{new})$ are given below.

```
Procedure New-Node($v_{new}$) begin
C = φ // C: set of colliding slots
for slot = 1 to M
    send NEW and C in header
    listen during T of the slot
    if collision is detected
        C = C ∪ slot
    else
        offset vector is received from $v_i$
        update $N^1(v_{new})$, $PG^2(v_{new})$ and $S_i$
if C ≠ φ // collision is detected
    wait until colliding neighbors reassign slots
    do ASSIGNING and send offset vector to neighbors
end
```

Theorem 2. *After the new node v_{new} is switched on, the slot reassignment procedure completes in (1) $(M+1)$ slots if no collision is detected at v_{new}, and (2) at most $((D+1)M+2\Delta+2)$ slots when collision is detected at v_{new}, where D is the diameter of the topology graph G in hops.*

Proof. First of all, it is guaranteed that the NEW messages are received by all nodes within the range of v_{new} as each of them listens during the H period of the slot assigned to it, in every cycle. This also ensures that v_{new} will eventually receive *offset vectors* from all nodes in $N^1(v_{new})$.

Let us assume that there is no collision during the first M slots of new node v_{new}. This implies that the slot assignment in G is consistent in presence of new node v_{new}. Also, v_{new} has received the slot assignment of nodes in $N^2(v_{new})$ via *offset vector* from $N^1(v_{new})$. Then v_{new} can immediately select a free slot and finish the slot assignment procedure in the next time slot. Therefore, the whole procedure completes in $(M+1)$ slots.

When collisions are detected at v_{new}, the colliding nodes identify themselves within the first $(M+1)$ slots. The SEARCH message initiated at a node v_i is received by all other colliding nodes within at most $D.M$ slots. Therefore, the colliding nodes can reassign their time slots after $((D+1)M+1)$ slots. Even if all 1-hop neighbors (at most Δ) of v_{new} need reassignment, their assignment can be finished within 2Δ slots as all other 1-hop neighbors of any colliding node v_i remain silent until v_{new} selects its own slot. This implies that the slot reassignment is completed within $((D+1)M + 2\Delta + 2)$ slots in the worst case. ∎

Procedure OnReceivingNewMsg(v_i, v_{new}) **begin**
$ready = false$; $N^1(v_i) = N^1(v_i) \cup \{v_{new}\}$
during T of $slot(v_i)$
    send *offset vector* to v_{new} and HOLD message to $N^1(v_i)$
wait to listen from v_{new} for next M slots
if collision at $slot(x_i)$
    $assigned = false$; $consistency := false$;
    $R = \{v_i\}$ // R: set of nodes to reassign slots
    send INCONSISTENT to v_j, $\forall v_j \in N^2(v_i)$
    wait until no NEW message
    broadcast $SEARCH(v_i, v_{new})$ message
    do for next D cycles
        if received SEARCH message from v_j
        $R = R \cup \{v_j\}$
        update $PG^2(v_i)$ by adding v_j as a neighbor of v_{new}
    $hN = \{v_j : v_j \in R, ID(v_j) > ID(v_i)\}$
    do in each slot of a cycle
        if $hN = \phi$
            do ASSIGNING - select first free slot and send *offset vector*
            $assigned = true$; $consistency := true$;
            send CONSISTENT message to all nodes in $N^2(v_i)$
        else
            do WAITING - listen for incoming message from v_{new}
            if received *offset vector* from v_{new}
                update S_i^2 and hN
wait until v_{new} assigns slot
$ready = true$ and send READY to $N^1(v_i)$
end

4.2 A Node Is Switched Off

Before the node v_i is switched off, it sends a *switching off* message in its slot. Knowing that v_i is getting switched off all nodes in $N^1(v_i)$ mark corresponding slot as available and inform their 1-hop neighbors to do the same thing. This also allows all 2-hop neighbors of v_i to mark the slot free.

5 Conclusion

A distributed technique for assigning time slots to the nodes of an ad hoc network is proposed here, assuming time is slotted and slot boundaries are synchronized. This allows collision-free transmission of packets by Spatial Time Division Media Access (STDMA) technique. An upper bound of $min\{(19\Delta - 18),$

$(\Delta^2 + 1)\}$ is established on the length of the time cycle assuming a constant bound Δ on the degree of each node for $\Delta \geq 2$. The assigned time slots are adjusted locally when topology changes due to mobility allowing a single addition within the 2-hop neighborhood of any node. The STDMA makes the scheduling predetermined and hence enables the nodes to remain in the sleep mode during the idle slots, saving energy significantly.

References

1. R. Nelson and L. Kleinrock: "Spatial-TDMA: A collision-free multihop channel access protocol", *IEEE Trans. Commun.*, vol. 33, no. 9, pp. 934-944, Sept. 1985.
2. S. Ramanathan: "A unified framework and algorithm for channel assignment in wireless networks", *Wireless Networks* 5(2) :81-94, 1999.
3. T Herman and S Tixeuil: "A distributed TDMA slot assignment algorithm for wireless sensor networks", *Proc. of the 1st Int. Workshop on Algorithmic Aspects of Wireless Sensor Networks*, ALGOSENSORS 2004, Springer LNCS 3121, pp. 45-58, July 2004.
4. H. L. Bodlaender, T. Kloks, R. B. Tan and J. van Leeuwen: "Approximations for coloring of graphs", *University of Utrecht, Department of Computer Science, Technical Report* 2000-25, 2000 (25 pages).
5. S. O. Krumke, M. V. Marathe and S. S. Ravi: "Models and approximation algorithms for channel assignment in radio networks", *Wireless Networks*, vol. 7, no. 6, pp. 575-584, 2001.
6. S. Ramanathan and E. L. Lloyd: "Scheduling algorithms for multi-hop radio networks", *IEEE/ACM Transactions on Networking*, vol. 1, no. 2, pp. 166-177, 1993.
7. A.-M. Chou and V. O. K. Li: "Slot allocation strategies for TDMA protocols in multihop packet radio networks", *Proc. of IEEE INFOCOM 1992*, pp. 710-716, 1992.
8. C. Zhu and M. S. Corson: "A five-phase reservation protocol (FPRP) for mobile ad hoc networks", *Wireless networks*, vol. 7, pp. 371-384, July 2001.
9. K. Sohrabi and G. J. Pottie: "Performance of a novel self-organization protocol for wireless ad hoc sensor networks", *Proc. of the IEEE 50th Vehicular Technology Conference*, pp. 1222-1226, 1999.
10. P. Bjrklund, P. Vrbrand and D. Yuan: "Resource Optimization of Spatial TDMA in Ad Hoc Radio Networks: A Column Generation Approach", *Proc. of IEEE INFOCOM 2003*, pp. 818-824, 2003.
11. J. Gronkvist: "Assignment methods for spatial reuse TDMA", *Proc. of IEEE Annual Workshop on Mobile and Ad Hoc Networking and Computing (MobilHOC)*, pp 119-124, 2000.
12. I. Chlamtac, A. Farago: "Making transmission schedules immune to topology changes in multi-hop packet radio networks", *IEEE/ACM Trans. on Networking*, vol. 2, pp. 23-29, Feb. 1994.

Efficient Algorithm for Placing Base Stations by Avoiding Forbidden Zone

Sasanka Roy[1], Debabrata Bardhan[2], and Sandip Das[1]

[1] Indian Statistical Institute, Kolkata - 700 108, India
[2] LSI Logic India Pvt. Ltd., Kolkata - 700 091, India

Abstract. Let P be a polygonal region which is forbidden in order to place a base station in the context of mobile communication. Our objective is to place one base station at any point on the boundary of P or two base stations at some specified edge and assign a range such that every point in the region is covered by those base stations and the maximum range assigned to these base stations is minimum among all such possible choice of base stations. Here we consider the forbidden region P as convex and base station can be placed on the boundary of the region. We present optimum linear time algorithms for these problems.

1 Introduction

Sometimes fixing a base station for mobile communication is difficult on some region say, water bodies, etc. However, we need to provide mobile service on that region. Here, in this paper we consider the region as convex.

Let P be a convex polygon. The vertices are $v_0, v_1, \ldots, v_{n-1}$ in anticlockwise order and the edge (v_i, v_{i+1}) is denoted by e_i.

In this paper, we are considering the following two problems in context of placing base station on boundary of polygon for covering that polygonal region. Main objective is to locate the position of base station with some additional constraints such that every point on that polygon is covered by those base stations and to minimize the maximum range of these base stations.

Problem $P1$: Locate a point α on the boundary of the polygon P such that the maximum distance from α to any point p inside polygon P is minimized.

Problem $P2$: Find two points γ and δ on a given edge e of the polygon and a length l such that every point x on the boundary of the polygon P is covered by the circles centered at γ or δ of radius l and the length of l is minimum for such choice of γ and δ.

We address these two problems in next two sections and proposed two different linear time algorithms described in each section. Although we consider these two problems as separate one, but solution technique in problem $P1$ gives some basic ideas for solving problem $P2$.

2 Problem $P1$

The motivation of this problem is to identify a location α on the boundary of a forbidden zone represented by convex polygon P for covering the region for mobile communication with minimum power consumption by reducing the size of radius of covering circle.

Euclidean 1-center problem is an well known similar type of problem which has a long history and was originally posed in 1857 by Sylvester [16]. The problem is to find the smallest circle that encloses a given set of n points. In that problem, there is no restriction on placement of the center of that circle. Shamos [12], Shamos and Hoey [13] and Preparata [11] initially proposed an $O(n \log n)$ time algorithms which are a considerable improvement over $O(n^2)$ solution proposed in [6]. Lee [9] proposed the furthest point Voronoi diagram structure and using that structure, the 1-center problem can be solved in $O(n \log n)$ time. Finally Megiddo [10] found an optimal $O(n)$ algorithm for solving this problem using prune-and-search technique.

While much has been done on such unconstrained versions of the classical problem, little has been done in constrained version. Megiddo in [10] studied the case where the center of the smallest enclosing circle must lie on a given straight line. In [7], Hurtado, Sacristan and Toussaint provided an $O(n + m)$ time algorithm for finding minimum enclosing circle with its center constrained to satisfy m linear constraints with the help of linear programming problem.

The constraints in the problem $P1$, we are addressing here are different. Instead of placing the center inside the convex region, we consider the center on the boundary of the region. A similar problem was first addressed in [4] where the center of the minimum enclosing circle lies on the boundary of a convex polygon of size n and cover a set of m points which may not lie on or inside the polygon, and provided an $O((n + m) \log(n + m))$ time algorithm for that problem. Here we derive some interesting geometric characterizations and propose an $O(n)$ time algorithm for problem $P1$ that avoids the linear programming techniques.

Let the smallest circle that cover the polygonal region P and have center on boundary of the convex region be $\mathcal{C}$. Suppose the radius of circle $\mathcal{C}$ is l and center lies at α on the boundary of convex polygonal region. Then we have the following observations.

Observation 1. *Circle $\mathcal{C}$ of radius l centered at α must passes through a vertex of polygon P, and all other points lie on or inside the circle.*

Observation 2. *Let e be the edge of polygon P that contains the point α. If the circle $\mathcal{C}$ is passing through a single vertex v of polygon P, then the line $\overline{v\alpha}$ is perpendicular to edge e at point α.*

Consider the furthest point Voronoi diagram $\mathcal{V}(V)$ for the set of n vertices V of the given polygon P. It partition the plane into convex regions, $V(p_1)$, $V(p_2)$, ..., $V(p_n)$, such that any point in $V(p_j)$ is farther from point p_j than from any other point in V. From observation 1, we can conclude that if p_i is on boundary of $\mathcal{C}$ then p_i is farthest vertex from α and hence α must be in $V(p_i)$. Sometimes the circle $\mathcal{C}$ may pass through more than one vertices of polygon P and in that case we have the following observation.

Observation 3. *If the circle C is passing through two vertices of polygon P, then α must be at some intersection point between an edge of farthest point Voronoi diagram $\mathcal{V}(V)$ and an edge of polygon P.*

From the above observations, we can conclude the following lemma.

Lemma 1. *If center α of circle C lies on edge e then α must be either a perpendicular projection of some vertex of P on edge e or an intersection point of edge e with an edge of furthest point Voronoi diagram.*

Proof: Lemma follows from observation 2 and 3. □

Therefore, to locate the circle C, we will identify the set of points A generated due to the intersection of the edges of furthest point Voronoi diagram with the edges of polygon P. We also consider each edge e of P, and identify those vertices of P, whose projection on e lie completely inside the edge e. That set of projected points on edges of the polygon is represented by set B. Note that, if the point α is from set B, then it must be a projection of some vertex v on some edge e and α is on the cell that corresponds v in farthest point Voronoi diagram. So, we only consider those points of B which lie in the farthest point Voronoi region of the corresponding projected vertex of the polygon. Hence, it becomes essential to construct the farthest point Voronoi diagram of the vertex set of polygon P and identify the intersection points with the edges of polygon P. These intersection points partition the boundary of polygon into a set of polygonal chain formed by consecutive sequence of polygonal edges bounded by points from set A. Each polygonal chain must lie on a single Voronoi region. Let us denote the set of polygonal chain as $\mathcal{B}(P)$.

While locating the point α, construction of Voronoi diagram itself will take $O(n \log n)$ time. Although the farthest point Voronoi diagram for the vertices of a convex polygon can be computed in linear time [1], computation of all the intersection points of Voronoi edges with polygonal boundary of convex polygon P needs $O(n \log n)$ time (as stated in [4]).

In [2], A. Aggarwal and Kravets introduce a linear time algorithm for finding all farthest neighbors for every vertex of a convex polygon. This result was obtained using quadrangle inequality that says, the sum of the diagonals of a quadrangle is strictly greater than the sum of two opposite sides. Using this fact, it can be shown that the matrix $M = \{m_{ij}\}$ where $m_{ij} = dist\ of\ i\ to\ (j \bmod n)$, $i < j < i+n$ and $m_{ij} = -\infty$ for other j corresponding to this convex polygon is a monotone matrix. Hence, using matrix searching technique all farthest neighbors of each vertex can be computed in linear time.

Here, instead of computing the farthest point Voronoi diagram, we present a simple $O(n)$ time algorithm for finding the set A. Let $u_0, u_1, \ldots, u_k$ be the points of set A and they are in anticlockwise order on the boundary of polygon P. These intersection points generate the set of polygonal chains $\mathcal{B}(P)$. Any chain c in $\mathcal{B}(P)$ is bounded by two consecutive points of u_i's and each one must lie on a single Voronoi cell. These will generate k polygonal chains $c_0, c_1, \ldots, c_k$, where chain c_i is bounded by points u_i and u_{i+1}. Each Voronoi cell can be represented by the respective farthest point which is a vertex of polygon P. Let the farthest vertex corresponds to the cell containing c_i be $v'_i \in \{v_0, v_1, \ldots, v_n\}$ for $0 \leq i \leq k$. Here we like to introduce a new function $index()$ as $index(v'_i) = j$ whenever $v'_i = v_j$. Below, we characterize the farthest point Voronoi diagram for the vertices of a convex polygon.

Lemma 2. *Each cell of a farthest point Voronoi diagram is unbounded convex region.*

Proof: Let any point in cell $V(p_j)$ be farther from point p_j than from any other point of the vertex set of polygon P. Therefore the point p_j must not be on that cell. Any point p on the boundary b of the cell identifies another vertex say, p_k of polygon P, such that distances between p to p_j and p_k are same. Here p_j must lie on opposite side of cell $V(p_j)$ along the boundary b. Therefore, p_j must lie on the intersection of all the half-planes defined by the lines generating the boundary of cell $V(p_j)$ and in opposite side of the cell. In case of bounded cell, no such region exists. For the proof of convexity, consider two points u and v in that cell. From simple geometry, it can be shown that any point on the joining line segment of u and v is farther from p_j than any other points of vertex set of P. □

Lemma 3. *Let e be any edge for the vertices of polygon P. The perpendicular bisector of e must define a boundary of a Voronoi cell $\mathcal{V}(V)$. Furthermore, this boundary is a half-line.*

Proof: Let the edge e be bounded by vertices u and v of polygon P. Consider l be the perpendicular bisector of edge e intersects e at point w. While moving along l from w on the direction where the polygon P belongs, the distance of u or v increases and after a certain point z, distance from u, v becomes farther than any other vertex of P. Hence, we can conclude that the half line of l from z is a Voronoi edge separating Voronoi cells correspond to vertices u and v. □

Lemma 4. *Let u, v and w be three consecutive vertices and $e_1 = (u, v)$ and $e_2 = (v, w)$ are two consecutive edges of the convex polygon P. If the perpendicular bisector of those two edges intersects outside the polygon, then there does not exist any point on boundary of P from which v is the farthest among all vertices of P.*

Proof: Let l_1 and l_2 be the perpendicular bisectors of e_1 and e_2 respectively and they intersect at point q outside the polygon. The Voronoi cell corresponds to point u and the Voronoi cell corresponds to point v are in the opposite half planes generated by line l_1. Similarly, the Voronoi cell corresponds to point w and the Voronoi cell corresponds to point v are in the opposite half planes generated by line l_2. Therefore the Voronoi cell corresponds to point v must be in the common region of two half plane as shown in Fig. 1. □

From the above lemma, we also conclude that the cardinality of set A is less than the cardinality of set V, that is, k is less than or equal to n. The following lemma indicates the arrangement of Voronoi cells along the boundary of the polygon.

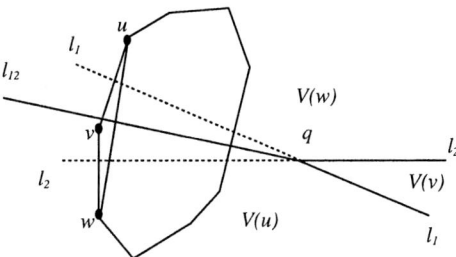

Fig. 1. Illustrating the proof of lemma 4

Lemma 5. *If $index(v'_r)$ is the least value among all index values of $v'_i (0 \leq i \leq k)$, then $index(v'_r) < index(v'_{r+1}) < \ldots, < index(v'_k) < index(v'_0) < \ldots < index(v'_{r-1})$*

Proof: The common boundary of the polygonal chains c_r and c_{r+1} is the point u_{r+1} on the perpendicular bisector (say l) of the line segment formed by joining vertices v'_r and v'_{r+1}. The vertex v'_r must lie on the half-plane generated by line l along the side containing polygonal chain c_{r+1}. The vertex v'_{r+1} is on anticlockwise direction of v'_r along the boundary of the polygon P as shown in Fig. 2. So, a circle centered at u_{r+1} with radius $dist(u_{r+1}, v'_r)$ must pass through v'_r, v'_{r+1} and polygon P is inside the circle. As the index of v'_r is least among all index values of $v'_i (0 < i < k)$, so $index(v'_r) < index(v'_{r+1})$. Note that any circle with center at boundary of P and contains polygon P does not intersect the arc (v'_r, v'_{r+1}) in the direction v'_r to v'_{r+1} (Fig. 2). If $index(v'_{r+1}) - index(v'_r) > 1$, then for all $\beta \in [index(v'_r), index(v'_{r+1})]$, there does not exist any point on boundary of polygon P from which v_β is farthest among all vertices of polygon P. Hence the lemma follows. □

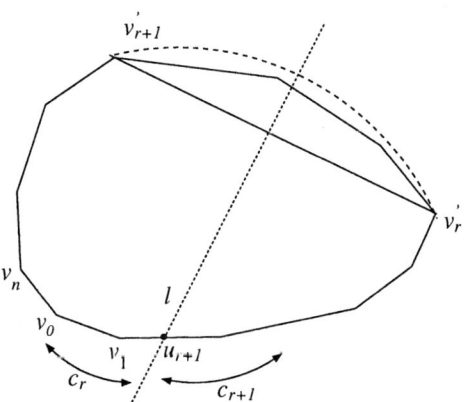

Fig. 2. Illustrating the proof of lemma 5

2.1 Algorithm

Now we devise an algorithm that generates the points $u_0, u_1, \ldots, u_k$. Using monotone matrix searching technique as in [2], we can compute the farthest among vertices of polygon P from each vertex of P in linear time. For each vertex v of V, we can map the representing vertex of Voronoi cell that contain vertex v using the allotment of farthest vertex from each vertices of P. Instead of locating the boundary of Voronoi cell, here we demarcate the Voronoi cell by the vertex which is farthest from any point on that cell. Note that some cell in farthest point Voronoi diagram may not contain any vertex of polygon P, and in that case, corresponding polygonal chain (if exists) is a straight line segment bounded by two consecutive points of $u_0, u_1, \ldots, u_k$ on some edge of P.

Let v_γ be the farthest point from v_0 and therefore, v_0 must be in the Voronoi cell that corresponds to vertex v_γ. Without loss of generality, we can assume that the vertex v_0 is in polygonal chain c_0. So, u_1 is a boundary of the polygonal chain c_0 which is in counter-clockwise direction of v_0. Here, u_1 is on the perpendicular bisector of the line segment joining v_γ and some vertex say v_δ of polygon P in counter-clockwise direction of v_γ. Then from lemma 4, we can conclude that the boundary of the polygon P is not intersected by the cells corresponding to vertices $v_{\gamma+1}, v_{\gamma+2}, \ldots, v_{\delta-1}$. To identify the point u_1, proceed along the vertices of P in anticlockwise direction from vertex v_0 until we locate v_i which is not in Voronoi cell of v_γ but v_{i-1} is in Voronoi cell of v_γ. Let us assume that v_i is in Voronoi cell corresponding to v_ψ. Let e denotes the edge between vertices v_{i-1} and v_i. To locate v_δ for computing u_1 and also to identify other u_i's on e, we proceed as follows:

Consider the vertices $v_{\gamma+1}, v_{\gamma+2}, \ldots, v_{\psi-1}, v_\psi$ in that order. Maintain a linklist $\mathcal{L}$ that stores the intersection points generated due to intersection between the edge $e = (v_{i-1}, v_i)$ and the boundary of Voronoi cells which are actually perpendicular bisectors of the joining line segments of two vertices from $v_\gamma, v_{\gamma+1}, v_{\gamma+2}, \ldots, v_{\psi-1}, v_\psi$. For generating this list $\mathcal{L}$, initially consider the perpendicular bisector of line segment $v_\gamma, v_{\gamma+1}$. Store the intersection point of perpendicular bisector with e in list $\mathcal{L}$. Consider next vertex $v_{\gamma+2}$. Compute the intersection point between perpendicular bisector of line segment $v_{\gamma+1}, v_{\gamma+2}$ with e. If the intersection point is in anticlockwise direction then push the intersection point in list $\mathcal{L}$ and repeat the process by considering next vertex say $v_{\gamma+3}$ and so on. On the contrary, if the intersection point is on clockwise direction of last inserted point in the list $\mathcal{L}$, then from lemma 4, we conclude that the Voronoi cell corresponding to vertex $v_{\gamma+1}$ must not intersect the polygon boundary and hence does not correspond any polygonal chain. In that case we pop the last inserted intersection point from list $\mathcal{L}$ and consider the perpendicular bisector of line segment joining $v_{\gamma+2}$ and v_γ which one is the previous vertex (in clockwise direction) of the dropped vertex. Here, in each such cases, we are effectively dropping one vertex from set $v_{\gamma+1}, v_{\gamma+2}, \ldots, v_{\psi-1}, v_\psi$. This process continues until we find list $\mathcal{L}$ empty or no more pop is required from list $\mathcal{L}$. If the list becomes empty after some pop operation, push the current intersection point into the list and consider next the vertex in set $v_{\gamma+1}, v_{\gamma+2}, \ldots, v_{\psi-1}, v_\psi$ and repeat the process. After consideration of all such vertices, list $\mathcal{L}$ outputs intersection points $u_0, u_1, \ldots, u_m$ generated due to intersection between the edge $e = (v_{i-1}, v_i)$ and the boundary of Voronoi cells in anticlockwise order. Note that, we can drop at most $n - k$ vertices, which are not contributing any chain, so this sorts of modification will be needed in at most $n - k$ cases and that will take $O(n - k)$ additional time. Therefore we can conclude the following theorem.

Theorem 1. *The intersection points between the edges of a convex polygon of n vertices with the Voronoi edges of the farthest point Voronoi diagram constituted by the vertices of the polygon can be determined in $O(n)$ time*

Proof: Follows from above discussion. □

3 Problem $P2$

Here we consider other variations of this problem. Instead of placing one center on the boundary, we like to place two circles in order to cover the region. Given a set S, of n points, the *2-center problem* for S is to cover S by two closed disks whose radius is as small as possible. In [14], Sharir presents a near-linear algorithm running in $O(n \log^9 n)$ time. Currently best algorithm for its solution is proposed by Chan [5]. They suggest a deterministic algorithm that runs in $O(n \log^2 n (\log \log n)^2)$ and a randomized algorithm that runs in $O(n \log^2 n)$ time with high probability. In general, the Euclidean p-center problem is NP-hard. A variation of this problem is the *discrete two-center problem* that finds two closed disks whose union cover the point set S and whose centers are at points of S. This problem is solved in $O(n^{4/3} \log^5 n)$ time by Agarwal et al. [3]. Recently, Kim et al. [8] solve both of the standard and discrete two-center problem for a set of points that are in convex positions in $O(n \log^3 n \log \log n)$ and $O(n \log^2 n)$ time respectively.

In this paper, we consider different variation of constraints in placing two circles for covering the convex polygonal region P. We consider the case, where only one side of the convex polygon is available for placing base stations in order to cover the region. Placement of a single base station on that edge with minimum range for covering that region can be done using the same technique as described in Problem $P1$ and therefore the base station location can be identified in $O(n)$ time. Now our objective is to find two points on that specified edge e for placing base stations such that the maximum range required for base stations to communicate any point on that region from at least one of these two base stations is minimum among all such possible choice of pair of points on edge e. Here we propose an $O(n)$ time algorithm for this problem $P2$.

Without loss of generality, we may assume that the edge e is on x-axis and e is the joining line segment of vertices v_0 and v_1, where v_0 is on left side of v_1 (see Fig. 3). Let $x(v)$ denotes the x-coordinate of vertex v. The distance function $dist(v, v')$ outputs the Euclidean distance between two points v and v'. Suppose C_1 and C_2 are two equal radius circles of optimum size covering the region P with their centers constrained to lie on edge e say at α and β respectively. Without

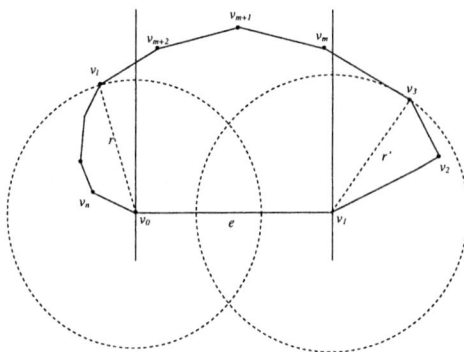

Fig. 3. Illustrating the proof of Observation 4

loss of generality, we also can assume that $x(\alpha)$ is less than $x(\beta)$, that is, C_1 is on left side of C_2. Then we have the following observations.

Observation 4. *Let r be the maximum distance from v_0 among all vertices of P whose x-coordinate is less than $x(v_0)$, and r' be the maximum distance from v_1 among all vertices of P whose x-coordinate is greater than $x(v_1)$. Then the radius of each circle C_1 and C_2 is greater than equal to $\max(r, r')$.*

Observation 5. *If a vertex v is in C_1 but not in C_2 and a vertex v' is in C_2 but not in C_1, then $x(v) < x(v')$.*

Note that, if a single minimum radius circle with center on e encloses the polygon P, then its radius is greater than equal to r and the radius of the circle is exactly equal to r if it is passing through only one vertex of P. This can be detected in linear time using the techniques described in previous. Now onwards, assume that the circles C_1 and C_2 are smaller than the single circle that covered the entire polygon P with center on edge e.

Let k and k' be the maximum and minimum index of v respectively such that v_k is not in C_1 and $v_{k'}$ is not in C_2. That is, the vertices $v_0, v_n, v_{n-1}, \ldots v_{k+1}$ of P are in C_1 and $v_1, v_2, \ldots v_{k'-1}$ are in C_2. Then from observation 5, we can conclude that $x(v_{k'}) < x(v_k)$.

The following lemma indicates the position of the centers of the enclosing circles.

Lemma 6. *Let C' and C'' be two minimum radius circles enclosing point set $\{v_1, v_2, \ldots v_s\}$ and point set $\{v_1, v_2, \ldots v_{s'}\}$ respectively among all such circles having center on edge e.*

1. *If $s' > s$ then the x-coordinate of the center of circle C' is greater than or equal to the x-coordinate of the center of circle C''.*
2. *If $s' > s$ then the radius of circle C' is less than or equal to the radius of circle C''.*

3. Suppose both the circle is passing through exactly two vertices of polygon P and $s' > s$. If C' is passing through the vertices v_a and v_b of polygon P with $a < b$ and C'' is passing through the vertices v_z and v_w of polygon P with $z < w$ then $z \leq a < b \leq w$.

Proof: First two statements follows from simple Euclidean geometry. Third statement can be proved using statement 2 and observation 3. □

Hence from lemma 6, we can conclude that if the radius of circle C' enclosing point set $\{v_0, v_n, v_{n-1}, \ldots v_s\}$ with $s \geq k+1$ is minimum among all such circles having center on edge e, then the center of the circle C' is on left side of point α. Similarly, if the radius of circle C'' enclosing point set $\{v_1, v_2, \ldots v_{s'}\}$ with $s' \leq k' - 1$ is minimum among all such circles having center on edge e, then the center of the circle C'' is on right side of point β.

Again from Lemma 1, we can conclude that the center of circle C'' is either on edge e with x-coordinate $x(v_i)$, $1 \leq i \leq s'$ or it is at some intersection point of e with an edge of the farthest point Voronoi diagram constituted by the point set $\{v_1, v_2, \ldots v_{s'}\}$. Similar things can be concluded for the center of circle C' covering point set $\{v_0, v_n, v_{n-1}, \ldots v_s\}$. Therefore we are interested about the intersection points of e with the edges of two farthest point Voronoi diagrams with point sets $\{v_0, v_n, v_{n-1}, \ldots v_s\}$ and $\{v_1, v_2, \ldots v_{s'}\}$.

Initially while preprocessing the point set, we do not have any prior information of s and s'. Therefore below we would like to propose a technique of dynamic updation of the intersection points of Voronoi edges with edge e while introducing a new point in the point set of farthest point Voronoi diagram.

Lemma 7. *Let $\{u_1, u_2, \ldots u_m\}$ be the set of points generated due to intersection between edge e and the edges of the farthest point Voronoi diagram constituted by $\{v_1, v_2, \ldots v_l\}$ where $x(u_1) \leq x(u_2) \leq \ldots \leq x(u_m)$. After introducing the vertex v_{l+1} in the point set of farthest point Voronoi diagram, if the intersection points of e with edges of farthest point Voronoi diagram constituted by $\{v_1, v_2, \ldots v_{l+1}\}$ are $\{u'_1, u'_2, \ldots u'_t\}$, where $x(u'_1) \leq x(u'_2) \leq \ldots \leq x(u'_t)$ then*
(1) $m + 1 \geq t$
(2) $u_1 = u'_1, u_2 = u'_2, \ldots, u_{t-1} = u'_{t-1}$.
Furthermore, if u_{t-1} is generated by the perpendicular bisector of the line segment joining vertices v_i and v_{i+j} ($i, j > 0$), then u'_t is the point generated due to intersection of edge e with the perpendicular bisector of line segment joining vertices v_{i+j} and v_{l+1}.

Proof: Follows from the property of farthest point Voronoi diagram and from Lemma 4 and 5. □

Lemma 8. *The amortized time complexity for reporting the intersection points between c and edge of the furthest point Voronoi diagram while introducing the vertices $\{v_{l+1}, v_{l+2}, \ldots, v_n\}$ in that order one at a time in the point set of a farthest point Voronoi diagram constituted by $\{v_1, v_2, \ldots v_l\}$ is $O(n)$.*

Proof: Proof follows from above discussion and from similar arguments for proof of Theorem 1. □

3.1 Algorithm

Now we are in position to describe the algorithm for computing minimum radius circles C_1, C_2 with centers α and β respectively on edge e for covering the region P. First we try to locate two minimum radius circles C' and C'' with centers on edge e such that all the vertices of P are on or inside one or both the circles C' and C''. In order to locate C' and C'', we follow an iterative method and have at most $O(n)$ iteration steps. We consider initial solution by circles C'_0 and C''_0 centered at vertices v_0 and v_1 respectively. C'_0 covers all the vertices $v \in V$ with $x(v) \leq x(v_0)$ and C''_0 covers all the vertices $v \in V$ with $x(v) \geq x(v_1)$. Suppose the circle C'_0 having radius r'_0 is passing through vertices a and b with $x(a) \leq x(b)$ and the circle C''_0 having radius r''_0 is passing through vertices z and w with $x(z) \leq x(w)$. Let w'_1 and w''_1 be two vertices among the uncovered vertex set that have minimum and maximum x-coordinate respectively. If r'_0 is smaller than r''_0, then we try to include w'_1 along with points of C'_0 as next iterative step and form a new minimum radius circle C'_1 having center at an edge e covering vertices $\{v_0, v_n, v_{n-1}, \ldots w'_1\}$. Circle C'_1 must passes through vertex w'_1. The center of circle C'_1 is either at projection of w'_1 on e or on left of that point and passing through another vertex η of P. From lemma 6, we can conclude that $x(a) \geq x(\eta)$. While determining the vertex η, we compute the intersection point of farthest point Voronoi diagram constituted by vertex set $\{v_0, v_n, v_{n-1}, \ldots w'_1\}$ with edge e. From lemma 8, we conclude that the complexity for generating these intersection points over all iteration is of $O(n)$. Here the center of C'_1 must be on edge e at Voronoi cell corresponds to vertex w'_1 and the center is on rightmost boundary of the partition on e due to cell representing vertex w'_1. Hence we can compute the radius of circle C'_1. If r'_0 is greater than r''_0, then w''_1 is included along points of C''_0 and form a new circle C''_1 using similar type of technique described above. This process continues until no vertex remains uncovered by these two circles.

While considering the last uncovered vertex, a typical situation may arise. Let C'_k and C''_k be two circles with radius r'_k and r''_k respectively after k iterative steps, covers all vertices except the last one. Without loss of generality, assume that $r'_k \leq r''_k$. Therefore in the next iteration, after consuming the last uncovered vertex, the circle C'_k turns a bigger circle and its radius may become even larger than the radius of modified circle C''_k after absorbing the last uncovered vertex. Therefore, we need to consider this case and generate the minimum radius circles C' and C'' with centers on edge e that cover all the vertices of polygon P.

Theorem 2. *A pair of circles C' and C'' with centers on edge e cover all the vertices of polygon P and maximum radius of these two circle is minimum among all such possible cover. Then these two circles can be located in $O(n)$ time.*

Proof: Result follows from above discussion and from Lemma 6, 7 and 8. □

But there is no guarantee that these two circles C' and C'' covers the polygonal region completely.

Observation 6. *Either circles C' and C'' together cover the polygon P completely, or only a segment of an edge among the boundary of polygon P is uncovered by these two circles.*

If the circles C' and C'' do not cover the the polygon completely, then the uncovered edge e' can be detected while computing these two circles. Therefore, for locating the optimum circles C_1 and C_2 covering the region P having centers at α and β respectively on edge e, we first identify the edge e' of P. Note that the circles C_1 and C_2 are of same size and must intersect at some point on edge e'. Let that point be denoted by π and the equation of the line corresponding to edge e' be $y = m.x + c$. Suppose a be the vertex of P which is on the boundary of circle C' having least x-coordinate value and w be the vertex of P which is on the boundary of circle C'' having greatest x-coordinate values. From Lemma 6, we can conclude that C_1 is passing through either vertex a or some other vertex on left side of a and similarly, C_2 is passing through either vertex w or some other vertex with greater x-coordinate value than w.

Observation 7. *The point π is the intersection point between the perpendicular bisector of the line segment joining point α and β with the edge e'*

Consider the coordinate of π as (x, y) and the coordinate of α is $(\epsilon, 0)$. From above observation, we can say that the coordinate of β is $(2x - \epsilon, 0)$. Assume that the circles C_1 and C_2 is passing through a and w respectively, whose coordinates are known constants. As both the circles are passing through π and have centers α and β respectively, we can solve x, y and ϵ by finding the roots of a four degree polynomial. In case the point α and β are not in the Voronoi cells correspond to vertex a and w respectively, then using the iteration technique described above we can locate the vertices on left of a or to the right of w that are on the circles C_1 and C_2. Hence we have the following theorem.

Theorem 3. *The minimum radius circles C_1 and C_2 covering the region P with centers on edge e can be computed in $O(n)$ time.*

References

1. A. Aggarwal, Leonidas J. Guibas, J. Saxe and P. Shor, A linear time algorithm for computing the Voronoi diagram of a convex polygon, *Proc. 19th Annu. ACM Sympos. Theory Comput.*, pages 39-45, 1987.
2. A. Aggarwal and Dina Kravets, A linear time algorithm for finding all furthest neighbours in a convex polygon, *Inf. Proc. Let.*, pp. 17-20, 1989.
3. P.K. Agarwal, M. Sharir and E. Welzl, The discrete 2-Center problem, *Proc. 13th Anno. ACM Sympos. Comput. Geom.*, pp. 147-155, 1997.
4. P. Bose and G. Toussaint, Computing the constrained Euclidean, geodesic and link center of a simple polygon with applications, *Proc. of Pacific Graphics International*, pp. 102-112, 1996.
5. T.M. Chan, More planar two-center algorithms, *Computational Geometry: Theory and Application*, vol. 13, pp 189-198, 1999.
6. J. Elzinga and D. W. Hearn, Geometrical solutions to some minimax location problems *Transp. Sci.*, vol. 6, pp. 379-394, 1972.
7. F. Hurtado, V. Sacristan and G. Toussaint, Facility location problems with constraints, *Studies in Locational Analysis*, vol. 15, pp. 17-35, 2000.

8. S.K. Kim, and C-S Shin, Efficient algorithms for two-center problems for a convex polygon, *Proc. 6th Int. Conf. Computing and Combinatorics*, pp. 299-309, 2000.
9. D.T. Lee, Furthest neighbour Voronoi diagrams and applications, *Report80-11-FC-04, Dept. Elect. Engrg. Comput. Sci., Northwestern Univ., Evanston, IL*, 1980.
10. N. Megiddo, Linear-time algorithms for linear programming in R^3 and related problems, SIAM J. Comput., vol 12, pp. 759-776, 1983.
11. F. Preparata, Minimum spanning circle, *Technical report, Univ. Illinois, Urbana, IL, in Steps into Computational Geometry*, 1977.
12. M. I. Samos, Computational geometry, *Ph D. thesis. Dept. Computer Sci., Yale Univ., New Haven, CT* , 1978.
13. M.I. Shamos and D. Hoey, Closest-point problem, *Proc. 16th Annual IEEE Sympos. Found. Comput. Sci.*, pages 151-162, 1975.
14. Micha Sharir, A Near-Linear Algorithm for the Planar 2-Center Problem, *Symposium on Computational Geometry*, pp. 106-112, 1996.
15. Chan-Su Shin, Jung-Hyun Kim, Sung Kwon Kim and Kyung-Yong Chwa, Two-Center Problems for a Convex Polygon, *Proc. of the 6th Annual European Symposium on Algorithms*, pp. 199-210, 1998.
16. J. J. Sylvester, A question in the geometry of situation, *Quarterly Journal of Matthematices*, pp. 1-79, 1857.

Secure Two-Party Context Free Language Recognition

Anshuman Singh, Siddharth Barman, and K.K. Shukla

Dept. of Computer Sc. and Engg., Institute of Technology, Banaras Hindu University,
Varanasi, India - 221005
anshum4n@yahoo.com, siddharth.barman@cse05.itbhu.org,
shukla@ieee.org

Abstract. The growth of the internet provides opportunities for cooperative computation, it also requires development of protocols that can accomplish this task among mutually untrusting parties. The aim is to develop methods which ensure both the correct evaluation of the function and privacy of individual inputs. Multiparty Computation protocols help to achieve the aim without using a trusted third party.

In this paper we consider the problem of context-free language recognition in a two-party setting. Alice has the description of a context-free language L while Bob has a secret string whose membership in L is to be checked. Neither Alice nor Bob is ready to disclose his/her input to the other. Here we propose a protocol which accomplishes secure two party context-free language recognition. The novelty of this paper lies in the use of formal languages based approach for multiparty computations.

1 Introduction

The development of computer networks and consequently the Internet has opened the wide area of distributed computation. Internet allows computers from far off places to interact and opens possibilities that were unknown before. A scenario is conceivable where some parties want to compute a function over data which is distributed among the parties, but none of the parties want to disclose their private data. A naive solution would be to send the data to a trusted party who performs the computation and returns the results to respective parties. However a trusted agency may not be available or affordable. In such a case we can use cryptographic techniques of Secure Multiparty Computation.

Secure multi-party computation (MPC) was introduced by Yao in [1]. It deals with the problem of securely computing an arbitrary function f over the private inputs of n players. Here security means guaranteeing the correctness of the output as well as the privacy of the player's inputs, even when some players cheat. Assuming we have inputs $x_1, x_2, \ldots x_n$ where player i knows x_i, we want to compute $f(x_1, x_2, \ldots x_n) = (y_1, y_2, \ldots y_n)$ such that player i is guaranteed to learn y_i, but can get no more information. A number of cooperative computation problems have been shown to be plausible, in a secure way, using multi party computational techniques [2, 5]. Generic solutions have been developed [3, 8] and much effort has been directed towards reducing the communication complexity [7] and round complexity [6] of these solutions.

In this paper we are concerned with Context Free Language Recognition (CFLR) in a two-party setting. In a traditional setting the problem of CFLR is to determine the membership of a string **w** in a context free language **L**. In the two party setting the problem remains the same but the inputs are distributed among two different parties, Alice and Bob. Now Alice has a private context free grammar **G** while Bob has a private string **w**. Bob wants to check the membership of **w** in **L(G)**, the language generated by **G**. Also neither of the two is willing to disclose his/her private input to the other.

CFLR is an interesting problem and has various applications. For instance, the problem of checking the syntactic correctness of a program can be posed as CFLR. Also pattern matching and recognition queries can be posed as CFLR. Numerous other decision problems can be solved using CFLR. The basic methodology is to describe some class of objects using a context free grammar **G**. When a new object is encountered, we determine it's membership in **L(G)**. This tells us whether the new object belongs to the same class or not. A solution for the two-party version of CFLR can be used to solve the above problems in a secure two-party manner.

It is the first time that a formal language based approach has been used for solving multiparty computation problems. The completeness of multiparty protocols has been shown in [2]. The solution given in [2] can be used to solve the membership question for recursive languages, i.e. the languages recognized by a turing machine. Since context free languages are a proper subset of recursive languages, CFLR can also be solved using such a method. However, the protocol that we present here generates a more efficient solution of membership question for context free languages than promised by the generic approach. This is because our solution utilizes the specific properties of context free grammars, used in description of a context free language.

2 Preliminaries

In this section we give the notation and definitions of the terms used in this paper. Most of the content of this section from basic formal language theory. We have endeavored to use standard notations throughout. A superscript on a vector, such as S^m, denotes the mth bit of it. Also $|V|$ represents the size of set V.

Formal Language Basics. A grammar $G = (V, T, S, P)$ is said to be context-free if all its productions are of the form $A \to x$ where $A \in V$ and $x \in (V \cup T)^*$. Here V is the set of variables, T is the set of terminals, S is the starting symbol and P are the production/rewrite rules. A language L is said to be context-free if and only if there exists a context-free grammar G, such that $L = L(G)$. Here $L(G)$ denotes the set of strings that can be produced by the grammar. This can also be written as "$L = \{w \in T^* | S \Rightarrow^* w\}$?" where the symbol '$\Rightarrow^*$' stands for 'derives'.

Given a context grammar G and a string w the problem of CFLR is to determine the answer to the following question "Does $w \in L(G)$?". We now give a definition for the two-party version of CFLR.

Secure Two-Party Context Free Language Recognition Protocol. Alice and Bob, determine whether Bob's secret string w is present in Alice's secret Context Free Language $L(G)$. At the end of the protocol the following properties must hold.

- Bob knows whether **w**$\in L(G)$
- Alice gains no information about **w**
- Bob gains only as much information about **L(G)** as can be determined from the output, i.e. whether **w** is accepted by **L(G)** or not.

Solving Context Free Language Recognition: The CYK Membership Algorithm. There are many existing algorithms for solving CFLR. One of the standard methods is the CYK membership algorithm [11]. It's time complexity is cubic in the size of the input. There exist some efficient (linear time) membership algorithms that can solve some restricted versions of CFLR. We selected CYK for it's generality. The CYK algorithm requires the context free grammar to be converted to chomsky normal form. A context free grammar $G = (V, T, S, P)$ is in chomsky normal form if all it's productions are of the form $A \to BC$ or $A \to a$ where $A, B, C \in V$ and $a \in T$. Any context-free grammar can be written in chomsky normal form following a straightforward set of rules [11]. The CYK algorithm first converts a given grammar in CNF and then utilizes it to determine membership. We now describe the CYK algorithm.

Assume that we have a grammar $G = (V, T, S, P)$ in Chomsky Normal Form and a string $w = w_1 w_2 ... w_n$. We define sub-string $w_{ij} = w_i ... w_j$ and subsets of V, $S_{ij} = \{A \in V : A \Rightarrow^* w_{ij}\}$. Clearly $w \in L$ if and only if $S \in S_{1n}$. To compute S_{ii}, observe that $A \in S_{ii}$ if and only if G contains a production $A \to w_i$. Therefore S_{ii} can be computed for all $1 \leq i \leq n$ by inspection of w and the productions of the grammar. To continue notice that for $j > i$, A derives w_{ij} if and only if there is a production $A \to BC$, with $B \Rightarrow^* w_{ik}$ and $C \Rightarrow^* w_{k+1j}$ for some k with $i \leq k < j$. In other words

$$S_{ij} = \bigcup_{k \in \{i, i+1, ..., j-1\}} \{A : A \to BC, \text{ with } B \in S_{ik}, C \in S_{k+1j}\} \quad (1)$$

An inspection of indices show that the above equation can be used to compute all the S_{ij}s if we proceed in the sequence

1. Compute $S_{11}, S_{22}, ..., S_{nn}$
2. Compute $S_{12}, S_{23}, ..., S_{n-1n}$
3. Compute $S_{13}, S_{24}, ..., S_{n-2n}$

and so on.

Cryptographic Assumptions and Oblivious Transfers. The security of our protocol is based on oblivious transfers. Oblivious Transfers are a basic cryptographic primitive that has proved necessary for many of the protocols [10]. It allows multiple parties to get individual secrets from a single seller. There are different definitions of oblivious transfers [4, 12]. In it's most primitive form, the sender has an input $(b_1, b_2, ..., b_k)$ and the receiver has an input $i \in \{1, 2, ..., k\}$. The goal is to transfer the ith bit to the receiver without letting the receiver obtain knowledge of any other bit and without letting the sender obtain the knowledge of the identity of the bit required by the receiver. Assuming the existence of trapdoor permutation, a protocol for the above functionality can be constructed as given in [12]. The above version of Oblivious transfer functionality is a main ingredient of our construction. The existence of trapdoor permutation [12] is the only assumption we make for security of our protocol.

3 The Protocol

Our protocol is a secure two-party version of the CYK Algorithm. Observe that if we can securely compute S_{ii} for $1 \leq i \leq n$ and provide a secure protocol to compute S_{ij} given S_{ik} and S_{k+1j} where $i \leq k < j$ we can use them to carry out CYK in a two party setting.

Let the context free grammar with Alice be $G = \{V, T, S, P\}$ where $V = \{V_1, V_2, \ldots V_{|V|}\}$, $T = \{T_1, T_2, \ldots T_{|T|}\}$, S is the starting symbol and P is the set of rewrite rules in chomsky normal form. The sets S_{ij}, as defined in (1), are maintained as a $|V|$ length 0/1 vector Γ_{ij} where $\Gamma_{ij}^m = 1$ if and only if $V_m \in S_{ij}$. Note that here (and in the remainder of the paper) a superscript m denotes the mth bit of the corresponding vector. These vectors are shared by a simple xor scheme such that if A_{ij} is Alice's share and B_{ij} is Bob's share, then $A_{ij} \oplus B_{ij} = \Gamma_{ij}$. The Γ_{ii}s in the first step are constructed using a 1-out-of-n Oblivious Transfer protocol as shown next.

Alice builds up a vector S_t for each of the terminal t. S_t^m is 1 if and only if $V_m \to t$. She also chooses a random 0/1 vector A_{ii} for each $1 \leq i \leq n$ which forms her share of Γ_{ii}. A_{ii} when xored with the S_t for each $t \in T$, yield a set of vectors $B_{ii} = \{B_{ii}^{t_1}, B_{ii}^{t_2}, \ldots B_{ii}^{t_{|T|}}\}$. Bob is allowed to select $B_{ii}^{w_i}$ from this set (depending upon his character w_i) using 1-out-of-$|T|$ oblivious transfer protocol. This forms his share of Γ_{ii}. Thus $S_{11}, S_{22}, ..., S_{nn}$ are shared between Alice and Bob.

The protocol now proceeds in phases and after each phase the new Γ_{ij}, as given in the sequence for CYK, are computed. Shares of Γ_{ij} can be computed provided Γ_{ik} and Γ_{k+1j} for all $k \in i, i+1, ..j-1$ have already been shared. For each production of the form $V_X \to V_Y V_Z$ Alice and Bob co-operatively update the xth bit of shares A_{ij} and B_{ij}. Let the new shares be called $A_{ij}^{x\ new}$ and $B_{ij}^{x\ new}$. Then the xth bit of the updated share can be written as

$$B_{ij}^{x\ new} = \left([(A_{ik}^y \oplus B_{ik}^y) \wedge (A_{k+1j}^z \oplus B_{k+1j}^z)] \vee [A_{ij}^x \oplus B_{ij}^x]\right) \oplus r^A \quad (2)$$

$$A_{ij}^{x\ new} = r^A, \text{ where } r^A \text{ is chosen randomly by Alice} \quad (3)$$

Equations (2) and (3) are the same as (1), except for the notations. $(A_{ik}^y \oplus B_{ik}^y)$ gives whether $V_y \in S_{ik}$ while $(A_{k+1j}^z \oplus B_{k+1j}^z)$ gives whether $V_z \in S_{k+1j}$. If both the above expressions evaluate to true Γ_{ij}^x must be one and otherwise it should remain as it is, as is emphasized by oring the above expression with $[A_{ij}^x \oplus B_{ij}^x]$. Finally, we xor it with a random term r^A chosen by Alice, which forms her private share(A_{ij}^x) for Γ_{ij}^x.

Equations (2) and (3) can be calculated using the general circuit evaluation protocol [3]. Finally, Alice and Bob check out whether Γ_{1n} contains the starting symbol S or not.

3.1 Initialization Step

1. Alice prepares vectors S_t for each $t \in T$ such that $S_t^k = 1$ if and only if $V_k \to t$.
2. Alice prepares random $|V|$ length vectors A_{ii} for each $1 \le i \le n$. These form her share of Γ_{ii}.
3. Alice constructs a set of vectors $B^j = \{B_{jj}^{t_1}, B_{jj}^{t_2}, \ldots B_{jj}^{t_{|T|}}\}$ for all $j \in \{1, 2, \ldots, n\}$ where $B_{jj}^{t_k} = S_{t_k} \oplus A_{jj}$.
4. For each $j \in \{1, n\}$, Bob selects a vector $B_{jj}^{w_j}$ from B^j using oblivious transfer protocol. This forms his share B_{jj}.
5. Thus Alice and Bob share the initial Γ_{jj} as A_{jj} and B_{jj} for $j \in \{1, n\}$. This completes the initialization step.

3.2 Computing Γ_{1n}

We now describe the crux of the protocol, the computation of Γ_{1n}. We give the description in pseudocode as it is easier to understand and more expressive this way.

1. for d= 1 to n-1 do
2.   for i = 1 to n-d do
3.   j=i+d
4.   for k = i to j-1 do
5.   for each Production $x \to yz$ with Alice do
6.   Alice chooses a random bit r^A
7.   Alice and Bob use secure circuit evaluation protocol to compute

$$B_{ij}^{x\ new} = \left([(A_{ik}^y \oplus B_{ik}^y) \wedge (A_{k+1j}^z \oplus B_{k+1j}^z)] \vee [A_{ij}^x \oplus B_{ij}^x]\right) \oplus r^A \quad (4)$$

$$A_{ij}^{x\ new} = r^A \quad (5)$$

8.   endfor
9.   endfor
10.   endfor
11. endfor

3.3 Final Step

Using the initialization step and then computing each of Γ_{ij} as above, Alice and Bob obtain the shares for Γ_{1n}. At this point Alice sends her share of the bit corresponding to the starting symbol S from A_{1n} to Bob. Bob xors it with the corresponding bit in his share. The result tells Bob whether $S \in S_{1n}$ and hence whether w is generated by Alice's grammar or not.

4 Security

We prove the security of our protocol in the semihonest model with passive adversary. Such a protocol can be compiled into a protocol secure against a dishonest party and in presence of malicious adversary [9] using verifiable secret sharing and zero-knowledge proofs [2]. It is a standard procedure to construct a secure protocol in semihonest model and then convert it to a secure protocol in malicious model. However such a conversion increases the communication and computation cost of the protocol. Below we give an informal proof of security for the proposed protocol.

The protocol consists of three distinct phases the initialization step, the updation step and the final step. Without loss of generality we can consider the case where the language $L(G)$ consists of only two alphabets 0 and 1. In the initialization step, Alice prepares B_{jj}^0 and B_{jj}^1 for $j \in \{1, 2, ..., n\}$. One of this is selected by Bob based on his input w_j using 1-out-of-2 oblivious transfer protocol. If oblivious transfers were carried out correctly, there is no information gain for Alice as she doesn't know whether Bob has chosen B_{jj}^0 or B_{jj}^1. Also Bob remains ignorant of the variables in S_{jj} as B_{jj} has been xored with a random vector A_{jj} which forms Alice's share. Hence there is no gain of information for either parties in the initialization step.

The updation step is based on the secure circuit evaluation protocol. During the computation of the circuit no information is revealed to either party. Finally the result of the evaluation $B_{ij}^{x\ new}$ is revealed only to Bob. But this is xored with a random bit r^A, known only to Alice. Hence the information content in $B_{ij}^{x\ new}$ is nil for Bob.

In the final step Alice sends the bit corresponding to S (starting symbol) in her share A_{1n} to Bob. This transfer doesn't increase her information in any way. Bob then xors this bit with the corresponding bit in his share to obtain one bit of information namely whether $w \in L(G)$. Hence during whole of the protocol the information gained by Bob is one bit.

Other Security Issues. One can say that after the protocol, Alice knows the length of Bob's string while Bob knows the exact number of variables, productions in Alice's automaton. This gives them some idea of the complexity of the other's input. However such information can easily be hidden. Alice can add some dubious variables and productions in G that do not affect the language $L(G)$ generated by G. Bob can also add some random symbols after/before his actual input string. In such an instant Alice allows Bob to choose one of the bits corresponding to S in A_{ij} for all $1 \leq i,j \leq n$ using 1-out-of-N oblivious transfer protocol. Bob will choose the bit in A_{ij}, w_{ij} being his actual string.

5 Analysis

The number of communication rounds required is $O(|w|^3)$ for each of S_{ij}. Also for the calculation of each S_{ij} the communication required is $O(|P|)$ where $|P|$ gives the number of productions in the grammar. Each round requires $O(|V|)$ communication for carrying out 1-out-of-$|V|$ oblivious transfers. Hence the total communication complexity of the protocol is $O(|w|^3|P||V|)$. Thus the multiparty version of CYK is slower by a factor of $O(|V|)$.

In an implementation over a data network, instead of running the protocol in a step by step manner, we can run steps 4 to 9 at once. Hence all the updates are made to the vectors concurrently. We can parallelize these steps because they are independent from each other and can be carried in any order we please. Taking network latency into account, this gives performance benefits over a network as sending chunks of data is more efficient than sending it bit by bit. The round complexity of the protocol is reduced to $O(|w|)$ without affecting the communication complexity. Thus the actual running time of the protocol is reduced.

6 Applications

A two-party CFLR, as discussed in this paper, can be used for providing web services over internet. It can also help in protecting intellectual property for both the parties. Consider a case where Alice has discovered the context free grammar that can accurately describe a disease. Using the protocol she can keep the discovery to herself while making it available for use through a web service. The interesting part of such a service would be that the patient can be diagnosed without revealing his syndromes. Also the result of the diagnosis would be known only to him. Such a protocol can be useful in a social scenario.

Another use for the protocol can be for providing a compilation service over the network where a user can submit his program to get it syntax checked. Our protocol is stricter than required for this case. In such a case the CFG is public and it is only the input that needs to be hidden.

References

1. A. Yao. Protocols for secure computations: In Proceedings of the twenty-third annual IEEE Symposium on Foundations of Computer Science, pages 160-164. IEEE Computer Society, 1982.
2. M. Ben-Or, S. Goldwasser, and A. Wigderson: Completeness theorems for non-cryptographic fault- tolerant distributed computation. In Proc. of 20th STOC, pp. 1-10, 1988.

3. A. Yao: How to generate and exchange secrets. In Proceedings of the twenty-seventh annual IEEE Symposium on Foundations of Computer Science, pages 162-167. IEEE Computer Society, 1986
4. Bruce Schneier: Applied Cryptography, 2nd Ed., John Wiley & Sons Pte Ltd, pp. 96, pp. 543
5. David Chaum, Claude Cropeau, and Ivan Damgard: Multiparty unconditionally secure protocols. In Proceedings of the twentieth annual ACM symposium on Theory of computing, pages 11-19. ACM Press, 1988.
6. D. Beaver, S. Micali, and P. Rogaway: The round complexity of secure protocols. In Proc. of 22nd STOC, pp. 503-513, 1990.
7. M. Franklin and M. Yung. Communication complexity of secure computation. In Proc. of 24th STOC, pp. 699-710, 1992.
8. O. Goldreich, S. Micali, and A. Wigderson: How to play any mental game (extended abstract). In Proc. of 19th STOC, pp. 218-229, 1987.
9. R.Canetti, U.Fiege, O.Goldreich and M.Naor: Adaptively Secure Computation, Proceedings of STOC 1996.
10. J.Kilian: Founding Cryptography on Oblivious Transfer, Proceedings of the Twentieth Annual ACM Symposium on Theory of Computing, pages 2031, Chicago, Illinois, 24 May 1988.
11. Peter Linz: An Introduction to Formal Languages and Automata, Narosa Publications.
12. O. Goldreich: Secure Multiparty Computation, Version 1.4, available at http://www.wisdom.weizmann.ac.il/~oded/PS/prot.ps

Autonomous Agent Based Distributed Fault-Tolerant Intrusion Detection System

Jaydip Sen and Indranil Sengupta

Department of Computer Science and Engineering,
Indian Institute of Technology, Kharagpur-721302
`sen_jaydip@yahoo.com, isg@iitkgp.ac.in`

Abstract. Because all vulnerabilities of a network cannot be realized, and penetration of the system cannot always be prevented, intrusion detection systems have become necessary to ensure the security of a network. The intrusion detection systems need to be accurate, adaptive, and extensible. Given these requirements and the complexities of today's network environments, the design of an intrusion detection system has become a very challenging task. A great deal of research has been conducted on intrusion detection in a distributed environment to circumvent the problems of centralized approaches. However, distributed intrusion detection systems suffer from a number of drawbacks e.g., high rates of false positives, low efficiency etc. In this paper, we propose the architecture of a fully distributed intrusion detection system that uses a set of autonomous but cooperating agents. The system has also the capability of isolating compromised nodes from intrusion detection activity thereby ensuring fault-tolerance in computation.

1 Introduction

An Intrusion Detection System (IDS) is a security mechanism that can monitor and detect intrusions into the computer systems in real time. IDSs can be either host-based (sources of data are operating system and applications audit trails), or network-based (monitor and analyze network traffic). Conventional approaches to intrusion detection involving a central unit to monitor the entire system have several disadvantages [1]. To circumvent the demerits of centralized IDSs, the research in the field of intrusion detection, over the last decade, has been heading towards a distributed framework of monitors that do local detection, and provide information to perform global detection of intrusions. In these systems, the local intrusion detection components look for local intrusions and pass their analysis results to the upper levels of the hierarchy. The components at the upper levels analyze the refined data from multiple lower level components and seek to establish a global view of the system state. Such intrusion detection systems are not truly distributed systems, because of the centralized data analysis performed at the higher levels of the hierarchy [1]. Moreover, these systems suffer from the problem of single point of failure.

In this paper, we describe the model of a distributed intrusion detection with the help of a large number of autonomous, but cooperating agents. The system performs intrusion detection activity by incorporating inter-agent communication, and distributed computation by the agents. The two primary goals of our model are: detection of intrusive activities, and identification and isolation of compromised hosts in the network. The rest of the paper is organized as follows. Section 2 describes the system architecture and various components of the system. Section 3 describes the distributed intrusion detection mechanism using Bayesian network framework. Section 4 presents the trust management among the peer hosts. Section 5 contains a very brief overview of the proposed implementation and testing of the model, and Section 6 concludes the paper.

2 Architecture of the System

In this section we describe the architecture of the overall system very briefly with particular attention to the agents.

2.1 System Architecture

We propose a distributed, lightweight, agent-based intrusion detection mechanism. Our model architecture is almost similar to what have been proposed in [3], but differs completely in the mechanism of trust management and fault-tolerance.

The agents are put into several subdomains. While the agents in the same subdomain communicate actively and frequently, communication between agents belonging to adjacent subdomains happens quite infrequently. The agents have knowledge about a Bayesian network model of the structures of well-known attack types as well as normal usage pattern, which is constructed offline from data repositories containing system logs from ongoing attacks. This global Bayesian network has been partitioned into multiple subnets based on the spatial locations of the agents. To ensure fault-tolerance in the system, every host has one special agent, called the *Distributed Trust Manager* (DTM), which continuously sends messages to its peers in other hosts. We will discuss more about this in Section 4.

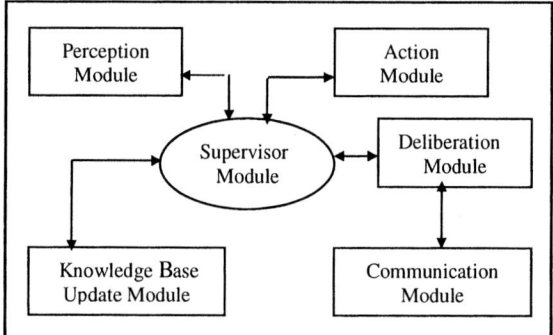

Fig. 1. Architecture of an agent embedded in a node

Figure 1 depicts the architecture of an agent. Each agent consists of six modules. The *supervisory module* coordinates the tasks of the other modules. The *perception module* collects the audit or network data from the agent's subdomain. The *deliberation module* analyzes the data collected by the perception module. The *communication module* allows an agent to communicate its belief, decisions, and knowledge to its peer agents. The *action module* takes appropriate actions when a possible intrusion is detected. The *knowledge-base update module* updates the attack signature knowledge base when an anomaly is detected for the first time.

2.2 Agent Communication Architecture

Figure 2 shows the interactions among different types of agents. The *System Monitoring Agents* collect, transform, and distribute intrusion specific data upon request. The *Intrusion Monitoring Agents* subscribe to beliefs published by the system monitoring agents. A *registry* maintains information about the monitored variables of each agent. For agents in the same host, we propose to use shared memory implementation of agent communication because of its efficiency.

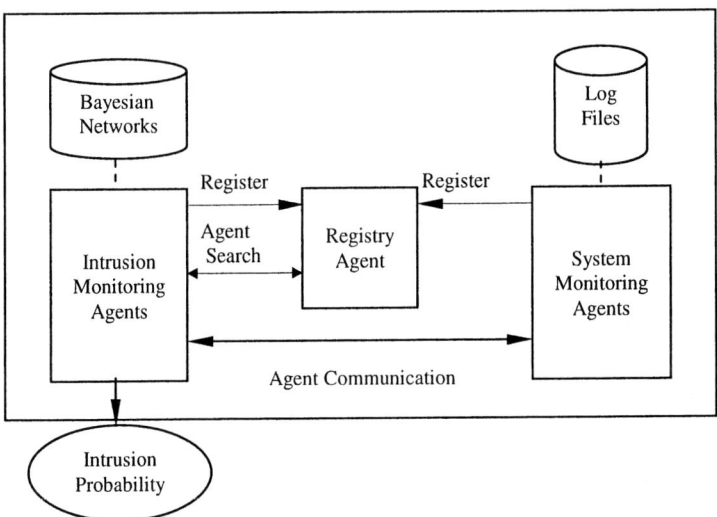

Fig. 2. Major components of the system

3 Intrusion Detection Using Bayesian Hypothesis

In this section we describe the use of Bayesian networks and Multiply Sectioned Bayesian Networks (MSBNs) in our model. We use Bayesian networks to model our system because a Bayesian network can represent causal dependency among a set of variables, which can help our system to combine *a priori* knowledge and observed data in taking a probabilistic decision. Also, a Bayesian network can allow us to detect novel attacks by the mechanism of belief updates. A global Bayesian network is first constructed from a database of known attacks, and then this network is partitioned into several subtrees following the principle of Multiply Sectioned Bayesian Networks (MSBNs) [4], and distributed among the agents.

Existing methods for multiagent inference in MSBNs are extensions of a class of methods for inference in single-agent Bayesian networks: *message passing in junction trees* [7]. The *linked junction forest* (LJF) method [5,6] compiles each subnet of a multiply connected network into a *junction tree* (JT). The algorithm performs message propagation over the JT or the *linkage tree* between a pair of adjacent nodes.

Figure 3 shows an MSBN with three subnets G_0, G_1, G_2 each having some agents in it. The LJF method has compiled each subnet into a JT (called a local JT), and has converted each d-sepset into a JT (called linkage tree). Figure 3 also illustrates the three local JTs and two linkage trees of the monitoring system. Local inference is performed by message passing in the local JT. Message passing between a pair of adjacent subdomains is performed using the linkage tree.

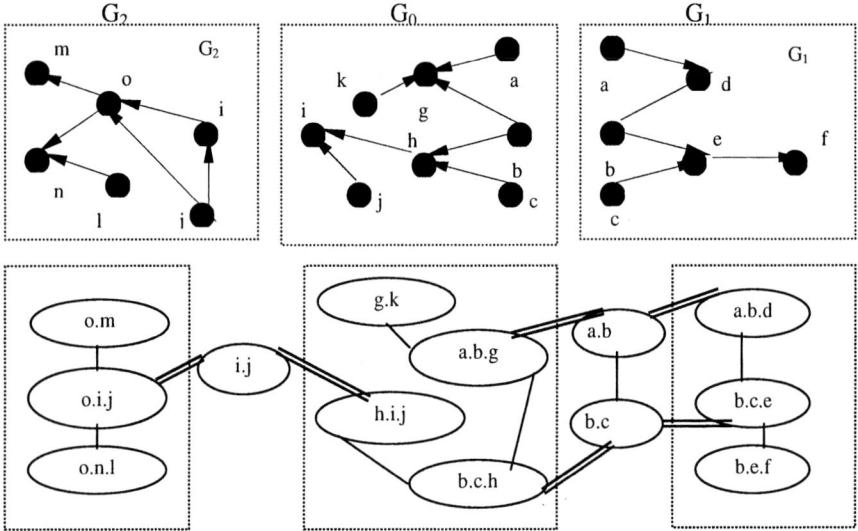

Fig. 3. The DAGs of the three subnets of an MSBN and JTs constructed from the subnet

4 Fault-Tolerance by Trust Mechanism Among Hosts

The agents in a distributed intrusion detection system are always vulnerable to attacks by intruders. If an intruder can compromise any host in the system, the detection capability of the entire system will be severely affected. The agents in a compromised host will attempt to influence the JT and their effect will be propagated in the entire system by the message passing mechanism among the agents unless the compromised host is detected and isolated promptly. To ensure early detection of any compromised host(s), we have developed a trust mechanism among the peer hosts using Byzantine Agreement Protocol. In the following section we briefly describe the protocol.

4.1 Byzantine Agreement Protocol –Signed Message Algorithm

Lamport et.al. described the Byzantine Generals Problem in [9]. Specifically, the problem formulation is as follows: Imagine that several divisions of a Byzantine army are camped outside an enemy city, each division commanded by its own general. The generals can communicate with each other only by messengers. After observing the enemy, they must decide upon a common plan of action. However, some of the generals may be traitors, trying to prevent the loyal generals from reaching an agreement. The generals must have an algorithm to guarantee that: All loyal generals decide upon the same plan of action. The loyal generals will all do what the algorithm asks them to do, but the traitors may do anything they wish. The loyal generals should not only reach an agreement, but should agree upon a reasonable plan.

The *Byzantine Agreement Protocol* (BAP) is essentially an algorithm designed to achieve consensus among a set of processes participating in a distributed computation. These processes achieve consensus if they all agree on some allowed values called the 'outcome'. A consensus algorithm terminates when all non-faulty (not compromised) processes know the outcome. If we substitute the generals for the hosts in the distributed system, and consensus for the need to agree on which agents are sane, then the problem of identifying and isolating compromised host(s) can be described as follows: Imagine in a distributed system with several hosts, and each host having a set of agents in it. The agents cooperate to detect intrusions into the system. Each host runs a special agent, the Distributed Trust Manager (DTM), which continuously sends messages to other hosts. The message that it sends has two possible values. They are: i) *Message A_1:* "Keep sane" or "0". ii) *Message A_2:* " I am potentially compromised" or "1".

The *Signed Message Algorithm* (SMA) proposed by Lamport [9] for solution of Byzantine Generals Problem, requires $O(n^2)$ messages to achieve a consensus. It works effectively if there are at most *n-2* number of traitors (compromised hosts). However, it will work correctly if we can guarantee certain conditions [9]. The communication mechanism between peer hosts in our system is secure enough to guarantee that all of those conditions are satisfied. Thus, SMA can be implemented in our system to establish a trust mechanism. In SMA, one of the hosts acts as the leader and sends an order to the other hosts. Whenever a host receives a message, it takes the order and puts it in a list. Then the receiver signs the message with its own signature and forwards it to all the hosts whose signature is not on the order. If a host receives a message with an order that is already in its list, it ignores the message. When message communication completes, the hosts all choose an order from the list of orders they have received. If only one order has been received, that order is chosen. Because any order that reaches a sane host will be forwarded to all other hosts who have not seen the order, all the sane hosts will have the same set of orders to choose from.

4.2 Distributed Trust Manager

The *Distributed Trust Manager* (DTM) is responsible for forming and maintaining *trust domains*. A trust domain is a set of hosts that share a charter and a security policy, and behave consistently according to the security policy. The hosts in the trust domain work together to prevent compromised hosts from joining the trust domain. If any host becomes compromised after joining the trust domain, other hosts in the trust domain will be able to detect it and isolate it from the trust domain.

We assume that at the beginning, the trust domain consists of hosts that are all sane. DTM tries to detect and remove any host that becomes compromised after it has joined the trust domain. Compromised host(s) in the trust domain is (are) identified by running n instances (n is the maximum number of hosts in the trust domain) of the SMA in parallel, assuming that the majority of the hosts in the trust domain are not compromised. If the "leader" of the SMA is not compromised, then after running the algorithm in parallel, all the hosts that are not compromised will know that the leader is not compromised. If the leader of an execution of the SMA is compromised, then any of the following cases can happen: (i) The leader sends 0 messages to all the sane hosts. In this case, all the sane hosts will assume the leader host to be compromised or dead. (ii) The leader sends 1 message to only some of the hosts are sane. In this case, the sane hosts that received 1 message from the leader are able to detect that there is a compromised host in the system. These hosts, then, send messages to other hosts informing about this suspected compromised host. On further investigation by message communication, the status of the suspected host will be understood. (iii) The leader sends 1 message to all the sane hosts. All the sane hosts understand that the message is wrong, and the leader host is compromised, if it contradicts the majority. If the message does not contradict the majority, it is not possible to conclude about the status of the leader, unless it sends a different message to at least one compromised host, which in turn forwards the message to a sane host. In this case the leader is compromised, and should be removed. However, it is not a critical problem, as it is not causing any damage at present. (iv) The leader sends two or more different messages to some sane hosts. All the sane hosts eventually see contradictory instructions, and understand that the leader is compromised. Thus the DTM can identify compromised hosts in the system in all possible cases.

5 Implementation and Experiments

We propose to develop a proof-of-concept prototype of our model using Java, C, and JADE. We plan to test its performance using the KDD Cup 1999 intrusion detection contest data [8]. We will select a large sample from this dataset, and use Bayesian Network Power Constructor (BNPC) [2] to generate a Bayesian network to distribute it among agents.

6 Conclusions

In this paper, we have presented the model of a distributed IDS that uses a collection of agents. By distributed computation and message passing between the agents, the model can detect intrusions and can identify and isolate compromised hosts in the system. We will build a prototype of the system, and evaluate its performance.

References

1. Gopalakrishna, R., Spafford, E.: "A Framework for Distributed Intrusion Detection System using Interest Driven Cooperating Agents." In *Proceedings of Recent Advances in Intrusion Detection, 4th International Symposium (RAID 2001)*, October 2001.
2. Cheng, J., Bell, D., Liu, W.: "Learning Bayesian Networks from Data: An efficient approach based on Information Theory." Technical Report, University of Alberta, Canada, 1998.
3. Ghosh, A., Sen, S.: "Agent-based Distributed Intrusion Alert System." In *6th International Workshop on Distributed Computing,* Kolkata, India, December 2004.
4. Xiang, Y., Poole, D., Beddoes, M.: "Multiply Sectioned Bayesian Networks and Junction Forest for Large Knowledge-Based Systems." *Computational Intelligence,* 9(2): 171-220, 1993.
5. Guo, H., Hsu, W.H.:"A Survey of Algorithms for Real-time Bayesian Network Inference." In *AAAI/KDD/UAI-2002 Joint Workshop on Real-time Decision Support and Diagnosis Systems,* Edmonton, July 2002.
6. Xiang, Y.: "Belief Updating in Multiply Sectioned Bayesian Networks without Repeated Local Propagation." *International Journal of Approximate Reasoning* 23: 1-21, 2000.
7. Jensen, F.V., Lauritzen, S.L., Oleson, K.G.: "Bayesian Updating in Causal Probabilistic Networks by Local Computations." *Computational Statistics Quarterly,* 4: 269-282, 1990.
8. Kddcup 99 Intrusion Detection Data Set. DARPA Intrusion Data Repository. http://kdd.ics.uci.edu/databases/kddcup99/kddcup.data_10_percent.gz.
9. Lamport, L., Shostak, R., Pease, M.: "The Byzantine General Problem." *ACM Transaction on Programming Languages and Systems,* 4(3): 382-401, July 1982.

Cleaning an Arbitrary Regular Network with Mobile Agents*

Paola Flocchini, Amiya Nayak, and Arno Schulz

School of Information Technology and Engineering,
University of Ottawa,
800 King Edward Avenue,
Ottawa, ON K1N 6N5, Canada
{flocchin, anayak, aschulz}@site.uottawa.ca

Abstract. In this paper, we consider a contaminated network with an intruder. The task for the mobile agents is to decontaminate all hosts while preventing a recontamination and to do so as efficiently as possible. We study under what conditions and what cost a team of mobile agents can do this in synchronous arbitrary regular graphs using the breadth-first-search strategy. Due to the nature of the experiment we use a genetic algorithm to find the minimum number of agents required to decontaminate a given network. The results show that there is a relation between the degree, the size of the graph, and the number of starting locations of the mobile agents. in particular, this relation demonstrates the possibility of improvements in reducing the number of mobile agents used depending on the number of starting location in arbitrary regular graphs.

Keywords: Mobile Agents, Intruder Capture, Graph Search, Mesh.

1 Introduction

1.1 The Problem

Consider a network where nodes represent hosts and edges represent connections between hosts. An *intruder* is a dangerous piece of software (e.g., a virus) that moves arbitrarily fast from host to host contaminating the nodes. The intruder capture problem consists of deploying a team of collaborative software agents to capture the intruder.

We can formulate the intruder capture problem equivalently in terms of a *decontamination (or cleaning)* problem in which each node of the network can be in one of three possible states: *clean, contaminated, guarded*. Initially all nodes are *contaminated* except for the nodes containing an agent (which are *guarded*). A node becomes *clean* when an agent passes by it, and an unguarded node becomes *contaminated* if one of its neighbors is contaminated. A guarded node is also

---

* Work partially supported by Natural Sciences and Engineering Research Council of Canada.

clean. The decontamination problem consists of reaching a situation where all the nodes are simultaneously *clean*. In particular, we are interested in *monotone* strategies of decontamination; i.e., we want that a node that becomes clean will never be contaminated again. In other words, we have to design cleaning strategies that "protect" clean node from recontamination; once a node is clean, all its neighbors must be clean or guarded.

An agent is a mobile entity that can move from node to a neighboring node. Agents can communicate by accessing local small whiteboard located at the nodes (whiteboards of size $O(\log n)$ are enough for our purposes). The whiteboard of a node will contain the state of the node (*clean, contaminated* or *guarded* and any other information the agents need to communicate to the other agents). Finally, we assume that an agent can "see" the state of its neighbors. The possible actions of an agent are:

- LOCAL COMPUTATIONS (or local actions): Each agent is provided with $O(\log n)$ of local memory to be used when performing local computations, where n is the number of nodes. Particular local action are: the observation of the neighbors' states; cloning (the agent can clone several copies of itself); termination (an agent can terminate its execution).
- MOVEMENTS from a host to a neighboring host: In this paper, we consider synchronous movements, i.e., it takes one unit of time for an agent to traverse a link. Moreover, we assume that the agents start simultaneously.

When designing a decontamination strategy, the efficiency is measured in terms of the number of agents deployed (maximum number of agents simultaneously active), number of moves, and the time it takes to clean a network. To determine the minimum number of mobile agents required to decontaminate a given network using this strategy, we use a genetic algorithm to find which combination of starting home bases will reduce the number of mobile agents used. The genetic algorithm provides a good estimate of the number of mobile agents required to clean a given network of fixed degree, size, and the number of starting home bases for the mobile agents.

1.2 Related Work

A variation of the intruder capturing (or decontamination) problem has been widely studied in the literature under the name of *graph search problem*. This problem was first introduced by Breish [3] and Parson [12] and was studied extensively under different variations (edge search, node search, mixed search) (e.g., see [4, 8, 9, 10, 11, 13]). The main goal of all these investigations was to determine the minimum number of agents required to perform the search. Determining such a number ("searching number") in an arbitrary network is an NP-complete problem.

In all the graph search variations studied in the literature, searchers may be removed from a node and placed on any other node of the graph being searched, i.e., they are allowed to *"jump"* while they perform the searching task.

However, in a networked environment, agents cannot jump, but can only move from node to neighboring node. Simulating the jump by neighboring moves may make the strategy non monotone.

A variation of the node/edge-search problem is called the *contiguous search problem* [1, 2] which adds the requirement that 1) the agents can move only from node to neighboring node without jumping, 2) the strategy is monotone, and 3) the decontaminated area is connected. This problem is harder than the non-contiguous one as it has been shown in [2] that there are networks where the contiguous searching number is strictly greater then the non-contiguous searching number. Finding the contiguous searching number is still an NP-complete problem for general graphs. A few specific topologies have been studied; for example, it has been shown that the problem can be solved in linear time in trees [1], meshes and tori [5]. Moreover, strategies and upper bounds have been studied only in hypercubes [6]. All the previous investigations have been carried out in asynchronous environment.

1.3 Our Result

In this paper, we consider the contiguous decontamination problem in a synchronous arbitrary regular network without the restriction that the decontaminated must be connected. We first describe a general strategy in which the agents perform the decontamination by moving in a breadth-first manner, making sure that no recontamination will occur. This technique can be applied to any arbitrary topology. This general strategy can be initiated by an arbitrary number of starting locations, and its efficiency depends on the number of starting places and their location.

Generally, starting from more locations will increase the number of agents but will decrease the time. An interesting question is: given a network and a number of starting agents what is the optimal placement of the agents? Even in symmetric networks, increasing the number of starting locations, the problem becomes quite complex; thus, in order to obtain minimum number of agents we resorted to simulations using a genetic algorithm. In fact, to choose good starting locations, we design a genetic algorithm that will find the solution that will use the least number of agents in a single step, for a given graph and a fixed number starting locations. Through experiments, we show that as the number of home bases increases, the number of agents required decreases in all network topologies considered.

2 The Strategy

The cleaning strategy (protocol CLEAN illustrated in Figure 1) is very simple. Initially, the agents are placed in arbitrary starting location. Each starting agent will try to move its clones on a breadth-first-search (BFS) tree of the network rooted at its starting position. More precisely, at each step, if an agent arrives to a node alone, it cleans the node, clones itself as many times as the number of contaminated neighbors, and sends them on the corresponding links. If, however, more than one agent arrives at a node simultaneously, only one of them survives, cleans the node, clones itself as many times as the number of contaminated neighbors, and sends them on the corresponding links; the other agents terminate here.

Protocol CLEAN (for an agent a arriving at node x)

If a is alone:
  Clean x.
  Check the state of neighbors.
  Let $N_{D(x)}$ be the set of decontaminated neighbors of x.
  Clone $|N_{D(x)}|$ agents.
  Send the cloned agents to the decontaminated neighbors.
If a is not alone:
  Locally choose a leader.
  If I am the leader:
    Clean x.
    Check the state of neighbors.
    Let $N_{D(x)}$ be the set of decontaminated neighbors of x.
    Clone $|N_{D(x)}|$ agents.
    Send the cloned agents to the decontaminated neighbors.
  Otherwise
    Terminate.

Fig. 1. Protocol CLEAN

The procedure *locally choose a leader* in Figure 1 consists in selecting one of the agents to continue the cleaning operation, the leader is the agent that first accesses the local whiteboard.

In a clean area, internal nodes are the nodes whose neighbors are all clean, border nodes have some clean neighbors and some contaminated neighbors.

Theorem 1. *Protocol* CLEAN *performs a monotone decontamination of the network.*

Proof. We want to prove by induction that once a node is clean, it will never be re-contaminated.

Basis. The starting locations of the agents are clean and since, by definition, enough agents are sent simultaneously to all their contaminated neighbors, they will not be re-contaminated in the subsequent step. Moreover, the border nodes are all guarded (in this case border nodes are just single nodes).

Induction. At step k, some nodes are clean and the border nodes are guarded. At step $k+1$ the agents that are on the border nodes will clone themselves, by definition of the algorithm, and then proceed to the contaminated nodes. As all contaminated neighbors receive at least one agent, the old border nodes become internal nodes, and thus cannot be re-contaminated in the subsequent step, while the border node are all guarded.

We have shown that once a node is clean, it will never be re-contaminated. Since the graph is connected, we have that all nodes will eventually be decontaminated. □

Notice that, for some specific topologies, it can be easy to compute the number of agents needed for decontamination, when considering a single starting location ("home base"). In this case, the number of steps is always equal to the diameter of the network, while the number of agents clearly depends on the topology. For example, in the case of the hypercube, the maximum number of agents simultaneously active would be equal to the maximum number of edges between levels of the broadcast tree (which is $(\lfloor \frac{n}{2} \rfloor + 1) \cdot (\lfloor \frac{\log n}{2} \rfloor + 1)$).

However, when we have more than one home base for the mobile agents, the nature of the problem becomes more complex with the added difficulty of finding the optimal configuration. Even in symmetric networks, adding multiple starting locations increases the complexity; thus, in order to obtain minimum number of agents we resorted to simulations using a genetic algorithm.

3 The Genetic Algorithm

3.1 Genetic Algorithm Background

The genetic algorithm as described by Goldberg [7] is a process composed of two elements: a population of strings and a fitness function. As can be seen in Figure 2, at each round of the genetic algorithm, the fitness function allows to pick the fittest individuals (the strings that achieve a better score according to the fitness function) and then uses them as a basis to generate a new generation. As each generation brings a new population generated from the fittest individuals from the previous generation, over the course of several generations, the individuals tend to get better and better fit, thus providing a good solution in a relatively short period of time as the least fit individuals are no longer considered. However, evolving the optimal solution is more difficult and will take more time as in the later generations. When there are many individuals with equal fitness, there is no bias towards any particular individual.

3.2 Our Implementation

For our experiment, we use individuals where each individual represents the starting positions of the mobile agents within the graph. The graphs are represented by a Boolean array where each entry of the array corresponds to a node in the graph. If the Boolean value corresponding to a node is true it means that the node is going to be a starting location for a mobile agent. These arrays are stored in matrix composed of 1024 individuals (the population size used by the genetic algorithm).

In order to have a starting point for the genetic algorithm, the initial population is generated in a random manner. Each individual, having the same number of agents, will place these agents in random positions of the array (if an agent

```
Genetic Algorithm:

For 52 generations do
    Set total fitness TS to 0.
    While there exists a candidate string out of 1024 candidates
        s = next candidate string.
        Evaluate s with the fitness function F(s).
        Add F(s) to TS.
    End While
    Create a biased wheel of size TS where for each s,
        a space corresponding to the F(s) fitness is allocated.
    Pick randomly 1024 candidate strings from the wheel.
End For
```

Fig. 2. Genetic Algorithm

is already there, another random position is selected until an empty position is found). Once the population has been generated, it is then passed on to the genetic algorithm which then runs 52 times, each time generating a new population (from the previous generation).

Each population that is passed on to the genetic algorithm is evaluated according to a "fitness" function. The fitness function used is the maximum number of agents that were used at any one step during the decontamination of the network. The fitness obtained is then stored in order to determine the maximum fitness and the best individual of each generation later on.

After all the fitnesses have been collected, the algorithm sets up a biased evolutionary wheel, that gives to each individual a percentage of the wheel proportional to its fitness compared to the total fitness of the population (note that the wheel represents the total fitness of the population). This favors the fittest individuals as they will represent a greater percentage. Thus, while creating a new generation, as the selection is done in a random manner, the fittest individuals are most likely to be selected. The new generation is then created using one of two techniques, *mutation* and *cross-over*, described below.

The *mutation* consists of selecting an individual randomly in the evolutionary wheel. We then change the position of one of the mobile agent's starting home base within the Boolean array which represents an individual (note that it is still possible for a selected individual not to get changed during the mutation).

The *cross-over* consists of selecting two individuals randomly in the evolutionary wheel and then creating two new individuals by switching the second half of each of the selected individuals. For example, if the two parts of the first selected individual is (x1, x2) and the second selected individual is (y1, y2), the cross-over process creates two new individuals with two parts as (x1, y2) and (y1, x2).

After the new generation has been bred, the best of this generation is then compared with the best of all previous generations; if the fitness is higher, the new champion individual is preserved. Finally the next generation is passed to the genetic algorithm, and the process is repeated until we reach the 52nd generation.

3.3 The Benefits and Restrictions of Genetic Algorithms

The advantage of using the genetic algorithm is that it allows us to narrow down to an acceptable solution for a given topology. Most importantly, it gives us a good approximation (if not the maximum number of agents required) for a particular network. We are also able to use it instead of doing an exhaustive search to evaluate each and every possible configuration of the mobile agents starting home bases for a given network topology.

There are two limitations with this approach. First, without resorting to an exhaustive search, it is not possible to confirm whether the results obtained by the genetic algorithm truly represent the optimal solution for a particular graph. Second, there is the possibility of premature convergence giving a local minima as a result instead of finding a lower minimum. To minimize the effects of these limitations, we run each configurations 300 times as explained in the following section.

4 Experimental Results

4.1 Methodology

Using the described genetic algorithm we are able to test specific arbitrary regular graph groups of given size, degree with different number of starting home bases for the mobile agents. For statistical significance, we run the genetic algorithm over 60,000 individual experiments. The entire experiment uses 200 different graph groups (five graph sizes with 512, 768, 1024, 1576, 2048 nodes; four degrees: 4, 8, 16, 32; and ten different numbers of home bases: 1, 2, 3, 4, 6, 8, 10, 12, 14, 16). Each graph group can be viewed as a set of graphs with parameters (size, degree, number of home bases); for example, (512, 4, 10) represents a graph group where all graphs have 512 nodes, degree 4, and 10 home bases. For each graph group, we run 300 experiments which is divided into 30 series of experiments, each series uses a different graph with the same set of parameters. Each series is then run 10 times. Each experiment yields two results: the number of mobile agents used and the number of steps used.

We observed that within a graph group, the variation of results for the number of mobile agents between individual experiments and between series of experiments is less than 3%. Occasional abnormalities in the results due to pre-mature convergence in the genetic algorithm are less than .5% and are ignored. For the number of steps, we also observed less than .5% abnormality (considered when the variation is not within ±1 step).

Once all the results have been collected for each graph group; the median is taken for both sets of results for each series of experiments (i.e., the number of mobile agents used and the number of steps used). We then take the median of all the medians within a graph group which is then plotted (please refer to Figure 4 for the number of mobile agents used and to Figure 3 for the number of steps used).

4.2 Number of Steps Used

Given the synchronous nature of the experiments, one of the interesting facts to consider is the number of steps taken by the mobile agents to decontaminate the network, and how it relates to the size, the degree of the network, as well as the number of starting home bases for the mobile agents.

The results are shown in Figure 3. These results were as expected due to the BFS strategy used by the mobile agents. At each step, in this strategy, it is possible to predict that the number of agents at the next step. For example, in a network of degree 4 with 512 nodes and one starting base, the number of mobile agents would roughly increase 4 fold at every step. One can then see that once we are at a step where the number of agents exceeds the number of nodes in the graph it would be the maximum of steps used for that graph.

Figure 3 shows that the number of steps varies between 2 and 9. The expected behavior can be seen for all graph groups; that is, as the number of home bases increases the number of steps taken decreases.

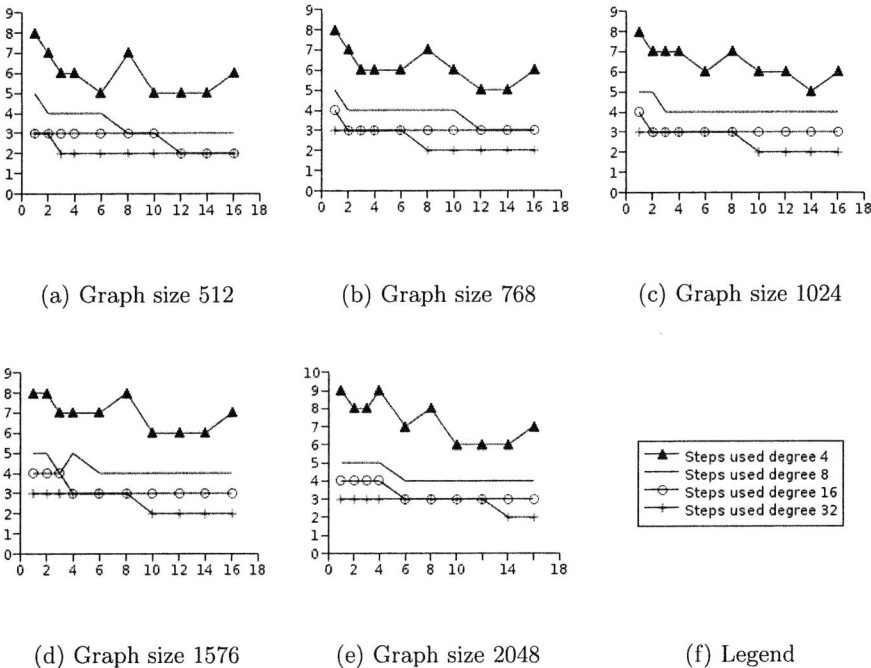

(a) Graph size 512   (b) Graph size 768   (c) Graph size 1024

(d) Graph size 1576   (e) Graph size 2048   (f) Legend

Fig. 3. Steps Used (x-axis: number of home bases; y-axis: number of steps)

4.3 Number of Agents Used

The main goal of this experiment was to determine the minimum number of mobiles agents used for decontaminating different networks with one or more home bases. The results for different graph groups are shown in Figure 4. We observe the following. First, for a given graph group, fewer agents are required for certain numbers of home bases. For example, the graph group (2048, 32, 2) uses fewer agents than the graph group (2048, 32, 1). Second, the variations of the number of agents used depends on the degree of the graph groups. The variation is larger for graph groups of higher degrees.

These results were expected. As we increase the number of home bases, we see a drop in the number of agents. This is true for all graph groups.

Due to the nature of the decontamination strategy based on BFS technique, there will always be an overuse of the number of agents. A contaminated node will always receive an agent from all its decontaminated neighbors. The overuse

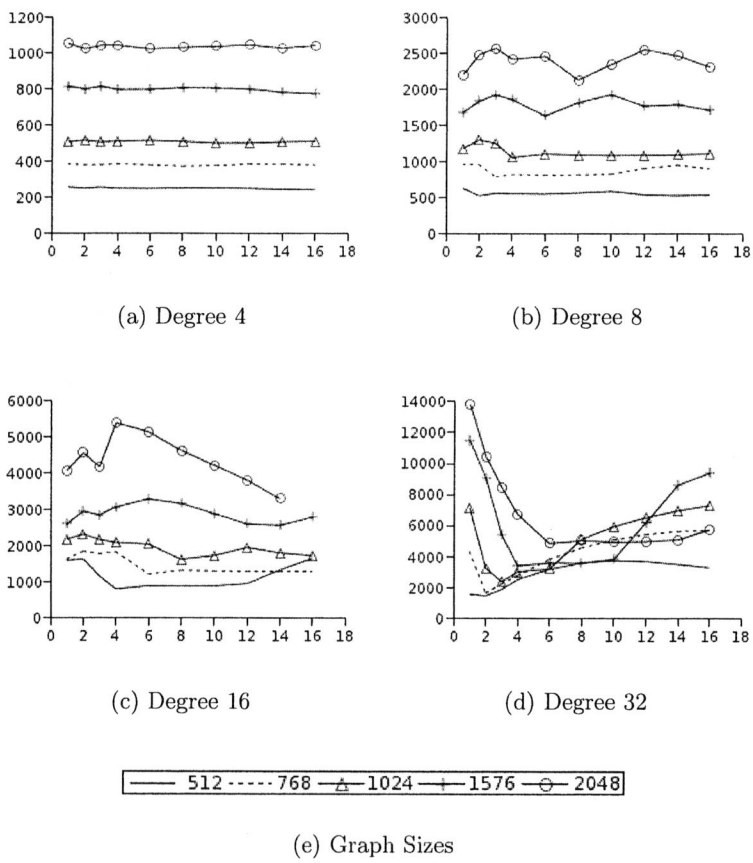

(a) Degree 4

(b) Degree 8

(c) Degree 16

(d) Degree 32

(e) Graph Sizes

Fig. 4. Agents Used (x-axis: number of home bases; y-axis: number of agents)

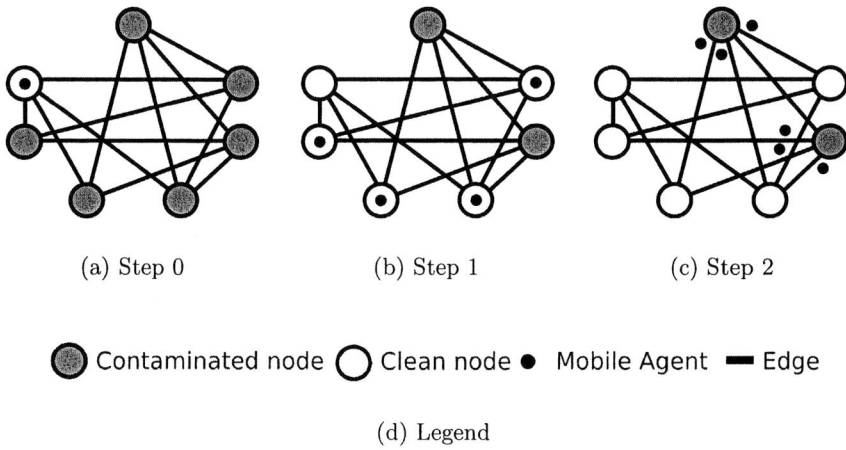

Fig. 5. Overuse of mobile agents

of agents is proportional to the ratio of decontaminated and contaminated nodes. Initially, the overuse is low as there are fewer decontaminated neighbors for each contaminated node. The overuse is highest in the last stage of decontamination as most of the neighbors of contaminated nodes have been decontaminated.

Figure 5 illustrates the propagation of the mobile agents, in the given graph of degree 4 with 7 nodes and 1 home base, through the network using the BFS technique. In the last step, while there are only 2 nodes left to be decontaminated, 6 agents are used by the algorithm. This example clearly shows the overuse of agents when using the BFS technique in a synchronous network.

5 Conclusions

In this paper, we considered the problem of decontaminating synchronous networks with mobile agents using BFS technique. We used a genetic algorithm to avoid exhaustive search. The genetic algorithm allowed to find a good approximation of the minimum number of agents needed to decontaminate the network. We considered various networks with different number of home bases to study the relationship between the number of home bases and the agents/steps required. The experiments allowed us to confirm that as the number of home bases increases, the number of agents required decreases in all network topologies considered. We observed that as the number of home bases increases the number of steps taken to decontaminate the network also decreases. The overuse of agents due to the BFS strategy increases with the decrease in the number of contaminated nodes.

Currently, we are investigating the use of global blackboard, other models to coordinate mobile agents, and asynchronous networks to see which model further reduces the number of mobile agents used. We will also consider simulating classic networks such as the hypercube, the mesh, and other networks to see if the use of several home bases can reduce the number of mobile agents required for one home base [6] when using the BFS strategy. Finally, we are considering the use of genetic algorithm to find the optimal number of home bases for a given network.

References

1. L. Barrière and P. Flocchini and P. Fraignaud and N. Santoro. Capture of an Intruder by Mobile Agents. *Proc. 14-th ACM Symposium on Parallel Algorithms and Architectures (SPAA)*, 200-209, 2002.
2. L. Barrière and P. Fraignaud and N. Santoro and D.M. Thilikos. Searching is not Jumping. *Proc. 29th Workshop on Graph Theoretic Concepts in Computer Science, (WG)* LNCS, vol. 2880, 34-45, 2003.
3. R. Breish. An intuitive approach to speleotopology. *Southwestern cavers*, **VI** (5), 72-28, 1967.
4. J.A. Ellis and I.H. Sudborough and J.S. Turner. The vertex separation and search number of a graph. *Information and Computation*, 113: 50-79, 1994.
5. P. Flocchini, L. Song, F. L. Luccio. Size Optimal Strategies for Capturing an Intruder in Mesh Networks, *Proc. of 2005 International Conference on Communications in Computing (CIC 2005)*.
6. P. Flocchini, M. J. Huang, F. L. Luccio. Contiguous Search in the Hypercube for Capturing an Intruder. *Proc. 19th IEEE International Parallel and Distributed Processing Symposium* (IPDPS 2005).
7. D.E. Goldberg, Genetic Algorithms in Search, Optimization, and Machine Learning. *Addison-Wesley.* , 1989.
8. L. M. Kirousis and C. H. Papadimitriou. Searching and pebbling. *Theoretical Computer Science*, **47**, 205-218, 1986.
9. A. Lapaugh. Recontamination does not help to search a graph. *Journal of the ACM*, **40** (2), 224-245, 1993.
10. N. Megiddo and S. Hakimi and M. Garey and D. Johnson and C. Papadimitriou. The complexity of searching a graph. *Journal of the ACM*, **35** (1), 18-44, 1988.
11. B. Monien and I.H. Sudborough. Min cut is NP-complete for edge weighted trees. *Theoretical Computer Science*, **58**, 209-229, 1988.
12. T. Parson. Pursuit-evasion problem on a graph. *Theory and applications in graphs*, Lecture Notes in Mathematics, Springer-Verlag, 426-441, 1976.
13. S. Peng and M. Ko and C. Ho and T. Hsu and C. Tang. Graph searching on chordal graphs. *Algorithmica*, **27**, 395-426, 2000.

Multi-attribute Hashing of Wireless Data for Content-Based Queries

Yon Dohn Chung[1] and Ji Yeon Lee[2]

[1] Department of Computer Engineering, Dongguk University, Seoul, Korea
ydchung@dgu.edu
[2] E-Government Team, National Computerization Agency, Seoul, Korea
jylee@nca.or.kr

Abstract. In mobile distributed systems data broadcasting is widely used as a data dissemination solution, where we need an indexing scheme in order to energy-efficiently access the wireless data. In conventional indexing schemes, they use key attribute values and construct tree-structured index. Therefore, the conventional indexing schemes do not support content-based retrieval queries such as partial-match queries, range-queries, and so on. In this paper we propose an index method which supports content-based retrieval queries on wireless broadcast data stream. For this purpose, we construct a tree-structured index which is composed of bit-vectors, where the bit-vectors are generated from data records through multi-attribute hashing.

1 Introduction

The wireless data broadcasting delivers data through public channels to unspecified clients in mobile distributed systems. Compared with the peer-to-peer communication between the server and mobile clients, the broadcasting approach is recognized as energy and bandwidth efficient [9, 10, 11]. In wireless data broadcasting, we consider two performance aspects, access time and tuning time. The access time is the duration from the time of query submission to that of complete retrieval of required data. The tuning time is the actual *tune-in* time for accessing the data, which is the duration when the devices remain in the *active* mode (i.e., high energy consumption mode) [9].

There have been many studies on wireless data broadcasting: data caching[2, 12] and non-uniform broadcasting approaches[2, 10] for reducing access time, broadcast data clustering approaches[5, 6, 14] for improving access time performance of partial and multi-point queries, indexing[3, 11] of wireless broadcast data stream for improving tuning time performance, the use of signatures[8, 10] for approximate retrieval of wireless data, and so on.

This paper focuses on the indexing approach for reducing tuning time. The index on the air means the addresses of data records, where the address is the time when the target data record arrives. The use of index on the wireless data stream is the most popular approach for improving tuning time performance. However, most of the conventional indexing approaches [3, 11] consider only *key-based* point queries, and hence they cannot effectively handle nonkey-based queries. In this paper, we propose an index method for content-based retrieval queries (CBQ) such as *partial-match queries* and *range queries*. For supporting content-based accesses, we represent data records as bit-vectors using multi-attribute hashing, and construct a bit-vector tree for wireless index structure.

2 Related Work and Motivation

There have been some index methods for wireless data stream, such as *(1, M) Indexing*, *Flexible Indexing*, *Distributed Indexing*[9, 11] for uniformly data set and *CF* and *VF* methods[3] for skewed data. Basically these index methods construct tree-structured index, *B-Tree* [9, 11] and *Huffman Tree* [3] for uniform and skewed data sets respectively, and organize the broadcast data stream with the data records and index records, where the index records are intermixed with data through tree traversal. However, these previous methods are not good at processing content-based queries (CBQ), where content-based queries access the wireless data stream by specifying some (non-key) attribute values or value ranges [1, 13, 14]. The CBQ is known as one of the most widely used query types in database and information retrieval systems [1, 7, 13]. In the below, we show an example of the use of CBQ in wireless information systems.

Example 1 [A Stock Information System for Mobile Clients]. The server repeatedly broadcasts current stock price records via a public channel. The stock record consists of four attributes: A_1 (*Company Code*), A_2 (*Amount of Sales*), A_3 (*Amount of Purchase*) and A_4 (*Price*). The clients possess portable terminals with wireless communication modules. So, they can move around and frequently access the stock price information via wireless communication. While some clients have interests on the stock price information that they hold, others may have interests on the stocks that have some specific patterns e.g., the stock whose *price* is greater than $50 and the *amount of sales* is less than ten thousands. After retrieving the stock price information, the mobile clients can issue some requests (i.e., sell or buy some stocks) via pre-assigned P2P communication channels, which may be *wireless* or *wired* ones. (We consider only the process of data retrieval. The remaining actions such as sending requests are not addressed in the paper.) ∎

In Example 1, the former clients use primary key (i.e., A_1 *Company Code*)-based point queries and the latter ones use CBQ. The CBQ is not applicable to the conventional key-based index structures [3, 11], since they do not include non-key attributes at all. If the broadcast data stream is indexed by a conventional one, we have to read all data records and check whether the data records are satisfied by the query, which requires huge tuning time.

3 The Proposed Method

In the proposed method, we define the bit-vector for each data record using the multi-attribute hashing which is a well-known content-describing technique [7]. After generating the bit-vectors, we construct an index tree of bit-vectors. Then, the broadcast data stream, intermixed with the bit-vector index information, enables the mobile clients to access the data with content-based queries (CBQ) in an energy-efficient way.

3.1 Bit-Vector Representation Using Multi-attribute Hashing

Using multi-attribute hashing, we represent data records as *data bit-vectors* and user queries as *query bit-vectors*. (We use the terms *data vectors* and *query vectors* for short.)

Definition 1. A data record R_j consists of k attributes $A_1, A_2, ..., A_k$. And, we assume there is a predetermined hash function h_i for each attribute A_i. Then, the data vector dv_j for data record R_j is $h_1(R_j(A_1)) \oplus h_2(R_j(A_2)) \oplus ... \oplus h_k(R_j(A_k))$, where '$\oplus$' denotes the bit stream concatenation operator.[1]

Definition 2. The query vector qv_j for query Q_j is $h_1(Q_j(A_1)) \oplus h_2(Q_j(A_2)) \oplus ... \oplus h_k(Q_j(A_k))$. Here, $Q_j(A_i)$ denotes the value of attribute A_i of the query. If the query does not contain specified value for A_i, the hashed bit stream of $h_i(Q_j(A_i))$ becomes "**...*", where the size is equal to $h_i(R_j(A_i))$ for any j. (The symbol '*' means "*don't care*".) ∎

We show an example of data and query vectors based on Example 1. Let us assume there are four hash functions as follows: (The sizes of hashed bit streams for the attributes are 2, 2, 2, and 3 respectively in this hashing scheme. And hence the size of the *data* (also *query*) vector is 9.)

$$h_{company}(x) = \begin{cases} 00 & \text{if } x \text{ is a financial company} \\ 01 & \text{if } x \text{ is a manufacturing company} \\ 10 & \text{if } x \text{ is a computer and communication company} \\ 11 & \text{otherwise} \end{cases}$$

$$h_{amount\ of\ sale\ (or\ amount\ of\ purchase)}(x) = \begin{cases} 00 & \text{if } x < 10000 \\ 01 & \text{if } 10000 \leq x < 20000 \\ 10 & \text{if } 2000 \leq x < 30000 \\ 11 & \text{if } 30000 \leq x \end{cases}$$

$$h_{price}(x) = \begin{cases} 000 & \text{if } x < 5 \\ 001 & \text{if } 5 \leq x < 10 \\ 010 & \text{if } 10 \leq x < 20 \\ 011 & \text{if } 20 \leq x < 30 \\ 100 & \text{if } 30 \leq x < 40 \\ 101 & \text{if } 40 \leq x < 50 \\ 110 & \text{if } 50 \leq x < 60 \\ 111 & \text{if } 60 \leq x \end{cases}$$

Then the *data vector* for a data record [*Company Code*=150 (a code for manufacturing company), *Amount of Sale*=13000, *Amount of Purchase*=2000, *Price*=22] is "*010100011* (= *01* ⊕ *01* ⊕ *00* ⊕ *011*)". The *query vector* can be generated similarly.

---

[1] The proposed approach is different from previous signature methods [5, 8]. The bit-vector uses the concatenation operator while the signature uses superimposed coding. And thus, there is no false-drop in the proposed method.

The *query vector* for a query [*Amount of Sale* ≥ 30,000, 10 ≤ *Price* < 20] is "**11**010". Since the attributes *Company Code* and *Amount of Purchase* are not specified in the query, the bit positions for the corresponding attributes are filled with '*'. Although the concept of 'bit' can represent only two states '0' and '1', we in the paper assume that one bit represents '0', '1', and '*' for the sake of convenience.

3.2 The Bit-Vector Tree (BV-Tree)

We construct a tree-structured hierarchical index with the *data vectors* generated in Section 3.1. We call the tree the *Bit-Vector Tree* (the *BV-Tree* in short), which is defined as follows:

Definition 3. Let l be the size of a bit vector. Then the *BV-tree* of l-bit bit-vectors is a tree such that:

(1) The *BV-tree* is a full binary tree with the height of '$l+1$'.
(2) The root node is "***…*", and the level of the root is '0'.
(3) A node in level 'i' is a bit-vector where upper (i.e., left) 'i' bits are '0' or '1' and the remaining '$l-i$' bits are '*'.
(4) A node in level 'i' ($i<l$) has two children at level '$i+1$', where the children bit-vectors are same to the parent bit-vector except that the left-most '*' bit in the parent is replaced by '0' or '1' in the children.
(5) The leaf nodes (level 'l') are fully-specified l-bit vectors (i.e., there is no '*' in the bit-vector).

3.3 The Structure of Index and Data Buckets

Since the basic unit of wireless communication is the bucket [11], we have to construct the broadcast data stream (including index information) into buckets. Basically all buckets (irrespective of their types) contain some control information such as the type of bucket, the link to the next index, and the start address of the next broadcast cycle.

Definition 4. The index bucket is organized as follows:

- *BUCKET_TYPE*: the Boolean field for indicating the bucket type (i.e., *index* or *data* bucket)
- *ARRAY_OF_ADDRESS_TUPLES[M]*: the array of M address tuples, where the address tuple is a pair of (index bit-vector, address of the target bucket).
- *LINK_TO_NEXT_INDEX*: the address of the next nearest index bucket
- *NEXT_BROADCAST*: the start address of the next broadcast cycle.

Definition 5. The data bucket is organized as follows:

- *BUCKET_TYPE*: the Boolean field for indicating the bucket type
- *ARRAY_OF_DATA_RECORDS[N]*: the array of N data records
- *CONTINUE_TO_NEXT_BUCKET*: the Boolean field for indicating whether the data records consecutively allocated in the next bucket; When the data records represented by a leaf node bit-vector are too many to fit into one data bucket, this field set as *TRUE*.
- *LINK_TO_NEXT_INDEX*: the address of the next nearest index bucket
- *NEXT_BROADCAST*: the start address of the next broadcast cycle. ∎

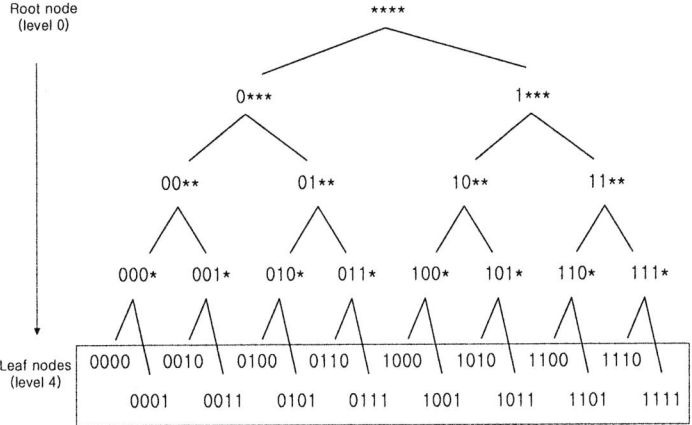

Fig. 1. The *BV-tree* for 4-bit bit-vectors - The leaf node of the *BV-tree* represents the data records whose contents are described by the corresponding bit-vectors through multi-attribute hashing. The intermediate nodes *cover*[2] their descendant nodes because each parent node *covers* their children nodes by the 4th condition in Definition 3. For example, the bit-vector '00**' *covers* '000*' and '001*', each of which *covers* their two children '0000' and '0001' and '0010' and '0011' respectively. Consequently, the root node *covers* all nodes in the tree.

When some system parameters (such as the bucket size, the size of a bit-vector, etc.) are determined, the value of M and N can be easily computed as follows:

$$N = \left\lceil \frac{\text{(the size of a bucket - the sum of all control information field sizes)}}{\text{the size of a data record}} \right\rceil$$

$$M = \left\lceil \frac{\text{(the size of a bucket - the sum of all control information field sizes)}}{\text{the size of an address tuple}} \right\rceil.$$

3.4 The Bucket-Based Bit Vector-Tree (B2V-Tree)

The *B2V-Tree* is constructed by merging *BV-tree* nodes according to the capacity M of the index bucket. However, we cannot use the value M directly. Since we have to preserve the property of *tree*, we set the *fan-out* of the *B2V-tree* as an exponential value of 2. Note that in a tree, there exists a unique path from the root to each leaf node. It means that a node covers all its children nodes and all children nodes are covered by a unique parent node. Since the *BV-Tree* is a full-balanced binary tree, the unique path property cannot hold when we use an arbitrary value (not an exponential value of 2) for the fan-out of the *B2V-Tree*. With the *tree* property, mobile clients effectively find their target data by traversing the *B2V-Tree*. Thus, we compute the fan-out of the *B2V-Tree* as follows using the value of M determined previously:

$$f = \text{Max. } 2^i \text{ such that } 2^i \leq M, \text{ (where } i \text{ is a positive integer).}$$

---

[2] The bit-vector v_1 *covers* v_2 if and only if all the '0/1' bit representations of v_2 is included by those of v_1, where the '0/1' bit representations means the enumeration of bit streams by replacing '*' bit positions of the given bit-vector into '0' or '1'.

Using f, we group the *BV-Tree* nodes into buckets and construct the *B2V-tree*. For brevity, the formal *B2V-Tree* construction algorithm is abbreviated in the paper. Instead, we show in Figure 2 a *B2V-tree* constructed from the *BV-tree* of Figure 1. Here, we assume f to be 4. The white rectangles denote index buckets of the *B2V-tree*, and the colored ones denote the data buckets.

We also show the wireless data stream intermixed with index information in the bottom of the figure. We used the depth-first traversal of the *B2V-Tree*, which is a common broadcast data generation method [2, 13]. Since the hierarchical structure of the proposed indexing scheme is the same to that of the previous one, the index replication approaches [4, 10] previously studied for tree-structured index can also be applied to our method. For example, if we apply the index replication strategy of the *Distributed Indexing* [10], then the wireless broadcast stream becomes as follows:

$<I_1, I_2, D_1, ..., D_5, I_1', I_3, D_6, ..., D_{13}, I_1'', I_4, D_{14}, ..., D_{19}, I_1''', I_5, D_{20}, D_{21}>$,

where I_i' is the second replica of I_i, I_i'' is the third replica of I_i, and so on.

In Figure 2, the link between data buckets means that there are too many records to fit into one data bucket, and thus they are stored contiguous buckets. The field *CONTINUE_TO_ NEXT _BUCKET* in Definition 5 handles this situation. The data bucket D_{20} is indicated by three address tuples, which is the result of post-optimization i.e., saving the space. In the post-optimization, we can merge data buckets pointed by some address tuples only when the address tuples are in one index bucket. We cannot merge D_{19} and D_{20} in the figure, although they are sparse enough to be merged into one, because their parents are in two distinct index buckets (I_4 and I_5).

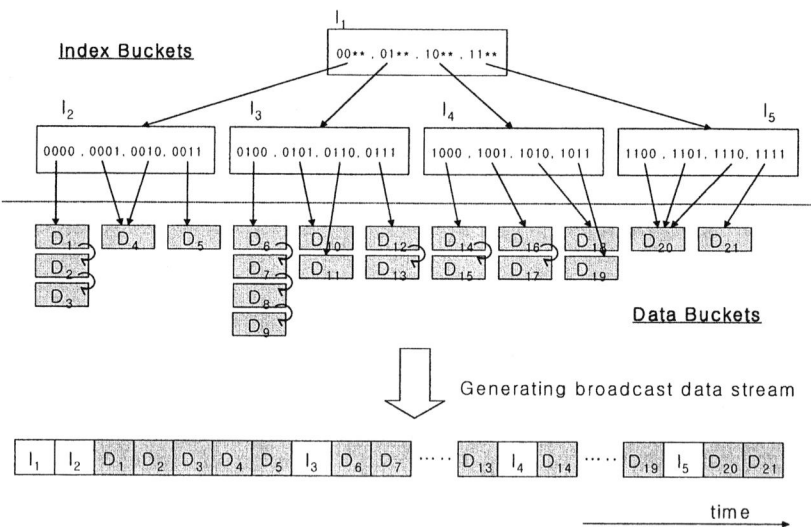

Fig. 2. The *B2V-Tree* for Figure 1 and its broadcast data stream - Since the height of *BV-Tree* is 5 and the fan-out is 4, the root node I_1 consists of four address tuples whose bit-vectors are '00**', '01**', '10**' and '11**', and these addresses are the links to the children sub-trees

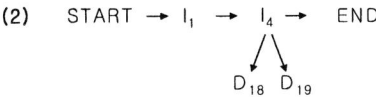
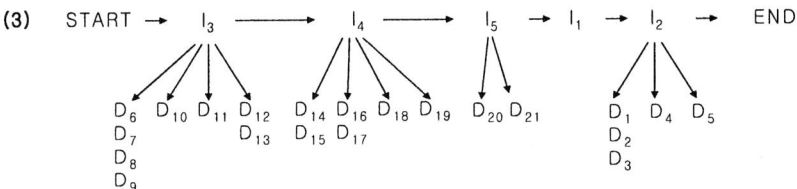

Fig. 3. Examples of data access steps

3.5 Accessing the Wireless Stream

For processing CBQs on the wireless data stream, the mobile client probes relevant index buckets through the bit-vector comparison between the query vector (QV) of the user query and the bit-vectors of address tuples in index buckets. Note that if the QV is not fully-specified (i.e., to the leaf level), then we may have to follow (in parallel) multiple paths of index probes, each of them reaching to corresponding leaf nodes. Instead of fully describing the access algorithm, we show in Figure 3 some examples based on Figure 2.

In Case (1) of Figure 3, a mobile client starts to retrieve data records for a CBQ "0111" at the time of D_5. Then the access steps are I_5, D_{12}, and D_{13}. Since a bit-vector ("0111") of an address tuple in I_5 is exactly matched with the QV, it can directly access the data records which are in D_{12} and D_{13}. In Case (2), the QV is "101*", and the query start time is at the time of I_1. The access steps are I_1, I_4, D_{18}, and D_{19}. Here, we have to follow two paths of index probing for D_{18} and D_{19}. It is because the QV "101*" includes two bit-vectors ("1010" and "1011"), and they are linked to D_{18} and D_{19} respectively. In the figure, we depict the multiple paths with vertical arrows whereas the horizontal arrows denote sequential probes. Case (3) shows the access steps for processing a QV "****" at the time of I_3. Because the current index bucket contains four address tuples all of which are included by the QV, we have to follow the four paths of index probes. And, for the bit-vectors not covered by I_3, we have to sequentially probe another relevant index buckets I_4, I_5 and I_2[3]. Arriving at each of the index buckets, we follow the data links and retrieve the data records.

4 Analysis and Experiments

In this section we analyze some properties of the proposed method, and experimentally evaluate its effectiveness with respect to the improvement of energy-efficiency

---

[3] If we apply the index replication strategies of [4], such as *SL(Sibling Link)* or *NL(Nephew Link)*, the access steps for Case 3 in Figure 3 will be changed such that the step for index bucket I_1 is removed.

compared with the previous index. For convenience of analysis, we assume that the data records are uniform, thus the number of data buckets pointed by each leaf-level bit-vector is the same and the *BV-tree* is fully balanced.

Observation 1. Let l be the number of bits for a bit-vector, ndb be the number of data buckets for a fully specified bit-vector, and f be the fan-out as computed in Section 3.4. Then, we can observe the followings:

1. the height of the *BV-tree* is $l+1$
2. the height of the *B2V-tree* is $\left\lceil \frac{l+1}{i} \right\rceil + 1$, where $i = \log_2 f$
3. the number of tuning steps for reading index buckets is $\left\lceil \frac{l+1}{i} \right\rceil + 2$ (i.e., the *height + 1*) in the worst case and *1* in the best case
4. the number of tuning steps for reading data buckets for a CBQ q is $2^w \times ndb$, where w is the number of '*' in q. ∎

Now, we compare the proposed indexing scheme with the previous index method. Firstly, in order to show the need of supporting CBQs, we compare the *Distributed Indexing* method and the proposed one in Table 1, which is the qualitative comparison

Table 1. Tuning performance comparison for each query type

Query Type	The Proposed Method	The *Distributed Indexing* Method
Point queries with the key attribute	- Partially Supported[4]	- **Completely Supported**
Point queries without the key attribute	-**Partially Supported** (same to the above; but **more efficient** than the *Distributed Indexing*	- Not Supported. (i.e., all data buckets must be read to be checked)
Partial-match queries with the key attribute	- **Efficiently Supported**	- Partially Supported if the key attribute is used for data access. - Not Supported otherwise
Partial-match queries without the key		- Not Supported
Range-queries with the key attribute		- Partially Supported if the key attribute is used for data access - Not Supported otherwise
Range-queries without the key attribute		- Not Supported

---

[4] We can improve the efficiency by assigning more bits to the key attribute when designing hash functions.

of tuning performance for various query types. (Signature techniques are not considered in this comparison since they are filtering approaches not indexing ones. Filtering mechanism can be added to conventional indexing methods and also our proposed method for further performance improvement.)

We consider 6 query types: (1) *point queries with the key attribute*, (2) *point queries without the key attribute*, (3) *partial-match queries with the key attribute*, (4) *partial-match queries without the key attribute*, (5) *range-queries with the key attribute* and (6) *range-queries without the key attribute*.

Now we experimentally compare the proposed method with the conventional *Distributed Indexing* method. We simulate the wireless media with a data stream on disks, that is, the server generates the broadcast data stream into a file, and client modules read the file according to the wireless data stream access protocol. The data set used for the experiment is as follows:

- Number of data records: 4096
- The contents of a data record: 4 attributes - company code, amount of sale, amount of purchase, and price (in this order), where the company code is the unique primary key attribute. The domain of each attribute is:
    - A1 (*company code*): 0 ~ 4096
    - A2 (*amount of sale*), A3 (*amount of purchase*): 0 ~ 2^{19}-1
    - A4 (*price*): 0 ~ 2^{10}-1
- The size of a data record: 16 bytes

We set the size of bucket as 128 bytes and the size of bit-vector as 16 bits. (We tested other bit-vector and bucket sizes, but result patterns were similar.) For each method, we measure the access time and tuning time performance for 10 test queries in Table 2. We in this experiment measure the access and tuning time when assuming the query processing begins at the root node.

Table 2. Queries used in the experiment

Query	Description	Remarks
Q1	code = 12	Point query with key attribute (low value)
Q2	code = 3210	Point query with key attribute (high value)
Q3	amount of sale = 100000	Point query with non-key (the 2nd) attribute
Q4	amount of purchase = 0	Point query with non-key (the 3rd) attribute
Q5	price = 100	Point query with non-key (the 4th i.e., the least significant) attribute
Q6	100 < code < 300	Range query with key attribute
Q7	amount of sale < 50000	Range query with non-key attribute
Q8	100000 < amount of sale < 200000	Range query with non-key attribute
Q9	code = 12 and amount of sale < 10000	Pointed by key attribute and ranged with non-key attribute
Q10	amount of sale = 100 and 100 < price < 200	Pointed by non-key attribute and ranged with non-key attribute

Figure 4 shows the experiment results of our method and the conventional method. As discussed in the above qualitative comparison, the proposed method outperforms the previous method except some primary key-based queries (e.g., *Q1*, *Q2*, *Q6*, and *Q9*). The results show that our method provides 80%~90% tuning time reduction with only 20%~30% access time increase. In case of *Q5*, the performance of our method is not so good. This is because the attribute '*price*' is the least significant one, and hence their bit representations are positioned at the right end in bit-vectors, which reduces index probing efficiency.

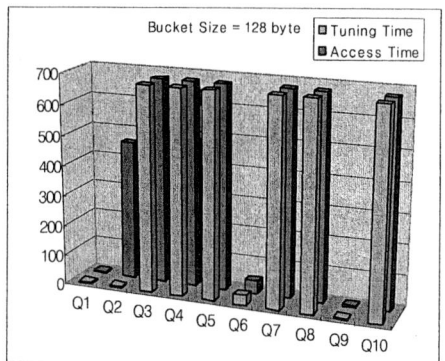 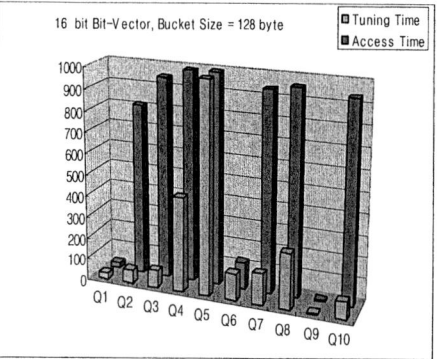

Fig. 4. Experiment Results of *Distributed Indexing* (left) and *Our Method* (right)

6 Conclusion

The broadcasting strategy is widely used in wireless information systems due to its various merits. However, the previous indexing methods for broadcast data mostly considered key-based point queries, which are so restrictive in their usage. In the paper we have proposed an index method for content-based queries on wireless data stream. The content-based queries retrieve data records from the wireless stream by specifying the contents of data not the key attribute values.

In the paper, we have used the multi-attribute hashing for bit-vector representation of data records and queries. The multi-attribute hashing is known as a popular method for content description. With the bit-vectors, we have constructed the *BV-tree*, which includes data bit-vectors in the leaf level and partially-specified (i.e.,'*') bit-vectors in the intermediate levels. After constructing the *BV-tree*, we have merged the *BV-tree* nodes in the unit of bucket for the index on the air, called the *B2V-tree*.

Through the analysis and experiments, we have described some properties of the proposed index structure and showed its effectiveness with respect to the improvement of tuning performance compared with the previous index method. Since the previous method uses the key attribute for tree-style index construction, they cannot effectively support content-based queries. In contrast, with the proposed method, the mobile clients are able to energy-efficiently process content-based queries such as partial-match and range-queries.

In the future, we will comprehensively experiment the proposed method considering various environmental settings such as data distribution, caching policies of mobile clients, error-rates of wireless communication and so on. The research on content-based query processing for non-uniform data streaming applications will also be of importance.

Acknowledgement

This work was done as a part of Information & Communication Fundamental Technology Research Program, supported by Ministry of Information & Communication in Republic of Korea.

References

1. Abdel-Ghaffar, K.A.S., Abbadi, A. E.: Optimal Disk Allocation for Partial Match Queries. ACM Transactions on Database Systems, 18(1), (1993) 132-156
2. Acharya , S., Alonso, R. , Franklin, M., Zdonik, S.: Broadcast Disks : Data Management for Asymmetric Communication Environments. In Proceedings of ACM SIGMOD Conference (1995) 199 - 210
3. Chen, M. S., Wu, K. L., Yu, P. S.: Optimizing Index Allocation for Sequential Data Broadcasting in Wireless Mobile Computing, IEEE Transactions on Knowledge and Data Engineering, 15(1), (2003) 161-173
4. Chung, Y. D., Kim, M. H.: An Index Replication Scheme for Wireless Data Broadcasting, Journal of Systems and Software, 51(3), (2000) 191-199
5. Chung, Y. D., Kim, M. H.,: A Wireless Data Clustering Method for Multipoint Queries, Decision Support Systems, 30(4), (2001) 469-482
6. Chung, Y. D., Kim, M. H.: Effective Data Placement for Wireless Broadcast. Distributed and Parallel Databases, 9 (2001) 133-150
7. Faloutsos, C.: Multiattribute Hashing Using Gray Codes. In Proceedings of ACM SIGMOD Conference (1986) 227 - 238
8. Hu, Q, Lee, W.-C., Lee, D. L.,: A Hybrid Index Technique for Power Efficient Data Broadcast. Distributed and Parallel Databases, 9 (2001) 151-177
9. Imielinski, T., Badrinath, B. R.: Data Management for Mobile Computing. SIGMOD RECORD, (1993) 22(1)
10. Imielinski, T., Viswanathan, S., Badrinath, B. R.: Power Efficient Filtering of Data on Air. In Proceedings of Extending Database Technology (1994)
11. Imielinski, T., Viswanathan, S., Badrinath, B. R.: Data on Air : Organization and Access. IEEE Transactions on Knowledge and Data Engineering 9(3), (1997)
12. Jing, J., Bakhres, O., Elmagarmid, A., Alonso, R.: Bit-Sequences : An Adaptive Cache Invalidation Method in Mobile Client/Server Environments. Mobile Networks and Applications (MONET), 2(2), (1997)115 - 127
13. Kim, M. H., Pramanik, S.: Optimal File Distribution for Partial Match Retrieval. In Proceedings of ACM SIGMOD Conference, (1998)173-182
14. Lee, J. Y., Chung, Y. D., Lee, Y. J. Kim, M. H.: Gray Code Clustering of Wireless Data for Partial Match Queries. Journal of Systems Architecture, 47 (2001), 445-458

A Tool for Automated Resource Consumption Profiling of Distributed Transactions

B. Nagaprabhanjan and Varsha Apte

Indian Institute of Technology Bombay, India
nagaprabhanjan@it.iitb.ac.in, varsha@cse.iitb.ac.in

Abstract. In this paper, we present a tool, called Autoprofiler, that automates the discovery of resource consumption by transactions on distributed systems. Such information is required as input to performance analysis tools, which may be used for capacity planning, for re-architecting a distributed system, or to identify potential bottlenecks. Deriving this information using existing tools is a tedious and error prone process. In contrast, our tool requires minimal human intervention, and brings down the time required to profile complex distributed systems to a few minutes. It does this by co-ordinating the process of load generation and server resource profiling. Our tool also works with a Java profiler, called LiteJava Profiler, which we have built, to fully automate the process of resource consumption discovery for J2EE servers.

1 Introduction

With the advent of the Internet, the trend of business transactions between customers and enterprises has changed drastically. Now, a customer expects to perform a business transaction within seconds from home through the Internet. The IT infrastructure of an enterprise should be robust enough to provide such service to its customers. As distributed computing systems have been proven to be a low cost and high performance alternative to centralized systems, most of the Internet based services are supported by distributed systems. An enterprise can also choose to consolidate all their applications and services in high-performance data centers. In either case, a typical transaction always accesses multiple nodes before completion. For example, a transaction to transfer money from one account to another may access the authentication server for verifying the credentials of a person, the database server to access the accounts and the application server for processing the business logic.

In such a scenario, it is necessary for an enterprise or the owner of a data center to make sure that the user performance requirements of a service, such as response time, throughput, connection loss rate etc. are met. At the same time, it is desirable that the IT infrastructure is utilized well and the systems operate close to their capacity. The process of sizing the infrastructure so that service performance requirements are met, is called "capacity planning". Capacity planning can be carried out if the resource requirements of individual applications are known, along with the usage volumes (or *load*) that the applications need to support.

One way to answer a capacity planning question, such as how many machines of a certain type are required to support a certain application, is the following: If resource utilization and load measurements are available from a system where this application is currently deployed, a simple linear scaling can be used for future capacity planning. E.g. if it is known that application server A deployed on Machine M, is supporting 1000 customers, with machine M's utilization level at 80%, then if the number of customers is projected to reach 2000, planning for one more machine of the same type will be needed.

However, this approach works only if the nature, or the *mix* of transactions coming to the system can be assumed to be unchanging. If the workload mix on a system changes, then linear scaling methods do not work. In such cases, a more detailed model of the system, and a fine-grained resource consumption profile of the transaction is required. That is, we need to know what the resource requirement of each *type* of transaction is, not the application server as a whole. More specifically, a complete resource consumption profile, such as the CPU time required by each transaction of the application, the memory requirement, the disk and network I/O, is required, along with a characterization of the workload (e.g. rate at which the requests for different transactions arrive). With these inputs, analytical queueing models (or simulation models), can be used to arrive at an optimal sizing and deployment configuration of the applications on the infrastructure [13].

Several modeling tools exist that accept the resource requirements, the message flows and the deployment configuration of applications on physical resources as inputs, and solve an underlying queueing model to provide performance measurements [13]. However, in realistic scenarios, these inputs may not be readily available, and effort must be made to explicitly discover them. Of the three mentioned above, the deployment details are the easiest to obtain; however, derivation of the message flows and resource requirement may be more involved. The process of discovering resource consumption for multiple transactions that access multiple servers can be quite tedious and error prone. Thus, there is a need for designing good software tools that make this process smoother, error-free and requiring minimal human involvement.

In this paper, we describe a tool that automates this process of resource usage profiling for distributed applications which have a Web-based front-end. Given a simple deployment description, and the URLs of the Web-transactions, the tool generates a resource consumption profile of all specified servers. The tool includes two components: the wrapper component, which we call the *Autoprofiler* which automates and co-ordinates the entire process; and a Java-specific profiler called the *LiteJava Profiler*. This was required since direct interaction with JVM internals is required to produce a fine-grained profile of a Java application.

We note here that none of the existing load generators are built for this purpose; they are primarily "performance testing" tools - a purpose which is distinctly different from resource profiling. In case of Java profilers, none of the exisiting Java profilers fit into the automated framework that we were building, therefore we built a custom profiler (LiteJava Profiler), which is flexible and scalable, to suit our requirements. In our experiments with **Autoprofiler** working with the LiteJava Profiler, the time required to profile a sample J2EE application called ECPerf reduced dramatically. Thus, our tool can significantly enhance the productivity of an IT enterprise.

The rest of the paper is as follows. In Section 2, we present some commonly available load generators and resource profilers and discuss their limitations. In Section 3 we present **Autoprofiler**, a framework to automate the process of load generation and resource profiling. We discuss the LiteJava Profiler in Section 4. In Section 5, we present the results of some preliminary experiments conducted with the tool and discuss some observations that we found in Java based applications. We conclude in Section 6 with a discussion on future work.

2 Background and Motivation

In order to better understand the need for automating the process of resource consumption profiling, consider the scenario in Figure 1. Here, we have deployed the *ECPerf* [1] application on the JBoss application server on one machine and the PostgreSQL database server on another machine. The *ECPerf* application supports services such as creating a new order, getting the status of an order, getting the status of a customer, cancelling an order, scheduling a work order, updating a work order etc. [1].

Now in order to find, for e.g., the CPU time consumed by each of the above transactions on each of the servers, we need to do the following:

– Generate the requests for a particular transaction using some load generator.
– After some warm-up time, start measurements on both machines to profile the corresponding processes.
– When the load generation is over, stop profiling the processes on the server machines.
– Collect the statistics from the load generator as well as the profiling processes. Correlate it (e.g. at request rate x, CPU utilization is y).

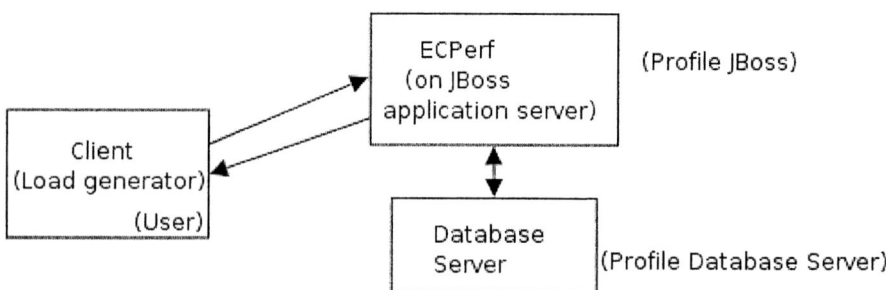

Fig. 1. A Resource Usage Profiling Scenario

- Carry out the calculations required to get the resource consumption values for a single request.
- Repeat these steps for each transaction that the application supports.

Currently, in order to carry out the above steps, we need two distinct kind of tools *viz. load generators* which generate load on the system and *server profiling tools* which give us the resource consumption measurements from the server. However, the co-ordination between the load generation and the server resource profiling process needs to be done manually. Furthermore, the actual calculations needed to derive per-transaction resource consumption, also must be done manually. This increases the time required to generate a complete resource consumption profile of the server and increases the possibility of errors that occur in the co-ordination process. As the service becomes more distributed in nature, with a large number of components, the process of manually profiling becomes more time consuming, tedious and error prone.

Most of the work mentioned above can and should be automated. This is what we have aimed for in our tool *viz.* Autoprofiler. The tool should generate the load for the transaction. After detecting sufficient warm up for the transaction, it should automatically start measurement at the server end. When the load generation process is over, it should get the resource consumption details from the servers, normalize the values and display the same. In case the server is a Java based server, the tool should also interact with the Java profiler to get fine grained details.

2.1 Existing Tools

There are a number of commercial Web load generators available in the market, e.g. *PureLoad*[2], *openSTA*[6] and *Httperf*[3]. Products such as *Silk Performer*[4] and Mercury LoadRunner[5] are commercially available enterprise class tools. However, these are all primarily *performance testing* tools that focus on recording and analyzing client-side performance measures. Although some do provide consolidated views of client-side performance measures along with server side resource utilization measures, none of them do any co-ordination or calculations necessary to provide per-transaction resource consumption details.

Some common OS utilities provide comprehensive resource consumption information. *Top* displays the dynamic values of the system state, such as CPU utilization, memory consumed etc. on a per process basis. Additionally, utilities such as *iostat, vmstat, netstat, sar, ps* provide information similar to *top*. The *Linux Trace Toolkit* [7] can give finer information such as time spent in I/O etc. by a process.

There are a number of profilers available for the Java environment. The *Extensible Java Profiler* (EJP)[8] is a Java profiling tool that enables developers to test and improve the performance of their programs running on the JVM. It has filtering capability allowing one to log only methods of specified packages. *Yourkit Java Profiler* (YJP) [9] gives useful profiling information regarding the heap (memory). Using this profiler, one can get the CPU and memory allocation information about the application. It has support for partial profiling which means that profiling can be enabled or disabled as and when required. Details about more profilers can be found in [10]. The main drawback of these profilers is that they are written for simple to moderate-sized applications, and meant to be used in an interactive manner by humans. Hence, for e.g., they have very user-friendly graphical interfaces. However, they fail to scale up when deployed and run in a J2EE environment, requiring overheads such as a long start-up time and a large amount of disk space for the large amount of data generated. Furthermore, they are not built for automation, which makes them unsuitable for our purpose.

3 Autoprofiler

The **Autoprofiler** is a distributed tool with a master-slave architecture, that co-ordinates the process of load generation and resource profiling. In master mode, the tool generates the load and is responsible for co-ordinating the process. In slave mode, the tool records the resource utilization information and sends this to the master when asked for. This basic co-ordination process for a general distributed system is depicted in Figure 2.

Here, the master resides at the client side and the slaves at the servers. The client side is the one where load is generated and the server side is the one where the application servers reside that serve the requests.

In the first version of the tool, we have focussed mainly on resource profiling. We aim to get only raw service times for requests and do not want to put the resources under contention. In order to ensure this, the tool generates the requests sequentially; that is, only after the reply for a request arrives, it generates

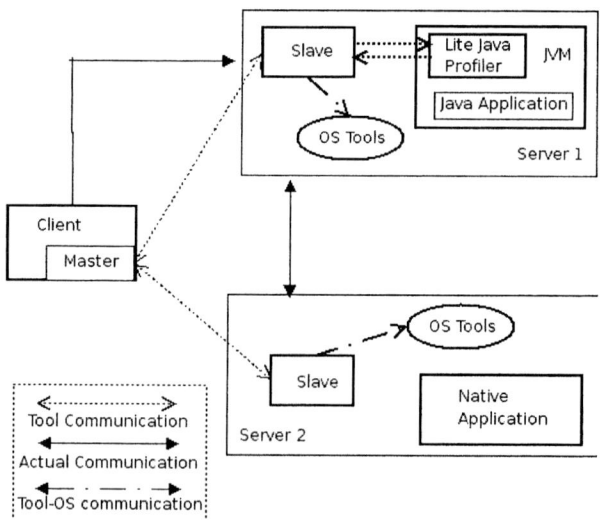

Fig. 2. Autoprofiler: Architecture and process co-ordination

the next request. These raw service times will serve as input to queueing models from which the performance attributes of the system such as the average number of jobs, average waiting time etc. can be derived.

We now discuss the architecture of the tool in detail. As the tool works in two modes viz. master and slave, we discuss their architectures seperately.

3.1 Master Architecture

The tool, as a master, does the following:

- Reads the information about the transactions from an XML file.
- Generates the corresponding HTTP requests.
- Co-ordinates the process of resource profiling by issuing commands to the slaves.
- Displays the resource profile summary on the master terminal.

We elaborate further on some of the elements of the Master.

Input Specification Formats: The tool needs inputs such as the description of the transactions, the software servers and their deployment details. We have created an XML DTD that allows us to specify this information. Figure 3 shows the XML DTD which we explain in detail as follows:

Transaction Specification: As can be seen from the DTD, the basic information about a transaction comprises of:

- The transaction name.
- The Web interface for the transaction.
- The information about the applications, and their deployment information, that are accessed by the transaction.

The Web interface comprises of the node and port on which the Web server is running. This information is given as **url** and **port** respectively. It also includes the Uniform Resource Identifier (URI) information which specifies what needs to be accessed.

Specification of URI: A static URI is specified as uri in the XML file. If variable URIs are to be sent (e.g. URIs with "name-value" pairs), the name of a file of such URIs is given instead, as uriFile in the XML specification.

Node information: The tool also needs to know the information about the nodes that are accessed by a particular transaction so that it can communicate with the slaves at the respective nodes. The tool identifies two different types of nodes. One is a *Java node* and the other one is a *native node*.

A *Java node* is one which hosts a Java based application server such as *Tomcat, JBoss* etc. On a *Java node*, we have the Java based profiler running inside the JVM which does profiling on a per method basis. A *native node* is one which hosts any other conventional application server. Irrespective of whether a node is a *Java node* or a *native node*, the name of the process which serves the transaction on that machine needs to be specified. If there is more than one process

```
<!DOCTYPE services [
<!ELEMENT services (TransInfo+)>
<!ELEMENT TransInfo (Name, WebInterface, NodesInfo+)>
<!ELEMENT WebInterface (url,port,(uri|uriInfoFile))>
<!ELEMENT NodesInfo (nativeNode|javaNode)>
<!ELEMENT nativeNode (Node, Process)>
<!ELEMENT javaNode (Node, Process, ComponentInfo?)>
<!ELEMENT ComponentInfo (Component+)>
<!ELEMENT Component (Name,Interface+)>
<!ELEMENT Node (#PCDATA)>
<!ELEMENT Process (#PCDATA)>
<!ELEMENT Name (#PCDATA)>
<!ELEMENT url (#PCDATA)>
<!ELEMENT port (#PCDATA)>
<!ELEMENT uri (#PCDATA)>
<!ELEMENT uriInfoFile (#PCDATA)>
<!ELEMENT Interface (#PCDATA)>
]>
```

Fig. 3. The XML DTD

serving the transaction on a given node, then the two processes are mentioned as seperate entries. If the node is a *Java node*, then more information is specified. We will discuss this in Section 4. If a node has both Java and native servers running on it and they need to be profiled, then they are specified as two separate entries in the XML file.

Procedures Done by the Master: After reading the input in the XML format, the Master carries out the following procedures:

Request Generation: The request generator generates the requests sequentially. It reads the transaction information and frames the URL accordingly depending on the type of transaction.

Warm up Detection: We use the technique of *moving average* to detect the steady state of the server. As the request generator receives the responses from the server, it records the response times. We define a window of size w and calculate and store the average of the last w values. If the normalized difference between the two averages is less than a given ϵ, then we conclude that the server has sufficiently warmed up and we start taking measurements from that point onwards.

If the value of w is small, then we may see too many fluctuations between successive values and if the value of w is large, then we may not see any fluctuations at all. We have chosen w to be 5, which successfully detected warm-up in our experiments. This method is loosely based on Welch's method for discarding the initial transient and detecting the steady state [11].

If the successive moving averages do not differ by more than 15%($\epsilon \leq 0.15$), then we conclude that the server has sufficiently warmed up.

Master-Slave Co-ordination: The main purpose of Autoprofiler is to co-ordinate the process of load generation with the resource profiling. When the load generator detects sufficient warmup of the server, commands are sent to the slaves to start profiling. When the load generation process is over, the master again sends commands to get the profiling data from the slaves.

The profiling process can be summarized as follows:

- Master reads the transaction information from the XML file.
- Master starts generating the load.
- When the server has warmed up, commands are sent to the slaves to start profiling.
- When the load generation process is over, commands are again sent to slaves to get Che profiling data.

As can be seen, the entire profiling process as described in Section 2, that was being done manually is now fully automated by the Autoprofiler.

3.2 Slave Architecture

The tool when working as a slave, interacts with the OS tools as well as the in-process Java profiler to control the profiling. It works in the passive mode; that is, it waits for the master to send commands and then acts on them.

Interaction with the OS tools: The resources that are profiled by the tool are CPU time consumed, disk I/O, network I/O. Since the tool is developed for a Linux environment, we use tools that are available with every Linux distribution. We use ps for the CPU time consumed, vmstat for the details about disk I/O and netstat for the details about network I/O. Since the values given by the tool are cumulative, the slave takes the snapshot of the values at the beginning of the profiling process and at the end of the profiling process.

Interaction with the Java profiler: The slave controls the in-process Java profiler. The slave is responsible for initializing and resetting the profiler state, sending the necessary data to the profiler and receiving the data from the profiler. The Java profiler is explained in detail in the next section. Figure 2 shows the overall architecture of Autoprofiler integrated with the Lite Java Profiler.

4 Lite Java Profiler (LJP)

We have developed an in-process Java profiler, called the LiteJava Profiler, (LJP), which can give fine grained information such as per method CPU information, memory allocated in the JVM and garbage collection information by using JVMPI [12]. LJP interacts with the AutoProfiler slaves, and hence fits into the overall automated framework. LJP is "lighweight"; i.e., it has low profiling overhead, does not generate unreasonably large amounts of data, and does not require disk I/O.

4.1 Features

We wrote LJP to overcome the limitations of the existing Java profilers. The enhanced features that are unique to our tool are:

- *Partial profiling:* This means that the profiling process can be stopped and started whenever required. This is necessary especially in J2EE kind of environments where continuous profiling can result in very large overhead which can affect the measurement process.
- *Remotely controllable:.* LJP can be controlled from a remote machine. This feature is required for automating the process of resource profiling.
- *Dynamic filter support:* LJP supports dynamic filtering. Filters are set to profile only selected methods and hence reduce the profiling overhead. The profilers we surveyed either had static filtering option where it obtains the filtering information once at start-up or provided filtering only at the display stage.
- *No File I/O:* LJP does not do any file I/O since it can cause unnecessary overhead. It maintains in-memory data structures to store all the intermediary data.
- *Garbage collection information:* As the garbage collection process happens asynchronously in the JVM, it can indeed affect the response time of a transaction. LJP separately profiles the garbage collection process and reports the statistics.

4.2 Implementation Details

Partial Profiling and Remote Controllability. When the JVM is started, the LJP spawns a separate thread and starts listening for commands from the master. The LJP works with the JVMPI, which generates various events. Only the class_load event is enabled in the beginning (i.e. before LJP is asked to start profiling). This lets LJP build the mapping between the method names and method IDs. This is stored internally by the LJP as a hash map, which is required because method events only include method IDs. Other events, such as method entry and exit, object allocation and garbage collection that are used for the actualy profiling are enabled and disabled based on commands from the master. Thus there is no unnecessary start-up overhead. The master communicates with the LJP through the slave. This "partial" profiling results in huge saving of overheads, since one can choose not to profile the thousands of methods that are called at start-up by the J2EE application server such as JBoss, and instead start profiling only when transactions start coming to the server.

Dynamic Filtering Support. Filters are necessary to avoid unnecessary profiling overhead, so that, for e.g., one can profile only the application-specific methods, and not the internal methods called by the application server. However, when profiling the server with minimal human interaction, the flexibility of changing the filter without re-starting the JVM and the application server, is required. Thus dynamic filtering support has been provided in LJP. It uses a set of in-memory data structures to maintain the filter information, thus no files need to be read. The filter information is provided in the form of class names and the corresponding method names. Whenever such a method executes, its execution time is recorded. The specific components and their corresponding methods are specifed in ComponentInfo element in the XML file.

Garbage Collection. As already mentioned, garbage collection can happen asynchronously during the load generation period and hence can affect the response time. We capture the garbage collection information and report it along with the other profile details. This is done by enabling the gc_start and gc_finish events in the JVMPI.

5 Experiments and Observations

To test the tool, we profiled *ECPerf*, a sample J2EE application which was written to serve as a benchmark for evaluating different J2EE servers. We deployed ECperf application on the JBoss application server. The experimental setup is as depicted in Figure 1.

The database server is hosted on a uni-processor Pentium 4 machine and the JBoss application server on a dual processor Pentium 4 machine. All transactions access the database server for retrieving data. The resource consumption details of various transactions for ECPerf are as shown in Table 1.

Table 1. Results

T_N	R_t (ms)	JBoss Server					PostgreSQL			
		S_t (ms)	N_i	N_o (bytes)	D_r	D_w	S_t (ms)	N_i	N_o (bytes)	D_r	D_w
Order Status	492.6	480.5	147.4	25.6	962.5	120.0	7.5	143.1	15.5	798.7	87.7
Customer Status	654.5	633.3	196.7	26.3	131.5	70.0	9.4	195.1	96.5	146.7	50.7
Cancel Order	620.8	616.5	196.4	28.6	172.5	30.0	3.5	184.1	11.5	652.7	273.7
Schedule Work Order	560.6	533.5	164.4	24.6	137.5	89.0	10.5	160.1	13.8	555.7	69.7
Update Work Order	572.4	566.67	168.4	26.6	106.5	49.0	6.5	165.12	10.5	603.7	47.7
Complete Work Order	1041.4	1033.3	302.4	45.6	233.5	273.0	10.5	304.12	19.5	1156.7	1501.7
Cancel Work Order	577.9	540.5	178.4	26.6	150.5	18.0	12.5	172.12	19.5	528.7	38.7

Here S_t is the service time in milliseconds per transaction, N_i and N_o are number of bytes sent and received on the network, D_r and D_w are number of disk bytes read from and written to disk[1]. The values given by the Java profiler for individual transactions are shown in Table 2.

The entire profiling process, which generated 8 set of resource consumption measures, for 7 transactions, on 2 servers, took less than 10 minutes with the

---

[1] vmstat and netstat give values on an overall basis - not per-process. Thus the values obtained from vmstat and netstat include background disk and network activity. In the future versions of the tool, this "noise" will be removed.

Table 2. Results from Java Profiler

Transaction Name	Method Info			GC Time (ms)
	Method Name	CPU time (ms)	Memory consumed (kilobytes)	
Order Status	getOrderStatus()	32.7	16	43
Customer Status	getCustomerStatus()	48	26	44
Cancel Order	cancelOrder()	43.6	33	43
Schedule Work Order	scheduleWorkOrder()	24	17	42
Update Work Order	updateWorkOrder()	30.6	17	42
Complete Work Order	completeWorkOrder()	81	45	42
Cancel Work Order	cancelWorkOrder()	43	24	45

aid of the tool. If done manually, this experimentation, and the generation of results, can consume days.

Resource profiles such as this one can lead to helpful insights about the bottlenecks in a distributed system. For example, let us compare the CPU time taken by the application methods in the JBoss server (as shown in Table 2), with the total time consumed by the *java* process (as shown in Table 1). We can derive the time taken by the JBoss server methods by calculating the difference in these two measurements. We conclude that the JBoss application server contributes a large CPU time overhead (90% of the total time) while servicing a request. Similarly, we can observe that garbage collection time is more or less the same for all transactions.

6 Conclusion and Future Work

In this paper, we presented a tool that automates the process of fine-grained resource consumption profiling of distributed transactions. We believe that this tool represents a different paradigm - one in which performance measurement is done for the purpose of performance *modeling* and *prediction*, not simply for the sake of performance "testing". Existing tools do not significantly ease the process of gathering inputs that a performance analyst or a modeling tool would need, if performance is to be predicted beyond that which the load generator can measure. Sophisticated capacity planning requires the use of performance models, and performance models require inputs such as per-transaction and per-server resource consumption details.

We have built such a tool, and demonstrated that it can significantly reduce the time to produce such data, which will result in greater productivity of the performance analyst, and ultimately will cut costs of running large data centers.

Our experimentation also showed that resource profiling can reveal valuable insights about the performance characteristics of the applications under study - e.g. that application server overhead in J2EE servers can be large.

The tool can be enhanced in several directions. First, we can add innumerable features to it which enhance its usability for realistic Web-based systems.

Second, the tool can be made more "intelligent" by having it automate several tasks that are a part of a measurement study; e.g. automatically characterize maximum throughput, find the bottleneck components, the maximum number of users that can be supported by the system, etc. Third, we can extend the tool so that it can work on high-level measurements obtained from a *production* environment. Generating resource profiles from measurements made in an uncontrolled environment is an interesting research problem that can be pursued further.

References

1. Sun Microsystems: The ECperf benchmark for evaluating J2EE servers (2003), http://java.sun.com/j2ee/ecperf/index.jsp.
2. Minq Software AB: Pure load (2003), http://www.minq.se.
3. David Mosberger: httperf (2003), http://www.hpl.hp.com/personal/David_Mosberger/httperf.html.
4. Segue Software Inc: Silk performer (2002), http://www.segue.com.
5. Mercury Interactive Corporation: LoadRunner (2002), http://www.mercury.com/us/products/.
6. openSTA: openSTA Software Testing Architecture (2002), http://www.opensta.org/.
7. OperSys: Linux Trace Tool kit (LTT) (2002), http://www.opersys.com/LTT.
8. Sabastien Vauclair: Extensible Java Profiler (2003), http://ejp.soureforge.net.
9. Yourkit: Yourkit Java Profiler (2003) http://www.yourkit.com.
10. B Nagaprabhanjan: Automated and Fine grained Resource Consumption Discovery of Distributed Transactions. Master's thesis, K.R.School of Information Technology, IIT Bombay (2004).
11. Law, A.M., Kelton, W.D.: Simulation modeling and analysis (2003).
12. Sun Microsystems: The Java Virtual Machine Programming Interface (JVMPI) (2004) http://java.sun.com/j2se/1.4.2/docs/guide/jvmpi/jvmpi.html.
13. Rolia, J.A., C.Sevcik, K.: The method of layers. In: IEEE Transactions on Software Engineering archive. Volume 21, Issue = 8 (August 1995). (1995) 689 – 700.

An Efficient Algorithm for Removing Useless Logged Messages in SBML Protocols

JinHo Ahn

Dept. of Computer Science,
College of Information Science, Kyonggi University,
San 94-6 Iuidong, Yeongtonggu,
Suwon-si Gyeonggi-do 443-760, Republic of Korea
jhahn@kyonggi.ac.kr

Abstract. To continuously log messages in the limited volatile memories of their sending processes, existing SBML protocols force the processes to periodically flush the message log into the stable storage or messages in the log to be useless for future failures and then removes them. But, these garbage collection algorithms may result in a large number of stable storage accesses or high communication and checkpointing overheads as inter-process communication rate increases. To address this problem, we propose an efficient algorithm to autonomously remove useless log information in its volatile storage by piggybacking only some additional information. It requires no extra message and forced checkpoint. Additionally, the algorithm efficiently supports fast commit of all output to the outside world. Simulation results show that our algorithm considerably outperforms the traditional algorithm with respect to the average elapsed time required until the memory buffer for message logging of a process is full.

1 Introduction

As message-passing distributed systems scale up, their failure rate may also increase. In particular, if long-running distributed and parallel applications are executed on the systems, process failure may become the most critical issue [1, 9]. To address the issue, the systems use log-based rollback recovery as a cost-effective and transparent fault-tolerance technique, in which each process periodically saves it local state by or without synchronizing with other processes [2, 6], and logs each received message [5]. If a process crashes, the technique creates a new process and allows the process to restore its consistent state and replay its previously received messages beyond the state.

Message logging protocols are classified into two approaches, i.e., sender-based and receiver-based message logging, depending on which process each message is logged by [5]. First, receiver-based message logging(RBML) approach [8, 11] logs the recovery information of every received message to the stable storage before the message is delivered to the receiving process. Thus, the approach simplifies the recovery procedure of failed processes. However, its main drawback is the high failure-free overhead caused by synchronous logging.

Sender-based message logging(SBML) approach [3, 4, 10] enables each message to be logged in the volatile memory of its corresponding sender for avoiding logging messages to stable storage. Therefore, it reduces the failure-free overhead compared with the first approach. But, the second approach forces each process to maintain in its limited volatile storage the log information of its sent messages required for recovering receivers of the messages when they crash. Therefore, the sender-based message logging approach needs an efficient garbage collection algorithm to have the volatile memory of each process for message logging become full as late as possible because, otherwise, the technique forces the message log in the memory to be frequently flushed to stable storage or requires a large number of additional messages and forced checkpoints for removing the log.

Existing SBML protocols use one between two message log management procedures to ensure system consistency despite future failures according to each cost. The first procedure just flushes the message log to the stable storage. It is very simple, but may result in a large number of stable storage accesses during failure-free operation and recovery. The second procedure forces messages in the log to be useless for future failures and then removes them. In other wards, the procedure checks whether receivers of the messages has indeed received the corresponding messages and then taken no checkpoint since. If so, it forces the receivers to take their checkpoints. Thus, this behavior may lead to high communication and checkpointing overheads as inter-process communication rate increases. This paper presents an efficient algorithm to autonomously remove useless log information in its volatile storage by piggybacking only some additional information. It requires no extra message and forced checkpoint. Additionally, the algorithm efficiently supports fast commit of all output to the outside world, which consists of everything that processes in the system can interact with that cannot be rolled back.

2 Basic Idea

The sender-based message logging approach has the feature that each failed process has to be rolled back to the latest checkpoint and replay the received messages beyond the checkpoint by obtaining the recovery information from their sender processes. From this feature, we can see that all the messages received before process p takes its latest checkpoint, are useless for recovering p to a consistent state in case of p's failure. For example, there are three processes $p1$, $p2$ and $p3$ in figure 1. In here, process $p1$ sends two messages $msg1$ and $msg3$ to $p2$ after having saved the log information of the messages in its volatile storage. Also, process $p3$ sends message $msg2$ to $p2$ in the same way. In this case, we suppose that process $p2$ takes its i-th checkpoint after it received the three messages like in this figure. Afterwards, even if $p2$ fails, it rolls back at most up to the i-th checkpoint. Thus, the log information of the three messages $msg1$, $msg2$ and $msg3$ becomes useless in case of future failures.

Therefore, our algorithm are designed to enable p to locally remove the useless logged messages from the volatile storage without requiring any extra message

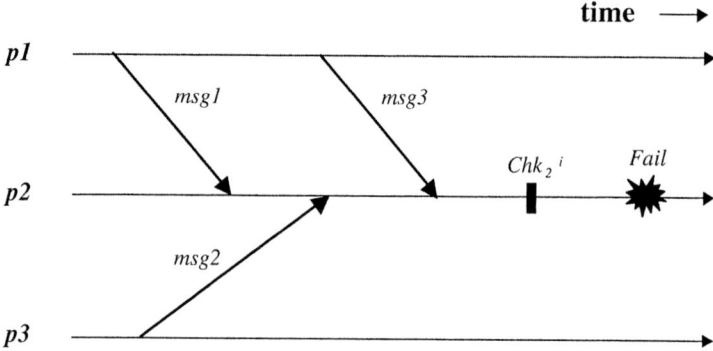

Fig. 1. What is useless log information in SBML protocols?

and forced checkpoint. For this purpose, each process p must have the following data structures in the proposed algorithm.

- $Sendlg_p$: a set saving $lge(rid, ssn, rsn, data)$ of each message sent by p. In here, lge is the log information of a message and the four fields are the identifier of the receiver, the send sequence number, the receive sequence number and data of the message respectively.
- Rsn_p: the receive sequence number of the latest message delivered to p.
- $RsnVector_p$: a vector in which $RsnVector_p[k]$ is the receive sequence number of the last message delivered to k before k has saved the last checkpointed state of k on the stable storage.

Informally, our algorithm is performed as follows. Taking a local checkpoint, p updates $RsnVector_p[p]$ to the receive sequence number of the latest message delivered to p. If p sends a message m to another process q, the vector is piggybacked on the message. When receiving the message with $RsnVector_p$, q takes the component-wise maximum of two vectors $RsnVector_p$ and $RsnVector_q$. Afterwards, q can remove from its message log $Sendlg_q$ all $lge(u)$s such that for all $k \in$ a set of all processes in the system, $lge(u).rid$ is k and $lge(u).rsn$ is less than or equal to $RsnVector_p[k]$.

To explain the algorithm more easily, figure 2 shows an example of a distributed computation consisting of three processes $p1$, $p2$ and $p3$ communicating with each other. In this example, the processes take their local checkpoints Chk_1^w, Chk_2^x and Chk_1^y. In this case, they update $RsnVector_1[1]$, $RsnVector_2[2]$ and $RsnVector_3[3]$ to each rsn of the last message received before taking its respective checkpoint. In here, we assume that values of Rsn_1, Rsn_2 and Rsn_3 are a, b and c. Afterwards, $p2$ receives four messages, $msg1$ and $msg5$ from $p1$ and $msg2$ and $msg4$ from $p3$. At this point, $p1$ keeps $lge(msg1)$ and $lge(msg5)$ in $Sendlg_1$, and $p3$, $lge(msg2)$ and $lge(msg4)$ in $Sendlg_3$. On taking the next local checkpoint Chk_2^{x+1}, $p2$ updates $RsnVector_2[2]$ to rsn of $msg5$ as $msg5$ is the last message received before the checkpoint. In this case, the value of Rsn_2 becomes (b+4). Then, it sends a message $msg7$ with $RsnVector_2$ to $p1$. When

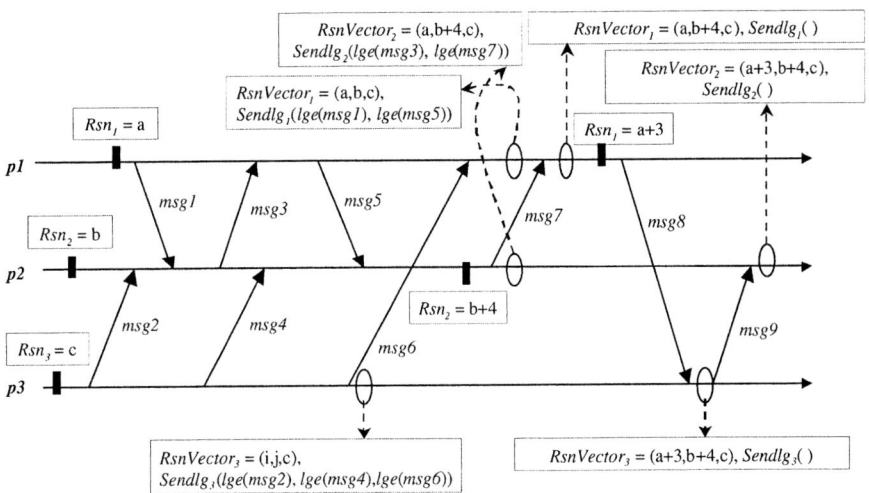

Fig. 2. An example of a distributed computation consisting of three processes $p1$, $p2$ and $p3$

receiving the message, $p1$ updates $RsnVector_1[2]$ to (b+4). Thus, it can remove useless log information, $lge(msg1)$ and $lge(msg5)$, from $Sendlg_1$ because rsn of message $msg5$ is equal to $RsnVector_1[2]$. Hereafter, it takes the next local checkpoint Chk_1^{w+1} and so sets the value of $RsnVector_1[1]$ to rsn of the last message, $msg7$, received before taking the checkpoint. In this case, $RsnVector_1[1]$ becomes (a+3). After that, it sends a message $msg8$ with $RsnVector_1$ to $p3$. On receiving the message, $p3$ updates $RsnVector_3$ to (a+3, b+4, c) by using the vector of $p1$ piggybacked on the message. It can remove $lge(msg2)$, $lge(msg4)$ and $lge(msg6)$ from $Sendlg_3$ because $rsns$ of messages $msg4$ and $msg6$ are less than $RsnVector_3[2]$ and $RsnVector_3[1]$ respectively. Then, $p3$ sends $p2$ a message $msg9$ with $RsnVector_3$. When $p2$ receives the message, $RsnVector_2$ becomes (a+3, b+4, c) after updating it. In this case, $p2$ can remove useless $lge(msg3)$ and $lge(msg7)$ from $Sendlg_2$. From this example, we can see that the algorithm allows each process to locally remove useless log information from its volatile storage with no extra messages and forced checkpoints.

3 Discussion

To evaluate performance of our algorithm($PGCA$) with that of traditional one ($TGCA$) [4], some experiments are performed in this paper using a discrete-event simulation language [7]. One performance index is used for evaluation; the average elapsed time required until the volatile memory buffer for message logging of a process is full(T_{full}). The performance index T_{full} is measured under the condition that the two algorithms perform no forced garbage collection procedure, i.e., incur no additional messages and no forced checkpoints. A simulated system consists of 10 hosts connected by a network, which is modelled

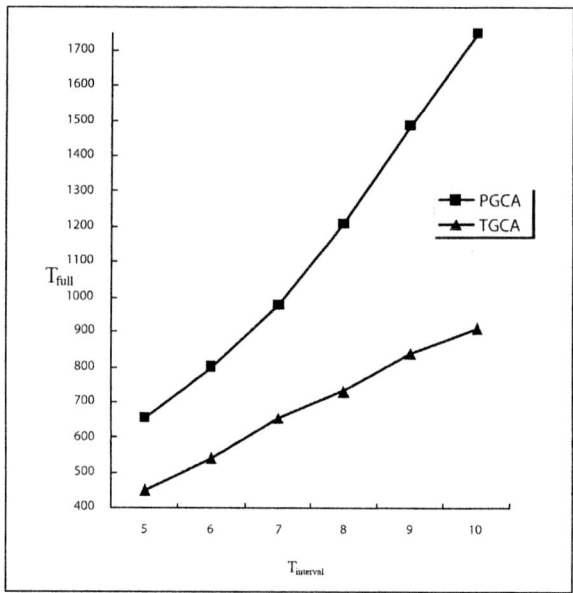

Fig. 3. Average elapsed time required until the volatile memory buffer for message logging of a process is full according to $T_{interval}$

as a multi-access LAN (Ethernet). The message transmission capacity of a link in the network is 100 Mbps. Nodes connected to the network are identical and uniformly distributed along the physical medium. For simplicity of this simulation, it is assumed each node has one process executing on it and 10 processes are initiated and completed together. For the experiments, it is also assumed that the size of each application message ranges from 50 to 200 Kbytes and the size of the memory buffer for logging of every process is 10Mbytes. Each process takes its local checkpoint with an interval following an exponential distribution with a mean $Ckpt_{time}$=3 minutes. The simulation parameter is the mean message sending rate, $T_{interval}$, following an exponential distribution. All simulation results shown in this section are averages over a number of trials.

Figure 3 shows the average elapsed time of the two algorithms required until the volatile memory buffer for message logging of a process is full for the specified range of the $T_{interval}$ values. In this figure, as their $T_{interval}$s of $PGCA$ and $TGCA$ increase, their corresponding T_{full}s also increase. The reason is that as each process sends messages more slowly, the size of its message log also increases at a lower rate. However, as it is expected, T_{full} of $PGCA$ is significantly higher than that of $TGCA$. In particular, as $T_{interval}$ increases, the increasing rate of the first rises more fast than that of the latter. This benefit of our algorithm results from its desirable feature as follows: it enables a process p to autonomously and locally eliminate useless log information from the buffer by only carrying a vector $RsnVector_p$ on each sent message whereas the traditional algorithm does not so.

References

1. A. M. Agbaria, R. Friedman. Starfish: fault-tolerant dynamic mpi programs on clusters of workstations. *In Proc. of the High Performance Distributed Computing Symposium*, pp. 31-40, Aug. 1999.
2. B. Bhargava and S. R. Lian. Independent checkpointing and concurrent rollback for recovery - An optimistic approach. *In Proc. of the Symposium on Reliable Distributed Systems*, pp. 3-12, 1988.
3. A. Bouteiller, F. Cappello, T. Hérault, G. Krawezik, P. Lemarinier and F. Magniette. MPICH-V2: a Fault Tolerant MPI for Volatile Nodes based on Pessimistic Sender Based Message Logging. *In Proc. of the 15th International Conference on High Performance Networking and Computing(SC2003)*, November 2003.
4. D. B. Johnson and W. Zwaenpoel. Sender-Based Message Logging. *In Digest of Papers: 17th International Symposium on Fault-Tolerant Computing*, pp. 14-19, 1987.
5. E. N. Elnozahy, L. Alvisi, Y. M. Wang and D. B. Johnson. A Survey of Rollback-Recovery Protocols in Message-Passing Systems. *ACM Computing Surveys*, 34(3), pp. 375-408, 2002.
6. R. Koo and S. Toueg. Checkpointing and rollback-recovery for distributed systems. *IEEE Transactions on Software Engineering*, Vol. 13, pp. 23-31, 1987.
7. R. McNab and F. W. Howell. simjava: a discrete event simulation package for Java with applications in computer systems modelling. *In Proc. First International Conference on Web-based Modelling and Simulation*, 1998.
8. M. L. Powell and D. L. Presotto. Publishing: A reliable broadcast communication mechanism. *In Proc. of the 9th International Symposium on Operating System Principles*, pp. 100-109, 1983.
9. J. T. Rough and A. M. Goscinski. The development of an efficient checkpointing facility exploiting operating systems services of the GENESIS cluster operating system. *Future Generation Computer Systems*, Vol. 20, No. 4, pp 523-538, 2004.
10. J. Xu, R.B. Netzer and M. Mackey. Sender-based message logging for reducing rollback propagation. *In Proc. of the 7th International Symposium on Parallel and Distributed Processing*, pp. 602-609, 1995.
11. B. Yao, K. -F. Ssu and W. K. Fuchs. Message Logging in Mobile Computing. *In Proc. of the 29th International Symposium on Fault-Tolerant Computing*, pp. 14-19, 1999.

Divide and Concur: Employing Chandra and Toueg's Consensus Algorithm in a Multi-level Setting

Rahul Agarwal[1,*], Mahender Bisht[2], S.N. Maheshwari[3], and Sanjiva Prasad[3]

[1] Computer Science Department, SUNY at Stony Brook, Stony Brook, NY 11794-4400, USA
ragarwal@cs.sunysb.edu
[2] INSEAD, 77305 Fontainebleau, France
[3] Department of Computer Science and Engineering, Indian Institute of Technology Delhi, Hauz Khas, New Delhi 110016, India

Abstract. We revisit the work of Chandra and Toueg on achieving *consensus* using *unreliable failure detectors* in an asynchronous system with crash stop failures. Following a brief review of their approach, we provide a probabilistic analysis of their consensus algorithm, which shows that the number of messages is exponentially proportional to the number of participating processes n. Based on our analysis, we study how their solution may be improved when we have *a priori* knowledge of the maximum number of process failures that may occur. Accordingly, we propose *multi-level consensus* as a generalization of the Chandra-Toueg algorithm, and give a probabilistic analysis of our algorithm. For n large relative to the bound on the number of failures k, this approach yields an improvement (in the expected case) in the message complexity.

Keywords: Distributed Consensus Algorithms, Algorithm Design, Failure Detectors, Probabilistic Analysis.

1 Introduction

Achieving consensus within a set of distributed processes is an important, arguably paradigmatic, problem in distributed computing. Consensus algorithms find diverse applications, *e.g.*, in fault-tolerant distributed systems and in realizing various distributed programming primitives. In the consensus problem, all correct processes propose a value and must reach a unanimous and irrevocable decision on some value related to the proposed values, in the presence of process failures. Solutions to the problem are required to satisfy the following conditions:

Termination – every correct process eventually decides on some value;
Uniform Integrity – every process decides at most once;
Agreement – no two correct processes decide differently; and
Validity – a value decided on by a process must have been proposed by some process.

The existence and nature of a solution to the distributed consensus problem depend very much on whether the model is *synchronous* or not[1] and on the *failure model* as-

---

* Corresponding author.
[1] A process is synchronous if there exist bounds on message delay, execution time of a step in the process and clock drift of local clocks at each process.

sumed. Most distributed systems are assumed to be be asynchronous. A variety of failure models have been studied: a process can stop and do nothing after that (*crash stop*), crash and recover (*crash recovery*), fail to send or receive messages (*send/receive omission*) or exhibit arbitrary behavior (*Byzantine failure*).

There is a well known *impossibility result* that "no deterministic algorithm solves consensus in an asynchronous system that tolerates even a single crash failure" [10]. To circumvent the impossibility result various approaches have been suggested: failure detectors[1, 5, 6, 8], randomized algorithms [2, 7] and partial synchrony models [3, 4, 9]. ([12] contains a detailed coverage of these various approaches). Note that in these results, all processes are assumed to be of the same status, and trivial "asymmetric" solutions which involve imposing the value proposed by an individual or a cabal of processes are precluded.

We adopt the concept of *Unreliable Failure Detectors* introduced by Chandra, Hadzilacos and Toueg [5], wherein the asynchronous model of computation has been augmented by each process having a *fallible external failure detection mechanism*, and examine Chandra and Toueg's algorithm for achieving consensus in a crash stop model [8], which relies on a simple *majority of correct processes*.

Informally, a failure detector is a module that outputs the set of processes which it currently suspects of having failed. Failure detectors are specified in terms of two abstract properties: (i) *completeness*, and (ii) *accuracy*. *Completeness* can be (a) *strong* – eventually every process that crashes is permanently suspected by every correct process, or (b) *weak* – eventually every process that crashes is permanently suspected by some correct process. *Accuracy* can be (a) *strong* – no process is suspected before it crashes, (b) *weak* – some correct process is never suspected, (c) *eventual strong* – there is a time after which correct processes are not suspected by any correct process, or (d) *eventual weak* – there is a time after which some correct process is never suspected by any correct process. Based on these properties, there exist eight failure detector classes. The weakest class is $\Diamond W$, which satisfies weak completeness and weak eventual accuracy and is the weakest class with which consensus can be solved in an asynchronous crash stop model. $\Diamond S$ failure detectors satisfy strong completeness and eventual weak accuracy. Chandra and Toueg show a transformation from weak complete to strong complete preserving accuracy is possible in the crash stop model at the expense of extra messages. Hence, as $\Diamond W$ is equivalent to $\Diamond S$, they solve consensus in an asynchronous crash stop model using a $\Diamond S$ failure detector.

The Chandra-Toueg consensus algorithm using $\Diamond S$ failure detectors (called $CT\Diamond S$ hereafter) involves each process going through possibly several asynchronous rounds; each round has a designated coordinator and comprises different phases which involve communicating with the coordinator. The algorithm relies on a majority of processes being correct, since that ensures that a value decided on by a correct process will be transferred to subsequent rounds (§2 provides an intuitive explanation of the algorithm but a reader interested in the details may refer to [8]).

The first question we address concerns the number of messages involved. We provide a probabilistic analysis of the algorithm and show that the expected number of messages required by the $CT\Diamond S$ algorithm is exponentially proportional to the number of processes involved (denoted by n).

Further, in the $CT\Diamond S$ algorithm, the coordinator waits for a majority of processes (required to ensure overlap) in each of the asynchronous rounds. We ask the question whether the algorithm can be "sharpened" and expected number of messages can be reduced by exploiting *a priori* knowledge of the maximum number of failures (hereafter denoted by k).

These observations lead us to explore a "divide-and-conquer" approach — reducing the number of processes participating in the consensus so as to reduce the expected number of messages — and refining our analysis explicitly incorporating the parameter k. What emerges is a "layered" consensus algorithm. We first formalize a two-level consensus algorithm, and then generalize this idea (in particular for cases where $k \ll n$) to formulate a *multi-level* consensus algorithm. Our multi-level algorithm can be viewed as a natural generalization of the Chandra-Toueg idea, and indeed their algorithm can be seen as the one-level case. Multi-level consensus is behaviorally adequate with respect to the Chandra-Toueg algorithm in that any consensus decision achievable using our multi-level algorithm can also be achieved using $CT\Diamond S$. Further, our analysis reveals that in our framework the expected number of messages is exponentially proportional to k rather than to n. When $k \ll n$, this leads to significant improvement in message complexity.

The idea of multi-level consensus algorithms and the probabilistic analysis of the expected number of messages should be seen as the main contributions of this paper. We must also mention that although in this paper we have motivated the development of multi-level consensus algorithms from an analysis of expected message complexity, there are several applications that naturally require multi-level consensus. A typical example is a decision-making system, wherein constituencies individually make their decisions and then delegate representatives to participate at caucuses to arrive at a common decision.

We conclude the paper by summarizing our results and mentioning directions for future work.

2 The Chandra and Toueg Consensus Algorithm

The $CT\Diamond S$ algorithm may involve several asynchronous rounds, each with a designated coordinator. A round consists of four asynchronous phases. In **phase 1**, each process sends to the current round's coordinator c_i its own current estimate of the decision value time-stamped with the round number in which it adopted this estimate. In **phase 2**, the coordinator c_i gathers $\lceil \frac{n+1}{2} \rceil$ such estimates (a majority), and selects one with the largest time-stamp, which it sends to all the processes as their new estimate, $estimate_{c_i}$. In **phase 3**, each process p may execute one of two alternatives:

(i) it receives $estimate_{c_i}$ from c_i and responds to c_i with an *ack*, indicating that it adopted $estimate_{c_i}$ as its own estimate, or
(ii) on checking with its failure detector module, p suspects that c_i may have crashed, and so sends it a *nack* and starts a new round.

In **phase 4**, c_i waits for $\lceil \frac{n+1}{2} \rceil$ replies (*acks* or *nacks*). If all these replies are *acks*, c_i knows that a majority of processes have changed their estimate to $estimate_{c_i}$ and thus $estimate_{c_i}$ is locked. It then "reliably broadcasts" this decided value to all processes.

If a process "reliably delivers" such a request from a coordinator, it is taken to have decided accordingly.

The algorithm works under the assumption that a majority of the processes are correct. The algorithm satisfies *validity* trivially since each process's estimate is either its own value or a value that it received from some other process. The *agreement* property of the algorithm follows from the fact that once a decision is received by any process in any given round then in any subsequent rounds, the remaining processes make the same decision. This fact is because the coordinator of each round waits for the estimate of a majority of the processes and selects the estimate with the highest time-stamp. Suppose a decision was received for the first time in a given round by any process j, Then, since the coordinator of the next round waits for a majority of the processes, at least one process i which had participated in the current round will also take part in the next round. Its estimate, which is the same as the value decided by j, is selected because its time-stamp is highest. The algorithm *terminates* as each process has a $\Diamond S$ failure detector and thus eventually there is a process which is not suspected by any other process and can be chosen as the coordinator. Since the majority of the processes are correct, this coordinator's wait for a majority of processes will not block forever.

We now analyze the number of messages required for consensus using the above algorithm by considering any process p_k. We should clarify here that we do not count messages from ("unconsummated") rounds that are initiated by some process but do not proceed beyond the initial phases[2].

Let X_i be a random variable denoting the number of messages that a particular process sent or received in round i of the $CT\Diamond S$ algorithm if it is not the coordinator of round i.

$$X_i = \begin{cases} 0 & \text{if } p_k \text{ is the coordinator for round } i \\ \text{number of messages } p_k \text{ sent or received in round } i & \text{if it is not the coordinator} \end{cases}$$

Since all messages are transmitted to or from the coordinator, we avoid counting any message twice.

Lemma 1. $E[X_i] = \left(\frac{n-1}{n}\right) b$ where b denotes the expected number of phases a process goes through in any consensus round and $1 \leq b \leq 4$.

PROOF: The probability of the process being a coordinator of the round is $\frac{1}{n}$ and not being a coordinator is $\left(\frac{n-1}{n}\right)$. Thus,
$E[X_i] = \left(\frac{n-1}{n}\right) b + \left(\frac{1}{n}\right) 0$
$= \left(\frac{n-1}{n}\right) b.$ □

Let x be the probability that a process does not suspect another process wrongly. We assume that this probability is the same for all processes, the same with respect to all processes throughout a given round, and also the same for all rounds. Let c be the probability that the leader fails during a given round.

---

[2] Note that the specification of the $CT\Diamond S$ algorithm allows processes to embark *asynchronously* on fresh rounds, mainly to avoid unwanted synchronization constraints. We observe that messages from unconsummated rounds are not germane to achieving consensus and termination — they can safely be omitted from any run of the protocol to obtain an equivalent run.

Lemma 2. *Under the assumption that the failure detector is near perfect, i.e. $x \simeq 1$, $E[r_p]$, the expected number of rounds in which at least a majority of the processes participated is given by $\frac{1}{1-c}x^{-n}$.*

PROOF: $Pr[r_p = t]$ denotes the probability that consensus is achieved in t rounds. Let y be the probability that the current round succeeds. y is Pr[leader didn't fail in the given round]$*Pr$[at least a majority didn't suspect the leader wrongly in this round]. Therefore,

$$y = (1-c)\left\{\binom{n}{\lceil\frac{n+1}{2}\rceil}x^{\lceil\frac{n+1}{2}\rceil}(1-x)^{\lfloor\frac{n-1}{2}\rfloor} + \binom{n}{\lceil\frac{n+3}{2}\rceil}x^{\lceil\frac{n+3}{2}\rceil}(1-x)^{\lfloor\frac{n-3}{2}\rfloor} + \ldots\right.$$
$$\left. + \binom{n}{n}x^n\right\} \quad (1)$$

$= (1-c)\theta,$

where

$$\theta = \binom{n}{\lceil\frac{n+1}{2}\rceil}x^{\lceil\frac{n+1}{2}\rceil}(1-x)^{\lfloor\frac{n-1}{2}\rfloor} + \binom{n}{\lceil\frac{n+3}{2}\rceil}x^{\lceil\frac{n+3}{2}\rceil}(1-x)^{\lfloor\frac{n-3}{2}\rfloor} + \ldots$$
$$+ \binom{n}{n}x^n \quad (2)$$

Let α denote the probability that a new round is started. α is Pr[leader failed in the current round] + Pr[leader didn't fail in the current round]$*Pr$[at least a majority of processes suspect the leader wrongly in the current round]. Therefore,

$$\alpha = c + (1-c)\left\{\binom{n}{0}(1-x)^n + \ldots + \binom{n}{\lfloor\frac{n-1}{2}\rfloor}(1-x)^{\lceil\frac{n+1}{2}\rceil}x^{\lfloor\frac{n-1}{2}\rfloor}\right\} \quad (3)$$

Note that $Pr[r_p = 1]$, the probability that the first round succeeds, is y. Also, $Pr[r_p = 2]$, the probability that a new round was started after the first round and the second round succeeded is given as αy. In general, $Pr[r_p = i] = \alpha^{i-1}y$. Hence, $E[r_p] = \sum_{i\geq 1} i(\alpha^{i-1}y) = \frac{y}{(1-\alpha)^2}$. Notice that when n is even, α can be written as

$$c + (1-c)\left\{\binom{n}{0}(1-x)^n + \ldots + \binom{n}{\frac{n}{2}-1}(1-x)^{\frac{n}{2}+1}x^{\frac{n}{2}-1}\right\}.$$

Using (2), we get

$$\alpha = c + (1-c)\left\{1 - \theta - \binom{n}{\frac{n}{2}}(1-x)^{\frac{n}{2}}x^{\frac{n}{2}}\right\}$$

$$= 1 - y - (1-c)\binom{n}{\frac{n}{2}}(1-x)^{\frac{n}{2}}x^{\frac{n}{2}}$$

As the failure detector is near perfect, i.e. $x \simeq 1$, α can be approximated as $(1-y)$. Therefore,

$$E[r_p] = \frac{y}{(1-(1-y))^2} = \frac{y}{y^2} = \frac{1}{y}.$$

Dropping the terms involving $(1-x)$ in (1) as $x \simeq 1$, we get

$$E[r_p] = \frac{1}{(1-c)} x^{-n}$$

The case for n odd is similar. □

Theorem 1. *Under the assumption that the failure detector is near perfect, the expected number of messages required for CT◇S algorithm is $(n-1)\frac{b}{1-c}x^{-n}$.*

PROOF: The total number of messages sent or received by $p_k = X = \sum_{i=1}^{r_p} X_i$, where r_p itself is a random variable denoting the last round in which p_k received the decision. The random variable r_p is a stopping time, since the value of r_p depends only on $X_1, X_2, \ldots X_{r_p-1}$. So, we can use Wald's equation to find $E[X] = E[X_i] * E[r_p]$ (each of the X_i's are i.i.d. random variables). From Lemmas 1 and 2, the total number of messages for a given process is $\left(\frac{n-1}{n}\right)\frac{b}{1-c}x^{-n}$. Hence, the total number of messages involved in consensus is:

$$n * E[\text{messages per process}] = (n-1)\frac{b}{1-c}x^{-n}.$$

□

Additionally, there are messages for a reliable bradcast, but the above number dominates. Hence the *total number of messages is exponentially proportional to the number of participants*.

3 Multi Level Consensus

We observed in the previous section that the number of messages required for the CT◇S algorithm is exponentially proportional to the number of processes participating in the consensus. The CT◇S algorithm assumes that at most half of the total participating processes can fail simultaneously. Even if the bound on the maximum number of failures in the system is known to be less than half of the total number of participating processes, the CT◇S algorithm does not take that into account. One natural question arises — "how can we make use of this knowledge of process failures to reduce the number of messages required for consensus?"

If k is the maximum number of process failures in the system and $k \ll n$, then it seems plausible that consensus can be obtained with fewer messages exchanged than those required by CT◇S. Since only k processes can fail, the CT◇S algorithm can solve consensus in a group of size $s = 2k+1$, as a majority of the processes $(k+1)$ are correct. Also, the coordinator needs to wait for only $(k+1)$ processes instead of $\lceil\frac{n+1}{2}\rceil$. Since $(2k+1)$ can be $\ll n$ we can achieve a significant reduction in the number of messages required for consensus.

Having said that consensus can be solved in a group of $(2k+1)$ processes when k is known, one approach to solve consensus for n processes would be to partition the n processes into groups of at least $(2k+1)$ processes, obtain consensus within each group, choose a process from each group to represent its group's decision and do another consensus amongst the representatives. When $(4k+1) < n < (2k+1)^2$ we show below that this approach solves consensus in two levels.

3.1 Two Level Consensus Algorithm

We assume that we have the $CT\diamond S$ algorithm available as a procedure $CT\diamond S(group, v_i)$. Each p_i in $group$ calls $CT\diamond S(group, v_i)$ which *returns* the consensus reached by processes in $group$. Note that, v_i is the value proposed by process p_i.

procedure $lower\_level\_consensus(val, level)$
  { group G of this process p_i is all processes p_j participating in the two-level consensus s.t.
  $\left\lceil \frac{j}{(2k+1)^{level}} \right\rceil = \left\lceil \frac{i}{(2k+1)^{level}} \right\rceil$ }
  $v_i \leftarrow CT\diamond S(G, val)$
  return v_i

end proc

procedure $upper\_level\_consensus(val, level)$
  { group G' of this process p_i is all processes p_j participating in the two-level consensus s.t.
  $j \bmod (2k+1)^{level} = 1$ or $\left\lfloor \frac{i}{(2k+1)^{level}} \right\rfloor \geq \left\lfloor \frac{n}{(2k+1)^{level}} \right\rfloor - 1$ }
  $v_i \leftarrow CT\diamond S(G', val)$
  if $\left\lfloor \frac{i}{(2k+1)^{level}} \right\rfloor \geq \left\lfloor \frac{n}{(2k+1)^{level}} \right\rfloor - 1$ and $i \bmod (2k+1)^{level} \leq k+1$ **then**
    (* i is one of the k+1 processes which is to disseminate the consensus value *)
    send v_i to all the processes not in this level

end proc

Each process p_i executes the following:

$level \leftarrow 1$ \hfill { level is initialized to 1 }

procedure $two\_level(v_p, level)$
  if $(\left\lfloor \frac{n}{(2k+1)^{level}} \right\rfloor < 2)$ **then**
    $CT\diamond S(G_0, v_p)$ \hfill { G_0 is the group of all n processes }
    terminate
  else
    if $\left\lfloor \frac{i}{(2k+1)^{level}} \right\rfloor < \left\lfloor \frac{n}{(2k+1)^{level}} \right\rfloor - 1$ **then**
      $v_p \leftarrow lower\_level\_consensus(v_p, level)$
      if $(i \bmod (2k+1)^{level} = 1)$ or $\left\lfloor \frac{i}{(2k+1)^{level}} \right\rfloor > \left\lfloor \frac{n}{(2k+1)^{level}} \right\rfloor - 1$ **then**
        $v_{2,dec} \leftarrow upper\_level\_consensus(v_p, level)$
    else
      wait for decision

end proc

Fig. 1. The Two-level Consensus Algorithm

If the number of processes $n \leq (4k+1)$, then a simple call to $CT\diamond S$ involving all the n processes is executed. If $(4k+1) < n < (2k+1)^2$ then there exist a, d, $(a, d < 2k+1)$ such that $n = a(2k+1) + d$. We partition the entire set into a groups,

$a - 1$ of which are of size $(2k + 1)$ and one group of size $(2k + 1) + d$. This partitioning is based on their process numbers (which are uniquely assigned initially). If $(i - 1) \equiv (j - 1)$ div $(2k + 1)$ then i and j belong to the same group. $(a - 1)$ groups execute $CT\diamondsuit S$ at the lower level (this involves calls to procedure *lower_level_consensus* in each of the $a - 1$ groups). One process from each of the $(a - 1)$ groups is chosen (we can choose the least numbered process of the group) to represent the decision of the group at the upper level and do a $CT\diamondsuit S$ consensus involving the $a - 1$ representatives and the remaining $(2k + 1) + d$ processes. Having reached a decision, $k + 1$ of the processes in the upper level (chosen by any arbitrary fixed rule, say the first $k + 1$ in the last group) disseminate the decision to all the processes not in upper level. Note that this algorithm differs from $CT\diamondsuit S$ in how the consensus value is disseminated – the latter uses reliable broadcast by the coordinator of the last round. In contrast in our algorithm, since all correct processes in the upper level have the consensus value, some $k + 1$ of them only need to simply send the value to the rest.

The detailed Two-level algorithm is given in Figure 1. Correctness of the two-level algorithm is based on the following observations:

Lemma 3. *The processes executing lower_level_consensus eventually decide on some value which is proposed by some process in their group.*

PROOF: In *lower_level_consensus*, the group members execute $CT\diamondsuit S$. The $CT\diamondsuit S$ algorithm requires that a majority of the processes be correct. Therefore, if the group size is $\geq 2k + 1$, we can be sure that a majority of the processes are correct as at most k can fail. As the $CT\diamondsuit S$ algorithm satisfies termination, validity and agreement, therefore processes in a group executing *lower_level_consensus* eventually decide on some value which has been proposed by a process in their group and no two processes in the given group decide differently. □

Lemma 4. *All processes which execute upper_level_consensus eventually decide on a value proposed by one of them and this is the consensus value arrived at by all the n processes and no two processes decide differently.*

PROOF: As in the proof of Lemma 3, all the processes executing *upper_level_consensus* eventually decide on some *valid* value in their group. After a value has been decided on, $k + 1$ processes send the decision to all the processes not in this group. As at most k of the processes can fail, there is at least one process which had decided in *upper_level_consensus* and did not fail. Therefore, every correct process eventually receives the decision. □

The validity, termination and agreement properties of the two-level consensus algorithm follow from Lemmas 3 and 4.

We now analyze the message complexity of the two-level consensus algorithm. The total number of messages used in *all* reliable broadcasts in all instances of $CT\diamondsuit S$ in this algorithm is $(a - 1)(2k + 1)^2 + (a + 2k + d)^2$, which is $\mathcal{O}(nk)$. For simplifying the presentation of the analysis, we leave out this term in the following results, since the complexity does not change.

Lemma 5. *The expected number of messages required by the two-level consensus is*

$$\leq \frac{b}{1-c} 4k^2 x^{-(2k+1)} + \frac{b}{(1-c)} 6kx^{-(6k+1)} + (k+1)(n - (2k+1))$$

when $(4k+1) < n < (2k+1)^2$.

PROOF: The number of messages required for two-level consensus is equal to the number of messages required for lower level consensus + the number of messages required for upper level consensus. The number of messages required at the lower level is given by number of groups * number of messages per group. Note that at the lower level we have $(a-1)$ groups of size $(2k+1)$. By Theorem 1 and using the fact that $a < 2k+1$, the number of messages required for lower level consensus $\leq \frac{b}{1-c} 4k^2 x^{-(2k+1)}$. In the upper level consensus, the maximum number of processes is $(2k+1) + (a-1) + d \leq (6k+1)$. Therefore by Theorem 1, the number of messages required for upper level consensus is $\frac{b}{(1-c)} 6kx^{-(6k+1)}$. While disseminating, $(k+1)$ processes send the decision to the processes not in the upper level. Since this number is at most $(n - (2k+1))$, messages for distribution are $\leq (k+1)(n - (2k+1))$. □

3.2 Multi Level Consensus Algorithm

If $n \gg 2k+1$ then the idea of two-level consensus can be recursively extended to formulate a *multi-level* consensus algorithm, given in Figure 2. The multi-level algorithm proceeds in a fashion similar to the two-level consensus. If n or the number of processes at any level $< (2k+1)^2$ the two-level consensus algorithm is executed. Otherwise, the multi-level consensus algorithm partitions processes at any level in groups of size $(2k+1)$ save one group which can have up to $(4k+1)$, and each group is represented by a process at the next higher level. The proof of correctness of the multi-level consensus algorithm is along the same lines as the two-level consensus algorithm, and is omitted here.

Note that the expected number of messages required by the multi-level consensus algorithm is equal to the expected number of messages required for $L-1$ levels + the expected number of messages required for two-level consensus at level L. Since the number of groups formed at level i $(i \leq L-1)$ is $\left\lfloor \frac{n}{(2k+1)^i} \right\rfloor$, the expected number of messages required for the first $L-1$ levels is

$\frac{b}{1-c} x^{-(2k+1)} 2k \left\{ \left\lfloor \frac{n}{2k+1} \right\rfloor + \left\lfloor \frac{n}{(2k+1)^2} \right\rfloor + \ldots + \left\lfloor \frac{n}{(2k+1)^{(L-1)}} \right\rfloor \right\} + \frac{b}{1-c}(L-1)$
$\{x^{-(4k+1)} 4k - x^{-(2k+1)} 2k\}$
$\leq \frac{b}{1-c} n x^{-(2k+1)} 2k + \frac{b}{1-c}(L-1)\{x^{-(4k+1)} 4k - x^{-(2k+1)} 2k\}$.

The expected number of messages required for the two-level consensus is

$\leq \frac{b}{(1-c)} 4k^2 x^{-(2k+1)} + \frac{b}{1-c} 6kx^{-(6k+1)} + (k+1)(n - (2k+1))$.

Hence, the number of messages required for multi-level consensus is bounded by

$\frac{b}{1-c} n x^{-(2k+1)} 2k + \frac{b}{1-c}(L-1)\{x^{-(4k+1)} 4k - x^{-(2k+1)} 2k\} + \frac{b}{(1-c)} 4k^2 x^{-(2k+1)} + \frac{b}{(1-c)} 6kx^{-(6k+1)} + (k+1)(n - 2k + 1)$.

Notice that this expression grows exponentially in k (since $x < 1$).

Summarizing these observations, we can state the following result about our multi-level consensus algorithm:

Each process p_i executes the following:
$level \leftarrow 1$ { the current level of consensus; initially 1 }
$L \leftarrow \lfloor log_{2k+1} n \rfloor$ { maximum number of levels of consensus }

   procedure $multi\_level(v_p, level)$
      if ($L = 1$ or $level = L$) **then**
         $two\_level(v_p, level)$
         terminate
      else
         { if $level = 1$ then all processes participate and process p_i belongs to group G whose members are p_j s.t. $j - 1 \equiv i - 1$ div $(2k + 1)$
         For other levels, process p_i belongs to group G whose members are p_j s.t.(j mod $(2k+1)^{level-1} = 1$ and $\left\lceil \frac{i}{(2k+1)^{level-1}} \right\rceil \neq \left\lfloor \frac{n}{(2k+1)^{level-1}} \right\rfloor + 1$) and $j \equiv i$ div $(2k+1)^{level}$.
         If $\left\lceil \frac{i}{(2k+1)^{level}} \right\rceil = \left\lfloor \frac{n}{(2k+1)^{level}} \right\rfloor + 1$) then it belongs to group number $\left\lfloor \frac{i}{(2k+1)^{level}} \right\rfloor$ }
         $dec \leftarrow CT \Diamond S(G, v_p)$
         if (i mod $(2k+1)^{level} = 1$ and $\left\lceil \frac{i}{(2k+1)^{level}} \right\rceil \neq \left\lfloor \frac{n}{(2k+1)^{level}} \right\rfloor + 1$) **then**
            $level \leftarrow level + 1$
            $multi\_level(dec, level)$
         else
            wait for decision.

end proc

Fig. 2. The Multi-level Consensus Algorithm

Theorem 2. *The multi-level consensus algorithm*
(i) satisfies termination, validity and agreement.
(ii) is sound with respect to the Chandra-Toueg algorithm using $\Diamond S$.
(iii) requires messages exponential in k, the maximum number of failures.

4 Conclusions and Future Work

To summarize, we have presented in this paper:

1. A probabilistic analysis of the Chandra-Toueg consensus algorithm. Our analysis shows that the expected number of messages grows exponentially in n, the number of processes.
2. Refining the analysis by introducing *a priori* knowledge of a bound on the number of failures as a parameter k, we have formalized a multi-level generalization of their consensus algorithm. Our algorithm exhibits an improvement in the expected number of messages, since it grows exponentially in the parameter k rather than in n.

3. The $CT\diamond S$ algorithm is interesting as it works with fallible failure detectors. Our analysis is for the interesting case when the failure oracles have only a small element of fallibility ($x \simeq 1$). However, one can also note that if the performance of the failure detectors deteriorates, the $CT\diamond S$ degrades rapidly as the terms neglected in the analysis begin to contribute to the message complexity.

There are several directions for further work. Some of these include:

- The algorithm we have presented is not behaviorally equivalent (in a "may" sense) to the Chandra-Toueg algorithm, since there may be executions of the latter which reach a consensus value that may not be reached by our algorithms — the failure of a representative of a group in the lower level consensus may result in the value decided by that group not being propagated to the upper level. There is, however, a naive approach to rectifying this lacuna: each group is represented by $k+1$ members at the next higher level, and thus its decided value is propagated. Of course, this modification increases the number of groups and levels. We are currently studying how to minimize the associated increase in the number of messages by exploring alternatives in the two level stage.
- We would like to explore whether the approach is also feasible when we look at different failure models, in particular crash recovery [1, 11]. Here, we clearly need a different notion of message complexity from that in crash stop models, since (i) processes may send unboundedly many "I have recovered" messages; (ii) in the presence of link failures, a process may have to reiterate the last message it send several times.
- The metric we have studied is the number of messages, which is adversely influenced by the fact that the model assumes a fully-connected point-to-point topology. Other metrics, communication topologies and models may require a different approach. We should, however, observe that it is the *number of rounds* in the $CT\diamond S$ algorithm that grows exponentially in n.
- We would also like to explore whether other interesting problems are also amenable to a similar multi-level approach.

References

1. Marcos Kawazoe Aguilera, Wei Chen and Sam Toueg, "Failure Detection and Consensus in the Crash Recovery Model". In *Proceedings of the International Symposium on Distributed Computing*, pages 231–245, 1998.
2. Michael Ben-Or, "Another advantage of free choice: Completely asynchronous agreement protocols", In *Proceedings of the Second Annual ACM Symposium on Principles of Distributed Computing*, page 27–30, August 1983.
3. Piotr Berman and Anupam A. Bharali, "Distributed consensus in semi-synchronous systems", In *Proceedings of the Sixth International Parallel Processing Symposium*, pages 632-635, 1992.
4. Piotr Berman and Juan A. Garay, "Cloture voting: $n/4$-resilient distributed consensus in $t+1$ rounds", *Mathematical Systems Theory*, vol. 26(1), pages 3-20, 1993.
5. Tushar Deepak Chandra, Vassos Hadzilacos and Sam Toueg, "Unreliable failure detectors for asynchronous systems", In *Proceedings of the 10th Annual ACM Symposium on Principles of Distributed Computing*, pages 325–340, 1991.

6. Tushar Deepak Chandra, Vassos Hadzilacos and Sam Toueg, "The Weakest Failure Detector for solving consensus", *JACM*, vol. 43(4), pages 685–722, 1996.
7. Benny Chor, Amos Israeli and Ming Li, "On processor coordination using asynchronous hardware", In *Proceedings of the Sixth Annual ACM Symposium on Principle of Distributed Computing*, pages 86–97, 1987.
8. Tushar Deepak Chandra and Sam Toueg, "Unreliable Failure Detectors for Reliable Distributed Systems", *JACM*, vol. 43(2) pages 225–267, 1996.
9. Cynthia Dwork, Nancy Lynch and Larry Stockmeyer, "Consensus in the presence of partial synchrony", *JACM*, vol. 35(2), pages 288–323, 1988.
10. M.J. Fischer, N.A. Lynch and M.S. Paterson, "Impossibility of Distributed Consensus with one faulty process", *JACM*, vol. 32(2), pages 374–382, April 1985.
11. Michel Hurfin, Achour Mostefaoui, and Michel Raynal, "Consensus in asynchronous systems where processes can crash and recover", In *Proceedings of the 17th IEEE Symposium on Reliable Distributed Systems*, pages 280–286, October 1998.
12. Nancy A. Lynch, *Distributed Algorithms*, Morgan Kaufmann Publishers, Inc., San Francisco, California, 1996.

Distributed Multiple Hypothesis Testing in Sensor Networks Under Bandwidth Constraint

Chandrashekhar Thejaswi PS and Ranjeet Kumar Patro

Honeywell Technology Solution Laboratory,
151/1, Doraisanipalya, Bannerghatta Road,
Bangalore, 560076, India
{Chandrashekhara.Thejaswi, Ranjeet.Patro}@honeywell.com

Abstract. In this paper, we consider the problem of multiple hypothesis testing by a bandwidth and power constrained sensor network with a fusion center. We propose a scheme, where each sensor is restricted to send a 1-bit message to fusion center and the fusion center collates the bits sent by all the sensors and makes a decision about the hypothesis. We analyze the performance of our scheme and illustrate it with an example.

1 Introduction

In recent years, rapid progress in sensor technology, microprocessor and wireless communication has lead to the emergence of a new paradigm for connecting the world called wireless sensor network. A wireless sensor network is a special network formed by large number of tiny nodes equipped with sensors, embedded processors and transceivers. These energy-constrained sensor nodes collaborate to accomplish task such as environment monitoring, surveillance of remote area, asset tracking and biological/chemical threat detection. An important challenge in the design of these wireless sensor network is that two key resources, communication bandwidth and energy, which are severely limited. Because of the hostile communication links and the various associated processing in RF and baseband domains, sensor devices dissipate a major part of their power budget in information transfer. In fact, the power incurred due to transmission of a bit is much higher than that it takes to process a single bit. Due to these limitations, it is difficult for sensor nodes to send their entire real-valued observations for fusion. This has drawn the attention of the research community for the development of theory and methods for collaborative signal processing of the data collected by different sensor nodes. Motivated by these challenges, in this paper, we address the problem of distributed detection of multiple hypothesis testing in wireless sensor networks consisting of a fusion center and a large number of geographically distributed sensors. We assumed that sensor node can communicate to the fusion center, but cannot communicate with each other. We propose a scheme of distributed detection where each sensor is constrained to transmit only one bit to the fusion center.

Researchers have been diligently pursuing the decentralized detection problems. There is a significant collection of literature in this field. Survey papers [1],

[2] and [3], provide excellent references to the earlier work in this field. A comprehensive review of the theories for decentralized detection is given in [2]. It is also shown that, under the assumption of conditional independence of the sensors' observations, local decisions made by the sensors obey likelihood ratio test. If there is no assumption of conditional independence among sensor's observations, then the problem of finding optimal decision strategy is NP-complete. The decentralized detection with the communication cost constraints were first studied by Rago et.al [5], where the sensors employ a "send/no-send" strategy depending on the likelihood function, thereby reducing the communication cost. In [4], the decentralized detection problem is formulated as a constrained optimization problem with the constraints on transmission and measurement costs. They obtain the optimal solution using randomization of the measurement and send/no-send transmission policies meeting the constraints. Decentralized detection problem with communication constraints is also studied in [6], where sensors transmit only a 1-bit message to the fusion center and an universal detection scheme is proposed.

In this paper we propose a scheme for distributed multiple hypothesis testing when the communication link between the sensors and the fusion center is severely constrained. The rest of the paper is organized as follows. In Section 2, we state the system model and made the assumptions. In Section 3, the problem is formulated and the outline of our solution to the problem is given. We detail out the performance measure with an example in section 4. Section 5 deals with some simulation results and finally we conclude the paper in section 6.

2 System Model

Consider the scenario using K number of sensors to detect a phenomenon taking M states, such that $M = \log_2 K$. The aim is to detect the state of the phenomenon by carrying out collaboration among these sensors. We formulate this detection problem as a Multiple Hypothesis Testing (MHT) problem on the observable vectors $\mathbf{y_k} = [y_k(0), y_k(1) \ldots y_k(N)], k = 0, 1, 2, \ldots, K-1$ recorded by the kth sensor observing the event, where N is the number of observations. Under the null hypothesis (H_0) it is assumed that the data consists of just the noise. Under the alternative hypotheses ($H_1, \ldots H_M$), the data consist of the signal pertaining to the corresponding hypothesis embedded in the background noise. The observation noise is assumed to be identical across all the sensors.

Thus, the observation vector for the kth sensor becomes

$$H_0 : \mathbf{y_k} = \mathbf{w_k}$$
$$H_i : \mathbf{y_k} = \mathbf{w_k} + A_i, i = 1, \ldots, M-1,$$

where A_i is the signal corresponding to the ith hypothesis and $\mathbf{w_k} \sim \mathcal{N}(0, \sigma_w^2.\mathbf{I}_N)$ is the noise vector corresponding to the observations of kth sensor. Noise vector is assumed to be identically and independently distributed across all the sensors. Let $P_i = P(H_i)$ be the apriori probability of the hypothesis H_i which are assumed to be known. The detection scheme should detect the occurance of an event or phenomenon, and correctly classify it. Each sensor is allowed to communicate only one bit of information to the fusion center.

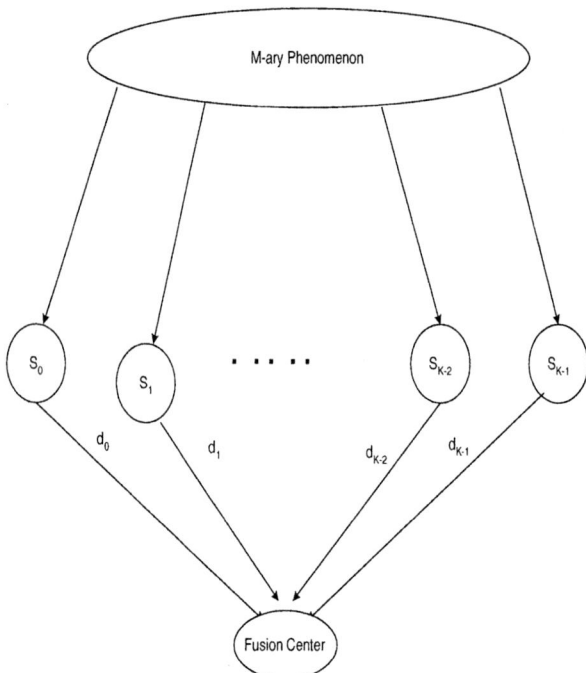

Fig. 1. Sensor Network Topology

3 Our Approach

Fig. 1 shows the topology of our system. Sensor k observes the data, makes decision on the event and transmits a single bit information d_k to the fusion center. Fusion center collects the bits $\{d_k\}_{k=0}^{K-1}$ sent by all the sensors and then makes the inference regarding the event. Let us investigate about how the scheme works. The entire scheme works in three steps.

- $M-$ary Hypothesis testing by the sensors.
- Mapping of the $M-$ary decision into a bit by each sensor.
- Final decision at the fusion center through single-bit sensor observations.

A. $M-ary$ Hypothesis testing by the sensors

Sensor k observes the data $\mathbf{y_k}$ associated with the event and perform $M-$ ary Hypothesis testing on the test statistic. Assuming that $\{P_i\}_0^{M-1}$ are known, each sensor uses the MAP criterion and decide in favor of one of the M hypotheses according to the following rule: Decide in favor of H_l whenever,

$$l = argmax_i P(H_i|\mathbf{y_k}) = argmax_i f(\mathbf{y_k}|H_i)P_i,$$

where $P(H_i|\mathbf{y_k})$ is the posteriori probability of H_i and $f(\mathbf{y_k}|H_i)$ is the likelihood function. We then say $\hat{h}_k = H_l$, where $\hat{h}_k$ denotes the decision made by the kth sensor. Let $\mathcal{Y}$ be the observation space which is divided into several mutually exclusive subspaces $\mathbf{Y_0},\ldots,\mathbf{Y_{M-1}}$ by assigning the points in each subspace to the corresponding hypothesis. The division is done in such a way that the probability of error is minimized. Thus the decision criteria becomes,

$$\hat{h}_k = H_l \text{ if } \mathbf{y_k} \in \mathbf{Y}_l.$$

B. Mapping of the $M-ary$ decision into single bit information by the sensor
After having performed the hypothesis testing, each sensor maps its decision either to a one or to a zero. It is done in the following way. Let us assume, integer i can be expanded as $i = \sum_{k=0}^{K-1} 2^k b_k(i)$, where $b_k(i)$ denote the value of the bit in the kth position of the binary representation of the number i. Assume that the kth sensor makes a decision in favor of the hypothesis H_l. Then, the corresponding sensor's mapping will be $d_k = b_k(l)$. That is, k^{th} sensor will transmit only the value of the kth bit location of the binary representation corresponding to the favored hypothesis's index.

C. Final decision at the fusion center through single-bit sensor observations
All the K sensors transmit their single bit decision to the fusion center. The fusion center collates the bits sent by all the sensors and makes a decision depending on the bit pattern. Thus, the estimated hypothesis at the fusion center is

$$\hat{H} = H_l,$$

where the index l is computed at the fusion center using the bit pattern $\{d_k\}_0^{K-1}$ as

$$l = \sum_{k=0}^{K-1} d_k 2^k.$$

Motivated by the work [5], we further improve our scheme by introducing a censor strategy. Each sensor transmits only when the information bit is non-zero and refrains from the transmission otherwise. The fusion center after waiting for few fixed slots, replaces the missing bits by zero bits to arrive at the final hypothesis. This method in fact, will also take care of the problem that otherwise would have occurred when there are more number of sensors than required to test the present set of hypothesis. That is, $K > \log_2 M$.

4 Performance Analysis

We will evaluate the performance of our proposed scheme. This is done through calculating two basic measures of performance. Probability of False Alarm (P_{FA}) and the probability of a correct decision (P_C).

A. Probability of False Alarm (P_{FA})
P_{FA} is defined as the probability of making decision in favor of the one of the non-zero hypothesis when the null hypothesis true. That is discovering falsely that an event has occurred when the 'no-event' case is the correct one. Thus we have

$$P_{FA} = P(\hat{H} = \bigcup_{l \neq 0} H_l | H_0)$$

$$= \sum_{l \neq 0} P(\hat{H} = H_l | H_0)$$
$$= 1 - P(\hat{H} = H_0 | H_0)$$
$$= 1 - \prod_{k=0}^{K-1} P(d_k = 0 | H_0), \qquad (1)$$

where the last equality is due to the fact that $\hat{H} = H_0$ only if a zero is transmitted by all the sensors. Consider the probability of transmitting zero from a sensor under the null hypothesis. Sensor k would decide it as the null hypothesis only when the observation vector falls in the region corresponding to the hypothesis whose index has a zero bit in its kth position. That is

$$d_k = 0 \text{ if } \mathbf{y}_k \in \bigcup_{i:b_k(i)=0} \mathbf{Y}_i.$$

Thus, the probability that the sensor k transmits a zero under the null hypothesis is

$$P(d_k = 0 | H_0) = P(\mathbf{y}_k \in \bigcup_{i:b_k(i)=0} \mathbf{Y}_i | H_0)$$
$$= \sum_{i:b_k(i)=0} P(\mathbf{y_k} \in \mathbf{Y}_i | H_0)$$

Thus equation 1 becomes

$$P_{FA} = 1 - \prod_{k=0}^{K-1} \sum_{i:b_k(i)=0} P(\mathbf{y_k} \in \mathbf{Y}_i | H_0). \qquad (2)$$

B. Probability of Correct Decision (P_C)

P_C is defined as the probability of correctly making a decision in favor of the one of the hypotheses when it is has actually occurred. Therefore,

$$P_C = \sum_{l=0}^{M-1} P(H_l) \cdot P(\hat{H} = H_l | H_l). \qquad (3)$$

We have,

$$P(\hat{H} = H_l | H_l) = P(l = \sum_{k=0}^{K-1} 2^k d_k | H_l)$$
$$= \prod_{k=0}^{K-1} P(d_k = b_k(l) | H_l)$$
$$= \prod_{k=0}^{K-1} \sum_{i:b_k(i)=b_k(l)} P(\mathbf{y_k} \in \mathbf{Y}_i | H_l)$$

To illustrate the performance of our scheme with an example, we consider an 8-ary phenomenon with each of its events corresponding to an 8-ary PAM system. Therefore we have $M = 8$ and $K = 3$. Assuming $N = 1$ and $w_k \sim \mathcal{N}(0,1)$, and the system equation as

$$H_0 : y_k = w_k$$
$$H_i : y_k = w_k + i.A, \quad i = 1, \ldots, 7,$$

for $k = 0, 1, 2$.

Let us evaluate P_{FA} of our scheme.

$$P(d_0 = 0|H_0) = P\left(w_0 \in \cup_{i=0}^{3} \mathbf{Y}_{2i}\right)$$
$$= Q(\tfrac{A}{2}) + \sum_{i=0}^{3} Q(\tfrac{(4i-1)A}{2}) - Q(\tfrac{(4i+1)A}{2}).$$
$$P(d_1 = 0|H_0) = P\left(w_1 \in \cup_{i:b_1(i)=0} \mathbf{Y}_i\right)$$
$$= Q(\tfrac{3A}{2}) + Q(\tfrac{7A}{2}) - Q(\tfrac{11A}{2}).$$
$$P(d_2 = 0|H_0) = P\left(w_2 \in \cup_{i:b_2(i)=0} \mathbf{Y}_i\right)$$
$$= Q(\tfrac{7A}{2}).$$

From (2) we have,

$$P_{FA} = 1 - P(d_0 = 0|H_0)P(d_1 = 0|H_0)P(d_2 = 0|H_0).$$

5 Simulation Results

We simulated our proposed scheme with that of a standard detection algorithm. The standard algorithm is based on the majority voting rule (MVR) which decides in favor of hypothesis H_l where

$$l = argmax_{i \in \{0,1\ldots,M-1\}} \left\{ \sum_{k=0}^{K-1} I(\hat{h}_k = H_i) \right\},$$

$\hat{h}_k$ is the hypothesis favored by sensor k and $I(\cdot)$ is the indicator function

$$I(a = b) = \begin{cases} 1 & \text{if } a = b \\ 0 & \text{otherwise.} \end{cases}$$

Table 1 shows comparison between our proposed scheme and the standard MVR scheme both incuring the same transmit power using a simple binary communication scheme. We considered a system with $M = 8, K = 3$. The apriori distribution of the events was chosen to be uniform. i,e. $P(H_i) = \tfrac{1}{M}$ $i = 0, \ldots 1$. The noise at each sensor was iid Gaussian with zero mean. The communication links were also assumed to be channels with AWGN. We varied the noise variance of both link and the sensors thus varying link SNRs and sensor SNRs respectively. The values of P_C is tabulated for different values sensor SNRs and the SNR of

Table 1. Comparison of *Probability of Correct Decisions* for the proposed distributed scheme (P_{Cd}) and MVR scheme (P_{CM})

Sensor SNR (in dB)	link SNR= 0dB		link SNR= 5dB		link SNR= 10dB	
	P_{Cd}	P_{CM}	P_{Cd}	P_{CM}	P_{Cd}	P_{CM}
0	0.3	0.26	0.398	0.392	0.582	0.602
4	0.4	0.32	0.592	0.5346	0.773	0.86
7	0.45	0.34	.7019	0.605	0.952	0.955

the communication link between sensor and the fusion center. It is obvious that P_C is also the measure of P_{FA} because $P_{FA} \propto 1 - P_C$.

One can observe that for a given link SNR, the performance of our scheme is superior than that of MVR scheme and both tend to be identical as the sensor SNRs decrease. At low link SNRs, one can see that our scheme performs better than MVR scheme. These observation can be reasoned out as follows. The MVR scheme is optimal in terms of detecting the hypothesis whereas our scheme is just suboptimal and hence its performance deteriorates at low sensor SNRs. However, when sensors have low noise, the effect of noise at the communication link will be dominant in fusion center in making a decision from the noisy observations transmitted by the sensors. Since, in our scheme each sensor transmits just a single bit, it can pump as much power in a single bit as a sensor in MVR scheme pumps to transmit K bits. Thus, the single bit messages will be more reliable than the K bit messages.

6 Conclusions and Future Directions

We addressed the problem of multiple hypothesis testing in sensor networks where the link between sensors and the fusion center is severely bandwidth constrained. A scheme was developed to accomplish this. We analyzed the performance of this algorithm and compared it with that of existing standard rule. We found that our scheme outperforms the latter when the communication link is power and bandwidth constrained. This kind of setup will be useful in many scenarios like target tracking, surveillance, event detection etc. As an extension to this problem, it will be interesting to consider the case when sensor noises are not identical. We can also look at the optimal fusion strategy, where the metric $|H_i - \hat{H}|$, the difference between the actual hypothesis and the detected hypothesis is minimized.

References

1. R.S. Blum, S.A. Kassam and H.V. Poor.: "Distributed Detection with Multiple Sensors: Part II - Advanced Topics," *Proceedings of the IEEE*, vol. 85, no. 1, pp. 64-79, January, 1997.
2. J.N. Tstsiklis.: "Decentralized Detection," *Advances in Statistical Signal Processing*, Vol 2, pp. 297-344, JAI Press, 1993.
3. R. Viswanathan and P.K. Varshney.: "Distributed detection with multiple sensors: Part I - fundamentals," *Proceedings of the IEEE*, vol. 85, no.1, pp. 54-63, January, 1997.
4. Appadwedula, S., Veeravalli and V.V. Jones, D.L.: "Energy-Efficient Detection in Sensor Networks," *IEEE JSAC*, vol. 23, Issue. 4, pp. 693- 702, April, 2005.
5. C. Rago, P. Willett, and Y. Bar-Shalom.: "Censoring sensors: A low-communication-rate scheme for distributed detection," *IEEE Transactions on Aerospace and Electronic Systems*, vol. 32, pp. 554- 568, April 1996.
6. Jin-Jun Xiao, Zhi-Quan Luo.: "Decentralized detection in a bandwidth constrained sensor network," *IEEE GLOBECOM '04*, vol. 1, pp. 123- 128, 2004.

A Scalable Multi-level Distributed System-Level Diagnosis

Paritosh Chandrapal[1] and Padam Kumar[2]

[1] Dept. of Electronics & Computer Engieering. IIT Roorkee,
Roorkee 247667, India
paritosh_pal@yahoo.com
[2] Professor, Dept. of Electronics & Computer Engieering. IIT Roorkee,
Roorkee 247667, India

Abstract. The purpose of distributed system-level diagnosis is to have each fault-free nodes determine the state of all nodes of system. The paper presents a Multi-level distributed system-level diagnosis, which considers the problem of achieving scalability and performance tuning for distributed diagnosis. Existing work is aimed to reduce either diagnosis latency or network utilization but scales poorly. A diagnosis algorithm, called Multi-level DSD, is presented to provide scalability, which controls both latency and network utilization in fully connected networks. The algorithm is scalable in the sense that it is possible to diagnose system with large number of processing elements (nodes) by tuning diagnosis parameters. The diagnosis algorithm allows tuning of diagnosis performance to lever latency message cost trade-off. Multi-level DSD divides system in clusters of nodes, where each cluster is either a single node or a group of clusters. Cluster diagnoses itself by running a cluster diagnosis algorithm between its sub clusters. Clusters at each level runs same cluster diagnosis algorithm.

1 Introduction

Traditional centralized network management solution does not scale to present-day large-scale computer networks. It has been recognized that distributed solutions can solve some of the problems associated with centralized solutions. The proposed diagnosis algorithm provides such a solution with use of multilevel paradigm. The term scalable suggests that diagnosis can be adapted for large-sized networks by tuning diagnosis parameters. The proposed algorithm Multi-level DSD (distributed system-level diagnosis) divides system in clusters of nodes, where each cluster is either a single node or a group of clusters. Each cluster diagnoses itself by running a diagnosis algorithm between its sub clusters called cluster diagnosis algorithm. Clusters at each level runs same cluster diagnosis algorithm. The diagnosis can be configured to adapt requirements through alteration of number of nodes and cluster diagnosis algorithms at different levels.

Performance of a distributed system-level diagnosis is described by several performance measures described as below. Diagnosis latency is the time from the detection of a fault event until all nodes can identify the event. If every single message over link costs then algorithm must reduce number of tests to be performed. Network utilization is measured as number of messages transmitted per diagnosis interval, called message cost. In case, where message size varies, network utilization is considered as number of diagnostic units (diagnostic information of single node). To measure scalability for a diagnosis algorithm, a performance measure Scale Factor (SF) is introduced, which is product of diagnosis latency in testing rounds and message cost per diagnosis interval. As total node increases, diagnosis latency as well as message cost per node increases, and consequently scale factor will increase for any diagnosis algorithm. Lower values of SF and less steeper SF graph suggests higher scalability.

Diagnosis latency can be measured in testing round where testing round is the period of time in which every fault free node in the system has tested another node as fault free, and has obtained diagnostic information from that node, or has tested all other nodes as faulty. A diagnosis interval is considered as a testing round in heartbeat-based mechanism.

2 Related Work

Related diagnosis algorithms for fully connected networks i.e. ADSD, Hi-ADSD, Heartbeat and ML-ADSD are described follow.

Adaptive testing and distributed diagnosis were incorporated into the Adaptive DSD algorithm (ADSD), developed and implemented by Bianchini and Buskens [1]. The Adaptive DSD implementation, which also incorporated practical implementation considerations, was the first practical online implementation of system-level diagnosis in an actual distributed environment. Unlike the SELF, ADSD is not bounded by number of faulty nodes. The diagnosis algorithm is meant for minimizing network resources. The diagnosis constructs a cycle of fault free nodes. ADSD has minimum message cost per diagnosis process of n than any existing diagnosis algorithm, but has maximum diagnosis latency of n-1 testing round.

The Hierarchical Adaptive Distributed System- Level Diagnosis (Hi-ADSD) algorithm is presented by E.P. Duarte [2, 3]. Hi-ADSD maps nodes to clusters, which are sets of nodes. Hi-ADSD employs a divide-and-conquer testing strategy. The system considered for Hi-ADSD is fully connected. In Hi-ADSD, nodes are grouped into clusters for testing. Clusters are sets of nodes. The number of nodes in a cluster is always a power of two. A cluster of n nodes, where n is a power of two, is recursively defined as either a node, in case n is one, or the union of two clusters. Hi-ADSD achieves diagnostic latency of $\log_2^2 n$ testing rounds, message cost of $n \log_2^2 n$ per diagnosis process and message cost of one message per diagnosis interval per node.

The Distributed System- Level Diagnosis algorithm in Dynamic Fault Environment is presented by A. Subbiah [4]. The algorithms are meant for achieving diagnosis under dynamic failures and repairs. Author assumes testing is accomplished via Heartbeat based mechanisms that have low cost. The base algorithm of Heartbeat is meant for completely connected networks, has both latency and state holding time equal to approximately one testing round, where one testing round can be considered as one heartbeat transmission round for smaller values of heartbeat period. The algorithm has minimum diagnosis latency than any diagnosis algorithm, but has high message cost of n (n-1) messages per diagnosis interval. The algorithm costs n (n-1) number of diagnostic units per diagnosis interval. Major drawback of these algorithms is that algorithms are non-scalable.

A multi-level adaptive distributed diagnosis algorithm by K Thulasiraman [5, 6] works for fully connected networks. The algorithm is called the ML-ADSD algorithm [5, 6]. The nodes are partitioned into clusters. Clusters are recursively partitioned into sub clusters. In each cluster, the node with the smallest id will be called the leader of that cluster. At cluster, all leaders will run ADSD diagnosis algorithm among them and exchange diagnostic information about nodes considered in sub clusters. The diagnosis method scales and works efficiently compare to ADSD and Hi-ADSD under system constraints. However, it introduces overhead of leader election in diagnosis latency. ML-DSD algorithm shows better performance than ML-ADSD.

3 System Model

To model system attributes, working environment for diagnosis algorithm is defined by different models like interaction model, fault model and communication model. Model is similar to model described by A. Subbiah [4].

3.1 Interaction Model

When system works in synchronous mode, responses from a server are guaranteed to come within a bounded known amount of time. Each step of a process has known lower & upper bounds. Each Process has a local clock whose drift rate from real time has a known bound. When system works in asynchronous mode, there is no time bound over response time, process execution time or clock drift rate. In this paper, system is considered with a synchronous interaction model. Physical clock at each node is sufficient to work. Clock drift rate at system nodes is assumed zero. The clock drift rate is relative rate at which a computer clock drifts away from a perfect reference clock.

3.2 Failure Model

Our approach considers PMC model [7] with distributed environment, which is used for most of the distributed diagnosis algorithms. The status of a node is modeled with two states, failed and working. Failed nodes do not send messages nor do they perform any computation. Working nodes faithfully execute the diagnosis procedure.

Proposed diagnosis algorithm considers only crash and permanent faults in nodes. Crash failure indicates that server works correctly, until it halts while permanent fault is one that continues to exist until the faulty component is repaired. If heartbeat based algorithm is converted to test based mechanisms than our assumption of crash fault can be extended for other kind of faults. Processing element is considered as fail-stop. The term fail-stop suggests that the server simply stops operating. Its halting can be detected by other processes. Environment is considered dynamic fault environment, where neither fault timing nor fault count is bounded.

The state holding time is the minimum time a node remains in the failed/working state before transitioning to the working/failed state. We assume that faults are restricted to nodes, i.e. the network delivers messages reliably.

3.3 Communication Model

Diagnosis algorithms can use either unicast or multicast communication. The proposed diagnosis algorithm considers unicast communication over UDP/IP for fully connected networks. In fully connected networks, there is a direct communication channel between every pair of nodes. The maximum message delay is the maximum message transmission times. The delay is used to calculate and set heartbeat intervals. Any message processing time on a receiving node is assumed included in the message delay. We assume that messages are encoded in such a way, e.g. using checksums, to enable incomplete messages to be detected and discarded.

3.4 Assumptions

ML-DSD assumes non-event driven approach, where diagnosis does not trigged by any event but diagnosis is done periodically after every Δ_D interval (diagnosis interval). We assume heartbeat-based algorithms work with the use of heartbeat messages, i.e. that each node periodically initiates a round of message transmissions to other nodes in order to indicate that the node is working (not crashed). Wherever test-based algorithms work with the use of test and test reply messages, i.e. each node periodically tests other nodes and working node sends test reply along with diagnostic information.

ML-DSD is a diagnosis algorithm in which both the heartbeat-based algorithms and test-based algorithms are used as cluster diagnosis algorithm. Heartbeat-based mechanism is more efficient because only one message is required instead of two in the standard testing model. In the standard testing model, while a node remains in the failed state, other node would periodically test it and therefore, generates additional messages. Test based mechanism have there own advantage that it can be used to identify all kind of faults unlike heartbeat mechanism which only identifies crash fault. It is assumed that heartbeat based diagnosis can be incorporated only at lowest level. If heartbeat based mechanism is introduced at higher levels, diagnosis fails to maintain fairness between system nodes. As number of nodes increases, size of diagnostic information increases and consequently system does instable diagnosis under unavailability of resources.

4 Multi-level DSD (ML-DSD)

Diagnosis algorithm works in the fully connected systems that satisfies model defined in previous section. Working of proposed algorithm can be explained in following steps.

4.1 System Partitioning

Proposed algorithm divides system of size N into p clusters of size N/p, where N and p are assumed power of 2. These clusters are divided into q clusters, each of size N/(p*q), where q is power of two. As N and p are power of two, N/p is also power of two. In this way, division continues up to L times, where L is total levels defined for diagnosis. Nodes at second level are leader of first level. Number of levels and cluster size at different level decides performance of diagnosis.

4.2 Cluster Diagnosis Algorithm Selection

Diagnosis of each of the cluster is independent. The proposed diagnosis method does not interfere in working of diagnosis inside the cluster. Cluster diagnosis algorithm is responsible for providing diagnostic information about all sub clusters to every sub cluster of same cluster. Cluster is made of sub clusters or single node. If cluster is made of sub cluster then leader node of each sub cluster will represent its sub cluster. Cluster diagnosis algorithm will be executed between leaders of all sub clusters inside cluster. On test, leader provides diagnostic information about all nodes in sub cluster. Cluster diagnosis algorithm can be any distributed diagnosis algorithm that works under system model defined in section 3. Diagnosis algorithm that uses heartbeat-based mechanism can be used as cluster diagnosis algorithm only at lower most level.

4.3 Leader Selection

At higher levels, diagnosis algorithm is executed between leaders of sub clusters. As no cluster node is free from faults, leader of cluster is selected dynamically. Cluster leader can be decided by running leadership algorithm between cluster nodes. In proposed algorithm, cluster leader is a fault free node of cluster having minimum identification number. Identification number of a node are defined statically or decided by node attribute like IP (Internet Protocol) number. Each node in cluster uses its gathered diagnostic information to find cluster leader. In case of leader becomes faulty, all nodes come to know about new leader of cluster after d_i time, where d_i is diagnosis latency of cluster diagnosis algorithm. As diagnosis algorithm provides correct diagnostic information after d_i time, cluster node correctly identifies cluster leader after d_i time. Cluster diagnosis algorithm is executed parallel to leadership algorithm, such that diagnosis process is not affected even in case of frequent switching of leaders. For cluster diagnosis algorithm, a sub cluster is considered as faulty if and only if all sub cluster nodes becomes faulty.

4.4 Diagnostic Information Management

Cluster diagnosis algorithm is responsible for providing diagnosis of cluster. To achieve the diagnosis, cluster leader attaches diagnostic information about nodes outside cluster, with its own diagnostic information every time it transmits its own diagnostic information to other cluster nodes. The diagnostic information is provided to every node of cluster within latency time of cluster diagnosis algorithm.

4.5 Pseudo Code

As shown in fig. 1, on recovery node calls `Recovery` procedure, during which node calls `Initialize` to initialize itself. On fault, node looses control as crash faults are considered. `Fault` procedure is presented to keep the diagnosis extensible for other type of faults, during which all timers are cancelled, and data structure used for cluster diagnosis algorithm are reset.

```
Algo[i] = cluster diagnosis algorithm at level i
$\Delta_D$     =Time interval between successive diagnosis
Procedure Recovery()
      Initialize()

Procedure Fault
      For each level i
            Reset datastructures used at level i
            Cancel all scheduled timers
      End For

Procedure Cluster_Initialize(i)
Procedure Cluster_Diagnosis(i)
Procedure Cluster_Test(nd, i)
Procedure Cluster_Test_Response(nd, i, msg)
Procedure Cluster_Test_Fail(nd, i)

Procedure Initialize()
      For each level i
        Cluster_Initialize(i)
      End For
      Schedule Diagnosis

Procedure Diagnosis()
      For each level i
        Cluster_Diagnosis(i)
      End For
      Schedule Diagnosis after $\Delta_D$ time

Procedure Test(nd, i)
      sc=cluster residing node nd at level i-1
      Test all nodes in cluster sc until first fault-free node
        found
      If (all nodes in cluster sc are faulty)
        Test_Fail(sc, i)
      End If

Procedure On_Test(nd, i)
      sc =cluster of nd at level i-1
      C =super cluster of sc
      Attach diagnostic information about all nodes in cluster
        sc with message msg
      If (sc=leader of cluster C)
        Attach diagnostic information about nodes outside
          cluster C with message msg
      End If
      Send the test-response containing msg

Procedure Test_Response(nd, i, msg)
      Retrieve attached diagnosis information
      Cluster_Test_Response(nd, i, msg)

Procedure Test_Fail(nd, i)
      Set status of nd as failed
      Cluster_Test_Fail(nd,i)
```

Fig. 1. Psuedo code for ML-DSD algorithm

Procedures with prefix cluster show independent working of cluster diagnosis algorithm at each level i. Cluster diagnosis algorithm specific code is not shown for the procedures. Cluster diagnosis algorithm works among leaders of sub clusters, during which leaders exchanges diagnostic information about thier sub clusters. As test on leader is performed for sub cluster, test on leader fails only if all the nodes in the sub cluster are faulty.

`Cluster_Initialize` procedure initializes data structure required for cluster diagnosis algorithm at level i. `Cluster_Diagnosis` procedure is called for each node at regular interval ΔD, which does diagnosis of its cluster at level i using corresponding cluster diagnosis algorithm. `Cluster_Test` procedure is called to test a leader of sub cluster, nd, at level i. Result of the test performed over nd, provided by `Cluster_Test_Response` procedure on success and by `Cluster_Test_Fail` procedure on failure of test. The three procedures for test, response and failure for sub cluster leader are implemented with the use of procedures `Test`, `Test_Response` and `Test_Fail` procedures described as below.

On initialize, node calls `Initialize` procedure, which subsequently calls `Cluster_Initialize` for each level i. `Diagnosis` procedure is called at regular interval ΔD to initialize diagnosis interval. The procedure consequently calls `Cluster_Diagnosis` for each level i. A test event for a cluster leader initiates `Test` procedure. Test, its response and failure of a cluster leader are fully handled by ML-DSD. Procedure `Test` initiates sequence of test for all nodes of its cluster until a fault free node found. On getting test response from any of the cluster nodes, `Test_Response` procedure is executed, which subsequently calls procedure `Cluster_Test_Response` for level i, at which test was performed. If all cluster nodes are faulty, `Test_Fail` procedure is executed, which subsequently calls `Cluster_Test_Fail` for level i, at which test was performed.

Procedure On_Test is executed on node nd on receiving test message from source. It attaches diagnostic information of nodes in cluster to message msg. If node is leader of super cluster of its cluster, then diagnostic information of nodes outside the super cluster of its cluster is attached to msg.

In Heartbeat based mechanism, test procedure does not executed, but `Cluster_Test_Response` procedure get executed on receiving heartbeat from a node and `Cluster_Test_Fail` called on expire of heartbeat timer. In Heartbeat based mechanism, On_Test procedure is executed before sending a heartbeat.

4.6 Algorithm Analysis

The size of cluster at level i is defined as si (i=1....L), in number nodes. System of n nodes is partitioned in L levels. Message cost considered in analysis is number of messages per diagnosis interval. Analysis is considered under worst-case scenario.

If cluster diagnosis algorithm at level i has worst-case diagnosis latency of d_i then worst-case diagnosis latency D for ML-DSD is defined by equation (1). d_i includes delay introduced by leader failure. In worst case, node x and node y are not a leader at any level and resides in different clusters at highest level. In such scenario, diagnostic information about node x traverse up to topmost level in $(d_1+d_2+... +d_{L-1})$ testing rounds. Highest-level cluster of node y grabs information after next d_L testing rounds.

Node y receives the information about node x up to bottom level after $(d_1+d_2+...+d_{L-1})$ testing rounds. Sum of all the above testing rounds gives worst-case diagnosis latency as in equation (1).

$$D = 2*(d_1+d_2+...+d_{L-1})+d_L \qquad (1)$$

If cluster diagnosis algorithm at level i has message cost of m_i then message cost M for ML-DSD is defined by equation (2). In each term $m_i*(n/s_i)$ shown in equation, (n/s_i) is number of clusters at level i for clusters at level i. Total message cost M is sum of such terms, which is message cost for all clusters.

$$M = \sum_{\text{for each level i}} m_i*(n/s_i) \qquad (2)$$

In fig. 2(a) and fig. 2(b), message cost and diagnosis latency in testing rounds for one diagnosis interval are shown for different diagnosis algorithms[1]. It can be seen that overall performance of ML-DSD is better than existing diagnosis algorithms.

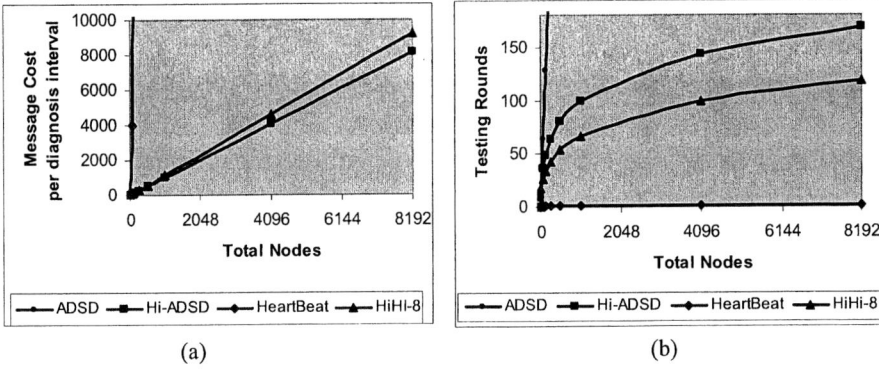

Fig. 2. Worst-case analysis for ML-DSD (a) Total nodes vs. Message cost (b) Total nodes Vs. Diagnosis Latency

5 Simulation Results and Discussions

All average-case results shown in this section, are taken from the simulation of ML-DSD algorithms over OMNeT++ (Object-oriented Modular Discrete Event Network Simulator) [8] simulation environment. Value of Δ_D is taken as 30 seconds, whereas link delay is uniformly distributed between 0.01 and 0.082 seconds. Each node retains its state at least for state holding time. State holding time is considered as 1000 seconds, whereas fault and recovery process are considered as poisson distribution with mean as 6000 and 3000 seconds for each node. It means that fault distribution decides time between two faults at same node and recovery distribution decides time for which node retains its fault-free state.

---

[1] ML-DSD configuration is identified by "A1A2.. AL-s1-s2-..-sL", where s1, s2.. sL are cluster sizes at each level and A1,A2,.. AL are short form for cluster diagnosis algorithm at each level. Short forms HI, HB and AD stands for Hi-ADSD, Heartbeat algorithm and ADSD.

5.1 Trade-off for Diagnosis Latency and Message Cost

In Fig 3(b) graph for diagnosis latency Vs. Number of Nodes is shown, where diagnosis latency is measured in testing rounds. In Fig 3(a) graph for message cost Vs. Number of Nodes is shown, where message cost is number of messages required per node for one diagnosis interval. It can be seen that as number of nodes increases, diagnosis latency and message cost increases for any diagnosis algorithm. Message cost can be reduced by reducing number of test performed by a node, but introduces inefficiency in diagnosis latency. Similarly, if diagnosis latency is reduced by increasing message cost. For higher value of nodes, if the both measure are not controlled, diagnosis process becomes unstable under unavailability of resources. ML-DSD considered is two-level ML-DSD with Hi-ADSD as cluster diagnosis algorithm at both levels, where cluster size is varied to get scalability. ML-DSD provides moderate values of diagnosis latency and message cost, while providing better scalability than other diagnosis algorithms. Graph shown in Fig 3(c) presents the fact that ML-DSD is more scalable than other diagnosis algorithms.

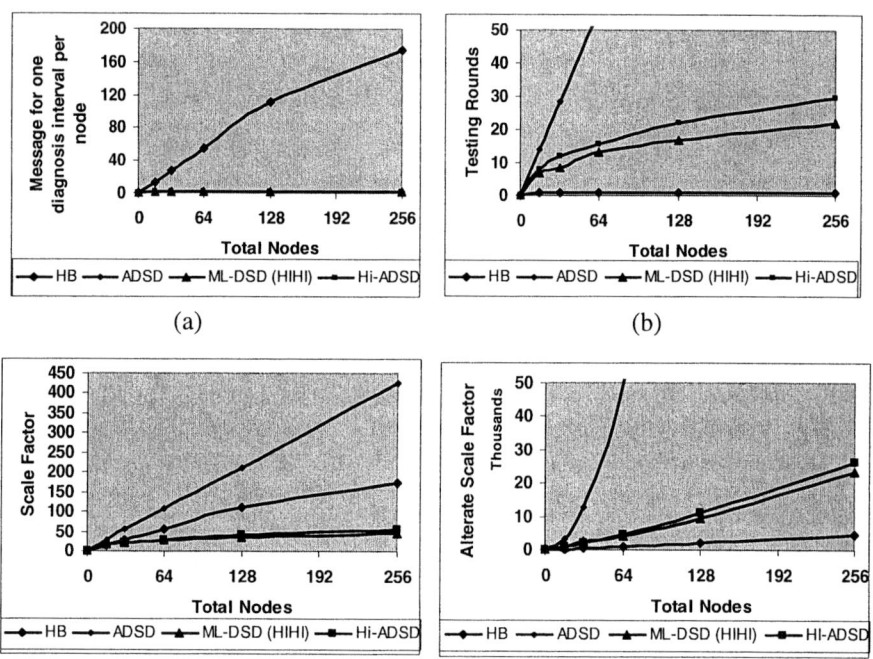

Fig. 3. Trade-off for Latency & Message cost (a) Total nodes vs. Message cost (b) Total nodes Vs. Diagnosis Latency (c) Total nodes vs. Scale factor (d) Total nodes vs. ASF

5.2 Effect on Latency Time and Diagnostic Units

As performance measures shown in above section never remained satisfactorily. The term latency time is unlike testing round, which does not depend on number of failed tests. The term diagnostic unit cost is unlike message cost, which does not consider size of message. However, the diagnostic unit cost looses its effect for lower diagnostic unit size, and latency time depends on diagnosis interval. Alternative scale factor (ASF) is the product of latency time and diagnostic unit cost. As shown in fig 3(d), ML-DSD is scalable than diagnosis algorithms except Heartbeat. However, ASF should not be considered as scalability factor, which presents Heartbeat as scalable algorithm.

5.3 Effect of Cluster Diagnosis Algorithm

Cluster diagnosis algorithm used at different level decides performance of algorithm. Cluster diagnosis algorithm can be any diagnosis algorithm satisfying system model described in section 3. Diagnosis algorithm like ADSD, Hi-ADSD and Heartbeat are among favorites due to their unique properties. However, in non-event-driven diagnosis ADSD gains no advantage than Hi-ADSD. Use any of the above diagnosis algorithm introduces effect from its unique property. I.e. introduces ADSD in one of the level reduces message cost, and introducing Heartbeat algorithm reduces diagnosis latency for diagnosis process. In fig 4, simulation results for latency, message cost and scale factor are shown for 256-node system.

In fig, 4, it can be noticed that ML-DSD introduces higher message cost on using Heartbeat as cluster diagnosis algorithm, but considerably reduces diagnosis latency. Using ADSD as cluster diagnosis algorithm in ML-DSD introduces less message cost at the cost of higher diagnosis latency. Whereas using Hi-ADSD as cluster diagnosis algorithm, optimizes performance for diagnosis latency and message cost. For any cluster diagnosis algorithm, too large or too small cluster size degrades performance. It can be seen that increment in levels degrades performance after reaching an optimum performance.

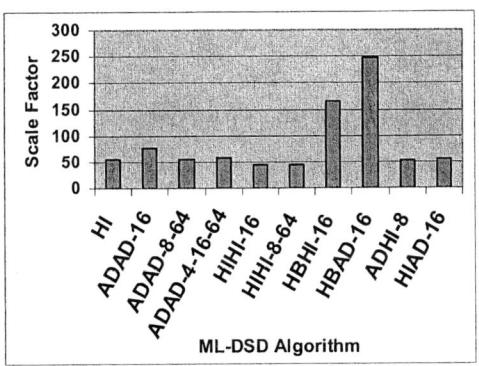

Fig. 4. Scale Factor for ML-DSD under different parameters

6 Conclusion

Using event-driven approach, ADSD provides minimum message-cost at the cost of higher diagnosis latency. If system with less number of nodes, it is beneficial to switch to Hi-ADSD algorithm, which exploits concept of divide, & conquer and achieves diagnostic latency of $\log_2^2$ n testing rounds. The algorithm ML-ADSD, introduces concept of multi-level paradigm and scalability, but diagnosis is done under constraints and diagnosis latency is higher than proposed algorithm with comparable message cost. On the other side, Heartbeat algorithms works over a different approach where diagnosis latency is given higher priority than number of tests performed, and it has achieved the diagnostic latency of approximately one testing round. It provides smallest value of diagnosis latency among all existing diagnosis algorithms.

ML-DSD achieves diagnosis of fully connected network, and is ready to use for network management and monitoring. It provides better scalability under optimum parameters than other diagnosis algorithms. ML-DSD can be tuned for diagnosis latency or message cost under predefined system constraints. The diagnosis can be extended to provide fairness among nodes by implementing in fully distributed way. In fully distributed way, though no leader is selected, each node has to perform predefined tests on cluster behalf.

The diagnosis algorithm can be used for network management and monitoring and fault tolerance for network. It can be extended to support SNMP protocol. The diagnosis algorithm is capable of performing system-level diagnosis for multiprocessors. Our work can also be extended for distributed load balancing by attaching performance measures (e.g. CPU utilization, memory utilization etc.) with fault status.

References

[1] Bianchini R. and Buskens R., "Implementation of On-Line Distributed System-Level Diagnosis Theory", IEEE Trans. Computers, vol. 41, pp. 616-626, May 1992.
[2] Duarte E.P. Jr. and Nanya T., "A Hierarchical Adaptive Distributed System-Level Diagnosis Algorithm", IEEE Trans. Computers, vol. 47, pp. 34-45, Jan. 1998.
[3] Duarte E.P. Jr., Brawerman A., and Albini L.C.P., "An Algorithm for Distributed Hierarchical Diagnosis of Dynamic Fault and Repair Events", Proc. Seventh Int'l Conf. Parallel and Distributed Systems, pp. 299-306, 2000.
[4] Subbiah A. and Douglas M., "Distributed Diagnosis in Dynamic Fault Environments", IEEE Transactions on Parallel and Distributed Systems, Vol.15, pp. 453-467, May 2004.
[5] Su M. S., Thulasiraman K. and Das A., "A Scalable On-line Multilevel Distributed Network Fault Detection/Monitoring System based on the SNMP protocol", IEEE GlobeComm2002, November 2002.
[6] Su M. S., Thulasiraman K., and Goel V., "The Multi-Level Paradigm for Distributed Fault Detection in Network with Unreliable Processors", ISCAS'03, Proc. of the 2003 Int'l symposium on Circuits and Systems, vol. 3, pp. III 862-865, May 2003
[7] Preparata F., Metze G. and Chien R., "On the connection assignment problem of diagnosable systems", IEEE Trans. Elect. Comput. EC-16, 6 (Dec.), pp. 848-854, 1967.
[8] Varga A., "Object-oriented Modular Discrete Event Network Simulator", OMNeT++ Community Site, www.omnetpp.org, January 2005

Analysis of Interval-Based Global State Detection

Punit Chandra and Ajay D. Kshemkalyani

Computer Science Department, Univ. of Illinois at Chicago, Chicago, IL 60607, USA
{pchandra, ajayk}@cs.uic.edu

Abstract. The problem of global state observation is fundamental to distributed systems. All interactions in distributed systems can be analyzed in terms of the building block formed by the pairwise interactions of intervals between two processes. Considering causality-based pairwise interactions by which two intervals at different processes may interact with each other, there are 40 possible orthogonal interactions. This paper examines the problem: "If a global state of interest to an application is specified in terms of the pairwise interaction types between each pair of processes, how can such a global state be detected?" A solution identifies a global state in which the relation specified for each process pair is satisfied. This paper formulates the specific conditions on the exact communication structures to determine which of the intervals being examined at any time may never satisfy the stipulated relation for that pair of processes, and therefore that interval must be deleted.

1 Introduction

The problem of global state observation is fundamental to distributed systems, as identified by Chandy and Lamport's seminal paper on recording global states [6]. It has been observed that all causality-based interactions in distributed systems can be analyzed in terms of the building block formed by the pairwise interactions of intervals between two processes [11]. A detailed analysis of the causality-based pairwise interactions by which two processes may interact with each other identified 29 (40) causality-based orthogonal interactions, denoted as $\Re$, between two processes under the dense (and nondense) time model, respectively [11]. This paper examines the state detection problem: "If a global state of interest to an application is specified in terms of the pairwise interaction types between each pair of processes, how can such a global state be detected?"

Central to the pairwise interactions studied in this paper is the notion of *time intervals* at each process. A time interval at a process is the local duration in which the process "interacts", or in which some *local* property of interest is true. The semantics of the interval are application-dependent [8, 9, 11, 12, 15, 18]; application areas such as sensor networks, distributed debugging, deadlock characterization [16], predicate detection [3, 4, 5], checkpointing [7, 10], and industrial process control model such intervals.

The above state detection problem was formulated as the following problem DOOR for the Detection of Orthogonal Relations [1, 12].

Problem DOOR. Given a relation $r_{i,j}$ from $\Re$ for each pair of processes i and j, devise a distributed on-line algorithm to identify the intervals, if they exist, one from each process, such that each relation $r_{i,j}$ is satisfied by the (i,j) process pair.

A solution satisfying the set of relations $\{r_{i,j}(\forall i,j)\}$ identifies a global state of the system [6, 14]. We showed [3] that this problem generalizes the global predicate detection problem [4, 5], and further that the solution to this problem is not more expensive than existing solutions to global predicate detection.

Devising an efficient on-line algorithm to solve problem DOOR is a challenging problem because of the overhead of having to track the intervals at different processes. Three solutions have been proposed to this problem so far. A distributed on-line algorithm to solve this problem was outlined in [1]. This algorithm uses $O(n \cdot \min(np, 4mn))$ number of messages with a message size of $O(n)$, where n is the number of processes, m is the maximum number of messages sent by any process, and p is the maximum number of intervals at any process. Another distributed algorithm requiring fewer messages, but at the cost of somewhat larger messages, was given in [2]. This algorithm uses $O(\min(np, 4mn))$ number of messages with a message size of $O(n^2)$. For both the algorithms, the total space complexity across all the processes is $\min(4n^2p - 2np, 10n^2m)$, and the average time complexity at a process is $O(\min(np, 4mn))$. A centralized on-line algorithm run at a server P_0 was given in [3]. For this algorithm, M = maximum queue length at P_0, $p \geq M$ as all the intervals may not be sent to P_0. The performance of the algorithms is summarized in Table 1.

Summary of Results and Contributions. The algorithms in [1, 2, 3] to solve DOOR were presented without any formal discussion or analysis of the theoretical basis, and without any correctness proofs. This paper makes the following contributions.

1. To devise any efficient solution, this paper formulates specific conditions on the structure of the exact causal communication patterns to determine which

Table 1. Comparison of space, message and time complexities

Centralized algorithm	Avg. time complexity at P_0	Total number of messages	Space at P_0 (= total msg. space)	Avg. space at P_i, $i \in [1,n]$
Fine_Rel [3]	$O(n^2 M)$ or $O(\min(n^2 p, 4mn^2))$	$O(\min(np, 4mn))$	$O(\min((4n-2)np, 10n^2m))$	$O(n)$
Distributed Algorithms	**Average time complexity/ proc.**	**Total number of messages**	**Message size**	**Total space**
Algorithm [1]	$O(\min(np, 4mn))$	$O(n \cdot \min(np, 4mn))$	$O(n)$	$O(\min(2np(2n-1), 10n^2m))$
Algorithm [2]	$O(\min(np, 4mn))$	$O(\min(np, 4mn))$	$O(n^2)$	$O(\min(2np(2n-1), 10n^2m))$

of two intervals being examined from processes i and j may never satisfy $r_{i,j}$, and therefore that interval(s) must be deleted. This result is embodied as:
 - a basic principle that we prove in Theorem 1 – the main result, and
 - Lemma 4, a useful lemma derived from the above theorem, and used by the algorithms in [1, 2, 3], that can be used to efficiently manage the distributed data structures.

The on-line algorithms [1, 2, 3] to solve problem DOOR indirectly used Lemma 4, but did not explain the principle or indicate how it was derived. This paper derives and explains the critical principle (Theorem 1) from scratch. Any future algorithms to solve DOOR will also have to be based on this principle.

2. Global state observation [6] and predicate detection [4, 5] are fundamental problems. The result provides an understanding of interval-based global state observation and predicate detection, in terms of the causal communication structure in an execution [15].

3. The process of devising this principle (Theorem 1) which guarantees that at least one of any pair of intervals being examined at any time can be deleted (Lemma 4), gives a deeper insight into the nature of reasoning with the structure of causality in a distributed execution. Schwarz and Mattern have identified this as an important problem [19].

Section 2 reviews the background. Section 3 gives the theory used to determine which of two given intervals at different processes can never be part of a solution set, thus allowing at least one of them to be deleted. Section 4 gives concluding remarks.

2 System Model and Background

We assume an asynchronous distributed system in which n processes communicate by reliable message passing over logical FIFO channels [11, 18]. A poset event structure $(E, \prec)$, where $\prec$ is an irreflexive partial ordering representing the causality or the "happens before" relation [17] on the event set E, is used as the model for the execution. E is partitioned into local executions at each process. Each E_i is a linearly ordered set of events executed by process P_i. An event e executed by P_i is denoted e_i. The set of processes is denoted by N.

A *cut* C is a subset of E such that if $e_i \in C$ then $(\forall e'_i)\, e'_i \prec e_i \implies e'_i \in C$. A *consistent cut* is a downward-closed subset of E and denotes an execution prefix. For event e, there are two special consistent cuts $\downarrow e$ and $e \uparrow$, defined next.

Definition 1. *Cut* $\downarrow e$ *is the maximal set of events* $\{e' \mid e' \prec e\}$ *that happen before* e. *Cut* $e \uparrow$ *is the set of all events* $\{e' \mid e' \not\succeq e\} \bigcup \{e_i, i = 1, \ldots, |N| \mid e_i \succeq e \bigwedge (\forall e'_i \prec e_i, e'_i \not\succeq e)\}$ *up to and including the earliest events at each process for which* e *happens before the events.*

The system state after the events in a cut is a *global state* [6]; if the cut is consistent, the corresponding system state is a consistent global state. The durations

Table 2. Dependent relations for interactions between intervals [11]

Relation r	Expression for $r(X,Y)$
R1	$\forall x \in X \forall y \in Y, x \prec y$
R2	$\forall x \in X \exists y \in Y, x \prec y$
R3	$\exists x \in X \forall y \in Y, x \prec y$
R4	$\exists x \in X \exists y \in Y, x \prec y$
S1	$\exists x \in X \forall y \in Y, x \not\prec y \wedge y \not\prec x$
S2	$\exists x_1, x_2 \in X \exists y \in Y, x_1 \prec y \prec x_2$

Table 3. The 40 orthogonal relations in $\Re$ [11]. The upper part gives the 29 relations assuming dense time. The lower part gives 11 additional relations for nondense time.

Interaction Type	Relation $r(X,Y)$						Relation $r(Y,X)$					
	R1	R2	R3	R4	S1	S2	R1	R2	R3	R4	S1	S2
$IA(=IQ^{-1})$	1	1	1	1	0	0	0	0	0	0	0	0
$IB(=IR^{-1})$	0	1	1	1	0	0	0	0	0	0	0	0
$IC(=IV^{-1})$	0	0	1	1	1	0	0	0	0	0	0	0
$ID(=IX^{-1})$	0	0	1	1	1	1	0	1	0	1	0	0
$ID'(=IU^{-1})$	0	0	1	1	0	1	0	1	0	1	0	1
$IE(=IW^{-1})$	0	0	1	1	1	1	0	0	0	1	0	0
$IE'(=IT^{-1})$	0	0	1	1	0	1	0	0	0	1	0	1
$IF(=IS^{-1})$	0	1	1	1	0	1	0	0	0	1	0	1
$IG(=IG^{-1})$	0	0	0	0	1	0	0	0	0	0	1	0
$IH(=IK^{-1})$	0	0	0	1	1	0	0	0	0	0	1	0
$II(=IJ^{-1})$	0	1	0	1	0	0	0	0	0	0	1	0
$IL(=IO^{-1})$	0	0	0	1	1	1	0	1	0	1	0	0
$IL'(=IP^{-1})$	0	0	0	1	0	1	0	1	0	1	0	1
$IM(=IM^{-1})$	0	0	0	1	1	0	0	0	0	1	1	0
$IN(=IM'^{-1})$	0	0	0	1	1	1	0	0	0	1	0	0
$IN'(=IN'^{-1})$	0	0	0	1	0	1	0	0	0	1	0	1
$ID''(=(IUX)^{-1})$	0	0	1	1	0	1	0	1	0	1	0	0
$IE''(=(ITW)^{-1})$	0	0	1	1	0	1	0	0	0	1	0	0
$IL''(=(IOP)^{-1})$	0	0	0	1	0	1	0	1	0	1	0	0
$IM''(=(IMN)^{-1})$	0	0	0	1	0	0	0	0	0	1	1	0
$IN''(=(IMN')^{-1})$	0	0	0	1	0	1	0	0	0	1	0	0
$IMN''(=(IMN'')^{-1})$	0	0	0	1	0	0	0	0	0	1	0	0

of interest at each process are the durations during which the process interacts, or during which the local application-specific predicate is true. Such a duration, also termed as an *interval*, at process P_i is identified by the corresponding events within E_i. Each interval can be viewed as defining an event of higher granularity at that process, as far as the local predicate of interest is concerned. Such higher-level events, one from each process, can be used to identify a global state [8, 13]. Intervals are denoted by capitals such as X. An interval X at P_i is also denoted by X_i.

It has been shown that there are 29 or 40 possible mutually *orthogonal* ways in which any two durations can be related to each other, depending on whether the *dense* or the *nondense* time model is assumed [11]. Informally speaking, with dense time, $\forall x, y$ in interval A, $x \prec y \implies \exists z \in A \mid x \prec z \prec y$. These orthogonal interaction types were identified by first using the six relations given in the

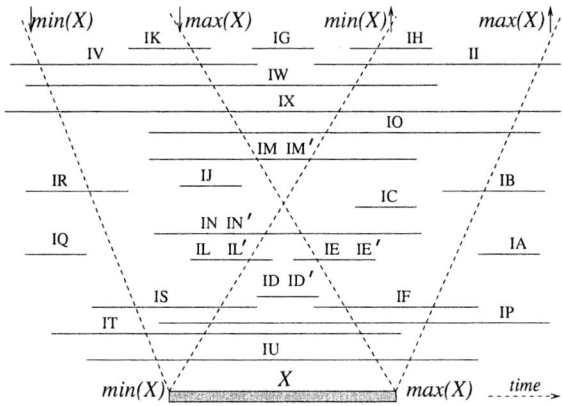

Fig. 1. Interaction types between intervals under the dense time model [11]

first two columns of Table 2. Relations R1 (strong precedence), R2 (partially strong precedence), R3 (partially weak precedence), R4 (weak precedence) define *causality conditions* whereas S1 and S2 define *coupling conditions*.

- (Dense time:) The 29 possible interaction types between a pair of intervals are given in the upper part of Table 3. The interaction types are specified using boolean vectors. The six relations R1-R4 and S1-S2 form a boolean vector of length 12, (six bits for $r(X,Y)$ and six bits for $r(Y,X)$). Of the 29 interactions, there are 13 pairs of inverses, while three are inverses of themselves. The interaction types are illustrated in Figure 1, where interval X is shown by a rectangle. Interval Y, indicated using horizontal lines, is in different positions relative to X. Each position of Y is labeled by an interaction type, IA through IX. The different types of interactions are identified by the various positions of Y relative to X. Five positions of Y have two labels each – the distinction between them is given in [11].
- (Nondense time:) The nondense time model which captures the reality that event sequences and real clocks are discrete permits 11 interaction types between a pair of intervals, defined in the lower part of Table 3, in addition to the 29 identified before. Of these, there are five pairs of inverses, while one is its own inverse. Illustrations are given in [11].

The set of 40 orthogonal relations is denoted as $\Re$.

Example specification of DOOR. Consider a system of three processes P_i, P_j, and P_k. The application wants to detect a global state in which the following relations are pairwise satisfied: (i) $IQ(X_i, Y_j)$ and $IA(Y_j, X_i)$, (ii) $IG(Y_j, Z_k)$ and $IG(Z_k, Y_j)$, and (iii) $IA(Z_k, X_i)$ and $IQ(X_i, Z_k)$.

Each of the 40 orthogonal relations in $\Re$ can be tested for using the bit-patterns for the dependent relations, as given in Table 3. The tests for the relations $R1 - R4$, $S1$, and $S2$ using vector timestamps are given in [1,2,3,12]. During an execution, the information about intervals at P_i is recorded in queue

Q_i. The intervals from the queues are examined pairwise across queues to check if the relation $r_{i,j}$ specified for P_i and P_j holds. In the algorithms in [1,2], the tests are collectively run in different distributed ways to solve **DOOR**, whereas in the algorithm in [3], they are run at a central server.

To understand the principle for designing these [1,2,3] and more efficient algorithms to process the queued intervals, we show our main result (Theorem 1) about when two given intervals may potentially satisfy a given interaction type we want to detect. This theorem in the form of Lemma 4 is used in practice by the algorithms [1,2,3] to solve **DOOR**.

3 The Elimination Conditions

Devising an efficient on-line algorithm to solve problem DOOR is a challenge because of the overhead of having to track the intervals at different processes. To devise any efficient solution, we formulate a basic principle that can be used to efficiently manage the distributed data structures. Specifically, we use the notion of a "prohibition" function [1,2,3] to show the main principle – Theorem 1 – and thereby Lemma 4 which is the condition for pruning of intervals from queues. We show that if the given relationship between a pair of processes does not hold for a pair of intervals being tested, then at least one of the intervals is deleted.

For any two intervals X and X' that occur at the same process, if $R1(X, X')$, then we say that X is a *predecessor* of X' and X' is a *successor* of X. We assume interval X occurs at P_i and interval Y occurs at P_j. Intuitively, for each $r_{i,j} \in \Re$, a *prohibition function* $\mathcal{H}(r_{i,j})$ is the set of all relations R such that if $R(X,Y)$ is true, then $r_{i,j}(X, Y')$ can never be true for some successor Y' of Y. $\mathcal{H}(r_{i,j})$ is the set of relations that prohibit $r_{i,j}$ from being true in the future.

Definition 2. *Prohibition function* $\mathcal{H} : \Re \to 2^\Re$ *is defined as* $\mathcal{H}(r_{i,j}) = \{R \in \Re \mid \text{if } R(X,Y) \text{ is true then } r_{i,j}(X,Y') \text{ is false for all } Y' \text{ that succeed } Y \}$.

Two relations R' and R'' in $\Re$ are related by the *allows* relation $\leadsto$ if the occurrence of $R'(X,Y)$ does not prohibit $R''(X,Y')$ for some successor Y' of Y.

Definition 3. *The "allows" relation* $\leadsto$ *is a relation on* $\Re \times \Re$ *such that* $R' \leadsto R''$ *if the following holds: if* $R'(X,Y)$ *is true then* $R''(X,Y')$ *can be true for some Y' that succeeds Y.*

Lemma 1. *If $R \in \mathcal{H}(r_{i,j})$ then $R \not\leadsto r_{i,j}$ else if $R \notin \mathcal{H}(r_{i,j})$ then $R \leadsto r_{i,j}$.*

Proof. If $R \in \mathcal{H}(r_{i,j})$, using Definition 2, it can be inferred that $r_{i,j}$ is false for all Y' that succeed Y. This does not satisfy Definition 3. Hence $R \not\leadsto r_{i,j}$. If $R \notin \mathcal{H}(r_{i,j})$, it follows that $r_{i,j}$ can be true for some Y' that succeeds Y. This satisfies Definition 3 and hence $R \leadsto r_{i,j}$. □

Given that $R'(A, B) \leadsto R''(A, B')$, where R' and R'' are orthogonal relations from $\Re$, the following lemma shows some relationships between interval pairs

A, B and A, B' in terms of the dependent set of causality relations $R1 - R4$. These relationships will be useful to show a critical relationship between R'^{-1} and R''^{-1} (Theorem 1) that allows efficient pruning of intervals on the queues in any algorithm to solve Problem **DOOR**.

Lemma 2. *If $R' \rightsquigarrow R''$, $R'(A, B)$ and $R''(A, B')$, where $R', R'' \in \Re$, then the statements in Table 5 are true.*

Proof. As $R' \rightsquigarrow R''$ and $R'(A, B)$ is true, we can safely assume that there can exist an interval B' that succeeds B and such that $R''(A, B')$ is true. Now consider axioms AL2, AL4, AL5 and AL6 given in Table 4. Applying the following transformations gives statements T1 to T4 of Table 5, respectively.

1. Substitute A, B, B' for X, Y, Z, respectively, in Table 4.
2. As B' succeeds B, hence substitute true for $R1(B, B')$, $R2(B, B')$, $R3(B, B')$, and $R4(B, B')$.

Consider axioms AL1, AL2, AL3 and AL4 given in Table 4. Applying the following transformations gives statements T5 to T8, of Table 5, respectively.

1. Substitute B, B', and A for X, Y, and Z, respectively in Table 4.
2. As B' succeeds B, hence substitute true for $R1(B, B')$, $R2(B, B')$, $R3(B, B')$, and $R4(B, B')$. □

We now show an important result between any two relations in $\Re$ that satisfy the "allows" relation, and the existence of the "allows" relation between their

Table 4. Axioms for the causality relations of Table 2 [11]. $\overline{R}$ stands for "R is $false$".

Axiom Label	$r_1(X,Y) \wedge r_2(Y,Z) \Longrightarrow r(X,Z)$
AL1	$R1(X,Y) \wedge R2(Y,Z) \Longrightarrow R2(X,Z)$
AL2	$R1(X,Y) \wedge R3(Y,Z) \Longrightarrow R1(X,Z)$
AL3	$R1(X,Y) \wedge R4(Y,Z) \Longrightarrow R2(X,Z)$
AL4	$R2(X,Y) \wedge R1(Y,Z) \Longrightarrow R1(X,Z)$
AL5	$R3(X,Y) \wedge R1(Y,Z) \Longrightarrow R3(X,Z)$
AL6	$R4(X,Y) \wedge R1(Y,Z) \Longrightarrow R3(X,Z)$
AL7	$R2(X,Y) \wedge R3(Y,Z) \Longrightarrow true$
AL8	$R2(X,Y) \wedge R4(Y,Z) \Longrightarrow true$
AL9	$R3(X,Y) \wedge R2(Y,Z) \Longrightarrow R4(X,Z)$
AL10	$R4(X,Y) \wedge R2(Y,Z) \Longrightarrow R4(X,Z)$
AL11	$R3(X,Y) \wedge R4(Y,Z) \Longrightarrow R4(X,Z)$
AL12	$R4(X,Y) \wedge R3(Y,Z) \Longrightarrow true$
AL13	$R1(X,Y) \Longrightarrow \overline{S1}(X,Y) \wedge \overline{S2}(X,Y) \wedge \overline{R4}(Y,X) \wedge \overline{S1}(Y,X) \wedge \overline{S2}(Y,X)$
AL14	$R2(X,Y) \Longrightarrow \overline{S1}(X,Y) \wedge \overline{R2}(Y,X)$
AL15	$R3(X,Y) \Longrightarrow \overline{R3}(Y,X) \wedge \overline{S1}(Y,X)$
AL16	$R4(X,Y) \Longrightarrow \overline{R1}(Y,X)$
AL17	$S1(X,Y) \Longrightarrow \overline{R2}(X,Y) \wedge \overline{R3}(Y,X) \wedge \overline{S2}(Y,X)$
AL18	$S2(X,Y) \Longrightarrow \overline{R1}(X,Y) \wedge \overline{R4}(X,Y) \wedge \overline{R1}(Y,X) \wedge \overline{R4}(Y,X) \wedge \overline{S1}(Y,X)$

Table 5. Given $R' \rightsquigarrow R''$, $R'(A,B)$ and $R''(A,B')$, for $R', R'' \in \Re$, statements between interval pairs A, B and A, B' using the dependent relations $R1 - R4$

Statement Label	Statements
T1	$R1(A,B) \Longrightarrow R1(A,B')$
T2	$R2(A,B) \Longrightarrow R1(A,B')$
T3	$R3(A,B) \Longrightarrow R3(A,B')$
T4	$R4(A,B) \Longrightarrow R3(A,B')$
T5	$R1(B',A) \Longrightarrow R1(B,A)$
T6	$R2(B',A) \Longrightarrow R2(B,A)$
T7	$R3(B',A) \Longrightarrow R1(B,A)$
T8	$R4(B',A) \Longrightarrow R2(B,A)$

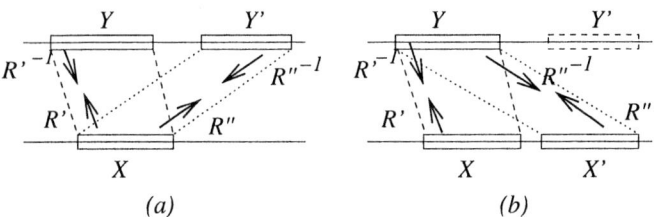

(a) $R'(X,Y)$, $R''(X,Y')$, and hence, R' allows R''

(b) From (a) we have $R'^{-1}(Y,X)$, $R''^{-1}(Y',X)$. But can $R''^{-1}(Y,X')$ hold? Theorem shows it cannot. Hence, R'^{-1} does not allow R''^{-1}

Fig. 2. Illustration of Theorem 1

respective inverses. Specifically, if R' allows R'' (and $R' \neq R''$), then Theorem 1 shows that R'^{-1} necessarily does not allow relation R''^{-1}. This theorem is illustrated in Figure 2. This theorem is used in deriving Lemma 4 which will be practically used in deriving solutions to problem DOOR, and to prove the correctness of such solutions.

Theorem 1. *For $R', R'' \in \Re$ and $R' \neq R''$, if $R' \rightsquigarrow R''$ then $R'^{-1} \not\rightsquigarrow R''^{-1}$*

Proof. We prove by contradiction. The assumption using which we show a contradiction is the following.

$$R'(X,Y) \text{ is true}, \; R'(X,Y) \rightsquigarrow R''(X,Y') \text{ and } R'^{-1}(Y,X) \rightsquigarrow R''^{-1}(Y,X') \tag{1}$$

As T1 to T8 must hold for both $R'(X,Y) \rightsquigarrow R''(X,Y')$ and $R'^{-1}(Y,X) \rightsquigarrow R''^{-1}(Y,X')$ we get two sets of constraints for intervals X, X', Y, and Y' in terms of the dependent causality relations $R1$ to $R4$.

Consider $R'(X,Y) \rightsquigarrow R''(X,Y')$. Instantiating A by X, B by Y, and B' by Y' in T1-T8, we have the following set of constraints that need to be satisfied.

C1: $R1(X,Y) \Rightarrow R1(X,Y')$
C2: $R2(X,Y) \Rightarrow R1(X,Y')$
C3: $R3(X,Y) \Rightarrow R3(X,Y')$
C4: $R4(X,Y) \Rightarrow R3(X,Y')$

C5: $R1(Y',X) \Rightarrow R1(Y,X)$
C6: $R2(Y',X) \Rightarrow R2(Y,X)$
C7: $R3(Y',X) \Rightarrow R1(Y,X)$
C8: $R4(Y',X) \Rightarrow R2(Y,X)$

Now consider $R'^{-1}(Y,X) \rightsquigarrow R''^{-1}(Y,X')$. Instantiating A by Y, B by X, and B' by X' in T1-T8, we have the following set of constraints that need to be satisfied.

C9: $R1(Y,X) \Rightarrow R1(Y,X')$
C10: $R2(Y,X) \Rightarrow R1(Y,X')$
C11: $R3(Y,X) \Rightarrow R3(Y,X')$
C12: $R4(Y,X) \Rightarrow R3(Y,X')$

C13: $R1(X',Y) \Rightarrow R1(X,Y)$
C14: $R2(X',Y) \Rightarrow R2(X,Y)$
C15: $R3(X',Y) \Rightarrow R1(X,Y)$
C16: $R4(X',Y) \Rightarrow R2(X,Y)$

From Equation 1, it can be seen that the interval pairs (Y',X) and (Y,X') both are related by the orthogonal relation R''^{-1}. Hence $r(Y',X) \Leftrightarrow r(Y,X')$, where r is any of the six dependent relations given in Table 2. Thus replacing $r(Y,X')$ by $r(Y',X)$ in C9 to C12, we have the following constraints.

C17: $R1(Y,X) \Rightarrow R1(Y',X)$
C18: $R2(Y,X) \Rightarrow R1(Y',X)$

C19: $R3(Y,X) \Rightarrow R3(Y',X)$
C20: $R4(Y,X) \Rightarrow R3(Y',X)$

From Equation 1, it can also be seen in a similar way that the interval pairs (X,Y') and (X',Y) both are related by the orthogonal relation R''. Hence $r(X,Y') \Leftrightarrow r(X',Y)$, where r is any of the six dependent relations given in Table 2. Thus replacing $r(X',Y)$ by $r(X,Y')$ in C13 to C16, we have the following constraints.

C21: $R1(X,Y') \Rightarrow R1(X,Y)$
C22: $R2(X,Y') \Rightarrow R2(X,Y)$

C23: $R3(X,Y') \Rightarrow R1(X,Y)$
C24: $R4(X,Y') \Rightarrow R2(X,Y)$

The two constraint sets (C1)-(C8) and (C17)-(C24) given above can be combined to obtain restrictions on the type of interactions (given in Table 3) that $R'(X,Y)$ can belong to. Combining constraints C1 to C4 with constraints C21 to C24 gives

$$R1(X,Y) \vee R2(X,Y) \vee R3(X,Y) \vee R4(X,Y) \Rightarrow R1(X,Y)$$

Note from the definitions in Table 2 that $R1(X,Y) \Rightarrow R2(X,Y) \wedge R3(X,Y) \wedge R4(X,Y)$. Thus,

$$\begin{aligned}R1(X,Y) \vee R2(X,Y) \vee R3(X,Y) \vee R4(X,Y) \Rightarrow \\ R1(X,Y) \wedge R2(X,Y) \wedge R3(X,Y) \wedge R4(X,Y)\end{aligned} \qquad (2)$$

The above implication implies that either relations $R1(X,Y)$, $R2(X,Y)$, $R3(X,Y)$, and $R4(X,Y)$ are all true or all false.

Using a similar approach, combining constraints C17 to C20 with constraints C5 to C8 gives

$$\begin{aligned}R1(Y,X) \vee R2(Y,X) \vee R3(Y,X) \vee R4(Y,X) \Rightarrow \\ R1(Y,X) \wedge R2(Y,X) \wedge R3(Y,X) \wedge R4(Y,X)\end{aligned} \qquad (3)$$

This means either relations $R1(Y,X)$, $R2(Y,X)$, $R3(Y,X)$, and $R4(Y,X)$, are all true or all false.

Implications (2) and (3) restrict the interaction type (given in Table 3) to which $R'(X,Y)$ can belong. We now examine all the restricted cases to which $R'(X,Y)$ can belong, i.e., when $R1(X,Y)$ to $R4(X,Y)$ are all true, and when $R1(X,Y)$ to $R4(X,Y)$ are all false, and show that $R'(X,Y)$ can not exist; which is a contradiction to Equation (1).

Case 1. $R1(X,Y)$, $R2(X,Y)$, $R3(X,Y)$, and $R4(X,Y)$ are all true.

From constraints C1 to C4, we get

$$R1(X,Y'),\ R2(X,Y'),\ R3(X,Y'),\ R4(X,Y') \text{ are true}. \qquad (4)$$

Using axioms AL13 to AL16 we get $R1(Y,X)$, $R2(Y,X)$, $R3(Y,X)$, $R4(Y,X)$, $S1(X,Y)$, $S2(X,Y)$, $S1(Y,X)$, $S2(Y,X)$ are all false. Now substituting X, Y' for X, Y in axioms AL13 to AL16, we get

$$R1(Y',X),\ R2(Y',X),\ R3(Y',X),\ R4(Y',X),\ S1(X,Y'),\ S2(X,Y'),$$
$$S1(Y',X),\ S2(Y',X) \text{ are false}. \qquad (5)$$

Using Table 3, the only possible combination by which to instantiate R' and R'' so that they satisfy Equations (4) and (5) is IA. Thus, we have $R'(X,Y) = R''(X,Y') = IA$. As $R' \neq R''$ by the theorem statement, this case cannot exist.

Case 2. $R1(X,Y)$, $R2(X,Y)$, $R3(X,Y)$ and $R4(X,Y)$ are all false.

This case has two subcases.

1. $R1(Y,X)$, $R2(Y,X)$, $R3(Y,X)$, and $R4(Y,X)$ are all true. From constraints C17 to C20, we get

$$R1(Y',X),\ R2(Y',X),\ R3(Y',X),\ R4(Y',X) \text{ are true}. \qquad (6)$$

Substituting Y, X for X, Y in axiom AL13 we get $S1(X,Y)$, $S2(X,Y)$, $S1(Y,X)$, $S2(Y,X)$, are all false. Now substituting Y', X for X, Y in axioms AL13 to AL16, we get

$$R1(X,Y'),\ R2(X,Y'),\ R3(X,Y'),\ R4(X,Y'),\ S1(X,Y'),\ S2(X,Y'),$$
$$S1(Y',X),\ S2(Y',X) \text{ are false}. \qquad (7)$$

Using Table 3, the only possible combination by which to instantiate R' and R'' so that they satisfy Equations (6) and (7) is IQ. Thus, we have $R'(X,Y) = R''(X,Y') = IQ$. As $R' \neq R''$ by the theorem statement, this case cannot exist.

2. $R1(Y,X)$, $R2(Y,X)$, $R3(Y,X)$, and $R4(Y,X)$ are all false. From constraints C5 to C8, we get

$$R1(Y',X),\ R2(Y',X),\ R3(Y',X),\ R4(Y',X) \text{ are false}. \qquad (8)$$

Table 6. $\mathcal{H}(r_{i,j})$ for the 40 independent relations in $\Re$. The upper part gives function $\mathcal{H}$ for dense time. The lower part gives the function $\mathcal{H}$ for the 11 additional relations for non-dense time.

Interaction Type $r_{i,j}$	$\mathcal{H}(r_{i,j})$	$\mathcal{H}(r_{j,i})$
$IA\ (=IQ^{-1})$	ϕ	$\Re - \{IQ\}$
$IB\ (=IR^{-1})$	$\{IA, IB, IF, II, IP, IO, IU, IX, IUX, IOP\}$	$\Re - \{IQ\}$
$IC\ (=IV^{-1})$	$\{IA, IB, IF, II, IP, IO, IU, IX, IUX, IOP\}$	$\Re - \{IQ\}$
$ID\ (=IX^{-1})$	$\Re - \{IQ, IS, IR, IJ, IL, IL', IL'', ID, ID', ID''\}$	$\Re - \{IQ\}$
$ID'\ (=IU^{-1})$	$\Re - \{IQ, IS, IR, IJ, IL, IL', IL'', ID, ID', ID''\}$	$\Re - \{IQ\}$
$IE\ (=IW^{-1})$	$\Re - \{IQ, IS, IR, IJ, IL, IL', IL'', ID, ID', ID''\}$	$\Re - \{IQ\}$
$IE'\ (=IT^{-1})$	$\Re - \{IQ, IS, IR, IJ, IL, IL', IL'', ID, ID', ID''\}$	$\Re - \{IQ\}$
$IF\ (=IS^{-1})$	$\Re - \{IQ, IS, IR, IJ, IL, IL', IL'', ID, ID', ID''\}$	$\Re - \{IQ\}$
$IG\ (=IG^{-1})$	$\Re - \{IQ, IR, IJ, IV, IK, IG\}$	$\Re - \{IQ, IR, IJ, IV, IK, IG\}$
$IH\ (=IK^{-1})$	$\Re - \{IQ, IR, IJ, IV, IK, IG\}$	$\Re - \{IQ, IR, IJ\}$
$II\ (=IJ^{-1})$	$\Re - \{IQ, IR, IJ, IV, IK, IG\}$	$\Re - \{IQ, IR, IJ\}$
$IL\ (=IO^{-1})$	$\Re - \{IQ, IR, IJ\}$	$\Re - \{IQ, IR, IJ\}$
$IL'\ (=IP^{-1})$	$\Re - \{IQ, IR, IJ\}$	$\Re - \{IQ, IR, IJ\}$
$IM\ (=IM^{-1})$	$\Re - \{IQ, IR, IJ\}$	$\Re - \{IQ, IR, IJ\}$
$IN\ (=IM'^{-1})$	$\Re - \{IQ, IR, IJ\}$	$\Re - \{IQ, IR, IJ\}$
$IN'\ (=IN'^{-1})$	$\Re - \{IQ, IR, IJ\}$	$\Re - \{IQ, IR, IJ\}$
$ID''\ (=(IUX)^{-1})$	$\Re - \{IQ, IS, IR, IJ, IL, IL', IL'', ID, ID', ID''\}$	$\Re - \{IQ\}$
$IE''\ (=(ITW)^{-1})$	$\Re - \{IQ, IS, IR, IJ, IL, IL', IL'', ID, ID', ID''\}$	$\Re - \{IQ\}$
$IL''\ (=(IOP)^{-1})$	$\Re - \{IQ, IR, IJ\}$	$\Re - \{IQ, IR, IJ\}$
$IM''\ (=(IMN)^{-1})$	$\Re - \{IQ, IR, IJ\}$	$\Re - \{IQ, IR, IJ\}$
$IN''\ (=(IMN')^{-1})$	$\Re - \{IQ, IR, IJ\}$	$\Re - \{IQ, IR, IJ\}$
$IMN''\ (=(IMN'')^{-1})$	$\Re - \{IQ, IR, IJ\}$	$\Re - \{IQ, IR, IJ\}$

Now substituting Y', X for X, Y in axioms AL13 to AL16, we get

$$R1(X, Y'), R2(X, Y'), R3(X, Y'), R4(X, Y') \text{ are false}. \qquad (9)$$

Using Table 3, the only possible combination by which to instantiate R' and R'' so that they satisfy Equations (8)-(9) is IG. Thus, we have $R'(X, Y) = R''(X, Y') = IG$. As $R' \neq R''$ by the theorem statement, this case cannot exist.

Hence there cannot exist a case where $R'(X, Y) \rightsquigarrow R''(X, Y')$ and $R'^{-1}(Y, X) \rightsquigarrow R''^{-1}(Y', X)$. This contradicts the assumption in Equation 1, proving the theorem. □

Example. $IC \rightsquigarrow IB \Rightarrow IV(=IC^{-1}) \not\rightsquigarrow IR(=IB^{-1})$, which is indeed *true*. Note that $R' \neq R''$ in the statement of Theorem 1 is necessary; otherwise $R' \rightsquigarrow R'$ leads to $R'^{-1} \not\rightsquigarrow R'^{-1}$ from the theorem, a contradiction.

Table 6 gives $S(r_{i,j})$ for each of the 40 interaction types in $\Re$. The table is constructed by analyzing each interaction pair in $\Re$. The following two lemmas are necessary to show the correctness of the algorithm in [1, 2, 3] and of any other algorithm to solve problem DOOR.

Lemma 3. *If the relationship $R(X, Y)$ between intervals X and Y (belonging to process P_i and P_j, resp.) is contained in the set $\mathcal{H}(r_{i,j})$, and $r_{i,j} \neq R$, then interval X can be removed from the queue Q_i.*

Proof. From the definition of $\mathcal{H}(r_{i,j})$, we get that $r_{i,j}(X, Y')$ cannot exist, where Y' is any successor interval of Y. Further, as $r_{i,j} \neq R$, we have that interval X can never be a part of the solution and can be deleted from the queue. □

The following final result, although simple in form, is based on the crucial Theorem 1 and shows that both $R \notin \mathcal{H}(r_{i,j})$ and $R^{-1} \notin \mathcal{H}(r_{j,i})$ cannot hold when $R \neq r_{i,j}$. Hence, by Lemma 3, if $R(X_i, Y_j) \neq r_{i,j}$ then at least one of the intervals X_i and Y_j being tested must be deleted.

Lemma 4. *If the relationship between a pair of intervals X and Y (belonging to processes P_i and P_j respectively) is not equal to $r_{i,j}$, then interval X or interval Y is removed from its queue Q_i or Q_j, respectively.*

Proof. We use contradiction. Assume relation $R(X, Y)$ ($\neq r_{i,j}(X, Y)$) is true for intervals X and Y. From Lemma 3, the only time neither X nor Y will be deleted is when $R \notin \mathcal{H}(r_{i,j})$ and $R^{-1} \notin \mathcal{H}(r_{j,i})$. From Lemma 1, it can be inferred that $R \leadsto r_{i,j}$ and $R^{-1} \leadsto r_{j,i}$. As $r_{i,j}^{-1} = r_{j,i}$, we get $R \leadsto r_{i,j}$ and $R^{-1} \leadsto r_{i,j}^{-1}$. This is a contradiction as by Theorem 1, $R \leadsto r_{i,j} \Rightarrow R^{-1} \not\leadsto r_{i,j}^{-1}$. Hence $R \in \mathcal{H}(r_{i,j})$ or $R^{-1} \in \mathcal{H}(r_{j,i})$, and thus at least one of the intervals will be deleted. □

Observe with reference to Table 6 that it is possible that both intervals being compared need to be deleted, e.g., when $r_{i,j} = IC$ and $R(X, Y) = IU$.

Significance of Theorem 1 and Lemma 4. Lemma 4 embodies a principle that underlies all solutions to problem DOOR. The algorithms given in [1, 2] use this result of Lemma 4 to efficiently manage and prune the local interval queues to solve problem DOOR in a distributed manner. Essentially, they examine the intervals in the queues, a pair of intervals from different processes, at a time. Lemma 4 guarantees that in each such test, at least one or both intervals being examined are deleted, unless $r_{i,j}(X_i, Y_j)$ is satisfied by that pair of intervals X_i and Y_j. The algorithms differ in the manner in which they construct the queues, and in how they process the intervals and the queues. The algorithm in [3] also relies on this result of Lemma 4 to process the interval information at a central server P_0 in an on-line manner. More efficient solutions to problem DOOR that may arise in the future will also have to use these results.

4 Conclusions

Causality-based pairwise temporal interactions between intervals in a distributed execution provide a valuable way to specify and model synchronization conditions and information interchange. This paper examined the underlying theory to solve the problem (problem DOOR) of how to devise algorithms to identify a set of intervals, one from each process, such that a given set of pairwise temporal interactions, one for each process pair, holds for the set of intervals identified. Devising an efficient on-line algorithm to solve problem DOOR is a challenge because of the overhead of having to track the intervals at different processes. For any two intervals being examined from processes P_i and P_j, this paper formulated and proved the underlying principle which identifies which (or both) of the intervals can be safely deleted if the intervals do not satisfy $r_{i,j}$. This principle can be used by any algorithm, such as those in [1, 2, 3] or any newer algorithms, to efficiently manage the local interval queues to solve problem DOOR.

Problem DOOR is important because it generalizes the global state observation and the predicate detection problems; further, solutions to problem DOOR which provide a much richer palette of information about the causality structure in the application execution (see [3]), cost about the same as the solutions to traditional forms of global predicate detection. The process of formulating the underlying principle of determining which intervals can be discarded as never forming a part of a solution that satisfies a specification of DOOR, also gave a deeper insight into the structure of causality in a distributed execution, and the global state observation and predicate detection problems.

References

1. P. Chandra, A.D. Kshemkalyani, Detection of orthogonal interval relations. Proc. 9th International High Performance Computing Conference (HiPC), LNCS 2552, Springer-Verlag, 323-333, December 2002.
2. P. Chandra, A.D. Kshemkalyani, Global state detection based on peer-to-peer interactions. Proc. IFIP International Conference on Embedded and Ubiquitous Computing (EUC), LNCS, Springer, Dec. 2005.
3. P. Chandra, A.D. Kshemkalyani, Causality-based predicate detection across space and time. IEEE Transactions on Computers, 54(11): 1438-1453, November 2005.
4. B. Charron-Bost, C. Delporte-Gallet, H. Fauconnier, Local and temporal predicates in distributed systems. ACM TOPLAS, 17(1): 157-179, 1995.
5. R. Cooper, K. Marzullo, Consistent detection of global predicates. Proc. ACM/ONR Workshop on Parallel and Distributed Debugging, 163-173, May 1991.
6. K.M. Chandy, L. Lamport, Distributed snapshots: Determining global states of distributed systems. ACM Transactions on Computer Systems, 3(1): 63-75, 1985.
7. E.N. Elnozahy, L. Alvisi, Y.-M. Wang, D.B. Johnson, A survey of rollback-recovery protocols in message-passing systems. ACM Comput. Surv., 34(3): 375-408, 2002.
8. J.M. Helary, A. Mostefaoui, M. Raynal, Virtual precedence in asynchronous systems: Concept and applications. Proc. WDAG, 170-184, LNCS 1320, Springer, 1997.
9. J.M. Helary, A. Mostefaoui, M. Raynal, Interval consistency of asynchronous distributed computations. J. Computer and System Sciences, 64, 329-349, 2002.
10. R. Koo, S. Toueg, Checkpointing and rollback-recovery for distributed systems. IEEE Trans. Software Eng. 13(1): 23-31, 1987.
11. A.D. Kshemkalyani, Temporal interactions of intervals in distributed systems. Journal of Computer and System Sciences, 52(2): 287-298, April 1996.
12. A.D. Kshemkalyani, A fine-grained modality classification for global predicates. IEEE Transactions on Parallel and Distributed Systems, 14(8): 807-816, Aug. 2003.
13. A.D. Kshemkalyani, A framework for viewing atomic events in distributed computations. Theoretical Computer Science, 196(1-2), 45-70, April 1998.
14. A.D. Kshemkalyani, M. Raynal, M. Singhal, An introduction to snapshot algorithms in distributed computing. Distributed Systems Engineering Journal, 2(4): 224-233, 1995.

15. A.D. Kshemkalyani, M. Singhal, Communication patterns in distributed computations. Journal of Parallel and Distributed Computing, 62(6): 1104-1119, June 2002.
16. A. D. Kshemkalyani, M. Singhal, On characterization and correctness of distributed deadlock detection. Journal of Parallel and Distributed Computing, 22(1): 44-59, July 1994.
17. L. Lamport, Time, clocks, and the ordering of events in a distributed system. Communications of the ACM, 558-565, 21(7), July 1978.
18. L. Lamport, On interprocess communication, Part I: Basic formalism; Part II: Algorithms. Distributed Computing, 1:77-85 and 1:86-101, 1986.
19. R. Schwarz, F. Mattern, Detecting causal relationships in distributed computations: In search of the holy grail. Distributed Computing, 7:149-174, 1994.

A Two-Phase Scheduling Algorithm for Efficient Collective Communications of MPICH-G2

Junghee Lee[1,2] and Dongsoo Han[1,*]

[1] Information and Communications University,
119 Munjiro, Yuseong-Gu, Daejeon, Korea
{lake, dshan}@icu.ac.kr
[2] Electronics and Telecommunications Research Institute,
161 Gajeong-dong, Yuseong-Gu, Daejeon, Korea
{lake@etri.re.kr}

Abstract. In this paper, we propose a packet-level parallel data transfer and a Two-Phase Scheduling(TPS) algorithm for collective communication primitives in MPICH-G2. The algorithms are characterized by two unique features: 1) a concurrent data transfer of packets from a source node to multiple destination nodes and 2) a scheduling of enhancing the performance of collective communications by early identification of bottleneck incurring nodes. The proposed technique is implemented and the performance improvement is measured. According to the performance evaluation, the proposed method has achieved about 20% performance improvement against conventional block data transfer methods when a binomial tree is used for the communication in LAN. In TPS algorithm, the distribution of messages to bottleneck incurring nodes is delayed to minimize the affection of the node to the total performance. Using TPS algorithm on WAN, significant performance improvement has also been achieved for various data sizes and number of nodes.

1 Introduction

Grids environment provides an enormous number of storage and computing resources connected to heterogeneous wide-area networks (WANs) or local-area networks (LANs). In Grids, computing resources constituting the GRID may have various capabilities and computing powers. In order to develop a communication schedule algorithm that enables effective access to such heterogeneous resources, both network bandwidth and latency should be considered as primary design factors. When we consider that the status of network frequently changes in WAN environment, the network status change should be considered also in improving the communication performance in the WAN environment [1].

Numerous researches have been done for the efficient scheduling of communications among computing resources. Heuristic algorithms such as FEF[1], ECEF[1], TTCC[2], and HLOT[3] were proposed for the fast construction of communication trees. However, these algorithms use only the latency factor for the construction of communication trees. Moreover, in the current MPICH-G2, a receiver node sends data of multiple

---

[*] Corresponding author.

packets to other nodes, only after they receive all packets from a sender node. In other words, in case of multi-chained data transmission, A→B→C, node B does not start sending data to node C, until it completes receiving the entire data from node A.

In this paper, we suggest two ideas for the frequently used collective communication primitive, MPI_Bcast of MPICH -G2, in order to overcome above two problems. First, we propose a packet-level parallel data transfer mechanism for LAN and WAN environments and a two-phase scheduling algorithm for WAN environment. In the packet-level parallel data transfer technique, each node sends individual packet to destination nodes on receiving a packet from a source node, and it simultaneously distributes the data to multiple destination nodes. The objective of this method is to improve the performance of the current data transfer method of the collective communication primitive of MPICH-G2 in Grids environment.

Second, we propose a two-phase scheduling algorithm(TPS) which uses transmission time for a tree construction metric. The algorithm improves the total performance by placing nodes, which are prone to bottleneck, to leaf nodes in a communication tree. The objective of this algorithm is to avoid a bottleneck caused by nodes with long transmission time and then to achieve performance improvement of the collective communication primitive.

In this paper, the performances of our methods are measured and the results are compared with the conventional methods. According to the performance evaluation for nodes connected to LAN, the packet-level parallel data transfer method has achieved about 20 % performance improvement against conventional data transfer methods. A binomial tree is used for the scheduling of the communication. According to the simulation of communications for nodes connected to WAN, the scheduling algorithm which uses both packet-level parallel data transfer and TPS algorithm has achieved overall performance improvement for various data sizes and number of nodes, against algorithms such as ECEF, HLOT, and flat tree.

This paper is organized as follows. In section 2 we describe the current status of MPICH-G2 and related work. Our proposed methods, packet-level parallel data transfer are explained in section 3 and our two-phase scheduling algorithm is explained in section 4, respectively. Then, we show the experimental results in section 5, and finally, we draw conclusion and describe future work in section 6.

2 Related Work

2.1 A Grid-Enabled MPI, MPICH-G2

Firstly, the current version of collective primitives of MPICH-G2 uses two-layered network topology-aware scheduling to reduce communication time, which just divides communication nodes into two divisions: nodes connected to LAN and nodes connected to WAN[4]. However, since it doesn't consider detailed network information upon constructing the communication tree, it may cause a relatively long communication time in WAN environment, which is characterized as a changeable network situations and long latency. Therefore, the schedule based on accurate network information has more opportunity in improving the performance of communication of MPICH-G2. Second, MPICH-G2 entrusts the control of data transmission to TCP/IP stack of the operating system, i.e., the current primitives of MPICH-G2 send data to the buffer of

TCP/IP stack and wait completion of operations. MPICH-G2 doesn't intervene in the transfer and wait until the sending is finished.

As a solution to fast data transmission of MPICH-G2, GridFTP[4] is provided. GridFTP in MPICH-G2 provides interfaces of opening multiple sockets between two endpoints, partitioning a large message into small packets, sending those packets in parallel using multiple sockets, and, lastly, re-assembling the large message. However, it is used not for collective operations but for collaborative environments. The facility provides a means of handling only two endpoints that have large blocks of data to send/receive, and it demands high-latency and high-bandwidth for efficient communications since the two endpoints transfer enormous data through multiple sockets. Moreover, some codes must be instrumented into MPI programs for the facility to be used in communicating programs. For example, user should set an attribute, assign two endpoints, and set the parameters such as the number of sockets and TCP buffer size.

2.2 Heuristic Algorithms

Many heuristic algorithms have been designed for collective operations of MPI(Message-Passing Interface): FEF(Fastest Edge First)[1], ECEF(Earliest Edge First)[1], TTCC(Two-Tree Collective Communication)[2], etc. FEF selects a node with the smallest communication cost from a root, and ECEF chooses the node with the minimum sum of communication cost and ready time of its sender[1]. TTCC transfers data with two communication trees made by ECEF algorithm[1]. HLOT is for WAN with comparatively very large latency, and after comparing its weight of edge with one of flat tree it decides if it uses a selected edge, or not. These algorithms intend to improve performance by using the schedule that considers network information. However, SPOC and FNF aren't well suited for Grid environments, and FEF and ECEF don't consider bandwidth or message size. When a parameter of algorithm is latency, the algorithms are suited for small messages. For a long message, bandwidth is also an important factor of data transmission. Moreover, these heuristic algorithms contain overheads for scheduling such as the creation cost of a tree, memory cost, managing cost for network information, etc. For example, TTCC can increase network loads since it creates two communication trees and sends along the two paths. It also assumes that TCP/IP can select one node out of two nodes, concurrently sending data. These heuristic algorithms are limited to scheduling only with network information. They don't consider the change of basic communication method.

3 Packet-Level Parallel Data Transfer

In this section, we propose packet-level data transfer and one-to-many communication using network information in MPICH-G2. This method, which uses these two ways, is named packet-level parallel data transfer.

3.1 Packet-Level Data Transfer

The current implementation of MPI_Bcast in MPICH-G2 is as follows: Each node doesn't start data transfer until receiving the entire data. We call this kind of data transfer blocking data transfer. To improve the performance of the current MPI_Bcast primitive, we propose a packet-level data transfer technique and it works as follows: In this technique, a node starts to send data to the next node immediately after receiving a packet unit from the source node. As a consequence, a node may send packets many times to the destination node while it receives the entire data from a source node. The technique is also used in cut-through routing[5].

Fig. 1 contrasts packet-level data transfer to blocking data transfer technique. Data is partitioned into 3 packets, and the path is simply represented with a linear tree with 4 nodes. The progress of data transfer is illustrated in Fig. 1. The packet-level data transfer technique finishes the communication within Time 4, whereas blocking method completes the communication within Time 6. In the packet-level data transfer, remarkable performance enhancement will be gained when the height of tree is high and the size of data is large. In this transfer, the size of packet should be carefully decided because prevailing of small-sized packets may cause network congestion. To prevent the network congestion, we set data size to be sent at one time to MTU(maximum transfer unit) of IP layer. Then, it is possible to reduce the completion time for the broadcast operation of MPICH-G2 without incurring any significant overhead.

	packet-level data transfer			blocking data transfer		
	Node 0	Node 1	Node 2	Node 0	Node 1	Node 2
Time 0	xyz			xyz		
Time 1		x			x	
Time 2		xy	x		xy	
Time 3		xyz	xy		xyz	
Time 4			xyz			x
Time 5						xy
Time 6						xyz

Fig. 1. Comparison packet-level data transfer with blocking data transfer

3.2 Parallel Data Transfer

If the capacity of the sender to transmit data could be sufficient enough, we can improve the performance of transmission with one-to-many data transfer. One-to-many data transfer means that one sender can simultaneously transfer data to multiple receivers. With this method, the increase of receivers can reduce available bandwidth of sender. Therefore, the optimal number of receivers should be determined considering both bandwidth and latency.

For instance, we suppose that data consist of 4 packets(w, x, y and z), each node has sufficient available bandwidth and a binomial tree with 8 nodes is used as a communication tree. The process of blocking data transfer is described in Fig. 2, and one of packet-level parallel data transfer illustrated in Fig. 3. Each node in Fig. 2 begins to transfer data only after the entire data, w, x, y and z are received from a source node. However, each one in Fig. 2 starts sending to destination nodes immediately after receiving packets, and transfers a packet simultaneously. At the Time 0, node 0 in Fig. 2 sends data only to node 4, and can forward data after Time 4, whereas, node 0 of Fig. 3 can send concurrently to node 4, 2, and 1, and node 4 can forward a packet immediately after receiving a packet from node 0. The data is completed in Time 6 as shown in Fig. 3. However, a broadcast operation in time depends on the depth and the width of the communication tree. When only the packet-level data transfer is applied, the tree with the large width will show worse performance than that with smaller width. However, when the available bandwidth is enough large, the better performance can be achieved using large width than small one of communication tree.

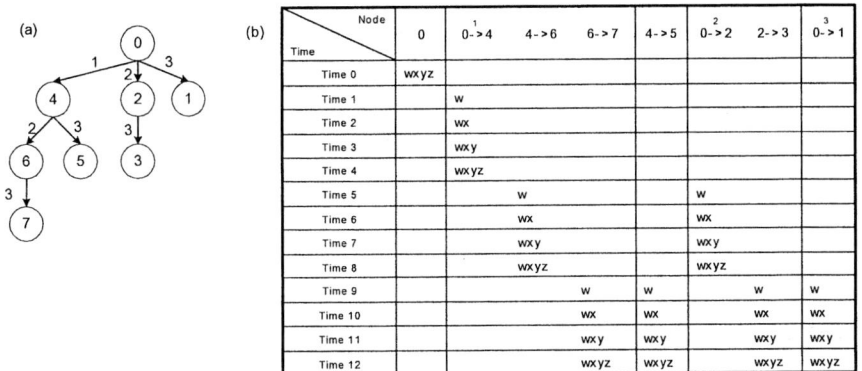

Fig. 2. Example of blocking data transfer: (a) communication tree (b) time table

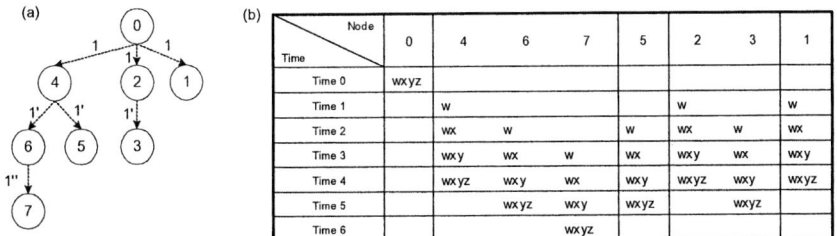

Fig. 3. Example of packet-level data transfer: (a) communication tree (b) time table

4 Proposed Algorithm

Algorithms of collective communications of MPI typically construct trees for the generation of a scheduling. However, finding an optimal tree for such an algorithm is known to be NP-hard problem. Many heuristic algorithms are proposed for collective communications of MPI. For example, flat tree is well suited for wide area networks, and binomial tree is almost optimal in local area networks [6]. Thus current implementation of MPI_Bcast in MPICH-G2 uses these two trees. Since LAN generally guarantees high speed and binomial tree works well in LAN, we focus on WAN environment in which it has relatively high latency and the status of network frequently changes. In this section, we develop a TPS tree algorithm for such WAN environment.

As noted earlier, our algorithm considers both latency and bandwidth between two nodes. We use completion time between two nodes as a target metric to be optimized. Completion time between two nodes is calculated with the following well-known equation, $completiontime_{i,j} = latency_{i,j} + \frac{messagesize}{bandwidth_{i,j}}$, and completion time of MPI_Bcast becomes the maximum time in the sums of completion time from root to every leaf node along a path. Nodes with long transmission are prone to incur bottlenecks of entire communication. If these nodes are placed in the middle of a tree, descendant nodes of these nodes will suffer from long communication delay. TPS tree algorithm identifies nodes with long transmission time, and tries to place such nodes to the leaves of a communication tree.

Fig. 4 shows TPS tree algorithm. Numbers on the edge of the tree denotes completion time. The algorithm sorts the values of $edge(j,i)$ for individual node i in V, where node i has not receive a message yet and node j has the message. Once all the values of $edge(j,i)$ are computed and sorted, node i can figure out which node can send the message to i in shortest completion time. Then, the algorithm selects number of k nodes with longest completion time. These nodes might incur bottlenecks. There are several ways to decide the number k, but we do not delve into details in this paper. Our method chooses nodes whose completion time is above the average of minimum completion time. At first, sender set A contains only a root node. Tree construction starts from the root. The algorithm finds fastest message arriving node j from node x

```
Two-Phase Scheduling Algorithm

Input:
V : set of nodes joining communication
B : set of nodes with long completion time
A : set of senders
root : root node

Output:
E := set of result edge

A := {root}
B := {}

Tree construction steps:
for i in V
      sort communication time from j to i where j in V and i <> j
B := k nodes with worst minimum time except root
//The first phase
while A <> V-B
      find j to which minimum edge from x where x in A, j in V-B-A, and x<>j
      add edge(x,j) to E
      add x to A
      x := j
//The second phase
for i in B
      find j minimizing weight of edge(j,i) + sum of weight from root to j in V-B
      add edge(j,i) to E
```

Fig. 4. Two-Phase Scheduling Algorithm

in A. Where node j is neither in A nor in B, and B contains number of k nodes. The chosen node j is added to sender set A and will receive data from its sender node. After finishing the first tree construction phase except k nodes, the insertion of k nodes is conducted at the second phase. TPS attaches the rest nodes in B to the tree so that the constructed tree achieves minimum completion time from root to the nodes in B. Through above two phases approach, we can prevent nodes with long completion time being placed in the middle of the tree. That is because our algorithm is named TPS algorithm. Time complexity of TPS is $O(N^2 \log N)$, where N is the number of nodes.

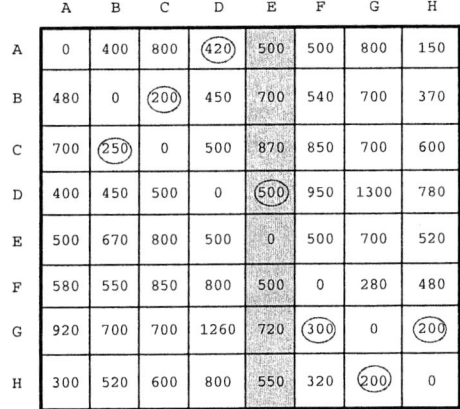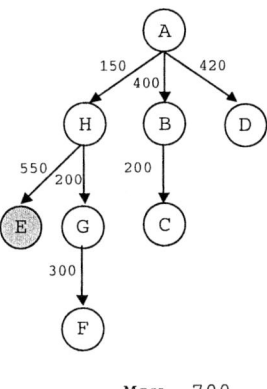

Fig. 5. Example of TPS

Fig. 5 shows an example of applying TPS algorithm to a tree. The completion time is used for the metric of tree construction. The completion time of every pair of nodes in the tree is computed and registered in a matrix. The values in red circle denote a pair with shortest completion time in each column. Then TPS finds the largest element among the values in red circle. In this example, node E has largest minimum completion time, 500. Note that, node D needs not to be considered in this case because it is already contained in the tree. In other words, node A and node D is already connected with each other when we consider node E. If we set k to 1, TPS constructs a tree with N- k nodes, i.e., 7 nodes using ECEF method. Then H, G, F, B, C, and D are picked in sequence, and lastly, TPS decides a node where it has to attach node E. Obviously, completion time of A-H-E is a minimum among other choices, so TPS attach node E to node H. As a result, the completion time of this broadcast becomes 700 ms. We contrast our tree algorithm to other algorithms in terms of environment, metric, and time complexity in Table 1.

Now, we analyze our algorithm via LogGP model[7]. LogGP model is suited for both short and long messages, whereas LogP model[8] is suited for a short message. LogGP model uses five parameters: latency, overhead, gap, gap per byte for long messages, and the number of processors. Since gap per byte for long messages,

Table 1. Comparison of tree algorithms

Tree	Environment	Metric	Time complexity
SPOC	LAN	Message initiation cost	$O(N\log N)$
FNF	LAN	Message initiation cost	$O(N^2)$
FEF	LAN/WAN	Communication time	$O(N^2 \log N)$
ECEF	LAN/WAN	Ready time$_i$ + Communication time$_{i,j}$	$O(N^2 \log N)$
Look-ahead	LAN/WAN	Ready time$_i$ + Communication time$_{i,j}$ + Look-ahead value$_i$	$O(N^3)$
TTCC	LAN/WAN	Ready time$_i$ + Communication time$_{i,j}$	$O(N^2 \log N)$
HLOT	LAN/WAN	Latency$_{i,j}$	$O(N^2 \log N)$
TPS	WAN	Completion time$_{ij}$	$O(N^2 \log N)$

G, is defined as the time per byte for a long message, it can be expressed by using bandwidth, $G = 1/bandwidth$. Then completion time of sending message with length k from process i to process j can be calculated as $o_s + \dfrac{k-1}{bandwidth} + L_{ij} + o_r$, where o_s is overhead of receiver, and L_{ij} is latency from i to j.

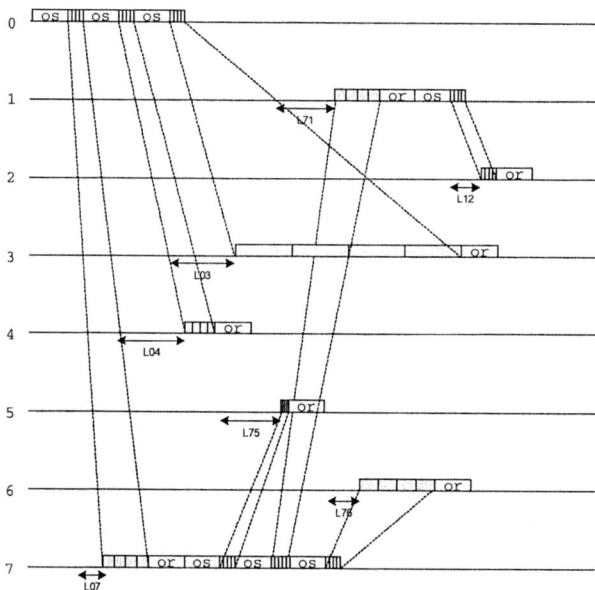

Fig. 6. Time diagram of Fig. 5

The completion time of broadcast is computed by equation, $completion\_time_B = Max\{completion\_time_l\}$, where l is the l-th leaf node of tree, and $completion\_time_l = \sum_{i=0}^{depth_i - 1} completion\_time_{st}$, where $depth_i$ denotes the depth of i-th leaf node, and *edge(s,t)* is a part of the path from root to *i*-th leaf node of tree. Completion_time$_{st}$ is computed by equation, $completion\_time_{st} = o_s + \frac{k-1}{bw_{st}} + L_{st} + o_r$, where bw_{st} is bandwidth from node *s* to *t*.

Fig. 6 depicts a timing diagram of Fig. 5 using LogGP model. The values of o_s and o_r are set with arbitrary numbers. Though the results may be changed when these values are changed, the pattern or appearances of the diagram will remain the same.

5 Evaluation

In this section, we present achieved performance enhancement on LAN through measurement, and expected performance enhancement on WAN through simulation. As explained earlier, communication performance on WAN is a dominant factor in deciding the performance of collective communications on WAN and LAN. In LAN, we use a binomial tree, which is known to be good for LAN. In WAN, TPS algorithm is used for a tree construction and we have tested the performance improvement through simulation. In this section, experiment environment, method of time measurement, and analysis result of the test are also explained.

5.1 Performance Measurement for WAN

Simulation Scenario. We apply our proposed tree algorithm on WAN. To evaluate the performance of the proposed algorithm, we use ns-2 simulator[9], which is a widely used network simulation tool. For the comparative study, we implemented TPS, ECEF[1], HLOT[3], and flat[6] algorithms. 220 nodes of transit-stub topology were generated using GT-ITM[10]. The delay and bandwidth of the network were randomly assigned. The scale of delay spans from 10 ms to 1000 ms, and the bandwidth spans from 10 Kbps to 10 Mbps, respectively. Two types of background traffic were used: CBR and FTP. Both of the traffics have randomly selected individual starting and ending time of exchanging messages for traffic generation. Consequently, the communication among grid nodes suffers from network congestion and burst of traffics while the background traffic is active. The detailed simulation steps are as follows:

1. Specified number of Grid nodes are randomly selected
2. Delays and bandwidths of the selected grid nodes are obtained. The obtained metrics are used for the construction of a tree.
3. Construct broadcast trees for collective communication, and perform a broadcast under the same topology and traffic condition as step 1.

The simulation process was repeated 15 times and average transmission time was computed.

Simulation Results. Fig. 7(a) shows the result of simulation. The completion time depending on the change of the number of selected nodes is illustrated in the graphs. The number of randomly selected nodes was varied from 10 to 60, hopping by 10 nodes. In every case, flat tree produced the worst results, and TPS was revealed to bring the best results. Fig. 7(b) shows the result of simulation depending on the change of data size. The size of data, 1 KB, 4 KB, 16 KB, and 256 KB, were used. For all data sizes, TPS outperformed other algorithms. As the size of data is getting bigger, the performance gap is much more conspicuous.

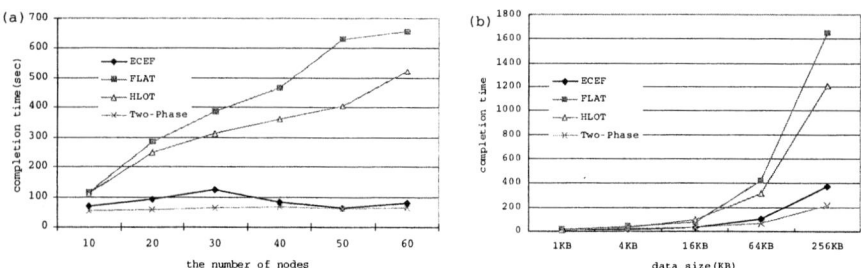

Fig. 7. Simulation results: (a) according to the number of nodes (b) according to data size

5.2 Performance Measurement for LAN

Since a binomial tree is known to be well suited for LAN, and network circumstances of LAN is more stable in terms of speed and variances than WAN environment, we used a binomial tree like current MPICH-G2. Here, we examine the effect of packet-level data transfer. First of all, we evaluated the effectiveness of using packet-level data transfer with a simple socket programming. The performance comparison between conventional block transfer method and the proposed method is conducted using multiplexing I/O. Fig. 8 depicts the testing environment. Node 0, 1, 2, and 3 connected to LAN are the components of the binomial tree.

To compare the performance between conventional block data transfer and our packet-level parallel data transfer, we measured the total elapsed time for broadcast. The completion time was measured as follows. Each node sends a completion message to the root when it receives the entire data, and the end time is determined by the message arrived last at the root node. Each packet contains both a header field and a

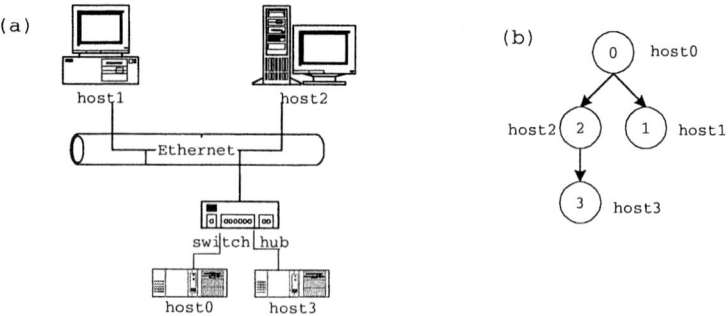

Fig. 8. (a) Test environment (b) binomial tree in LAN

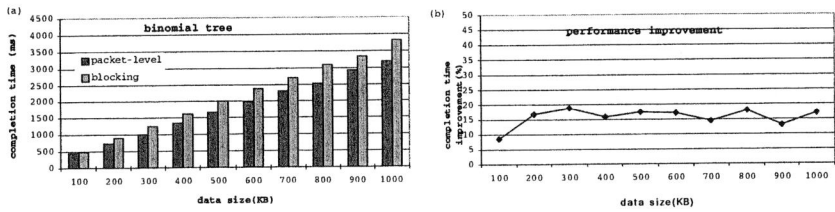

Fig. 9. Binomial tree with 4 nodes: (a) Completion time (b) ratio of completion of (a)

data field. The header field contains information such as header size, total data size, current data size, etc. The time attribute holds the information of end time of processing. Note that, the time required in sending an end message is negligible if the total data size is large enough. The size of a packet that can be transmitted to the network at a time is limited to MTU. Finally, to guarantee that only one packet is delivered at a time, the next packet is transmitted only after the transmission of the previous packet is completely ended. MTU was set to 1024 bytes and data size was varied from 100KB to 1000KB with 100KB intervals. The scale of time unit was *ms*. Fig. 9 shows the results of experiment using a binomial tree. In Fig. 9(a), packet-level parallel data transfer is revealed to show better performance than blocking data transfer for all levels of data size. With the involvement of 4 nodes, about 18.9% performance improvement is gained. In the Fig. 9, when the data size became large, i.e., when the necessary packet number was increased, the performance gain was evident. Since there is additional overhead of packet-level parallel data transfer, we can conclude that the benefits of using packet-level data transfer method pay the cost of it. The extents of performance improvement is higher on LAN environment than on WAN, because the available bandwidth on LAN is more stable than on WAN. As revealed in the result of the measurement, if the data size grows, more significant performance enhancement was achieved. Furthermore, when the available bandwidth grows, the completion time is expected to be shortened.

6 Conclusion and Future Work

In this paper, we proposed a method to improve the performance of collective communication primitives in MPICH-G2, which is an interface of MPI. We devised TPS algorithm as a tree algorithm and propose a packet-level parallel data transfer for collective communication of MPICH-G2.

In TPS, we use completion time as a metric of tree, and completion time is calculated with $latency + \frac{messagesize}{bandwidth}$. That is, we consider message size and bandwidth as well as latency. TPS is object to reduce completion time and to avoid bottleneck. It first selects k nodes with the largest weight. These k nodes with great possibility of bottleneck are put in leaf nodes. There are several ways to decide k. We use an average minimum completion time of each node as a way to select k nodes. We thought that nodes with minimum completion time accessing average time have high possibility to bottleneck. Running time of proposed algorithm takes $O(N^2 logN)$. The effect of the proposed method was theoretically analyzed and experimentally showed by implementing and testing the technique. According to the test, the proposed method showed a better performance than the current conventional version of collective operations in MPICH-G2.

In a packet-level parallel data transfer method, each node sends the packet to other multiple destination nodes in receiving packets from source node. In the experiment in the real network of LAN, the packet-level parallel data transfer demonstrated superior performance to the conventional entire data transfer. And, according to the simulation results of TPS, we can confirm a performance enhancement of TPS compared to ECEF, HLOT, and flat tree. The performance enhancement of TPS is larger as the number of nodes is increased and the size of data is enlarged.

In future, we are planning to implement the technique into MPICH-G2 collective communication primitives and test the performance. Finally, the number of k nodes in TPS should be clarified with accompanied by theoretical analysis.

References

1. P.B. Bhat, C.S. Raghavendra, and V.K. Prasanna, "Efficient collective communication in distributed heterogeneous systems," 19th IEEE International Confer-ence on Distributed Computing Systems, 1999.
2. Kwangho Cha, Dongsoo Han, and Chansu Yu, "Two-tree collective communication", Proceedings of the IASTED International Conference on Networks, Parallel and Distributed Processing and Applications, pp.30-35, Oct. 2003, Japan
3. Kyunglang Park, Hwangjik Lee, Younjoo Lee, Ohyoung Kwon, et la., "An Efficient Collective Communication Method for Gridi Scale Networks," ICCS 2003, LNCS 2660, pp. 819-828, January 2003.
4. http://www.hpclab.niu.edu/mpi
5. Peter S. Pacheco, Parallel Programming with MPI, Morgan Kautmann Publishers, Inc. 1997.
6. Thilo Kielman, Rutger F. H. Hofman, Henri E. Bal, Aske Plaat, and Raoul A. F. Bhoedjang, "MAGPIE: MPI's Collective Communications Operations for Clustered Wide Area Systems", Seventh ACM SIGPLAN Symposium on Principles and Practice of Parallel Programming, pp. 131-140, 1999
7. N. Karonis, M. Papka, J. Binns, J. Bresnahan, J. Insley, D. Jones, and J.Link, "High-Resolution Remote Rendering of Large Datasets in a Collaborative Environment," Future Generation of Computer Systems (FGCS), Vol. 19, No. 6, pp. 909-917, August 2003
8. Albert Alexandrove, Mihai F. Ionescu, Klaus E. Schauser, Chris Scheiman, "LogGP: Incorporating Long Messages into the LogP Model- One step close towards a realistic model for parallel computation", 7th Annual ACM Symposium on Parallel Algorithms and Architectures, CA, pp. 95-105, July 1995.
9. David Culler, Richard Karp, David Patterson, Abhijit Sahay, et la., "LogP: Towards a Realistic Model of Parallel Computation", Proceedings Symposium on Principles and Practice of Parallel Programming, CA, pp. 1-12, May 1993.
10. http://www.isi.edu/nsnam/ns/
11. Ellen W. Zegura, "GT-ITM: Georgia Tech Internetwork Topology Models", http://www.cc.gatech.edu/projects/gtitm.

Towards an Agent-Based Framework for Monitoring and Tuning Application Performance in Grid Environment

Sarbani Roy and Nandini Mukherjee

Department of Computer Science and Engineering,
Jadavpur University, Kolkata 700 032, India
sarbani_roy77@yahoo.co.in, nmukherjee@cse.jdvu.ac.in

Abstract. The essence of grid computing lies in the efficient utilization of a wide range of heterogeneous, loosely coupled resources in an organization. In a computational grid environment, regular monitoring of the execution of applications and taking actions for improving their performance in real time can achieve this. This paper presents the design of a multiagent framework for performance monitoring and tuning of an application executing in a Grid environment.

Keywords: Grid Monitoring, Application Performance Tuning, Multi-agent framework.

1 Introduction

An application running on a Grid needs to be adaptive to its current execution environment so that it can efficiently utilize the available resources. Maintaining the Quality of Services (QoS) and restraining the system from overprovisioning are also issues that need to be tackled in Grid environment. The basic technique can be regular monitoring of the infrastructure and the application performance and improving the performance of the application by using optimization techniques or adding more (or removing in case of overprovisioning) resources to its execution environment or simply by migrating the application or its components to other suitable Grid sites. This paper presents a multiagent framework for on-the-fly performance tuning of an application executing on Grid.

2 High Performance Computing and Grids

Computational resources on a Grid together can solve very large problems requiring more resources than is available on a single machine. An application is benefited from a Grid environment when the resource requirement cannot be fulfilled (either quantitatively or qualitatively) from the resources owned by the user. Thus, a Grid provides a good basis of creating a collaborative environment for high performance computing.

2.1 Performance Evaluation in Grid Environment

Mapping application processes to the resources in order to fulfill the requirement of the application in terms of power, capacity, quality and availability forms the basis of

Grid performance evaluation. The huge amount of monitoring data generated in a Grid environment is used to perform fault detection, diagnosis and scheduling in addition to performance analysis, prediction and tuning [1]. Due to the very dynamic and heterogeneous nature of a Grid, performance monitoring in Grid environment can be characterised as follows [2]:

- The execution environment in a Grid is not known beforehand and may change during execution or from one execution to another execution.
- Real-time performance analysis is thus essential in Grid environment.
- Performance tuning of applications during runtime is complicated and different from conventional techniques.
- New performance problems emerge out of the very different nature of the Grid.
- New performance metrics need to be defined which have not yet been taken care of.
- Grid information services, resource management and security policies add additional overhead to the execution of an application.

The Grid monitoring data may be used for detection of faults in system components and applications, for detection of performance bottlenecks in complex distributed systems, for real-time performance monitoring of applications and for determining performance characteristics of applications.

2.2 Application Performance Tuning in Grid

This section examines the requirements for application performance tuning in Grid environment. We divide the performance problems into two categories:

a) **Local Performance Problems:** When components of an application run on specific resources, there may be some performance problems, which can be (completely or partially) solved by adding more local level resources or by applying local level optimization techniques.

b) **Global Performance Problems:** When some global-level decisions need to be taken to counter a performance problem, the problem may be considered as global performance problem. This may be exemplified by using the following simple scenarios:
 Scenario 1 – Some faults are detected in the system or some performance bottlenecks are observed causing performance degradation of the application
 Scenario 2 – Observed performance of a component is not at par with the expectation.

In order to tackle the above two scenarios on the basis of real-time performance monitoring data and for efficient resource management, we propose a multi-agent framework which is described in the next section.

3 A Multi-agent Framework for Performance Tuning

In this section we describe the design of a multi-agent-based performance tuning framework for Grid applications. The framework is implemented on top of the Globus Toolkit [3]. It comprises four different components, which work in an integrated manner. These four components are: (a) *A resource broker (b) A Job Controller (c) An analyzer (d) A performance tuner.*

The *Resource Broker* acts as an intermediary between the application and a set of resources. It is the responsibility of the Resource Broker to negotiate and find suitable resources according to the application's resource requirement. The *Job Controller* is responsible for controlling the execution of the application at the local level. It also maintains a glob al view of the application's runtime behavior, as well as functioning of the infrastructure and performs control actions for improving the performance whenever the *service-level agreement* (SLA) [7] is violated. The *Analyzer* component monitors individual resources and gathers performance monitoring data related to application execution and infrastructure functioning. The performance data helps in evaluation of performance properties and identification of regions showing performance problems [4, 5]. *Performance Tuner* is responsible for tuning the performance of an application at local level. It receives a *service-level agreement* from the job controller and takes necessary actions for improving the application performance whenever the agreement is violated.

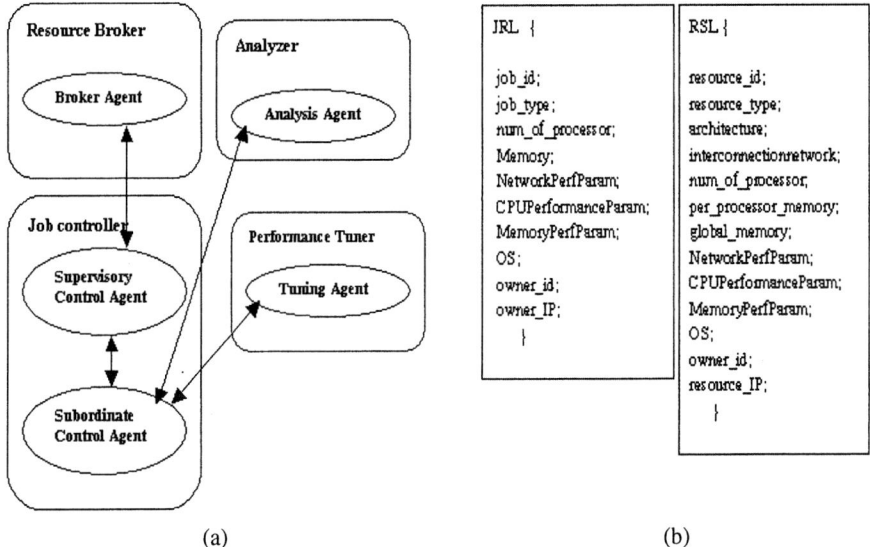

Fig. 1. (a) Components with agents (b) JRL and Resource Specification Template

3.1 The Agents in the System

This section presents a brief overview of the agents used in our framework. We distinguish the agents in two different categories: (i) functional agents and (ii) control agents. Each type of agents is part of either the Resource Broker, or the Job Controller or the Analyzer, or the Performance Tuner as shown in Figure 1 (a). The functional agents in our framework perform specific tasks, which are entrusted to them. Our system uses three types of *functional agents,* which are described below.

The *Broker Agent* resides in the Resource Broker component. The Broker agent receives a Job Requirement List (JRL) in which the basic requirements for a job are described. The Broker Agent consults the Grid Information Services (GRIS/GIIS,

MDS of Globus [6]) in order to obtain information about available resources and prepares a Resource Specification Table (RST). The information about a single resource provider willing to provide computational service is stored as a Resource Specification Template and the collection of several such templates is stored in a Resource Specification Table (RST). Figure 1 (b) shows the fields in a JRL and a Resource Specification Template. *Analysis Agents* reside on each of the resource providers, evaluate performance properties and detect performance problems. In addition to the resource-based analysis agents, there are agents that monitor the overall performance of the Grid. Thus an agent hierarchy is formed in which the lowest level agents monitor individual resources and the higher level agents collect data from the local agents and analyses the data in order to detect any performance bottleneck in the system. *Tuning Agents* also reside on each resource provider. This agent is responsible for local tuning of a running job on a specific resource provider.

Two types of *Control Agents* control the execution of an application. One is designated as supervisory type and it globally looks after the execution of all parallel jobs of an application. It is responsible for taking all global decisions, including rescheduling and establishing new SLAs. The *Supervisory Control Agent* maintains a list of resource provider addresses for each job for future rescheduling. Other control agents are subordinate to the supervisory agent. Each *Subordinate Control Agent* is associated with one of the parallel jobs of the application. It acquires the job along with an SLA from the Supervisory Control Agent and carries the job to the resource provider through a Grid Scheduling Service. The agent then resides on the resource provider. Whenever the agent is alerted by the analysis agent regarding some performance problem, it either activates the tuning agent for local tuning or consults the supervisory agent. It also performs any action directed to it by the supervisory agent. For example, if rescheduling is required, the supervisory agent takes the decision, selects next resource provider, establishes new SLA and directs the subordinate agent accordingly. The subordinate agent carries the job to the new resource provider. The subordinate control agents are lightweight, mobile agents that, under the directives of the supervisory agent, independently carry the jobs to the resource providers, submit the jobs and monitor their execution.

3.2 Interactions Among the Agents

A Grid application development environment on the client side accepts the application and decomposes it into a number of parallel jobs, which are placed in a job pool. Figure 2 demonstrates how a job is initially scheduled on the Grid.

The Broker agent acquires the next job from the job pool and prepares the Job Requirement List (JRL) and performance contract, as shown in figure 2. The JRL and the contract are built on the basis of a performance model and some input from the user, and form the basis of setting up *Service-Level Agreements* (SLAs) [7]. The Broker agent also consults the Grid Information Services (GRIS/GIIS of Globus [3]) with the help of MDS & SLA Management Service to obtain information about the available resources and prepares Resource Specification table (RST). The JRL and RST are matched by the Broker agent to find suitable resources with ability of meeting the requirements of the submitted job. A list of selected resource providers along with their SLA is then forwarded to the Supervisory Control Agent. The Supervisory Agent selects a resource provider (RP) from the list on the basis of some pre-assigned priority and establishes an SLA with the selected resource provider.

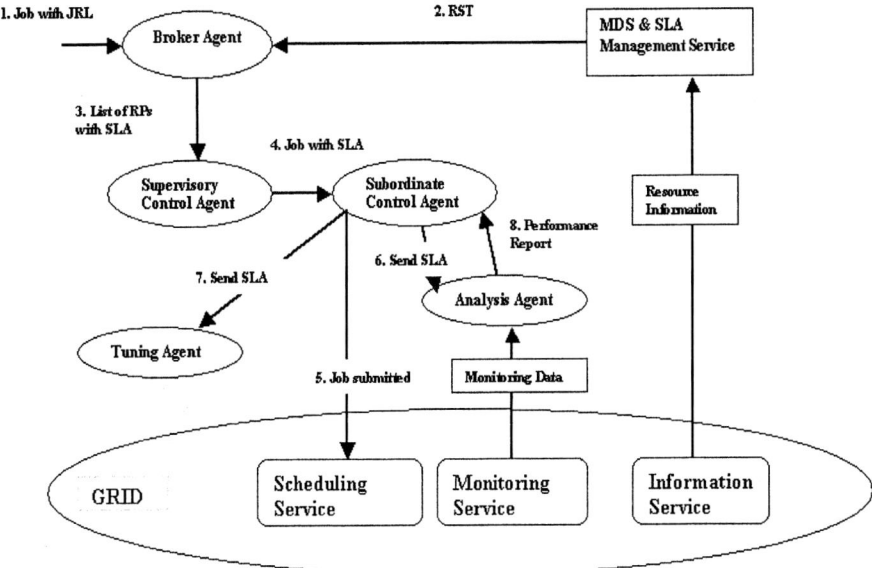

Fig. 2. Interaction among the agents at the time of initial scheduling

A Subordinate Agent, which is a mobile agent, carries the job and the SLA from the Supervisory Agent and gets deployed on the resource provider through a Grid scheduling service. The Subordinate Agent sends the SLA to the Analysis agent, which immediately starts monitoring the execution of the application. Analysis Agent interacts with Grid monitoring service (such as MDS) for monitoring data. A push data delivery model is used, i.e. the Subordinate Agent subscribes the events and obtains the analysis report periodically.

When any fault is detected or a resource provider cannot meet the performance contract, the analysis agent raises warning. On the basis of the report the Subordinate Agent either invokes the local Tuning Agent or requests advice from the Supervisory Agent. The Supervisory Agent, which maintains a list of resource providers for the particular job, selects the next resource provider from the list and establishes a new SLA. While establishing the new SLA it checks whether the selected resource provider is still in the list of valid resource providers. The Supervisory Agent then instructs the Subordinate Agent about the new SLA and the Subordinate Agent in turn carries the job to the new resource provider. At the time of rescheduling, the Subordinate Agent first checkpoints the job and then migrates.

4 Related Work

One of the major objectives of research in Performance Engineering is maintaining performance QoS for individual applications. In the ICENI project, application performance is achieved by an application mapper, which selects the "best" component implementations for the available resources, based on component meta-data [8].

In the GrADS project, each application has an application manager that monitors the performance of that application for QoS achievement. Failure to achieve QoS contract causes a rescheduling or redistribution of resources [9]. Active monitoring in Grid environment using mobile agent technology has been described in [10]. This paper, in contrast to the above mentioned systems, focuses on a multi-agent framework for enhancing the performance of an application at runtime.

5 Conclusion

The paper presents a multiagent framework for performance tuning of applications in Grid environment. Our multiagent framework works on top of the available Grid middleware (such as Globus Toolkit [3]), and uses the services available with it. A brief discussion about the design of the framework is presented in this paper. The discussion elaborates how the agents interact within the framework to improve the performance of an application during run-time.

References

1. Balaton Z., P. Kacsuk, N. Podhorszki and F. Vajda, *Comparison of Representative Grid Monitoring Tools*, Report of the Laboratory of Parallel and Distributed Systems, Computer and Automation Research Institute of the Hungarian Academy of Sciences, 2000.
2. Nemeth Z., *Performance Evaluation on Grids: Directions, Issues, and Open Problems*, Report of the Laboratory of Parallel and Distributed Systems, Computer and Automation Research Institute of the Hungarian Academy of Sciences, 2002.
3. Globus http://www.globus.org.
4. Fahringer T., M. Gerndt, B. Mohr, F. Wolf, G. Riley, J. L. Träff, *Knowledge Specification for Automatic Performance Analysis*, APART Technical Report, http://www.fz-juelich.de/apart, August 2001
5. Furlinger K and M. Gerndt, *Distributed Configurable Application Monitoring on SMP Clusters*, Proceedings of EuroPVM/MPI 2003, Venice, 2003
6. Aydt R. and D. Quesnel compiled *Performance Data Usage Scenarios (Draft 1)*, Grid Forum Performance Working Group, October 2, 2000.
7. Czajkowski K., I. Foster and C. Kesselman, *Resource and Service Management*, The Grid 2: Blueprint for a New Computing Infrastructure (Chapter 18) by Ian Foster and Carl Kesselman, Morgan Kaufmann; 2 edition (November 18, 2003)
8. Furmento N., A. Mayer, S. McGough, S. Newhouse, T. Field and J. Darlington, *ICENI: Optimisation of Component Applications within a Grid Environment*, Proceedings of Supercomputing 2001. http://www-icpc.doc.ic.ac.uk/components.
9. Kennedy K., et al, *Toward a Framework for Preparing and Executing Adaptive Grid Programs*, Proceedings of the International Parallel and Distributed Processing Symposium Workshop (IPDPS NGS), IEEE Computer Society Press, April 2002.
10. O. Tomarchio, L. Vita, and A. Puliafito. Active monitoring in GRID environments using mobile agent technology. In *2nd Workshop on Active Middleware Services (AMS'00) in HPDC-9*, Pittsburgh (Pennsylvania (USA)), August 2000.

GDP: A Paradigm for Intertask Communication in Grid Computing Through Distributed Pipes

D. Janakiram, M. Venkateswara Reddy, A. Vijay Srinivas,
M.A. Maluk Mohamed, and S. Santosh Kumar

Distributed & Object Systems Lab, Dept. of Computer Science & Engg.
Indian Institute of Technology Madras, Chennai, India
{djram, venkatm, avs, maluk, santosh}@cs.iitm.ernet.in
http://dos.iitm.ac.in

Abstract. Existing grid models target purely data parallel applications without inter-task communication. This paper proposes a transparent programming model to support communicating parallel tasks in a wide area grid. The proposed grid model with Distributed Pipes (DP) abstraction named as, GDP, enables location independent intertask communication among processes on machines spread over a wide area distributed system. This approach enables anonymous migration of communicating parallel tasks adjusting to grid dynamics. The proposed model supports sequential load to coexist with parallel load. A prototype of the proposed model has been implemented over clusters of nodes spread across the Internet. A steady state equilibrium engineering problem was studied over the model. Performance studies show linear to super linear speed up for the application.

1 Introduction

The concept of cluster computing became popular due to the better price to performance ratio over supercomputers. Models for cluster computing include Network Of Workstations (NOW) [1], Batrun [2], ARC [3] etc. Distributed Pipes [4] model was proposed to enable inter-task communication for clusters. This approach also enabled migration of communicating parallel tasks according to runtime conditions. Computational grids are realized across cluster of clusters located in different geographically distributed administrative domains [5]. These grids involve a higher degree of complexity, especially at the middleware layer, to run, administer, manage, and use these distributed computing resources.

1.1 Related Work and Motivation

Several grid environments exist, like Globus [6], Optimal Grid [7], and Legion [8]. Globus is more of a toolkit or infrastructure support for building the grid. Optimal Grid supports inter-task communication, which is based on T Spaces, a realization of Linda-like tuple space. However, the scalability of Optimal Grid is limited by the scalability of T Spaces. T Spaces may not scale, as scalability is not one of the key design considerations nor has T Spaces been proved scalable.

Further, since T Spaces does not address fault tolerance explicitly, the fault tolerance of Optimal Grid is also limited. Legion Grid is an object-based, meta-systems software project that addresses issues such as scalability, programming ease, fault tolerance, security, site autonomy etc.

A number of applications related to scientific problems like finite difference, finite element and finite volume methods require intermediate results to be exchanged for every iteration. This requires intertask communication. To the best of our knowledge the research that has gone into grid computing does not address such tasks. Further, existing grid computing research is more towards providing static load balancing across machines. This implies that the set of machines on which the task is started is the same on which the task completes, even if load fluctuates on those nodes. The task is restarted in case of failures. The proposed model focuses on task level load balancing, enabling balancing at runtime efficiently. The set of nodes on which computation starts can be quite different from the set on which it completes.

In this context, we propose GDP, a grid model that supports intertask communication, which is essential in several scientific applications such as Pizo-electrical coupled problems, electro-magnetic coupled problems and thermo-elastic problems. The model enables runtime task mobility to handle grid dynamics. GDP is built with Distributed Pipe (DP) abstraction to provide intertask communications among subtasks executing on different nodes. The proposed solution inherits the simple abstraction provided by DPs but redesigns it to scale over large networks.

The rest of the paper is organized as follows. Section 2 gives an overview of the proposed GDP model. Section 3 gives the case study for our proposed model. Section 4 gives the performance studies for the model and Section 5 concludes the paper.

2 Overview of GDP: Grid with DP Abstraction

The model employs the master-worker kind of computation similar to [4]. The model consists of a user process and several donor processes. The user process is a process which initiates the computation. Donor processes are on the participating nodes, which spawn the subtask process.

The model solves the finite element problems by decomposing the domain and assigning the sub domains to donor processes. The values after every iteration among the donor processes can be exchanged through the Distributed Pipes. The results are returned to the user process after the computation. The subtasks can be migrated to donors anonymously.

The grid is virtualized as cluster of clusters. Each cluster has a coordinator. The coordinator handles domain decomposition, pipe creation among donors, load balancing, anonymous migration of subtasks, list of friend clusters, history of the computation, result collection and aspects related to fault tolerance.

The Acceptor handles the security related issues like single sign-on and global policies. User process always communicates with the system coordinator through the Acceptor. It is the only entry point into the grid. Metering the resource usage is also possible due to single entry point.

The advantage of this model is anonymous migration of the tasks. This enables the system to adapt to dynamic load changes. The pool of the participating nodes vary dynamically based on runtime conditions. The model handles architecture heterogeneity with the help of the XDR model.

The figure 1 describes the proposed grid model. Circles represent the donors, acceptor, system-coordinator and user process. Ellipse represents the subtask processes. Thin lines represents the Unix stream socket connections where as thick lines represents TCP/IP connections. Dotted lines represents the distributed pipes abstraction which helps to exchange boundary values among subtasks.

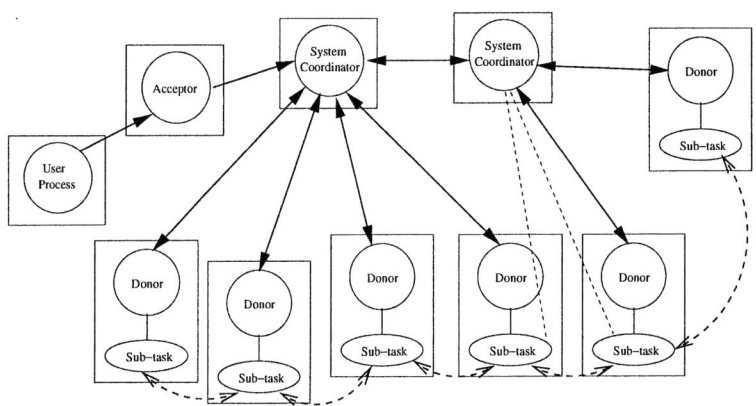

Fig. 1. GDP: Grid with Distributed Pipes Abstraction

The user submits the iterative computing class of application to the grid through user process. The user process collects the available nodes for the grid computation by initiating a request to the coordinator. Coordinator collects the load information from the available donors and choose the potential donors from the available donors based on the capability of the donor node. Based on the donor availability, the coordinator splits the domain of computation into sub domains. The coordinator initiates grid computation and pipe creation. The coordinator sends the results after computation to the user process. The design and implementation details are not given here due to space constraints and are available in the full paper, available at http://dos.iitm.ac.in/Publications/iconferences.html.

3 Case Study

Steady state equilibrium problem from fluid dynamics is considered for our case study. Here the problem is used to compute the intermediate temperature flux distribution of a rod whose both ends are kept in constant temperature bath.

Similar computational problems exist in many engineering disciplines to compute pressure distribution, composition distribution, etc.

The problem computes the temperature values at each part of the rod, for each time period, and in each iteration. The temperature values of a part in a time period is affected by that of the values in the previous time period and also with adjacent part's values in the previous time period. This accounts for the temperature flux by conduction. The problem considers temperature flux in only one dimension. The points at which the temperature is to be computed are evenly spaced. Also, the temperature of the part of the rod is evaluated at regular intervals in time. The data dependency among the adjacent parts is

$$T_{g,t} = f(T_{g-1,t-1}, T_{g,t-1}, T_{g+1,t-1})$$

where $T_{i,j}$ is the temperature of the slice i during the time j.

Temperature values of the fixed temperature baths, length and distance between adjacent grid points, and time interval between two successive computations are the data furnished at the beginning of the run. The equations that characterize the flow of temperature are space-time domain equations. The programming APIs and other details are not given here due to space constraints and are given in the full paper.

4 Performance Analysis

A prototypical GDP Model was implemented to study the performance. Experiments were conducted on two different test beds to analyze how the speedup will vary with wide-area network latency. One such test bed was within our own institute consisting of about 50 heterogeneous machines. The other was a wide area testbed, with 3 nodes from our institute and 2 nodes from IIIT Bangalore. The grain size of the problem is 10,00,00,000 grid points. The problem needs to be run for a certain number of iterations. After each iteration, the subtasks exchange their boundary values with neighbors on either side.

4.1 Effect of Memory Scaling

The iterative grid computation problem is memory intensive. When the problem is run on a single machine, it is necessary to maintain a secondary storage. But access to the secondary storage is slow compared to that of primary storage. In our model as the problem is divided into subtasks, the memory requirements are also divided among the subtasks. As less amount of memory is required, the swapping between the memories decreases thereby increasing the performance. The first graph in figure 2 presents the case.

4.2 Speedup – Grid Within the Same Organization

Linear speedups can be achieved by parallel execution over a sub domain. But in our model *super-linear speedup* was achieved as depicted in the second graph of

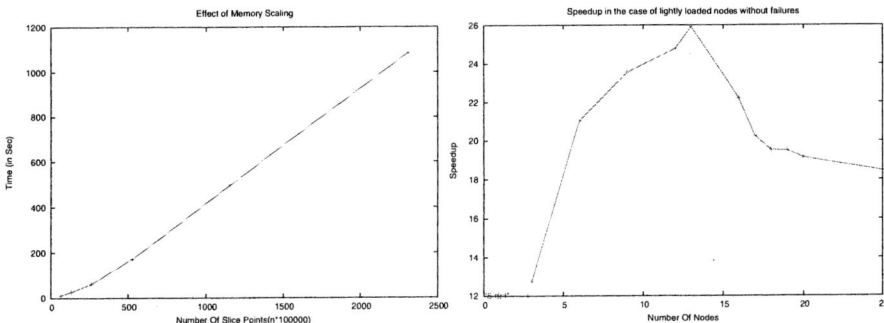

Fig. 2. (a) Effect of Memory Scaling and (b) Speed up in the case of lightly loaded nodes without failures

figure 2. This is because of parallelism and reduced memory requirements. These super linear speedups can be achieved as long as the problem runs on optimal number of nodes with appropriate grain size. If the grain size of the sub domain is small, the communication overhead increases, reducing the speedup. The grain size of a subtask is the number of slice points allotted to a subtask. Task time of a subtask is the time taken for computation of the subtask which is the sum of actual CPU time of the subtask and synchronization delay suffered by subtask. Speedup is defined as the ratio of parallel execution time of the problem to its sequential execution time.

4.3 Performance Saturation

The prototype results as shown in table 1 have shown that the speed up increases super-linearly as we increase the number of nodes. But this increase is limited up to some extent. The speedup increased when the number of nodes increased to 13. But the speedup decreased as the number of nodes was further increased and remained almost constant showing a saturation point. This was observed when the number of nodes was more than 18. The inference of the result was that, with less number of nodes the communication overhead is less than the computation overhead and also the synchronization delay is minimum. As the number of nodes increases, number of subtasks increases, reducing the grain sizes. Due to smaller grain sizes the communication overhead is more and the synchronization delay increases, resulting in performance saturation.

4.4 Speedup – Internet Scale Grid

When the same computing problem with same grain size was executed on WAN test bed, more synchronization delay between subtasks was observed. This is mainly due to communication latencies. When the computation is run on the Institute test bed, higher speedups are obtained. However, even in the wide area testbed, we were able to obtain super linear speedup for sufficiently large problem sizes. This is mainly due to scaled down memory requirements. The graph in figure 3 shows a case.

Table 1. Speed up with increasing nodes: Performance saturation

No. of Nodes	Grain Size	Total Task Time(Sec)	Speedup
1	10,00,00,000	1489.621789	-
3	3,30,00,000	116.876431	12.745273
9	1,11,11,000	63.254592	23.549623
13	76,92,307	57.496331	25.908119
16	62,50,000	67.106057	22.198023
17	58,82,352	73.605719	20.237854
18	55,55,555	76.353495	19.509543
20	50,00,000	77.887006	19.125421
25	40,00,000	80.708851	18.456734

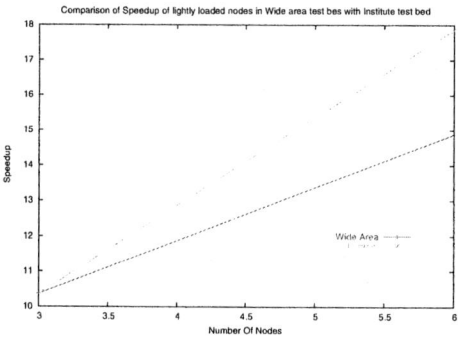

Fig. 3. Comparison of Speedup in the case of two different test beds

5 Conclusions

This paper has presented GDP, a model that enables transparent programmability of communicating tasks in a grid environment. Existing grid models do not provide support for communicating tasks. Performance studies over a prototypical implementation for a steady state problem confirm the feasibility of running such tasks in a grid environment. We were able to achieve linear to super-linear speed up even with wide-area latencies and load dynamics. However, we have not addressed fault-tolerance issues, which become important, especially in a wide area context. We are currently designing a Peer-to-Peer middleware layer in order to handle fault-tolerance and scalability issues for the grid.

References

1. D.Patterson Anderson T, David Culler. Case for now (network of work-stations). *IEEE Micro*, 15(1):1–20, Dec 1994.
2. Fredy Tandiary, Suraj C. Kothari, Ashish Dixit, and E. Walter Anderson. Batrun: Utilizing Idle Workstations for Large-Scale Computing. *IEEE Concurrency*, 4(2):41–48, Summer 1996.

3. D. Janakiram Rushikesh K. Joshi. Anonymous remote computing: A paradigm for parallel programming on interconnected workstations. *IEEE Trans. on Software Engineering*, 25(1):75–90, Jan/Feb 1999.
4. Binu K. Johnson, R. Karthikeyan, and D. Janaki Ram. Dp: A paradigm for anonymous remote computation and communication for cluster computing. *IEEE Transactions on Parallel and Distributed Systems*, 12(10):1052–1065, 2001.
5. Ian Foster, Carl Kesselman, and Steven Tuecke. The Anatomy of the Grid: Enabling Scalable Virtual Organizations. *International Journal on Supercomputer Applications*, 15(3), 2001.
6. C. Kesselman Foster. Globus: A metacomputing infrastructure toolkit. *Intl J. Supercomputer Applications*, 11(2):115–128, Fall 1997.
7. Tobin J. Lehman and James H. kaufman. Optimal Grid: Middleware for Automatic Deployment of Distributed FEM Problems on an Internet-Based Computing Grid. In *Proceedings of the IEEE International Conference on Cluster Computing (CLUSTER'03)*, 2003.
8. Andrew Grimshaw, Adam Ferrari, Frederick Knabe, and Marty Humphrey. Wide-Area Computing: Resource Sharing on a Large Scale. *IEEE Computer*, 32(5):29–37, May 1999.

Internet Technology Track Chair's Message

Sanjay K. Madria

University of Missouri-Rolla, USA

Abstract. Internet Technology Track received around 60 papers and the papers were reviewed by the International program committee and finally 9 papers have been selected for presentation (6 full and 3 short papers). As the track chair, I would like to thank all the authors who submitted their papers in this track and all the PC members who reviewed the papers in timely fashion. The paper presentation in this track is organized into three sessions, (1) Internet Search and Query, (2) E-commerce, (3) Web Browsing. I hope you enjoyed your presence in these sessions.

Rewriting Queries Using View for RDF/RDFS-Based Relational Data Integration

Huajun Chen

College of Computer Science, Zhejiang University, Hangzhou 310027, China
huajunsir@zju.edu.cn

Abstract. We study the problem of answering queries through a target RDF-based ontology, given a set of view-based mappings between one or more source relational schemas and this target ontology. Particularly, we consider a set of RDFS semantic constraints such as rdfs:subClassof, rdfs:subPropertyof, rdfs:domain, and rdfs:range, which are present in RDF model but neither XML nor relational models. We formally define the query semantics in such an integration scenario, and design a novel query rewriting algorithm to implement the semantics.[1]

1 Introduction

The Semantic Web is aimed at providing a common framework allowing data to be shared and reused across application, enterprize, and community boundaries. It is based on the Resource Description Framework (RDF), which is a language for representing web information in a minimally constrained, flexible, but meaningful way so that web data can be exchanged and integrated without loss of semantics. Most of existing data, however, is stored in relational databases. Thus, for semantic web to be really useful and successful, major efforts are required to offer methods and tools to support integration of heterogeneous relational databases using RDF model.

This paper is devoted to the problem of answering queries through a target RDF-based ontology, given a set of semantic mappings between one or more source relational schemas and this target ontology. In essence, this is the problem of uniformly querying many disparate data sources through one common virtual interface. A typical approach, called answering query using view [6][5], is to describe data sources as precomputed views over a mediated schema, and reformulate the user query, posed over the mediated schema, into queries that refer directly to the source schemas by query rewriting.

While most of the preceding work has been focused on the relational case [7][5][8], and the XML case [9][10], we consider the problem of answering RDF queries using RDF views over relational databases. In particular, we consider a set of extra RDFS semantic constraints such as rdfs:subClassof,

---

[1] The work is funded by China 973 project: Fundamental Approach, Model, and Theory of Semantic Grid, and subprogram of China 863 project : TCM Virtual Research Institute, and China NSF program (NSFC60503018): Research on Scale-free Network Model for Semantic Web and High Performance Semantic Search Algorithm.

rdfs:subPropertyof, rdfs:domain, and rdfs:range, which are present in RDF model but neither XML nor relational models. These constraints are of great importance in RDF-based data integration. Take a simple example, suppose there is a statement in the RDF ontology saying: *foaf:schoolHomepage* **rdfs:subPropertyOf** *foaf:homepage*. Suppose a semantic mapping from a column of a relational table T to the property *foaf:schoolHomepage* has been defined, and a semantic query referring the property *foaf:homepage* is given, the rewriting algorithm should automatically infer that T can also be used to generate rewritings since *foaf:schoolHomepage* is a subproperty of *foaf:homepage*. On the other hand, if a triple like *:aaa foaf:schoolHomepage :bbb* is generated as a query result, the system should automatically infer that the triple *:aaa foaf:homepage :bbb* is also a query result. As a matter of fact, *rdfs:subPropertyOf* sets an extra constraints that the query result should satisfy, and extensively enhances the query rewriting.

In this paper, we formally define the problem of answering queries using views for RDF/RDFS-based relational data integration. We define a *Target RDF Instance* that satisfies all the requirements with respect to the given views and RDFS semantic constraints on the ontology, and take the query semantics to be the result of evaluating the query on this *Target RDF Instance*. It then becomes a requirement that any query rewriting algorithm must satisfy. In addition, a RDF-inspired query rewriting algorithm is also implemented according to the formal query semantics.This algorithm extends earlier relational and XML techniques for rewriting queries using views,with consideration of the features of RDF model. Intuitively, it rewrites the target RDF queries into a set of source SQL queries. Evaluating the union of these rewritings on the data sources has essentially the same effect as running the RDF query on the *Target RDF Instance*.

This paper is laid out as follows: Section 2 mentions some related work. Section 3 introduce the RDF view by some examples. Section 4 formally discusses the problem of answering RDF queries using RDF views. Section 5,6 introduces the rewriting algorithm. Section 7 serves as a conclusion.

2 Related Works

In the context of semantic web research, there are a lot of works that concern mapping RDF with relational model. Some of them deal with the issue of using RDBMS as RDF triple storage, such as Jena or Sesame's relational storage component. This issue is not considered in this paper.

Some Others deal with the issue of integrating relational data using RDF, such as D2RMap [4], KAON REVERSE[2], D2RQ system [1] and RDF Gateway[3]. However, none of them consider the issue of RDFS semantic constraints, and the formal aspects such as query semantics, query complexity is not considered. Another issue they did not consider is the incompleteness of legacy database. For example, both of D2RQ and RDF Gateway define a declarative language

---

[2] http://kaon.semanticweb.org/alphaworld/reverse/view
[3] RDF Gateway: http://www.intellidimension.com

to describe mappings. However, the mappings, as they defined, are simple and equivalent mappings: it consists of statements asserting that some portion of relational data is equivalent to some portion of the RDF data.In contrast, the RDF views that we consider involves incomplete mappings, where each statement asserts that a relational source is a incomplete, partial view of the big model.

Piazza [2] consider the mapping of XML-to-XML and XML-RDF. [3]considers the problem of answering query using views for semantic web, but their approach is more description-logic-oriented.

3 RDF View

We start with a simple example: suppose both *W3C* and *Zhejiang University* (abbreviated as ZJU) have a legacy relational database about their employees and projects, and we would like to integrate them by the FOAF ontology[4], so that we can query these relational databases by formulating RDF queries upon the FOAF ontology.

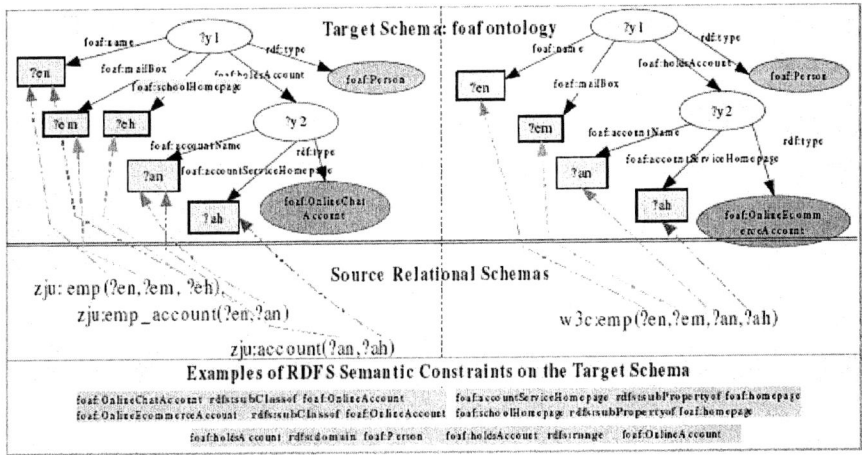

Fig. 1. Semantic Mapping from Relational Tables to RDF classes and properties : The symbols ?en; ?em; ?eh; ?an; ?ah are variables and represent, respectively, "employee name","employes email"," employes homepage at school","account name","account services homepage". ?y1; ?y2 are existential variables. Notice the account information in the first one is mapped to foaf:OnlineChatAccount, and the second one is mapped to foaf:OnlineEcommerceAccount.

The mapping scenario in Fig. 1 illustrates two source relational schemas (W3C, and ZJU), a target RDF schema (a part of the foaf ontology), and two mappings between them. Graphically, the mappings are described by the arrows that go between the mapped schema elements. The extra RDFS Semantic Constraints state that both foaf:schoolHomepage and foaf:accountServiceHomepage

---

[4] The FOAF project:http://www.foaf-project.org/

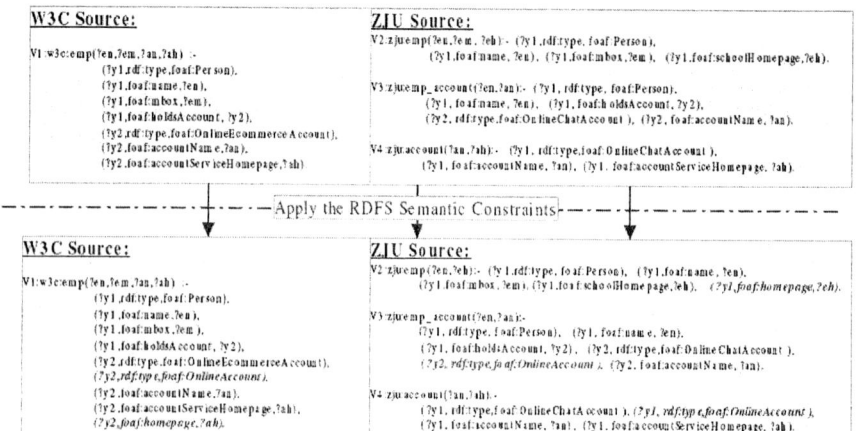

Fig. 2. RDF Views examples. Upper part is the set of original views, lower part is the set of views after applying RDFS semantic constraints(see Section 4.2). The newly added triples are italicized.

are subproperty of foaf:homepage, and both foaf:OnlineChatAccount and foaf:OnlineEcommerceAccount are subclass of foaf:OnlineAccount.

Mappings are often defined as views in conventional data integration systems, often in the form of GAV (globalas- view), LAV (local-as-view), or, more generally, GLAV (global-and-local-as-view) assertions. We take the LAV approach, i.e., we define each relational table in the source as a view over the RDF ontologies. We call such views as RDF Views. For formal discussion, we express such RDF views in a Datalog-like notation.

As the examples in Fig. 2 illustrates, a typical RDF view consists of two parts. The left part is called the view head, and is often a relational predicate. The right part is called the view body, and is often a set of RDF triples. In general, the body can be viewed as a RDF query over the target schema, and it defines the semantics of the relational predicate from perspective of the RDF ontology. Being similar to conventional view definitions expressed in Datalog, there are two kinds of variables for RDF view. The variables appearing in the view head is often called distinguished variable. The variables appearing only in the view body but not in the view head are called existential variables. In our examples, y1, y2,..., are existential variables.

4 The Query Answering Problem

4.1 RDF Queries

We then shift our focus onto RDF queries we would like to deal with in this paper. We start with an example again. Q1 is a query specified in terms of foaf ontology.

```
Q1: SELECT ?en ?em ?eh ?y2 ?an ?ah where
    ?y1 rdf:type foaf:Person.     ?y1 foaf:name ?en.
    ?y1 foaf:mbox ?em.        OPTIONAL ?y1 foaf:homepage ?eh.
    ?y1 foaf:holdsAccount ?y2.    ?y2 rdf:type foaf:OnlineAccount.
    ?y2 foaf:accountName ?an.     ?y2 foaf:homepage ?ah.
```

The query is written in SPARQL[5] query notation. It is to find the person name (?en), the mail box (?em), the homepage (?eh), his/her online account (?y2), the account name (?an), the homepage of the account service (?ah).We note that there is an Optional Block in Q1. According to the SPARQL specification, the OPTIONAL predicate specifies that if the optional part does not lead to any solutions, the variables in the optional block can be left unbound. As can be seen in Section 4, OPTIONAL predicate has an effect on the possible number of valid query writings that the algorithm can yield.

4.2 Answering Queries Using Views

The fundamental problem we want to address is : *given a set of source instances I, i.e., a set of source relations, and a set of RDF views such as V1, V2, plus a set of RDF semantic constraints such as rdfs:subClassof, what should the answers to a target RDF query such as Q1 be?*.

One possible approach that has been extensively studied in the relational literatures, is to consider the target instance, which is yielded by applying the view definitions onto the source instances, as an incomplete databases [6]. Often a number of possible databases D are consistent with this incomplete database. Then the query semantics is to take the intersection of Q(D) over all such possible D. This intersection is called the set of the certain answers [6]. This approach can not be applied directly to our case, since we need to consider extra semantic constraints on the target schema. Thus, we take a similar but somewhat different approach, which is more RDF-inspired.

In general, we define the semantics of target query answering by constructing a Target RDF Instance G based on the view definitions and RDFS semantic constraints.We then define the result of answering a target RDF query Q1 using the views to be the result of evaluating Q1 directly on G. There are two phases in this construction process:

1. Applying constraints onto RDF views. Before constructing G, an extra inference process is firstly applied onto the RDF views. For the examples illustrated in Fig. 2, five extra triples are added into the view defintions by applying the RDFS constraints in Fig. 1. For instance, applying the constraint (foaf:accountServiceHomepage rdfs:subPropertyof foaf:homepage) to the triple (?y2 foaf:accountServiceHomepage ?ah) will yield a new triple (?y2 foaf:homepage ?ah).

2. Applying RDF views onto source instances. In this process, for each tuple in the source instance, we add a set of RDF triples in the target such

---

[5] W3Cs SPARQL query language specification : http://www.w3.org/TR/rdf-sparql-query/

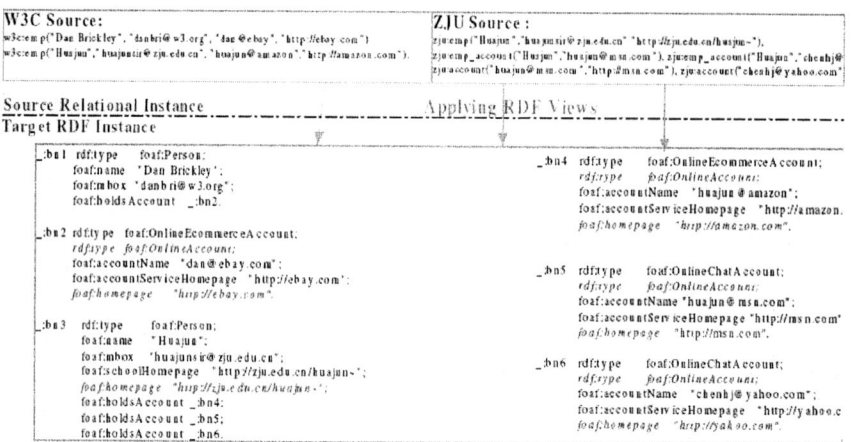

Fig. 3. The Source Relational Instance and Target RDF Instance. In the target instance, :bn1, :bn2, and so on, are all newly generated blank node IDs. The italicized triples are generated because of the RDFS semantic constraints. The triples are represented using N3 notation.

that the view-based mapping is satisfied. One important notion of the process is the skolem functions we introduced to generate the blank node IDs in the target RDF instance. As can be seen in Fig. 3, corresponding to each existential variable ?y in the view, we generate a new blank node ID. For examples, _:bn1, _:bn2 are both newly generated blank node IDs corresponding to the variables ?y1, ?y2 in V1. This treatment of the existential variable is in accordance with the RDF semantics, since blank nodes can be viewed as existential variables [6]. The evaluation of Q1 on this target RDF instance produces the tuples in Table1. In general, we associate each RDF class in the target ontology with a unique Skolem Function that can generate blank node ID at that type. For instances, we associate the two RDF classes in Fig. 1 with the following skolem functions respectively:

foaf:Person - SF1(?en); foaf:OnlineAccount - SF2(?an);

The choice of function parameters depends on the constraints user want to set on the target schema. For example, SF1(?en) set a new constraint that says: if two instances have the same value for the property foaf:name, then they are equivalent and same blank node ID is generated for both of them. This is somewhat similar to the Primary Key Constraint, and is useful for merging instances stemming from different sources. Take the examples in Fig. 3 again, for person name Huajun, the same blank node ID _:bn3 is generated for both W3C and ZJU sources, so that the data from different sources can be merged together.

We finally give the formal specification of the query semantics. We adopt this semantics as a formal requirement on query answering using RDF view over

---

[6] W3C RDF Semantics :http://www.w3.org/TR/rdf-mt/

Table 1. Query answers after evaluating Q1 on the Target RDF Instance in Fig. 3. Note the variable ?eh (Person.homepage) is left unbound, namely, is nullable, but other variables MUST have a binding.

Person.name	Person.mail-box	Person.homepage	Account	Account.name	Account.homepage
Dan Brickley	danbri@w3.org	NULL	_:bn2	dan@ebay	http://ebay.com
Huajun	huajunsir@zju.edu.cn	http://zju.edu.cn/huajun	_:bn4	huajun@amazon.com	http://amazon.com
Huajun	huajunsir@zju.edu.cn	http://zju.edu.cn/huajun	_:bn5	huajun@msn.com	http://msn.com
Huajun	huajunsir@zju.edu.cn	http://zju.edu.cn/huajun	_:bn6	huajun@yahoo.com	http://yahoo.com

relational schema, although not necessarily as an implementation strategy. In fact, we show in the next section how to implement this semantics, without materializing the Target RDF Instance,but instead by query rewriting.

Definition 2 Query Semantics. Let q be a RDF query, then the set of the query answer of q with respect to a set of relational source instance I, a set of RDF views V, plus a set of RDFS semantic constraints C, denoted by $answer_{V,C}(q, I)$, is the set of all tuples t such that $t \in (G)$ where G is the Target RDF Instance.

This query semantics is different from the certain answer [2] in relational literatures for two practical reasons: a)The query answer can contain nulls during evaluation, because of the OPTIONAL predicate used in RDF query; b)The query answer can contain newly generated blank node IDs which can be viewed as existential variables.

5 Query Rewriting Algorithm

We describe next the basic algorithm we developed to answer RDF queries using RDF views under RDFS semantic constraints. Basically, the algorithm can be divided into two phases : preprocessing views, and query transformation.

5.1 Preprocessing Views

The purpose of this phage is two fold. Firstly, RDFS Semantic Constraints are applied onto views, so that more types of query can be answered by using the extended views. Secondly, the view definitions are turned into a set of smaller rules called Class Mapping Rules, so that target query expressions can be more directly substituted by relational terms.

Applying constraints has been introduced in Section 4.2. Fig. 2 illustrates the examples of views after applying the RDFS semantic constraints. This extra inference process is valuable because it enables the rewriting algorithm to answer more types of query. For example, without this process, Q1 can not be answered by rewriting the views, because the query terms foaf:OnlineAccount and foaf:homepage do not appear in any view definitions at all. Generating class

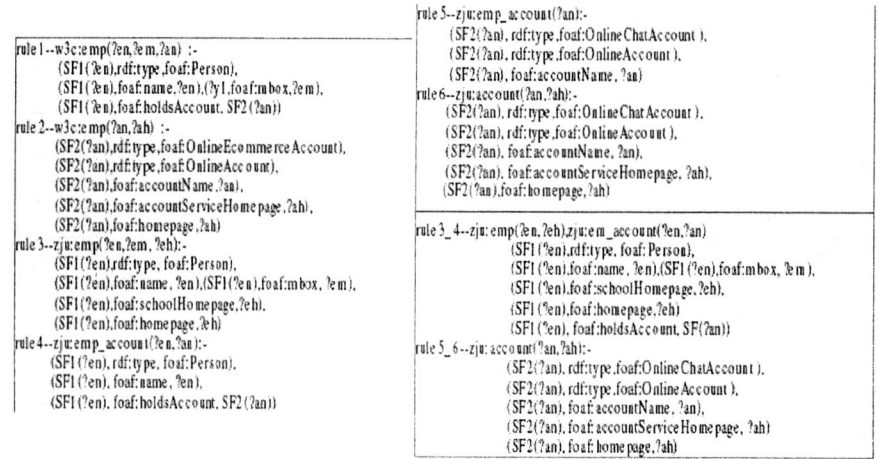

Fig. 4. Examples of Class Mapping Rules

mappings rules is somewhat more complex. The complete algorithm is illustrated in the left part of Fig. 5. In general, the algorithm can be divided into four steps.

1. Grouping Triples. The algorithm starts by looking at the body of views, and group the triples by subject name, i.e., a separate group is created for each set of triples that have same subject name. For example, three such triple groups are created for V 1 as illustrated in Fig. 4. In the first group, three triples share the same subject name ?y1 which will be replaced by the skolem function name SF1(?en).

2. Skolemizing Triples. Next, the algorithm replaces all existential variables $?yn \in Y$ with corresponding Skolem Function Names. As introduced in Section 4.2, we associate each RDF class with a unique Skolem Function to generate blank node IDs for that type. For example, the ?y1, ?y2 in V1 are replaced by skolem function name SF1(?en); SF2(?pn) respectively.

3. Constructing Class Mapping Rules. Next, for each triple group, a new class mapping rule is created. The rule head is the original relational predicate, and the rule body the triples of that group.

4. Merging Class Mapping Rules. At last, some mapping rules are merged. There are two kinds of cases when rules need to be merged. One is the case of redundant rule. For example, as illustrated in Fig. 4, rule5 and rule6 will be merged into the rule5 6 because rule5 is a redundant rule. Another case is: if there is a referential constraints between two relational tables, then their corresponding rules will be merged. For example, rule3 and rule4 will be merged into the rule3 4 because there are referential constraints between zju:emp(?en,?eh) and zju:em account(?en,?an).

```
Algortihm 1: Class Mapping Rule Generation
-------------------------------------------
1. Input: set of RDF view V

2. Initialize mapping rules list M;

3. For each v in V
4.    Group the triples in v.body by subject name;
5.    Replace variables in v with corresponding skolem function;
6.    Let L be the set of triple groups of v.body:

7.    For each triple group g in L
8.       create a new mapping rule m;
9.       m.head=v.head
10.      m.body=g;
11.      add m to M
12.   End For
13. End For

14. Merge those rules that are about same RDF class;

15. Output: mapping rule list M;
```

```
Algortihm 2: Query Transformation
---------------------------------
1. Input: target query q, set of mapping rules M
2. Initialize rewriting list Q;
3. Group the triples in q.body by subject name;
4. Replace variables in q.body with corresponding skolem function;
4. Let L be the set of triple groups of q.body;

5. Add q to Q;
6. For each triple group g in L
7.    Let AM=the set of mapping rules applicable to g;
8.    For each q in Q
9.       remove q from Q;
10.      For each rule m in AM
11.         For each OPTIONAL triple t in g
12.            Let x be the variable in t and x in q.head;
13.            q.head=q.head[x/x=null];
14.         End For
15.         q=q[g/m.head];
16.         Add q' to Q;
17.      End For
18.   End For
19. End for
20. Output: rewriting list Q;
```

Fig. 5. The Algorithms. We use "q=q[a/b]" to denote replacing all occurrence of "a" in "q" with "b", and use "q.head" and "q.body" to denote the head and body of q

5.2 Rewriting Queries Using Class Mapping Rules

In this phase, the algorithm transforms the input query using the newly generated mapping rules, and outputs a set of valid rewritings.

Similarly, the algorithm starts by looking at the body of the query and group the triples by subject name. For example, there are three such groups for Q1. In the first group, three triples share the same subject name ?y1.

Next, the algorithm replace all variables ?yn with corresponding Skolem Function Names. For example, the ?y1, ?y2 in Q1 are replaced by skolem function name SF1(?en); SF2(?an) respectively.

Next, the algorithm begins to look for rewritings for each triple group by trying to find an applicable mapping rules. If it finds one, it replaces the triple group by the head of the mapping rule, and generate a new partial rewriting. After all triple groups have been replaced, a candidate rewriting is yielded. If a triple t in Q1 is OPTIONAL and no triple in the mapping rule is mapped to t, the variable in t is set to NULL as default value. Fig. 6 illustrates the rewriting process for query Q1. Because of the space limitation, only r1 and r4 are illustrated.

Definition 3 Triple Mapping. Given two triples $t1, t2$, we say $t1$ maps $t2$, if there is a variable mapping φ from $Vars(t1)$ to $Vars(t2)$ such that $t2 = \varphi(t1).Vars(t1)$ denotes the set of variables in $t1$.

Definition 4 Applicable Class Mapping Rule. Given a triple group g of a query Q, a mapping rule m is a *Applicable Class Mapping Rules* with respect to g, if there is a triple mapping τ that maps every *non optional* triple in g to a triple in m.

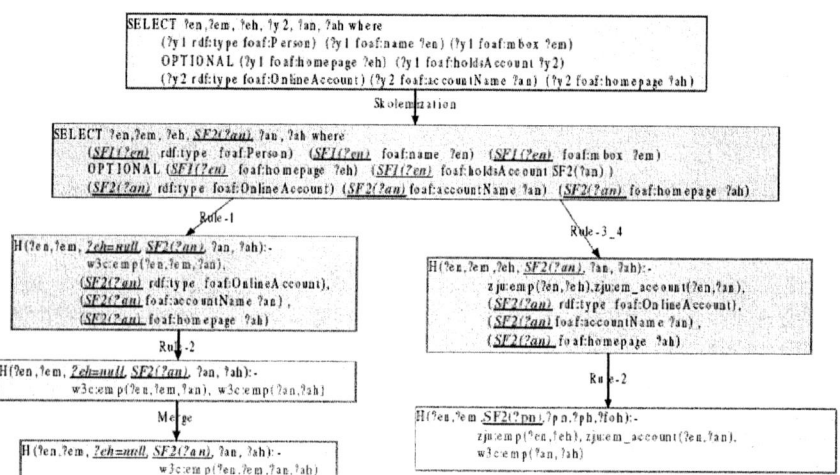

Fig. 6. The query rewriting example. The final rewriting is expressed using Datalog like notation which can be easily transformed into a SQL query.

6 Experimental Evaluations

The first goal of our experiment is to validate that our algorithm can scale up to deal with large mapping complexity . We consider two general classes of relational schema: chain schema and star schema. In these two case, we consider queries and views that have the same shape and size. Moreover, we also consider the worst case in which two parameters are looked upon: (1)The number of triple groups of query, (2)The number of sources. The whole system is implemented in Java and all experiments are performed on a PC with a single 1.8GHz P4 CPU and 512MB RAM, running Windows XP(SP2) and JRE 1.4.1.

Chain Scenario. In a chain schema, there are a line of relational tables that are joined one by one with each other. The chain scenario simulates the case where multiple inter-linked relational tables are mapped to a target RDF ontology with large number of levels (depth). The panel A of Fig. 7 shows the performance in the chain scenario with the increasing length of the chain and also the number of views. The algorithm can scale up to 300 views under 10 seconds.

Star Scenario. In a star schema, there exists a unique relational tables that is joined with every other tables, and there are no joins between the other tables. The star scenario simulates the case where source relational tables are mapped to a target RDF graph with large branching factor .The panel B of Fig. 7 shows the performance in the star scenario with the increasing branching factor of the star and also the number of views. The algorithm can easily scale up 300 views under 1 seconds. The experiments illustrate that the algorithm works better in star scenario.

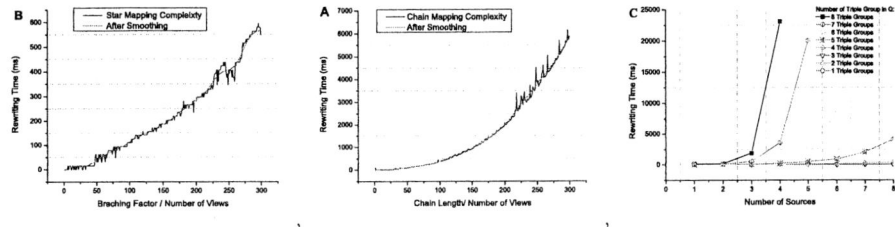

Fig. 7. Mapping Complexity Experiment. A. Chain Scenario, B. Star Scenario, C. Worst Case Analysis.

Worst Case Analysis. The worst case happens when for each RDF class, there are a lot of class mapping rules generated for them, and the number of triple groups in the query is also large. In this case, for each triple group of the query, there are a lot of applicable mapping rules. Thus, there would be many rewritings, since virtually all combinations produce valid rewritings, and complete algorithm is forced to form an exponential number rewritings. In the experiment illustrated in C in Fig. 7, we set up 10 sources, and for each source, 8 chained tables are mapped to 8 RDF classes respectively. The figure shows the cost of rewriting increases quickly as the number of triple groups and number of sources increases. As can be seen, in the case of 8 groups, the cost reaches 25 seconds with only 4 sources.

7 Summary and Future Work

This paper study the problem answering RDF queries using RDF views over incomplete relational databases under RDFS semantic constraints. We define a Target RDF Instance that satisfies all the requirements with respect to the given views and RDFS semantic constraints such as rdfs:subClassof, rdfs:subPropertyof, rdfs:domain, and rdfs:range, which are present in RDF model but neither XML nor relational models, and take the semantics of query answering to be the result of evaluating the query on this Target RDF Instance. With our approach, we highlight the important role played by the RDF blank nodes in representing incomplete information of relational data. The implementation of a visual semantic mapping tool and the application in the TCM domain are also reported. Some of the open questions that remain to be answered are: extension to a more expressive RDF-based query languages such as:inverse role, recursive queries, functional property etc.. And how to make the mappings evolve if the ontology evolves with time is also an important issue we are taking into consideration.

References

1. Christian Bizer, Andy Seaborne. D2RQ -Treating Non-RDF Databases as Virtual RDF Graphs.Poster at ISWC2004.
2. Alon Y. Halevy, Zachary G. Ives, Peter Mork, Igor Tatarinov. Peer Data Management Systems: Infrastructure for the Semantic Web.WWW2003.

3. Francois Goasdoue. Answering Queries using Views: a KRDB Perspective for the Semantic Web. ACM Transaction on Internet Technology.June 2003, P 1-22.
4. Chris Bizer, Freie. D2R MAP - A Database to RDF Mapping Language.WWW2003.
5. A. Y. Halevy. 2001. Answering queries using views: A survey. Journal of Very Large Database, 2001; 10(4), 75-102.
6. Serge Abiteboul. Complexity of Answering Queries Using Materialized Views. PODS1998, 254-263.
7. X. Qian. Query folding. ICDE1996, 48-55.
8. Rachel Pottinger ,Alon Y. Halevy. 2001. MiniCon: A Scalable Algorithm for Answering Queries Using Views.Journal of Very Large Database 2001; 10(2-3), 182-198.
9. Cong Yu and Lucian Popa. Constraint-based XML Query Rewriting for Data Integration.SIGMOD 2004, 371-382.
10. A. Deutsch and V. Tannen. MARS: A system for publishing XML from mixed and redundant storage. VLDB2003

An Effective Searching Method Using the Example-Based Query

Kil Hong Joo and Jaeho Lee

Dept. of Computer Education,
Gyeongin National University of Education, Gyodae Street 45,
Gyeyang-gu, Incheon, Korea, 407-753
{khjoo, jhlee}@ginue.ac.kr

Abstract. An efficient searching system is needed to offer the exact result of diverse web information to the user. Due to this reason, it is important to extract and analyze the user requirements in the distributed information environment. The searching method proposed in this paper uses the keyword as well as its context information for effective searching. Moreover, the proposed searching method is extracted keywords by using the new keyword extraction method also proposed in this paper, and it is executed web searching based on keyword mining profile generated by the extracted keywords. Unlike the conventional searching method, which searched for information by representative words, the proposed searching method is more efficient and exact. This is because data are searched by the example-based query including the content information as well as the representative words. Moreover, this searching method makes a domain keyword list for a quick search. The domain keyword is the representative word of a special domain. The performance of the proposed algorithm is analyzed in a series of experiments to identify its various characteristics.

1 Introduction

In searching for web document, the structured document plays an important role in a searching system. This means that the accuracy of searching can be improved if the structured document is considered. It is important to extract the keyword that represents the characteristic of a document for efficient web searching. Therefore, words are extracted as keywords by the style-based keyword extracting method presented in this paper. This is because a word with a different style has an important or an emphasized meaning.

A profile is generated by keywords extracted using the style-based keyword extracting method, and the web searching is performed by the generated profile. In this paper, the web searching based on the keyword mining profile is used. The web searching based on the keyword mining profile can be performed according to the following steps. First, the web searching offers an example-based query according to web documents which include contents similar to requirement information to users. Second, a log is extracted by the example-based query. Third, a profile is generated by a data mining technique that is applied to the extracted log. Finally, documents similar to the profile are found out through web searching. In this method, the query is performed by the example-based query. This query differs from that of a conventional searching system. The example-based query is composed of selected pages after the direct visit to the web pages. Consequently, this paper proposes the style-based keyword extraction method. Several experiments verify the efficiency and the accuracy of the style-based keyword extraction method. Moreover, this paper designs and implements a keyword mining-based web searching system based on the style-based keyword extraction method.

This paper consists of seven parts. Section 2 describes related works and Section 3 introduces the method of a web document and the style-based keyword extraction method based on the structured document. In Section 4, a profile generation method based on the extracted keyword and the web searching based on a keyword mining profile are shown. In Section 5, the method described in Sections 3 and 4 are analyzed in a series of experiments to identify its various characteristics. Finally, Section 6 draws overall conclusions.

2 Relate Work

For each word used in a structured document, its term weight is calculated to choose the keywords of the document. For this purpose, the *TF*IDF* (Term Frequency Inversed Document Frequency) [3, 4] is used widely to reflect the importance of a specific word in a document. The term frequency (TF) of a word in a document is the number of occurrences of the word in the document. The inverse document frequency (IDF) of a word is the number of documents containing the word, and it indicates how commonly the word is used in the documents of the data set. When the IDF of a word is high, the usage of the word is localized to a small number of documents in the data set. According to the TF*IDF method, the weight $tfidf_{ij}$ of a word w_j in a document d_i is defined as follows:

$$tfidf_{ij} = tf_{ij} \times \ln \frac{N}{df_i}$$

where N is the total number of documents in a data set and the term frequency tf_{ij} denotes the frequency of a word w_j occurred in a document d_i. In addition, the document frequency df_j denotes the number of documents that the word w_j appears in the data set. The *TF*IDF* function means that the possibility that a specific word represents the key concept of a particular document is proportional to the frequency of the word in the document. At the same time, it is also inversely proportional to the number of documents that contain the word. In other words, a word can be one of keywords for a document if it appears frequently in a small number of documents in a data set. However, the *TF*IDF* function suffers from the following weak point: As the number of documents in a data set becomes larger, the effect of the *IDF* of a word on the term weight of the word in each document increases, especially when most of the documents contain a small number of words as in web documents.

Generally, the document length normalization is used by the maximum frequency normalization and the cosine normalization [5]. The maximum frequency normalization is defined by dividing the frequency of each word by the maximum frequency in a document. The cosine normalization has been widely used in a vector space model. In the cosine normalization, given a vector $V = \{v_1, v_2, ..., v_n\}$, each element of the vector is divided by a cosine normalization element $\sqrt{v_1^2 + v_2^2 + ... + v_n^2}$. This cosine normalization makes it possible to normalize the length of a document based on the frequencies of all words in a document.

The studies for the example-based query have been performed with a document clustering and a categorization [9, 10, 11]. In order to express the example-based query, it is important to consider the association rule among words in a document based on data mining [12]. Association rule [13] is a powerful method for so-called *market basket analysis*, which aims at finding regularities in the shopping behavior of customers of supermarkets, mail-order companies, and the like. With the association rules one tries to find sets of products that are frequently bought together, so that from the presence of certain products in a shopping cart one can infer (with a high probability) that certain other products are present. The association rule is defined in a frequent itemset which satisfies the minimum support [13]. If a frequent itemset and an items support are known, the association rule can be easily found. Accordingly, the study [14, 15] on searching a frequent itemset has been actively carried out. The main problem of association rule is that there are so many possible rules. For example, for the product range of a supermarket, which may consist of several thousand different products, there are billions of possible association rules. It is obvious that such a vast amount of rules cannot be processed by inspecting each one in turn. Therefore, efficient algorithms are needed to restrict the search space and check only a subset of all rules, but, if possible, without missing important rules. Such algorithms are an Apriori algorithm [14], a DHP algorithm [15], a partition algorithm [16] and a DS algorithm [17].

3 Style-Based Keyword Extraction Method

A document keyword is the most important factor to structurize document in a web searching system. Since the keyword of a document represents the contents of the document, the efficiency of the web searching system can be improved if it extracts exact keywords. To overcome the weak points of the conventional frequency-based keyword extraction method, this paper proposes a new keyword extraction method considering a weight support based on styles of a document. Since the words that are different from the rest of the words that complete the whole document style have an important meaning or emphasis, the style-based keyword extracting method extracts keywords according to the difference of styles. For example, if the size of a font point of a word is 15 when the size of a font point of the overall style is 10, it is recognized as an emphasis word. In addition, if the font color of a word is blue when the overall font color is black, it is also recognized as an emphasis word.

Text Formatting tags among HTML tags represent how an applied word should be expressed in the browser. Several tags can be applied to a single word, and the word style can be decided by the integrated results of tags. Therefore, the keyword weight of the style-based keyword extracting method is calculated by the style expressed on the browser as a final result. In this paper, the style of a word is composed of 7 measures presented in [12], and the word is calculated by each measure. The keyword of document is decided by the frequency of word in the document. All conventional keyword extracting methods got the same weight as frequency. However, the style-based keyword extracting method presented in this paper does not regard the frequency as the same one and calculates frequency by the weight of applied styles. The frequency is calculated by considering the weight of words after adding up normalizing weights calculated by 7 style measures in the table 1. In this paper, a document word extracting method is used by presented in [13] and the style actually applied in the document is defined as a style instance. For example, if the font sizes in a document are 12, 14 and 24, those style instances become 12, 14 and 24. The style instance of the font style can become italic, normal, and oblique.

Let SW_i and SV_i denote the weight and the value of a style instance i respectively. The style weight SW_i is defined as two kinds of styles. First, the weight is calculated by the mean value of relevant SV_i to decide the relative importance in the document since the more SV_i is, the more important it is. If the SV_i becomes bigger than the mean value, a positive weight is given, and if the SV_i smaller than that, a negative weight is given. In addition, when the value is getting increasingly farther from the mean value, the weight is getting bigger. In the first method, the normalization of SV_i is carried out by making the value divided by the standard deviation. In addition, let SC_i denote the count of words in which the style instance i is applied, the mean value of the style instance i is defined as the representative value of SV_i. The mean value and the standard deviation are calculated by regarding SC_i as a frequency. The first style weight can be defined by Equation (1).

$$SW_i = \frac{SV_i - SC_{avg}}{SC_{sd}} \quad (1)$$

where SC_{avg} and SC_{sd} denote a mean value and a standard deviation respectively.

The second method decides the importance based on the count of words in which style instance is applied when it is difficult to decide the importance by the style instance values such as font family, font style, color, text align and text decoration. In other words, as the number of the applied word is decreased, the word is more important. For this reason, the representative value of a style instance is contrasted with total word count of document, and this is defined as the ratio of the count of words to which a relevant style instance is applied. The count of words to which a style instance is applied is defined as a frequency, and a mean value and a standard deviation are calculated. Given the total word count of document TC, the value of a style instance i SV_i denotes SC_i/TC. Therefore, the second style weight can be defined by Equation (2). Unlike the Equation (1), Equation (2) gets negative number because SV_i is not important.

$$SW_i = \frac{SV_i - SC_{avg}}{SC_{sd}} = \frac{SC_{avg}}{SC_{sd}} - \frac{SC_i}{TC \cdot SC_{sd}} \quad (2)$$

Given the set of applied tag instance T, the occurrence frequency of word w_i, in which instance j is given, can be defined as $fv_{i,j}$. The occurrence frequency $fv_{i,j}$ is calculated by adding the sum of weight of applied style instance and sum of 1 in Equation (3).

$$fv_{i,j} = 1 + \sum_{k \in T} SW_k \qquad (3)$$

Given instance set of word w_i I, the total sum of occurrence frequency fv of instances of w_i becomes an occurrence frequency fv_i whose weight of word w_i is applied, and it is defined by Equation (4).

$$fv_i = \sum_{j \in i} fv_{i,j} \qquad (4)$$

The frequency F_i in which a normalized weight of word w_i is applied should be calculated by carrying out normalization after supposing that fv_i values make the standard normal distribution. Let FV_{avg} and FV_{sd} denote a mean value and a standard deviation of fv_i values respectively. F_i can be defined by Equation (5). As a result, F_i becomes style weight of word w_i.

$$F_i = P(Z < a), \quad a = \frac{fv_i - FV_{avg}}{FV_{sd}}. \qquad (5)$$

4 Web Searching Based on a Keyword Mining Profile

A web searching based on a keyword mining profile provides users with necessary web documents, which includes contents similar to information that users need using an example-based query. Therefore, a query is evaluated by the example-based query without the direct input of keyword.

4.1 Target and Context Profiles

The web searching based on a keyword mining profile is carried out by the following steps. First, the web documents, which include contents similar to the information users want are provided to the example-based query and a log is extracted. Second, a profile is generated by applying a data mining technique to the extracted log. Third, similar documents are searched based on the generated profile. The query method is performed by the example-based query and it does not need direct input of the keyword that is performed in the conventional searching system. The query is completed with the selection of pages that belongs to the query after the visit of the real web pages that represent the necessary contents. A web site indicates more than one subject, and the subject should be composed of detailed subjects. For instance, the documents on the newspaper web site are news articles. However, they are also divided into political, social, economic, and sports articles in detail. Therefore, the documents required through the web site belong to the web site subject or its detailed subjects, and the subject in which necessary documents are included is regarded as the context of necessary content.

In the conventional searching method, if a user provides a keyword which represents the necessary document, *Target*, pages showing the searching words are shown as its result. However, these methods have the common weak point that the meaning of a searching word should be different according to the subject used by users. For example, when the word "environment" is inputted as a searching word, its meaning should be different according to subjects that belong to: politics, economics, academy and education. As a result, the searching word will be included in the searched results but unwanted meaning can also exist. Given the overall web document set U and the set of documents that included the searching words S in Figure 1, C is the subset of S ($C \subset S$). The set C is equal to a set of searching results. In addition, the difference set $P(=S-C)$, the complement of C in S, is the set in which not only the searching word but also unnecessary searching results due to the various meanings of words are included. In this paper, a set of documents that include unnecessary results is called the negative error set. The aim of this paper is to reduce the negative error set.

The negative error set can be reduced if the users search words using not only a keyword but also the context which belongs to the keyword. Hence, this paper should be considered both the Target query and the Context query including the Target query. *Target* represents the contents like the objective searching word used in the conventional searching method. Since *Context* means the context information including *Target*, the exact meaning of *Target* in *Context* can be defined and the negative error set can be reduced. In addition, the searching method proposed in this paper used the related meaning between *Context* and *Target* for exact searching. Accordingly, the searching method proposed in this paper carried out searching based on a Context profile, a Target profile and a Context-Target profile.

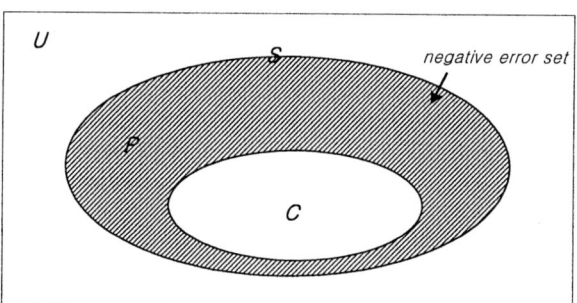

Fig. 1. A set of web documents

4.2 Generation of the Profile Based on *Target* and *Context*

In the searching method proposed in this paper, a query is composed of selected pages, and each page is composed of words. In addition, keywords extracted from the keyword extraction method represent a page within a query. As a result, the keyword is the basic unit that makes a query and the site is the basic unit that represents contents that a user finds since *Target* and *Context* should be chosen together in defining a query. If keywords shown in various sites are extracted at the same time when the keyword is extracted, the exact information can be provided to the user. If the query is composed of a single page, the keyword set which represents a page can be decided by the profile. To increase the accuracy of searching method, this paper shows a useful summary from much information by choosing a number of examples as queries. At this time, an Apriori algorithm [13], one of data mining techniques, is used for the generation of the profile. The steps in which the profiles are generated by the example-based query consist of four steps with Figure 2.

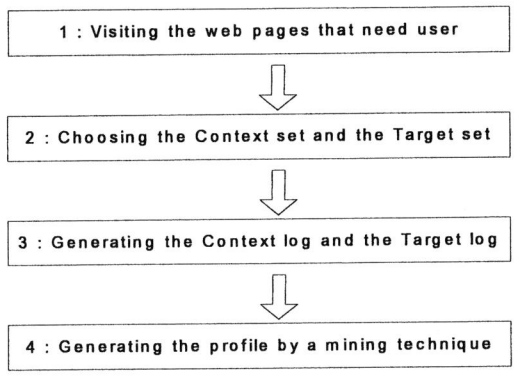

Fig. 2. The generation procedure of a profile

In Figure 2, steps 1 and 2 are the defining steps of queries. In the case of searching for *Context* or *Target* page which users want in visiting web pages, a keyword is extracted from the representative page or the needed region in a page. If the region which needs to be extracted exists in discrete several regions, it is selected and extracted in order. A query is defined applying repeatedly about all pages. After the query definition, a log generation process is carried out in step 3. In step 3, the link structure among web pages selected from *Context* and *Target* and the log for making profile of *Context* and *Target* from key sets of each page are generated. Logs generated in this step are a Context log, a Target log and a Context-Target log respectively. The Context log is a keyword list of pages decided as *Context* by each site. The Target log is also a keyword list of pages decided as *Target* by each site. The visiting order of pages in the generating Context-Target log depends on a depth-first searching method. At this time, the starting page of visiting is page selected by *Context* or *Target*.

4.3 Comparison Measures Between a Log and a Pattern

A frequent itemset is composed of a keyword and the support of the keyword. The frequent itemset is defined as a pattern. A profile is generated by this pattern, and then the pattern must be decided in accord with sites by the generated profile. Whether it corresponds with a query site which users want to search must also be checked. The generated log should be compared with the profile after generating logs by sites. When all the words of any patterns of the profile are included to the log, this pattern is called as a *complete match*. In addition, when more than half of all the words of any patterns of the profile are included to the log, this pattern is called as a *partial match*. The ratio of words which represent the agreement in contrast with the count of the total words of the pattern is called as a matching ratio of the pattern on a log. When a single log on the site satisfies more than a regular length, it is regarded as a log which satisfies the profile. This paper proposes 6 comparison measures such as a matched pattern ratio(MPR), a match word count(MWC), a pattern support(PS), a match pattern point ratio(MPRR), a pattern matching ratio in an interval(PMRI) and a word matching ratio in an interval(WMRI). These measures increase the accuracy of the matching ratio between the log and the pattern.

First, the matched pattern ratio (MPR) means a ratio whose pattern has among profiles. Second, the matched word count (MWC) describes the mean count of patterns when they match the complete match or the partial match. In other words, it shows how many word patterns which satisfy logs correspond with on average. Third, the pattern support (PS) is the mean support of patterns when they match the complete match or the partial match. It means how much support patterns they have on average. For the definition of the matched pattern point ratio (MPPR), a pattern point and a matched pattern point are defined by the definition 1 and the definition 2 respectively.

Definition 1. Pattern Point (PP)
In order to integrate a pattern which is characterized as a word and a support into a single value, a pattern point is defined as follows. Given a word count which belongs to a pattern to be a pattern length, a pattern point is defined by multiplying a pattern length by a pattern support. It is decided at the time of the generation of a profile.

$$PP = PL \times PS .$$ ∎

Definition 2. Matched Pattern Point (MPP)
Since a pattern can be the partial matching, a matched pattern point is defined as follows so that it may be ranked by a matched ratio. The matched pattern point is defined by multiplying a matched ratio by a pattern point defined by Definition 1.

$$MPP = \sum_{i \in rule} PP_i \times m_i$$ where m_i is a matching ratio of a pattern i. ∎

Therefore, the fourth measure, the matched pattern point ratio (MPPR) is defined by Equation (6). In other words, the MPPR is the ratio of a matched pattern point among total pattern points.

$$MPPR = \frac{MPP}{\sum_{i \in rule} PP_i} \qquad (6)$$

Fifth, the pattern matching ratio in an interval (*PMRI*) is the ratio of a matched pattern among the total patterns in an interval obtained after dividing patterns into a support interval. Finally, the word matching ratio in an interval (*WMRI*) is the ratio of matching word according to the pattern in an interval. The *PMRI* and the *WMRI* increase the accuracy of a searching result and obtain an exist information because of observation in detail in an interval. To make a criterion to decide the similarity with the query, the observation of the query sites is carried out. It is based on above 6 comparison measures. The value of each item is calculated in sites, and then the mean and the standard variation of the whole query sites are calculated. The similarity with the query is decided on the basis of the calculated mean and standard variation. Given the constant of a searching system n and the standard deviation of a matching ratio δ, when the mean of each matched item is allotted as a base value, it is matched in case it is less than matched region $n \times \sigma$ from the base value.

5 Experiments

In order to illustrate the performance of the proposed searching method, this section presents several experimental results. In this paper, a domain is considered to identity the effect of the proposed searching method. The domain is denoted by *DOMAIN* whose dormitory is in the USA. All experiments on the *DOMAIN* are executed with a total of 281 web pages in 18 dormitory sites randomly. The domain is searched by Yahoo search engine. The server support of a keyword is the ratio of a site that includes a keyword among total sites. In these experiments, the minimum server support is 0.6.

To verify this efficiency, Keyword Extraction based on the Style (KES) proposed in this paper is compared with Keyword Extraction based on the Frequency (KEF), the conventional method. In addition, the keyword is extracted from each page in *DOMAIN*, and the extracted keywords are divided into *KES* method and *KEF* method. Therefore, they are compared based on both *KES* and *KEF* methods. Both quantitative and qualitative comparisons are done on all experiment results to achieve more accurate results. The quantitative comparison is the ratio of domain keywords among extracted keywords. As this ratio becomes higher, the accuracy of a keyword extraction becomes higher. The qualitative comparison computes the average order in keywords which include domain keywords. As the average order becomes smaller, the accuracy of a keyword extraction becomes higher since the domain order of the extracted keyword becomes higher.

Figures 3 and 4 represent the result of a quantitative comparison and that of a qualitative comparison for the *DOMAIN* respectively. The threshold of a page keyword is varied from 0 to 0.9. As shown in Figure 3, as the threshold of a page keyword becomes higher, the accuracy of *KES* method is enhanced. As shown in Figure 4, as the threshold of a page keyword becomes higher, the average order of *KES* method is more decreased. Therefore, *KES* method provides more exact

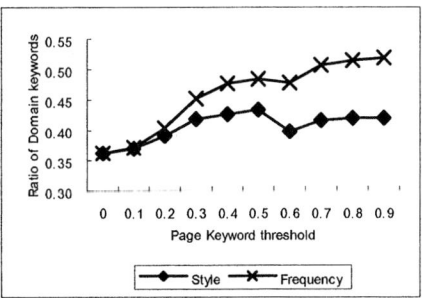

Fig. 3. A quantitative comparison

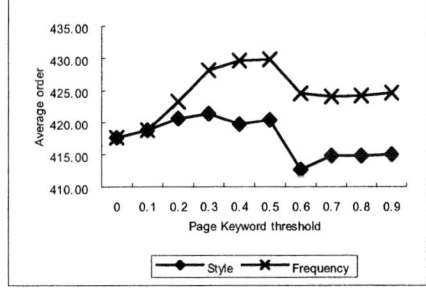

Fig. 4. A qualitative comparison

information than *KEF* method in both quantitative comparison and qualitative comparison since *KES* method extracts the keyword with much higher order.

To verify the accuracy of a profile, the profile-based decision method proposed in this paper is applied into three kinds profiles, such as a Target profile, a Context profile and a Context-Target profile. In addition, four kinds of comparison measures described in Section 4.3, such as a match pattern rate (MPR), a match word count (MWC), a pattern support (PS) and a match pattern point ratio (MPPR) are compared with the method based on only keyword. In *DOMAIN*, the Context profile is set to the notice and the bulletin board in 18 dormitories. The coefficient of a standard deviation is varied from 0.25 to 3. Figures 5, 6 and 7 show experiment results according to the context profile, the target profile and the context-target profile respectively. Y-axis means a rate of sites decided to an error. As it becomes smaller, the accuracy of a result is enhanced since it is executed in a query site. X-axis is the coefficient of a standard variation to decide the matching range and help recognize the distribution of a matched site.

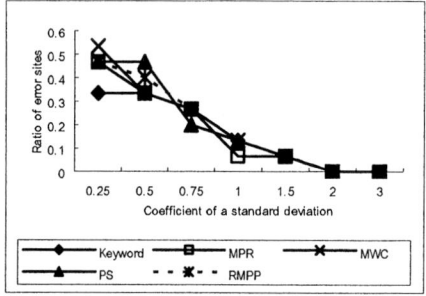
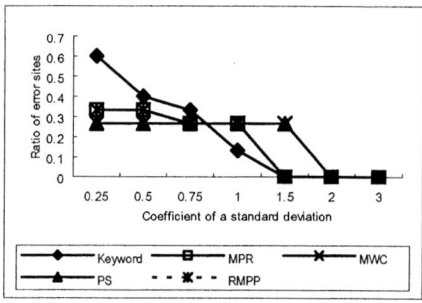

Fig. 5. Experiment result of a *Conte*xt profile   **Fig. 6.** Experiment result of a *Target* profile

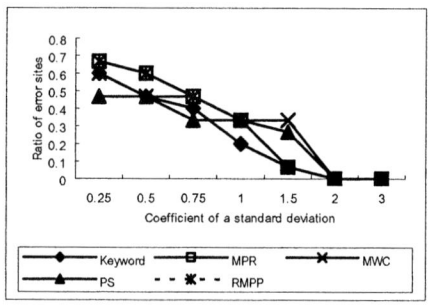

Fig. 7. Experiment result of a *Context-Target* profile

As shown in Figure 5, the result of the profile-based decision method is much better than or equal to that of the keyword-based decision method in the Context profile. Figure 6 according to the Target profile is the same with Figure 5. In Figure 7, if the coefficient of a standard deviation is less than 1, the matching ratio of the profile-based decision method is better than that of the keyword-based decision method in the Context-Target profile. Otherwise, it is smaller than the keyword-based decision method. For every profile, the gradient of the profile-based decision method is less than that of the keyword-based decision method. Therefore, the profile-based decision method is close to a base value and densely distributed. This means that the result of the profile-based decision method in a query sites is excellent, and the profile is a representative in a query site.

6 Conclusion

This paper proposes a style-based keyword extraction method to extract exact keywords. It is based on the conventional frequency-based keyword extraction method. The style of a document is analyzed by the style-based keyword extraction method. Based on the analyzed style, the importance is decided and the weight is imposed. To verify the effect of the style-based keyword extraction method, it is compared with the frequency-based keyword extraction method quantitatively and qualitatively. It was verified that the style-based keyword extraction method was even more efficient. Since it is certified that extracting keywords with a superior quality is more exact than extracting an amount of keywords by a series of experiment, the style-based keyword extraction method is superior The profile with Context information of a word is generated based on the style-based keyword extraction method. Based on the generated profile, this paper proposes and implements the web searching system based on the keyword mining profile. In this system, a query is not word-based but example-based. It is possible to search and define with the query. To verify the efficiency of the keyword mining profile, the comparison experiment is performed in the sites using the query. As a result, the keyword mining profile that considers context information of a word proved to be much more efficient than that with only a keyword.

References

1. E. shakshuki and H. Ghenniwa, "A multi-agent system architecture for information gathering". *Database and Expert Systems Applications, 2000. Proceedings. 11th International Workshop on*, pp. 732-736
2. Ricardo Baeza-Yates and Berthier Ribeiro-Neto. "Modern Information Retrieval". ADDISON WESLEY, pp. 29-30, 1999.
3. I. Aalbersberg,. "A Document Retrieval Model Based on Term Frequency Ranks". *17th international ACM SIGIR Conference on Research and Development in Information Retrieval*, 163-172, 1994
4. Amit Singhal, Chris Buckley, and Mandar Mitra. "Pivoted Document Length Normalization". *Proceedings of 19th ACM International Conference on Research and Development in Information Retrieval*, 1996
5. Cazalens S., Desmontils S., Jacquin C., and Lamarre P.. "A Web site indexing process for an Internet information retrieval agent system". *Web Information Systems Engineering 2000. Proceedings of the First International Conference on, Volumn: 1*, pp. 254-258 vol.1, 2000

6. M. Scmidt and U. Ruckert, "Content-based information retrieval using an embedded neural associative memory". *Parallel and Distributed Processing 2001 Proceedings. Ninth Euromicro Workshop on*, pp. 443-450
7. Weifeng Li, Baowen Xu, Hongji Yang, Cheng-Chung Chu W., and Chih-Wei Lu at Dept. of Compt. Sci. & Eng. Southeast Univ., Nanjing, China. "Application of genetic algorithm in search engine". *Multimedia Software Engineering, 2000. Proceedings. International Symposium on*, pp. 366-371
8. R. Weiss, B. Velez, M. Sheldon, C. Nemprempre, P. Szilagyi, and D. K. Gifford, HyPursuit: A hierachical Network engine that exploits content-link hypertext clustering. In *Proc. Of the 7th ACM Conference on Hypertext and Hypermedia*, pp. 180-193, Washington, DC, USA, 1996
9. A. Broder, S. Glassman, M. Manasse, and G. Zweig. Syntactic clustering of the web. In *6th Int. WWW Conference*, pp 391-404, Snata Clara, CA, USA, April 1997.
10. C-H. Chang and C-C. Hsu. Customizable mulit-engine search tool with clustering. In *6th Int. WWW Conference*, Santa Clara, Ca, USA, April 1997.
11. Jiawei Han, "Data Mining". Encyclopedia of Distributed Computing, Kluwer Academic Publisher.
12. R. Agrawal and R. Srikant, "Mining association rules betweensets of items in large databases. Proceeding of the ACM SIGMOD Conference on Management of Data, pp 207-216, Washington, D.C., May 1993
13. R. Agrawal and R. Srikant, "Fast algorithms for mining association rules", In Proceedings of the 20th VLDB Conference, Santiago, Chile, Sept., 1994
14. J.S. Park, M-S. Chen, and P.S. Ui, "An effective hash-based algorithm for mining association rules", In Proceedings of ACM SIGMOD Conference on Management of Data, pp.175-186, San Jose, California, May, 1995.
15. A. Savasere, E. Omiencinsky and S. Navathe, " An efficient algorithm for mining association rules in large databases ", In Proceedings of the 21th VLDB Conference, pp 4320444, Zurich, Swizerland, 1995.
16. J.S. Park, P.S. Yu, and M.-S. Chen, "Mining Association Rules with Adjustable Accuracy", In Proceedings of ACM CIKM 97, pp.151-160, Las Vegas, Nevada, November, 1997.
17. S.Brin, R. Motwani, J.D. Ullman, and S. Tsur, "Dynamic itemset Counting and Implication Rules for Market Basket Data", In Proceedings of ACM SIGMOD Conference on Management of Data, Tucson, Arizona, pp. 255-264, May, 1997.

On Communicating with Agents on the Network

Rajat Shuvro Roy[1] and M. Sohel Rahman[2]

[1] BRAC University, Department of Computer Science and Engineering,
Dhaka, Bangladesh
rajatshuvroroy@yahoo.com
[2] Bangladesh University of Engineering and Technology,
Department of Computer Science and Engineering,
Dhaka, Bangladesh
sohel_rahman_joy@yahoo.com

Abstract. We define an agent to be any node in the network that is prepared to provide some services to other parties when requested. Such services may be required for various purposes and then, searching and establishing communication with the agent will be necessary. The agent search may be oriented along a particular direction to reduce network load and optimize overall performance. Such oriented algorithms already exist. In this paper we have given a communications protocol that may use such oriented algorithm, defined its request and response packet formats and shown the simulation results for overhead incurred in such communication.

1 Motivation

The internet began as a communications network for researchers who used it to exchange information among themselves. With its growing popularity, its use is expanding into newer and newer spheres. The size and complexity of the internet is growing at an exponential rate. At one point it was assumed that all internet communications will know the destination machine. But in some cases we may not know exactly who we want to communicate with. The following examples will help to clarify the problem.

1. <u>Multicast retransmission node for reliable multimedia stream:</u> Usually the source of the stream redirects the client to the retransmission node. But in a dynamically changing network the best retransmission agent cannot be statically defined. And since the client wants the service, it may be in a better position to search and determine the best retransmission agent. Such nodes may be searched along the path to the source of the multimedia stream.
2. <u>Application gateway to convert data between incompatible clients:</u> The internet is a network of networks. Different networks may use different data and packet formats. If the two communicating parties have incompatible data formats they might need a gateway to convert the data for them. From the perspective of performance measure, it would be preferable to find a gateway along or around the shortest path between the two parties.

3. <u>Mirror Web Sites:</u> Many popular websites in the world use mirror websites to distribute load and enhance performance. When a request comes in, it is redirected to the nearest possible site. But it would have been more convenient if the client could have automatically detected a mirror site in its neighborhood without bothering for redirection from the main website.

With the never-ending increase of the nature and number of services in the Internet, knowing in advance which service provider (agent) will provide a service is a burden for the client. Moreover, in a dynamically changing web, a 'static agent' selection may not always give the best performance. For increasing the efficiency or facilitating newer functions on the internet, we need to take intermediaries into account and find an efficient way to communicate with them. The most important point to note here is that the "agent" is initially unknown.

In this paper we try to define a protocol to establish connection with agents for all types of service request and propose the oriented search of [1] as a good agent search mechanism. We present the reply methods of the responding agents (based on their classification) as well as the optimization of these replies messages to the source. Once the replies are collected, we have to select the best agent if more than one is found. We have addressed this issue. The protocol implementation of the oriented agent search algorithm and the reply methods have been proposed. The resulting agent search and communication protocol may serve many network protocols and facilitate many different types of interactions which require a topologically smart-placed intermediary. Finally, we show how much overhead traffic is required for using the protocol.

2 Agent Search and Communication

We often use agents on the internet. But the problem is, the identity of the agent we are using (in the form of IP address or any other form) has to be specified in advance. This can cause serious performance drawbacks as is evident from the following scenario:

Suppose *user 1* wants to communicate with *user 2* (Figure 2.1). The communication needs the mediation of an agent. *User 1* knows that *AGENT 1* can provide him with the required service. But unfortunately, the path via *AGENT 1* is far from the shortest path. Using this path will result in a considerable loss in performance. But unknown agents (Agent2) may exist near the shortest path. So, we need a method of discovering and communicating with (initially) unknown agents which may be near the shortest path.

Please note that by shortest path we always mean the path selected by the underlying unicast routing algorithm.

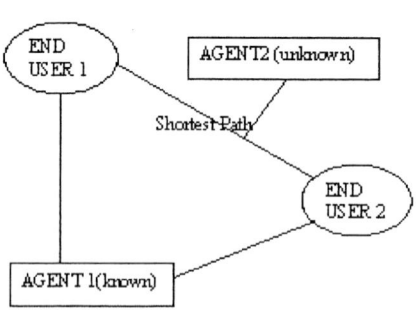

Fig. 2.1

2.1 Agent Search Algorithm

The classical technique currently used for agent search is the expanding ring search (ERS) combining the idea of Reverse Path Forwarding (RPF) [7]. For more detail please see [1, section 2]. It is important to note that, a request packet propagated by an ERS by a source S does not take into account the position of the other actors of the communication and floods surrounding nodes in all directions. For efficiency, controlling the flooding and finding a smart placed agent is very important.

However, in most cases, if not all, we could find a special target node serving as a beacon for the search area. We believe, an agent search protocol based on the oriented framework, which uses this information (e.g. that of [1]), could give the client the possibility to find a topologically smart-placed intermediary in the network. The basic idea of the algorithm is described in brief in the following paragraphs. For more detail please see [1,section 3].

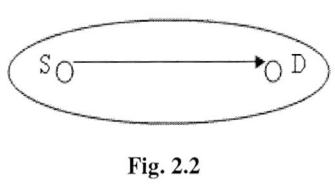

Fig. 2.2

Let S be the source node and D be the destination node. S and D are communicating (Figure 2.2) along the path connecting S and D (from here on referred to as S-D). They need an agent to assist in their communication. What the algorithm will do is to conduct a limited search in and around the shortest path (as indicated by the oval boundary).

There are many variants of this searching algorithm which will produce different shapes of the searching area (see [1, section 3] for details). The agent searching packets contain a special field called the *'range'*. As long as the packet travels along the shortest path between S and D, it is broadcasted on every link of the node except the arrival link and the range is not decreased. When it goes out of the shortest path S-D, the broadcasting policy depends on the parameter settings of the algorithm. It is clear that the total area of broadcast can be carefully controlled by the way we handle the parameter *'range'*.

2.2 Classification of Agents

After the service request has been sent out the next steps of establishing connection will depend on the service requested and agent's capabilities. We believe a classification of the agents based on these factors will make the process more efficient.

TYPE 1: The agent has everything that the client wants and is prepared to start providing the service immediately (e.g. proxy servers or mirror web sites).

TYPE 2: The agent is capable of providing the service but it cannot immediately start doing so. The service might need accumulation, compilation and computation of data depending on the request (e.g. a search engine, a simulator, etc).

TYPE 3: Both the client and the agent needs to be identified (e.g. an online sale house may have to identify itself to the income tax agent and vice versa).

TYPE 4: The agent is either too busy or unable to provide the service. So, it simply redirects the request to another agent who might provide the service.

2.3 Reply Methods

Once a service has been requested and an agent has received the request, the agent and the user must communicate. We present a mechanism which will enable such a communication without any parties having any specific prior knowledge of the other. When the request packet is seen by an agent, willing to provide the service, the first response packet will contain the following data for agent type 1, 2 & 3:

1. The type of the agent (based on the type shown above).
2. The encoding of the challenge string that will validate the agent. How such a technique may work will be discussed in section 2.4.
3. Quality of Service Parameters (QOS: Total travel time, Total queue time, Bandwidth, etc), that indicate how fast a service may be provided to the client.

Apart form the data above, according to the specific type of the agent, the following steps should follow.

TYPE 1 Agent: If there is space left in the 1st packet, some data may be piggybagged. The agent will wait for an ACK/NAK form the client. The client on getting the response will decide which agent to use (see sec 2.5).

TYPE 2 Agent: Since, the service needs to be provided by first preparing the results, a rough estimate of the time to prepare the service should be provided in the 1st packet. If the request packet contains enough data for preparing the results, the agent may simultaneously start processing the request so that if it is selected, it can provide the service quickly. If the client later rejects this agent, the prepared service, in some cases, may be cached to be quickly utilized elsewhere.

Note that in both the above cases, the chosen agent will be sent an ACK (Acknowledgement), the others a NAK (Negative Acknowledgement). . The agent will wait for an ACK for a specific time and if there is no reply form the client within that time, it will terminate the communication with a NAK.

TYPE 3 Agent: The 1st response packet will also contain a challenge byte stream that the client will encode to prove its identity. No data may be transferred at this stage. After receiving the first packet, if the user decides to use this agent, it will send the 2nd packet with its proper identification (possibly by encoding the challenge string). If the agent is satisfied with the client's authentication, the agent may establish the communication by sending an ACK. If the client makes an unusual delay, the agent will assume the communication to be dead and will terminate with a NAK to the client.

TYPE 4 Agent: The agent will simply redirect the request packet it has received by encapsulation (IP-within-IP Encapsulation Protocol, [6]), to another agent, who it believes, may be able to provide the service. This strategy may be employed if the agent is too busy or unable to provide the service. This would of course require cooperation among the agents. The client will have nothing to do with it.

Please note that, at any point any party may terminate the communication by sending a NAK packet.

2.4 Authentication

We assume that a Public Key Infrastructure (PKI) [3,sec8.7.5] exists with a directory structure that hand over the certificates for public keys. The PKI has multiple components, including users, Certification Authorities, directories, etc. With this structure we may authenticate Clients and agents as follows. The client sends out a random byte stream (B_a) that the agent will encrypt. The Agent encrypts B_a producing cipher text $E_a(B_a)$, and sends with it another random byte stream B_c that the client will encode to prove its identity. The client gets the agent's decryption key (D_a) which is public and stored at the PKI directory, and decrypts the encoded byte stream of the agent. If $D_a(E_a(B_a))= B_a$ then the agent is valid. To prove its identity, now the client encrypts the byte stream B_c sent by the agent with its encryption key producing cipher text $E_c(B_c)$. The agent, on receiving the cipher text from the client, will get the decryption key D_c form the directory and decrypt the cipher text. If it is identical with B_c, then the client is validated.

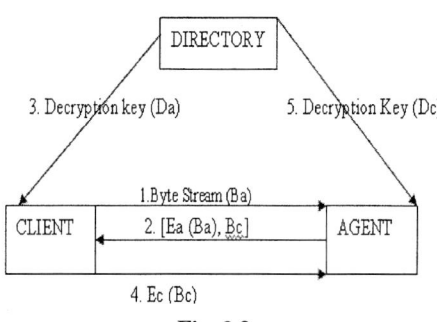

Fig. 2.3

2.5 Multiple Agent Scenarios

Multiple agents may respond to the service request. In such circumstances, it is the responsibility of the user, to choose one agent from the responding agents based on the service parameters in the reply packets. The selected agent is sent an ACK and the rejected ones a NAK. We have identified three parameters (QOS) that may be accumulated in the reply packet as it makes its way to the client form the agent. This list may grow in the future. The parameters are described below:

Total travel time of the Packet: This parameter will give the total travel time of the packet (i.e. how long the packet has been on the wires) from the responding agent.

Total Queue Wait Time: This is an estimation of how long the response packet has been in queue. The Queue time is an indication of congestion in the network.

Minimum Bandwidth: As we know, if a path is divided into many segments, each with a different throughput, then the ultimate throughput will be given by the minimum bandwidth of all these segments. This field will be checked by each hop and updated if necessary. Thus it will give the ultimate bandwidth of the connection.

The use of these parameters in selecting the best agent is a non-trivial problem. The solution depends on the type of service that is in question and the volume of data to be transferred. If the service will be provided in small bursts of packets at regular interval, where speed is necessary (interactive in nature), the user should rely heavily on the travel time and queue wait time parameters. On the other hand, if the service is such that the packets will contain large volume of data, ensuring a good bandwidth may be more important. If the client wants real time service where jitter is an issue, the user should avoid using path with high queuing delays. If the service is such that the agent will take some time to prepare it, then the efficiency of the agent should also be taken into account.

A responsible client should also send NAK to the agents it is rejecting. This will help to avoid unnecessary packets from being released on the net which may already be congested. Instead of relying totally on the clients, an agent may also use timeouts to determine if it should keep communicating with the user. This can be a serious issue in defining the dynamic aspects of the protocol and ensuring that the service providers do not put unnecessary load on the network.

3 Protocol

The routers usually know what services they are hosting. So, for efficiency, we will define the protocol in Network Layer using IPv6 extension headers, since IPv6 is the upcoming standard for network layer packets. Note carefully that in our protocol we are assuming the algorithm given in [1]. The extension headers that we are going to describe below are both Hop-by-Hop Options header.

REQUEST EXTENSION HEADER FORMAT

Next Header	Hdr Ext Len=1	Option Type=X	Opt Data Len=6
Algorithm bits	Initial Range	Function ID	Distance Covered
Len of challenge str	Range	Request ID	
PAYLOAD(not part of the ext. header) (The whole payload contains the random challenge byte stream)			

Next Header, Hdr Ext Len, Option Type, Opt Data Len: Please see [2] for detail.
Algorithm Bits: Bit fields (6 bits) required for the agent search algorithms of [1].
Initial Range: Defines the initial range value of a packet [1].
Function ID: Identifies the function or service searched by the source.
Distance_covered: Number of hops already covered.
Len of Challenge Str: Length of the Challenge string that is in the payload field.
Range: Integer used to define the degree of multicasting [1].
Request ID: This will be a unique number that will identify each request and will help the client identify a request and associated responses.

REPLY EXTENSION HEADER FORMAT

Next Header	Hdr Ext Len=1	Option Type=X	Opt Data Len
Function ID	Agent Type (T)	(For Type 3) Length of new Challenge String (For other types) Length of Piggy Bagged Data	Length of reply to challenge string
Request ID		(if T=2) Response Processing Time	
Total Travel Time(m sec)		Total Queue Time(in mSec)	
Min. Bandwidth of path(Kbps)			
PAYLOAD(not part of the ext. header) (The payload contains reply to challenge string and new challenge string if T=3. Else the agent might piggy bag some data)			

Next Header, Hdr Ext Len, Option Type, Opt Data Len, Function ID, Request ID: Same as in request extension header.

Agent Type: 4-bit selector, identifies the type of the agent as described in section 2.2. If the agent type is 3, it means that the user needs to be identified in order to be provided with the service. In that case the next 12 bits will give the length of the new challenge string that will be sent to the user for identifying itself. For other cases, if the agent feels that the service may be provided immediately, it may piggy bag some data in the payload of the IP packet. In such cases this 12-bit field will give the size of the piggy bagged data.

Response Processing Time: In case of Agent type 2, the response needs to be prepared. The agent will provide an estimate of the time required in this field.

Total Travel Time, Total Queue Time, Min Bandwidth : As defined in Section 2.5.

We can safely assume that the packet processing time at each hop is negligible compared to the travel time and queue time. Based on these parameters the source will have to derive an idea about the line condition between itself and the agent. It is very important to realize that the packet parameters are giving information about the path AS i.e. from the Agent to the client. But not the other way round. That is, we have no information about the path Client-Agent (SA). Although this is definitely an important issue to further look into, in many cases we can reasonably assume symmetric behavior and hence can approximate the information of the SA path form the information of AS path. This is very important when the service to be provided is such that a lot of data will travel along SA. Also in such cases, the source may use its own routing table to know about the line condition leading up to A.

4 Overhead Simulations

All network traffic in excess of the service being provided is considered overhead. So, all packets for service request, agent searching and selecting are overhead. We here perform the simulation on the first 3 types of agents. Note that, Type 4 agents merely redirect the request packets to known agents.

4.1 Simulation Environment

We have coded the simulation for overhead calculation using the JAVA programming language. In each iteration, we generate a random number of agents and random amount of data for service (both within their selected group limits). Each agent runs as a separate thread. The client (another thread) generates request packets and sends them to the agent threads. The communication then follows the steps as described in section 2.3. The sizes of all packets are recorded until an agent is finally selected for service. This gives the overhead of the current communication session. Twenty Thousand (20000) such communications have been aggregated to provide the final result for each agent type and data set (each bar in the bar chart and each entry in the table). We ran the simulation on a single-processor 300 MHz Pentium II WindowsXP desktop with 192MB RAM.

4.2 Simulation Results

Data Classes: We have divided the services in to four groups based on their data volume as follows:

Data Group	1	2	3	4
Data Size	1 KB to 4 KB	4 KB to 10 KB	10 KB to 1 MB	1 MB to 10 MB

Number of Agents Hit: The overhead incurred in an agent search and communication is directly proportional to the number of agents hit. So, we have performed simulation separately for different number of agents hit. The agent groups are as follows:

Group	1	2	3
Number of Agents	1 to 5	1 to 8	1 to 16

Table 1. Overhead for Agent type 1

Agent Group	1 to 16	Overhead ratio	1 to 8	Overhead ratio	1 to 5	Overhead ratio
Authentication	No		No		No	
Data Set	1	0.651303	1	0.297927	1	0.199701
	2	0.192156	2	0.089052	2	0.09018
	3	0.003143	3	0.001473	3	0.002895
	4	3.08E-04	4	1.33E-04	4	3.27E-04
Authentication	Yes		Yes		Yes	
Data Set	1	1.130803	1	0.523498	1	0.348711
	2	0.324915	2	0.150102	2	0.158767
	3	0.005219	3	0.002532	3	0.004965
	4	4.71E-04	4	2.31E-04	4	5.66E-04

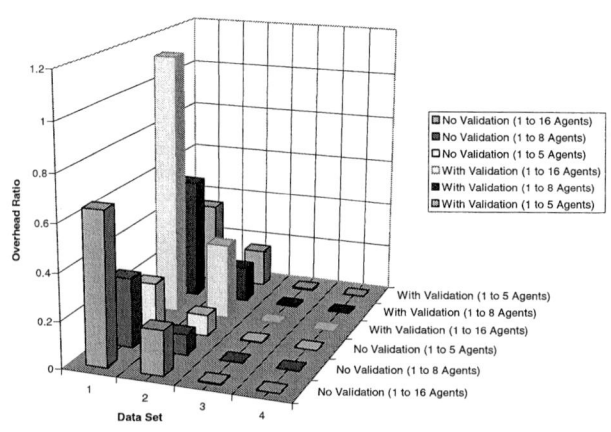

Table 2. Overhead for Agent type 2

Agent Group	1 to 16	Overhead ratio	1 to 8	Overhead ratio	1 to 5	Overhead ratio
Authentication	No		No		No	
Data Set	1	0.594139	1	0.300399	1	0.198723
	2	0.170445	2	0.136944	2	0.090371
	3	0.002876	3	0.00423	3	0.002835
	4	2.67E-04	4	4.88E-04	4	3.28E-04
Authentication	Yes		Yes		Yes	
Data Set	1	1.032231	1	0.522339	1	0.345247
	2	0.300126	2	0.23413	2	0.159326
	3	0.005041	3	0.00735	3	0.005001
	4	4.50E-04	4	8.33E-04	4	5.60E-04

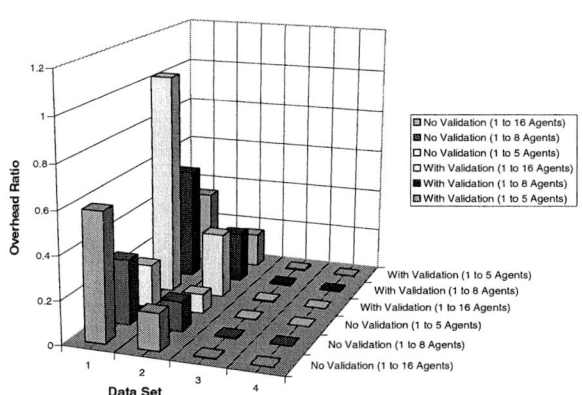

Agent Type 2

Table 3. Overhead for Agent type 3

Agent Group	1 to 16	Overhead ratio	1 to 8	Overhead ratio	1 to 5	Overhead ratio
Authentication	No		No		No	
Data Set	1	0.930572	1	0.49792	1	0.350326
	2	0.271326	2	0.226069	2	0.157163
	3	0.004578	3	0.007038	3	0.004952
	4	4.17E-04	4	8.15E-04	4	5.65E-04
Authentication	Yes		Yes		Yes	
Data Set	1	1.363299	1	0.727958	1	0.504469
	2	0.394607	2	0.332561	2	0.227699
	3	0.00636	3	0.010078	3	0.007161
	4	6.19E-04	4	1.19E-03	4	8.10E-04

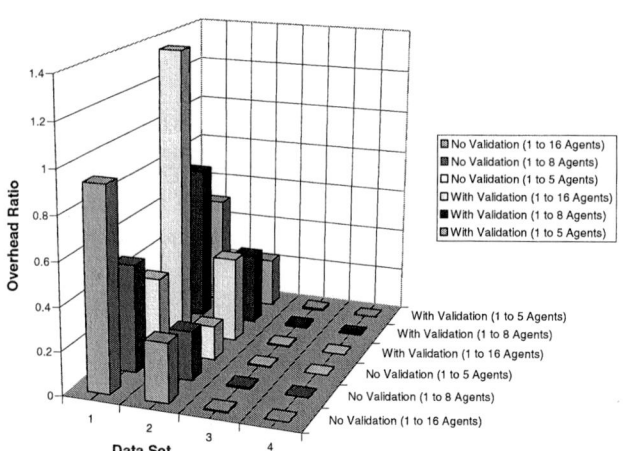

Authentication Overhead: Authentication is a stage that, in ideal situation, should not exist. However practical situations cannot be overlooked and so authentication can not be omitted. In the simulation we, therefore, show overhead both with and without authentication of agents.

In the following bar charts, overhead ratio (overhead incurred/actual data transferred) is plotted against specific data group both with and without authentication.

We highlight a few observations regarding the simulation results as follows:
- For any number of agents, the overhead incurred for small data traffic is quite substantial for Agent Type 1. For small data, many agents and authentication it is as high as 113%. But since agents are usually rare in the network, we can take the results with 1 to 8 agents as standard. Another point is that since small traffic such as 1KB to 4KB is not the usual case, we may consider 10KB to 1MB group as standard. This gives only 0.7% overhead with authentication.
- Agents of type 2 are those which offer sophisticated services (e.g. river morphology simulation). These agents are usually very rare. So, number of agents hit may be safely assumed to be 1 to 5. Authentication is important. But note that the data size may be small. E.g. the service request to solve a linear equation may consist of a small request and a small reply. So, a 1KB to 4KB data size seems plausible. Then the overhead is 34.5%. Though it is high, we must keep in mind that the utility of the service being offered far outweighs the cost of such overhead.
- Since agents of type 3 need authentication of the clients too, hence it is natural that this type of communication incurs more overhead than the other types.
- Regardless of the number of agents, for large data, the overhead is almost zero.

5 Concluding Remarks

In this paper we gave a protocol for client-agent communication. The resulting agent search and communication establishment protocol may serve many network protocols and facilitate many different types of interactions which require a topologically smart-placed intermediary. There remains, however, a number of issues that need serious considerations as follows.

- The agent or the client after releasing a packet cannot wait for ever for the response to come in. Again, too small a wait time may miss some of the more appropriate/better responses. Future research may be directed to finding appropriate timing criteria for both the agents and the clients.
- We have proposed to address the issue of choosing from among multiple responding agents basically by using three "Quality of Service" (QoS) parameters (and also "Time to Process a Response" for type 2) along and the service required. We have assumed that the client is free to use them as they please. Future works should be directed to more investigations in this regard.
- Another important point to note is that since we are relying entirely on the underlying unicast system to route the packets, the path AS (Agent-Client) may not always be the same. Due to the dynamic nature of the network, it may change at any time and thus the best agent candidate may change. If this kind of changes happens in the middle of an established communication, choosing another agent means restarting the whole process, which may not be feasible in most of the cases. Identifying those cases when a complete restart would be feasible is another issue for further consideration. For the time being, however, we ignore this issue.

Acknowledgement

The authors would like to express their gratitude to the anonymous reviewers whose helpful comments helped to improve the quality and presentation of the paper.

References

1. D. Magoni and J-J Panisot, Oriented Multicast Routing Algorithm Applied to Network-level Agent Search, *Discrete Mathematics and Theoretical Computer Science, 4, 2001, pp. 255-272.*
2. S.Deering and R.Hinden, RFC-2460 ,Internet Protocol, Version 6 (IPv6) specification, *April, 2003.*
3. A.S. Tanenbaum, Computer Networks (4th edition), *Prentice Hall, 2001.*
4. 4. Blumenthal, M.S., and Clark, D.D., Rethinking the design of the Internet: The end to end Argument vs. the brave new world. *ACM Transactions on Internet Technology 1,(August 2001).*
5. Davod D. Clark, Sollins, Wroclawski, Braden, Tussle in Cyberspace: Defining Tomorrow's Internet, *SIGCOMM'02, August 2002.*
6. RFC 1700, ASSIGNED NUMBERS.
7. Yogan Dalal and Robert Metcalfe. Reverse path forwarding of broadcast packets. *Communications of the ACM,* 21(12):1040–1048, December 1978.

Applying Fuzzy Logic to Recommend Consumer Electronics

Yukun Cao, Yunfeng Li, and Xiaofeng Liao

Department of Computer Science, Chongqing University,
Chongqing 400044, P.R. China
marilyn_cao@163.com

Abstract. Depending on the type of the product, different kinds of personalized recommender systems can be built to guide the consumers in a large product feature space. In the approach, we present a fuzzy-based recommender system for those products that a general consumer does not buy very often, especially for consumer electronic products. For those consumer electronic products, it is difficult and not necessary to reason a customer's previous preferences because there may not be enough information about the customer's past purchases and the customer may have his specific requirements in each single purchase. Hence the system has specific domain knowledge and capability to interact with the consumer. Experimental results show the promise of our systems.

1 Introduction

One way to overcome the problem of information overload on Internet is to develop intelligent recommender systems to provide personalized information services [1]: retrieving the information a consumer desires and helping him determine which one to buy. The purpose of personalized information services is to adjust strategies of promotion and advertisement to fit customer interests [2]. As there is a great deal of products on Internet, it is impossible to recommend all kinds of products in one system. But few existing recommendation systems distinguish the type of products, i.e. the recommendation method for books or CDs is the same method for computer or digital camera. We believe that the personalized recommendation system should be build according the special features of a certain kind of products, thereby forming professional recommendation systems for different products.

Depending on the type of the product, different kinds of personalized recommender systems can be built to guide the consumers in a large product feature space. For some type of product that a consumer may purchase frequently, such as books, CDs, or DVD films, recommender systems can be developed to reason his personal preferences by analyzing his personal information, his browsing history, and the products he has purchased through the Internet in the past. Yet, for those products such as computers or digital cameras that a general consumer does not buy very often as the other kinds just mentioned, it is difficult and not necessary to reason a customer's previous preferences because there may not be enough information about the customer's past purchases and the customer may have his specific requirements in each single purchase. In this situation, advises from domain experts are strongly demanded. Recommender systems are thus expected to have specific domain knowledge and capability to interact with the consumer. Consequently the systems can acquire and analyze a customer's current needs on the kind of product he has identified, and then evaluate the relevant products to help him recognize the optimal ones.

In the approach, we present a fuzzy-based recommender system for those products that a general consumer does not buy very often, especially for consumer electronic products, such as laptop, cell phone, digital camera, video games computer and so on. As the majority of purchasers of consumer electronics could use computer masterly, they might buy products through Internet frequently. Many B2C e-commerce enterprises concentrate on the sale of consumer electronic products. For example, the majority of electronic products sold by Amazon.com are consumer electronic products. And the system isn't only applied to e-commerce as an assistant system, but also could be an independent system for the real-life business.

The remainder of the paper is organized as follows. Section 2 presents the theoretical background. Implementation issues and the results of empirical studies are presented respectively in Section 3 and Section 4. Finally, the conclusion can be found in Section 5.

2 Theoretical Background

2.1 Linguistic Definition and Fuzzy Numbers

Based on the proposed system, the consumer needs and the candidate product features can be expressed in an appropriate way. In the approach, we use triangular fuzzy numbers to character consumer needs and product features.

A triangular fuzzy number is a particular case of fuzzy sets. It has a triangle-shaped membership function, which can be viewed as possibility distribution. It is supposed that $\tilde{q}$ is a triangular fuzzy number with membership function $\mu_{\tilde{p}}(x)$, and is denoted as $\tilde{q} = (q_1, q_2, q_3)$, where q_1, q_2 and q_3 are real numbers with $q_1 \leq q_2 \leq q_3$. To help consumers easily express their judgments, and domain experts easily evaluate product features, the linguistic terms are used to linguistically evaluate the importance of customer needs and ratings of product features. Seven linguistic sets, (1) Very Low (0,1,2), (2) Low (1,2,3), (3) Medium Low (2,3,4), (4) Medium (3,4,5), (5) Medium High (4,5,6), (6) High (5,6,7), (7) Very High (6,7,8), are allowable to describe the variables with one's subjective judgment.

2.2 Similarity Measure of Triangular Fuzzy Numbers

In the study, we utilize Euclidean fuzzy near compactness between two fuzzy numbers to measure the similarity between consumer needs and product features.

Suppose $\tilde{q}_A = (q_A^1, q_A^2, q_A^3)$ is a compared triangular fuzzy number, while $\tilde{q}_B = (q_B^1, q_B^2, q_B^3)$ is the target triangular fuzzy number. Then the Euclidean fuzzy near compactness between $\tilde{q}_A$ and $\tilde{q}_B$ is defined as follows:

$$N_E(\tilde{q}_A, \tilde{q}_B) = 1 - \frac{1}{\sqrt{3}} \left(\sum_{j=1}^{3} \left| q_A^j - q_B^j \right|^2 \right)^{1/2} \tag{1}$$

The above equation denotes one kind of similarity degree by calculating the Euclidean fuzzy near compactness between two triangular fuzzy numbers. While the near compactness between $\tilde{q}_A$ and $\tilde{q}_B$ gets smaller, then $\tilde{q}_A$ is more similar to $\tilde{q}_B$.

Furthermore, assume there are two sets of triangular fuzzy numbers, $\tilde{X} = (\tilde{x}_1, \tilde{x}_2, \cdots, \tilde{x}_n)$ and $\tilde{Y} = (\tilde{y}_1, \tilde{y}_2, \cdots, \tilde{y}_n)$. In fuzzy number set $\tilde{X}$, each fuzzy number $\tilde{x}_i$ is individually compared with a target fuzzy number $\tilde{y}_i$ in fuzzy number set $\tilde{Y}$. Because every fuzzy number in fuzzy number sets, $\tilde{X}$ and $\tilde{Y}$, represents a consumer need or a product feature actually, each fuzzy number in a fuzzy number set has different importance for identifying the consumer needs or the product features. Hence, by assigning a different weight according to the importance of the fuzzy number in a set, we can achieve better results. In the approach, a location weight vector $(v_1, v_2, \cdots, v_n)$ is assigned to $\tilde{X}$ and $\tilde{Y}$, what is normalized as $\sum_{i=1}^{n} v_i = 1$. And the fuzzy near compactness between the fuzzy number set $\tilde{X}$ and $\tilde{Y}$ is described as following:

$$N_E(\tilde{X}, \tilde{Y}) = \sum_{i=1}^{n} \left(N_E(\tilde{x}_i, \tilde{y}_i) \times v_i \right) \tag{2}$$

where v_i is the corresponding weight for the *ith* triangular fuzzy numbers. From the above equation, the smaller value for $N_E(\tilde{X}, \tilde{Y})$ denotes the higher synthetic similarity to the target fuzzy number set while the individual values of $N_E(\tilde{x}_i, \tilde{y}_i)$ and v_i get larger.

3 Implementation Methods

Because collecting and analyzing a consumer's personal needs is basis of the system. Our aim is to establish a transformation model for translating customer needs into optimal combination suggestions of applicable alternatives. To establish this model, the relationship between customer needs and product features needs to be constructed. Utilizing fuzzy operation, optimal alternative searching is performed based on the consumer's subjective needs. The procedure for establishing this system is described below.

3.1 Establishing and Weighting Customer Needs

In the approach, a laptop computer is taken as the objective product to demonstrate the effectiveness of the recommendation method. The interface in Fig. 1 presents some specially designed questions about the products for consumers. Presumably the consumer does not have enough domain knowledge to answer quantitative questions that concern about the specifications of the product, the system has to inquire some qualitative ones instead. For example, it is relatively difficult for an on-line game player to indicate the speed and the type of processor he prefers, but it is easy to express his need on the feature of multi-media. Therefore the qualitative questions are advanced according the consumer's job, hobby and other aspects what consumer is concerted about. Each consumer is represented by a qualitative features vector $(\tilde{q}_1, \tilde{q}_2, \cdots, \tilde{q}_3)$, where $\tilde{q}_i$ is a triangular fuzzy number representing ith consumer need.

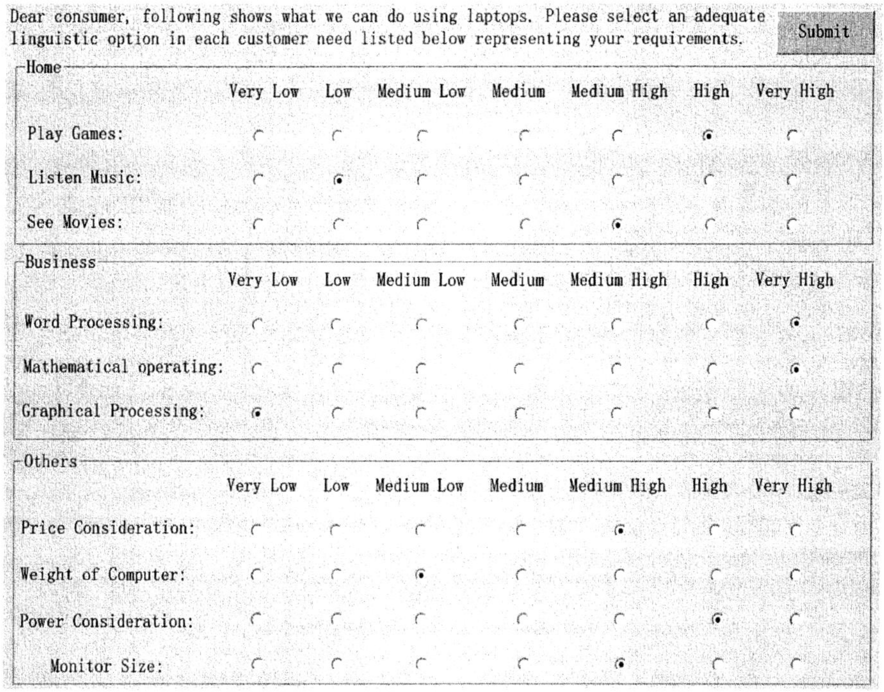

Fig. 1. Consumer Interface

After gathering the consumer's qualitative needs, the interface can then deliver them to the weight consumer needs model that is capable of conducting certain mapping between the needs and the quantitative product features from the expert agent to find the ideal products.

3.2 Establishing and Weighting Product Features

A product is specified by a set of critical components and different vendors have their own ways to categorize their products. For example, a laptop can be described by processor, memory, monitor, etc. And the processors could be named as Pentium 4 or AMD each with special meaning. In the approach, the technical data about products (i.e. laptops) is collected from Internet by hand and stored in the product feature database. A product P_i is represented as a series of critical component names, and the majority of components have some technical features. The technical features here are selected by domain experts to consider the quality of the component from different views. For instance, the technical features of a processor include process frequency, process type, cache size, etc.

It should be notes that different component has different technical features. Therefore each component is represented as a vector of technical features names $(c_i^1, c_i^2, \cdots, c_i^n)$. Then each component of a certain product is converted to a vector of feature functional values $\tilde{F}_i = (\tilde{f}_i^1, \tilde{f}_i^2, \cdots, \tilde{f}_i^n)$, in which each $\tilde{f}_i^j = (f_i^{j1}, f_i^{j2}, f_i^{j3})$ is a triangular fuzzy numbers (shown in Table 1), representing the quantitative ability value of jth technical feature of ith component. Because different technical feature has different influence on the capability of a component, a feature weight vector $(w_i^1, w_i^2, \cdots, w_i^n)$ is assigned to the technical features functional vector. Hence, we could calculate the component capability value of a component as following equation, $\tilde{p}_i = (p_i^1, p_i^2, p_i^3)$, what is shown as a triangular fuzzy number too.

$$p_i^k = \sum_{j=1}^n \left(f_i^{jk} \times w_i^j \right) \tag{3}$$

where $f_i^{jk} \in \tilde{f}_i^j$, $p_i^k \in \tilde{p}_i$ and $k = 1,2,3$. The component capability vector $\tilde{P} = (\tilde{p}_1, \tilde{p}_2, \cdots, \tilde{p}_n)$ is composed by the quantitative capability values of all components, what represents the quantitative ability of the critical components.

To analyze the product features of a laptop computer, two domain experts are employed to select technical features for each critical component of a laptop according the quality of the component from different views. Different products where analyzed to determine the more important features and these where laid out into a hierarchy structure, shown as table 1.

In the table, 10 critical components of a laptop, 25 technical features, its corresponding feature weight and the candidate value of those components are listed, where the feature weights is identified by the domain experts according the importance to the capability of corresponding component.

Once a product P_i has been characterized as a vector of functional values $(f_i^1, f_i^2, \cdots, f_i^n)$, each value f_i^j can be further transferred to a rank that represents the relative performance of the product, among all the products collected, in this dimension of the functional value i. As a result, P_i is finally represented as a triangular fuzzy number $\tilde{p}_i = (p_i^1, p_i^2, p_i^3)$ according equation (3).

Table 1. Technical features of Critical Component in a laptop

Component	Feature weight (w_i^j)	Technical feature	Candidates
CPU	0.45	Frequency	1.2 GHz, 2.0GHz, 2.4GHz, etc.
	0.25	L2 Cache	512KB, 1MKB, etc.
	0.1	Type	Power PC G4, Petium 4, etc.
	0.15	FSB	400MHz, 600MHz, etc.
	0.05	Manufacturer	Intel, AMD, IBM, etc.
Motherboard	0.7	Chipset Type	Intel 925, nVIDIA Force4, etc.
	0.3	Chipset Manufacturer	Intel, nVIDIA, SiS, VIA, etc.
Memory	0.7	Size	256MB, 512MB, etc.
	0.3	Type	DDR, SDRAM
Graphics	0.6	Graphic Card	ATI Mobility Radeon 9200, ATI Mobility Radeon X600, etc.
	0.4	Graphic RAM	64MB, 128MB, etc.
Hard Driver	0.1	Size	20GB, 30GB etc.
	0.45	Type	Ultra ATA, etc.
	0.3	REV	5400,7200,etc.
	0.15	Manufacturer	Portable, Samsung, etc.
Sound	1	Speaker	Built-in stereo speakers, etc.
Connectivity	0.2	Modem	56 Kbps, etc.
	0.8	Network Connection	10-/100-Mbps Ethernet, 54g 802.11b/g WLAN with 125HSM/SpeedBooster support, etc.
Display	0.8	Type	WXGA Display with XBRITE technology, etc.
	0.2	LCD Native Resolution	1024×768, etc.
Screen Size	1	Screen Size	12.1 inches, 17.0 inches, etc.
Weight	1	Weight	2kg, 3kg, etc.
Price	1	Price	800$, 1000$,1500$ etc.
Power	1	Time	4 Hours, 3 Hours, etc.

3.3 Measure Similarity Between Consumer Needs and Product Features

To estimate the optimality of each product for a consumer, a quantitative way to represent customer qualitative needs could facilitate the following similarity measure. Shown as fig.3, there is an interface for a consumer, who is asked to express his needs on some qualitative questions. Three types question are listed in the interface, including job, hobby and other aspects a consumer might be concerted in. Through those questions, we could become aware of the purpose a consumer buy a laptop. For instance, a consumer is a game player, so the laptop he needed should have higher capability on features concerning about some critical components in a laptop, including memory, graphic card, screen and so on. Furthermore the candidate answers of those questions are divided into seven levels, the qualitative needs of a consumer is expressed in a quantitative way. Owing to the capabilities of critical components in a laptop could be represented by triangular fuzzy numbers as mentioned before, it is convenient for the similarity measure between the product capabilities and the consumer needs.

In the system, the qualitative needs of a certain consumer is converted to a vector of consumer need values $\tilde{R} = (\tilde{r}_1, \tilde{r}_2, \cdots, \tilde{r}_n)$, in which $\tilde{r}_i$ is a triangular fuzzy number, representing the answer of ith qualitative question in fig. 1, i.e. the quantitative denotation of ith qualitative customer need.

Table 2. The relationship between the consumer qualitative need and the critical component

Consumer Qualitative need	Ability weight (v_i^j)	Critical Components
Play Games	0.2	CPU
	0.1	Memory
	0.1	Motherboard
	0.25	Graphics
	0.05	Hard Driver
	0.15	Sound
	0.15	Screen
Listen Music	1	Sound
See Movies	0.3	Graphics
	0.3	Sound
	0.3	Screen
	0.1	Hard Driver
Word Processing	1	CPU
Mathematical Operating	0.5	CPU
	0.15	Motherboard
	0.35	Memory
Graphical Processing	0.2	CPU
	0.2	Memory
	0.25	Graphics
	0.1	Hard Driver
	0.25	Screen
Price Consideration	1	Price
Weight Consideration	1	Weight
Power Consideration	1	Power
Screen Size	1	Screen

Since consumer's opinions on customer needs are quantified as fuzzy number vectors, there should be a manner to translate the vectors into product feature.

As the qualities of critical components are the key factors in the capability of a laptop, each qualitative need of a certain consumer is correlative to a number of critical components of a laptop. Therefore, assume that the corresponding components of ith customer need are represented by a component capability vector $\tilde{P}_i = (\tilde{p}_i^1, \tilde{p}_i^2, \cdots, \tilde{p}_i^n)$, where

$\tilde{p}_i^j$ is a triangular fuzzy number calculated by equation (3), representing the quality of *jth* component. Considering different component has different influence on the capability of a laptop in a certain customer need, an ability weight vector $\tilde{V} = (v_i^1, v_i^2, \cdots, v_i^n)$ is assigned to the component capability value vector. Hence we could measure the synthetical capability value of a laptop about a certain customer need. The *ith* synthetical capability is represented by a triangular fuzzy number $\tilde{q}_i = (q_i^1, q_i^2, q_i^3)$ and calculated by the following equation.

$$q_i^k = \sum_{j=1}^{n} \left(p_i^{jk} \times v_i^j \right) \quad (4)$$

where $p_i^{jk} \in \tilde{p}_i^j$, $q_i^k \in \tilde{q}_i$ and $k = 1, 2, 3$. Based on the previous method, a vector $\tilde{Q} = (\tilde{q}_1, \tilde{q}_2, \cdots, \tilde{q}_n)$ is obtained, what denotes the synthetical capability values of a laptop. The *ith* fuzzy number $\tilde{q}_i$ in the vector represents the integrative ability of a product for the *ith* qualitative need $\tilde{r}_i$ of a consumer.

To evaluate the capability of laptops based on customer needs, relationships between consumer needs and product components have to be developed with the ability of product to measure customer needs. In the study, domain experts judge the relations between customer needs and product features. Table 2 lists the detail of the relationship between the qualitative needs of a consumer and the critical components of a laptop.

Based on the previously obtained vectors $\tilde{R}$ and $\tilde{Q}$ respectively representing the quantified consumer needs and the synthetical abilities of a product, we could calculate the fuzzy near compactness of the two fuzzy number vectors according equation (1) and (2). For each laptops in the product database, the synthetical capability vector and its fuzzy near compactness with the consumer need vector could be calculated based on the previous method. And the smaller near compactness denotes the higher synthetic similarity to the qualitative needs of a certain consumer, i.e. the laptops with smaller near compactness are the ideal alternatives for the customer. The mechanism for the most ideal alternative combination to suit consumer's needs is summarized as follows.

Step 1: The Domain experts rate the technical features of *ith* laptop in the product database and give the *ith* feature functional vector $\tilde{F}_i$ for the technical features of the critical components.

Step 2: Calculating the corresponding component capability value and the component capability vector $\tilde{P}_i$ according the equation (3).

Step 3: Through answering the qualitative question shown in Fig. 1, the consumer could obtain the consumer need vector $\tilde{R}$, what quantifies the qualitative needs.

Step 4: Calculating the product synthetical capability vector $\tilde{Q}$ according equation (4), in which each fuzzy number denotes the compositive ability of a laptop on a certain consumer need.

Step 5: Calculating the fuzzy near compactness value s between $\tilde{R}$ and $\tilde{Q}$ according equation (1) and (2). If s is smaller than the predetermined threshold, then the laptop should be recommended to the customer.

Once the currently available products have been ranked by the above equations, the products with the smallest 10 ranks are then recommended to the customer. If the customer is not satisfied with the items recommended by the system, he can increase or decrease his requirements in different need feature dimensions. The modified specifications are used to calculate the optimality for each product again, and those products with smallest ranks are thus recommended to the customer.

4 Experiment and Results

The proposed system also could be applied to recommend the products that a consumer generally does not often buy in a short period of time and has his specific needs in each single purchase. In the experiment, the recommendation system proposed in the approach is utilized to recommend laptops that best satisfy the consumer's current needs and with the optimal quality. As performance measures, we employed the standard information retrieval measures of recall (r), precision (p), and F1 ($F1=2rp/(r+p)$).

4.1 Experiment Data Set

The purpose of the experiment is to test the effects of the recommendation system in this research. We collect a data set of laptops from Amazon.com, which contains 128 laptops of different brands, including Sony, Apple, IBM, Compaq, and so on. To compare the products or components of different vendors, domain expert knowledge is required to define the common criteria. For example, we can set the performance value of the 13.3 inches screen to *medium* and the 10.6 inches screen to *low*, where *medium* and *low* are two triangular fuzzy number. For the recommendation system presented here, as an example, four technical feature criteria of CPU are listed in Table 3, what includes the technical parameters of the familiar notebook CPU in market.

4.2 Simulation Results

The recommendation system described above is to recommend products that best satisfy the consumer's current needs and with the optimal quality. Therefore the experiments concentrate on evaluating the system behaviors. 7 consumers use our experimental system and give their opinion about it, what illustrates in Table 4. And the corresponding *recall, precision and F1* values are listed in Table 5. The average of *precision, recall and F1* measures are 83.82%, 87.57%, 85.39%, respectively. Furthermore, Fig. 2 shows the typical recommendation results corresponding to the consumer needs, in which fifteen laptops in all 138 laptops are recommended to the customer, according the fuzzy near compactness value between the consumer qualitative need and the product synthetical capability.

Table 3. Common Criteria of CPU Technical Features

Frequency	Type	L2 Cache	FSB	Manu-facturer	Feature value
Upwards of 3.0GHz (include 3.0GHz)	Intel Pentium4 M (Dothan), AMD Athlon 64-M	—	—	—	VH
2.4GHz—3.0GHz (include 2.4GHz)	Intel Mobile Pentium4 Supporting HT, PowerPC G5	2MB	533MHz	Intel	H
1.8GHz—2.4GHz (include 1.8GHz)	Intel Pentium4 M (Centrino), AMD Athlon XP-M, Power PC G4	1MB	—	AMD	MH
1.5GHz—1.8GHz (include 1.5GHz)	Intel Mobile P4	512KB	400MHz	IBM	M
1.2GHz—1.5GHz (include 1.2GHz)	Intel Mobile Pentium4 M	256KB	—	—	ML
1.0GHz—1.2GHz (include 1.0GHz)	Intel Celeron-M	128KB	133MHz	—	L
Downward of 1.0GHz (Not include 1.0GHz)	Intel Mobile Celeron	—	100MHz	—	VL

Table 4. The evaluation of seven consumers

	User1	User2	User3	User4	User5	User6	User7
The number of products what satisfy a certain user in the 15 recommended products.	12	13	13	12	11	14	13
The number of products what satisfy a certain user in the other 123 products.	2	3	2	1	1	3	1
The number of products what don't satisfy a certain user in the ten recommended products.	3	2	2	3	4	1	2

Table 5. The three measures' values

	Recall	Precision	F1
User 1	80%	85.7%	82.75%
User 2	86.7%	81.25%	83.89%
User 3	86.7%	86.7%	86.7%
User 4	80%	92.3%	85.71%
User 5	73.3%	91.7%	81.47%
User 6	93.3%	82.4%	87.51%
User 7	86.7%	92.9%	89.69%
Average	**83.82%**	**87.57%**	**85.39%**

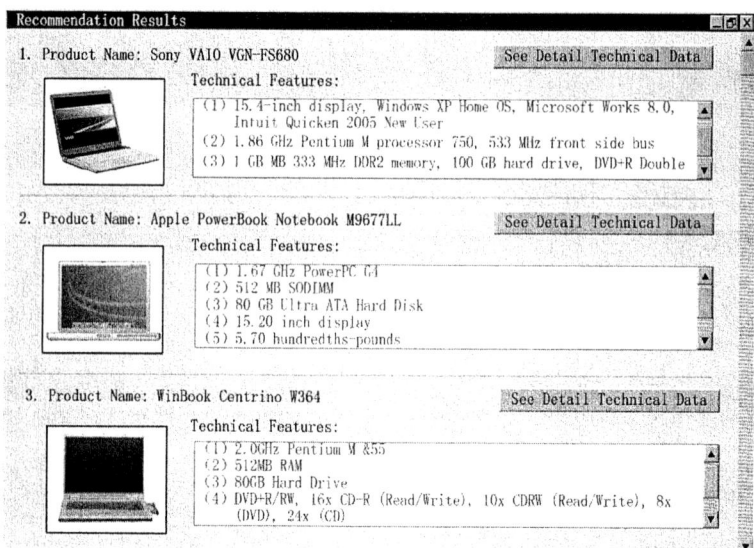

Fig. 2. Typical recommendation results

5 Conclusions

In the paper, we explain the need for Internet enterprises to provide personalized information services in making a successful Internet business, in addition to developing or improving the software and hardware equipment directly related to the Internet infrastructure. We have also suggested that developing personalized recommendation system is a promising way to achieve this goal. Therefore in this work, we present a personalized recommendation system for the digital products.

Because the digital products (such as laptops, digital cameras, etc.) are expensive opposite those commodities, and a general customer does not buy frequently, we can not built to reason about a customer's personal preferences from his purchasing history and provide the appropriate information services to meet his needs. And those recommendation system based on the consumer's preferences are not proper to recommend the kind of products. Hence it is required to construct a new recommendation system for the digital products. The system proposed in the approach concentrates on finding optimal products for a consumer by using the ephemeral information provided by him and the domain expert knowledge. In the system, different interfaces are developed to interact with the consumer, transfer external domain knowledge for internal use, and calculate the optimality of each product. Here a multi-attribute decision making method is used to recommend optimal laptop computer for a customer, based on his needs and the quality of the product. Experimental results have shown the promise of our systems. And the system isn't only applied to e-commerce as an assistant system, but could be an independent system for the real-life business.

Our future works will concentrate on consummating the fuzzy logical algorithm utilized in the paper, and investigating how the product knowledge from experts can be derived more easily.

References

1. Schafer, J.B., Konstan, U.: E-commerce recommendation applications, Journal of Data Mining and Knowledge Discovery, (2001)
2. S.W. Hsiao, M.C. Huang: A neural network based approach for product form design, Design Studies, 23 (1) (2002) 67-84
3. C.H. Hsieh, S.H. Chen: A model and algorithm of fuzzy product positioning, Information Sciences, 121(1999) 61-82
4. J. Sun, D. K. Kalenchuk: Design candidate identification using neural network based fuzzy reasoning, Robotics and Computer Integrated Manufacturing, 16 (2000) 383-396
5. Hung-Cheng Tsai, Shih-Wen Hsiao: Evaluation of alternatives for product customization using fuzzy logic, Information Sciences, 158 (2004) 233-262
6. Wei-Po Lee, Chih-Hung Liu: Intelligent agent-based systems for personalized recommendations in Internet commerce, Expert Systems with Applications, 22 (2002) 275-284
7. Tung-Lai Hu, Jiuh-Biing Sheu: A fuzzy-based customer classification method for demand-responsive logistical distribution operations, Fuzzy Sets and Systems, 139 (2003) 431-450
8. Jae Kyeong Kim, Yoon Ho Cho: A personalized recommendation procedure for Internet shopping support, Electronic Commerce Research and Applications, 1 (2002) 301–313.

Generic XML Schema Definition (XSD) to GUI Translator

V. Radha, S. Ramakrishna, and N. Pradeep Kumar

[1] Institute for Development and Research in Banking Technology (IDRBT),
Road No 1, Castle Hills, Masab Tank,
Hyderabad-50057, India
vradha@idrbt.ac.in,
{sramakrishna, npkumar}@mtech.idrbt.ac.in

Abstract. Organizations are seeking for a special kind of browser for exchanging structured information across business entities. In this paper, we present a generic solution called as XML Schema Definition (XSD) [6] to GUI translator. This translator processes data model defined in XML schema document and then generates user interface dynamically. This translator generates user interfaces in different rendering languages such as Java swings, HTML and WML.

Keywords: XML, XSD, WML.

1 Introduction

The presence of a standardized modeling language is a must for generating graphical user interface dynamically. An accurate description of the data structures i.e. data model is needed to exchange data effectively. These data structures represent relations and rules of the data to be exchanged. The XML Schema Definition specification [6] serves the purpose of modeling XML data [5]. It describes the structure and defines constraints of XML documents and is the key element in exchanging XML based data.

XML-based GUI description languages like XHTML, XForms or WML are easily generated from XML schema definition. XML based languages are also device-compliant as well as platform-compliant, so they can be adaptable to any platform and device.

2 Objectives

The main objective of this paper is to develop generic software that can generate user interfaces dynamically from any XSD document in different rendering languages such as (X)HTML, WML, Java, etc. This software also creates XML instance document once the user inputs the data through UI and validates instance document with the given XSD document. We intend to develop a special browser for exchanging structured information in the form of XML documents.

3 XSD to GUI Translator

In this section, we present how the translator is implemented by using XSD specification as reference. The workflow of the solution is as follows:

- Dynamic transformation from XML schemas to various types of user interface elements in rendering languages such as Java swings, HTML, WML.
- Culling of information from the user through generated interface
- Creation of XML document after data is entered completely
- Validation of the XML document with the associated XSD document
- Serialization

Schema document is parsed with DOM parser bundled with Apache Xerces-J as XSD itself is an XML document. The resultant of this step is a DOM tree representation of nodes, which correspond to elements, and attributes of given document. In DOM, both elements and attributes are treated as nodes. The nodes represent the schema vocabulary containing description about instance data nodes.

The nodes of DOM tree are to be interpreted according to their context i.e. functionality, structure and etc. Then they are to be transformed into instance with out values as well as GUI components using DOM API. We discuss underlying logic in transforming schema to GUI in the next section.

3.1 Transformation from XSD to GUI

Every XSD document does have one root element *schema*, also called as document element. The *schema* node contains global elements, global types, groupings and annotations as immediate children that include *element, complexType, simpleType, group, attributeGroup, annotation* nodes. One of global elements is the actual root element in the instance document. The following conditions need to be checked in selecting a root element for instance if there are many global elements.

1. It must not be an empty element
2. If more than one global element is present (one with simple and other with complex type), then the element of complex type is to be taken as root.
3. It should not be referred from non-global elements using *ref* attribute.

Once the root element of instance is identified, it is inserted into a new DOM tree (or document) say *Instance* created using *DocumentBuilderFactory* class. It will serve as DOM representation for XML instance for the given schema and also allows the application to insert data when the user enters data later.

We designed a recursive algorithm (Fig.1) to navigate the entire DOM tree of schema document until all the nodes are transformed into GUI components and whole XML instance is created. For *Transform* method, the global element identified as root node is passed as input. The *Transform* method in turn has one handler for each and every element type of schema vocabulary. The node passed as parameter is an *element* node, so it is handled by *element_handler* method (Fig.2).

Element_handler. In this handler, elements are classified into two types. They are global elements and non-global elements. The distinction is that global elements don't have ref attribute and occurrence constraints. So, they are handled separately. Initially,

Algorithm: Transform (Node node)	Comments
Begin 1: **If** (node->name **equals** "element") 2: Element_handler(node); 3: **If** (node->name **equals** "complexType") 4: ComplexType_handler(*node*); 5: **If** (node->name **equals** "simpleType") 6: SimpleType_handler(*node*); 7: **If** (node->name **equals** "attribute") 8: attribute_handler(node); **End**	**node** – represents a node in DOM tree of schema Handler for each element of schema vocabulary of w3c specification

Fig. 1. Transform Algorithm

Algorithm: Void Element_handler (Node node)	Comments
Begin 1: elem-name:=**Lookfor_name_attribute**(node); 2: comp-node:=**Lookfor_type_attribute_node**(node); 3: ref-node:=**Lookfor_ref_attribute_node**(node); 4: oldprefix:=prefix; 5: prefix:=prefix+":"+elem-name; 6: **If** (node->childs==null **And** comp-node==null **And** ref-node==null) 7: **If** (elem-name!=null) 8: Add node with *elem_name* to the *domdoc* DOM tree 9: type-info:=**Lookfor_type_attribute_name**(node); 10: Add GUI components w.r.t to simple type element 11: **If** (*type-info* is one of simple types of schema) 12: E(); 13: **Else If** (comp-node <> **null And** elem-name 14: <> null //C; 15: Add node with *elem_name* to *domdoc* DOM tree 16: **Transform** (comp-node); 17 **Else If** (ref-node <> null) {**Transform**(ref-node)}; 18: **Else** Child:=node->FirstChild; 19: **While** (child <> null) 20: Add node with *elem_name* to *domdoc* tree 21: **Transform**(child); 24: child:=child->NextSibling; 25: **End while** 26: Prefix:=oldprefix; **End**	**Lookfor_name_attribute()** - Returns the value of *name* attribute of node **Lookfor_type_attribute_node()** - Returns the node defined using *type* attribute of *node* **Lookfor_ref_attribute_node()** - Returns the node referenced using *ref* attribute of node **Lookfor_type_attribute_node()** - Returns the value of *type* attribute of *node* E() - Enforce a mechanism to ensure that data entered conforms to *type-info;* C - It is a complex type node i.e. having child nodes and/or attributes. It declares complex type definition defined with a name specified in *type* attribute value

Fig. 2. Element_handler algorithm

element_handler is called with root element. An *element* may be of different types as per schema specification. The handler first checks for *type* attribute of document element. If type attribute is not present, it will look for child (i.e. *complexType*) and then it calls *complexType_handler* to further explore sub elements. Otherwise, it finds the node with the name as specified in *type* attribute. For non-global elements, the handler calls *Lookfor_type_attribute*, *Lookfor_ref_attribute* methods, which return the complex type definition node/referenced node if the current *element* is complex type or referencing another *element*. Only label component is added to interface, but it will not add text box for data entry. If the returned values are null, it indicates that element is simple type. So the label and text box components are added to the interface.

ComplexType_handler. In this handler, the structure of *xsd:complexType* is analyzed. Generally, every complex type has one of the following three basic structures:

Sequence: P-> abc i.e. consecutive elements, denoted by the *xsd:sequence* element.

Repetition: B-> b* i.e. elements that occur n times (with $0 <= min <= n <= max <= infinity$), specified by the minOccurs, maxOccurs attributes in *xsd:element* of the schema document respectively.

Alternative: D->(e|f), denoted by *xsd:choice* elements

Arbitrary order: The sub elements of *xsd:all* tag can appear in any order in the instance document.

After processing these structures, further attributes are looked for and if there are any attributes or attribute groups, then it will invoke *attribute_handler* or *attribute-group_handler* for further transformation.

SimpleType_handler. A simple type element is one with no child or attribute elements. A *simpleType* element can occur as child of *element* or *attribute* and it can also be defined as a global type. Accordingly, it is handled and transformed into interface.

Similarly we handled other handlers like **Attribute Group handler, Restriction handler, Sequence_handler, Choice_handler, Enumeration_handler** etc for corresponding constructs defined the XML schema definition.

3.2 Creation of XML Instance

Each received parameter is a pair of parameter name and parameter value. The parameter name is divided into tokens using *stringTokenizer* class. Each token represents a node name in the partially created instance DOM tree (i.e. without values). For each parameter, it will navigate from root of the DOM tree as per tokens in parameter name until the end of the tokens is reached. Then the parameter value will be inserted as text node in the DOM tree. This is repeated until all parameters are inserted into DOM tree of *Instance*. The procedure for accomplishing this phase is also given in algorithm *insertNode* (Fig.3).

We used JAXP API as part of Xerces parser to validate the instance document with the corresponding schema. We implemented a *SchemaValidator* class that takes XML instance and its schema document as parameters and. Then it reads the XML instance using SAX API and validates it with schema. We used *XMLSerializer* class to serialize

Algorithm: Void insertNode (Node *node*, String *nodename*, String *text*)	Comments
1: desirednode:=*node*	*node* – denotes the document element (i.e. root) of XML instance
2: **For each** *token_i* **of** *nodename*	
3: **Begin**	
4: **If** (desirednode->name *equals token_i*)	
5: **If** (there exists no further token)	*nodename* – a prefix (node name) that contains collection of nodes separated by colon in hierarchical tree fashion (top to bottom)
6: desirednode:=desirednode -> FirstChild;	
7: **Else** textnode->value:=*text*;	
8: desirednode->appendChild:=textnode;	
9: **End if**	
10: **Else** desirednode:=desirednode->NextSibling;	
11: **While** (desirednode !=**null**)	*text* - the data to be inserted at the last node represented in *nodename*
12: **Begin**	
13: **If** (desirednode->name *equals token_i*)	
14: **If**(there exists no further tokens)	
15: desirednode:=desirednode->FirstChild;	**desirednode** - node object used to navigate the DOM tree
16: **Else** textnode->value:=*text*;	
17: desirednode->appendChild:=textnode;	
18: **break;**	
19: **End while** // C;	C - If match is not found for token in current DOM level, then it checks for names of attributes to find a match
20: **If** (token does not find a match in current DOM	
21: level nodes)	
22: parent:=desirednode->ParentNode;	
23: **If** (there exists any attributes)	
24: **For each** *attr_i* **of** Attrs[i]	
25: **If** (*attr_i* *equals token_i*)	
26: *attr_i* ->value:=*text*;	
27: **End else End for**	

Fig. 3. InsertNode Algorithm

XML instance document from the *Instance* DOM tree to make an XML file. We also set certain parameters for this class such as output format details, file name and etc.

5 Results and Conclusions

We present screenshot of this translator corresponding to transformation from XSD to Java swings.

We showed how to generate GUIs dynamically from composite schema documents and also developed a generic translator that consists of three modules that corresponds to XSD to HTML transformation for PCs and PDAs, XSD to Java swings transformation for PCs, XSD to WML transformation for mobile devices. The XSD to HTML, WML transformation modules are web based tools and the third one, XSD to Java Swings transformation, is a stand-alone offline client.

Generic XML Schema Definition (XSD) to GUI Translator

```xml
<?xml version="1.0" encoding="UTF-8"?>
<xsd:schema xmlns:xsd='http://www.w3.org/2001/XMLSchema'>

 <xsd:element name="employees">
  <xsd:complexType>
   <xsd:sequence>
    <xsd:element ref="employee" minOccurs='0' maxOccurs='unbounded'/>
   </xsd:sequence>
  </xsd:complexType>
 </xsd:element>


 <xsd:element name="employee">
  <xsd:complexType>
   <xsd:sequence>
    <xsd:element name="name" type="personType" />
    <xsd:element name="payrollNumber" type="xsd:positiveInteger"/>
    <xsd:element name="hourlyRate" type="xsd:decimal"/>
    <xsd:element name="casual" type="xsd:boolean" minOccurs='0'
    <xsd:element name="startDate" type="xsd:date"/>
 <xsd:element name="Bike">
  <xsd:simpleType>
   <xsd:restriction base="xs:string">
    <xsd:enumeration value="Hero Honda Karizma" />
    <xsd:enumeration value="Yamaha Enticer" />
    <xsd:enumeration value="Eliminator" />
    <xsd:enumeration value="TVS Victor" />
   </xsd:restriction>
  </xsd:simpleType>
 </xsd:element>

   </xsd:sequence>
  </xsd:complexType>
 </xsd:element>

<xsd:complexType name="personType" >
 <xsd:sequence>
  <xsd:element name="first" type='xsd:string' />
  <xsd:element name="last"  type='xsd:string' />
 </xsd:sequence>
</xsd:complexType>

</xsd:schema>
```

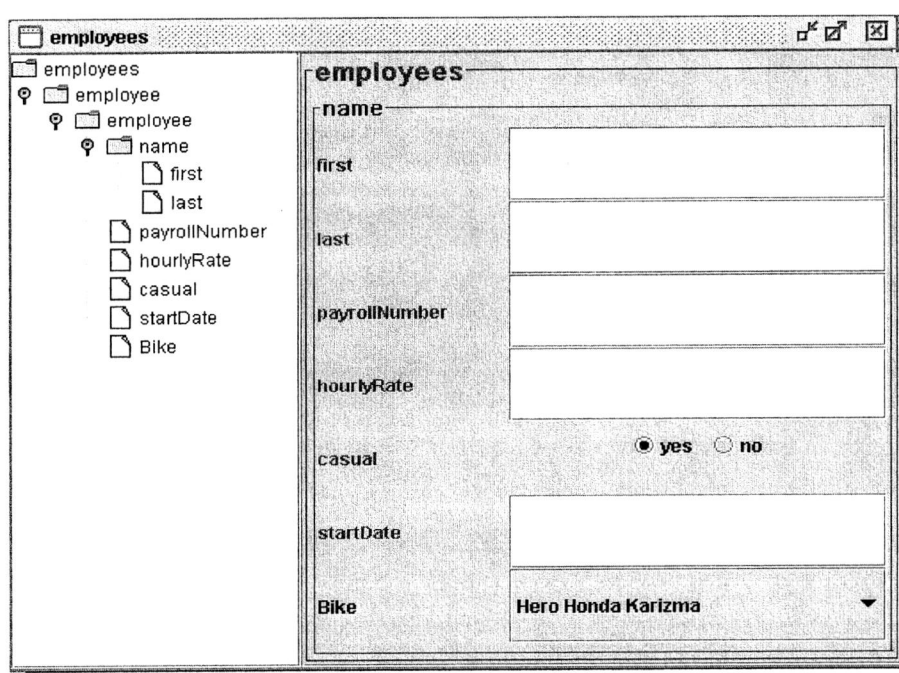

Fig. 4. Employee XSD and corresponding GUI

References

1. Luyten, K. und Coninx, K. "An XML-based runtime user interface description language for mobile computing devices", Lecture Notes in Computer Science: Interactive Systems: Design, Specification, and Verification: 8th Int. Workshop, DSV-IS 2001, Glasgow, Scotland, UK. 2220:1.15. 2001
2. Giulio Mori, Fabio Paterno, and Carmen Santoro, "Design and Development of Multi device User Interfaces through Multiple Logical Descriptions", IEEE Transactions on Software Engineering, Vol.30, No.8, August 2004
3. Pureta, A, "Issues in automatic generation of user interfaces in model-based systems", In: Vanderdonckt, J. (Hrsg.), Proceedings of the 2nd International Workshop on Computer-Aided Design of User Interfaces (CADUI'96) Namur, 5-7 June 1996
4. F. Paterno and C.Santoro, "One Model, Many Interfaces", Proc Fourth Int'l Conference on Computer-Aided Design of User Interfaces, pp 143-154, 2002
5. T. Bray, J. Paoli, C. M. Sperberg-McQueen and E. Maler, "Extensible Markup Language (XML) Version 1.0 (Second Edition)", http://www.w3c.org/TR/2000/REC-xml-20001006/, W3C Recommendation, October 2000
6. David C. Fallside, Priscilla Walmsley, "XML Schema Definition (XSD) Version 1.0", http://www.w3.org/TR/2004/REC-xmlschema-0-20041028/, W3C Recommendation.

Off-Line Micro-payment System for Content Sharing in P2P Networks

Xiaoling Dai[1] and John Grundy[2,3]

[1] Department of Mathematics and Computing Science,
The University of the South Pacific, Laucala Campus, Suva, Fiji
dai_s@usp.ac.fj
[2] Department of Electrical and Computer Engineering,
University of Auckland, Private Bag 92019, Auckland, New Zealand
[3] Department of Computer Science,
University of Auckland, Private Bag 92019, Auckland, New Zealand
john-g@cs.auckland.ac.nz

Abstract. Micro-payment systems have the potential to provide non-intrusive, high-volume and low-cost pay-as-you-use services for a wide variety of web-based applications. We propose an extension, P2P-NetPay, a micro-payment protocol characterized by off-line processing, suitable for peer-to-peer network services sharing. Our approach provides high performance and security using one-way hashing functions for e-coin encryption. In our P2P-NetPay protocol, each peer's transaction does not involve any broker and double spending is detected during the redeeming transaction. We describe the motivation for P2P-NetPay and describe three transactions of the P2P-NetPay protocol in detail to illustrate the approach. We then discuss future research on this protocol.

1 Introduction

A peer-to-peer architecture is a type of network in which each workstation generally has equivalent capabilities and responsibilities. Peer-to-peer networks are often simpler than client-server but they usually do not offer the same performance under heavy loads. A P2P network relies on computing power at the ends of a connection rather than from within the network or dedicated servers.

A Central Indexing Server (CIS) is sometimes used to index all users who are currently online. This server does not host any content itself but provides support for peers to locate content from other peers. Queries on the index server are used to find other connected users with content required and when a match is found the central server will tell clients where to find the requested content. Users can then choose a result from the search query and their peer will attempt to establish a connection with the computer hosting the information requested.

In a P2P CIS system, peers cooperate to search the relevant information in the system. However, in some peer-to-peer systems, peers often cannot find suitable services since many peers choose to decline requests from others for security or other reasons. This problem characterises the "free rider" problem in P2P – users who search and use content but don't allow others to use their client for services.

A natural approach to control free riding is to introduce a payment protocol into CIS systems, in which each peer has to pay for the services it receives from others, e.g., [11]. However, traditional heavy weight macro-payment protocols are unsuitable in this domain of high-volume, low cost-per-item searches and information downloads. We propose an off-line micro-payment protocol, P2P-NetPay, to address this common *free-rider* problem. Our protocol allows peers to buy "E-coins", worth very small amounts of money, from a broker and spend these E-coins at various peers to pay for large numbers of searches and digital files of small value each. P2P-NetPay shifts the communication traffic bottleneck from a broker and distributes it among the peers by using transferable E-coin Touchstones and Indexes, much in the same way as micro-payment in client-server network applications [2].

In this paper, we briefly describe Ppay protocol and the NetPay micro-payment protocol with the three kinds of e-wallets in the client-server networks. We then proposal an off-line micro-payment protocol called P2P-NetPay to control free riding problem in peer-to-peer networks. We conclude with an outline of our further plans for research and development in this area.

2 Motivation

While there is an emergence of new technologies and applications to enable users to exchange content over P2P networks, the success of such systems depend on users' willingness to share computing resources and exchange content. One of the first and most well-known P2P file-sharing systems, Napster [15], has attracted great public attention for the P2P systems as well as at one time having tens of millions of users. Napster was designed to help its users to trade music files, however, P2P applications could exchange any kind of digital document. The file sharing is free by peers in most current P2P systems. Since peers do not benefit from serving files to others, many users decline to provide services to others. In fact, a recent study of the Gnutella network found that more than 70% of its peers have made no contribution to the P2P system [12]. This emerging phenomenon of "selfish" individuals in P2P systems has been widely studied, and is known as the *free-rider* problem. There is a trend towards charging peers for access CIS or charging for every file download in order for peers make direct profit from files they upload [12].

One payment model for peer-to-peer systems is a subscription-based method. In this approach the CIS charges a membership fee per time period as a way of recovering the overhead involved in running its services. The subscription charge does have an impact on peers' decisions about whether or not to participate in the P2P network. However, the contribution to the system of such a fee is irrelevant to their efforts to maximize utility when they have made this decision. Most importantly, the fact that subscription fees are unrelated to peers' behavior implies that they still give rise to a free rider problem.

In order to encourage peers to balance what they take from the system with what they contribute to the system we present an on-line micro-payment approach used to charge peers for every download and to reward peers for every upload [11]. For each registered peer the Central Indexing Server tracks the number of files downloaded and the number of files uploaded during the time period. Each time a file is successfully exchanged between two peers, the server increments the download count of the peer who downloaded the file and the upload count of the peer who uploaded it. Observe that in such a model server involves all such transfers and it's an on-line, client-server brokered system.

A point-based mechanism that is similar to the micro-payment mechanisms discussed above is introduced in [11]. In order to make use of an internal currency, peers are allowed to buy points either with money or with contributions to the network, but peers are not allowed to convert points back into money. Since peers cannot "cash out" their points, the mechanism must allow them to maintain a balance from one time period to the next. This system also uses an on-line mechanism. There are a number of micro-payment systems for client-server networks in various stages of development from proposals in the academic literature to systems in commercial use [1], [7], [8], [9], [10]. Micro-payment systems can be used to support payment of vendors from customers in client-server networks. In peer-to-peer applications, there is not any clear distinction between vendors and customers. There are simply peers which can be vendors or customers or both. Ppay is an example off-line micro-payment system in peer-to-peer networks [14].

3 Ppay: A Peer-to-Peer Micro-payment Protocol

The Ppay micro-payment system was proposed by Yang and Garcia-Molina [14]. The concept of floating and self-managed currency is introduced, so each peer's transaction does not involve any broker. The coins can float from one peer to another peer and the owner of a given coin manages the currency itself, except when it is created or cashed. Fig. 1 shows key Ppay interactions.

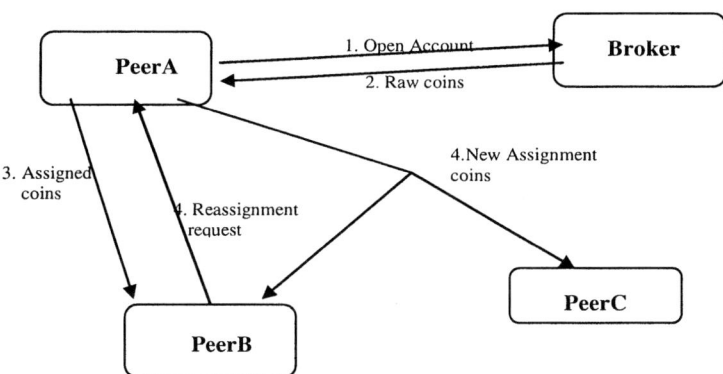

Fig. 1. Ppay protocol participant interactions [based on 14]

- *Open an account with a broker:* The PeerA opens an account with the broker scrip at start of the day and the broker returns initial raw coins to the PeerA. Now PeerA is the owner of the coins.
- *Assigned coins*: when PeerA wants to purchase an item or a service from PeerB, PeerA will send the assigned coins to PeerB. Now PeerB is the holder of the coins. PeerB can decide to cash them or re-assign them to another peer (PeerC).
- *Reassignment request*: If PeerB wants to re-assign the coins, PeerB sends the reassignment request to PeerA.
- *New assigned coins*: after receiving the request, PeerA PeerA processes and sends the new reassignment to PeerB and PeerC.

The problem with this approach is that PeerA can be down when PeerB wants to reassign his own coins. A peer can be down with almost 97% probability, on average, when a payment must be made, so a *downtime protocol* is presented in Ppay [14]. In the downtime protocol, the Broker generates the newly assigned coins and sends the assigned coins back to PeerA when PeerA comes back online in order to detect frauds committed. Key drawback with downtime protocol includes: the broker must be on-line when the peers wish to re-assign the coins and the broker has to check when peers came back on-line. Due to the high percentage of off-line periods for a peer, the broker' load significantly grows up.

In order to avoid the above problems, a concept of *layered coins* is used in the Ppay protocol. The layered coins are used to float the coins from one peer to another. Each layer represents a reassignment request and the broker and the owner of the coins can peel off all the layers to obtain all the necessary proofs. The layered coins introduce the delay of the fraud detection and the floating coins growing in size.

4 NetPay in Client-Server Networks

We developed a protocol called NetPay that provides a secure, cheap, widely available, and debit-based protocol for an off-line micro-payment system [1]. We have developed NetPay-based systems for client-server broker, vendor and customer networks [3], [4]. We have also designed three kinds of "e-wallets" to manage e-coins in our client-server NetPay systems [3], [4], [5]. In one model the E-wallet is hosted by vendor servers and is passed from vendor to vendor as the customer moves from one site to another. The second is a client-side application resident on the client's PC. The third is a hybrid that caches E-coins in a web browser cookie for debiting as the customer spends at a site.

The client-side e-wallet is an application running on the client PC that holds e-coin information. Customers can buy article content using the client-side e-wallet at different sites without the need to log in after the e-wallet application is downloaded to their PC. Their e-coins are resident on their own PC and so access to them is never lost due to network outages to one vendor. The e-coin debiting time is slower for a client-side e-wallet than the server-side e-wallet due to the extra communication between vendor application server and customer PC's e-wallet application. In a client-side e-wallet NetPay system, a Touchstone and an Index (T&I) of a customer's e-wallet are passed from the broker to each vendor. We designed that the broker application server communicates with vendor application servers to get the T&I to verify e-coins. The vendor application servers also communicate with another vendor application server to pass the T&I, without use of the broker. The main problem with this approach is that a vendor system cannot get the T&I if a previous vendor system down.

5 P2P-NetPay Protocol in Peer-to-Peer Networks

Based on the client-side e-wallet NetPay protocol, we propose an adaption to a P2P-NeyPay protocol that is suitable for P2P-based network environments. Our P2P-NetPay protocol uses touchstones that are signed by the broker and an e-coin index signed by requesting peers. The signed touchstone is used by a supplying peer to verify the electronic currency – paywords, and signed Index is used to prevent double spending from peers and to resolve disputes between peers. In this section, we describe the key transactions in P2P-NetPay protocol in P2P networks.

In this section, the details of a peer-to-peer micro-payment NetPay model are discussed. Consider a trading community consisting of Peers and Broker (B). The CIS system can also act as a Broker in the P2P networks. Assume that the broker is honest and is trusted by the peers. The peers may be or may not be honest. The peers open accounts and deposit funds with the broker. The payment only involves Peers and Broker is responsible for the registration of peers and for crediting the peer's account and debiting the peer's account. In a P2P-NetPay system, there are three transactions which are requesting peer-broker, requesting peer – supplying peer1, and peer - broker transactions. How the NetPay protocol works in each transaction will now be described in more detail. We adopt the following notations:

IDa --- pseudonymous identity of any party A in the trade community issued by the broker.
PK-a --- A's public key.
SK-a --- A's digital signature.
{x}SK-a --- x signed by A.
   {x}PK-a --- x is encrypted by A's public key.
   {x}SAK-a --- x signed by A using A's asymmetric key.

There are a number of cryptography and micro-payment terminologies used in the P2P-NetPay micro-payment protocol. The details of these terminologies are given as follows

1. ***One-way Hash Function.*** The one-way hash function MD5 used in the NetPay implementation is an algorithm that has the two properties. It seems impossible to give an example of hash function used in hash chain in a form of normal functions in mathematics. The difficulties include:
   - The value of a mathematical function is a real or complex number (a data value for hash function);
   - It is always possible to compute the set $X = \{x | x = h^{-1}(y)\}$ for a given y for a mathematical function h (not satisfying the two properties of the hash function).
2. ***Payword Chain.*** A "payword chain" is generated by using a one way hash function. Suppose we want to generate a payword chain which contains ten "paywords". We need randomly pick a payword seed W_{11} and then compute a payword chain by repeatedly hashing

   $W_{10} = h(W_{11})$, $W_9 = h(W_{10})$,
   ......,
   $W_1 = h(W_2)$, $W_0 = h(W_1)$

where h(.) is a hash function such as MD5 and W_0 is called the root for the chain. The MD5 (Message Digest) algorithm is one of the series of messages in hash algorithms and involves appending a length field to a message and padding it up to a multiple of 512 bit blocks. This means that every payword W_i is stored as a 32 length string in a database. A payword chain is going to be used to represent a set of E-coins in the P2P-NetPay system.

5.1 Transaction 1: Requesting Peer1 – Broker

Before a Requesting Peer1 (RP1) asks for service from the Supplying Peer2 (SP2), she has to register and send an integer n (M1), the number of paywords in a payword chain the RP1 applied for, to the broker (Fig. 2). The broker completes two actions:

- Debits money from the account of RP1 and creates a payword chain $W_0, W_1, W_2,...,W_n, W_{n+1}$ which satisfy $W_i = h(W_{i+1})$, where $i = n, ..., 0$. (here h(.) is a one way hash function). Root W_0 is used to verify the validity of the paywords $W_1, W_2, ..., W_n$ by peers and the broker. Seed W_{n+1} is kept by the broker to be used to prevent the peer1 from overspending and forging paywords in that chain. The peer1 only receives ID_e (e-coin ID) and paywords $W_1, W_2,...,W_n$ that are encrypted by RP1's public key from the broker (M2) as shown in Fig. 2.

$$M2 = \{ ID_e, W_1, W_2, ... ,W_n \}_{PK\text{-}RP1}$$

The broker computes the touchstone for the payword chain:

$$M3 = T = \{ID_e, W_0\}_{SK\text{-}broker}$$

and sends it to RP1.

- Save ID_e, W_0, W_{n+1}, and amount to the broker database.

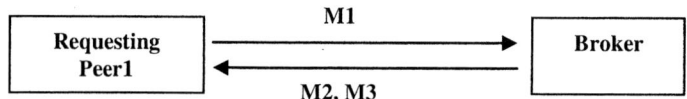

Fig. 2. Requesting Peer buys e-coins transaction

For example, the requesting peer sends n=50 to the broker who generates the $ID_e=1$ and payword chain $\{W_0, W_1, W_2, ... ,W_{50}, W_{51}\}$. The RP1's e-wallet is thus $\{ID_e, W_1, W_2, ... ,W_{50}\}$ and T. The broker saves ID_e, W_0, W_{n+1}, and 50 to its database.

The requesting peer - broker transaction guarantees no overspending and forging. The broker selects the seed W_{n+1} to create the payword chain which satisfy $W_n = h(W_{n+1})$, $W_{n-1} = h(W_n)$, ..., $W_1 = h(W_2)$, $W_0 = h(W_1)$ and keep the seed W_{n+1} secretly. It is impossible to forge the paywords in that chain by peers and attackers, since they do not have the seed W_{n+1}, i.e. it is impossible to generate other paywords in a chain by knowing some of them in the chain since h() is a truly one-way hash function [16].

5.1 Transaction 2: Requesting Peer1 – Supplying Peer2

The following sequence of messages describes a transaction between a requesting peer and a supplying peer1 in the course of a download of information from Peer1 to Peer2. The requesting peer1 (RP1) and supplying peer2 (SP2) needs to agree on the amount that RP1 pays.

When a RP1 find a desired file that belongs to SP2, the RP1's e-wallet sends message M4 and T to the SP2.

$$M4 = \{ ID_e, paywords\}$$

where paywords = $\{W_1, W_2, ..., W_m\}$. For example, to make a 2cs (m=2) payment, the peer1 sends the paywords W_1, W_2: Paywords = $\{W_1, W_2\}$ to the SP2. The RP1 also signs the following transmission message:

$$Index = \{ID_e, i\}_{SAK\text{-}RP1}$$

and transmits them to SP2, where i is the index of the last payword SP2 received. The Index is used to prevent double spending from RP1 and may be used for disputes between the peers. The touchstone authorises SP2 to verify the paywords using root W_0 and redeems the paywords with the broker as shown in Fig. 3.

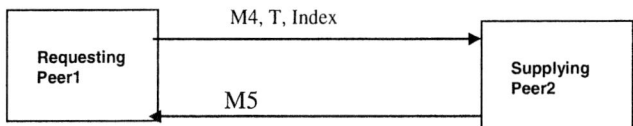

Fig. 3. Requesting peer buys digital file transaction

The paywords are verified by taking the hash of the paywords in the order W_1 first, then W_2, and so on. The paywords W_1 and W_2 are valid if the hash matches the root of the chain (W_0) in the touchstone ($h(W_1)=W_0$, $h(h(W_2))=W_0$). This works because the hash function with the property $W_{i-1}= h(W_i)$ (i = 1, 2, ..., n) and SP2 gets W_0 from the broker.

On the other hand, it is hard for SP2 to create W_1 even though he knows W_0 since the generation of a value that would hash to W_0 is computationally infeasible due to the nature of the one-way hash function [16]. For the same reason, it is also hard for an attacker to generate valid paywords in the chain even if he knows W_0 or some paywords except for the seed W_{n+1} [16], [17].

If the paywords are valid, they will be stored for a later offline transaction with the broker. The RP1 downloads the file from SP2 (M5). Multiple payments can be charged against the length of the payword chain, until the payword chain is fully spent or the RP1 no longer requires files with other peers [16].

When the RP1 wishes to purchase files with supplying peer2, RP1 repeats the transaction2 with M4, M5, and M6.

For example, the RP1 requests to buy a file which costs 3cs. The RP1 sends M4 = $\{IDe, W_1W_2W_3\}$, T and signed Index to the SP2. The current state of the RP1 e-wallet database is shown in Fig. 4.

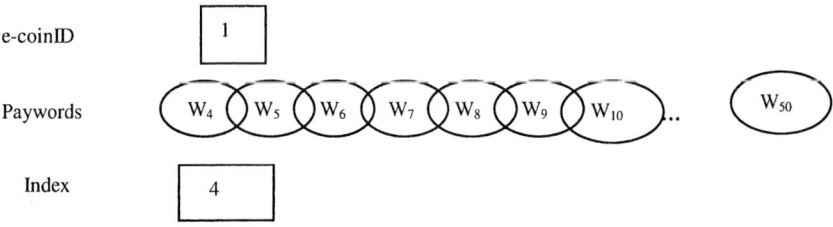

Fig. 4. Example of RP1's e-wallet database after first transaction

The SP2 gets T from the RP1 and then verifies W_1, W_2, W_3 by using W_0 such as $h(W_1)=W_0$, $h(h(W_2))=W_0$, $h(h(h(W_3)))=W_0$. If the paywords are valid, the RP1 download the file from SP2 (M6) and saves IDe=1, index=4, price=3, W_0, paywords= $W_1W_2W_3$ in a redeem database as shown in Fig. 5.

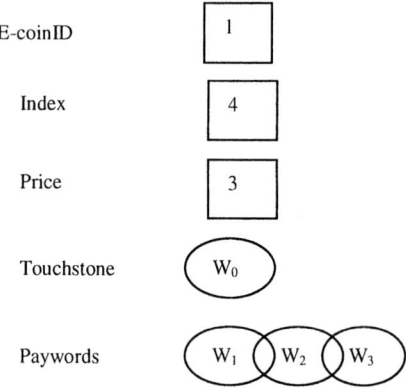

Fig. 5. Example of redeem database after first transaction

The RP1 continues to buy another file which costs 2cs, the RP1 sends M4 = {IDe, W_4W_5}, T and Index=6 to the SP2. The current state of the RP1's e-wallet database is shown in Fig. 6.

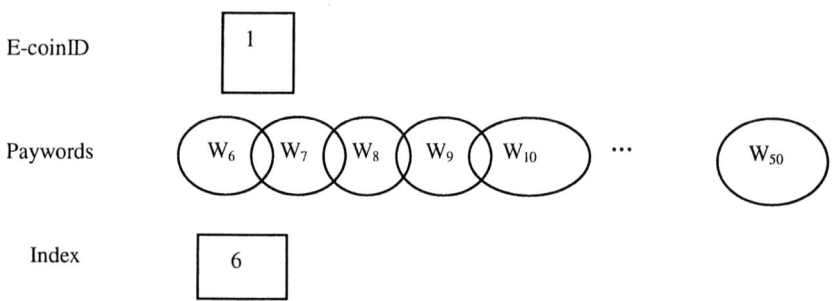

Fig. 6. Example of the e-wallet database after second transaction

The SP2 verifies W_4, W_5 by using W_0 obtained before. If the paywords are valid, RP1 downloads the file from SP2 (M6) and saves IDe, index=6, price=2, W_0, paywords= W_4W_5 to the redeem database as shown in Fig. 7.

When PP1 wishes to make a purchase at a different peer RP3, he/she sends M4, T (where T = {IDe, W_0} $_{SK\text{-broker}}$) and Index to the SP3. RP1 can download the file if the paywords are valid.

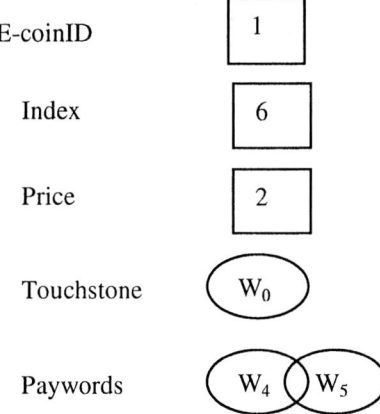

Fig. 7. Example of redeem database after second transaction

5.3 Transaction 3: Peer – Broker Offline Redeem Processing

At the end of each day (or another suitable period), for each payword chain, all supplying peers need to send all paywords that they received from requesting peers to the broker and redeem them for real money. To do this a supplying peer must aggregate the paywords by each e-coinID and send the following message to the broker

$$M6 = \{IDp, IDe, Payments\}$$

The broker needs to verify each payword received from the peer by performing hashes on it and counting the amount of paywords. If all the paywords are valid, the broker deposits the amount to the peer's account, and then sends an acknowledgement

$$M7 = \{Balance\ Statement\ of\ the\ peer's\ account\}$$

to the supplying peer as shown in Fig. 8.

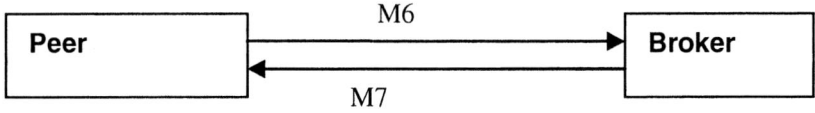

Fig. 8. Peer-redeem transaction

The protocol is credit based. There is no protection mechanism to prevent a peer from double spending. Double spending is detected at the time of the redeeming process. The broker checks the peer's paywords whether they are already in the database or not. Once double spending is detected, the malicious peers are penalized by terminating to use P2P-NetPay and access the peer-to-peer networks.

For example, at the end of each day, SP2 aggregates two payments as shown in Fig. 5 and Fig. 7 for IDe=1 and sends ID_{SP2} and IDe along with 6 (index), 5 (price),

$W_1 W_2 \ldots W_5$ (paywords) (M7) shown as Fig. 9 to the broker. The broker verifies the paywords ($W_1 W_2 \ldots W_5$) by using W_0, index (6) and price (5). If they are valid, the broker deposits 5cs to the SP2's account and send the balance to the SP2 (M8).

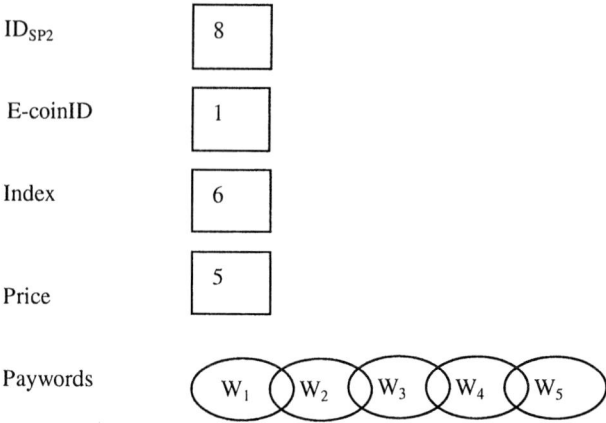

Fig. 9. SP2 aggregates two payments

6 Discussion

As we discussed in Section 3, existing P2P micro-payment protocols like Ppay have a down time protocol which is almost an on-line micro-payment system. The use of layered coins of Ppay protocol introduces the delay of the fraud detection and the floating coins growing in size. We have presented a real off-line and credit-based protocol suitable for micropayments in peer-to-peer networks. The protocol prevents peers from double spending using after-fact policy and any internal and external adversaries from forging, so it satisfies the requirements of security that a micropayment system should have. The protocol is economical since it does not involve public-key operations per purchase. Netpay can easily handle more transactions between peers. The major thrust of Netpay protocol is that it shifts the communication traffic bottleneck from the broker and distributes it among the peers, thus placing some processing burden on the requesting peer when a requesting peer wishes to purchase from a supplying peer. Work is underway to implement a trading community on the proposal protocol to evaluate its feasibility using our client-server based NetPay e-wallets and e-coin purchase/redemption as a prototype infrastructure.

References

1. Dai, X. and Lo, B.: NetPay – An Efficient Protocol for Micropayments on the WWW. Fifth Australian World Wide Web Conference, Australia (1999)
2. Dai X. and Grundy J.: Architecture for a Component-based, Plug-in Micro-payment System, In Proceedings of the Fifth Asia Pacific Web Conference, LNCS 2642, Springer, April 2003, pp. 251-262.

3. Dai, X., Grundy, J.: Architecture of a Micro-Payment System for Thin-Client Web Applications. In Proceedings of the 2002 International Conference on Internet Computing, Las Vegas, CSREA Press, June 24-27, 444--450
4. Dai, X. and Grundy J.: Customer Perception of a Thin-client Micro-payment System Issues and Experiences, Journal of End User Computing, 15(4), pp 62-77, (2003).
5. Dai X. and Grundy J., Three Kinds of E-wallets for a NetPay Micro-payment System, The Fifth International Conference on Web Information Systems Engineering, November 22-24, 2004, Brisbane, Australia. Lecture notes in Computer Science 3306, pp. 66 - 77
6. Gabber, E. and Silberschatz, A.: Agora: A Minimal Distributed Protocol for Electronic Commerce, Proceedings of the Second USENIX Workshop on Electronic Commerce, Oakland, California, November 18-21, 1996, pp. 223-232
7. Gabber, E. and Silberschatz, A.: "Micro Payment Transfer Protocol (MPTP) Version 0.1". *W3C Working Draft*, 1995. http://www.w3.org/pub/WWW/TR/WD-mptp
8. Herzberg, A. and Yochai, H. : Mini-pay: Charging per Click on the Web, 1996 http://www.ibm.net.il/ibm_il/int-lab/mpay
9. Manasse, M.: The Millicent Protocols for Electronic Commerce. First USENIX Workshop on Electronic Commerce. New York (1995)
10. Rivest, R. and Shamir, A.: PayWord and MicroMint: Two Simple Micropayment Schemes. Proceedings of 1996 International Workshop on Security Protocols, Lecture Notes in Computer Science, Vol. 1189. Springer (1997) 69—87
11. Golle, P., Leylton-Brown, K. and Mironov, I.: Incentives for sharing in peer-to-peer networks. In Proc. of Second workshop on Electronic Commerce (WELCOM'01), Heidelberg, Germany, November, 2001.
12. Shneidman, J. and Parkes, D.: Rationality and self-interest in peer-to-peer networks. In Proc. of 2nd International Workshop on Peer-to-Peer Systems (IPTPS '03), Berkeley, CA, USA, February 2003.
13. Eytan Adar and Bernardo Huberman. Free riding on Gnutella. First Monday, 5(10), 2000.
14. Yang, B. and Garcia-Molina, H.: Ppay: micropayments for peer-to-peer systems. In prooc. Of the 10th ACM conference on computer and communication security, pages 300-310. ACM press, 2003.
15. The Napster home page, http://www.napster.com/
16. Rivest, R.: "The MD5 Message-Digest Algorithm". RFC 1321, Internet Activities Board, 1992.
17. Menezes, A. J., Oorschot , P. C. and Vanstone, S. A.: Handbook of Applied Cryptography. New York, 1997.

FlexiRank: An Algorithm Offering Flexibility and Accuracy for Ranking the Web Pages

Debajyoti Mukhopadhyay[1] and Pradipta Biswas[2]

[1] Cellular Automata Research Lab, Techno India,
(affiliated to W.B. University of Technology),
EM 4/1 Salt Lake Sector V, Calcutta 700091, India
debm@vsnl.com
[2] Indian Institute of Technology, School of Information Technology,
Kharagpur 721302, India
pbiswas@sit.iitkgp.ernet.in

Abstract. The existing search engines sometimes give unsatisfactory search result for lack of any categorization. If there is some means to know the preference of user about the search result and rank pages accordingly, the result will be more useful and accurate to the user. In the present paper a web page ranking algorithm is proposed based on syntactic classification of web pages. The proposed approach mainly consists of three steps: select some properties of web pages based on user's demand, measure them, and give different weightage to each property during ranking for different types of pages. The existence of syntactic classification is supported by running fuzzy c-means algorithm and neural network classifier on a set of web pages. It has been demonstrated that, for different types of pages, the same query string has produced different page ranking.

1 Introduction

Web page ranking algorithms are used to order web pages according to their relevance. Exactly what information the user wants is unpredictable. So the web page ranking algorithms are designed to anticipate the user requirements from various static (e.g., number of hyperlinks, textual content) and dynamic (e.g., popularity) features. The goal of the present paper is to introduce an algorithm called FlexiRank to offer some flexibility to the user while searching the web pages. A search engine interface is incorporated with some option buttons to fine-tune the options while sending the query to the search engine. The option buttons are easy to use for naïve users and not as complicated as some of the existing advanced search engine interfaces.

2 Related Work

Among the existing page ranking algorithms the most important algorithms are Kleinberg's HITS algorithm, Brin & Page's PageRank algorithm, SALSA algorithm,

CLEVER Project etc. The AltaVista Search Engine implements HITS algorithm. But the HITS (Hyperlink Induced Topic Search) is a purely link structure-based computation, ignoring the textual content [1]. According to PageRank algorithm used in Google [2], a page has a high rank if the sum of the ranks of its back-links is high. CLEVER project [3] mainly emphasizes on enhancements to HITS algorithm, hypertext classification, focused crawling, mining communities, modeling the web as a graph. The weight assignment to hyperlinks is more exploited in [4] where each link gets a weight based on its position at the page, length of anchor text and on the tag where the link is inserted. In [5] the links of a web page are weighted based on the number of in-links and out-links of their reference pages. In [6] a new approach of dissecting queries into crisp and fuzzy part has been introduced. In [7], a parameter viz. query sensitiveness is measured which signifies the relevance of a document with respect to a term or topic. In [8], the damping factor of PageRank algorithm is changed to a parameter viz. confidence of a page with respect to a particular topic. The confidence is defined as the probability of accessing a particular page for a particular topic.

3 Our Approach

Approach taken in this paper is to make a classification of web pages based on only syntax of the page. This type of classification is independent to the semantics of the content of a page. The search engine interface is incorporated with some option buttons to take the proper class of a page along with the query topic. The web page classification will be like Index page, Home Page, Article, Definition, Advertisement Pages etc. As for example, if a search topic is given like "Antivirus Software" and given category of page is "Homepage" then the homepages of different Antivirus companies will get higher ranking. If for the same query, the category given is "Article", then the pages giving general description of Antivirus Software will get higher ranking. Again if the given category is "Index" then a page having large number of links to different antivirus software vendors will get higher ranking. Thus in the proposed page-ranking algorithm for a single query term, a particular page can get different ranking based on users' demand.

4 Parameters Used for Ranking

In this section different parameters, selected for web page ranking, are discussed. The page ranking will be done by taking a weighted average of all or some of the parameters. The weight given to a particular parameter will depend upon the category of the page. In the proposed algorithm a single query may give different ranking to a page depending on the category of the page-which is not possible in any existing search engines. The algorithm is flexible in the sense that just by changing the weights, the same algorithm satisfies user demands for different types of pages.

4.1 Relevance Weight

Relevance weight measures the relevance of a page with respect to a query topic by counting the number of occurrences of the query topic or part of the query topic within the text of the document. In the present paper, the page relevance algorithm used has taken an approach of the Three Level Scoring method. In the proposed algorithm, firstly the words in "Stop List" are removed from the search string. After proper stemming, the relevant keywords or terms are extracted from the search string. Next, the occurrence of each term is found out, and a weightage is given to it as the ratio of its length to the length of the given query topic. As for example, for a query string "data mining," the term "data mining" will get a weightage of "1" whereas the term "mining" will get a weightage of "6/11" i.e., 0.545. Finally the algorithm is as follows:

```
function Calc_Relev_Wt(File F: A Text File, String S: The
Search String)
return Relev_weight
/* relevance of textual content of file F w.r.t. Search
string S */
var KEYWORD_SET[1…N]
/* To store the subset of relevant strings within the search
string */
var CNT /*Number of relevant substrings */
var OCCURRENCE[1…N]
/* OCCURRENCE[I]= Occurrences of substring KEYWORD_SET[I]
within file F */
KEYWORD_SET=Set of relevant substrings within S
CNT=|KEYWORD_SET|
For (I=1 to CNT)
OCCURRENCE[I]= Number of Occurrences of substring
KEYWORD_SET[I] within file F
For (I=1 to CNT)
Relev_Weight=Relev_Weight+(Length(KEYWORD_SET[I])/Length(S))*
OCCURRENCE[I]
```

4.2 Hub and Authority Weight

Authorities are pages that are recognized as providing significant, trustworthy, and useful information on a topic. Hubs are index pages that provide lots of useful links to relevant content pages. The authority value of page p is the sum of hub scores of all the pages that points to p and the hub value of page p is the sum of authority scores of all the pages that p points to. It has been observed that the small number of pages with the largest authority converged value should be the pages that had the best authorities for the topic.

4.3 Link Analysis of a Page

The HITS algorithm analyzes the link structure information of a web graph. The hyperlink information of a single page (e.g., number of hyperlinks, anchor text and positions of the pages in the domain tree with respect to a particular page) are also found to give useful information during syntactic categorization of a web page. The number of hyperlinks of a page is calculated by getting the total number of *a href* tags. For getting the exact number of hyperlinks the number of *frame src* tags should be added to the number of *a href* tags and links to the same page should be excluded. By analyzing anchor text the glossary pages can very easily be identified. It has been found the portals have large number of hyperlinks pointing to same level nodes in the domain tree rooted at the next higher level node of the source of the page; e.g., if source is **a.b.com** nature of hyperlinks is **x.b.com** or **y.b.com**. The site maps and home pages have large number of hyperlinks pointing to lower level nodes in the domain tree rooted at the source of the page; e.g., if source is **a.b.com** nature of hyperlinks is **a.b.com/x, a.b.com/y**.

4.4 Types of Content

The syntactic analysis of the content also gives useful properties about the type of a page. Examples of this type of properties are: number of images in a page; proportion of text length to number of images; relevance weight of the query string within special tags like header tag, title tag, etc.

5 The FlexiRank Algorithm

The FlexiRank algorithm operates on a set of web pages returned by a web crawler and gives a ranking of the pages as output. It operates according to the following steps:

- **Select attributes based on user demand:** Based on the users' demand the algorithm chooses a set of properties of a web page. Some properties are chosen irrespective of the users' demand. Examples of such mandatory properties are Relevance weight, Hub weight and Authority weight. The other attributes are chosen based on user demand to provide an accurate ranking. Examples of such optional attributes are number of hyperlinks, number of images, properties of anchor text, etc.
- **Measure the attributes:** The selected attributes are measured for each web page.
- **Calculate rank:** The rank is calculated by taking a weighted average of the measured values. The weight assigned to each attribute is based on users' demand.

The algorithm provides flexibility in two grounds:

- **In selection of properties:** As for example when the users' demand is index type pages, number of hyperlinks of a page will be measured whereas number of images or text to image proportion will not be measured.
- **In determining weightages of properties:** The selected attributes get different weightage for difference in user demand. As for example, for article type of pages, relevance weight and authority weight will get highest weightage whereas for advertisement type of pages, number of thumbnails (i.e., number of images) and hub weight will get higher weightage.

Due to these varying selections of properties and their corresponding weightages, the algorithm provides more flexibility to the user and also gives more accurate result.

6 Experimental Results

The experiment has been done in two parts. In the first part, several web pages are downloaded and classified according to the proposed properties. In the second part, some web pages are downloaded again from an existing search engine and ranked according to the FlexiRank algorithm. Each of these parts is discussed below.

6.1 Clustering the Web Pages

In this part about 50 web pages are downloaded from Google search engine. The pages are clustered according to different properties like Relevance weight, Number of Images, Number of Links, Document Length etc. For clustering purpose, Fuzzy c-means algorithm is used. Cluster validation is done by Classification Entropy. With c = 4, we got a hint of the existence of syntactic classification. To confirm the existence of syntactic classification, we use a neural network software viz. NeuNet Pro downloaded from http://www.cormactech.com. Using this software we define a feed forward neural network with 5 hidden nodes and use back-propagation learning algorithm for classifying 30 web pages downloaded from Google. After completing 1000 cycles with learning rate=60 and verify rate=10 (these rates are defined by the software internally) we get the following scatter graph in Fig. 1 and time series graph in Fig. 2. Since the classification is carried on using only 7 properties, we do not get a very accurate classification. Still the result of the fuzzy clustering algorithm and the less than 20% R.M.S. error in classification confirm the existence of syntactic classification of web pages.

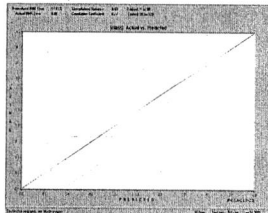 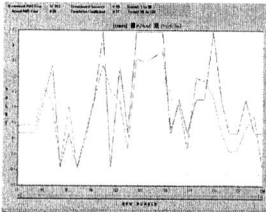

Fig. 1. Scatter graph for Syntactic Classification

Fig. 2. Time Series Graph for Syntactic Classification

6.2 Ranking the Web Pages

For testing the actual change in ranking for different types of pages, the proposed ranking algorithm is run on top 30 pages downloaded using Google search engine with the search topic "Human Computer Interaction". The screenshot of the proposed interface of a search engine is shown in Fig. 3. When the type of page is given as index, the following three pages get first three ranks:

1. http://is.twi.tudelft.nl/hci/
2. http://dmoz.org/Computers/Human-Computer_Interaction/
3. http://www-hcid.soi.city.ac.uk/

The first two pages are literally index pages while the third one is the home page of Centre of HCI Design, City University London. The page contains a lot of hyperlinks. Again when the type of page is given as article the following three pages get first three ranks:

1. http://sigchi.org/cdg/cdg2.html
2. http:// www.cs.cmu.edu/~amulet/papers/uihistory.tr.html
3. http://www.id-book.com/

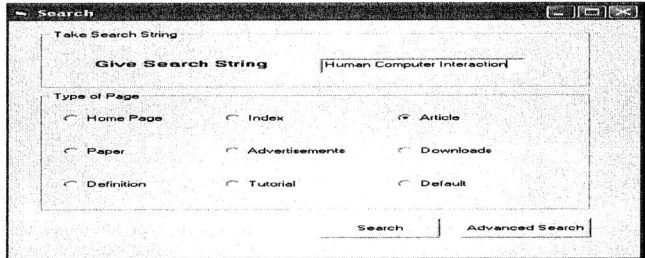

Fig. 3. Screenshot of the Proposed Interface of a Search Engine

Here also, the first two sites are text intensive articles. As can be seen in the interface a default option is also being kept for ranking all types of pages.

7 Conclusion

The present paper discusses a web page ranking algorithm, which consolidates web page classification with web page ranking to offer flexibility to the user as well as to produce more accurate search result. The classification is done based on several properties of a web page which are not dependent on the meaning of its content. The existence of this type of classification is supported by applying fuzzy c-means algorithm and neural network classification on a set of web pages. The typical interface of a web search engine is proposed to change to a more flexible interface which can take the type of the web page along with the search string.

References

1. Kleinberg, Jon; "Authoritative Sources in a Hyperlinked Environment;" Proc. ACM-SIAM Symposium on Discrete Algorithms, 1998; pp. 668-677
2. Brin, Sergey; Page, Lawrence; "The Anatomy of a Large-Scale Hypertextual Web Search Engine;" 7th Int. WWW Conf. Proceedings, Brisbane, Australia; April 1998
3. Chakrabarti, S. et. al.,; "Mining the link structure of the World Wide Web;" IEEE Computer, 32(8), August 1999
4. Baeza-Yates,Ricardo; Davis, Emilio; "Web page ranking using link attributes," Proceedings of the 13th international World Wide Web conference on Alternate track papers & posters, May 2004
5. Xing, W.; Ghorbani, A.; "Weighted PageRank algorithm;" Proceedings of the Second Annual Conference on Communication Networks and Services Research, 19-21 May 2004; pp. 305 – 314
6. Dae-Young Choi ; "Enhancing the power of Web search engines by means of fuzzy query" Decision Support Systems, Volume 35, Issue 1, April 2003, pp. 31-44
7. Wen-Xue Tao; Wan-Li Zuo;" Query-sensitive self-adaptable web page ranking algorithm" International Conference on Machine Learning and Cybernetics, Vol. 1, 2-5 Nov. 2003; pp. 413 - 418
8. Mukhopadhyay, Debajyoti; Giri, Debasis; Singh, Sanasam Ranbir; "An Approach to Confidence Based Page Ranking for User Oriented Web Search;" SIGMOD Record, Vol.32, No.2, June 2003; pp. 28-33

Adaptable Web Browsing of Images in Mobile Computing Environment: Experiments and Observations

Atul Kumar[1], Anjali Bhargava[1], Bharat Bhargava[1], and Sanjay Madria[2]

[1] Department of Computer Science, Purdue University, West Lafayette, IN
[2] Department of Computer Science, University of Missouri-Rolla, MO

Abstract. In this paper, we report some experiments and observations to make browsing of images more adaptable using small devices. We highlight the usability of such an alternative in mobile e-commerce and bandwidth-constrained systems.

1 Introduction

The cellular phones, wearable PCs, personal digital assistants (PDA) being mobile, wireless and small, pose new challenges for browsing. Some issues include low bandwidth availability, limited memory, limited display area, frequent disconnection, fast changing locations etc [4]. In addition there is a problem of redundant information which becomes all the more costly in the context of limited resources. Full quality and high-resolution images may not be needed when the user just wants the stock quote of a company on his cell phone screen. Why burden a user with high quality thumbnail images for choices when the content provider is sure that the user will like to see in more detail and in better quality, the particular items he/she is more interested in?

New features started appearing in the widespread browsers including offline browsing and also some type of filtering. But they are not flexible enough in the sense that they can not download a web page with varying levels of compression on the fly so that the user can select what is suitable in current context nor can they offer choices with multi-resolution display of a page. Content based editing is difficult because of the inherent difficulty in understanding the semantics of the contents. The methodologies in this category offer text-only version or fixed pre-decided contents. An example is a text-based technology called "*Web Clipping*" developed by 3Com for its wireless Palm [16]. *Web Clipping* allows mobile users to download short bursts of text information from Web sites that have tailored content for 3Com's technology but it doesn't allow users to surf the Web at large.

We propose experimental observations [11] that can result in savings in download time and in easing the strain on the network bandwidth. We consider a novel approach to bridge the gap between the time required to download a website in its entirety and the time, the user is ready to wait for that website, by offering information at various levels of quality. These various levels of qualities are made possible by compressing the inline images at different ratios. Our solution is scalable as it can add on many other filtering criteria and can support various modes of compression as well as selective compression. We didn't emphasize on algorithm of compression as many standards and effective compression techniques [5] are now supported in most of the high level languages. The solution is 'robust and scalable' in the sense that it can service a large number of these small devices in parallel without a loss of generality. It is 'transparent' in the sense that the user is totally unaware of the calculations going at the server side and it appears as if the user is directly connected to the actual web server. The scheme will work effectively with the new media streaming applications such as [4,5,9].

In trying to cut down the download time for the entire web site, we compress all the inline images in it. It warranties trapping all the multiple HTTP requests issued in effect while trying to access a single URL. We decided to enhance the existing applications by adding adaptability features in the browsing software (or more appropriately by changing the way the clients would browse a site) rather than building a complete new one. This decision is based on following pragmatic assertion: most users want to use their traditional browsers to surf even on their portable devices in a fashion similar to their desktop browsers.

2 Background and Relevant Work

Different research groups are developing prototypes to suggest the adaptable features and the tradeoff between the cost and applicability [1,13]. *NetBlitz* [1] is a multiresolution -based system for the WWW. This involves setting up a proxy server housing the URL cache and the multiresolution techniques. It dynamically generates different versions and delivers them to the users. It focuses on multiresolution as the parameter for quality of service. We concentrate on compressing many details and embedded information in fine quality images that can be taken off without any loss of generality of the image but in turn savings in the download time. [7] discusses about techniques to provide dynamic distillation of image and video over the web. Work is going on in the direction of transcoding images and content negotiation amongst the web community. We have not come across browsers that support vast adaptability criterion suitable for hand-held devices. [15] discussed methodologies to adapt multimedia traffic which is basically based on the idea of the application having some knowledge about the underlying network and the network having some knowledge of the kind of application currently running. It tries to fragment packet semantically rather than using the current IP fragmentation scheme. We observe that the above scheme when applied to our technique of compressing the images can help in guaranteeing much better QoS for the application.

2.1 Mobility Issues and Constraints

Providing Internet and WWW services on a wireless data network presents many challenges [2,3,8]. Mass-market, hand-held wireless devices present a more constrained computing environment compared to desktop computers. The wireless data networks present a more constrained communication environment compared to wired networks. Because of fundamental limitations of power, available spectrum, and mobility, wireless data networks tend to have less availability, stability, and bandwidth as well as greater latency. Mobile networks are growing in complexity and the cost of providing new value-added services to wireless users is increasing.

3 Experimental Set Up

The experimental set up consists of setting our own proxy server. This proxy server ideally should be a powerful workstation servicing many mobile devices in parallel. All these devices here configure their client browser to talk to this server instead of directly connecting to the actual web server. The paradigm is a standard client-server model [1].

The compression engine, CE, is responsible for compressing the in-line images on the fly. The cache is supported in proxy to speed up the computation and performance of our adaptable web browser in the case where the compressed image is already in the cache. The experiment consists of directing the browsers (i.e. clients) to talk to the proxy server, which is waiting infinitely for clients' connections. The server dispatches a thread to handle each request to minimize loss of any client request. Now each request consist of multiple HTTP messages being sent to server. From the HTTP request format (e.g. using the content-type and content-length), the proxy makes decisions whether to compress the image or let it go as it is. The compression ratio in our case is determined by the available bandwidth at the client side. So the users can select the browsing speed at which they want to browse a particular web page. Based on the browsing speed selected, a compression ratio ranging from 0.0 to 1.0 (lower quality image implies more compression or equivalently more compression ratio) is determined by the proxy using JPEG image compression algorithms.

3.1 Experiments and Observations

We conducted an extensive set of experiments on popular websites especially sites related to e-commerce to evaluate our proposed model. The sites were downloaded at different browsing speeds and hence at different image compression levels. Compressing the image results in reduction of the sizes, this finally leads to reduction in time because of transporting smaller files across the network. There have been many other researchers in this direction [1,10]. We computed the savings in download time with different network connection speed. The sample data presented in Table 1 has been collected at two different speeds – 28.8 kbps and 56.6 kbps. Note that this can be easily extended to any other types of connectivity and speed.

The leftmost column represents all the files present on a single web page. The next column represents the uncompressed sizes of the files. Measurements for two different levels of compression were taken. The figure 'COMPR 1' represents maximum compression without losing the sense of images while the next compression level 'COMPR 2' is the compression level which the end user will gladly accept. The idea was to prove that even at the 2nd compression level, there are substantial savings in the download time. So the end user can carry out e-business or any other applications without substantial loss of quality in a much lesser time. The next column shows the download time that each file takes assuming 28.8 kbps connection speed. There are three time measurements under that category. Time 0 represents the download time for uncompressed image. Time 1 is the time for maximally compressed images (hence the smallest time) while Time 2 represents time for lesser compression level, a better quality level. Exactly similar calculations were made out assuming 56.6 kbps connection. Finally the sum totals were calculated.

Table 2 shows a sample data and the corresponding graph depicting the reduction in size with varying quality of image. The image is one of the pictures of the planet Mars posted on the NASA website. The same experiment was carried on large variety of images and on different kinds of web sites. We took in consideration images varying from very detailed fine quality to the ones having courser appearance. Also the sample images were chosen to be representative of largely varying sizes. The resulting graph was basically of the same nature confirming our experiments.

Table 1. Measurements for the embedded images and text files

					File Name: URL:	UBID Main Page http://www.ubid.com					
								Connections			
FILES	SIZE	COMPR1	SIZE1	COMPR2	SIZE2	28.8 kbps			56.6 kbps		
	(KB)		(KB)		(KB)	Time0	Time1	Time2	Time0	Time1	Time2
00_120x60.gif	5	68%	1.6	56%	2.2	1.39	0.44	0.61	0.71	0.23	0.31
00_AOLSeal.gif	2	50%	1	44%	1.12	0.56	0.28	0.31	0.28	0.14	0.16
00_BBLLogo.gif	5	73%	1.35	66%	1.72	1.39	0.38	0.48	0.71	0.19	0.24
00_ClickTabs2.gif	2	20%	1.6	20%	1.61	0.56	0.45	0.45	0.28	0.23	0.23
00_Desktops.gif	2	55%	0.9	42%	1.17	0.56	0.25	0.32	0.28	0.13	0.16
00_diamond.gif	2	35%	1.3	26%	1.48	0.56	0.36	0.41	0.28	0.18	0.21
00_logo2.gif	5	63%	1.85	56%	2.2	1.39	0.51	0.61	0.71	0.26	0.31
00_Notebooks.gif	2	45%	1.1	31%	1.38	0.56	0.31	0.38	0.28	0.16	0.20
00_pcmall.gif	2	53%	0.94	43%	1.14	0.56	0.26	0.32	0.28	0.13	0.16
00_quote.gif	2	49%	1.02	27%	1.46	0.56	0.28	0.41	0.28	0.14	0.21
00_SecureIcon.gif	2	79%	0.43	74%	0.52	0.56	0.12	0.14	0.28	0.06	0.07
00_tabs.gif	4	39%	2.44	24%	3.04	1.11	0.68	0.84	0.57	0.34	0.43
00_ThisHour.gif	1	21%	0.79	21%	0.79	0.28	0.22	0.22	0.14	0.11	0.11
00_Top10.gif	1	23%	0.77	23%	0.77	0.28	0.21	0.21	0.14	0.11	0.11
00_blank.gif	1	12%	0.88	12%	0.88	0.28	0.24	0.24	0.14	0.12	0.12
00_dss.gif	3	55%	1.35	36%	1.92	0.83	0.38	0.53	0.42	0.19	0.27
00_GoldenGavel.gif	6	47%	3.18	40%	3.6	1.67	0.88	1.00	0.85	0.45	0.51
00_July4thPromo.gif	2	58%	0.84	46%	1.08	0.56	0.23	0.30	0.28	0.12	0.15
00_SummerPromo.gif	3	51%	1.47	33%	2.01	0.83	0.41	0.56	0.42	0.21	0.28
40411.jpg	4	50%	2	16%	3.36	1.11	0.56	0.93	0.57	0.28	0.47
40725.jpg	3	47%	1.59	16%	2.52	0.83	0.44	0.70	0.42	0.22	0.36
47616.jpg	3	62%	1.14	60%	1.2	0.83	0.32	0.33	0.42	0.16	0.17
52228.jpg	8	60%	3.2	58%	3.36	2.22	0.89	0.93	1.13	0.45	0.47
52431.jpg	6	76%	1.44	72%	1.68	1.67	0.40	0.47	0.85	0.20	0.24
53224.jpg	9	58%	3.78	54%	4.14	2.50	1.05	1.15	1.27	0.53	0.59
advert1.gif	2	25%	1.5	7%	1.86	0.56	0.42	0.52	0.28	0.21	0.26
advert2.gif	14	11%	12.5	1%	13.9	3.89	3.46	3.85	1.98	1.76	1.96
index.html	27	0%	27	0%	27	7.50	7.50	7.50	3.82	3.82	3.82
TOTALS	128		76.92		89.07	35.56	21.9	24.74	18.09	11.16	12.59

Table 3 and 4 shows the effect of trying to compress the original image as well as image conceived when we extrapolate to better quality size. We found out that many images are not put at their best quality but are at reduced quality due to the same underlying assumption as ours i.e. sacrificing quality a bit does not lead to appreciable

Table 2. Size of the image as a function of the quality

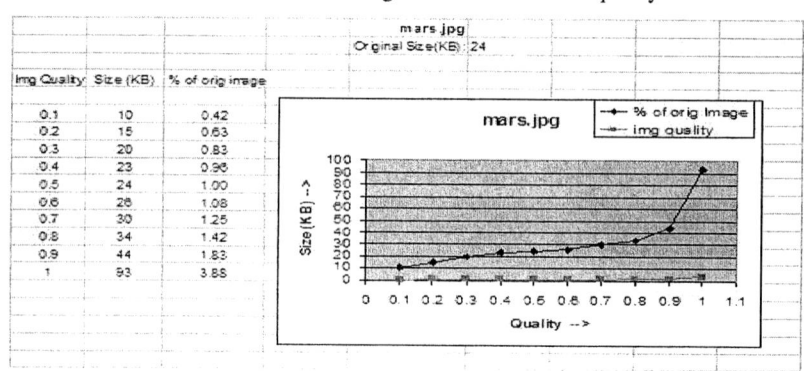

Table 3. Compression at original size and quality of image

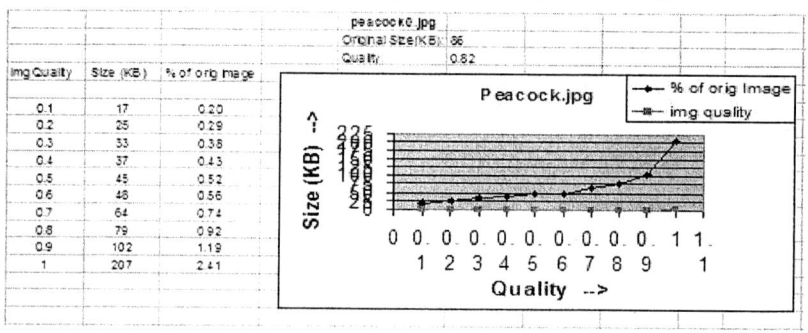

distortion of the image. The original image (peacock.jpg), for example, here was between quality 0.8 and 0.9. We tried to extrapolate the image to a better quality (and hence larger size) and then apply our techniques on that trying to compress it at different levels. We observe the same trends in the resulting graph. This was repeated for different original starting quality and hence different initial sizes.

We make the following observations from the sample data. Definitely, compressing the images result in savings of download time as well as the amount of storage required to cache the inline images. The obvious drawback is the loss in visual quality of the images [2,3,6,12]. But this is immaterial here, to an extent, because most of the times (especially in e-commerce web sites), the user is more concerned with the contents of the web page rather than the quality of images e.g. the quality of the various icons or the quality of the images that external advertiser embed in the web page. This is more pertinent in cases of mobile devices supporting browsers. A more subtle question is the tradeoff between the overhead associated with the compression and the final savings in download time. We argue on the basis of the table 2, 3, 4 and the corresponding graphs that, we get substantial savings in the size of image with a sacrifice in the quality of image. These savings in turn reflect in the savings in the download time. Compressing every image even to correspond to just 1 lower level of quality can benefit us with an appreciable savings in download time. We justify that this kind of application is primarily aimed for users doing lots of e-business and also assuming that they have a slower Internet connectivity, even though they have top-of-line fast computers (in terms of processing power). Even with faster network connectivity, the problem envisioned is the rate at which network bandwidth is being hogged. Since the available bandwidth is, more or less, constant but the applications consuming them are burgeoning, it might result that even with a faster link, people have to suffer considerable delay because of network congestion. Hence it makes sense to bear the overhead of image compression. Also with now more and more support being built in programming languages for images, this can be done on the fly. In other words, this adaptability makes sense if the client is being supported on mobile devices or it has a low bandwidth connection to the network. Also it is most effective for sites where we can achieve significance compression without major sacrifice in visual quality. Another adaptable browser based on multi-resolution [8], has been studied and it also deduces similar conclusions based on different set of experiments and setup.

Table 4. Compression at extrapolated size and quality of image

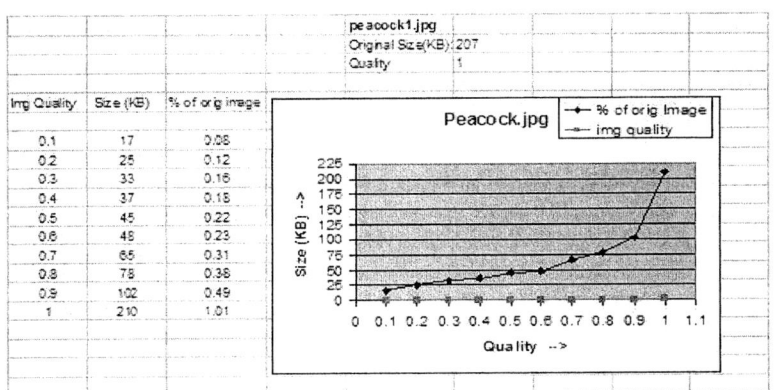

4 Conclusions and Future Research

We reported some experiments and observations for mobile application requirements such as Web browsing. The experimental results show the huge savings in time that can be achieved by compressing high resolution and big inline images. This approach is a step in the direction of making browsing more user-friendly and easing the constraints on system resources. We also discuss the tradeoff associated with it and the favorable factors under which proposed solution works best. For future work, we are using finer criterion for compressing the images. The compressed images should also be effectively cached at the proxy servers to avoid duplication of work in compression of same images. This work can be extended to support all the image types and even the text portion of the pages as they form a major chunk in many of the web-sites. This would result in further savings of the download time.

References

[1] Swarup Acharya, Henry Korth & Viswanath Poosala. Systematic Multiresolution and its Application to the World Wide Web, ICDE, 1999, pp. 40-49.

[2] Bharat Bhargava, Shunghe Li et al. Impact of Codec Schemes on Multimedia Communications, In Proceedings of the IETE International Conference on Multi-media Information Systems (MULTIMEDIA 96)}, Feb., 96, New Delhi, India, Published by McGraw Hill, pp. 94-105..

[3] Bharat Bhargava, Shunghe Li et al. Performance Studies for an Adaptive Video Conferencing System. In Proceedings of the IETE International Conference on Multi-media Information Systems MULTIMEDIA 96)}, Feb., 96, New Delhi, India, Published by McGraw Hill, pp 106-116.

[4] Bharat K. Bhargava, Changgui Shi, Sheng-Yih Wang: MPEG Video Encryption Algorithms. Multimedia Tools Appl. 24(1): 57-79 (2004).

[5] Bharat K. Bhargava, Changgui Shi, Sheng-Yih Wang: MPEG Video Encryption Algorithms. Multimedia Tools Appl. 24(1): 57-79 (2004).

[6] Ron Frederick. Experiences with Real-time Software Video Compression. In proceedings of the packet video workshop, Portland, Oregon, 1994.

[7] A. Fox, S. D. Gribble, E. A. Brewer, and E. Amir. Adapting to Network and Client Variability via On-demand Dynamic Distillation. ASPLOS Proceedings, Oct. 1996.

[8] Martin Gaedke, Michael Beigl, Hans-Werner Gellersen, Christian Segor: Web Content Delivery to Heterogeneous Mobile Platforms. ER Workshops 1998: 205-217

[9] Mohamed Hefeeda, Bharat K. Bhargava, David K. Y. Yau: A hybrid architecture for cost-effective on-demand media streaming. Computer Networks 44(3): 353-382 (2004)

[10] Van Jacobsen. Congestion Avoidance and Control. In proceedings of Symposium on Communications Architectures and Protocols (SIGCOMM'88)

[11] Atul Kumar, Adaptable Web Browsing, Project Report, Purdue University, 2000.

[12] Overview of the MPEG-4 Standard. International Organization for Standardization for Coding of Moving Pictures and Audio, March 1999.

[13] Standards for Mixed Media Communications. Lucent Technologies, June 1997.

[14] Sanjay Madria, Mukesh Mohania, Sourav Bhowmick, Bharat Bhargava. Mobile Data and Transaction Management, Information Science Journal, 2002.

[15] Sheng-Yih Wang, Bharat Bhargava. An adaptable network architecture for multimedia traffic management and control, IEEE International Conference on Multimedia and Expo (III) 2000: 1615-1618.

[16] Web Clipping. URL: http://cnn.com/TECH/computing

An Incremental Document Clustering Algorithm Based on a Hierarchical Agglomerative Approach

Kil Hong Joo and SooJung Lee

Dept. of Computer Education, Gyeongin National University of Education,
Gyodae Street, 45, Gyeyang-gu, Inchon, Korea, 407-753
{khjoo, sjlee}@ginue.ac.kr

Abstract. Document clustering is classifying a data set of documents into groups of closely related documents, so that its resulting clusters can be used in browsing and searching the documents of a specific topic. In most cases of such as application, a set of new documents are incrementally added to the data set and there can be a large variation in the number of words in each document. This paper proposes an incremental document clustering method for an incrementally increasing data set of documents. The normalized inverse document frequency of a word in the data set is introduced to cope with the variation of the number of words in each document. Furthermore, an average link method for document clustering instead of using one similarity measure used in two similarity measures: a cluster cohesion rate and a cluster participation rate. Furthermore, a category tree for a set of identified clusters is introduced to assist the incremental document clustering of newly added documents. In this paper, the performance of the proposed method is analyzed by a series of experiments to identify their various characteristics.

1 Introduction

Various methods and techniques for processing unstructured data such as textual data are introduced in the field of information retrieval (IR). Basically, the main purpose of these techniques is to construct a large set of well-categorized documents automatically for effective searching and browsing [1]. For this purpose, *document clustering* and *classification* are actively studied [2] since they can play an important role in helping an information retrieval system with a huge number of documents. Given a predefined set of document classes, document classification is identifying the appropriate class of a particular document [3]. Traditionally, the document classification is carried out manually. In order to assign a document to an appropriate class manually, a user should analyze the contents of the document. Therefore, a large amount of human effort would be required. There has been some research work on automatic document classification. One approach is learning appropriate text classifiers by machine learning techniques [4, 5] based on a training data set containing positive and negative examples. The accuracy of a resulting classifier is highly dependent on the fitness of the training data set. However, there are lots of terms and various classes of documents. In addition, many new terms and concepts are introduced everyday. Consequently, it is quite impossible to learn a classifier for each document class in such a manner.

In order to group a set of related documents automatically, clustering techniques [6, 7, 8] have been widely employed. The attractiveness of these cluster techniques is that they can find a set of similar data objects as a cluster directly from a given data set without relying on any predefined information such as training examples provided by domain experts [6, 7]. In most cases of such an application, a set of new documents is incrementally added to the data set.

This paper proposes an incremental document clustering method. The characteristics of a document are represented by a set of keywords that are extracted by evaluating the term weight of each word in the document. The term weight of each keyword for a document indicates the relative importance of the keyword in the document. Given a finite data set of documents, most document clustering algorithms use a TF*IDF function [12] to find the term weight of a word in a document. The term frequency (TF) of a word in a document is the number of occurrences of the word in the document. The inverse document frequency (IDF) of a word is the number of documents containing the word and it indicates how commonly the word is used in the documents of the data set. When the IDF of a word is high, the usage of the word is localized to a small number of documents in the data set. However, the TF*IDF function is not suitable for an incremental document clustering algorithm due to the following reasons: (1) A word with a relatively low document frequency tends to have a high term weight, so that a large number of document clusters can be generated potentially. (2) As the number of documents in a data set becomes larger, the effect of the IDF of a word on the term weight of the word in each document is increased specially when most of the documents contain a small number of words as in web documents. This is because the TF of a word in a document becomes small relative to its IDF. Furthermore, if document clustering should be performed in an incremental way, this effect is amplified since the value of IDF is increased continuously. For these reasons, a normalized inversed document frequency (NIDF) is used instead in this paper.

Given an initial set of documents, the initial clusters of similar documents are found by a seed document clustering method called SCUP (Seed Clustering Using Participation and cohesion) in this paper. The SCUP algorithm is a kind of an average link method of hierarchical agglomerative clustering [9, 10]. In a hierarchical agglomerative clustering algorithm, two clusters of the highest similarity are merged in each step. However, there may be a more similar cluster in the future when a set of new documents is incrementally added. Accordingly, the accuracy of a cluster can be degraded in the future. To resolve this problem of a hierarchical agglomerative clustering algorithm, this paper proposes two similarity measures: a cluster cohesion rate and a cluster participation rate. The cluster participation rate is examined to merge a new document with current set of clusters. By using the cluster participation rate, the accuracy of end cluster can be guaranteed at any time. In addition, the hierarchical agglomerative clustering algorithm generally requires a great amount of memory space since it is proportional to the square of the number of documents in a data set [11]. In order to minimize the usage of memory space, the SCUP algorithm produces dendrogram. The resulting dendrogram of the SCUP algorithm is used by an incremental document clustering algorithm (IDC) proposed in this paper in order to construct the category tree of identified clusters. Consequently, as a new document is incrementally added to the data set, the most appropriate cluster for the document can be found in the IDC algorithm based on the category tree efficiently.

Figure 1 illustrates the overall procedure of the proposed seed clustering SCUP algorithm. The SCUP algorithm is composed of the following steps. First, the keywords of each document in the initial set of documents are selected by the TF*NIDF method. Second, the proposed SCUP algorithm is performed to generate a set of initial clusters. Finally, a category tree for the resulting clusters is generated to be used by the incremental document clustering (IDC) algorithm for a new document.

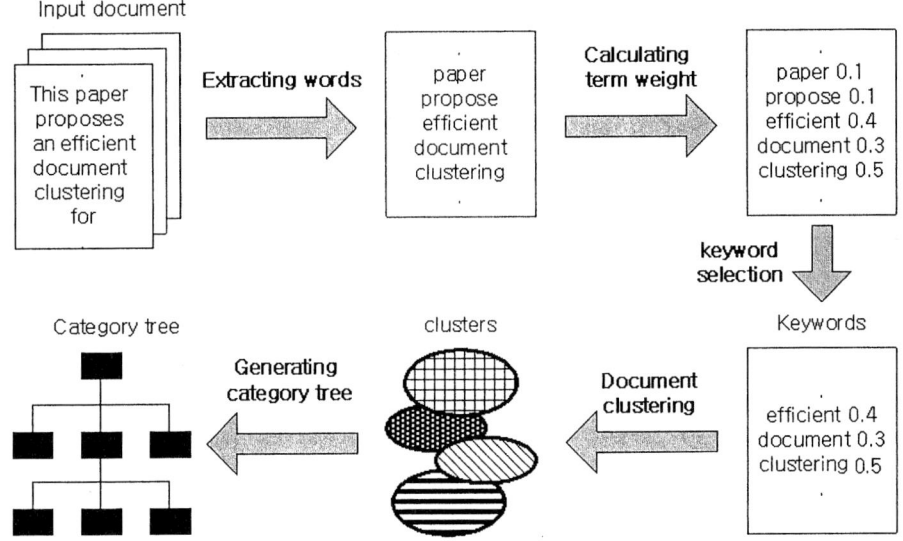

Fig. 1. Procedure of the SCUP algorithm

This paper is organized as follows. Section 2 introduces how the term weight of a word for a document in a dataset of documents is calculated to choose the keywords of the document. In Section 3, the proposed SCUP algorithm is presented in detail. Furthermore, the structure of a category tree for identified clusters is described. In Section 4, an incremental document clustering (IDC) algorithm is proposed. Section 5, several experiment results are comparatively analyzed to illustrate the various characteristics of the proposed algorithms. Finally, Section 6 draws overall conclusions.

2 Extraction of Keywords by Normalized Term Weight

For each word used in a document of an initial data set, its term weight is calculated to choose the keywords of the document. For this purpose, the TF*IDF (Term Frequency Inversed Document Frequency) [12] is used widely to reflect the importance of a specific word in a document. According to the TF*IDF method, the weight $tfidf_{ij}$ of a word w_j in a document d_i is defined as follows:

$$tfidf_{ij} = tf_{ij} \times \ln \frac{N}{df_j} \qquad (1)$$

where N is the total number documents in a data set and the term frequency tf_{ij} denotes the frequency of a word w_j occurred in a document d_i. In addition, the document frequency df_j denotes the number of documents that the word w_j appears in the data set. Equation (1) means that the possibility of a specific word representing the key concept of a particular document is proportional to the frequency of the word in the document. As the same time, it is also inversely proportional to the number of documents that contain the word. In other words, a word can be one of keywords for a document if it appears frequently in a small number of documents in a data set.

However, as the total number of documents N becomes larger, the effect of the inversed document frequency on a term weight is increased. This is because the term frequency of a word in a document is usually in a certain range specially for a short document. On the other hand, the IDF has the range of [0, lnN], and hence the value of the IDF is greatly influenced by the total number of documents in a data set. Furthermore, when new documents are incrementally added to a data set continuously, the number of documents N is continuously increased. In order to avoid this, the value of the IDF should be confined within a certain range regardless of N. This paper introduces a TF*NIDF (Term Frequency Normalized Inversed Document Frequency) function in which the maximum value of the IDF is normalized within a range [0, μ] for a fixed value of μ. The IDF idf_j of a word w_j is represented as follows:

$$idf_j = \ln \frac{N}{df_j} = \ln N - \ln df_j$$

the target range of its normalized inversed document frequency (NIDF) $nidf_j$ is $[0, \mu]$, so that $nidf_j$ can be represented like idf_j as follows:

$$nidf_j = \mu - \ln y$$

where y is a certain linear function of df_j. Given the range of df_j $[1, N]$, the following function makes the value of $\ln y$ be the range $[0, \mu]$.

$$y = \frac{e^\mu - 1}{N - 1}(df_j - 1) + 1$$

Based on the above function y, the term weight $tfnidf_{ij}$ of a word w_j in a document d_i is defined by Equation (2).

$$tfnidf_{ij} = tf_{ij} \times \left\{ \mu - \ln\left(\left(\frac{e^\mu - 1}{N - 1}\right) \times (df_j - 1) + 1\right) \right\} \qquad (2)$$

A word in a document is chosen as a keyword of the document if the term weight TF*NIDF of the word is larger than the average term weight of words in the document. Since the number of words in each document can be different, the range of the term frequency TF of a word in each document is not the same. In other words, when a word appears frequently in a long document, the TF of the word becomes large. As a result, its term weight can become large even though its NIDF is relatively small. To prevent this, the length of a document should also be normalized.

To normalize the number of words in a document, the maximum frequency normalization [13] can be considered. In this method, it uses the ratio of the frequency of each word in a document over the most frequently used word in the document. However, this can cause a problem when the frequency of a specific word is exceptionally large. This paper uses a cosine normalization which has been widely used in a vector space model. In the cosine normalization, given a vector $V = \{v_1, v_2, ..., v_n\}$, each element of the vector is divided by a cosine normalization element $\sqrt{v_1^2 + v_2^2 + ... + v_n^2}$. This cosine normalization makes it possible to normalize the length of a document based on the frequencies of all words in a document together. In this paper, the normalized term weight of a keyword k_j in a document d_i containing n distinct words represented by the cosine normalization is denoted by $t(d_i, k_j)$ as follows:

$$t(d_i, k_j) = \frac{tfnidf_{ij}}{\sqrt{\sum_{k=1}^{n} tfnidf_{ik}^2}}. \tag{3}$$

3 Seed Clustering Using a Participation and Cohesion Method

Given an initial data set of documents, the SCUP algorithm finds the initial clusters of the data set. Although the SCUP algorithm can be solely used as a clustering method for a set of documents, it can also provide an initial set of document clusters for an incrementally growing data set of documents. It is basically the same as the hierarchical agglomerative clustering algorithm [10] but uses different similarity measures defined in Definition 1 and Definition 2.

Definition 1. Document Similarity
Given two documents d_i and d_j with their keyword sets K_i and K_j respectively, their document similarity measure $s(d_i, d_j)$ is defined as follows:

$$s(d_i, d_j) = \frac{1}{2} \left(\frac{\sum_{w \in K_i \cap K_j} t(d_i, w)}{\sum_{w \in K_i} t(d_i, w)} + \frac{\sum_{w \in K_i \cap K_j} t(d_j, w)}{\sum_{w \in K_i} t(d_j, w)} \right) \tag{4}$$

∎

The above document similarity measure can provide the rate of similarity between only two documents. As a similarity measure for all the documents of a cluster, a *cluster cohesion* measure is defined in Definition 2. A cluster cohesion measure indicates how tightly the documents of a cluster are related in terms of their keywords. It is the average of the document similarities of all pairs of documents in a cluster.

Definition 2. Cluster Cohesion

Given a cluster C, let $|C|$ denotes the number of documents in C and $s(d_i, d_j)$ denotes the document similarity of two documents d_i and d_j in the cluster C. The cluster cohesion rate $h(C)$ of the cluster C is defined as follows:

$$h(C) = \frac{\sum_{d_i \in C} \sum_{d_j \in C - \{d_i\}} s(d_i, d_j)}{|C| C_2} \quad (5)$$

■

In the conventional agglomerative approach, a cluster is forced to be merged with another cluster until a predefined number of clusters are left. However, the SCUP algorithm is intended to be used in an incrementally growing set of documents. Consequently, clusters should be carefully merged. In other words, a cluster should not be merged with another cluster unless the documents of the two clusters are similar enough to be merged. If a cluster can not find another cluster that is eligible to be merged in the current set of clusters, it should not be merged. This is because there may be a more similar cluster in the clusters of incrementally added documents in the future. For this purpose, a cluster participation measure between two clusters of documents is defined in Definition 3. The union of the document keyword sets of all documents in a same cluster is named as the *cluster keyword set* of the cluster.

Definition 3. Cluster Participation

Given two clusters C_m and C_n of documents with cluster keyword sets CK_m and CK_n, a cluster participation rate $CP(C_m | C_n)$ of the cluster C_n to the cluster C_m is defined as follows:

$$CP(C_m | C_n) = \frac{\sum_{d_i \in C_m} \sum_{w \in CK_m \cap CK_n} t(d_i, w)}{\sum_{d_i \in C_n} \sum_{w \in CK_n} t(d_i, w)} \quad (6)$$

■

Given a minimum cluster participation rate *MinClPar* and a minimum cluster cohesion rate *MinClCoh*, two clusters C_m and C_n are eligible to be merged into one cluster C_{mn} which contains all the documents of the two clusters if the following conditions are satisfied.

(i) $CP(C_m | C_n) \geq MinClPar$ and $CP(C_n | C_m) \geq MinClPar$ and
(ii) $h(C_{mn}) \geq MinClCoh$

Among the pairs (C_m, C_n) of clusters that satisfy the above two conditions, the one with the highest cluster cohesion rate $h(C_{mn})$ merged into one cluster. The dendrogram [9] of the SCUP algorithm is used as a category tree. It is widely used to represent the hierarchical cluster structure of a data set. It is generated by keeping merging two similar clusters repeatedly until all documents of the data set are grouped into one cluster. A node of a category tree represents a category. It contains its *category keywords* which are the union of the cluster keyword sets of all the clusters of its sub-tree. A category tree can be used as an index in searching and browsing a specific cluster.

4 Incremental Document Clustering (IDC)

Most conventional document clustering algorithms [10, 14] are not intended to be used in an incrementally growing set of documents. Therefore, whenever a set of new documents is added incrementally, all documents in the enlarged data set should be reclustered from scratch. To avoid this, this section presents an incremental document clustering algorithm (IDC) based on the result of the SCUP algorithm presented in Section 4. When a new document is added to a data set of documents, among the current clusters, the most appropriate cluster is identified by traversing the category tree of the clusters starting from the root node of the category tree. The node participation rate of a new document d_l for a node N in the category tree defined in Definition 4 is used to traverse the tree.

Definition 4. Node Participation in the category tree
Given a new document d_m with its keyword set K_m and a node N of a category tree, let NK denote the set of category keywords in the node N. The node participation rate $NP(d_m \mid N)$ of the document d_m for the node N is defined as follows:

$$NP(d_m \mid N) = \frac{\sum_{d_i \in N} \sum_{w \in NK \cap K_m} t(d_i, w)}{\sum_{d_i \in N} \sum_{w \in NK} t(d_i, w)} \quad (7)$$

■

For a newly added document d, starting from the root node of a category tree, a document d recursively searches down to its corresponding leaf node based on the node participation rate of each node in its path from the root node. Figure 2 illustrates how a newly added document is incrementally clustered.

Whenever visiting a node of the category tree for a new document d, among the children of the node N, the one with the highest node participation rate for the document is identified. If the highest node participation rate is greater than or equal to a predefined minimum node participation rate, the corresponding child node is visited. Otherwise, the document is regarded as a noise document temporarily. This traversal is performed repeatedly until a document d visits a leaf node. When a leaf node is visited successfully, the document d is inserted to the cluster of the leaf node if the document d is greater than or equal to a predefined minimum cluster cohesion rate. If the above condition is not satisfied, the document is regarded as a noise document too. When a considerable number of noise documents are collected, the SCUP method is performed to generate a set of new clusters from the set of noise documents and the category tree is modified accordingly. On the other hand, when a document in a

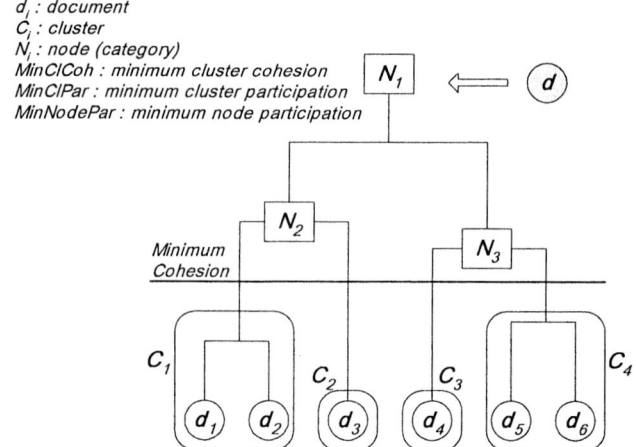

(a) Search an eligible cluster in a category tree

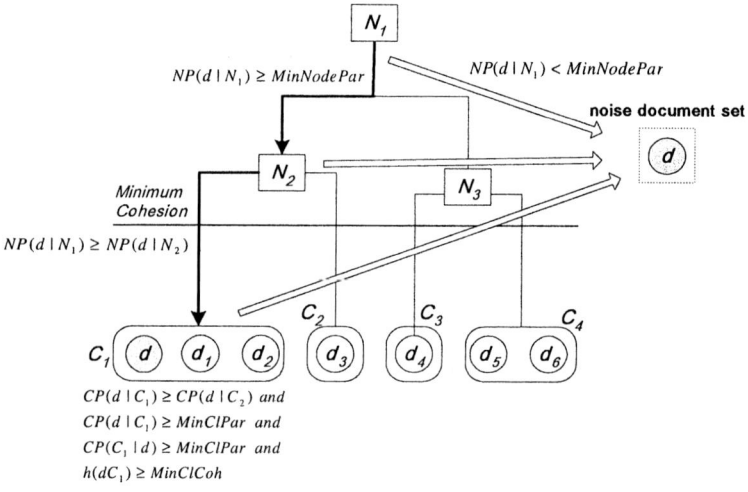

(b) Insert into the most eligible cluster

Fig. 2. Example of an incremental document clustering

cluster is deleted, if the updated cluster cohesion rate of the cluster becomes less than a minimum cluster cohesion rate, the documents of the cluster are reclustered by the SCUP algorithm to partition the documents into groups of more similar documents.

5 Experiments and Analysis of Result

To illustrate the performance of the proposed method, several experiment results are presented in this section. Among news categories provided in 'Yahoo', documents in

10 different domains such as business, science, politics and society are extracted as a data set of documents to be used in these experiments. For each domain, the average number of documents is 1026 and the average number of words in a document is 800.

In Figure 4, the clustering result of the SCUP algorithm is compared with that of the hierarchical agglomerative clustering algorithm (HAC). To show the relative effectiveness of the proposed clustering algorithm the same similarity measures as described in Section 4 is used for the hierarchical agglomerative clustering algorithm. The resulting number of clusters generated by each algorithm is compared in Figure 4-(a). The average number of documents in a cluster is compared in Figure 4-(b). In addition, the average cluster cohesion rate is compared in Figure 4-(c). The number of clusters generated by the proposed SCUP algorithm is much smaller than that by the hierarchical agglomerative clustering algorithm. However, their order is reversed in terms of the average number of documents in a cluster. However, the average cluster cohesions of two algorithms are almost the same.

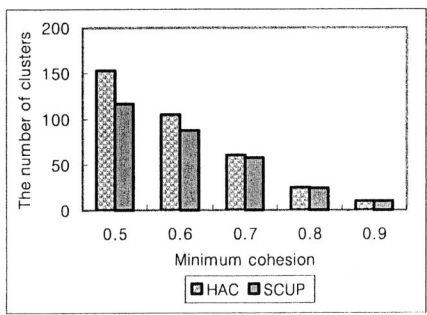

(a) The number of clusters

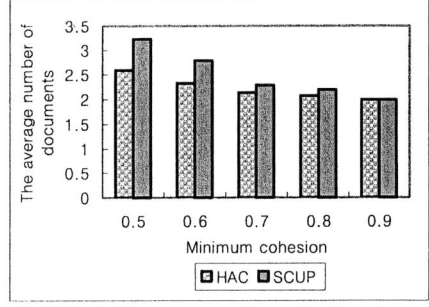

(b) The average number of documents in a cluster

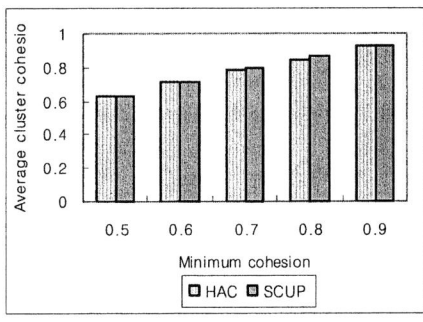

(c) Average cohesion of clusters

Fig. 4. Performance of the SCUP algorithm

About 10000 documents in the business domain of Yahoo are used to illustrate the performance of the proposed IDC algorithm. The proposed IDC algorithm requires a minimum cluster participation rate additionally. When the value of a minimum cluster participation rate is set to 0.2, the IDC algorithm shows the best result. When the value of a minimum cluster participation rate is set 0.2, in Figure 5, the result of the IDC algorithm is composed with the HAC algorithm. Since the HAC clustering is not an incremental algorithm, all documents of the data set are clustered together at the same time in terms of the number of generated clusters and the average number of documents in a cluster by varying the value of a minimum cluster cohesion rate.

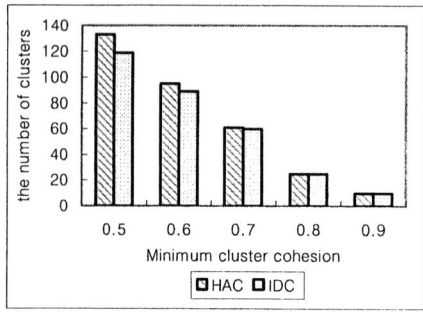
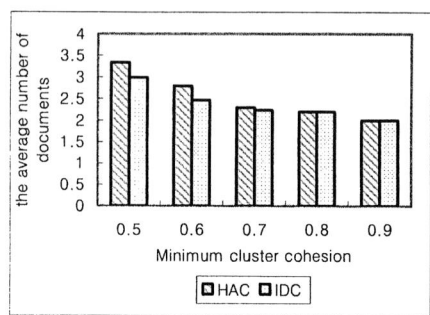

(a) The number of clusters

(b) The average number of documents in a cluster

Fig. 5. Performance of the IDC algorithm

Given a set of document clusters $HC = \{p_1, p_2, ..., p_m\}$ generated by the HAC algorithm and a set of document clusters $IC = \{q_1, q_2, ..., q_n\}$ generated by the IDC algorithm, let $sim(q_i, HC)$ denote the ratio of the number of common documents of a cluster q_i ($1 \leq i \leq n$) in the IC and a cluster p_j ($1 \leq j \leq m$) in the HC over the number of documents in the cluster q_i. The cluster p_j includes most documents belonging to a cluster q_i among clusters in HC. Accordingly, $sim(q_i | IC, HC)$ is defined by Equation (8).

$$sim(q_i, HC) = \max\left(\frac{|q_i \cap p_j|}{|q_i|}\right) \quad (\forall p_j \in HC \ (1 \leq i \leq m)) \tag{8}$$

Based on this, the similarity $sim(IDC, HAC)$ between the result of the *HAC* algorithm and that of the *IDC* algorithm is defined by Equation (9).

$$sim(IDC, HAC) = \frac{1}{n}\sum_{i=1}^{n} sim(q_i, HC) \tag{9}$$

Hence, the difference δ between the result of the *HAC* algorithm and that of the *IDC* algorithm is defined by Equation (10).

$$\delta = 1 - sim(IDC, HAC) \tag{10}$$

In Figure 6, the difference is illustrated when the values of a minimum cluster participation rate and a minimum cluster cohesion rate are varied from 0.5 to 0.9. As the value of a minimum cluster cohesion rate becomes higher, the results of the two algorithms become more similar. By varying the number of documents, the processing times of the *HAC* algorithm and the IDC algorithm are compared in Figure 7. As the number of documents is increased, the processing time of the *HAC* algorithm is increased more rapidly since the HAC algorithm is not incremental.

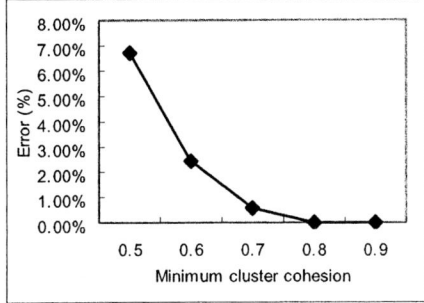

Fig. 6. Difference ratio between *HAC* and *IDC*

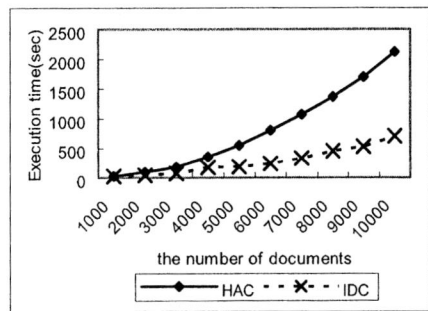

Fig. 7. Processing times between *HAC* and *IDC*

6 Conclusion

A TF*NIDF function is introduced to overcome the weak points of the TF*IDF function since the SCUP algorithm should be performed in an incremental way. This paper proposes the SCUP algorithm to find the initial clusters of similar documents in a set of document based on a cluster cohesion rate as well as a cluster participation rate. This paper introduces a category tree for incremental hierarchical document clustering, so that it is used by the incremental document clustering (IDC) algorithm to find the most appropriate cluster if any efficiently. In the IDC algorithm, a newly added document is examined to be clustered to the most appropriate cluster in the category tree. By comparing the IDC algorithm with the HAC algorithm, the cluster accuracy of the IDC algorithm is more similar relatively to the HAC algorithm. However, the processing time of the IDC algorithm is faster than that of the HAC algorithm when the number of document is increased.

References

1. Zamir, O. and Etzioni, O. "Web Document Clustering: A Feasibility Demonstration", SIGIR, pp. 46-54, 1998
2. Wai-cjiu Wong and Ads Wai-chee Fu, Incremental Document Clustering for Web Page Classification, In Proceedings of 2000 International Conference on Information Society in the 21st Century: Emerging Technologies and New Challenges (IS2000), Aizu-Wakamatsu City, Fukushima, Japan November 5-8, 2000
3. C. J. Van Rijsvergen, "Information Retrieval", Butterworth, London, 2nd edition, 1979

4. Wai Lam and Chao Yang Ho. Using a generalized instance set for automatic text categorization. In Proceedings of the 21th annual international ACM SIGIR conference on Research and development in information retrieval, p.81-89, Melbourne, Australia, August 1998.
5. Sean Slattery and Mark Craven, Combining statistical and relation methods for learning in hypertext domains. In proceedings of the 8th International Conference on Inductive Logic Programming, Madison, Wisconsin, USA, July 1998.
6. David D. Lewis, Robert E. Schapire, James P.Callan, Ron Papka, "Training Algorithms for Linear Text Classifiers", *Proceedings of 19th ACM International Conference on Research and Development in Information Retrieval*, 1996
7. Eui-Hong (Sam) Han, George Karypis, and Vipin Kumar, "Text Categorization Using Weight Adjusted k-Nearest Neighbor Classification", *5th Pacific Asia Conference on Knowledge Discovery And Data Mining*, 2001
8. Yiming Yang, "Expert Network: Effective and efficient learning from human decisions in text categorization and retrieval", *17th ACM SIGIR Conference on Research and Development in Information Retrieval*, 13-22, 1994
9. B. W. Frakes and R. Baeza-Yates, "Information Retrieval: Data Structures & Algorithms", Prentice Hall, 1992
10. Jain, A. K. and Dubes, R. C., "Algorithms for Clustering Data", Prentice Hall, 1988
11. Arnard Ribert, Abdel Ennaji, Yves Lecourtier, An Incremental Hierarchical Clustering, Vision Interface '99. Trois-Rivieres, Canada, 19-21 May, p.586-591.
12. G. Salton, C. Buckley, "Term-weighting approaches in automatic text retrieval", *Information Processing and Management*, Vol. 24 No. 5 pp. 513-523, 1988
13. Amit Singhal, Chris Buckley, and Mandar Mitra, "Pivoted Document Length Normalization", *Proceedings of 19th ACM International Conference on Research and Development in Information Retrieval*, 1996
14. Drug fisher, Iterative Optimization and Simplification of Hierarchical Clusterings, Journal of Artificial Intelligence Research, 1995

System Security Track Chair's Message

Indrajit Ray

Colorado State University, USA

Abstract. The objectives of the System Security track of the 2nd International Conference on Distributed Computing and Internet Technology were to discuss in depth the current state of the research and practice in computer security with emphasis on network and distributed systems security, enable participants to benefit from personal contact with other researchers and expand their knowledge and disseminate the research results. This volume contains the 10 papers that were presented at the System Security track of the conference. These papers which had been selected from 77 submissions were rigorously reviewed by members of the Program Committee comprising of internationally recognized researchers in the area of computer security. The topics covered include a broad range of sub-areas - from emerging areas such as security issues in mobile and ad-hoc networks, security policy integration and code fingerprinting, to more traditional areas such as digital watermarking, intrusion detection and defense against virus and worms. These papers, the program committee believes, address some of the most pressing needs of the day for computer security. We would like to thank all the authors for submitting reports of their leading edge research to this conference and making it a success. A special thank you goes to the members of the System Security track program committee and other external reviewers who helped with the review process in spite of their busy schedule.

A Game Based Model of Security for Key Predistribution Schemes in Wireless Sensor Network

Debapriyay Mukhopadhyay and Suman Roy

Honeywell Technology Solutions Lab Pvt Ltd.,
151/1, Doraisanipalya, Bannerghatta Road,
Bangalore 560076, India
{debapriyay.mukhopadhyay, suman.roy}@honeywell.com

Abstract. Many random key predistribution schemes have been proposed for pairwise key establishment in sensor networks recently. A general model of security under which these key predistribution techniques can be formally analyzed for correctness is required. In this paper, we have made such an attempt. We use the well known computational model of probabilistic turn based $2\frac{1}{2}$-player games to model the key predistribution schemes and have shown how this model can be translated in formally specifying a property that these schemes should have. To the best of our knowledge this is the first work where we show the significance of probabilistic turn based $2\frac{1}{2}$-player games in modelling security requirement of key predistribution schemes.

1 Introduction

Distributed sensor networks are now being widely deployed to monitor and protect different targeted infrastructures including life-critical applications such as wildlife monitoring, military target tracking, home security monitoring and scientific exploration in hazardous environments. Sensor nodes are typically small, battery powered, and resource constrained devices. They usually communicate with each other through wireless links and the fundamental nature of communication is broadcast.

As one of the most fundamental security services, pairwise key establishment enables the sensor nodes to communicate securely with each other using cryptographic techniques. But, because of the resource constrained nature of sensor nodes and lack of trusted infrastructure, public key cryptography and trusted server based pairwise key establishment techniques are not feasible to be used in sensor network. A third way of establishing pairwise key is through key predistribution, where (secret) key information is pre-distributed to all sensor nodes prior to deployment. Such schemes are most appropriate for distributed sensor networks. Many random key predistribution schemes [8, 10, 11] for pairwise key establishment in sensor networks have been proposed recently. The main idea here is to let each sensor node randomly pick a set of keys from a key pool before the deployment so that any two sensor nodes have certain probability to share at least one common key.

A wide range of security protocols have been found to have flaws years after their publication - the most well known example being Needham-Schroeder's protocol [1]. For this reason, it has been realized that formal methods can be useful for the analysis of the security of the cryptographic protocols. Two major approaches in this area are logic analysis and attack construction and a formal computational model of the protocol under test forms the backbone of both. Games provide a powerful mathematical framework with a well-developed theory and rich models of computation. Many problems of computer science can be seen as a game between two or more players, which occur naturally in many computational settings. As for example, in a network a set of compromised nodes may join hand to compromise the whole network, so we can conceive it as a game between the set of compromised nodes and the set of uncompromised nodes. Games provide versatile models of computation which naturally captures the interplay between the involved players. From this observation a new direction of research to model cryptographic protocol interactions as games to obtain a powerful notion of security against adversaries has emerged and has been found to have made some steady progress in last few years [3, 4, 5].

Again, it has been identified [2] that its not just enough to abstract the protocol actions through a model for its formal specification and analysis; one should also have means of formally specifying the properties that a protocol must have. This essentially means modelling the security requirements of a protocol as it provides with a language for precise specification of the properties to be verified. In this paper, we have made an attempt to model the security requirement of random key predistribution schemes for wireless sensor network. We use the well known computational model of probabilistic turn based $2\frac{1}{2}$-player games to model the key predistribution schemes and have shown how this model can be translated in formally specifying a property that these schemes should have. To the best of our knowledge this is the first work where we show the significance of probabilistic turn based $2\frac{1}{2}$-player games in modelling security requirement of key predistribution schemes. In the security definition of random key predistribution schemes adversary is considered as a polynomial time algorithm that may exploit oracles and security requirement is defined in terms of probability of adversary's success. Proposed model can exactly capture this definition of an adversary and also being probabilistic in nature helps in precise specification of the security requirement (of key predistribution protocol) and thereby formal verification of the requirement being possible.

We organize the paper as follows. In Section 2, we introduce the probabilistic turn based $2\frac{1}{2}$-player game and also describe some of the properties associated with this game. We also introduce Message Authentication Code in this section, as it will be needed in subsequent sections. A general framework of security in which to analyze the random key predistribution schemes for wireless sensor network is detailed in Section 3. We describe in Section 4 a random key predistribution scheme and illustrate how security of such a scheme can be analyzed under the general framework discussed in Section 3. The applicability of the probabilistic turn based $2\frac{1}{2}$-player game in modelling security requirement of random key predistribution schemes and also its relevance in formally verifying it is justified in Section 5. Conclusions of our work and the future line of research are described in Section 6.

2 Preliminaries

2.1 Probabilistic Turn Based $2\frac{1}{2}$ Player Game

A turn-based probabilistic $2\frac{1}{2}$-player game graph $G = ((S, E), (S_1, S_2, S_O), \delta)$ consists of a directed graph (S, E), a partition (S_1, S_2, S_O) of the finite set S of states, and a probabilistic transition function $\delta : S_O \to D(S)$, where $D(S)$ denotes the set of probability distributions over the state space S. The states in S_1 are the player 1 states, where player 1 decides the successor state; the states in S_2 are the player 2 states, where player 2 decides the successor state; and the states in S_O are the probabilistic states, where the successor state is chosen according to the probabilistic transition function δ. We assume that for $s \in S_O$ and $t \in S$, we have $(s, t) \in E$ iff $\delta(s)(t) > 0$. Sometimes we designate by s_0 the "start state" and indicate the game graph by G_{s_0}. s_0 can only belong to S_1 or S_2 and if $s_0 \in S_i$, then the player i starts the game, for $i = 1, 2$.

Plays and Strategies: A play in the game graph G_{s_0} is an infinite sequence $\alpha = <s_0, s_1, \ldots, s_k, s_{k+1}, \ldots>$ of states such that $(s_k, s_{k+1}) \in E$ for all $k \in N$. For each $k \in N$, we denote by $\alpha(k)$ the kth state in the sequence α, i.e., $\alpha(k) = s_k$. For a state $s_0 \in S$, we write Ω_{s_0} for the set of all plays that start from s_0. A strategy for player 1 is a function $\rho : S^*.S_1 \to D(S)$ (or $\rho : S^+.S_1 \to D(S)$, if $s_0 \notin S_1$) that assigns a probability distribution to all finite sequences $w \in S^*.S_1$ (or $w \in S^+.S_1$) of states ending in a player1 state. A strategy must prescribe only available moves, i.e., for all $w \in S^*$ (or $w \in S^+$), $s \in S_1$, and $t \in S$, if $\rho(w.s)(t) > 0$, then $(s, t) \in E$. The strategies for player 2 can be defined analogously. We denote by Σ and Π the set of all strategies for player 1 and player 2 respectively.

Once a starting state s_0 and strategies $\rho \in \Sigma$ and $\pi \in \Pi$ for the two players are fixed, the outcome of the game is a random walk $\alpha_{s_0}^{\rho,\pi} \in \Omega_{s_0}$ for which the probabilities of events are uniquely defined, when an event $E \subseteq \Omega_{s_0}$ is a measurable set of paths. For the start state s_0 and an event $E \subseteq \Omega_{s_0}$, we denote by $Pr_{s_0}^{\rho,\pi}(E)$ the probability that a path belongs to E if the game starts from the state s_0 and the players follow the strategies ρ and π, respectively. The strategies that do not use randomization are called pure. A player1 strategy ρ is pure if for all $w \in S^*$ (or $w \in S^+$) and $s \in S_1$, there is a state $t \in S$ such that $\rho(w.s)(t) = 1$. A strategy that is not necessarily pure is called randomized. A strategy ρ for player 1 is called memoryless if ρ is a map from S_1 to $D(S)$, i.e., $\rho : S_1 \to D(S)$. Memoryless strategy for player 2 can be defined similarly. Thus, a strategy which doesn't depend on the whole history of the play, but only on the current state(vertex of G_{s_0}) is called a memoryless strategy. A *pure memoryless* *strategy* of player 1 is thus a function $\rho : S_1 \to S$ such that $(s, \rho(s)) \in E$ for all $s \in S_1$. Note that in the game graph G_{s_0} if player 1 follows a pure memoryless strategy ρ, then that can be interpreted as an $1\frac{1}{2}$-player game played on the game graph $G_{s_0}^\rho$, where $G_{s_0}^\rho$ is a subgraph of the game graph G_{s_0} obtained by removing the edges $(s, t) \in E$ of G_{s_0} such that $\rho(s) \neq t$.

Objectives: The decision who wins a play in the game G_{s_0} is fixed by an ω-regular set $\Phi \subseteq \Omega_{s_0}$, and is referred as the winning objective the game. Objectives of the two players are complementary, i.e., if the objective of one player is Φ, then the objective of the other player is Ω_{s_0}/Φ. For a play $\alpha = < s_0, s_1, s_2, \ldots >$, let $Inf(\alpha)$ be the set $\{s \in S : s = s_k \text{ for infinitely many } k \geq 0\}$ of states that occur infinitely often in α. For a set F of final states, *reachability* objective in the game G_{s_0} is defined as $Reach_F = \{\alpha = < s_0, s_1, s_2, \ldots > \in \Omega_{s_0} : s_k \in F \text{ for some } k \geq 0\}$, and *Büchi* objective in the game G_{s_0} is defined as $Büchi_F = \{\alpha \in \Omega_{s_0} : Inf(\alpha) \cap F \neq \emptyset\}$. Let, p be a function $p : S \to \{0, 1, 2, \ldots, d\}$ assigning a priority $p(s)$ to every state $s \in S$, where $d \in N$. The *even parity* objective is defined as $Even(p) = \{\alpha \in \Omega_{s_0} : \min_{s \in Inf(\alpha)} \{p(s)\} \text{ is even}\}$, and the *odd parity* objective can be equivalently defined. Büchi objective can be derived from an even parity objective with priority function $p : S \to \{0, 1\}$ such that $p(s) = 0$ iff $s \in F$, and $p(s) = 1$ otherwise, and reachability objective comes as a special case of Büchi objective, where all states of F are absorbing, i.e., if $s \in F$, and $(s, v) \in E$, then $s = v$. In this paper, we only consider reachability objective for our purpose. But still we make special mention of Büchi and parity objectives, for, certain results that hold for $2\frac{1}{2}$-player parity game thus holds good for $2\frac{1}{2}$-player reachability game too.

Given reachability objective $Reach_F \subseteq \Omega_{s_0}$ for player 1 and $\Omega_{s_0}/Reach_F$ for player 2 corresponding to the game G_{s_0}, we define $Val^1(Reach_F)(s_0)$ and $Val^2(\Omega_{s_0}/Reach_F)(s_0)$ for players 1 and 2, respectively, as follows, $Val^1(Reach_F)(s_0) = \sup_{\rho \in \Sigma} \inf_{\pi \in \Pi} Pr_{s_0}^{\rho,\pi}(Reach_F)$, and $Val^2(\Omega_{s_0}/Reach_F)(s_0) = \sup_{\pi \in \Pi} \inf_{\rho \in \Sigma} Pr_{s_0}^{\rho,\pi}(\Omega_{s_0}/Reach_F)$. In other words, $Val^1(Reach_F)(s_0)$ gives the maximal probability with which player 1 can achieve her objective $Reach_F$ from "start state" s_0, and analogously for player 2. Form the determinacy result of $2\frac{1}{2}$-player parity games [7], following then can be written for the game graph G_{s_0} with reachability objective.

Theorem 1. *For a $2\frac{1}{2}$-player game with reachability objective, played on the game graph G_{s_0}, we have $Val^1(Reach_F)(s_0) + Val^2(\Omega_{s_0}/Reach_F)(s_0) = 1$.*

A strategy ρ in the game graph G_{s_0} for the player 1 is called optimal for the objective $Reach_F$ if $Val^1(Reach_F)(s_0) = \inf_{\pi \in \Pi} Pr_{s_0}^{\rho,\pi}(Reach_F)$. The optimal strategies for player 2 can be analogously defined. Computing the values of $Val^1(Reach_F)(s_0)$ and $Val^2(\Omega_{s_0}/Reach_F)(s_0)$ for players 1 and 2 respectively, is referred as the *quantitative* analysis of the game. The *quantitative decision problem* for the game graph G_{s_0} is, given a real number $\epsilon \in (0, 1]$, to determine whether $Val^1(Reach_F)(s_0) > \epsilon$. It has been shown in [6] that pure memoryless optimal strategies exist for quantitative $2\frac{1}{2}$-player parity games and hence holds true for the $2\frac{1}{2}$-player game played on the game graph G_{s_0} with reachability objective, for it being a special case of the former. Once a pure memoryless strategy for a $2\frac{1}{2}$-player parity game is fixed, we then have a $1\frac{1}{2}$-player parity game, for which the following result is known.

Theorem 2. *Quantitative $1\frac{1}{2}$-player parity games can be solved in polynomial time by solving a linear program.*

A detailed description on the procedure of finding the quantitative solution of $1\frac{1}{2}$-player parity games can be found in [6].

2.2 Message Authentication Code

We now describe what it means for a MAC to be secure, but we start by defining MAC which are keyed hash functions. A hash family is a four tuple $(\mathcal{X}, \mathcal{Y}, \mathcal{K}, \mathcal{H})$, where $\mathcal{X}$ is a set of possible messages, $\mathcal{Y}$ a set of authentication tags, $\mathcal{K}$ a finite set of possible keys and $\mathcal{H}$ a set of hash functions. For each $K \in \mathcal{K}$, there is a hash function $h_K \in \mathcal{H}$ such that $h_K : \mathcal{X} \to \mathcal{Y}$. We assume that $\mathcal{X}$ and $\mathcal{Y}$ are both finite sets and such that $|\mathcal{X}| \geq 2|\mathcal{Y}|$. A pair $(x, y) \in \mathcal{X} \times \mathcal{Y}$ is said to be valid under the key K if $h_K(x) = y$.

The objective of an adversary is to try to produce a pair (x, y) that is valid under an unknown but fixed key, $K \in \mathcal{K}$. The adversary is allowed to request (up to) q valid MACs on messages $x_1, x_2, \ldots, x_q$ of his own choice. Adversary thus obtains a list of valid pairs (under the unknown key K): $(x_1, y_1); (x_2, y_2); \ldots; (x_q, y_q)$ by querying the oracle with messages $x_1, x_2, \ldots, x_q$. Then, the adversary outputs the pair (x, y), it is required that $x \notin \{x_1, x_2, \ldots, x_q\}$. If this pair (x, y) comes out to be a valid pair with respect to the unknown key K, then the pair is said to be a forgery. If the probability that the adversary outputs a forgery is at least ϵ, then the adversary is said to be an (ϵ, q) forger for the given MAC. For a particular value of q, let us now define the deception probability Pd_q to be the maximum value of ϵ such that (ϵ, q) forger exists. Suppose, $(x_1, y_1); (x_2, y_2); \ldots; (x_q, y_q)$ is a set of valid pairs under the unknown but fixed key K. Now, let $x' \in \mathcal{X}$, where $x' \neq x$. Define $p_K\{(x', y')|(x_1, y_1); (x_2, y_2); \ldots; (x_q, y_q)\}$ to be the probability that (x', y') is a valid pair under the key K, given that $(x_1, y_1); (x_2, y_2); \ldots; (x_q, y_q)$ are also valid pairs under the same key. Then, it can be computed as follows:

$$p_K\{(x', y')|(x_1, y_1); (x_2, y_2); \ldots; (x_q, y_q)\} = \frac{|K \in \mathcal{K} : y' = h_K(x'), y_1 = h_K(x_1), \ldots, y_q = h_K(x_q)|}{|K \in \mathcal{K} : y_1 = h_K(x_1), \ldots, y_q = h_K(x_q)|}.$$

We can then compute Pd_q using the following formula: $Pd_q = max\{p_K : K \in \mathcal{K}\}$.

3 A Security Framework for Key Predistribution Schemes

In this section, we describe a general framework in which to analyze the security of random key predistribution schemes, borrowed from [8]. We first define key predistribution schemes and the "basic" level of security desired from them, which essentially captures the idea that an adversary should (except with low probability) be unable to determine the key shared by some pair of nodes. A stronger notion of security is then imposed on these schemes by requiring that an adversary remains unsuccessful in inserting a bogus message which gets accepted as legitimate by one of the nodes. Adversary's attempt to deceive a node by inserting a bogus message can be seen as an attack against message authentication code and a successful attack thus defeats the purpose of key predistribution schemes. This justifies why such a stronger notion of security is required - a formal definition of which is given in sequel.

Key predistribution schemes can be seen as being composed of algorithms for key generation, key distribution, and key derivation. In the randomized key generation phase, some master secret information S is established. Given S and a node identity i, a key distribution algorithm randomly picks a subset S_i of S and generates information k^i which will be stored by node i. Finally, during the key derivation phase, two distinct nodes i and j holding k^i and k^j respectively, execute an algorithm Derive and output a shared key $K_{ij} \in \{0,1\}^l$ or $\perp$ if no such key can be established. Execution of the algorithm by node i is denoted as $\mathsf{Derive}(k^i, i, j)$ and such that $\mathsf{Derive}(k^i, i, j) = \mathsf{Derive}(k^j, j, i) = K_{ij}$. It is not mandatory for every pair of nodes i and j to be able to establish a key $K_{ij} \neq \perp$ and the probability with which i and j can establish such a key $K_{ij}(\neq \perp)$ is called the *connectivity probability* of the scheme. Let's now assume that adversary has compromised x randomly-selected nodes $\{i_1, i_2, \ldots, i_x\}$ and thus the piece of information he has access to is $I = \{(i_1, k^{i_1}), (i_2, k^{i_2}), \ldots, (i_x, k^{i_x})\}$. Adversary's aim is then to output (i, j, K), where $i, j \notin I$ and $K \in \{0,1\}^l$ represents its "guess" for the key K_{ij}. Basic level of security demanded from these key predistribution schemes is then to ensure that probability of adversary's success in correctly guessing the key K_{ij} has to be negligibly small.

In order to define a stronger notion of security, in [8] key predistribution schemes have been augmented with an additional *message authentication* algorithm and *message verification* algorithm. For the sake of simplicity, we consider here that these algorithms are implemented as *Message Authentication Codes(MACs)*. Therefore, once nodes i, j establish a shared key $K_{ij} \neq \perp$, node i can authenticate its communication to node j (j can authenticate its communication to node i similarly) by sending the pair (m, tag), where $tag = h_{K_{ij}}(m)$ for some hash function h. On receiving (m, tag) node j checks whether tag is really equal to $h_{K_{ij}}(m)$ or not. If it is, then accepts the message, otherwise rejects. For completeness, we define $h_\perp(m) \neq tag$ for all m, tag.

Cryptographic key predistribution then can be defined by the following game. We assume as before that adversary has compromised x randomly selected nodes, and has learnt the information $I = \{(i_1, k^{i_1}), (i_2, k^{i_2}), \ldots, (i_x, k^{i_x})\}$. Additionally, an adversary can make unbounded number of message authentication requests of the form $\bar{h}(m, i', j')$, with the effect that node i' authenticates message m for node j' (using key $K_{i'j'}$) and returns the resulting $tag = h_{K_{i'j'}}(m)$ to the adversary. One standard practice to study security of MAC is to provide the adversary with a random oracle which it can query to get message-tag pairs valid under a secret key. So, adversary's ability to make message authentication requests of the form $\bar{h}(m, i', j')$ can be justified by saying that it has access to some random oracle and we consider q as the bound on the number of oracle queries that it can make. Fixing this bound q limits the computational capabilities of the adversary since making unbounded number of message authentication requests is impossible otherwise.

Adversary then attempts to output (i, j, m^*, tag^*) and its success depends on satisfaction of the following two conditions: (1) $h_{K_{ij}}(m^*) = tag^*$ (this requires, $K_{ij} \neq \perp$), and (2) he had never requested $\bar{h}(i, j, m^*)$ or $\bar{h}(j, i, m^*)$. So, adversary's ability to "insert" a bogus message m^* which gets accepted as valid by one of the nodes i and j even though neither has authenticated this message is considered as its success. Let us now denote probability of adversary's success conditioned on the values of S and I by $Pr[Succ|S,I]$. A scheme will be called $(\lambda, \epsilon, \delta)$-secure *cryptographic key predistribution scheme* if, for any adversary running in time T we have,

$$Pr_{S,I}[Pr[Succ|S,I] \leq \epsilon] \geq 1 - \delta$$

as long as the number of compromised nodes is less than λ. In this paper, we attempt to formally model this security requirement of key predistribution scheme.

4 A Key Predistribution Scheme and Its Security Analysis

4.1 Polynomial Pool Based Key Predistribution Scheme

Polynomial-based key predistribution protocol was first described in [9]. A t-degree symmetric bi-variate polynomial $f(x, y) = \sum_{i,j=0}^{t} a_{ij} x^i y^j$ over a finite filed F_q, where q is a large prime, is randomly chosen by the key setup server. It is assumed that each sensor node has a unique ID. For each node i, the setup server computes $f(i, y)$ and this single variate polynomial share is predistributed to node i. Thus, for any two sensor nodes i and j, node i can compute the key $f(i, j)$ by evaluating $f(i, y)$ at point j, and node j can compute the same key $f(j, i) = f(i, j)$ by evaluating $f(j, y)$ at point i. This scheme is t-collusion resistant since a coalition of up to t compromised sensor nodes can not reveal the bivariate polynomial and hence the pairwise key between any two non-compromised nodes still remains secure.

A random key predistribution technique based on the polynomial based scheme described above, called *polynomial pool based key predistribution* [10], is what we consider here in this paper as an example. In this scheme, pairwise key establishment is done in three phases: *setup, direct key establishment*, and *path key establishment*.

Setup: Setup server randomly generates a pool S of bi-variate t-degree symmetric polynomials over the finite field F_q such that $|S| = s$, where $|.|$ denotes the cardinality of a set. For each sensor node i, setup server then randomly picks a subset S_i of S with $|S_i| = s'$, and for each $f \in S_i$, assigns the polynomial share $f(i,y)$ to node i. It is recommended that this random selection of subsets should be evenly distributed over S.

Direct Key Establishment: The main issue in this phase is the polynomial share discovery problem, which specifies how to find a common bi-variate polynomial of which both nodes have polynomial shares. One simplest way to do so is to let two sensors exchange the IDs of polynomials of which they both have shares, and then to identify the common polynomial. This method of establishing key reveals the subset assignment (S_i) pattern among nodes to the adversary. Alternate method which hides this information from an adversary is called private shared-key discovery and goes as follows. Sensor node i that initiates the process establishing key with node j sends to j an encryption list α, $E_{K_v}(\alpha)$, where $K_v = f_v(i,j)$, for $v = 1, 2, \ldots, |S_i|$, is a potential pairwise key between them and α is a challenge. Node j then attempts to decrypt $E_{K_v}(\alpha)$ with $K'_v = f_v(j,i)$, for $v = 1, 2, \ldots, |S_j|$, and the value of K'_v for which the challenge α gets revealed is considered as the pairwise key between them, since that ensures existence of some $v = m$, such that $K_v = f_v(i,j) = f_v(j,i) = K'_v$. A pairwise key established in this phase is called a direct key and henceforth the secure link established using this key is referred as *direct link*.

Path Key Establishment: If two sensors fail to establish a direct key, then they need to start path key establishment phase. To establish a pairwise key with node j, sensor node i needs to find a sequence of nodes between itself and node j such that any two adjacent nodes in this sequence can establish a direct key. Such a sequence of nodes is called a key path and the key established in this way is called an indirect key and henceforth the secure link established using this key is referred as *indirect link*. In this context, we assume that two adjacent nodes in a path not only can establish direct key, but also they are neighbors of each other with respect to wireless communication range.

4.2 Security Analysis

A graph formed out of the nodes in a sensor network as vertices and with edges connecting a pair of nodes if and only if (1) they can establish a direct key, and (2) within wireless transmission region they can reach each other. This graph is called a key sharing graph. We assume here that key sharing graph is fully connected and the probability that an edge exists between a pair of vertices is denoted by p (also called *connectivity probability*). Security of the polynomial pool based key predistribution scheme can then be calculated in probabilistic terms for two different cases.

Two nodes share a direct key: When two nodes can establish a direct key for secure message authentication then that essentially means that two nodes share a common bivariate polynomial. Now, in this case an adversary can achieve success in either of the following two ways - 1) by compromising the common bivariate polynomial between the sensor nodes, and 2) by launching a successful attack on MAC.

The probability of launching a successful attack on MAC when adversary is allowed to make q oracle queries is given by Pd_q, which has already been discussed in an earlier section. We will now calculate the probability that a bivariate polynomial (common key space) is compromised and will denote this probability by P_{cd}. From the security analysis in [9], it follows that an attacker can only determine non-compromised keys established with a polynomial only when he/she has compromised more than t sensor nodes that have shares of this polynomial. Assume an attacker has compromised x sensor nodes out of total N nodes in a network. Thus, for $x \leq t$, $P_{cd} = 0$. Lets now consider the case when $x > t$. Let f be any polynomial in S. The probability of f being chosen for a sensor node is $\frac{s'}{s}$, and the probability of this polynomial being chosen exactly i times among x compromised sensor nodes is,

$$P[\text{i compromised shares}] = \frac{x!}{(x-i)!i!}(\frac{s'}{s})^i(1-\frac{s'}{s})^{(x-i)}.$$

Thus, the probability of a particular bivariate polynomial being compromised (when $x \geq t$) is $P_{cd} = 1 - \sum_{i=0}^{t} P[\text{i compromised shares}]$.

Let A denote the fact that two nodes share a direct key, B denote that common key space between them is compromised, and C denote the fact that an attack against the MAC is successful. The independence between the events B and C can be safely assumed. Then, the probability that a direct link between two non-compromised nodes is not compromised is given by,

$$P_{direct} = P(A).P(B^c \cap C^c) = p(1 - P_{cd})(1 - Pd_q).$$

Two nodes share an indirect key: When two sensor nodes will fail to establish a direct key, then they will establish an indirect key through path discovery. In this context, we assume that topology of the network gurrantees that such a pair of nodes will always be able to find an intermediate node with which both the nodes can establish a direct key and thus helping key establishment through path discovery being possible. Now, an adversary can achieve success through any one of the following ways - 1)by compromising the intermediate node facilitating the key establishment, 2)by compromising the common bivariate polynomial between intermediate node and at least one of the sensor nodes (who are trying to establish the key), and 3) by launching a successful attack on MAC. Let A denote the fact that two nodes share an indirect key, B denote that intermediate node is compromised, C denote the fact that common bivariate polynomial of the intermediate node with at least one of the sensor nodes is compromised, and D denote the fact that an attack against the MAC is successful. The independence between the events B, C, and D can be safely assumed. Then, the probability that an indirect link between two non-compromised nodes is not compromised is given by,

$$P_{indirect} = P(A).P(B^c \cap C^c \cap D^c) = (1-p)(1-\frac{x}{N})(1-P_{cd})^2(1-Pd_q).$$

Therefore, the probability that any secure link (direct or indirect) between two non-compromised nodes is not compromised can be estimated by,

$$P_{secure} = P_{direct} + P_{indirect} = (1 - P_{cd})(1 - Pd_q)\{p + (1-p)(1 - \frac{x}{N})(1 - P_{cd})\}.$$

5 Modelling Security of Key Predistribution Schemes

In this section, we show how $2\frac{1}{2}$-player probabilistic game discussed in Section 2 finds its application in modelling security requirement of random key predistribution schemes for wireless sensor network. Let there be N nodes in a wireless sensor network and out of which $x (\leq N)$ nodes are compromised by an adversary. We denote the remaining $N - x$ uncompromised nodes as $1, 2, \ldots, N - x = k$, and let $U = \{1, 2, \ldots, k\}$. We have already described that adversary's success corresponds to its ability in inserting a bogus message which gets accepted as valid by one of the uncompromised nodes i and j even though neither has authenticated this message. Without loss of generality, let us fix this node to be k which accepts the bogus message as valid and considers as if it has been sent by some other node j from the set of uncompromised nodes U.

An adversary's attempt to cheat a node by sending bogus message, can be seen as a game played between the adversary and the set of uncompromised nodes, where a win in the game corresponds to adversary's success. We thus consider adversary as player 1, the set of nodes comprising $U - \{k\}$ as player 2, and the node k, adversary's target as player random. The game will be played on the game graph $G_{s_0} = ((S, E), (S_1, S_2, S_O), \delta)$ (Figure 1) where

1. $S = \{s_0, s_1, s_2, s_3\}$ with $S_1 = \{s_0, s_1\}$, $S_2 = \{s_2\}$ and $S_O = \{s_3\}$ are the set of states with S_1, S_2, S_O denoting the corresponding states of player 1, 2 and random respectively.
2. The set E of directed arcs consists of the following $E = \{(s_0, s_2); (s_2, s_0); (s_0, s_3); (s_3, s_0); (s_3, s_1); (s_1, s_1)\}$. The state $s_0 \in S_1$, is the start state of the game and hence player 1(the adversary) starts the game.
3. The probabilistic transition function $\delta : S_O \to D(S)$ is such that $\delta(s_3) = \mu(\mu \in D(S))$ such that $\mu(s_0) = P_{secure}$ and $\mu(s_1) = 1 - P_{secure}$. The term P_{secure} has already been explained in Section 4.

For this game to be played on the game graph G_{s_0}, we consider here a reachability objective with $F = \{s_1\}$ as the set of final states. Note that because of the directed arc $(s_1, s_1) \in E$ the states in F are absorbing.

The game gets started at state s_0 by the adversary who aims to cheat node k by sending bogus message. In the process, it could have chosen any node from the set $U - \{k\}$ to obtain valid message-tag pairs. In order for that it sends message m to node $j \in U - \{k\}$ and this we model in the game as player 1 from state s_0 chooses the successor state as s_2. On receiving the message m, node j computes $tag = h_{K_{jk}}(m)$ and sends it back to the adversary. This can be interpreted in the game as player 2 chooses the successor state as s_0. In order to cheat k, adversary outputs the pair (m^*, tag^*) and sends it to node k. Thus,

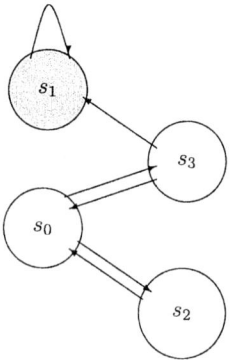

Fig. 1. Probabilistic $2\frac{1}{2}$-player game graph G_{s_0}

from state s_0, player 1 can also select s_3 as the successor state. Now, whether node k will accept the pair (m^*, tag^*) as valid or not depends on whether the secure link (direct or indirect) between the nodes j and k is compromised or not. From the analysis given in Section 4, it therefore follows that the pair (m^*, tag^*) is accepted as valid with probability $1 - P_{secure}$, while it gets rejected with probability P_{secure}. This we model in the game as player random from state s_3 can select the successor states as s_0 or s_1 with $\mu(s_0) = P_{secure}$ and $\mu(s_1) = 1 - P_{secure}$ respectively, depending on whether the pair (m^*, tag^*) gets rejected or not. Correspondingly, when player random selects the successor state as s_1, game then stays there forever. This thus ensures that reachability objective is met since s_1 is the only final state in the game and hence player 1 wins.

From the game graph its evident that at any point of time in a play, from state $s_2 \in S_2$, player 2 can only select s_0 as the successor state. This can alternatively be stated as - player 2 is following a pure memoryless strategy $\pi : S_2 \to S$ such that $\pi(s_2) = s_0$. Whereas in any move of player 1, it can select any one of the state from the set $\{s_2, s_3\}$ as the successor state. Player 1 thus can adopt randomized strategy to win the game and also its strategy may depend on the history of the game. The reason for this discrimination in strategy is that we are interested in seeing how good a strategy of player 2 is against any possible sequence of moves of player 1 and thus helping us to analyze the robustness of the key predistribution scheme.

From Theorem 1, it follows that the above defined game to be played on the game graph G_{s_0} (Figure 1), being a probabilistic turn based $2\frac{1}{2}$-player game with reachability objective is determined. Again, since player 2 is following a pure memoryless strategy, so we can consider this to be an $1\frac{1}{2}$-player game and as such from Theorem 2 it follows that the game can be solved for its quantitative solution in polynomial time. Note that, the value of $Val^1(Reach_F)(s_0)$, here in this context gives the maximum probability with which player 1 can succeed in cheating node k by sending bogus message. Since quantitative optimal strategies exist, so we assume here that adversary will play the game using this strategy to increase his chances of success to a maximum to attain the value $Val^1(Reach_F)(s_0)$ and this of-course is true when an adversary can play the game for an unbounded amount of time. But, in the definition of the $(\lambda, \epsilon, \delta)$-property its given that adversary is running in time T. So, what we essentially need to look for is the maximum probability with which player 1 can meet its winning objective within time bounded by T.

Since we only need to account for the running time of an adversary, so in the context of our game, we assume that time used by player 1, and not player 2 or player random, is counted as the time used by the game. We also assume here that player 1 spends unit time in selecting the successor state from each of its state in S_1. For any $\alpha \in \Omega_{s_0}$ and for any $k \in N$, we define, $Index_k^\alpha = \{i \in N : i < k \text{ and } \alpha(i) \in S_1\}$. Note that, for any $\alpha \in \Omega_{s_0}$, we have $Index_0^\alpha = \emptyset$. Given that player 1 is running in time bounded by T, we can partition the winning objective $Reach_F$ as $Reach_F^{\leq T} \cup (Reach_F - Reach_F^{\leq T})$, where $Reach_F^{\leq T} = \{\alpha \in \Omega_{s_0} : \alpha(k) \in F \text{ for some } k \geq 0 \text{ such that } k = min\{k' \in N : \alpha(k') \in F\} \text{ and } |Index_k^\alpha| \leq T\}$. Its now clear that $Reach_F^{\leq T}$ consists of those plays from $Reach_F$, for which player 1 can ensure a win in the game within time bounded by T. In a similar line, we can then define $Val^1(Reach_F^{\leq T})(s_0)$ as the maximum probability with which player 1 can ensure a win in the game graph G_{s_0} (Figure 1) with reachability objective within time bounded by T and that is exactly what we need for the purpose of specifying the $(\lambda, \epsilon, \delta)$-property. In this paper, we don't deal with the problem of computing the value of $Val^1(Reach_F^{\leq T})(s_0)$ for any probabilistic $2\frac{1}{2}$-player game and also don't attempt to answer the question whether optimal strategies exist for that or not. We leave these questions as open.

Since $Val^1(Reach_F^{\leq T})(s_0) < Val^1(Reach_F)(s_0)$, and if $Val^1(Reach_F)(s_0) \leq \epsilon$, then it necessarily implies that probability of success for any adversary running in time T is bounded above by ϵ. But, if $Val^1(Reach_F)(s_0) > \epsilon$, then $Val^1(Reach_F^{\leq T})(s_0)$ can either be greater than or less that equal to ϵ. The fact that $Val^1(Reach_F)(s_0)$ can assume different values can be justified by saying that with the value of x varying, the probability with which the random player selects the successor state also changes, since in the definition of P_{secure} the term x is involved. So, with each value of $x \in [0, N]$, we can associate $Val^1(Reach_F^{\leq T})(s_0)$ as the probability of adversary's success conditioned on the values of S, I and also when the adversary is running in time T. $Pr_{S,I}[Pr[Succ|S, I] > \epsilon]$ can then be calculated as the fraction of the values of $x \in [0, N]$ for which $Val^1(Reach_F^{\leq T})(s_0) > \epsilon$. Let, y be the number of different values of x for which $Pr[Succ|S, I]$ is greater than ϵ and as such, we have $Pr_{S,I}[Pr[Succ|S, I] > \epsilon] = \frac{y}{N+1}$.

Note that, $(\lambda, \epsilon, \delta)$ security property of a random key predistribution scheme can be equivalently written as $Pr_{S,I}[Pr[Succ|S, I] > \epsilon] \leq \delta$. Hence, from above, we should have, $\frac{y}{N+1} \leq \delta$ and hence $y \leq \delta(N + 1)$. Since, the probability of adversary's success monotonically increases with each additional node being compromised, so corresponding to each $y \leq \delta(N + 1)$, we have a set of values of x for which $Pr[Succ|S,I] > \epsilon$ and we denote this set by X_y. Note that, $X_0 = \emptyset$ and $X_{y-1} \subset X_y$ for all $0 \leq y \leq \lfloor \delta(N+1) \rfloor$ and thus $X_{\lfloor \delta(N+1) \rfloor}$ containing all possible values of x for which $Pr[Succ|S,I] > \epsilon$. Average of the values of $x \in X_{\lfloor \delta(N+1) \rfloor}$ then can be considered as an estimate for λ and hence we set $\lambda = \lfloor \frac{\sum_{x \in X_{\lfloor \delta(N+1) \rfloor}} x}{|X_{\lfloor \delta(N+1) \rfloor}|} \rfloor$. Its clear now from the above discussion that as long as the number of compromised nodes is less than equal to $\lfloor \frac{\sum_{x \in X_{\lfloor \delta(N+1) \rfloor}} x}{|X_{\lfloor \delta(N+1) \rfloor}|} \rfloor$, $Pr_{S,I}[Pr[Succ|S,I] > \epsilon] \leq \delta$ and hence justifying our claim that this value can indeed be considered as an estimate for λ.

6 Conclusion

We have thus shown that how probabilistic $2\frac{1}{2}$-player turn based games can be used to model random key predistribution schemes in wireless sensor network and have also demonstrated how this model facilitates in precise specification of $(\lambda, \epsilon, \delta)$ security property desired out of these schemes. We emphasize that the framework presented here is a work in progress and much work remains to be done. Our work also leaves few questions as open. First, for a probabilistic $2\frac{1}{2}$-player turn based games with reachability winning objective how to evaluate the maximum probability with which a player 1 can force a win in the game within time bounded by T, i.e., how to calculate the value of $Val^1(Reach_F^{\leq T})(s_0)$. We also have provided a means to estimate the value of λ given ϵ and δ. Naturally, the next question is how good this estimate for λ is and whether we can improve upon this.

References

1. Lowe, G.: An attack on the Needham-Schroeder Public-Key Authentication Protocol. Information Processing Letters **56(3)** (1995) 131–133
2. Syverson, P.F., Meadows, C.: Formal Requirements for Key Distribution Protocols. In: Santis, A. D.(eds): Advances in Cryptology, Eurocrypt 94. LNCS, vol. **950**. Springer-Verlag (1995) 320–331
3. Kremer, S., Raskin, J.-F.: A game-based verification of non-repudiation and fair exchange protocols. CONCUR 2001 - Concurrency Theory. LNCS, vol. **2154**. Springer-Verlag (2001) 551–565
4. Morselli, R., Katz, J., Bhattacharjee, B.: A Game-Theoretic Framework for Analyzing Trust-Inference Protocols. 2nd Workshop on Economics of Peer-to-Peer Systems Cambridge MA USA (2004)
5. Mahimkar, A., Shmatikov, V.: Game-Based Analysis of Denial-of-Service Prevention Protocols. 18th IEEE Computer Security Foundations Workshop (CSFW05) (June 2005) (to appear)
6. Chatterjee, K., Jurdziński, M., Henzinger, T. A.: Quantitative stochastic parity games. SODA'04 SIAM (2004) 114–123
7. de Alfaro, L., Majumdar, R.: Quantitative solution of omega-regular games. STOC'01 ACM Press (2001) 675–683

8. Du, W., Deng, J., Han, Y. S., Varshney, P. K., Katz, J., Khalili, A.: A Pairwise Key predistribution Scheme for Wireless Sensor Networks. ACM Transactions Information and System Security (TISSEC) **8(2)** (2005) 228–258
9. Blundo, C., Santis, A. D., Herzberg, A., Kutten, S., Vaccaro, U., Yung, M.: Perfectly-Secure Key Distribution for Dynamic Conferences. In Proceedings of the 12th Annual International Cryptology Conference on Advances in Cryptology. LNCS, vol. **740**. Springer-Verlag (1992) 471–486
10. Liu, D., Ning, P.: Establishing pairwise keys in distributed sensor networks. In Proceedings of the 10th ACM conference on Computer and communication security (2003) 52–61
11. Eschenauer L., Gligor, V. D.: A key-management scheme for distributed sensor networks. In Proceedings of the 9th ACM Conference on Computer and Communications Security (2002) 41–47

E-mail Worm Detection Using the Analysis of Behavior[*]

Tao Jiang[1], Wonil Kim[2,**], Kyungsuk Lhee[1], and Manpyo Hong[1]

[1] Digital Vaccine and Internet Immune System Laboratory,
Graduate School of Information and Communication, Ajou University,
Suwon, Korea
{taojiang, klhee, mphong}@ajou.ac.kr
http://iislab.ajou.ac.kr
[2] College of Electronics and Information Engineering, Sejong University,
Seoul, Korea
wikim@sejong.ac.kr
http://dasan.sejong.ac.kr/~wilkim

Abstract. With the appearance of a number of e-mail worms in recent years, we urgently need a solution to detect unknown e-mail worms rather than using the traditional solution: signature-based scanning which does not deal with the new e-mail worms well. Our collected data shows that the quantitative trend of e-mail worms is really exploding. In this paper, we propose an e-mail worm Detection System that is based on analysis on human and worm behavior for detecting unknown e-mail worms. Message data such as e-mail or short messages are the result of human behavior. The proposed system detects unknown worms by assessment of behavior in communication because human behavior and worm behavior have different projection on data.

1 Introduction

An obvious trend of Internet worms is the application of mass-mailing [2,5]. Almost all of the major virus and worms have utilized mass-mailing since March 1999 of Melissa accident. Kaspersky Lab presents the most active top 20 virus for several months in 2004 and the report indicates that More than 70% of them employ the approach of mass-mailing [1,2].

E-mail worms are malicious e-mails which contain an executable attachment or script and propagate themselves to other user's e-mail box by tricking victim users into running the malicious functions. Since an e-mail worm is extremely simple to create, a huge amount of e-mail worms and their variants are active in the Internet with rapid birth of new sorts of worms. The collected data showing the exploding trend of e-mail worms are presented in Table 1 [5]. The traditional solution, the signature-based detection, depends on the manually created signatures which are effective only for known e-mail worms. In order to detect varied e-mail worms, we should focus on the mechanism which is able to detect the unknown worm.

---

[*] This research is supported by the ubiquitous Autonomic Computing and Network Project, the Ministry of Information and Communication (MIC) 21st Century Frontier R&D Program in Korea.
[**] Author for correspondence: +82-2-3408-3795.

Table 1. Observed worms from 1998 to 2003

Category	1998	1999	2000	2001	2002	2003
Conventional Worm	1	1	0	10	3	4
E-mail Worm	1	18	44	93	159	192

Many systems are proposed in an attempt to detect unknown e-mail worm, such as Bayesian Classifier of email, Sandbox for suspicious code, and auto analysis of attachment of email [8]. However, the content of message is not the nature of worm and examination of the purpose of the executable code is an extremely complex work.

To overcome these weaknesses, we advance a new approach here: because e-mail messages are data strongly related to human will, by comparing the characteristics of user behavior and worm behavior at the client side, we could recognize whether a host is infected by any e-mail worm.

The rest of the paper is organized as follows: we describe related work in Section 2. In Section 3, we present the proposed unknown e-mail worm detection system. Next, in Section 4, we give details on how to conduct a characteristic formulation and some created formulations. Further simulation data is showed in Section 5. Finally, we summarize our work in Section 6.

2 Related Work

To protect Internet from the threat of e-mail worms, a number of solutions have been proposed by researchers.

The Malicious Email Filter, MEF, is a system integrating with UNIX mail server and detects malicious Windows attachments [12]. Its core idea is that by using data-mining, knowledge of known malicious executables can be generalized to detect unknown malicious executables. The detection rate of the MEF is up to the relevance between the known malicious executable and the unknown malicious executable. The weakness is that the e-mail worm maker could change the code byte sequence easily to make it different from the appeared pattern of the malicious code. Especially considering various versions of compilers existed in Windows platforms, which could produce different bytes, the detection relying on data mining on pattern of malicious code may not be effective in discovering the e-mail worms with unknown code patterns.

A system that relies on the observation that e-mail worms send messages at a high rate is designed to limit the propagation of e-mail worms [11]. The system is deployed on mail server to throttle the rapid e-mails from a particular user. Therefore, a weak point is that the system could be fooled on the estimation of a particular user when e-mail worms use a fake sender address. On the other hand, if the e-mail worms slow down the propagation speed under the threshold value, the system would not try to throttle it.

Our contribution is that we do not consider data semantic of e-mail attachment which most of existing detection systems used. Judgment on e-mail attachment is usually relevant to platform implementation and prior knowledge on appeared e-mail worms. The proposed detection system focuses on the deviation between worm behavior and user behavior. Moreover, we base our approach on macro view of whole system activity and communication caused by user.

3 Proposed Worm Detection System

In nature, human beings have spirit or life, but worm is machine code. Different nature decides that worm's behavior and human being's are destined to be different. Our behavior comparison works effectively on a data strongly relating to human's activation. In other words, the characteristics of data are decided by human beings and are affected by individual's habit. For instance, E-Mail and an Instant message in ICQ are such kind of data. Another point of crucial importance is that comparison occurs between a single user's behavior and worm's behavior. Different users have different habits so the corresponding communication shows difference. However, worm's behavior will interrupt projection of human's habits and show its own particular characteristic so we construct our comparison on a basis of knowledge of user's behavior. Each person has his own habit of using email or other message techniques. Some would like to send all e-mails on morning. Some keep frequent correspond with old friend or boss. Some use only one e-mail account. These are human's personal habit. We can see other common habits among people: different friends have different communication frequency; different style of the words of the message. Some research even report that it is possible to judge the gender of the sender of an e-mail by the content recognition [10].These human's habit are mapped on data of e-mail in the form of time, size, name, frequency etc.

When worm is active, the characteristic of data will show a difference, contrast with the human's habits. We consider this variation of value of the characteristics as the evidence of worm infection.

The proposed worm detection system presented in Figure 1 is made up of four components: *data gathering*, *characteristic evaluation*, *profile of user behavior* and *behavior comparison*. The data gathering component is responsible for watching

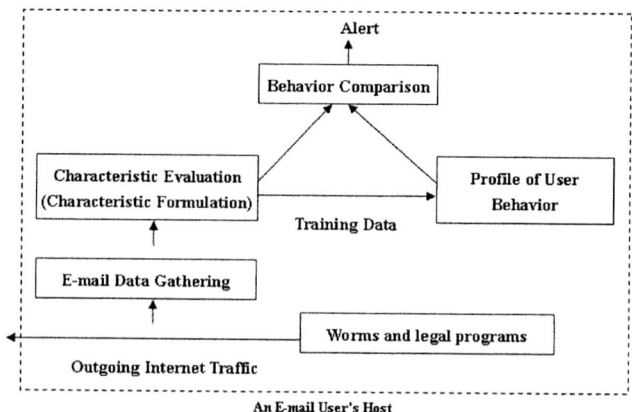

Fig. 1. Components Diagram of the Worm Detection System

Internet traffic and gathering data under the definition of characteristic formulations. The characteristic evaluation component receives the selected data from data gathering component and calculates the characteristic value under the definition of the characteristic formulation. Next, it will submit the characteristic value array to the behavior comparison component or to the profile of user behavior as an updating data. Profile of user behavior is a database recording the characteristic value representing user behavior. In the behavior comparison component, the characteristic value from both characteristic evaluation component and profile of user behavior component are compared to decide whether an ongoing behavior is following the user behavior.

Our worm detection system starts to work through three stages. First stage, *the formulation stage*, we formulate the data characteristics which are distinct from human and worm and describe these characteristics with equations (discussed in Section 4). Second stage, *the training stage*, we learn a user's history behavior and record these characteristics with the equations. In this stage, we are actually to record the characteristic of user's habit. Third stage, *the work stage*, we reply on user's recorded characteristic which is a reference to monitor the user's communication data. In other words, after getting the user's characteristic data in second stage, then we enter the comparison stage. If behavior characteristics being monitored deviate from our recorded data (user's characteristic), then we conclude that a worm has infected user's machine. Our method mainly detects whether a host is infected or not. Here, we are to focus on how to detect E-mail worm via our comparison theory.

4 Characteristic Formulation

We consider a typical user who uses e-mail for work. He/she receives or sends e-mails to others everyday. It may seem nothing special here, but it reveal an important characteristic: when e-mail was send out, recipient is already in user's address book or recipient comes from an e-mail in in-box. We define that all address in the user's address book and those from an e-mail of in-box are in 'Former Address' class. Thus, all other recipients that appear in user's e-mail communication belong to 'New Address' class. Usually, they send email to 'Former Address' most of the time and 'New Address' sometimes, but 'Former Address' make up the majority of e-mails [13]. To the contrary the e-mail worm would try to spread as vast as possible by mass-mailing, usually including an e-mail address harvest technique [2]. After the load of worm code, it will search all directories in the machine to absorb all possible address for spreading so we can deduce that proportion of 'New Address' will increase, when worm begins to spread. To describe this characteristic, we define function *AddrRatio*().

AddrRatio()=*Number of New Address/Number of Former Address* . (1)

We also consider user's own mailbox account (sender address). When users use Outlook, they can choose which e-mail account to send their mail (if users have more than one e-mail account). For typical users, they have several different e-mail accounts for business and private. While a worm is transporting malicious e-mail to e-mail server, it is not easy for the worm to get what the user's own address is. The worms have to create or randomly choose an email address in user's computer as a fake 'sender' [2]. We treat 'sender' that appeared in the user behavior learning stage (second stage) as 'Former Sender'. Thus, all other 'sender's that appear in user's communication in comparison stage belong to 'New Sender' class. To describe this characteristic, we define function *SenderRatio()*.

$$SenderRatio()=Number\ of\ New\ Sender/Number\ of\ Former\ Sender\ . \qquad (2)$$

When users download or send e-mail via user's server at company or a website such as Hotmail, normally, they set up a server for receiving and a server for sending for each corresponding account in user's client. When users are sending a e-mail, user's e-mail client will connect with the mail server according to user's configuration and user's mail are buffered in the server and sent to destination by the server. This process always comprises an authentication part so usually a worm can not take advantage of user's sending service server but has to use its own server list or connect directly to the recipient's server [2]. We deduce that there would be more MTA(Message Transfer Agent) servers connected when a worm is active [7]. To describe this characteristic, we define function *Server()*.

$$Server()=Number\ of\ Server\ /\ Time\ . \qquad (3)$$

One of the common characteristics of viral e-mail is that these mails contain attachment with same size and same content. Actually, this attachment is the body of worm [2]. Of course human's behavior can also cause mail communication with this characteristic. Considering users do not do this all the time, we still use this characteristic as one of the worm's behavior characteristics. To describe this characteristic, we define function *AttachSizeVar(k)* which means the variation of size of attachment.

$$AttachSizeVar(k)= (Attach\ Size_K - (\sum^K Attach\ Size/k))^2\ . \qquad (4)$$

When trying to connect with a message transfer server, the client will execute a request of mail exchange record [7]. Since most of e-mail worm send e-mail by directly connecting with recipient's server [2], we treat the variation of the quantity of MX(Mail eXchange) request as another characteristic of worm's behavior. To describe this characteristic, we define function *MXReq ()*.

$$MXReq()=Number\ of\ MX\ Request/\ Time\ . \qquad (5)$$

A typical user sends a certain number of mails during a day. Worm also do the same job during a day while the quantity would be considerably different. We could imagine that it is easy for a worm to send out hundreds of mails in a minute [2]. Obviously, this is not a human behavior. To describe this characteristic, we define function *Mail()*.

$$Mail()=Number\ of\ Mail/\ Time\ . \qquad (6)$$

By putting further research on both human behavior and worm behavior, we can create more characteristics implying worms' action in the future work.

5 Simulation

In the simulation, we trace and record the communication data of active worm and a user, then make comparisons. We select NetSky.C and MyDoom.M because they are two of most active e-mail worms in the recent months [1, 3, 4].

A client is supposed to be an infected computer on which we run worm code and the network monitor for recording data [6]. This client also includes some other application and internet cache, which contains useful address for worm. An address book with 50 contacts and in-box filled with 40 mails from "Former Address" are established in the Outlook. We ask the user to use this client freely for a week, gathering normal e-mail communication for comparison. All measures here are to best simulate a typical user's computer.

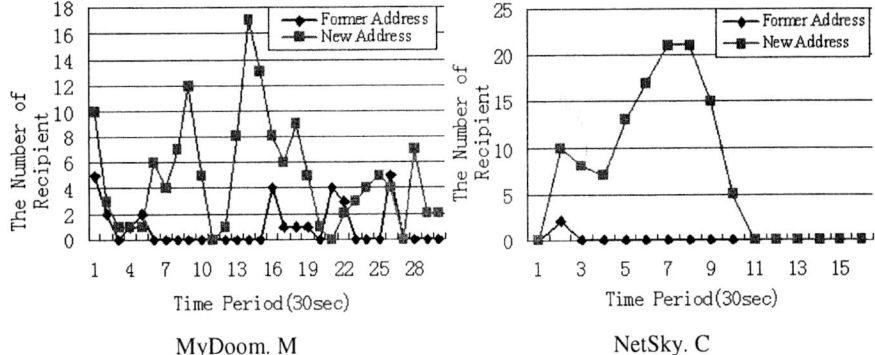

Fig. 2. The number of Former Address and New Address

Fig.2 show that the value of *RatioAddr()* is much larger than 1 since the number of "New Address" actually overwhelm the number of "Former Address". In the contrast, the user's value of *RatioAddr()* is less than 0.2.

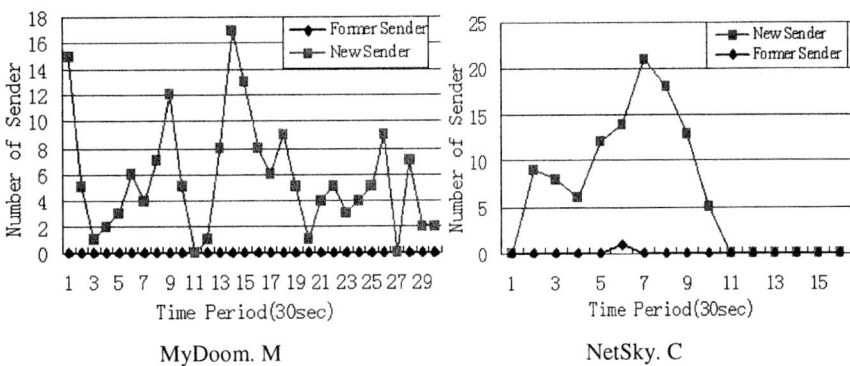

Fig. 3. The number of Former Sender and New Sender

Fig.3 shows that the value of *RatioSender()* is almost infinite because the number of 'Former Sender' is nearly zero and the number of 'New Sender' is relatively big. In contrast, the user's value of *RatioSender()* is zero since the user always uses the same two e-mail accounts of his own. Further, note that the huge number of "New Sender" is apparent viral behavior.

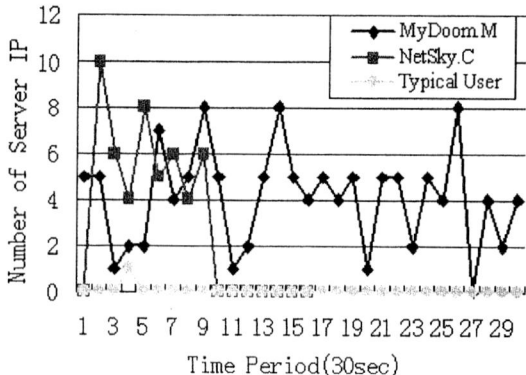

Fig. 4. The number of MTA server

Fig.4 means how many IP address of MTA servers appeared in a period (30 seconds) [7]. The value of *Server()* is much diverse from the user to worms. The main reason is that worms in the simulation establish a direct connection to recipient's server. In contrast, the user is connecting with only one MTA server in a short period [7].

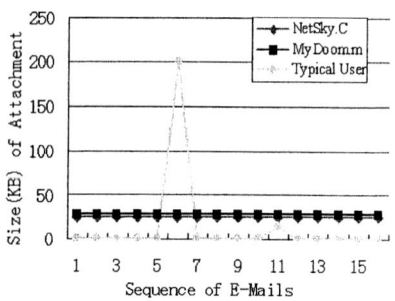

Fig. 5. The size(KB) of email attachment

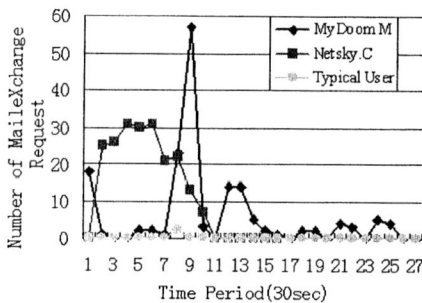

Fig. 6. The number of Mail Exchange request

Fig.5 shows that the value of *AttachSizeVar()* of worms is zero as they send themselves by e-mail and each e-mail carries a file of same size [3, 4] because *AttachSizeVar()* calculates the value of variation of attachment size. Contrarily, the size of the user's attachment shows great variation.

Before establishing a connection to recipients' server, worms send a large number of MX requests to get IP address of MTA server [7]. As for the user, the mail client sends a single MX request by the user's server configuration when client tries to send user's e-mail. Thus, at the Fig.6, the value of *MXReq()* is very large for worms but reasonably small for the user.

As we have seen in Fig.7, the value of *Mail()* is very distinguishable from worms to the user [11]. The user's e-mail is at a very low speed, compared to the high speed of worm which is at the average level of 5~10 e-mails per 30 seconds.

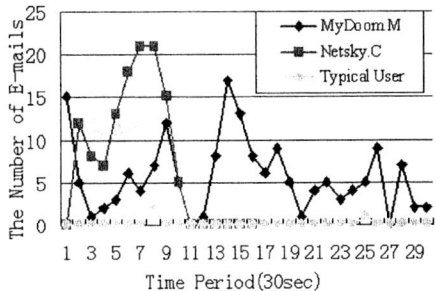

Fig. 7. The Number of E-mail

6 Conclusions

In this paper, we propose an unknown worm detection system based on comparison of worm behavior and user's behavior. The core of proposed system is that we should create characteristic formulations indicating characteristics which distinguish human being's behavior from worm's behavior. Our contribution is that our mechanism takes into account the difference between human behavior and worm behavior. We also advise some characteristics for e-mail worm detection. As we have seen in simulation, the proposed system works effectively since our carefully chosen characteristics changed significantly between user's behavior and worm's behavior. Such unknown worm detection system on the basis of analysis of behavior is effective when the objective of comparison is the data strongly relating to user's will and habit, such as e-mail, instant message, and short message.

References

1. Kaspersky Lab, Virus Top Twenty for (October, September, August) 2004, Http://www.viruslist.com/ en/analysis?pubid (154331948,153837339,153837687)
2. Kaspersky Lab, Network Worms, http://www.viruslist.com/en/viruses/encyclopedia?Chapter=152540408
3. Kaspersky Lab, Mydoom.m, http://www.viruslist.com/en/viruses/encyclopedia?virusid=57410
4. Kaspersky Lab, Netsky.C, http://www.viruslist.com/en/viruses/encyclopedia?Virusid=22746
5. Darrell M. Kienzle and Matthew C. Elder," Recent Worms: A Survey and Trends," Proceedings of the WORM 03, 2003
6. Microsoft Corp, About Network Monitor 2.0, http://msdn.microsoft.com/library/default.asp? url=/library/en-us/netmon/netmon/about_network_monitor_2_0.asp
7. W.Richard Stevens, "TCP/IP Illustrated Volume 1 the Protocols," Addison-Wesley Press, 2001
8. InSeon Yoo and Ulrich Ultes-Nitsche,"How to Predict Email Viruss Under Uncertainty," Proceedings of the 23rd IEEE International Performance, Computing and Communications Conference, 2004

9. Matthew M. Williamson, "Throttling Viruses: Restricting propagation to defeat malicious mobile code, " Proceedings of the 18th Annual Computer Security Applications Conference, 2002
10. Malcolm Corney, Olivier de Vel, and Alison Anderson1 George Mohay, "Gender-Preferential Text Mining of E-mail Discourse," Proceedings of Computer Security Applications Conference (ACSAC'02), 2002
11. Matthew M. Williamson, "Design, Implementation and Test of an Email Virus Throttle," Proceedings of the 19th Annual Computer Security Applications Conference, 2003
12. Matthew G. Schultz, Eleazar Eskin, Erez Zadok, Manasi Bhattacharyya, and Salvatore J. Stolfo, "Malicious Email Filter - A UNIX Mail Filter that Detects Malicious Windows Executables," Proceedings of USENIX Annual Technical Conference, 2001
13. Tao Jiang, Wonil Kim and Manpyo Hong, "Unknown Worm Detection via Behavior Comparison," Proceedings of the Workshop on Information Security Application, 2005

Verifiably Encrypted Signature Scheme Without Random Oracles

M. Choudary Gorantla and Ashutosh Saxena

Institute for Development and Research in Banking Technology,
Road No. 1, Castle Hills, Masab Tank, Hyderabad - 500057,
Andhra Pradesh, India
gmchoudary@gmail.com, asaxena@idrbt.ac.in

Abstract. Verifiably encrypted signature is a useful mechanism for fair exchange especially, for online contract signing. In this paper, we propose a verifiably encrypted signature scheme using bilinear pairings. The scheme is secure against existential forgery under chosen message attack and extraction, without random oracles.

Keywords: Fair Exchange, Verifiably Encrypted Signature, Bilinear Pairings, Random Oracles.

1 Introduction

Electronic commerce is conducting business communications over networks and through computers. It usually involves two distrusted parties exchanging items with each other, for instance a payment via an electronic check for a digital movie over the Internet. When commercial transactions are conducted in such distributed environments, it is difficult to assess the counter-party's trustworthiness. Fair exchange is the problem of exchanging data in a way that guarantees that either all participants obtain what they want, or none do [1].

Contract signing is a particular form of fair exchange, in which the parties exchange commitments to a contract; typically, containing the terms of the deal. In the case of online contracts, a commitment is often identified with the party's digital signature on the contract. The main properties a contract signing protocol should guarantee are *fairness* and *timeliness* [2], [3]. A protocol between Alice and Bob is fair for Alice if, in any situation where Bob has obtained Alice's commitment, Alice can obtain Bob's commitment regardless of Bob's actions. Optimistic fair exchange protocols [4] that employ a "time-out" mechanism, either leaves one player "hanging" for an unacceptably long time (if the time-out is too long), or exposes the other player to an unacceptable risk of being cheated (if the time-out is too short). Not only this is a great inconvenience, but also leads to a real loss in the case of time-sensitive data like forex and stock quotes.

A Verifiably Encrypted Signature (VES) enables optimistic fair exchange [5], [6] over the Internet, especially online contracts. It relies on a trusted third party called Adjudicator, in an optimistic way, that the adjudication is only needed in cases where one participant attempts to cheat the other or simply crashes. Another key feature of VES is that a participant can always force a fair and timely termination, without the cooperation of the other participants. It uses no "time-out" mechanism and neither party can be left hanging or cheated so long as the adjudicator is available.

A VES enables the verifier to test that a given ciphertext is the encryption of a signature on a given message. Alice creates a VES on a message by using her private key and an Adjudicator's public key. The verifier, Bob is convinced that the encrypted signature is indeed of Alice, which he verifies using the public keys of Alice and the Adjudicator. Even though Bob does not have the capability of decrypting the VES, the verification is performed without deducing any information about Alice's signature. At a later stage on agreed terms, Bob can either obtain the original signature from Alice or approach the adjudicator with the VES, in case of dispute. The adjudicator extracts and gives Alice's signature to Bob, if the given VES is valid.

VES schemes using bilinear pairings were proposed by Boneh et al. [6] and Zhang et al. [7] with security proofs in random oracle model [8]. Roughly speaking, a random oracle is a hash function $H : X \rightarrow Y$ chosen uniformly at random from the set of all functions $\{h : X \rightarrow Y\}$ (assuming Y as infinite set). It is observed that the security proofs in the random oracle model do not always imply the security of the actual scheme in the "real world" and "behaving like a random oracle" is not a property that can be realized in general [9]. Moreover, to this day nobody was able to formalize precisely the requirements on the cryptographic hash functions in the schemes [8], [10], [11], which are using random oracle model.

Boneh and Boyen [12] proposed a short signature scheme which is secure against existential forgery under chosen message attack without random oracles. Based on this short signature, we propose a new verifiably encrypted signature scheme using bilinear pairings. To the best of our knowledge, our scheme is the first verifiably encrypted signature scheme secure against existential forgery under chosen message attack and extraction, without random oracles.

The organization of the paper is as follows: Section 2 briefly describes the necessary background concepts. Section 3 presents the proposed verifiably encrypted signature scheme. Section 4 analyzes the scheme. Finally, we conclude our work in Section 5.

2 Background Concepts

In this section, we first briefly describe bilinear pairings and some related mathematical problems, which form the basis of security for our scheme. Later, we review the base signature scheme [12].

2.1 Bilinear Pairing

We use cryptographic bilinear pairing, which is a modified Weil pairing [13] to construct our scheme. The pairing is defined as $e : G_1 \times G_1 \rightarrow G_2$ where G_1 is an additive cyclic group of prime order p, G_2 is a multiplicative cyclic group of the same order and P is an arbitrary generator of G_1. A cryptographic bilinear pairing has the following properties:

Bilinear: For any $R, S \in G_1$, $e(aR, bS) = e(R, S)^{ab}$ $\forall\ a, b \in Z_p^*$. This can be restated as, for any $R, S, T \in G_1$, $e(R+S, T) = e(R, T)e(S, T)$ and $e(R, S+T) = e(R, S)e(R, T)$.

Non-degenerate: There exists $R, S \in G_1$ such that $e(R, S) \neq I_{G_2}$, where I_{G_2} denotes the identity element of the group G_2.

Computable: There exists an efficient algorithm to compute $e(R, S)$ $\forall R, S \in G_1$.

The group G_1 is a subgroup of the additive group of points of an elliptic curve E/F_p and the group G_2 is a subgroup of the multiplicative group of a finite field $F_{p^2}^*$.

2.2 Discrete Logarithm Problem

The Discrete Logarithm Problem (DLP) in G_1 is defined as: Given $\langle P, Q \rangle$ for some $Q \in G_1^*$, compute a such that $Q = aP$ for some $a \in Z_p^*$.

The DLP in G_1 is assumed to be computationally hard and can be efficiently reduced to DLP in G_2 [14].

2.3 The Strong Diffie-Hellman Assumption

The q-Strong Diffie-Hellman Problem (q-SDH) problem in (G_1, G_2) is defined as: Given a $(q+1)$-tuple $(P, aP, a^2P, ..., a^qP)$ as input, compute a pair $(c, 1/(a+c)P)$, where $c \in Z_p^*$. An algorithm $\mathcal{A}$ has an advantage ϵ in solving q-SDH in G_1 if

$$\Pr\left[\mathcal{A}(P, aP, ..., a^qP) = (c, \frac{1}{a+c}P)\right] \geq \epsilon$$

q-SDH Assumption. For any probabilistic, polynomial time algorithm the probability of solving q-SDH problem is negligible [6].

2.4 Short Signature Without Random Oracles

The short signature scheme without random oracles proposed in [12] is described as below.

Let (G_1, G_2) be bilinear groups where $|G_1| = |G_2| = p$ for some large prime p and let the message to be signed m, is an element of Z_p^*. Note that the message domain can be extended to all $\{0, 1\}^*$ using a collision resistent hash function $H : \{0, 1\}^* \longrightarrow Z_p^*$. The signature scheme is described as below.

Key Generation: Pick a generator $P \in G_1$ and $x, y \in Z_p^*$, randomly. Compute $u = xP, v = yP \in G_1$ and $z = e(P, P) \in G_2$. The private key is (x, y) and public key is (P, u, v, z).

Sign: Given a private key $(x, y) \in Z_p^*$ and a message $m \in Z_p^*$, pick a random $r \in Z_p^*$ and compute $\sigma = \frac{1}{(x+m+yr)}P \in G_1$. Here, $\frac{1}{(x+m+yr)}$ is computed modulo

p. In the unlikely event that $x + m + yr = 0$, we try again with a different r. The signature is (σ, r).

Verify: Given a public key (P, u, v, z), a message $m \in Z_p^*$ and a signature (σ, r), accept the signature as valid if the below equation holds and reject otherwise.

$$e(\sigma, u + mP + rv) = z$$

In [12], the authors proved that the scheme is secure against existential forgery under chosen message attack without random oracles, assuming the hardness of q-SDH problem.

3 Proposed VES Scheme

A VES scheme consists of three entities:

Signer: Creates the VES using his private key and adjudicator's public key
Verifier: Verifies the VES using the public keys of signer and adjudicator and obtains the original signature either from signer or from adjudicator at a later stage
Adjudicator: Trusted entity who can extract the original signature of the signer in the case of disputes.

Now, we present our VES scheme, which is based on the short signature scheme in Section 2.4. Our scheme has seven phases namely, *KeyGen*, *Sign*, *Verify*, *AdjKeyGen*, *VES-Creation*, *VES-Verification* and *Adjudication*. The *KeyGen*, *Sign* and *Verify* phases correspond to Key Generation, Sign and Verify of the base scheme respectively. *AdjKeyGen* generates key pair of an adjudicator using the Key Generation of the base scheme. Given the private key of the signer and the public key of adjudicator, a VES is generated in the *VES-Creation* phase. The verification of the VES is performed in the *VES-Verification* phase using the public keys of the signer and adjudicator. In the *Adjudication* phase, an adjudicator extracts the original signature on the message from the VES using his key pair and signer's public key.

Let the user's private key be $(x, y) \in Z_p^*$ and public key be $(P, u, v, z) \in G_1$. Similarly, let the adjudicator's private key be $(x_{Ad}, y_{Ad}) \in Z_p^*$ and public key be $(P_{Ad}, u_{Ad}, v_{Ad}, z_{Ad}) \in G_1$.

VES-Creation: The signer generates a VES on a message $m \in Z_p^*$ using his private key (x, y) and adjudicator's public key $(P_{Ad}, u_{Ad}, v_{Ad}, z_{Ad})$ as follows:

1. Selects a random $r \in Z_p^*$
2. Computes $\sigma_{VES} = \frac{1}{x+m+yr}(u_{Ad} + rv_{Ad})$

The VES on the message m, $\langle \sigma_{VES}, r \rangle$ is sent to the verifier.

VES-Verification: The verifier checks the validity of the VES $\langle \sigma_{VES}, r \rangle$ on a message m using the signer's public key (P, u, v, z), and adjudicator's public key $(P_{Ad}, u_{Ad}, v_{Ad}, z_{Ad})$. He accepts it, if and only if the following equation holds:

$$e(\sigma_{VES}, u + mP + rv) = e(u_{Ad} + rv_{Ad}, P).$$

At a later stage on agreed terms, the verifier requests the signer for the original signature. The signer executes the *Sign* phase and gives the original signature $\langle \sigma, r \rangle$ to the verifier. The verifier can verify $\langle \sigma, r \rangle$ by executing the *Verify* phase. If the signer is reluctant to cooperate with the verifier, the verifier approaches the adjudicator with the VES $\langle \sigma_{VES}, r \rangle$ for adjudication service.

Adjudication: When disputes arise between two participating entities, the adjudicator first ensures that the VES $\langle \sigma_{VES}, r \rangle$ on a message m is valid, by executing the *VES-Verification* phase. Then he extracts the original signature using his private key (x_{Ad}, y_{Ad}) as below:

$$\sigma = \frac{1}{x_{Ad} + ry_{Ad}}(\sigma_{VES})$$

The adjudicator gives the extracted original signature $\langle \sigma, r \rangle$ to the verifier. The verifier can check its validity by executing the *Verify* phase.

4 Analysis

In this section, we first justify the validity of the scheme and subsequently analyze its security.

4.1 Validity

The correctness of the VES verification equation is justified as below:

$$e(\sigma_{VES}, u + mP + rv)$$
$$= e\left(\frac{1}{x+m+yr}(u_{Ad} + rv_{Ad}), xP + mP + ryP\right)$$
$$= e\left(\frac{1}{x+m+yr}(u_{Ad} + rv_{Ad}), (x + m + yr)P\right) = e(u_{Ad} + rv_{Ad}, P)$$

The above equality implies *VES-Verification(m, VES-Creation)* is true. The verification of the signature extracted from the given VES $\langle \sigma_{VES}, r \rangle$, in the adjudication phase holds good as shown below.

$$e\left(u + mP + rv, \frac{1}{x_{Ad}+ry_{Ad}}\sigma_{VES}\right)$$
$$= e\left(u + mP + rv, \frac{1}{(x_{Ad}+ry_{Ad})(x+m+yr)}(x_{Ad} + ry_{Ad})P\right)$$
$$= e\left((x + m + ry)P, \frac{1}{(x+m+yr)}P\right) = e(P, P)$$

The above equality means *Verify(m, Adjudication(VES-Creation(m)))* is true i.e. the verification of the signature extracted from the given VES in the adjudication phase holds good. Hence, our VES scheme is valid.

4.2 Security Analysis

We show that the scheme is secure against existential forgery and extraction without random oracles.

Assertion 1. *If the base signature scheme is secure against existential forgery, our VES scheme is also secure against existential forgery.*

Proof. To prove the above, we show that if our VES scheme is existentially forgeable, then the base signature scheme is also forgeable. That is if there exists a probabilistic polynomial time adversary $\mathcal{A}$ existentially forging our VES scheme with a non-negligible probability, then using $\mathcal{A}$, we can construct a new probabilistic polynomial time adversary $\mathcal{A}'$ such that $\mathcal{A}'$ can forge the base signature scheme with non-negligible probability.

We adopt the security model given by Boneh et al. in [6]. The adversary $\mathcal{A}'$ sets up a VES scheme using the base scheme as follows: $\mathcal{A}'$ generates the key pair $\langle (x_0, y_0), (P_0, u_0, v_0, z_0) \rangle$ which serves as that of the adjudicator. Suppose there exists a probabilistic polynomial time adversary $\mathcal{A}$ for our VES scheme. Then, $\mathcal{A}'$ starts the attack by running $\mathcal{A}$ on the VES. If $\mathcal{A}$ succeeds in generating a forged VES $\langle \sigma'_{VES}, r \rangle$ on a message m' then $\mathcal{A}$ generates a forged signature $\langle \sigma', r \rangle$ of the base signature scheme on the message m' as $\sigma' = \frac{1}{x_0 + ry_0} \sigma'_{VES}$.

But, as the base signature scheme [12] is secure against existential forgery under chosen message attack (without random oracle) assuming q-SDH problem is hard, our verifiably encrypted signature scheme is unforgeable.

Assertion 2. *If the base signature scheme is secure against existential forgery and the DLP in G_1 is hard, our VES scheme is secure against extraction.*

Proof. We say that a VES on a message m is secure against extraction if, an adversary $\mathcal{A}$ cannot compute the original signature $\langle \sigma, r \rangle$ on the message from the given $\langle \sigma_{VES}, r \rangle$. The adversary $\mathcal{A}$ can get the signature $\langle \sigma, r \rangle$ on the message m either by forging it directly (under the public key (P, u, v, z)) or by extracting it from the VES $\langle \sigma_{VES}, r \rangle$, such that it satisfies the verification process.

Note that the base scheme [12] is proven secure against existential forgery under q-SDH assumption without random oracles. Hence, a direct forging of the signature is computationally hard. Now, we show that extracting the original signature $\langle \sigma, r \rangle$ (that satisfies the verification condition), from the VES $\langle \sigma_{VES}, r \rangle$ is equivalent to solving DLP. We have the VES satisfying the below equation:

$$e(\sigma_{VES}, u + mP + rv) = e(u_{Ad} + rv_{Ad}, P) = e(P, P)^{x_{Ad} + ry_{Ad}}$$

Due to *Bilinearity*, from the above equation, we have

$$e\left(\frac{1}{x_{Ad} + ry_{Ad}} \sigma_{VES}, u + mP + rv\right) = e(P, P)$$

Further, due to *Non-Degeneracy*, from the verification condition of the original signature and from the above equation we have $\sigma = \frac{1}{x_{Ad} + ry_{Ad}} \sigma_{VES}$. To compute the original signature $\langle \sigma, r \rangle$, the adversary $\mathcal{A}$ must know the component $x_{Ad} + ry_{Ad}$, which is discrete logarithm of $(u_{Ad} + rv_{Ad})$ to the base P in G_1. As given in section 2.2, calculating $x_{Ad} + ry_{Ad}$ is computationally infeasible. Hence, our VES scheme is secure against extraction.

5 Conclusions

The fair exchange problem especially online contract signing can be efficiently handled by verifiably encrypted signatures. In contrast to the schemes in [6], [7] which are secure in random oracle model, we proposed a verifiably encrypted signature scheme which is secure without random oracles. We analyzed the scheme for its validity and showed that it is secure against existential forgery and extraction.

References

1. Asokan, N., Shoup, V., Waidner, M.: Optimistic Fair Exchange of Digital Signatures (extended abstract). In: Advances in Cryptology-Eurocrypt'98. Volume 1403 of LNCS. (1998) 591–606
2. Norman, G., Shmatikov, V.: Analysis of Probabilistic Contract Signing. In: Formal Aspects of Security-FASeC'02. Volume 2629 of LNCS., Springer (2003) 81–96
3. Ray, I., Ray, I.: Fair exchange in E-commerce. SIGecom Exch. **3** (2002) 9–17
4. Ben-Or, M., Goldreich, O., Micali, S., Rivest, R.L.: A Fair Protocol for Signing Contracts (extended abstract). In: Proceedings of ICALP'85. Volume 194 of LNCS., Springer (1985) 43–52
5. Ateniese, G.: Efficient verifiable encryption (and fair exchange) of digital signatures. In: ACM conference on Computer and Communications Security-CCS'99, ACM Press (1999) 138–146
6. Boneh, D., Gentry, C., Lynn, B., Shacham, H.: Aggregate and Verifiably Encrypted Signatures from Bilinear Maps. In: Advances in Cryptology-Eurocrypt'03. Volume 2656 of LNCS., Springer (2003) 416–432
7. Zhang, F., Safavi-Naini, R., Susilo, W.: Efficient Verifiably Encrypted Signature and Partially Blind Signature from Bilinear Pairings. In: Progress in Cryptology-Indocrypt'03. Volume 2904 of LNCS., Springer (2003) 191–204
8. Bellare, M., Rogaway, P.: Random oracles are practical: a paradigm for designing efficient protocols. In: ACM conference on Computer and Communications Security-CCS'93, ACM Press (1993) 62–73
9. Canetti, R., Goldreich, O., Halevi, S.: The random oracle methodology, revisited (preliminary version). In: STOC'98, ACM Press (1998) 209–218
10. Bellare, M., Rogaway, P.: The Exact Security of Digital Signatures - How to Sign with RSA and Rabin. In: Advances in Cryptology-Eurocrypt'96. Volume 3027 of LNCS., Springer-Verlag (1996) 399–416
11. Pointcheval, D., Stern, J.: Security Proofs for Signature Schemes. In: Advances in Cryptology-Eurocrypt'96. Volume 1070 of LNCS., Springer (1996) 387–398
12. Boneh, D., Boyen, X.: Short Signatures Without Random Oracles. In: Advances in Cryptology-Eurocrypt'04. Volume 3027 of LNCS., Springer (2004) 56–73
13. Boneh, D., Franklin, M.K.: Identity-Based Encryption from the Weil Pairing. In: Advances in Cryptology-Crypto'01. Volume 2139 of LNCS., Springer-Verlag (2001) 213–229
14. Menezes, A., Okamoto, T., Vanstone, S.A.: Reducing elliptic curve logarithms to logarithms in a finite field. IEEE Transactions on Information Theory **39** (1993) 1639–1646

An Improved Intrusion Detection Technique for Mobile Adhoc Networks

S. Prasanna[1] and V. Vetriselvi[2]

[1] Member Technical Staff, Sun Microsystems India Pvt Ltd,
Bangalore, India
Prasanna.Seshadri@sun.com
[2] Lecturer, School of Computer Science,
College of Engineering, Anna University,
Chennai, India
vetri@cs.annauniv.edu

Abstract. In this paper, we propose a Distributed Intrusion Detection System to protect Mobile Adhoc Networks from intruder-induced attacks. The highly dynamic, decentralized nature of these networks and a lack of infrastructure means that these networks are exposed to various kinds of security threats like spoofing, DOS attacks etc. We propose a new procedure to circumvent the intruder node and a technique to detect the intruder node in a co-operative manner based on the history of the failed paths due to intrusion. The experimental setup and the obtained results are presented discussing the various performance and security issues in the proposed protocol.

1 Introduction

A mobile ad hoc network is a group of wireless mobile nodes capable of communicating without the use of network infrastructure or any centralized administration [1]. These kinds of networks are typically deployed in emergency situations like disaster recovery, battlefield systems used by military, etc. The absence of a proper infrastructure and the decentralized nature of these networks mean that the nodes are unattended and exposed to various kinds of security threats like spoofing, DOS attacks, etc. Moreover the intruder is also a part of the network unlike in wired networks where the intruder may be an insider within the network or from the external network. The highly dynamic nature of these networks means that the topology changes with time making traditional security mechanisms for wired networks, obsolete.

The kind of intruder-induced attacks can be classified into two types as discussed in [2]. 1. Attacks on the flow of data traffic and 2. Attacks on the flow of routing traffic. In the former kind of attack, the intruder corrupts, drops, delays and replays data packets passing by, leaving all the routing control packets unharmed. In the latter kind of attack the intruder attacks the routing control packets. Attack on data traffic can be further classified into two types namely the flow disruption attack and resource depletion attack. Flow disruption attack is one in which the intruder corrupts, drops, delays and replays data packets passing through it. A resource depletion attack occurs when an intruder injects spurious packets into the network there by denying the flow of legitimate traffic. In the attack on data traffic, since the intruder exchanges all routing control information with its neighbors like link status, forwarding route requests, etc but harms only data packets, existing routing algorithms won't detect path failure due to such intrusions [3]. They are designed only to handle path failures due to node movements and node crashes. This work presents an improved solution to overcome the former kind of attack, namely the attack on data traffic.

2 Related Work

There are two approaches to protect a mobile Adhoc network from intruder-induced attacks. One approach is to circumvent or avoid the intruder by employing multi path routing [4]. The obvious disadvantage with this approach is that the redundant path consumes more bandwidth and not all current routing algorithms support multipath routing. Another approach to overcome flow disruption attack and also to identify the malicious node is to detect suspicious activities by snooping or overhearing neighbor's transmission. The disadvantage of this approach is that the nodes should keep track of every packet snooped to make sure that it was not modified during the transit, which is an additional overhead and also node movements and node crashes will have a worst effect on the system in the sense that node movements and node crashes affect the flow of traffic and hence leads to false alarms, resulting in innocent nodes being detected as intruders.

Ramanujan et al [3] proposes a novel approach to overcome the attack on data traffic induced by a malicious intruder node using three techniques which operate on the network layer namely distributed wireless firewalls, overlay routing and path failure detection. It deals about the attack on data traffic while all the routing control packets are left unharmed. The limitation in [3] is that the mechanism used to find an intruder free path upon detecting a path failure due to intrusion (Overlay routing) does not guarantee an intruder free path (at the best) and also only the intrusive path is detected but not the intruder node. We present a more improved and robust technique to detect an alternate path, which is intruder free (at the best), and also a technique to detect the intruder node in a co-operative manner based on the history of paths failed due to intrusion.

3 Distributed Wireless Firewalls

We briefly summarize the working of the distributed wireless firewall as proposed in [3] with an example topology as shown below. We assume that all the links are bi-directional.

The firewall table of all the nodes would contain the source address, destination address and a lifetime for that entry as shown below. Initially there will be no entry in the firewall table.

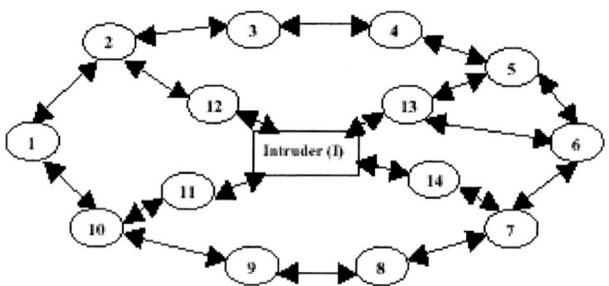

Fig. 1. Sample Wireless Adhoc Network Topology with bi-directional links

Table 1. Firewall table maintained by a node

Source Address	Destination Address	Lifetime
123.4.5.6	134.5.6.6	40 sec
124.4.5.6	135.6.7.8	50 sec

In the above topology if node 1 establishes a route to node 6 via the intruder node (I), say 1 - 2 - 12 - I - 14 - 7 - 6, the sender sends a FLOW_REQUEST packet to the receiver before transmitting the data packets. If the receiver authenticates the sender, it sends a FLOW_REPLY packet to the sender, which takes the reverse of the route between 1 and 6. All intermediate nodes in the route between 1 to 6 snoops the FLOW_REQUEST and FLOW_REPLY packets and the firewall entries of all intermediate nodes in the path between 1 and 6 (including 1 and 6) will be configured i.e. they will add the address of 1 as source and address of 6 as destination with a finite lifetime for that entry, which means that the nodes will transfer all packets from 1 to 6 and reject all other packets (assuming that there is only one flow in the network i.e. from 1 to 6). Now if the intruder injects spurious packets to one of the nodes say 5, then that packet will be rejected within the neighborhood of the intruder node since it is not a valid flow.

It has to be noted that till the end of the session, the sender and the receiver will have to refresh the firewall entries by sending some refresh and reply packets since the firewall entries are maintained in a soft state. This dynamic nature of the firewall is useful because even if the intruder node moves, the firewalls in the neighborhood region of the intruder will prevent the intruder from sending spurious packets and the current firewalls will time out. But if the intruder attacks the data traffic from 1 to 6 by corrupting, replaying, dropping and delaying data packets, the current firewalls will still allow the packets to pass through, because the flow between 1 and 6 is valid. In such a case the receiver node will use some IPSEC techniques to detect these activities. For example, the receiver can verify the checksum of the packet to detect packet corruption, sequence numbers to detect packet losses and replayed packets, message authentication code to verify the integrity of the packets, etc. Finally when the attack threshold exceeds a predefined value, the receiver assumes that the current path had failed due to intrusion.

Once the receiver has detected a path failure due to intrusion, it will stop replying the refresh packet sent by the sender at periodic intervals of time. Subsequently the sender will invoke a procedure to find a new path to the destination to circumvent the intruder (assuming that the current path failed due to intrusion on not getting a response after some tries). Meanwhile the current firewalls will timeout and the firewalls in the new path will be configured. [3] uses a concept of buddy nodes to select an alternate path (a buddy node is a list of random neighbors, a node can have). In the above case, the buddy node for 1 may be 5 and the alternate path may be 1 - 2 - 3 - 4 - 5 and 5 - 6 (i.e. 1 - 2 - 3 - 4 - 5 - 6) which is intruder free. The disadvantage of this approach is that two routes have to be found and there is no guarantee this mechanism will cicumvent the intruder node (say a path 1 - 10 - 11 - I - 13 - 5 and 5 - 6) in which case the procedure has to be repeated again. Moreover only the intruder path is found and not the intruder node.

4 Proposed Technique

Our work is inspired based on the concept of distributed wireless firewall and IPSEC techniques for detecting the intruder path as discussed in [3]. However our approach differs from that of [3] in the following ways. We propose a new approach to find an intruder free path and also to detect the intruder node based on the history of the suspects detected from the failed paths due to intrusion, by different nodes. If a node is able to detect a single suspect from the history of the failed paths due to intrusion, then that node is the intruder and the details of the intruder is broadcast to all nodes in the network so that all nodes remove the intruder from their neighbor list and the intruder will be denied the network resources. But if the number of suspects detected is a group of nodes, then the nodes exchange information about their suspects with other nodes so as to eliminate innocent nodes from their suspect list and pass their updated suspect list to all other nodes and so on. Finally if any one node manages to find a single suspect in common from the information exchanged, it is detected as the intruder. This kind of technique to detect the intruder is more robust in the sense that the intruder detected is based on the information (about suspects) from all other nodes and will be agreed by all nodes; also the technique to detect the intruder node is based on elimination so that there is no chance of an innocent node being detected as intruder.

In our approach we have two modes of operation namely 1) Normal mode and 2) Intruder mode. In the normal mode, all routing algorithms operate as usual forwarding route requests, finding a route, transmitting data packets, etc. Once a path failure due to intrusion is detected by the receiver using some IPSEC techniques, the intruder mode of operation comes into picture, where the algorithms we developed to circumvent the intruder path, to detect the intruder node based on the history of the failed paths due to intrusion comes into action.

In our approach, the task of cooperatively finding an alternate path, which is intruder free, depends both on the sender and the receiver. Once the receiver detects an intruder induced path failure, the sender and the receiver nodes co-operatively determine an alternate path and ensures (at the best) that the alternate path selected is intruder free. In general the techniques we discuss to circumvent the intruder path and to detect the intruder node can work above any routing algorithm as an extension.

i.e. all existing routing algorithms work as usual in the normal mode with all techniques implemented to work in the intruder mode acting as an extension, monitoring the flow. Once an intruder induced path failure is detected, the node switches to the intruder mode where the techniques used to circumvent the intruder path and to detect the intruder node takes full control. In short, there is no need to modify the existing routing algorithms to incorporate these techniques but implement them as an extension to these routing algorithms so that they monitor the flow in normal mode and takes full control once an intruder induced path failure is detected.

4.1 Detailed Working of the Proposed Technique

In the proposed technique, as noted earlier, once the receiver detects a path failure due to intrusion, both the sender and the receiver determine the alternate path co-operatively. The alternate path is designed to be intruder free. For finding the alternate path, we define two additional routing control packets, which are as follows.

1. ALTERNATE_ROUTE_REQUEST packet, which will contain a list of the address of all the nodes in the previous path, which has failed due to intrusion (excluding the sender and the receiver). We call this list as the prohibited list; also all prohibited lists will be recorded in a log, which we call the intruder log.
2. ROUTE_FORWARD packet whose functionality will be explained below.

We define the terms *prohibited list*, *intruder log* and *suspect list* for easier understanding of the technique as explained below. All the participating nodes maintain these three lists.

Prohibited list. A *prohibited list* is a list of nodes in the current path, which has failed due to intrusion. Once a path to a particular destination is found it is stored and once that path fails due to intrusion, the list of nodes involved in that path (excluding the source and the destination) becomes the current *prohibited list*.

For example if the source node is 1 and the destination node is 6 as in the above topology, and a path from 1 to 6 is $1 - 2 - 12 - I - 13 - 5 - 6$ (an intruder path), then when a path failure due to intrusion is detected the prohibited list will be *Prohibited list* $= 2 - 12 - I - 13 - 5$.

Intruder log. The Intruder log is a list of *prohibited lists*. Once a prohibited list is determined from a path failure due to intrusion, it is appended to the intruder log. For example as determined above in the path $1 - 2 - 12 - I - 13 - 5 - 6$, which is an intruder path.

Prohibited list $= 2 - 12 - I - 13 - 5$ and *Intruder log* $= 2 - 12 - I - 13 - 5$

If there is a flow from 1 to another destination 6 say via the path, $1 - 10 - 11 - I - 14 - 7 - 6$ which is also an intruder path it will be detected and the current prohibited list will be *Prohibited list* $= 10 - 11 - I - 14 - 7$ which will be appended to the intruder log. Now the intruder log will be

Intruder log
$2 - 12 - I - 13 - 5$
$10 - 11 - I - 14 - 7$

Suspect list. A *Suspect list* is a list of suspected intruder nodes determined from the intruder log. It is determined from the number of nodes common in all individual lists of the intruder log. For example, the above Intruder log contains node I in common. Therefore node I is detected as the intruder. If more than one node is common in all lists or occurs in maximum number of times from all lists, then they are called as suspects (but not the intruders). These suspect nodes are exchanged between all the nodes in the network to determine the exact intruder node (by eliminating innocent nodes) as will be explained below.

We now explain the proposed scheme with the sample Adhoc Network topology shown above. We assume that each of the two packets discussed above has a Route record associated with it containing a unique request_id and the list of nodes in the current route i.e. the list of nodes traversed in the current route.

The proposed scheme can be best explained by considering the sample Adhoc network topology as in figure 2a below. Here we assume that node 1 is the source and node 6 is the destination. Assuming that the route from 1 to 6 is 1 - 2 - 12 - I - 14 - 7 - 6, node 1 sends the FLOW_REQUEST packet to 6 and after authenticating the sender, node 6 sends a FLOW_REPLY packet to the sender. The FLOW_REQUEST and FLOW_REPLY packets will be snooped by all the intermediate nodes 2, 12, I, 14, 7 and they all add a firewall entry (including 1 and 6) similar to the one shown above.

The path from 1 to 6, i.e. 1 - 2 - 12 - I - 14 - 7 - 6 is not an intruder free path. The intruder will corrupt, drop, replay and delay all the data packets, leaving all routing

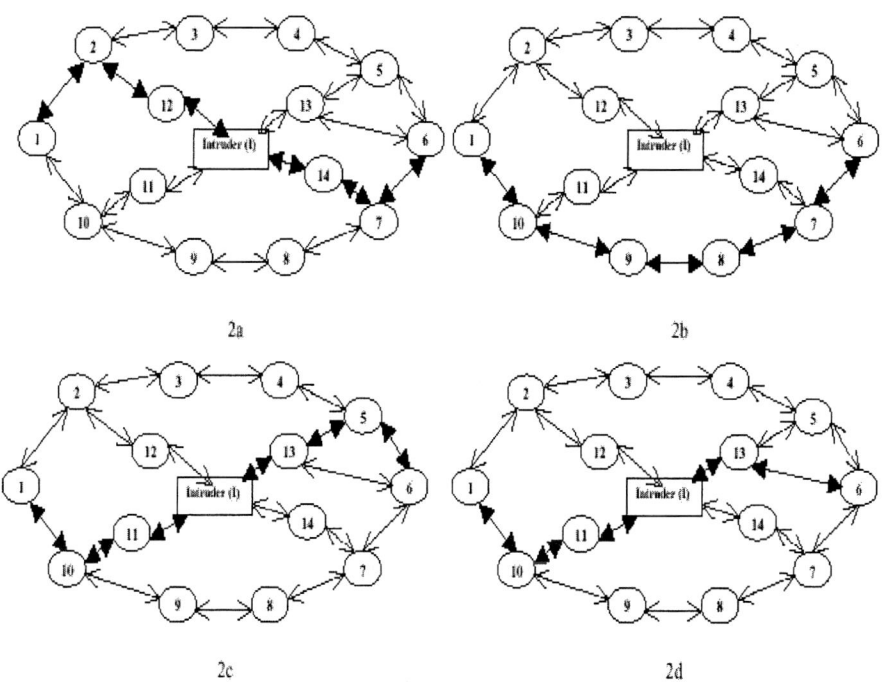

Fig. 2. (2a) Path from 1 to 6 via the Intruder node I. (2b, 2c, 2d) Three possible alternate routes from 1 to 6 via the ROUTE_REDISCOVERY procedure.

control packets unharmed. In this case, the receiver will use IPSEC techniques to detect these activities as discussed above. Finally when the attack threshold exceeds a predefined value, the receiver assumes that the current path had failed due to intrusion and hence it will stop responding to the refresh packets from the sender. The sender then switches to the intruder mode where the algorithms implemented to detect the intruder comes into action. Meanwhile the firewall entries in the current path will time out.

Now both the sender and the receiver will append the path 2 - 12 - I - 14 - 7 in their *intruder log* and the current *prohibited list* is 2 - 12 - I - 14 - 7 (excluding the source and destination). It has to be noted that both the sender and the receiver will keep track of the current route between them and it becomes the *prohibited list* once a path failure due to intrusion is detected. The sender will invoke ROUTE_REDISCOVERY procedure (We assume some encryption techniques are available to make sure that the suspect lists are exchanged securely.)

Now node 1 will check whether any of its neighbors are in the *prohibited list*. Node 2 is in the *prohibited list* so node 1 will send an ALTERNATE_ROUTE_REQUEST packet to all its neighbors except node 2 (in this case to node 10). Also node 1 will append its entry in the route list (list of nodes traversed) of the current route record.

Node 10 receives the ALTERNATE_ROUTE_REQUEST packet and checks whether any of its neighbors are in the *prohibited list*. Now node 10's neighbors 11 and 9 (except 1) are not in the prohibited list. Therefore node 10 will forward an ALTERNATE_ROUTE_REQUEST packet to 11 and 9 (appending its entry in the route list). Now two interesting case arises.

Case 1. Node 9 gets the ALTERNATE_ROUTE_REQUEST from 10 and forwards it to 8, but node 8 has no neighbors, which are not there in the *prohibited list* (excluding the source from which this request came from i.e. node 9). In this case it forwards a ROUTE_FORWARD packet to all its neighbors, which are in the *prohibited list* (to node 7 in this case). Now node 7 receives the ROUTE_FORWARD packet and forwards it to all its neighbors and tries to find a route to 6 [1]. We assume that one such route is 1 - 10 - 9 - 8 - 7 – 6 (Fig 2b). Now node 6 keeps track of this route waiting for more possible routes.

Case 2. Node 11 gets the ALTERNATE_ROUTE_REQUEST from 10 finds that it has no neighbors other than 10, which are not in the *prohibited list*. In this case it forwards a ROUTE_FORWARD packet to all its neighbors, which are in the *prohib-*

---

[1] Note: If a node receives a ROUTE_ FORWARD packet it forwards it to all its neighbors to find a path to the destination. The procedure employed to find the route to the destination is similar to that used in routing algorithms like AODV [5] and DSR [6] in which all nodes process a request once. But the significance of the ROUTE_FORWARD packet is that irrespective of whether a route to a destination exists in a node's routing table or not, it has to append its address to the list of nodes traversed in the route record and forward the ROUTE_FORWARD packet to all its neighbors so that all possible alternate paths reach the destination. All the nodes will process the ROUTE_FORWARD packet only once and duplicates will be discarded based on the unique identifier in the route record. This procedure is very useful to detect the intruder free path from many options and also to detect the intruder node in case of multiple path failures as will be discussed.

ited list (to node I in this case). Now node I receive the ROUTE_FORWARD packet and forward it to all its neighbors to find a route to 6 (assuming that it participates correctly in the routing protocol). We assume that two such routes are 1 - 10 - 11 - I - 13 - 5 - 6 (Fig 2c) and 1 - 10 - 11 - I - 13 – 6 (Fig 2d). It should be noted that route 1 - 10 - 11 - I - 14 - 7 - 6 is not possible because node 7 has already received the ROUTE_FORWARD packet from 8 (assuming that node 7 received the ROUTE_FORWARD packet from 8 before 14) in the previous case and hence it ignores the duplicate request. By a similar analogy we assume that there are no other possible routes.

Therefore the receiver node 6 receives three ROUTE_FORWARD packets (ROUTE_FORWARD and ALTERNATE_ROUTE_REQUEST packets are treated as same by the receiver) from node. (The receiver waits for a finite amount of time making sure that all possible alternate routes are got. Once the timer expires further routes will be discarded). The three routes are

Route 1: 1 - 10 - 9 - 8 - 7 – 6,
Route 2: 1 - 10 - 11 - I - 13 - 5 - 6
Route 3: 1 - 10 - 11 - I - 13 – 6

The receiver compares three routes with each prohibited list entry in the intruder log. Now the intruder log contains only one prohibited list, namely 2 - 12 - I - 14 - 7. The first route (excluding the source and the destination) is compared with the prohibited list. i.e. 10 - 9 - 8 - 7 with 2 - 12 - I - 14 - 7. Now only one node (node 7) matches since it is in both the entries. Coming to the second route, 10 - 11 - I - 13 - 5 and 2 - 12 - I - 14 - 7, in this case also there is only one match, namely node I. The third route 10 - 11 - I - 13 also has one match with 2 - 12 - I - 14 - 7.

Now all the three routes have one node, which matches an entry in the prohibited list, but Route 2 (1 - 10 - 11 - I - 13 - 5 - 6) has 6 hops whereas the other two routes only have 5 hops. Therefore Route 2 is not favored. Now both routes, Route 1 and Route 2 have one node, which matches an entry in the prohibited list and also have the same number of hops (5). In this case the receiver selects a random route among them and replies via that route to the sender. Now two special cases arise

Route 1. The receiver selects the route 1 - 10 - 9 - 8 - 7 - 6 and replies it to the sender via the reverse path. The sender will get this route and since this route is intruder free and the sender will transmit all packets to the destination. Thus an intruder free path is got. In this case all the nodes, which are there in this intruder free path, are deleted from the *suspect list* maintained by the sender and the receiver.

Route 3. The receiver selects the route 1 - 10 - 11 - I - 13 - 6. As obvious, this route is not free from the intruder. Once again, this route will fail due to intrusion and the receiver will detect this path failure due to intrusion. Now the current *prohibited list* for both the sender and the receiver will be 10 - 11 - I - 13 (excluding source and destination). Both the sender and the receiver will append it to their *intruder log*. Therefore the intruder log of node 1 and 6 contains the following routes.

Intruder log of 1	Intruder log of 6
2 - 12 - I - 14 - 7	2 - 12 - I - 14 - 7
10 - 11 - I - 13	10 - 11 - I - 13

Current *prohibited list* is 10 - 11 - I - 13

Now since there is more than one *prohibited list* in the *intruder log*, the sender and the receiver will try to detect the exact intruder node by finding the common entry in the prohibited lists recorded so far. As obvious, the intruder node I figures in both the prohibited lists and hence the sender and the receiver have detected the intruder node *authoritatively*. The sender and the receiver can invoke an alarm and transmit the intruder node details to all other nodes in the network so that all the nodes can remove the intruder node's address from their neighbor list and the intruder node will be denied the network resources. The system now returns to the normal mode.

It is also possible that more than one node might also figure in the entire *prohibited list* or occurs in the maximum number of times in common (in different topologies*)*. In that case, the exact intruder node cannot be determined. But the lists of nodes, which are common in all the prohibited lists in the intruder log, are called as suspects. All the nodes exchange information about the suspects to other nodes in the network periodically and nodes compare their suspects with suspect lists received from other nodes to find a common entry in the suspect lists. This can also be used to eliminate innocent nodes if any from the suspect list (i.e. nodes which are not in common). Finally if any one node manages to find a single suspect (or common suspects which can't be eliminated) from the information exchanged, it is detected as the intruder(s).

5 Experiments

For experiments, we have developed an Ad hoc network simulator in python and tested our IDS on different topologies. Experiments were performed to

1. Detect the intrusive behavior on a given path (using IPSEC principles, for example, end to end authentication of packets).
2. Study how effectively the proposed technique detects an alternate path, which is intruder free.
3. Detection of the intruder node based on the history of previous path failures due to intrusion.

The success of the proposed Intrusion Detection System is determined by its ability to send a predefined number of data packets to the destination circumventing the intruder. The performance of the IDS is measured in terms of

1. The quality of the intruder free path selected (in terms of the number of hops)
2. The total time taken to send all data packets to the destination circumventing the intruder node (this is equal to the sum of the time taken to detect a path failure due to intrusion and the time taken to send all packets to the destination intact in the intruder free path selected)
3. The probability of a false path being selected as an intruder free path (which should be ideally zero or negligible)
4. Effect of Mobility on the proposed system
5. Impact of the proposed scheme on Network performance.

The experimental setup and the obtained results were summarized below.

5.1 Experimental Setup

1. Number of nodes: 8 to 30
2. Firewall entry refresh time: 13 seconds (every 13 seconds, the sender should send a ROUTE_REFRESH packet to the destination for which the receiver should send a ROUTE_REFRESH_REPLY packet which will be snooped by all the intermediate nodes in the path to refresh the firewall entry).
3. Total number of data packets sent to the destination: 200 packets with one second delay between every packet sent.
4. Routing algorithm: Any Mobile ad hoc Network routing algorithm (DSR, AODV, etc).
5. Attack threshold: 20 (i.e. if more than 20 packets are dropped, corrupted or replayed), the destination node decides to abort the current transmission (by not responding to the ROUTE_REFRESH packet sent by the source at frequent intervals)

Making certain nodes to disrupt the flow of data traffic and also to inject spurious packets into the network simulated intruders. The attacks simulated were spurious packet injection into the network, replay attack, dropping, delaying and corrupting data packets corrupting data packets (modifying the headers, checksum, etc).The obtained results were summarized below.

5.1.1 Quality of the Intruder Free Path Selected

Since the intruder free path selected is based on the route with the least number of matches in the *prohibited list* with the least number of hops, the alternate path selected doesn't impose any additional overhead on the number of hops. In general, the number of hops in the intruder free path is designed to be the shortest possible path from the source to the destination, which is intruder free. This is the exact reason

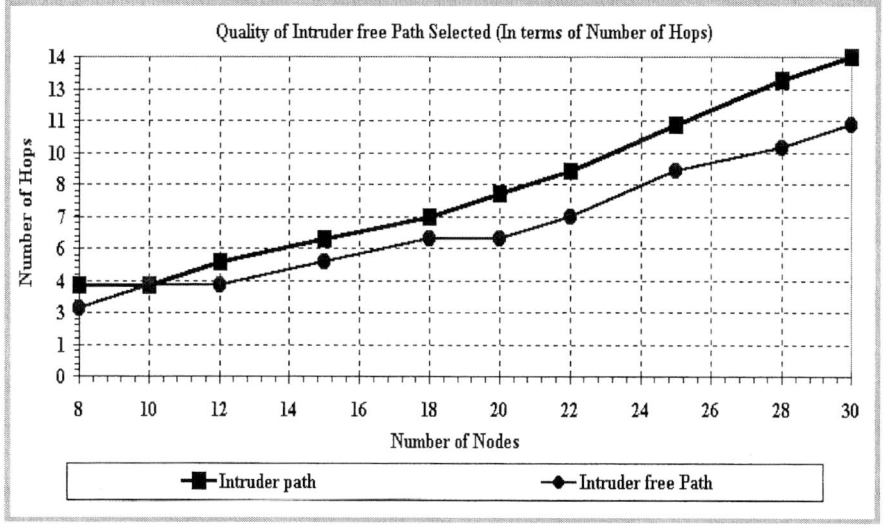

Fig. 3. Quality of the Intruder free path in terms of number of hops

behind the use of the ROUTE_FORWARD packet so that all possible alternate path reaches the destination and the destination selects the path with the least number of hops and least number of matches in the current *prohibited list* and replies to the sender via this path.

As shown in the graph, the number of hops in the intruder free path is less than or equal to the number of hops in the intruder path. Since in finding the intruder free path, the least number of matches in the current *prohibited list* is taken into account, therefore a path in which there is less or no match with the current *prohibited list* takes priority. And from such paths selecting a path with the less number of hops generally has a very high probability of having the less number of hops than that contained in the intruder path.

5.1.2 Performance of the IDS

This is crucial to the functioning of the proposed system. To ensure that the performance of the proposed system is acceptable, it has to be ensured that the alternate path has less number of hops than the intruder path and also the chances of a false path being detected is nearly zero. As noted from the results, in almost all cases, the alternate path selected is intruder free, failing which the performance of the system gets affected drastically (The two tall lines in the middle). At the very worst case, it has to be ensured that an alternate path selected is intruder free at least after one failure.

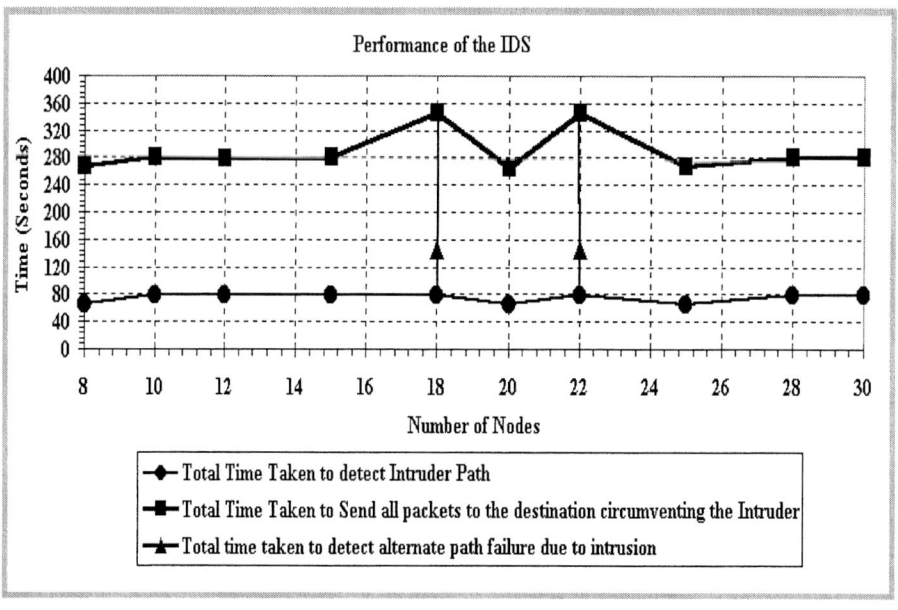

Fig. 4. Performance of the IDS

5.1.3 Security Ratio

The security ratio of the proposed system depends on its ability to determine an intruder free path effectively. As discussed above the probability of a false route being selected as intruder free path selected should ideally be zero. From the simulation results as noted above, it has been found that 84% of the alternate path found to circumvent the intruder is intruder free. The reason for an alternate path being a false path is because when an alternate path is found, the node with the least number of hops and least number of matches in the *prohibited list* is taken into consideration although priority is given to the least number of matches in the *prohibited list*. But if there are two paths with the same number of hops and the same number of matches with the current *prohibited list* entry, any one path is selected in random. It has to be noted that a false route being selected as an alternate path aids in determining the intruder quickly. As explained in the example above if there is a false route selected as intruder free route, it will only increase the number of paths failed due to intrusion and therefore the number of suspects will be narrowed down (since there is already a path failed) resulting in faster detection of the intruder.

Intruder log
2 - 12 - I - 14 - 7 (First *prohibited list*)
10 - 11 - I - 13 (Current *prohibited list* which is added)

As obvious from the above two entries in the intruder log, the node I is the only node, which figures, in both the prohibited lists. Therefore it is detected as the intruder. Therefore at the worst case if the alternate path selected is a false path (intruder path), it will only aid in determining the intruder node faster.

5.1.4 Effect of Mobility on the Proposed System

The effect of mobility on the proposed scheme only aids in determining the intruder node quickly. This is obvious from the fact that if the intruder node moves and disrupts different flows, it will figure in the suspect lists of different nodes, which will only help in detecting the intruder node quickly.

5.1.5 Impact of the Proposed Scheme on Network Performance

The two main overheads introduced in the proposed scheme are maintaining and refreshing the firewall entries frequently and exchanging suspect lists among the nodes to detect the intruder. As obvious any security scheme involves a performance penalty but given the limited power constraints of Mobile ad hoc Networks, it should be at a minimum. To ensure that the overheads involved are minimum and acceptable, the following steps can be taken

1. The firewall entry refresh time can be increased
2. Suspect lists can be exchanged at a slower rate (at longer periods of time). This will also ensure that the suspects maintained by a node will be narrowed down in case the same node experiences multiple path failures due to intrusion (for different destinations) and hence the chances of the same node detecting the intruder will be very high without even exchanging the suspect list or if at all the suspect list is exchanged, it will aid in detecting the intruder at a faster rate since the suspects are narrowed down.

Another important advantage of the proposed system is that it is somehow resilient to attack on routing traffic also (especially in the intruder mode). Since the intruder participates correctly in the routing protocol, the neighboring nodes will not suspect the intruder, since the intruder corrupts, replays, drops and delays only the data packets. This means that the intruder will also forward the ROUTE_FORWARD packet. But on the other hand even if the intruder drops the ROUTE_FORWARD packet or replays the ROUTE_FORWARD packet in the intruder mode of operation, it will not affect the proposed protocol. If the intruder drops the ROUTE_FORWARD packet, then the alternate path traveling via the intruder will not reach the destination, even if the intruder replays the ROUTE_FORWARD packet, since a node will accept a ROUTE_FORWARD packet only once, duplicates will be discarded and it will be filtered out within the nearest neighbor of the intruder node, thus preventing the attack traffic from seeping through the network.

6 Conclusion

In this paper, we have presented a new approach to overcome intruder-induced attack on data traffic. The intruder node is also identified in a co-operative manner based on the suspects detected by different nodes from the history of the previously failed paths due to intrusion. The above techniques can work above all routing algorithms i.e. in the normal mode the existing routing algorithms will function as usual with all techniques to detect an intruder induced path failure acting as extension, monitoring the flow. But once an intrusive path is detected, the system switches to the intruder mode where the techniques implemented to circumvent the intruder takes full control and finally when an intruder free path is detected, the system again switches to the normal mode In future, these techniques can easily extended to prevent attacks on routing traffic also, which is a serious security threat in these kinds of networks.

References

1. RFC 2501 - Mobile Ad hoc Networking (MANET): Routing Protocol Performance Issues and Evaluation Considerations
2. R. Ramanujan, A. Ahamad, J. Bonney, R.Hagelstrom, and K. Thurber, "Techniques For Intrusion-Resistant Ad Hoc Routing Algorithms (TIARA)," Proc. MILCOM'2000, October 2000.
3. R. Ramanujan, S. Kudige, S. Takkella, T. Nguyen, F.Adelstein, "Intrusion resistant ad hoc wireless networks," Proc. MILCOM'2002.
4. A.Nasipuri and S.R. Das, "On-Demand Multipath Routing for Mobile Ad Hoc Networks," Proceedings of the 8th International Conference on Computer Communications and Networks, October 1999.
5. Charles E. Perkins and E. M. Royer. "Ad hoc on demand distance vector routing," In IEEE WM-CSA'99, 1999.
6. David B. Johnson, David A. Maltz, Yih-Chun Hu, "The Dynamic source routing protocol for mobile ad hoc networks," Internet draft, April 2003

User Revocation in Secure Adhoc Networks*

Bezawada Bruhadeshwar and Sandeep S. Kulkarni

Department of Computer Science and Engineering, Michigan State University,
East Lansing MI 48824 USA
Tel: +1-517-355-2387, Fax: 1-517-432-1061
{bezawada, sandeep}@cse.msu.edu

Abstract. We focus on the problem of user revocation in secure adhoc networks. The current approach to achieve security in adhoc networks is to use a secret instantiation protocol in which, each user is given a subset of secrets from a common secret pool. To communicate securely, a pair of users use the secrets that are common to both of them. However, when users are compromised, some of these secrets are also compromised. Hence, to revoke the compromised users, the secrets known to these users need to be updated. Many group key management solutions exist for revocation of users from a group. However, due to the limitations in adhoc networks, i.e., lack of efficient broadcast mechanisms and lossy links, revocation of users is a challenging problem. In this paper, we propose a revocation algorithm that combines the secret instantiation protocols with group key management protocols. Depending on the combination of protocols used, our revocation algorithm provides deterministic or probabilistic guarantees for revocation. We illustrate our revocation algorithm by combining the square grid protocol and the logical key hierarchy protocol.

Keywords: Secure Adhoc Networks, User Revocation, Secret Instantiation Protocols, Group Key Management Protocols.

1 Introduction

Information security is necessary for users in an adhoc network. The current approach to achieve adhoc network security, including confidentiality and authentication, is to load each user with a random [1] (respectively, deterministic [2,3]) subset of secrets from a common secret pool at initial deployment. Using these shared secrets, the users establish the necessary session secrets at run-time. However, in this approach, if some users are compromised, it is necessary to revoke these users to protect the security of the remaining users. Due to the limitations, i.e., lack of efficient broadcast mechanisms and lossy links, revocation of users is difficult in adhoc networks. With this motivation, in this paper, we address the problem of user revocation in secure adhoc networks.

---
* This work is partially sponsored by NSF CAREER 0092724, ONR grant N00014-01-1-0744, DARPA contract F33615-01-C-1901, and a grant from Michigan State University.

Revocation of users from a group has been addressed by group key management protocols [4,5,6,7]. In these protocols, the users of the group share a group key and use it to encrypt the data. When membership of the group changes, a group controller distributes a new group key to revoke (respectively, add) the corresponding users. However, the group key management protocols assume an efficient broadcast primitive and rely on the group controller for distributing the new group key. Hence, these protocols, in their native form, are not suitable for adhoc networks.

An alternate approach for distributing the group key is to initially send the group key to a subset of users [8]. Now, this subset of users distribute the group key securely to the other users in the group. However, for such group key distribution, the users in the adhoc network need to be able to communicate securely among themselves. This problem of establishing secure channels among users in adhoc networks is addressed by secret instantiation protocols [2,1,9,3].

In this paper, for user revocation, we propose an algorithm that combines the secret instantiation protocols [1,3,2,9] and the group key management protocols [4,5,6,7]. Depending upon the protocols used for secret instantiation and group key management, we get different properties for revocation. Our contributions are as follows:

- We describe a revocation algorithm for adhoc networks by combining secret instantiation protocols and the group key management protocols. Our algorithm is generic in nature and can be used to revoke users from any adhoc network that uses secret instantiation protocols.
- We illustrate our algorithm by combining the square grid protocol (secret instantiation protocol) [3] and the logical key hierarchy protocol (group key management protocol) [6]. For this combination of protocols, we show that it is possible to achieve deterministic security for user revocation.
- We consider group key distribution in two scenarios of user communication capabilities. In the first scenario, there is an underlying support for routing messages in the network. In the second scenario, a user can only communicate with users in its neighborhood. Using simulation results, we show that, it is possible to achieve complete group key distribution in both these scenarios.

Organization of the paper. In Section 2, we describe the problem of revocation in adhoc networks. In Section 3, we describe our revocation algorithm. In Section 4, we describe an instance of our revocation algorithm by combining the square grid protocol and the logical key hierarchy protocol. In Section 5, we evaluate group key distribution in two scenarios: with routing support and without routing support. In Section 6, we present related work and conclude in Section 7.

2 Problem of Revocation

Secret instantiation protocols [1, 2, 3, 9] are used to achieve initial security in adhoc networks. In such a network, if users are compromised then it is necessary to revoke them. Therefore, the secrets known to the revoked users need to be updated. Furthermore, this update needs to be done in such a way that, all the uncompromised users sharing a secret before the revocation, possess the same updated shared secret after the revocation. And, the compromised users do not know the updated secret. There are two approaches for updating the shared secrets in a consistent manner. In the first approach, the group controller transmits these secrets securely to the users. However, this approach is undesirable as it requires the transmission of a large number of messages. In the second approach, the users receive a group key, k'_g, securely from the group controller and use the following technique to update the shared secrets: $k'_x = f(k'_g, k_x)$, where k_x is the old shared secret, k'_x is the new shared secret and, f is a one-way function. Using this technique, only those current users who knew the old shared secret, k_x, will be able to get the new shared secret, k'_x. Since the same group key is distributed to all the users, this technique guarantees consistent update of the shared secrets. This technique was also used in [5, 8, 7]. In our work, we adopt the second approach and focus on group key distribution to revoke users from secure adhoc networks.

We note that, group key distribution is relatively easy when users are added to the group. In the group key management protocols, the group controller uses the old group key, which not known to the new users, to send the new group key. The users use the one-way function approach we described above, to compute the new shared secrets. The new user receives the new group key and the shared secrets from the group controller through a secure unicast channel. We note that, the same approach can be used for adding users in adhoc networks and hence, we only focus on revocation of users.

In this paper, we describe an algorithm for revocation in secure adhoc networks. The attractive feature of our algorithm is that the group controller is only briefly involved in establishing the group key and the bulk of the group key distribution is done by the users themselves. In Section 3, we describe our revocation algorithm. In Section 4, we illustrate an instance of our revocation algorithm.

3 Combining Secret Instantiation with Group Key Management

The goal of the secret instantiation protocol is to provide an initial collection of secrets to users such that the users can utilize them to communicate securely. These protocols can be probabilistic [1] or deterministic [2, 3]. Furthermore, these protocols may require communicating nodes to depend on intermediate users [1] or they may assume that intermediate users are not trusted [2, 3]. (By trust in intermediate users, we mean that they can (or are required to) decrypt and re-encrypt messages they forward. In all the algorithms [2, 1, 3], the intermediate users are trusted to *route* the messages. However, in [2, 3], they cannot decrypt them.)

In the group key management protocol, a group of users shares a group key — known to all the users, along with some other secrets —shared by different subsets of users. When one or more users are revoked from the group, the group key should be changed in such a way that only the remaining users in the group can access the new group key. The distribution of this new group key is facilitated by the other secrets that the remaining users possess. Additionally, these protocols change any other secrets that the revoked users had in such a way that the changed secrets are not available to the revoked users. Examples of these protocols include [4,5,6,7].

In our approach, we combine the secret instantiation protocol and the group key management protocol as follows: initially, each user is associated with secrets from both protocols. Now, the users utilize the secrets from the secret instantiation protocol to establish secure communication. When users are revoked, in the first step, the group controller uses the group key management protocol to send the new group key. However, instead of sending the new group key to all users, the group controller sends it selectively to a subset of users. Especially, in adhoc networks it is desirable to minimize the number of messages sent by the group controller as broadcast is an unreliable operation in these networks. Subsequently, in the second step, other users can obtain the group key from this subset of users using the secrets from the secret instantiation protocol. Since the secret instantiation protocol enables two users to establish a common secret for communication, it can be used to provide authentication and confidentiality. Finally, the compromised secrets (i.e., secrets from the secret instantiation protocol and the group key management protocol that are known to the revoked users) are changed locally (cf. Section 2) so that the revoked users cannot access them. Note that the second step of the group key distribution can now occur in parallel.

We only consider those group key management protocols that ensure that only the remaining users get the new group key and any other secrets they shared with revoked users (e.g., [4,5,6,7]). Now, depending upon the protocol used for secret instantiation, the resulting protocol will provide probabilistic/deterministic security where intermediate nodes are trusted/untrusted. Specifically, if we use the deterministic protocol from [2,3], where intermediate users are not trusted, then the resulting revocation algorithm will guarantee that after revoking users (upto a certain limit) the remaining users can communicate with deterministic security. Likewise, if we use the probabilistic protocol from [1], where intermediate users are trusted, then the resulting algorithm will guarantee that, after revoking users, the remaining users can communicate with probabilistic security.

4 Instance of Revocation Algorithm

In this paper, we illustrate an instance of our revocation algorithm in which we use the square grid protocol from [3] for secret instantiation and the logical key hierarchy [6] protocol for group key management. We show that, our algorithm retains the property of deterministic security. We proceed as follows. In Section 4.1, we describe the square grid protocol [3]. In Section 4.2, we describe the logical key hierarchy protocol [6]. In Section 4.3, we describe the combination of these two protocols.

4.1 The Square Grid Protocol

In the square grid protocol [3], n users are arranged in a *logical* square grid of size $\sqrt{n}$ x $\sqrt{n}$. Each location, $\langle i,j \rangle$, $0 \leq i,j < \sqrt{n}$, in the grid is associated with a *user* $u_{\langle i,j \rangle}$ and a *grid secret* $k_{\langle i,j \rangle}$. Each user knows all the grid secrets that are along its row and column. For example, in Figure 1, the grid secret associated with $\langle 1,1 \rangle$ is known to users at locations $\langle j,1 \rangle, \langle 1,j \rangle, 0 \leq j \leq 3$. Additionally, each user maintains a direct secret with users in its row and column. This direct secret is not known to any other user. For example, user $u_{\langle 1,2 \rangle}$ shares a direct secret with user, $u_{\langle 1,3 \rangle}$, which is located in the same row (cf. Figure 1).

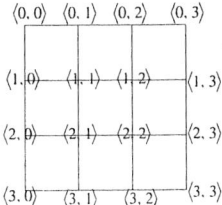

Fig. 1. Square grid protocol: A node marked $\langle j,k \rangle$ is associated with user $u_{\langle j,k \rangle}$ and grid secret $k_{\langle j,k \rangle}$

Now, consider the case where user A wants to set up a session key with user B. Let the locations of A and B be $\langle j_1, k_1 \rangle$ and $\langle j_2, k_2 \rangle$ respectively. In this case, A selects the session key and encrypts it using the following secret selection protocol.

Secret selection protocol for session key establishment
for users at $\langle j_1, k_1 \rangle$ and $\langle j_2, k_2 \rangle$
// If users are neither in same row nor in same column
If $(j_1 \neq j_2 \ \wedge \ k_1 \neq k_2)$
 Use the *grid secrets* $k_{\langle j_1, k_2 \rangle}$ and $k_{\langle j_2, k_1 \rangle}$
Else
// If users are in the same row or column
 Use the *direct secret* between $u_{\langle j_1, k_1 \rangle}$ and $u_{\langle j_2, k_2 \rangle}$

Along with the encrypted session key, A also sends its own grid location (in plain text) to B. If multiple secrets are selected by A then a combination of those secrets (using hash functions like MD5) is used to encrypt the session key.

Theorem 1. The above secret selection protocol ensures that the collection of secrets used by two communicating users is not known to any other user in the system. Hence, the above protocol can be used for establishing the session key. (cf. [3] for proof.) □

4.2 Logical Key Hierarchy

In the logical key hierarchy [6] protocol, the secrets are arranged as the nodes of a rooted tree and the users are associated with the leaf nodes of this tree. Each

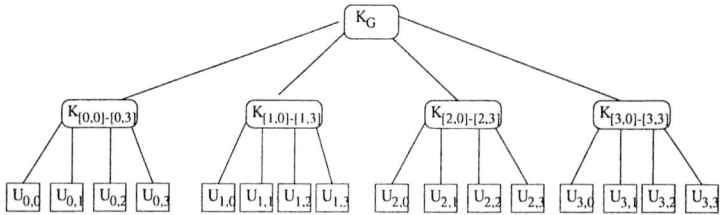

Fig. 2. Logical Key Hierarchy

user receives the secrets that are on the path from itself to the root node. As an illustration, in Figure 2, we show the logical key hierarchy for the system of 16 users from the square grid of Figure 1. Thus, in this arrangement, user $U_{\langle 0,0 \rangle}$ receives the secrets $K_{[0,0]-[0,3]}$ and K_G.

4.3 Combining of Square Grid with Logical Key Hierarchy

To combine the algorithms in Sections 4.1 and 4.2, we arrange the users in the square grid and the logical key hierarchy protocols[1]. The users receive secrets from both these protocols. As an illustration, we consider the square grid arrangement in Figure 1, which consists of 16 users. Each user receives $O(\sqrt{n})$ secrets from the square grid protocol.

Next, we instantiate a logical key hierarchy of degree 2 in two steps. In the first step, we treat an entire row of users, from the square grid protocol, as a leaf node in the logical key hierarchy i.e., a leaf node is a row of users from the square grid. As an illustration, in Figure 3(a), we show the first step of this instantiation in which each of leaf node is associated with an entire row of users from the square grid protocol (cf. Figure 1). For example, in this arrangement, the row users $U_{\langle 0,0 \rangle} - U_{\langle 0,3 \rangle}$ are given the secrets, $K_{[0,0]-[0,3]}$, $K_{[0,0]-[1,3]}$ and K_G.

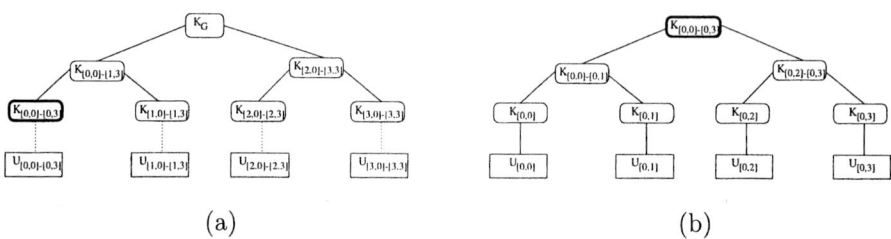

Fig. 3. Instantiation of Logical Key Hierarchy in Two Stages. Note that, the root node, $K_{[0,0]-[0,3]}$, of the hierarchy in (b) is the same as the key $K_{[0,0]-[0,3]}$ in (a).

In the second step, we instantiate the logical key hierarchy for each row of the users, i.e., each leaf node is a single user from a row in the square grid

---

[1] Note that, the user organization in the grid and key hierarchy is *logical*. This organization does not affect the *physical* deployment of users.

protocol and all the leaf nodes are from the same row. As an illustration, in Figure 3(b), we show the second step of instantiation for the users $U_{\langle 0,0 \rangle}$ – $U_{\langle 0,3 \rangle}$, who are in the first row of the square grid protocol in Figure 1. For example, in this instantiation, user $U_{\langle 0,0 \rangle}$ is given the secrets, $K_{[0,0]}$, $K_{[0,0]-[0,1]}$ and $K_{[0,0]-[0,3]}$. The number of secrets a user receives in the logical key hierarchy is $\log n$. Hence, the total number of secrets that the user needs to store in our revocation algorithm is still $O(\sqrt{n})$.

5 Evaluation

We consider two scenarios of revocation. In the first scenario (cf. Section 5.1), there is an underlying support for routing e.g., from [10,11], and hence, a user can send messages to any other user. In the second scenario (cf. Section 5.2), we consider the case where the users can only send messages to their neighbors. In the former case, the group controller can use the routing support to transmit the group key to the initial set of users. In the latter case, to transmit the group key, the group controller can use the multicast tree (e.g., built using a protocol such as described in [12]), if such a tree is available. Otherwise, the group controller broadcasts the encrypted group key. Although all the users may receive this message, only the subset of users who know the appropriate shared secret, with which the group key is encrypted, can obtain the group key.

5.1 Group Key Distribution with Routing Support

We consider two cases of revocation for the scenario when users are able to communicate with any other user in the network with the help of underlying routing layer. In the first case, the revoked users are located in $r < \sqrt{n}$ rows and in the second case, the revoked users are located in $r = \sqrt{n}$ rows. Also, we consider a special case of revocation when the square grid is only partially full, i.e., some locations in the grid are not assigned to any user.

Case 1. Since the number of rows containing revoked users is $< \sqrt{n}$, there will be at least one row in the square grid which does not contain any revoked users. To distribute the group key, we observe that, if users along a row in the square grid know the group key, they can send the group key to other users in their columns using the direct secrets. Since the direct secrets are unique for any given pair of users, this technique guarantees deterministic security. The group controller selects a row(s) of users not containing revoked users and uses the shared secret of this row(s) to transmit the group key. Specifically, the group controller uses the shared secrets from the logical key hierarchy shown in Figure 3(a).

As an illustration, we consider revocation of the users, $U_{\langle 0,0 \rangle}$, $U_{\langle 1,1 \rangle}$, and $U_{\langle 2,2 \rangle}$, from the square grid shown in Figure 1. Now, to transmit the group key, the group controller selects a row of users, in this example $U_{\langle 3,0 \rangle}$-$U_{\langle 3,3 \rangle}$, which does not contain any revoked users and uses the corresponding shared secret, $K_{[3,0]-[3,3]}$ (cf. Figure 3(a)). Once these users receive the group key, they use the direct secrets along their respective columns in the square grid to send it to other non-revoked users. For example, to send the group key, user $U_{\langle 3,0\rangle}$ uses the direct secret between itself and user $U_{\langle 2,0\rangle}$. Similarly, users $U_{\langle 3,1\rangle}$-$U_{\langle 3,3\rangle}$, send it to users in their columns.

To reduce the work done by each user for sending the group key, we use a divide and conquer approach. When a user U_i receives the group key from the group controller, it partitions the users in its column into two parts and sends the group key, along with the partition information, to a user U_j. Now, U_i is responsible for sending the group key to the first part. And, U_j is responsible for sending the group key to the second part. Continuing divide and conquer in this manner, it suffices for a user to send at most $\log n$ messages. Note that, in this approach, some users may receive multiple copies of the group key, but the number of messages sent by each user is bounded by $\log n$. Furthermore, the group controller includes an authentication message (cf. Section 5.3) which is used by the users in the network to verify the authenticity of the group key they receive from other users.

Theorem 2. *The above revocation process guarantees deterministic security if the revoked users are located in at most $r < \sqrt{n}$ rows.* □

Case 2. When every row contains at least one revoked user, the group controller cannot use any shared secrets associated with the rows (cf. Figure 3(a)). For this case, the group controller sends the new group key to the users in a selected row using a shared secret from the logical key hierarchy of that row (cf. Figure 3(b)). Towards this, the group controller locates a shared secret that is known to a maximum number of non-revoked users from the same row. The group controller uses this secret to send the group key to these users. As an illustration, we consider the revocation of users, $U_{\langle 0,0\rangle}, U_{\langle 1,1\rangle}, U_{\langle 2,2\rangle}$ and $U_{\langle 3,3\rangle}$, from the network.

In this example, the group controller selects the shared secret $K_{[0,2]-[0,3]}$ from the logical key hierarchy associated with the row of users $U_{\langle 0,0\rangle} - U_{\langle 0,3\rangle}$. The group controller sends the group key to $U_{\langle 0,2\rangle}$ and $U_{\langle 0,3\rangle}$ using this shared secret. Now, these users use the direct secrets along their row and columns to send the group key to the other non-revoked users. In the worst case scenario of revocation, where users from a single row are not able to cover the entire group, the group controller sends the group key to users in different rows.

To evaluate the effectiveness of our group key distribution, we have conducted experiments on the revocation of 50, 100 and 880 users from a group of size 1024 users arranged in a 32x32 grid. The results are as shown in Figure 4(a). We note that, when the number of revoked users is less than 85% of the group size, the group controller only needs to send the group key to a single non-revoked user to achieve 100% group key distribution. In the extreme case of revocation, say for 880 users, the group controller needs to send the group key to a small number of users from different rows, to achieve complete group key distribution.

Special Case. We consider a special case of revocation in the grids that are only partially filled with users, i.e., some grid locations are empty. This case occurs when a higher grid size, greater than the initial set of users, is chosen for accommodating new users who may join the network at a later stage. We have

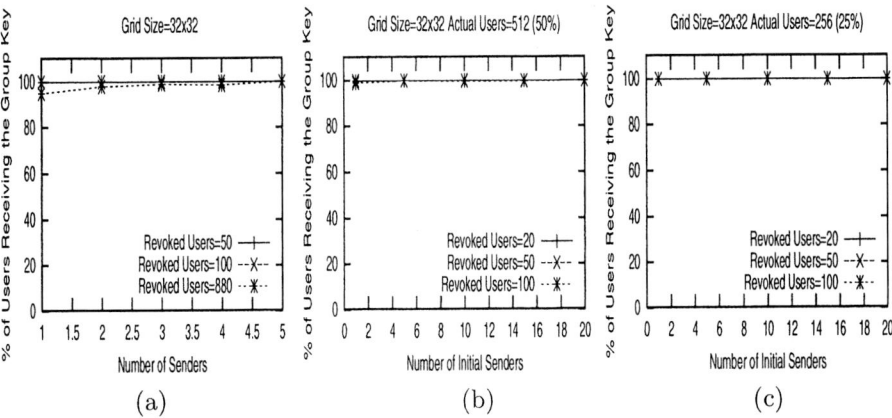

Fig. 4. Group Key Recovery with Routing Support for Grids 100, 50 and 25% full

considered the grids that are 25 and 50% filled and, simulated the revocation of 20, 50 and 100 users. We show the results of our experiments in Figures 4(b)-(c). We note that, even for such grids, the group key recovery is 100%.

5.2 Local Group Key Distribution

In this section, we consider group key distribution when a user is limited to sending messages to only users in its neighborhood. We use the term *neighborhood* to denote users within a certain hop distance, typically, $1 - 3$ hops from a user. A user can learn about these nodes by querying its immediate neighbors for a list of their neighbors. Thus, the number of nodes in the neighborhood depends upon the network density and the number of hops.

Now, depending on the information available with the group controller, we consider two cases. In the first case, the group controller has no knowledge about the neighborhood relations of the users, i.e., the group controller does not know which users are in the neighborhood of a user. In the second case, the group controller knows which users are in the neighborhood of a user.

Case 1. To send the group key, initially, the group controller randomly selects a set of non-revoked users. The number of these selected users is based on the average neighborhood size of the users. Once the selected users receive the group key, they transmit the group key to users in their neighborhood with whom they share direct or grid secrets from the secret instantiation protocol.

To illustrate our technique, we have considered revocation of 20, 50, and 100 users from a group of 1024 users arranged in a 32x32 square grid. We note that, to revoke 20 users, the group controller can use the technique we described in Section 5.1 as the revoked users are along < 32 rows. However, complete group key distribution may not be guaranteed due to the limited communication capabilities of the users. We show the results of our experiments for different neighborhood sizes in Figures 5(a)-(c). When the neighborhood of users is around $5 - 10$ users, for a sparse network, the number of users recovering the group key

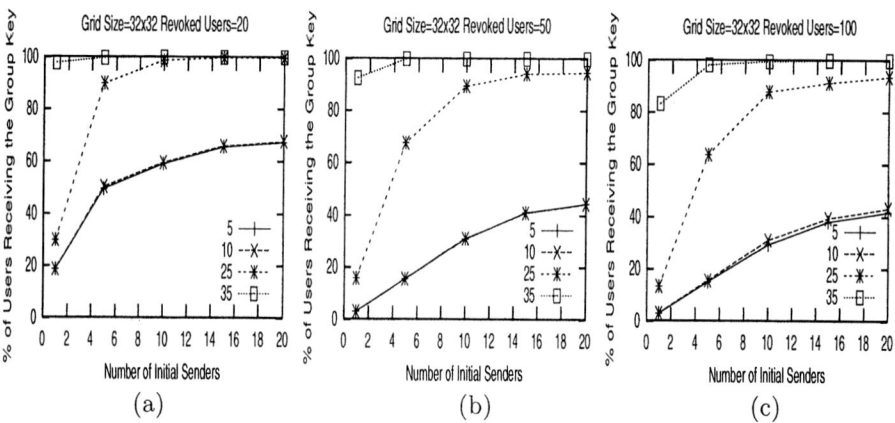

Fig. 5. Group Key Recovery with Only Local Transmissions

is only around 3 − 60%. When the neighborhood size is around 25 − 35 users, the group key recovery is 100%, depending on the number of revoked users and the number of initial senders contacted (cf. Figure 5(a)-(c)). Thus, to obtain 100% distribution of group key, the neighborhood size should be 25 − 35 users. This can be achieved by contacting neighbors within a certain hop distance until the number of nodes in this neighborhood increases to the desired value. Also, note that a user only contacts a subset of the users in this neighborhood; it only has to contact nodes with whom it can communicate securely in spite of possible collusion among the revoked users.

Case 2. When the group controller has information about the neighborhood of users, to send the group key, the group controller chooses the initial set of users in such a way that the users they can reach is non-overlapping. Towards this, first, the group controller selects a non-revoked user and computes all the users who are covered by this user and, its neighbors. Now, to select the next sender, the group controller selects a non-revoked user who is not in the set covered by the previous sender and its neighborhood. Further, the group controller repeats this process until the entire group is covered and then, transmits the group key to the set of the selected users.

As in Case 1, we have considered the revocation of 20, 50, and 100 users from the same network topology consisting of 1024 users arranged in the 32x32 grid. From the results in Figure 6, we observe that, for a neighborhood size of 25 users, the group controller achieves 100% group key recovery by contacting only a small set of initial senders.

5.3 Authentication

Note that, based on the properties of the square grid and the logical key hierarchy protocols, our revocation algorithm ensures confidentiality. We have not addressed the issue of authentication in specific detail as there are several approaches [13,8] to achieve authentication. Depending on the application requirements, the group controller selects the appropriate authentication protocol.

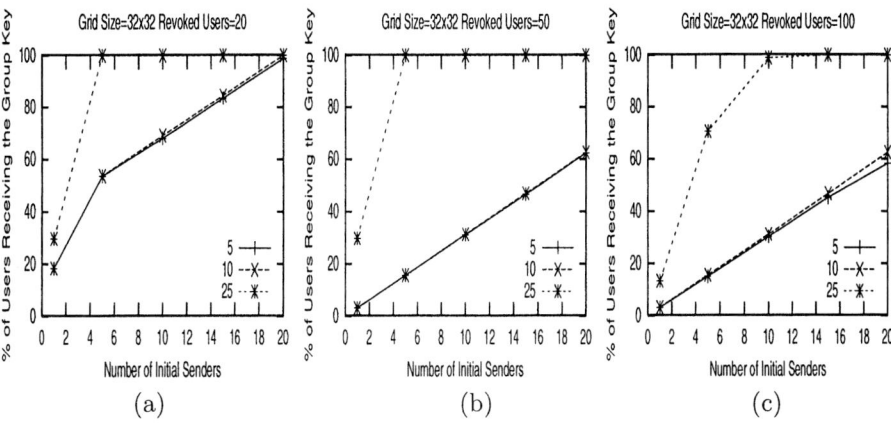

Fig. 6. Group Key Recovery in Local Transmissions with Neighborhood Information

6 Related Work

Approaches for distributing group keys in secure groups are described in [4,5,6,7]. These approaches, however, cannot be applied directly to adhoc networks as they are intended for a wired network model. Furthermore, these approaches are stateful, in that, they require the users to receive specific key updates in order to recover the group key. However, such a requirement cannot be easily satisfied in adhoc networks where the network links are unreliable and there are no guarantees of message delivery. To the best of our knowledge, the only work that considered revocation in adhoc networks is the GKMPAN protocol described in [8].

In GKMPAN, group key distribution is done by using the shared keys from the random key distribution protocol described in [1]. As the random key distribution protocol provides probabilistic guarantees of security, the group key distribution in GKMPAN is probabilistic in nature. In the random key distribution protocol [1], the users are given a random set of keys from a common key pool. The users establish session keys with their neighbors using the shared keys they have in common. These session keys are used to communicate securely between a pair of users. However, the shared keys used to establish the session keys may not be unique to a pair of users. Hence, in GKMPAN, the security of the group key distribution among the users is probabilistic. In contrast, in our revocation algorithm, we have shown that it is possible to provide deterministic guarantees.

7 Conclusion

In this paper, we described a revocation algorithm that combined the secret instantiation [1, 2, 3, 9] and group key management protocols [4, 5, 6, 7]. In our algorithm, the security of the revocation depends on the combination of the protocols used.

We illustrated an instance of our revocation algorithm by combining the square grid protocol [3] and the logical key hierarchy [6] protocol. Furthermore, we considered two scenarios of group key distribution. In the first scenario, routing support exists in the network and the user can send messages to any other user in the network. In the second scenario, no routing support exists and a user can transmit to only users in its neighborhood. Using simulation results, we showed that, it is possible to achieve complete group key distribution in both scenarios. Currently, we are evaluating the group key distribution in other instances where different secret instantiation protocols [1, 9] and different group key management protocols [5, 7] are used.

References

1. Laurent Eschenauer and Virgil D. Gligor. A key-management scheme for distributed sensor networks. In *ACM CCS*, pages 41–47, 2002.
2. Li Gong and David J. Wheeler. A matrix key-distribution scheme. *Journal of Cryptology*, 2(1):51–59, 1990.
3. Sandeep S. Kulkarni, Mohamed G. Gouda, and Anish Arora. Security instantiation in ad-hoc networks. *Special Issue of Elsevier Journal of Computer Communications on Dependable Wireless Sensor Networks*, 2005.
4. Debby M. Wallner, Eric J. Harder, and Ryan C. Agee. Key management for multicast: Issues and architectures. RFC 2627.
5. Isabella Chang, Robert Engel, Dilip Kandlur, Dimitrios Pendarakis, and Debanjan Saha. Key management for secure internet multicast using boolean function minimization techniques. In *Proceedings IEEE Infocomm*, pages 689–698, 1999.
6. Chung Kei Wong, Mohamed Gouda, and Simon S. Lam. Secure group communications using key graphs. *IEEE/ACM Transactions on Networking*, 2000.
7. Sandeep S. Kulkarni and Bezawada Bruhadeshwar. Rekeying and storage cost for multiple user revocation. In *12th Annual Network and Distributed System Security Symposium*, pages 45–54, San Diego, California, February 2005.
8. Sencun Zhu, Sanjeev Setia, Shouhuai Xu, and Sushil Jajodia. Gkmpan: An efficient group rekeying scheme for secure multicast in ad-hoc networks. In *MobiQuitous*, pages 42–51. IEEE Computer Society, 2004.
9. Donggang Liu and Peng Ning. Establishing pairwise keys in distributed sensor networks. In *Proceedings of the 10th ACM CCS , Washington, DC, USA*, 2003.
10. David B. Johnson and David A. Maltz. Dynamic source routing in ad hoc wireless networks. *Mobile Computing*, 5:153–181, 1996.
11. G. Chakrabarti and S. Kulkarni. Load balancing and resource reservation in ad-hoc networks. *Ad-Hoc Networks*, 2004. To Appear.
12. Elizabeth M. Belding-Royer and Charles E. Perkins. Multicast operation of the ad-hoc on-demand distance vector routing protocol. In *MOBICOM*, 1999.
13. Adrian Perrig, Ran Canetti, J. D. Tygar, and Dawn Xiaodong Song. Efficient authentication and signing of multicast streams over lossy channels. In *IEEE Symposium on Security and Privacy*, pages 56–73, 2000.

A Hybrid Method to Intrusion Detection Systems Using HMM

C.V. Raman and Atul Negi

University of Hyderabad, Gachibowli, Hyderabad, India
chvenkataraman@gmail.com
atulcs@uohyd.ernet.in

Abstract. IDS use different sources of observation data and a variety of techniques to differentiate between benign and malicious behaviors. In the current work, Hidden Markov Models (HMM) are used in a manner analogous to their use in text categorization. The proposed approach performs host-based intrusion detection by using HMM along with STIDE methodology (enumeration of subsequences) in a hybrid fashion. The proposed method differs from STIDE in that only one profile is created for the normal behavior of all applications using short sequences of system calls issued by the normal runs of the programs. Subsequent to this, HMM with simple states along with STIDE is used to categorize an unknown program's sequence of system calls to be either normal or an intrusion. The results on 1998 DARPA data show that the hybrid method results in low false positive rate with high detection rate.

1 Introduction

Anomaly Intrusion Detection methods make use of profiling normal behavior of programs which are found to be stable and consistent during program's normal activities [1]. Forrest et al [1] have found that short sequences of system call traces produced by the execution of the programs are a good discriminator between the normal and abnormal operating characteristics of programs. There are various ways in which these short sequences of system call traces could be used to construct a "normal" profile and test for deviations.

Short sequences of system call traces follow temporal ordering, so Markovian methods like the Hidden Markov Model (HMM) can be used to model the normal behavior. An IDS based on HMM for modelling and evaluating invisible events based on system calls was designed by Warrender et al [2] and later on developed by Qiao et al [3], Hui et al [4], Cho et al [5]and Hoang et al [6].

Sequence of system calls can also be modelled using the text processing metaphor, treating each system call as a 'word 'and the whole sequence as a 'document 'and then applying text categorization techniques to differentiate between the normal and abnormal behaviors. This method allows one to bypass the need to build separate databases and learn individual program profiles. For example, Vemuri et al [8] and Pradeep et al [9] have used the k-Nearest Neighbor method as the text categorization technique on the DARPA Data set and established its effectiveness.

In the current work, we propose a hybrid approach to Host-based Anomaly Intrusion Detection based upon STIDE and HMM concepts, using short sequences of system calls of the process as the characterizing feature between the benign and malicious behaviors. The main disadvantage with HMM is the high training time and need for large amount of computational resources. We use the HMM with simple states [12], which requires reduced training time and resources. In Section 2, we describe the proposed hybrid method of using HMM along with STIDE. Section 3 presents the experimental setup and Results. We conclude our work in section 4.

2 Description of Methodology

2.1 STIDE and HMM in IDS

STIDE. Forrest et al [10] in 1998 proposed a method called Sequence Time Delay Embedding (STIDE) in which the profile of normal behavior of system calls is built. STIDE gives very good results with low False Positive Rates and high Detection Rates, but the problem is in knowing and fixing the suitable window length (fixed at 6 empirically for their data set). t-STIDE, is an extension to the STIDE method [2] where the rare sequences are considered anomalous. This may increase the false positive rates. Authors in this paper compared STIDE, t-STIDE, HMM and RIPPER methods and concluded that HMM is giving best accuracy on average among the compared methods, but has a higher computational cost.

Maxion et al [11] compared Markov Models with STIDE methodology and proved that STIDE has blind regions i.e. it can not detect some attacks even in their presence. They state that the Minimum Foreign Sequence present in one of the intrusion trace of UNM datasets is six and hence the window of length '6' gave good results for STIDE. They have also shown that Markov Models get rid of the problem of suitable window size.

HMM. As the short sequence of system calls follow a temporal ordering, the Hidden Markov Models (HMM) are best suited to build the normal behavior of programs. Warrender et al [2] used HMM in anomaly intrusion detection by modelling the number of states of HMM to be roughly corresponding to the number of unique system calls used by their programs. They tested each system call, by finding unusual state transitions and/or symbol outputs depending upon predefined thresholds. Our work is different from other works like those of Qiao et al [3], Hui et al [4], Hoang et al [6] who have also used HMM for anomaly detection with the number of unique system calls as the number of states. They test a new sequence for anomaly based on its probability of occurrence from the trained HMM and then check with threshold limits. They all take the number of states of HMM as the number of unique system calls following Warrender et al [2]. Cho et al [5] work is also on the similar principle, but uses 5-15 states with sequence lengths ranging from 20-30. In our opinion none of these methods represent the semantics of HMM faithfully and have not utilized the capability of HMM completely.

2.2 Improved Semantics for HMM in IDS

In our opinion the true way to model HMM behavior is by making the states as hidden and producing only the visible observation symbols outside. We can achieve this functionality of HMM as making the system calls as observation symbols. So one must decide on the number of states of HMM before applying HMM to IDS.

The best way to fix the number of states of HMM is to make them equal to the length of the sliding window used to prepare normal sub sequences. This follows the semantics of HMM more faithfully by keeping the states as hidden and making the system calls as observation symbols. This approach follows the semantics used in speech processing etc., application areas.

So, the important thing to know is how to fix the best window length and consequently the number of states of HMM. As the minimum sliding window length is '2', we use a 2-state HMM for intrusion detection and use system calls as observation symbols. The trained HMM as we have described above classifies the subsequences for normal and abnormal behavior very well [12], but with some exceptions because of the doubly embedded stochastic process. This is due to a situation as described in the following.

Let a, b represent system calls, consider the subsequence of length '2' as $\langle a, b \rangle$ where individually a, b have appeared many times in the normal trace. However, the subsequence $\langle a, b \rangle$ has not occurred even once in the normal training data base. That is they have never *co-occurred*. In such a case, the normal trained HMM gives a very high likelihood probability. To take care of such situations we propose the Hybrid Algorithm as described below.

2.3 Proposed Hybrid Algorithm

Here we apply the positive features of STIDE and HMM to improve intrusion detection. While HMM learns the normal behavior of short subsequences, the text categorization approach gives us the freedom from having to maintain separately the normal profiles of each individual applications.

The current implementation uses HMM with two states as described in the previous section. The proposed algorithm tests the new execution sub sequences for anomalies and exits either on finding an intrusion or on completion. The algorithm is as follows:

1. Initialize anomaly_count = 0
2. Initialize the A and B matrices of HMM, λ with the unique normal sub sequences.
3. Train the HMM, λ with all the sub sequences of normal data.
4. Propose the k least likelihood probabilities of normal sequences from HMM, λ as the suitable candidates of probability thresholds.
5. Fix the Probability threshold, P_{th} from one of the proposed thresholds to check for anomaly.
6. Fix the Count threshold, $Count_{th}$ value to test for intrusion.
7. Fix the Rare threshold, $Rare_{th}$ value to test for rare sequences.
8. **For** each sub sequence, ss prepared from test sequence
9. **do**
10.   **IF** ss is not present in the normal sub sequences
11.   **Then**
12.   Increment anomaly_count by 1
13.   **Else**
14.   Find the frequency $Freq$ of ss.

15.   **If** $Freq < Rare_{th}$
16.   **Then**
17.   Find the probability P of the sub sequence ss from the HMM, λ
18.   **If** $P < P_{th}$
19.   **Then**
20.   Increment anomaly_count by 1
21.   **End if**
22.   **End if**
23. **End if**
24. **If** $anomaly\_count > Count_{th}$
25. **Then**
26.   Abort the process as `Intrusion`.
27. **End if.**
28. **End for.**

Step 4. above gives us k possible probability threshold limits. One of them is chosen as a probability threshold limit for intrusions. This method is a novel means for selection of the best possible candidates for a threshold, [12] unlike the previous methods which do not suggest any values for the probability thresholds.

Three sensitive parameters are required for proper operation of the above method. First is rare threshold ($Rare_{th}$), used for rare sub sequences (tests for anomalies with HMM). The second is a probability threshold (P_{th}), to differentiate normal and abnormal behavior with HMM. Third is a count threshold ($Count_{th}$), to differentiate anomalies from intrusions.

The algorithm takes the sub sequences of the new execution trace and checks for its presence in the normal sub sequences database just like as tested in STIDE method. If the test sub sequence is not found then anomaly_count is incremented else its frequency of occurrence in the normal database is computed and checked for rare sub sequence with rare threshold ($Rare_{th}$) as followed in t-STIDE method. If the test sub sequence is a rare sub sequence then it is checked for anomaly using HMM. The likelihood probability of the test sub sequence is found using the normally trained HMM, and tested with prefixed probability threshold P_{th}, to find anomaly. If anomaly is found, then anomlay_count is incremented. If the anomaly_count exceeds the Count threshold $Count_{th}$ at any point of execution, then the execution sequence is labelled as intrusion and the process is aborted. The variation in count-threshold ($Count_{th}$) values helps in detecting true intrusions instead of considering anomalies as intrusions which otherwise increases the false positive rate (FPR).

3 Experimental Setup and Results

In this section we present the details of results on 1998 DARPA data set, and the achieved false positive rate and detection rate.

Data sets. To evaluate the proposed hybrid method, 1998 DARPA data set is used. We compare the proposed method with those of Vemuri et al [8] and Pradeep et al [9]. We use the data set used in their schemes: (from *www.ll.mit.edu/IST/ideval/data/*).

This has 605 unique processes as training data set and uses 5285 normal processes for testing. It has 55 intrusive sessions as test data to find the efficiency of the methods. The complete description of 55 attacks is available on [8, 9].

From the 55 attacks they have used, we remove three and consider only 52 attacks. The removed attacks are *2.2_ it_ ipsweep* (port sweep), *test.1.5_ processtable* (Denial of Service) as both these attacks provide the same sequence of system calls as that of normal one and are network based attacks, detected easily by an NIDS. The attack *4.4_ it_080514warezclient_test* is a duplicate attack, same as *4.4_ it_080514warezclient* and is used to test the performance of Misuse Detection methodology and hence is removed from the testing data.

The normal data base used for our algorithm is as follows: (1) The number of sub sequences of length '2': 169494. (2) The unique number of sub sequences of length '2': 320. (3) The number of system calls : 50.

3.1 Results

We have considered twenty list of possible threshold limits. The following table describes the affect of FPR and DR with variation of count threshold ($Count_{th}$), probability threshold (P_{th}) and rare threshold ($Rare_{th}$).

The following Table-1 describes the threshold values at which the attacks are detected as intrusions with Rare threshold ($Rare_{th}$) value at 0.00005. Here we provided results for some thresholds until we get 100% DR and 0% FPR. The table indicates clearly that the count threshold $Count_{th}$ also plays a major role in DR and FPR. This is supporting the fact that "all the anomalous events may not be intrusions". The 15th probability threshold ($P_{index} = 15$) has given better results than all with FPR of 2.91% at 100% Detection Rate.

Table 1. Results of DARPA Data sets with hybrid-HMM with $Rare_{th}$=0.00005

P_{index}	P_{th}	$Count_{th}$	Detection of Attacks	DR	FPR
1	-5.442993	1	49	94	0.4
		2	44	85	0.11
		3	38	73	0.076
		4	34	65	0.038
		5	26	50	0.019
		6	25	48	0.019
		7	18	35	0
..	...	..	..	..	..
15	-4.756277	1	52	100	4.6
		2	52	100	2.91
		3	51	98	0.076
		4	50	96	0.038
		5	50	96	0.019
		6	47	90	0.019
		7	45	86	0

We have done the same experimentation with $Rare_{th}$ value at 0.0005 (Table 2). The best result is found at 8th probability threshold ($P_{index} = 8$) with the count threshold value being 3 ($Count_{th} = 3$).

Table 2. Results of DARPA Data sets with hybrid-HMM with $Rare_{th}$=0.0005

P_{index}	P_{th}	$Count_{th}$	Detection of Attacks	DR	FPR
1	-5.442993	1	49	94	0.4
..	...	..	..	..	..
8	-5.090818	1	52	100	7.1
		2	52	100	2.6
		3	52	100	0.68
		4	51	98	0.17
		5	49	94	0.13
		6	44	85	0.13
		7	35	67	0.09
		8	33	63	0.09
		9	24	46	0

Receiver Operating Characteristics Curve (ROC). The ROC curve is a plot of intrusion Detection Rate (DR) against the False Positives Rate (FPR). False Positive Rate is defined as percentage of false positives that means, the number of normal processes detected as abnormal divided by the total number of normal processes. In intrusion detection, the Receiver Operating Characteristics (ROC) curve is usually used to measure the performance of the method. For testing purposes, we have considered all the available normal data as test data. ROC curve gives an idea of the trade off between FPR and DR achieved by a classifier. An ideal ROC curve would coincide with the DR axis. The ROC curve for the current proposed algorithm is as follows:

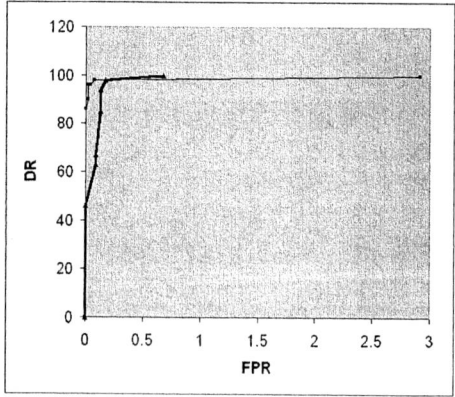

Fig. 1. ROC curve of the hybrid-HMM algorithm Thin line : Result with $Rare_{th} = 0.00005$ & Thick line: Result with $Rare_{th} = 0.0005$

In the ROC curve (Figure 1), note that with rare threshold value at 0.00005 ($Rare_{th}$ = 0.00005), the FPR is zero upto a DR value of 86%. At a DR of 100% the FPR is 2.91%. Whereas when the rare threshold value is increased to 0.0005 ($Rare_{th}$ = 0.0005), 100% DR is achieved at a lower FPR of 0.68% but the FPR is zero up to a DR of 46% only.

We have compared the performance of proposed method with k-NN using S^3 metric by Pradeep et al [9] which has used k-NN method with Sequence and Set Preserving Metric as it is giving best performance among the k-NN methods to DARPA Data set. The following Table-3 describes the FPR and DR of both methods. From the table it is evident that the proposed method has achieved 46% DR at 0% FPR which is far better than the k-NN method with SSS metric which has achieved only 27% DR at 0% FPR. The current proposed method is also outperforming in achieving 100% DR at 0.68% FPR, while k-NN method achieves 100% DR at 0.83% FPR. So the proposed hybrid method using HMM and STIDE is seen to be better than the existing methods for this data set.

Table 3. Comparison between k-NN and hybrid-HMM

k-NN with SSS		hybrid-HMM	
FPR	DR	FPR	DR
0	27	0	46
0.0189	36	0.09	63
0.0946	76	0.09	67
0.189	89	0.13	85
0.245	93	0.13	94
0.4162	93	0.17	98
0.491	95	0.68	100
0.756	95		
0.8325	95		
0.8325	100		

k-NN : k-Nearest Neighbor
SSS : Sequence and Set Similarity metric

4 Concluding Remarks

In this paper, we have proposed a hybrid algorithm using both the positive features of HMM, STIDE and applying them in text categorization scenario to Intrusion Detection field. The proposed method works independent of the length of the intrusion trace and also of the length of the window size. We have considered a window size of '2'as it is the minimum possible window size.

The proposed approach detects Network based attacks only at high false positive rates as the processes in those attack scenarios behave similar to the normal behavior. So it is advised to use NIDS to detect Network based attacks. The current method is also unable to detect TOCTTOU (Time Of Check To Time Of Use) attacks and mimicry attacks as they also behave similar to normal processes in system call invocations.

References

1. Hofmeyr, S.A. Forrest, S. and Somayaji, A. Intrusion detection using sequences of system calls. In *Journal of Computer Security*, Vol. 6, pages 151–180, 1998.
2. Forrest, S., Warrender,C., and Pearlmutter, B. Detecting intrusions using system calls : Alternative data models. In *IEEE Symposium on Security and Privacy*, pages 133–145, 1999.
3. Bin, Y., Qiao, Y., Xin, X.W., and Ge, S. Anomaly intrusion detection method based on HMM. In *IEEE Electronic letters Online No : 20020467*, volume 38, pages 663–664, 2002.
4. Hui-Ye Ma Bo Gao and Yu-Hang Yang. HMMs based on anomaly intrusion detection method. In *Proceedings of First International Conference on Machine Learning and Cybernetics*, Volume 1, pages 381–385, 2002.
5. Sung Bae Cho and Hyuk Jang Park. Efficient anomaly detection by modelling privilege flows using HMM. In *Computers & Security*, Vol. 22, pages 45–55, 2003.
6. Hu, J., Hoang, X.D., and Bertok, P. A multi layer model for anomaly intrusion detection using program sequences of system calls. In *IEEE International Conference on Networks*, 2003.
7. Rabiner L R. A tutorial on hidden Markov models and selected applications in speech recognition. In *Proceedings of the IEEE*, Vol. 77, pages 257-286, 1989.
8. Liao, Yihua, and Vemuri, V. Rao, Use of k-nearest neighbor classifier for intrusion detection. In *Networks and Security*, Vol. 21, pages 438–448, 2002.
9. Radha Krishna, P., Raju, S. Bapi, Arijit Laha, Pradeep Kumar, M. Venkateswara Rao. Intrusion detection system using sequence and set preserving metric. In *IEEE International Conference on Intelligence and Security Informatics, ISI*, pages 498–504, 2005.
10. Hofmeyr, Steven A., Forrest, S, and Somayaji, A. Intrusion detection using sequences of system calls. In *Journal of Computer Security*, Vol. 6, pages 151–180, 1998.
11. Tan, K.M.C., and Maxion, R A. Why 6? defining the operational limits of STIDE, an anomaly based intrusion detector. In *Proceeding of the 2002 IEEE Symposium on Security and Privacy*, pages 188, 2002.
12. Raman, C.V., Project work "Intrusion Detection using HMM with improved semantics"submitted to *University of Hyderabad*, Hyderabad, June, 2005.

Enhanced Network Traffic Anomaly Detector

Suresh Reddy and Sukumar Nandi

Department of Computer Science and Engineering,
Indian Institute of Technology, Guwahati 780139, India

Abstract. Network intrusion detection systems often rely on matching patterns that are learned from known attacks. While this method is reliable and rarely produces false alarms, it has the disadvantage that it cannot detect novel attacks. An alternative approach is to learn a model of normal traffic and report deviations, but these anomaly models are typically restricted to modeling IP addresses and ports. We describe an anomaly detection system which models all the fields of network, transport layer and payload of a packet at the byte level, by giving more weight to the most anomalous attributes. We investigated all the attributes and assigned weights to the attributes based on their anomalous behavior. We detect 144 of 185 attacks in the DARPA off-line intrusion detection evaluation data set [1] at 10 false alarms per day (total 100 false alarms), after training on one week of attack-free traffic. We investigate the performance of the system when attack free training data is not available.

1 Introduction

One important facet of computer security is intrusion detection - simply knowing whether a system has been compromised or an attack has been attempted. IDS's are classified as Network IDS or host based IDS depending on the source of data it monitors. IDS's can also be classified as signature based or anomaly based, depending on the detection strategy it uses. A *signature* detector examines traffic for known attacks using rules written by security experts, where as an *anomaly* detector examines traffic for deviation from the normal traffic.

In this paper, we focus on network anomaly detection. Most network anomaly systems such as ADAM [2], NIDES [3], and SPADE [4] monitor only the attributes like IP addresses, ports, and TCP state. This catches user misbehavior, but miss attacks on public servers or the TCP/IP stack that might otherwise be detected because of anomalies in other parts of the protocol. PHAD [5], NETAD [6] monitors all fields of the packet header without any preconceptions about which fields might be useful. Our system also monitors all fields of network, transport, and starting bytes of application layer, but gives more weight to the most anomalous attributes, which increases the detection rate for the same false alarm rate. We evaluate our system on the DARPA IDS evaluation data set [1] to investigate its performance.

2 Related Work

Early work in anomaly detection was host based. Forrest et.al [7] demonstrated that the system call sequences for processing attack packets deviate significantly from the normal pattern of system calls. Forrest detected these attacks by training an n-gram model (n=3 to 6) as the system ran normally.

Network intrusion detection is typically rule based. Systems like SNORT [9] and BRO [10] use hand written rules to detect signatures of known attacks. When a new type of attack is detected, new rules must be added to these systems. Anomaly detection systems such as SPADE [4], ADAM [2], and NIDES [3] learn a statistical model of normal network traffic, and flag deviations from this model. Models are usually based on the distribution of most anomalous attributes like addresses and ports per transaction. These systems use frequency-based models, in which the probability of an event is estimated by its average frequency during training.

The recent anomaly detection systems like PHAD [5], ALAD [11], LEARD [12], NETAD [6] monitor all fields of the packet header unlike SPADE, and ADAM (monitor only IP addresses and ports). These systems use time-based models, in which the probability of an event depends on the time since its last occurrence, in contrast to SPADE, and ADAM (use frequency-based models). NETAD also considers the frequency of events along with time-based model.

3 Proposed NIDS System

The proposed system detects anomalies in network packets at byte level. Similar to NETAD [6], it operates at two stages. In the first stage it filters out the uninteresting traffic, which is likely to generate false alarms. As most attacks are initiated against a target server, it is sufficient to examine only the first few packets of incoming server requests. Hence it filters out all non IP packets, the entire out going traffic, traffic related to the TCP connections initiated from internal network to outside the network, packets to high numbered ports, and packets not in the near start of TCP connection.

In the second stage our system models the most common protocols (IP, TCP, telnet, FTP, SMTP, HTTP) at the packet byte level, like NETAD , to flag events (byte values) that have not been observed for a long time. It models 48 attributes, consisting of the first 48 bytes of the packet starting with the IP header. If the packet is less than 48 bytes long, then the extra attributes are set to 0. However it defers from NETAD as follows:

1. anomaly score is modified to consider the frequency of novel events
2. weighted attribute model is used to evaluate the anomaly score of a packet.

3.1 Anomaly Score

Time based modeling of attributes was first used in PHAD. It assigns the score $t*n/r$ to anomalous attributes, where t is the time since the attribute was last anomalous (in training or testing), n is the number of training instances, and r is the number of allowed values (up to 256). NETAD made three improvements to the above anomaly score. First, n is set back to zero when an anomaly occurred during training. Second improvement is to decrease the weight of rules when r is near the maximum of 256. Third is that it considers the frequency of normal (not anomalous) events. Thus the NETAD anomaly score for an attribute is $t*n_a(1-r/256)/r + t_i/(f_i+r/256)$, where n_a is the number of training packets from the last anomaly to the end of the training period, t_i is the time (packet count in the modeled subset) since the value i (0-255) was last observed (in either training or testing), and f_i is the frequency in training, the number of times i was observed among training packets.

Though NETAD considers the frequency of normal events it ignores the frequency of anomalous events. If a value does not occur at least once during training period, it is treated as anomalous value. NETAD assigns maximum score, through first component $t*n_a(1-r/256)/r$, to all further occurrences of that value during testing period, ignoring its frequency. Our system considers the frequency of the anomalous values during testing period. We add another factor to the NETAD anomaly score, $T_i/(F_i+r/256)$, where T_i is the time(packet count) since the value $i(0-256)$ was last observed during testing, and F_i is the frequency in testing, the number of times i was observed among the packets occurred till that time from the beginning of testing period. This model assigns highest score for values that occur rarely (small F_i) and lowest score for values that occur frequently (large F_i). Thus it reduces the anomaly score for normal values that have not occurred at least once during training period, but occur frequently during testing period. Hence the possibility of generating false alarms is reduced. Thus the anomaly score S of an attribute is given by equation (1).

$$S = t*n_a(1-r/256)/r + t_i/(f_i+r/256) + T_i/(F_i+r/256). \qquad (1)$$

3.2 Weighted Attribute Model

Traditional anomaly systems like ADAM, (NIDES,) and SPADE monitor only the most anomalous attributes of the packet like IP addresses, ports, and TCP/IP flags. This misses the attacks that might otherwise be detected because of anomalies in other fields of the packet. PHAD and NETAD monitor all the fields of the packet at data link (PHAD only), network, transport, and part of application layer (NETAD only).

A criticism of PHAD and NETAD is that they do not have any preconceptions about which fields might be useful, and hence they give equal weight to all the attributes. This causes more false alarms to be generated because of uninteresting fields. To correct this we introduced weighted attribute model, in which we assign weights to the attributes based on their anomalous behavior. So that most anomalous attributes, like source IP address and TCP flags, get more weight and uninteresting attributes get less weight. We assign zero weight to the TTL field (simulation artifact). This reduces the false alarms score and increases the correct alarms score, so that more number of detections are possible at a given false alarm rate. Thus the anomaly score for a packet is given by equation (2), where W_j is the weight and S_j is the score of jth attribute.

$$\Sigma W_j * S_j. \tag{2}$$

4 Experimental Results

Our system examines only the inside network traffic logs of [1] because the inside data contains the evidence of attacks both from inside and outside the network, although we miss outside attacks against the router. Although there are 201 labeled attacks, the inside traffic is missing for one day (week 4, day 2) containing 12 attacks, leaving 189. There is also one unlabeled attack (*apache2*) and there are five external attacks (one *queso* and four *snmpget*) against the router which are not visible from inside the local network. This leaves 185 (189 + 1 − 5) detectable attacks, of which 68 were poorly detected in 1999.

We trained our system on week 3 (7 days of attack free traffic) of the inside tcpdump files, then tested the system on weeks 4 and 5 of the inside tcpdump files. We used the same evaluation criteria for our system as was used in the original evaluation. If there is more than one alarm identifying the same target within a 60 second period, then only the highest scoring alarm is evaluated and the others are discarded.

We zeroed out the TTL (time to live) field value, which we believe to be the simulation artifact. Although small TTL values might be used to elude an IDS by expiring the packet between the IDS and the target [13], this was not the case because the observed values were large, usually 126 or 253. Such artifacts are unfortunate, but probably inevitable, given the difficulty of simulating the Internet [14].

Table 1 shows that applying weighted attribute model to NETAD attributes, increases the detection rate for a given false alarm rate. The detection rate is not effective at 20 false alarms because majority of them are generated by the attributes with more weight. But the detection rate is very effective at 50-500 false alarms. This is because later the false alarms are generated by uninteresting attributes, whose weight is less in our model.

Table 1. Attacks detected at 20 to 5000 false alarms using weighted attribute model

Model	20	50	100	500	5000
NETAD: $\Sigma(tn_a/r + t_i/(f_i + r/256))$	66	97	132	148	152
Weighted attribute: $\Sigma W_j * (tn_a/r + t_i/(f_i + r/256))$	57	109	143	152	154

Table 2 shows the effects of change to the anomaly score function. It shows that the improvement, modeling frequency of anomalous events $(T_i/(F_i+r/256))$, to the anomaly score function of NETAD described in section 3.1, reduces the score of false alarms so that the detection rate is improved for a given false alarm

Table 2. Attacks detected at 20-5000 false alarms using various scoring functions

Scoring Function	20	50	100	500	5000
$\Sigma W_j * tn_a/r$	56	89	118	148	152
$\Sigma W_j * tn_a(1 - r/256)/r$	60	92	120	149	152
$\Sigma W_j * t_i/(f_i + 1)$	33	52	81	130	158
$\Sigma W_j * t_i/(f_i + r/256)$	78	115	127	142	156
$\Sigma W_j * t_i/(F_i + 1)$	82	91	96	124	154
$\Sigma W_j * t_i/(F_i + r/256)$	91	108	110	121	150

rate. It is clear from the table that the detection rate is improved at 20-100 false alarms, though it's unchanged beyond 500 false alarms.

To study the performance of our system in real network settings, we evaluated our system for two cases. In first case we assumed that the rate of attacks is low (compared to the volume of normal traffic) and ran our system in the training mode for all the three weeks. Second case is the more realistic case where attacks might occur at any point of time. For this we ran our system in the training mode during the attack period (weeks 4-5) with out using attack free data (week 3).

Table 3 shows the results for both the cases described above. If we run the system in training mode during attack period (weeks 4-5), then the anomalies present in the traffic will be added to the model and further instances of the same or similar attacks might be missed. There are 58 types of attacks present in the DARPA data set. If all the instances of these attacks have the identical signatures, then we should not expect to detect more than one instance of each. But our system can detect 110 instances (at 100 false alarms) when it is left in training mode for all three weeks, and 94 instances for the second and more realistic case, which indicates that there are subtle differences between instances of the same type.

Table 3. Number of attacks detected at 20 to 5000 false alarms when our system is left in training mode

	Week 3	Week 4-5	20	50	100	500	5000
Normal	Train	Test	59	115	144	152	154
Case 1	Train	Train	63	99	110	120	154
Case 2	Not used	Train	44	72	94	121	153

Table 4 lists the number of detections (at 100 false alarms) for each category of attack described by Kendall [15]. Our system performs well on probe, DOS, and R2L attacks. Like most other network intrusion detection systems, it performs poorly on U2R attacks. Detecting such attacks requires the IDS to interpret user commands, which might be entered locally or hidden by using a secure shell. Our system detects most of these attacks by anomalous source address. The category *poorly detected* includes the 74 (68 detectable) instances of attack types for which none of the original 18 evaluated systems in 1999 were able to detect more than half of the instances. Our system detects these at the same rate as other attacks, indicating that there is not a lot of overlap between the attacks detected by our system and by other techniques (signature, host based, etc.). This suggests that integrating our system with existing systems improves the overall detection rate.

Table 4. Attacks detected by category

Attack Category	Detected at 100 False Alarms
Probe	32/36 (89%)
Denial of Service (DOS)	50/63 (79%)
Remote to Local (R2L)	43/49 (88%)
User to Root (U2R)	18/33 (55%)
Data	1/4 (25%)
Total	144/185 (78%)
Poorly Detected in 1999	46/68 (68%)

Five of 58 attack types are not detected. *Httptunnel* is a back door which disguises its communication with the attacker as web client requests. Our system misses this because it does not monitor outgoing traffic or incoming client responses. *Selfping* and *ntfsdos* generate no traffic directly, but could theoretically be detected because they reboot the target, interrupting TCP connections. *Snmpget* is an external router attack, not visible on the inside sniffer. *Loadmodule* is U2R, thus hard to detect.

5 Conclusion

We described a network anomaly detection system that is unique in using weighted attributes to improve the detection rate for a given false alarm rate. We investigated all the attributes and assigned weights to the attributes so that most anomalous attributes got more weight and uninteresting attributes got less weight. This reduces the anomaly score of false alarms generated by uninteresting fields and improves the score of true positives. Hence the detection rate increases for a given false alarm rate.

Our system performs well on the DARPA IDS evaluation data set, detecting 78%of the total attacks. It detects those attacks that were poorly detected in the original evaluation at the rate 70%. None of the original systems detected more than half of the poorly detected attacks. This indicates, integrating our system with the systems participated in the original evaluation might improve the detection rate considerably.

We must note that DARPA's data is synthetic and therefore great care was taken to make the background traffic realistic. Furthermore, we have assumed that attack free traffic is available for training. This would not be true in a real environment. We have evaluated the system in training mode on the attack data (weeks 4,5) without using attack free data to train the system and found that there is a 35% decrease in the detection rate.

References

1. Lippmann, R., et al., "The 1999 DARPA Off-Line Intrusion Detection Evaluation", Computer Networks 34(4) 579-595, 2000.
2. Barbar, D., N. Wu, S. Jajodia, "Detecting Novel Network Intrusions using Bayes Estimators", First SIAM International Conference on Data Mining, 2001.
3. Anderson, D. et. al., "Detecting unusual program behavior using the statistical component of the Next-generation Intrusion Detection Expert System (NIDES)", Computer Science Laboratory SRI-CSL 95-06 May 1995.
4. SPADE, Silicon Defense, http://www.silicondefense.com/software/spice/.
5. Mahoney, M., P. K. Chan, "PHAD: Packet Header Anomaly Detection for Identifying Hostile Network Traffic", Florida Tech. technical report 2001-04.
6. M. Mahoney, "Network Traffic Anomaly Detection Based on Packet Bytes", Proc. ACM-SAC, 346-350, 2003.
7. Forrest, S., S. A. Hofmeyr, A. Somayaji, and T. A. Longstaff, "A Sense of Self for Unix Processes", Proc. of IEEE Symposium on Computer Security and Privacy, 1996.
8. L Zhuowei, A Das and S Nandi, "Utilizing Statistical Characteristics of N-grams for Intrusion Detection", International Conference on Cyberworlds, Singapore, December 2003.
9. Roesch, Martin, "Snort - Lightweight Intrusion Detection for Networks", Proc. USENIX Lisa '99, Seattle: Nov. 7-12, 1999.
10. Paxson, Vern, "Bro: A System for Detecting Network Intruders in Real-Time", Lawrence Berkeley National Laboratory Proc, 7'th USENIX Security Symposium, Jan. 26-29, 1998.
11. Mahoney, M., P. K. Chan, "Learning Models of Network Traffic for Detecting Novel Attacks", Florida Tech. technical report 2002-08.
12. Mahoney, M., P. K. Chan, "Learning Nonstationary Models of Normal Network Traffic for Detecting Novel Attacks ", Edmonton, Alberta: Proc. SIGKDD, 2002, 376-385.
13. Ptacek, Thomas H., and Timothy N. Newsham, "Insertion, Evasion, and Denial of Service: Eluding Network Intrusion Detection", January, 1998, ttp://www.robertgraham.com/mirror/Ptacek-Newsham-Evasion-98.html.
14. Floyd, S. and V. Paxson, "Difficulties in Simulating the Internet." IEEE/ACM Transactions on Networking Vol. 9, no. 4, pp. 392-403, Aug. 2001.
15. Kendall, Kristopher, "A Database of Computer Attacks for the Evaluation of Intrusion Detection Systems", Masters Thesis, MIT, 1999.

Statistically Secure Extension of Anti-collusion Code Fingerprinting

Jae-Min Seol and Seong-Whan Kim

Department of Computer Science, University of Seoul, Jeon-Nong-Dong, Seoul, Korea
`seoleda@hotmail.com`, `swkim7@uos.ac.kr`

Abstract. Fingerprinting schemes use digital watermarks to determine originators of unauthorized/pirated copies. Multiple users may collude and collectively escape identification by creating an average or median of their individually watermarked copies. We present a collusion-resilient code, which improves anti-collusion fingerprinting (AND-ACC) scheme using statistically secure matrix. Our approach improves the robustness for non-linear attacks, and can be scalable for large number of users. We experiment our approach using HVS based watermarking scheme, for standard test images, and the results show better collusion detection performance over average and median collusion attacks.

1 Introduction

A digital watermark or watermark is an invisible mark inserted in digital media, and fingerprinting uses digital watermark to determine originators of unauthorized/pirated copics. Multiple users may collude and collectively escape identification by creating an average or median of their individually watermarked copies. An early work on designing collusion-resistant binary fingerprint codes for generic data was based on marking assumption, which states that undetectable marks cannot be arbitrarily changed without rendering the object useless. However, multimedia data have very different characteristics from generic data, and we can use embed different marks or fingerprints in overall images, which biased strict marking assumption. Recently, an improvement was to merge the low level code (primitive code) with the direct sequence spread spectrum embedding for multimedia and extend the marking assumption to allow for random jamming [1]. W. Trappe et al. presented the design of collusion-resistant fingerprints using code modulation. They proposed a (k-1) collusion-resistant fingerprints scheme, and the (k-1) resilient AND-ACC (anti-collusion codes) is derived from (v, k, 1) balanced incomplete block designs (BIBD) [2]. The resulting (k-1) resilient AND-ACC code vectors are v-dimensional, and can represent $n = (v^2 - v) / (k^2 - k)$ users with these v basis vectors. However, the AND-ACC cannot identify large number of fingerprinting users.

We present a collusion-resilient code, which improves anti-collusion fingerprinting (AND-ACC) scheme using statistically secure matrix. We also present a scalable fingerprinting design scheme, which extends the collusion-resilient code for large number of user support. Instead of simply replicating codes, we designed a systematic approach to increase the number of fingerprint users. We evaluated our fingerprints on standard test images, and shows good collusion detection performance over average and median collusion attacks.

2 Related Works

An early work on designing collusion-resistant binary fingerprint codes was presented by Boneh and Shaw in 1995 [1], which primarily considered the problem of fingerprinting generic data that satisfy an underlying principle referred to as the marking assumption. Figure 1 illustrates a fingerprinting example for Log 5 value in logarithm table. As shown in Figure 1, a fingerprint consists of a collection of marks, each of which is modeled as a position in a digital value (denoted as boxes) and can take a finite number of states. A mark is considered detectable when a coalition of users does not have the same mark in that position. The marking assumption states that undetectable marks cannot be arbitrarily changed without rendering the object useless; however, it is considered possible for the colluding set to change a detectable mark to any state (collusion framework).

Correct value   0.6987000433601880478626110527551

Value for User A 0.6987000433601880478627110427541

Value for User B 0.6987000433601880478627110327531

Value for User C 0.6987000433601880478625110427531

Fig. 1. Fingerprint for log 5 in logarithm table

Min Wu presented the design of collusion-resistant fingerprints using code modulation [2]. The fingerprint signal wj for the j th user is constructed using a linear combination of a total of v orthogonal basis signals {ui} as (1)

$$w_j = \sum_{i=1}^{v} c_{ij} \mathbf{u}_i \qquad (1)$$

Here the coefficients $\{c_{ij}\}$, representing the fingerprint codes, are constructed by code vectors with $\{\pm 1\}$. Anti-collusion codes can be used with code modulation to construct a family of fingerprints with the ability to identify colluders. An anti-collusion code (ACC) is a family of code vectors for which the bits shared between code vectors uniquely identifies groups of colluding users. ACC codes have the property that the composition of any subset of K or fewer code vectors is unique. This property allows for the identification of up to K colluders. A K-resilient AND ACC is such a code where the composition is an element-wise AND operation. It has been shown that binary-valued AND-ACC can be constructed using balanced incomplete block designs (BIBD) [2]. The definition of (v, k, λ) BIBD code is a set of k-element subsets (blocks) of a v-element set χ, such that each pair of elements of χ occur together in exactly λ blocks. The (v, k, λ) BIBD has a total of n = $(v^2 - v)/(k^2 - k)$ blocks, and we can represent (v, k, λ) BIBD code using an v x n incidence matrix, where M(i, j) is set to 1 when the i th element belongs to the j th block, and set to 0 otherwise. The corresponding (k − 1)-resilient AND-ACC code vectors are assigned as the bit complements (finally represented using -1 and 1 for the 0 and 1, respectively) of the columns of the incidence matrix of a (v, k, 1) BIBD. The resulting (k-1) resilient AND-ACC code vectors are v-dimensional, and can represent n = $(v^2 - v) / (k^2 - k)$ users with these v basis vectors.

3 Design of Anti-collusion Code Using Statistically Secure Matrix

We embed the fingerprint codes over R selected regions as shown in Figure 2. Fingerprinting regions (blocks) are chosen based on the HVS (Human Visual System) characteristics and we used NVF (Noise Visibility Function) model [3]. Each user's fingerprint w_j, is embedded in the host image blocks using (2).as shown in Figure 2.

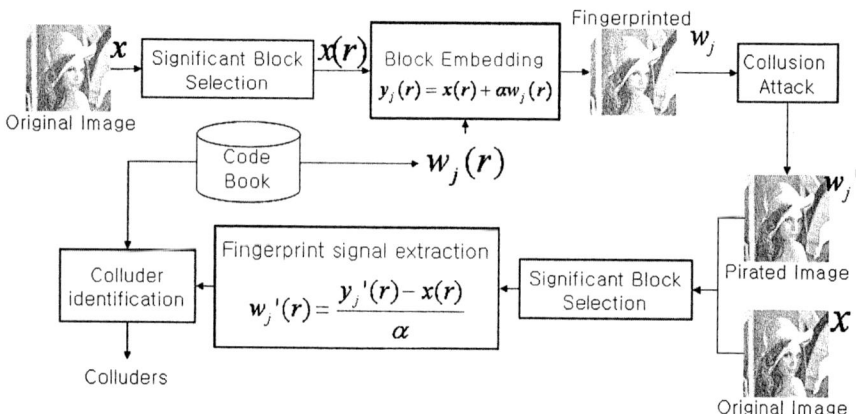

Fig. 2. Fingerprinting scheme: embedding and extraction of fingerprint w_j for user j

Each user's fingerprint f_l, is embedded in the host image blocks using the equation: $y_i = x + \alpha \cdot w_i$ .as shown in Figure 2. We design the statistically secure matrix which is modified version of C-matrix using random variable as (2) and (3). The coefficient of statistically secure matrix (s_{ij}) is sum of c_{ij} which is element of C matrix from Anti-collusion Code and $m_{ij}r$ (m_{ij} is coefficient from incident matrix form constructed from BIBD, and r is a random variable and it has a Gaussian distribution) The greater random variables increase, the more robustness increase against a median attack, but the detector will decode falsely. To achieve both robustness against median attack and detection performance, we use repetition and permutation techniques like Boneh and Shaw's scheme.

$$y_j = x + aw_j = x + (1-NVF)\sum_{i=1}^{v} s_{ij}\mathbf{u}_i. \tag{2}$$

$$\text{where} \quad NVF = \frac{1}{1+\sigma^2(i,j)}$$

$$w_j = \sum_{i=1}^{v} s_{ij}\mathbf{u}_i. \tag{3}$$

$$\text{where,} \quad s_{ij} = c_{ij} + m_{ij} \cdot r, \quad r \sim N(0, \sigma_r^2)$$

Figure 3 shows an example of S-matrix construction from (7, 3, 1)-BIBD. The element of S matrix whose value is -1 is changed using random variable r (i.i.d.).

$$S = \begin{pmatrix} -1 & -1 & -1 & 1 & 1 & 1 & 1 \\ -1 & 1 & 1 & -1 & -1 & 1 & 1 \\ 1 & -1 & 1 & -1 & 1 & -1 & 1 \\ -1 & 1 & 1 & 1 & 1 & -1 & -1 \\ 1 & 1 & -1 & -1 & 1 & 1 & -1 \\ 1 & -1 & 1 & 1 & -1 & 1 & -1 \\ 1 & 1 & -1 & 1 & -1 & -1 & 1 \end{pmatrix} \begin{pmatrix} 1 & 1 & 1 & 0 & 0 & 0 & 0 \\ 1 & 0 & 0 & 1 & 1 & 0 & 0 \\ 0 & 1 & 0 & 1 & 0 & 1 & 0 \\ 1 & 0 & 0 & 0 & 0 & 1 & 1 \\ 0 & 0 & 1 & 1 & 0 & 0 & 1 \\ 0 & 1 & 0 & 0 & 1 & 0 & 1 \\ 0 & 0 & 1 & 0 & 1 & 1 & 0 \end{pmatrix} + \begin{pmatrix} r & r & r & r & r & r & r \\ r & r & r & r & r & r & r \\ r & r & r & r & r & r & r \\ r & r & r & r & r & r & r \\ r & r & r & r & r & r & r \\ r & r & r & r & r & r & r \\ r & r & r & r & r & r & r \end{pmatrix}$$

$$= \begin{pmatrix} -1+r & -1+r & -1+r & 1 & 1 & 1 & 1 \\ -1+r & 1 & 1 & -1+r & -1+r & 1 & 1 \\ 1 & -1+r & 1 & -1+r & 1 & -1+r & 1 \\ -1+r & 1 & 1 & 1 & 1 & -1+r & -1+r \\ 1 & 1 & -1+r & -1+r & -1+r & 1 & -1+r \\ 1 & -1+r & 1 & 1 & -1+r & 1 & -1+r \\ 1 & 1 & -1+r & 1 & -1+r & -1+r & 1 \end{pmatrix}$$

Fig. 3. The construction of statistically secure matrix using (7, 3, 1)-BIBD

We embed the same w_j repetitively for the R selected blocks, for fingerprint robustness, and we can interpret that we embed $W_j = (w_j(1), w_j(2), \cdots, w_j(R))$ for R selected blocks. All the $w_j(i)$ are the same, however, the resulting watermark should be different, depending on the α, which considers the local HVS masking characteristics. We used non-blind scheme for fingerprint detection. To detect collusion, we used the collusion detection vector T, which can be computed using the same equation as Min Wu's [2]. Averaging individual marks, we can decrease variance of r ($\overline{r} \sim N(0, \sigma_r^2/R)$), but attacker does not know permutation sequence, therefore the attacker cannot distinguish each w_j.

4 Experimental Results

We tested our collusion-resistance code using statistically secure matrix for various collusion attacks (average, median, min, max, min-max, modified negative, randomized negatives) for the test images. Average and median collusions are widely used collusion attack [4], because it is efficient to attack fingerprints, and also it makes better image quality after collusion (usually it increases 2-3 dB). S matrix is

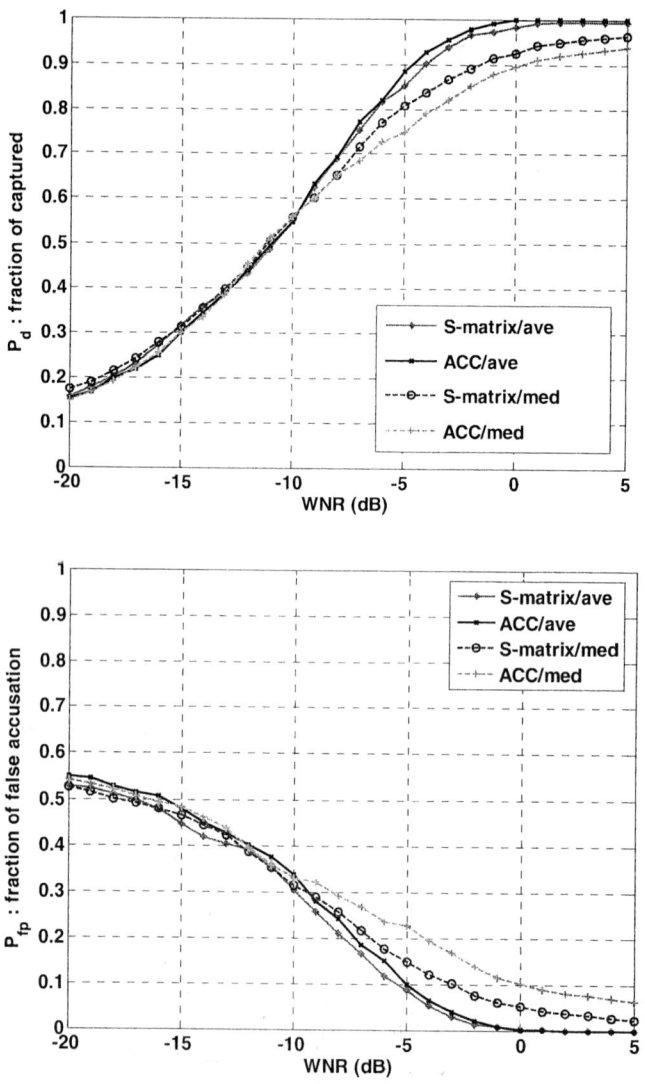

Fig. 4. The performance compared with ACC using 64 dimensions basis

constructed from (16, 4, 1)-BIBD, and we used the Hadamard matrix for code matrix S, because it is orthogonal, secure, and widely used in MPEG-4 Part 10 AVC (Advanced Visual Coding: H.264) video compression. The repetition factor is 4, setting threshold to 0.6. Figure 4 shows the simulation results, where we randomly select 3 users (acting as colluders) from 20 users, and combine their signals using average and median attack (the dimension of basis signal set to be 64). The fraction of captured means that at least one colluder is captured. Mathematically, it says $D \neq \varnothing, D \subseteq R$ (D: Detected colluders, R: Real colluders). The fraction of false accusation means that innocent users are captured ($D \not\subseteq R$). Figure 4 shows that the collusion-resilient code based on statistically secure matrix is more robust against median attacks, and shows comparable performance for average attack. The watermark-to-noise ratio (WNR) is defined as $WNR = 20\log_{10} \frac{\|w_i\|}{\|d_i\|}$.

5 Conclusions

In this paper, we present the modified anti-collusion code which improves anti-collusion fingerprinting (AND-ACC) scheme using statistically secure matrix To improve the detection performance, we repeated the fingerprints r multiple times. We evaluated our fingerprints on standard test images, and shows good collusion detection performance over average and median collusion attacks.

References

1. Boneh, D., Shaw, J.: Collusion-secure fingerprinting for digital data. IEEE Trans. Inform. Theory, vol. 44, Sept. (1998) 1897–1905
2. Wu, M., Trappe, W., Wang, Z. J., Liu, K. J. R.: Collusion-Resistant fingerprinting for multimedia IEEE signal processing magazine, Mar. (2004) 15-26
3. Voloshynovskiy, S., Herrige, A., Baumgaertner, N., Pun, T.: A stochastic approach to content adaptive digital image watermarking. Lecture Notes in Computer Science: 3rd Int. Workshop on Information Hiding, vol. 1768, Sept. (1999) 211-236
4. Zhao, H., Wu, M., Wang, Z. J., Liu, K. J, R.: Nonlinear collusion attacks on independent fingerprints for multimedia. Multimedia and Expo, 2003. ICME '03. Proceedings. 2003 Int. Conf. vol. 1, Jul (2003) 6-9

An Improvement of Auto-Correlation Based Video Watermarking Scheme Using Perceptual Masking for Motion

Hyun-Seong Sung and Seong-Whan Kim

Department of Computer Science, University of Seoul,
Jeon-Nong-Dong, Seoul, Korea
{wigman, swkim7}@uos.ac.kr

Abstract. Video watermarking hides information (e.g. ownership, recipient information, etc) into video contents. Video watermarking research is classified into (1) extension of still image watermarking, (2) use of the temporal domain features, and (3) use of video compression formats. In this paper, we propose a watermarking scheme to resist geometric attack (rotation, scaling, translation, and mixed) for H.264 (MPEG-4 Part 10 Advanced Video Coding) compressed video contents. We analyzed our perceptual model for video watermark in maximal capacity aspects, and experimented with the standard image and video sequences. Simulation results show that our video watermarking scheme is robust against H.264 video compression (average PSNR = 31 dB) and geometric attacks (rotation with 0-90 degree, scaling with 75-200%, and 50%~75% cropping).

1 Introduction

A digital watermark or watermark in short, is an invisible mark inserted in digital media such as digital images, audio and video so that it can later be detected and used as evidence of copyright infringement. However, insertion of such invisible mark should not alter the perceived quality of the digital media (it is the transparency requirement) while being extremely robust to attack (it is a robust requirement) and being impossible to insert another watermarks for rightful ownership (it is a maximal capacity requirement). Watermark attacks are classified into (1) intentional attacks, and (2) unintentional attacks. Basic requirements for video watermarking are geometric attack robustness (intentional attacks) and H.264 video compression (unintentional attacks). There are four major researches for geometric attack robustness, (1) invariant transform, (2) template based, (3) feature point based, and (4) auto-correlation based [1]. Invariant transform approach is to embed the watermark in an invariant domain, like Fourier-Mellin transform [2], whereby geometric transform is still a linear operation. Template approach is to identify the transformation by retrieving artificially embedded references [3]. Feature point based approach is an embedding and detection scheme, where the mark is bound with a content descriptor defined by salient points [1]. Finally, Auto-correlation approach is to insert the mark periodically during the embedding process, and use auto-correlation during the detection process [4, 5]. We designed an auto-correlation based watermark detection scheme for geometric attack robustness, and present a video watermarking scheme, which is robust on geometric attack (scaling, cropping, rotation, and mixed) and H.264 video compression.

2 Payload Embedded Watermarking on H.264 INTRA Frames

H.264 is a widely used video compression standard, in which it uses different coding techniques for INTRA (reference) and INTER (motion predicted) frames. We designed two watermarking schemes for INTRA and INTER frames, respectively. We embed the auto-correlated watermark in H.264 reference (INTRA) frames, because INTRA frames are used for reference frames of motion predicted (INTER) frames, and they are usually less compressed than INTER frames. Assuming we know which frame is the INTRA frame, Figure 1 shows the auto-correlation based watermark embedding scheme for INTRA coded frames. Watermark embedding for H.264 INTRA frames can be summarized in the following equation (1). I' is watermarked frame (I + W), and the watermark is composed of w_p (payload watermark) and w_s (synchronization watermark), which is multiplied by λ (weighting factor derived from perceptual masking model). As shown in Figure 1, we embedded the 64*64 block-wise watermarks repeatedly over whole image, thereby we can restore watermark even from 128x128 cropped image blocks.

Embedding $$I' = I + \lambda NW = I + \lambda N(w_p + w_s) \qquad (1)$$

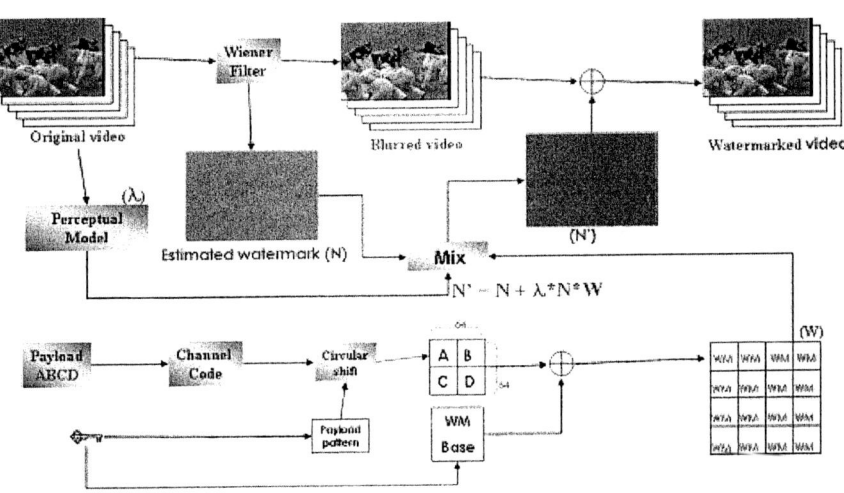

Fig. 1. Watermark embedding for H.264 INTRA frames

We improved auto-correlation based watermark embedding scheme as [6] using a different JND (just noticeable difference) model, which is based on the entropy. For each 64x64 blocks, we adjusted the watermark strength as image complexity using a mixed perceptual model of NVF (noise visibility function) and entropy masking [7, 8, 9, 10]. We used the following equations for our watermark embedding, and we experimentally set the multiplication factor of entropy model as 3.0. Also the A and B values are set to 5.0 and 1.0.

| Watermark strength | $\lambda = \max(\lambda_N, \lambda_E)$ | (2) |

NVF model λ_N

$$\lambda_N = (1 - NVF) * A + NVF * B, \text{ where}$$

$$NVF = \frac{1}{1+\sigma^2}$$

Entropy Masking model λ_E

$$\lambda_E = 3.0 * E, \text{ where } E = \sum_{x \in N(X)} p(x) \cdot \log \frac{1}{p(x)}$$

To detect watermark, we used auto-correlation function to estimate the geometric transform, and used Wiener filter to estimate the watermark in blind manner. We based on the auto-correlation based watermark detection approach as [6], and we used a different payload coding techniques to improve the payload detection. We used the smaller auto-correlation block size 64x64 than 128x128. In our experience, decreasing auto-correlation block size makes multiple auto-correlated blocks to be folded, and it increases the watermark robustness. Watermark detection and payload extraction for H.264 INTRA frames can be summarized in the following equations.

Detection
$$w_s \cdot w' = w_s \cdot (I' - E'), \text{ where } E' = \text{Wiener}(I')$$
$$= w_s \cdot (I + \lambda N w_p + \lambda N w_s + \delta)$$
(3)

Payload extraction
$$w_p \cdot w' = w_p \cdot (I + \lambda N w_p + \lambda N w_s + \delta).$$
(4)

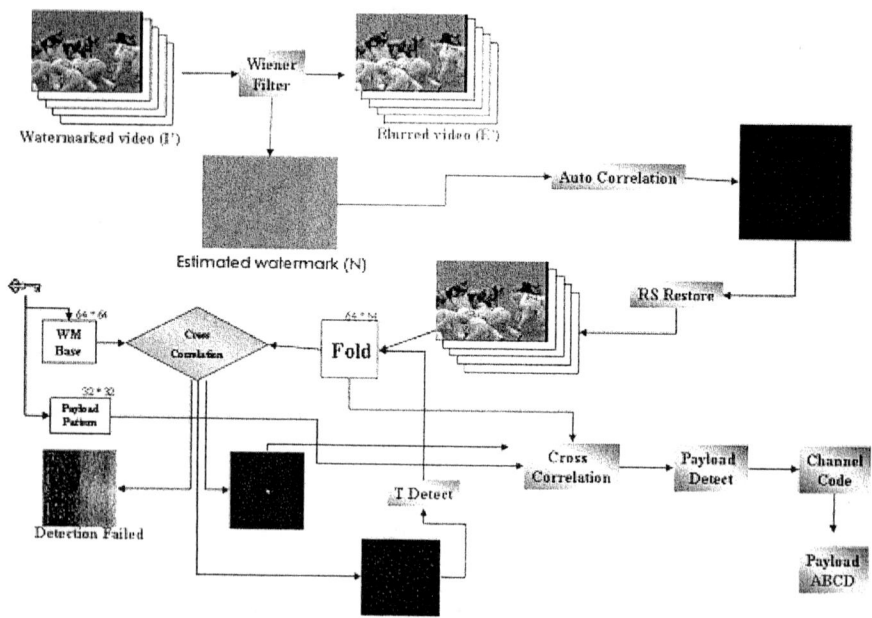

Fig. 2. Watermark detection for INTRA frames

3 Robust Watermarking on H.264 INTER Frame

INTER frames are usually more compressed than INTRA frames, and used INTER frames to show watermark detection purpose only. Figure 3 shows the INTER frame watermark embedding scheme. We used Hadamard transform to embed watermark, and we designed a perceptual model for the transform domain. INTER frames are more compressed than INTRA frames, and it is highly dependent on the transform used.

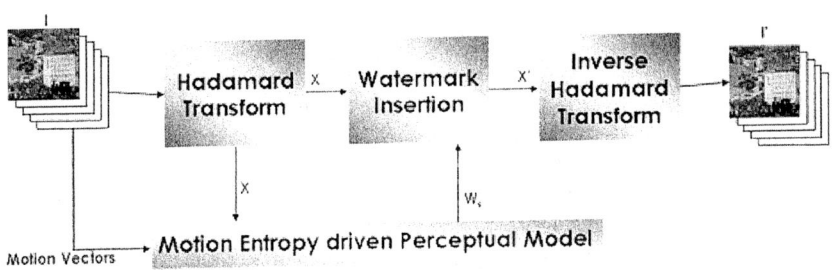

Fig. 3. Watermark embedding for INTER frames

In our watermark scheme, we chose 4x4 Hadamard transform because it is robust against the H.264 compression, and shows good performance to preserve security information. We assume the same geometric transform as the INTRA frame, and we do not consider geometric robustness in INTER frame watermarks. Watermark embedding for H.264 INTER frames can be summarized in the following equation (5). In INTER frame watermarking, we embedded watermark in 4x4 Hadamard transform domain, and we denote the Hadamard transform as H.

Embedding
$$I' = H^{-1}(H(I) + \lambda w_s) \approx I + H^{-1}(\lambda w_s) \quad (5)$$

Although INTER frames cannot show good performance to carry payload, INTER frames are motion predicted and we designed a perceptual model of motion entropy using the H.264 generated motion vectors. Motion entropy is a HVS derived features and we can embed much stronger watermark as follows.

Luminance Sensitivity
$$L_{u,v,b} = F_{u,v} \left[\frac{X_{0,0,b}}{X_{0,0}} \right]^{\alpha} \quad (6)$$

Contrast Masking
$$C_{u,v,b} = \max[L_{u,v,b}, |X_{u,v,b}|^{\beta_{u,v}} (L_{u,v,b})^{1-\beta_{u,v}}]$$

$$V_{u,v,b} = \max[C_{u,v,b}, |C_{u,v,b}| \cdot (E_{u,v,b})^{\gamma}], \text{ where}$$

Entropy Masking
$$E_{u,v,b} = \sum_{x \in N(X_{u,v,b})} p(x) \cdot \log \frac{1}{p(x)}$$

Motion Entropy

$$W_{u,v,b} = \max[V_{u,v,b}, |V_{u,v,b}| \cdot M^{\eta M_b}]$$, where

$$M_b = p(C(b)) \cdot \log \frac{1}{p(C(b))}$$

As shown in Figure 4, we estimate the watermark using Wiener filter, and performed Hadamard transform to compute correlation between w_s and detected watermark w' on Hadamard transform domain.

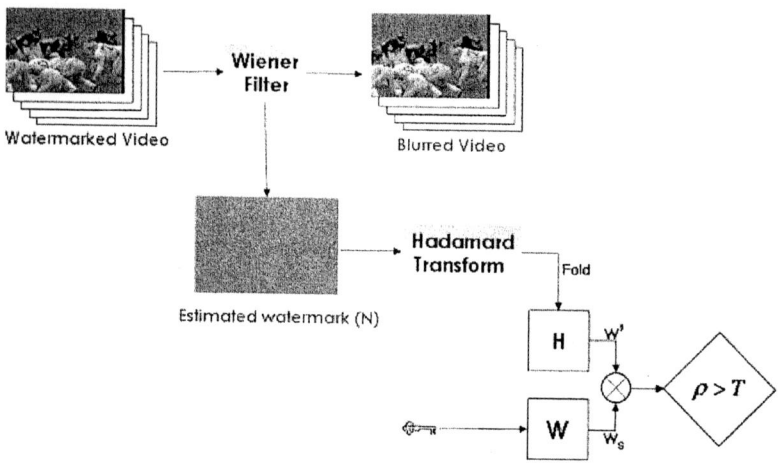

Fig. 4. Watermark detection for INTER frames

Watermark detection and payload extraction for H.264 INTER frames can be summarized in the following equation (7). To optimize the detection threshold, we used the same threshold selection strategy as [11], and set 3.97 for k.

Detection

$$\rho = \frac{1}{64^2} \sum \sum w' w_s > T \text{, where}$$
$$w' = H(I' - E') \text{ and E' = Wiener (I')} \tag{7}$$
$$T = k\sqrt{2 * T_1} \text{, } T_1 = \frac{1}{64^2} \sum \sum (w')^2.$$

4 Simulation Results

We experimented with the standard test image sequence from VQEG (Video Quality Expert Group) as shown in Figure 5 [12]. To experiment the geometric attack, we used Stirmark 4.0 [13] geometric attack packages for various geometric attacks (rotation with 0-90 degrees, scaling with 75-200%, cropping with 50-75%, and mixed). We experimented with five cases: (case 1) rotation with 1, 2, and 5 degree clockwise; (case 2) case 1 rotation and scaling to fit original image size; (case 3) cropping with

Fig. 5. VQEG test sequences

50% and 75%; (case 4) scaling with 50%, 75%, 150%, and 200%; and (case 5) median, Gaussian, and sharpening filter attacks.

Table 1 showed robustness result for the various geometric attack on INTRA frames, and shows successful payload detection results in most geometric attack cases, and shows some misses under combined attack of rotation and scaling.

Table 1. Payload detection after geometric attack (only for INTRA frames)

	Case 1: Rotation			Case 2: Rotation + Scaling			Case 3: Cropping	
	1	2	5	1	2	5	50	75
I1	100%	100%	67%	50%	34%	50%	100%	100%
I2	100%	100%	100%	67%	83%	67%	100%	100%
I3	100%	100%	67%	50%	50%	67%	100%	100%
I4	100%	100%	50%	100%	100%	100%	100%	100%
I5	100%	100%	83%	100%	100%	83%	100%	100%
I6	100%	100%	100%	67%	100%	50%	100%	100%
I7	100%	100%	100%	50%	83%	50%	100%	100%
I8	100%	100%	83%	67%	83%	50%	100%	100%
J1	100%	100%	67%	67%	67%	100%	100%	100%
J2	100%	100%	100%	67%	100%	100%	100%	100%
J3	100%	100%	100%	50%	50%	67%	100%	100%

J4	100%	100%	83%	34%	67%	100%	100%	100%
J5	100%	100%	67%	34%	50%	83%	100%	83%
J6	100%	100%	100%	100%	83%	100%	100%	100%
J7	100%	100%	100%	100%	83%	83%	100%	100%
J8	100%	100%	67%	67%	83%	83%	100%	100%
J9	100%	100%	100%	100%	100%	100%	100%	100%
J10	100%	100%	83%	83%	67%	100%	100%	100%

	Case 4: Scaling				Case 5: Median, Gaussian, Sharpening			
	50	75	150		M	G	S	
I1	100%	100%	100%		100%	100%	100%	
I2	100%	100%	100%		100%	100%	100%	
I3	100%	100%	100%		100%	100%	100%	
I4	100%	100%	100%		100%	100%	100%	
I5	100%	100%	100%		100%	100%	100%	
I6	100%	100%	100%		100%	100%	100%	
I7	100%	100%	100%		100%	100%	100%	
I8	100%	100%	100%		100%	100%	100%	
J1	100%	100%	100%		100%	100%	100%	
J2	100%	100%	100%		100%	100%	100%	
J3	100%	100%	100%		100%	100%	100%	
J4	100%	100%	100%		100%	100%	100%	
J5	100%	100%	100%		100%	100%	100%	
J6	100%	100%	100%		100%	100%	100%	
J7	100%	100%	100%		100%	100%	100%	
J8	100%	100%	100%		100%	100%	100%	
J9	100%	100%	100%		100%	100%	100%	
J10	100%	100%	100%		100%	100%	100%	

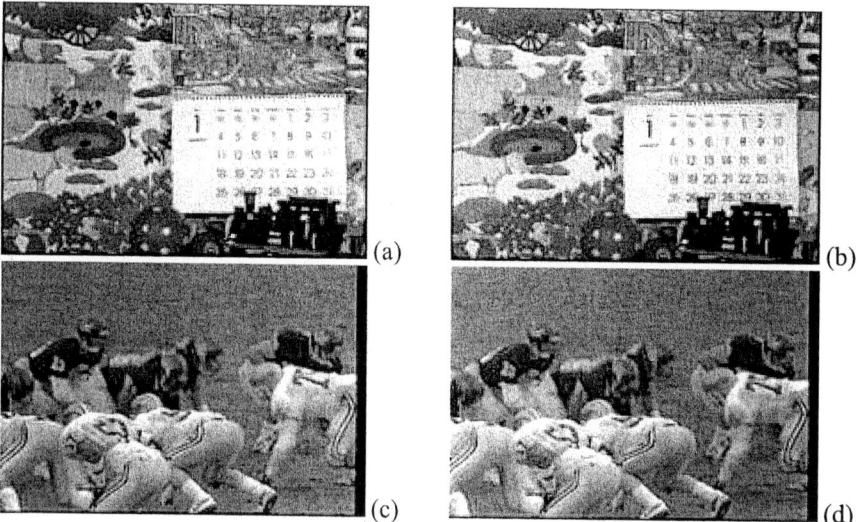

Fig. 6. Original and watermarked frames from: (a-b) Mobile&Calendar (PSNR=32.03) and (c-d) Football (PSNR=31.80) sequences

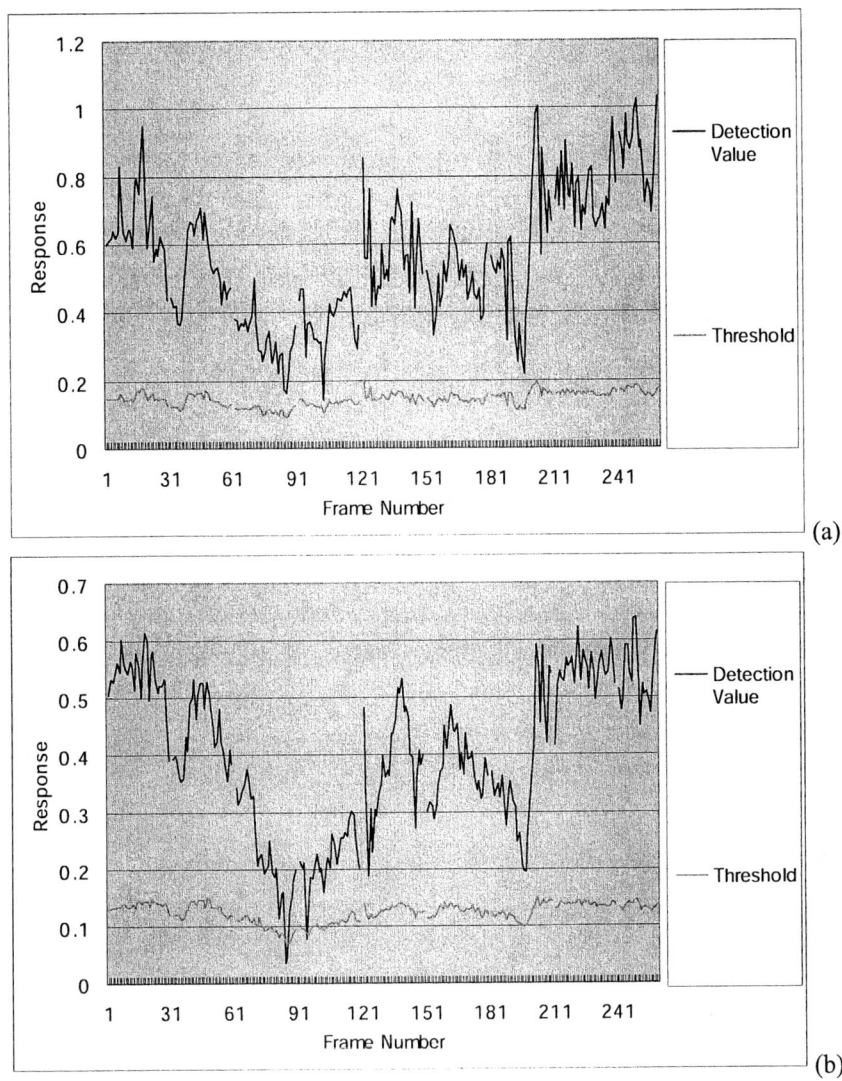

Fig. 7. Robustness for H.264 compression: (a) QP=28 and (b) QP=34 (Football sequence)

After INTRA frame watermark embedding, the watermarked images show good subjective quality. Figure 6 shows the original and watermarked frames for Mobile&Calendar and Football test sequences, and the average PSNR for two test sequence's INTRA frames are 32.03 and 31.80, respectively.

We used H.264 INTRA frames for geometric attack estimation, and H.264 INTER frames for watermark detection. INTER frames are highly compressed, and we used motion entropy masking model for Hadamard transform coefficients to make stronger watermark. Figure 7 shows the experimental watermark detection result for Football test sequence, and shows robustness over H.264 video compression with QP=28 and QP=34 (average PSNR = 34.0 dB). Figure 8 shows the experimental watermark detection result for Mobile&Calendar test sequence, and shows the average detection value 1.0 which is higher than Football test sequence, because Football test sequence has more INTRA coded blocks in H.264 video compression.

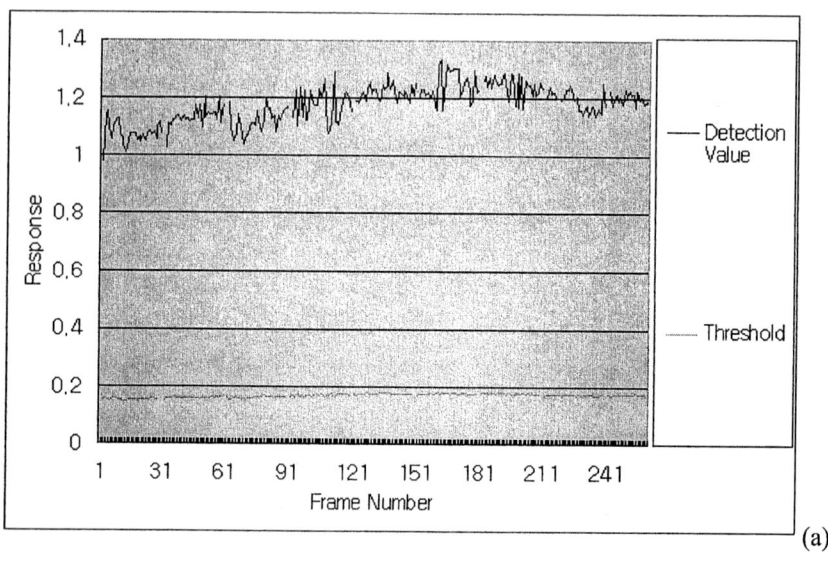

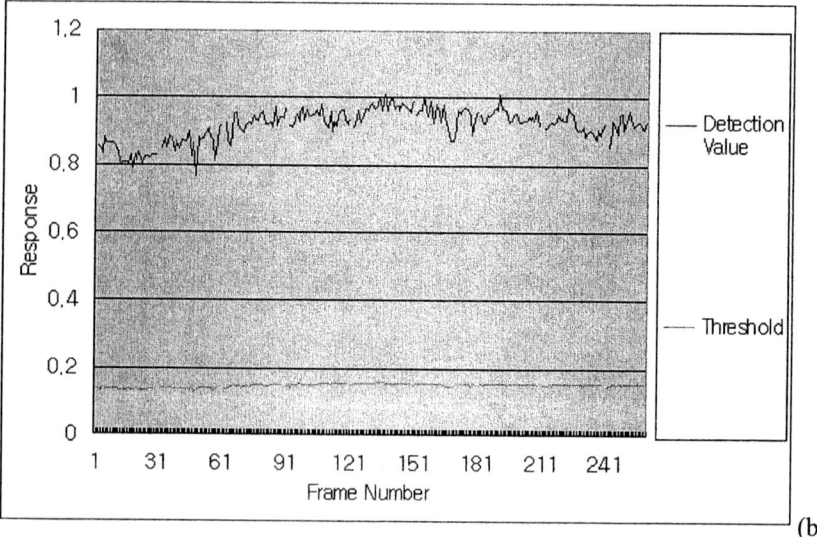

Fig. 8. Robustness for H.264 compression: (a) QP=28 and (b) QP=34 (Mobile&Calendar sequence)

5 Conclusions

In this paper, we presented a robust video watermarking scheme, which uses auto-correlation based scheme for geometric attack recovery, and uses human visual system characteristics for H.264 compression. Our video watermarking scheme is robust against H.264 video compression (average PSNR = 31 dB) and geometric attacks (rotation with 0-90 degree, scaling with 75-200%, and 50%~75% cropping).

References

1. Bas, P., Chassery, JM, Macq, B.: Geometrically invariant watermarking using feature points. IEEE Trans. Image Proc., vol. 11, no. 9 (2002) 1014–1028
2. O'Ruanaidh, J.J., Pun, T.: Rotation, scale and translation invariant digital image watermarking. Proc. IEEE Int. Conf. Image Proc.(1997) 536 -539
3. Pereira, S., Pun, T.: Robust template matching for affine resistant image watermarks. IEEE Trans. Image Proc., vol. 9, no. 6 (2000)
4. Kutter, M.: Watermarking resisting to translation, rotation, and scaling. Proc. of SPIE Int. Conf. on Multimedia Systems and Applications, vol. 3528 (1998) 423-431.
5. P.-C. Su and C.-C. J. Kuo, "Synchronized detection of the block-based watermark with invisible grid embedding," Proc. SPIE Electronic imaging (Security and Watermarking of Multimedia Contents III), 2001.
6. Su, P.-C., Kuo, C.-C. J.: Synchronized detection of the block-based watermark with invisible grid embedding. Proc. SPIE Electronic imaging (Security and Watermarking of Multimedia Contents III) (2001)
7. Lee, C. H., Lee, H. K., Suh, Y. H.: Autocorrelation Function-based Watermarking with Side Information. IS&T/SPIE, 15th Annual Symposium Electronic Imaging Science and Technology: Security and Watermarking of Multimedia Contents, San Jose, USA. (January 2003) 20-24
8. Voloshynovskiy, S., Herrige, A., Baumgaertner, N., Pun, T.: A stochastic approach to content adaptive digital image watermarking. Lecture Notes in Computer Science: 3rd Int. Workshop on Information Hiding, vol. 1768 (1999) 211-236
9. Watson, A. B., Borthwick, R., Taylor, M.: Image quality and entropy masking. Proc. SPIE Conf. Human Vision, Visual Processing, and Digital Display VI (1997)
10. Podilchuk, C., Zeng, W.: Image adaptive watermarking using visual models. IEEE J. Selected Areas in Communications, vol. 16, no. 4 (1998.)
11. Kim, S.W., Suthaharan, S., Lee, H.K., Rao, K.R.: An image watermarking scheme using visual model and BN distribution. IEE Elect. Letter, vol. 35 (3) (1999)
12. Barni, M., Bartolini, F., Cappellini, V., Lippi, A., Piva, A.: A DWT based technique for spatio frequency masking of digital signatures. Proc. IS&T/SPIE Conf. Security and watermarking of multimedia contents, vol. 3657 (1999) 31-39
13. http://www.its.bldrdoc.gov/vqeg/
14. http://www.petitcolas.net/fabien/watermarking/stirmark/

Validation of Policy Integration Using Alloy*

Manachai Toahchoodee and Indrakshi Ray

Department of Computer Science,
Colorado State University,
Fort Collins CO 80523-1873
{toahchoo, iray}@cs.colostate.edu

Abstract. Organizations typically have multiple security policies operating together in the same system. The integration of multiple policies might be needed to achieve the desired security requirements. Validating this integrated policy is a non-trivial process. This paper addresses the problem of composing, modeling and validating the security policies. We show how the various approaches for composing security policies can be modeled and verified using Alloy, a lightweight modeling system with automatic semantic analysis capability.

1 Introduction

Organizations typically enforce multiple policies to achieve security. For instance, each department in a hospital will have its own policy about disclosing the information of a patient. To get the information of a patient belonging to multiple departments, we need to combine the existing policies and check whether the requesters have enough permission to receive the information they need. Manually analyzing whether the integrated policy's behavior complies with the given requirement for a large-scale application is a tedious and error-prone process. Towards this end, we show how the process can be automated to some extent.

Our approach consists of developing a model of the system whose policies we are verifying. A model is an analyzable representation of a system. To be useful, it must be simpler than the system itself, but faithful to it. In our approach, we use the Alloy language [5, 6, 8, 10] to specify the model. The specification in Alloy can be automatically verified using the Alloy Analyzer. We show how the policy composition approaches proposed by Bonatti et al. [2] can be verified using Alloy.

The rest of this paper is organized as follows. Section 2 discusses some work on policy composition. Section 3 contains summary of the principle and the features of Alloy system. Section 4 describes algebra for composing access control policies and its representation in Alloy language. Examples are provided in section 5. Section 6 concludes the paper and gives some future directions.

2 Related Work

Several researchers have worked on the problem of policy composition. Hosmer [3] identified shortcomings in the unified security policy paradigm, such as inflexibility,

---

* This work was partially supported by AFOSR under Award No. FA9550-04-1-0102.

difficulty in exchanging data between systems having different policies, and poor performance. These shortcomings are eliminated in multipolicy paradigm proposed by the author. Bidan and Issarny [1] proposed a solution for reasoning about the coexistence of different security policies and how these policies can be combined. The authors also address issues pertaining to the completeness and the soundness of the combined security policy. Jajodia et al. [7] authors introduce the *Flexible Authorization Framework* (FAF) that allows users to specify policies in a flexible manner. The language allows the specification of both positive and negative authorizations and incorporates notions of authorization derivation, conflict resolution, and decision strategies. Such strategies can exploit the hierarchical structures in which system components are organized as well as any other relationship that the system security officer (SSO) may wish to exploit. Bonatti et al. [2] proposed an algebra for representing and composing access control policies. Complex policies are formulated as expressions of the algebra. Different component policies can be integrated while retaining their independence. This framework is flexible and keeps the composition process simple by organizing compound specifications into different levels of abstraction. Our work is based on this work. Siewe et al. [9] have developed a compositional framework for the specification of access control policies using specific language called ITL. Complex policies are created by composition using several operators. Multiple policies can be enforced through composition, and their properties reasoned about. The effect of the combined policy can be understood by using the simulator called Tempura. Zao et al. [10] and Schaad et al. [8] have investigated how Alloy can be used for verifying Role-Based Access Control (RBAC) policies. But none of these work address how to verify integrated policies.

3 Alloy Lightweight Modeling System

Alloy ([4], [5], [6], [10]), is a textual language developed at MIT by Daniel Jackson and his team. Unlike a programming language, an Alloy model is declarative. This allows very succinct and partial models to be constructed and analyzed. It is similar in spirit to the formal specification languages Z, VDM, Larch, B, OBJ, etc, but, unlike all of these, is amenable to fully automatic analysis in the style of a model checker.

Z was a major influence on Alloy. Unlike Z, Alloy is first order, which makes it analyzable but is also less expressive. Alloys composition mechanisms are designed to have the flexibility of Z's schema calculus, but are based on different idioms: extension by addition of fields, similar to inheritance in an object-oriented language, and reuse of formulas by explicit parameterization, similar to functions in a functional programming language. Alloy is a pure ASCII notation and does not require special typesetting tools.

The Alloy Analyzer's analysis is fully automatic, and when an assertion is found to be false, the Alloy Analyzer generates a counterexample. It's a "refuter" rather than a "prover". When a theorem prover fails to prove a theorem, it can be hard to tell what's gone wrong: whether the theorem is invalid, or whether the proof strategy failed. If the Alloy Analyzer finds no counterexample, the assertion may still be invalid. But by picking a large enough scope, you can usually make this very unlikely. The tool can generate instances of invariants, simulate the execution of operations (even those defined implicitly), and check user-specified properties of a model.

4 An Algebra for Composing Access Control Policies and Its Representation in Alloy

Bonatti et al. [2] propose an algebra for composing access control policies. In this section, we show how these policy expressions can be represented in Alloy.

4.1 Definitions Used in Bonatti's Work

We begin by giving some definitions used in Bonatti's work.

Definition 1. [**Authorization Term**] *Authorization terms are triples of the form* (s,o,a), *where s is a constant in S or a variable over S, o is a constant in O or a variable over O, and a is a constant in A or a variable over A where S, O, and A represent the set of subjects, objects, and actions, respectively.*

At a semantic level, a policy is defined as a set of ground (i.e., variable-free) triples.

Definition 2. [**Policy**] *A policy is a set of ground authorization terms. The triples in a policy P state the accesses permitted by P.*

The algebra (among other operations) allows policies to be restricted (by posing constraints on their authorizations) and closed with respect to inference rules.

- An *authorization constraint language* L_{acon} and a semantic relation *satisfy* $\subseteq (S \times O \times A) \times L_{acon}$; the latter specifies for each ground authorization term (s,o,a) and constraint $c \in L_{acon}$ whether (s,o,a) satisfies c.
- A *rule language* L_{rule} and a semantic function *closure*: $\wp(L_{rule}) \times \wp(S \times O \times A) \to \wp(S \times O \times A)$; the latter specifies for each set of rules R and ground authorizations P which authorizations are derived from P by R.

These languages have been chosen with the goal of keeping the presentation as simple as possible, focusing attention on policy composition, rather than authorization properties and inference rules.

Compound policies can be obtained by combining policy identifiers through the algebra operators. Let the metavariables P_1 and P_2 range over policy expressions.

Addition/Union (+). It merges two policies by returning their union. Formally, $P_1 + P_2 = P_1 \cup P_2$. Intuitively it means that if access is permitted by either of the policies, then the access will be allowed by the resulting composed policy.

Conjunction/Intersection (&). It merges two policies by returning their intersection. Formally, $P_1 \& P_2 = P_1 \cap P_2$. This means the access will be permitted only if both the component policies allow access.

Subtraction (−). It restricts a policy by eliminating all the accesses in a second policy. The formal definition is $P_1 - P_2 = P_1 \setminus P_2$. The resulting policy permits access only if the access is allowed by P_1 and not by P_2.

Closure (∗). It closes a policy under a set of inference (derivation) rules. Formally, $P * R = closure(R, P)$. It basically signifies the set of policies that can be generated from the policy P given the derivation rule R.

Scoping restriction (^). It restricts the application of a policy to a given set of subjects, objects, and actions. Formally, $P^\wedge c = \{(s,o,a)\theta \mid (s,o,a)\theta \in P, (s,o,a)\theta \text{ satisfy } c\theta\}$ where $c \in L_{acon}$ and θ is a ground substitution for variables s,o,a. Scoping is particularly useful to "limit" the statements that can be established by a policy and to enforce authority confinement. Intuitively, all authorizations in the policy that do not satisfy the scoping restriction are ignored, and therefore ineffective.

4.2 Representation of the Integrated Access Control Policy in Alloy

We apply the following rules in order to represent policies in Alloy:

Base Elements. Each base element in the access control policy (that is, the set of subjects, objects and actions) is represented by using signature (see example 1 for details).

Authorization Term. The authorization term is expressed using a special signature that comprises subject, object and action (see Example 1 for details).

Policy. Policy is described using a special signature which is composed of the set of authorization terms (see example 1 for details).

Closure. We define closure as a fact in Alloy. This feature ensures that all elements in our model must satisfy the predefined rules in the fact section. Fact content can be either attached to or separated from the content of the signature. If we attach fact to the signature, this means the fact is applied to the signature only (see example 2 and 7 for details).

Policy expressions. Other policy expressions, such as, scoping restriction, addition, conjunction and subtraction, are represented using predicates. We can think of a predicate as a function that will change the value of parameters (if any) according to the expressions stated in the predicate's context, and return true or false. Using predicates allows us to verify our integrated access control policy in the following ways:

- Model consistency check: We can check from the predicate whether there exists an input for our model or not by using run command in Alloy. If there is any input that satisfies the model, Alloy will show it. Otherwise it will report an error.
- Model correctness check: The correctness of the policy composition can also be validated by using test cases. The test cases are specified using the assert feature. In the assert part, we define the result we expect from the policy composition and use check command in Alloy to evaluate it. If the assertion does not hold, a counterexample is produced. To define the expected result in the assert part, we define the preconditions and the expected post conditions then concatenate them by the imply operator ($\Rightarrow$).

5 Example Scenario

We illustrate our approach by using an example application. Consider a hospital composed of three departments, namely, *Radiology*, *Surgery*, and *Medicine*. Each department is responsible for granting access to data under their authority domains, where domains are specified using scoping restrictions. In addition there are administrators who may or may not be a member of a department. These relationships are shown in Figure 1.

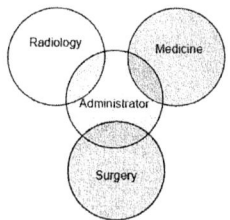

Fig. 1. Hospital policy relationship diagram

Example 1. We represent the set Subject, Object, and Action as signatures in Alloy. The authorization term is represented as a signature whose constituent elements are members of the set of subject, object and action, respectively. This specification given below shows how the authorization term and policies are represented in Alloy.

```
sig Subject {}
sig Radiology, Surgery, Medicine extends Subject {}
sig Administrator in Subject {}
sig Object
{
    owner: Subject
}
sig File, Form extends Object {}
sig Action {}
sig ReadOnly, Write, Execute extends Action {}
sig AuthorizationTerm
{
    subject: Subject,
    object: Object,
    action: Action
}
sig Policy
{
    auth: set AuthorizationTerm
}
```

Example 2. Every authorization term in the hospital policy must satisfy a set of ground rules. These ground rules will be used when computing the closure of some policy. The ground rules are as follows.

- The elements of set *Subject* must come from the union of the elements from the set *Radiology*, *Surgery*, *Medicine* and *Administrator* only.
- The elements of set *Object* must come from the union of the elements from the set *File* and *Form* only.
- The elements of set *Action* must come from the union of the elements from the set *ReadOnly*, *Write* and *Execute* only.

- Every department has their own *administrators*.
- There must be at least one member for each department.

The specification given below shows how these can be represented as facts in Alloy.

```
fact PolicyGroundRules
{
    // Specify the elements in the universe (Subject, Object, Action)
    Subject = Radiology + Surgery + Medicine + Administrator
    Object = File + Form
    Action = ReadOnly + Write + Execute
    // Every departments have administrators
    Radiology & Administrator != none
    Surgery & Administrator != none
    Medicine & Administrator != none
    // Each subset of subject must not empty
    Radiology != none
    Surgery != none
    Medicine != none
    Administrator != none
}
```

Example 3. To represent the scope restriction, we use Alloy's predicate feature to represent the scope operation. We can check whether the combination of each condition in the predicate can generate the output or not by using command run in the Alloy Analyzer. If there are any conflicts of conditions, the analyzer will send an error message. If the analyzer can find valid input for the predicate, it will show the graph of the input as in Figure 2.

After we have created the predicate, we can verify the correctness of our operation (in this case, the scoping restriction) by using the assert feature in Alloy. Assert will try to find the counterexample for our predicate and show us the counterexample graph if any counterexample exists as in figure 3.

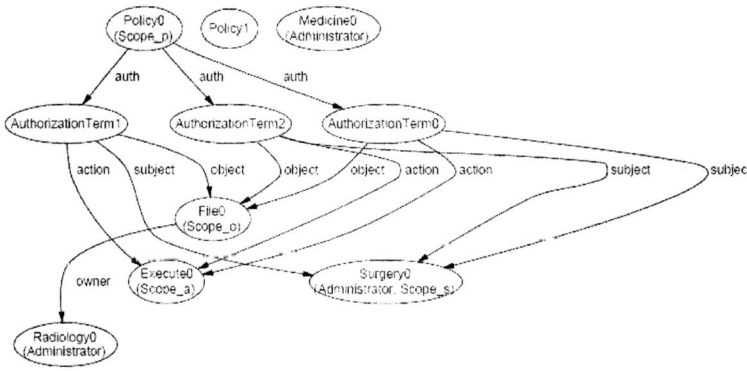

Fig. 2. Example of input for Scope

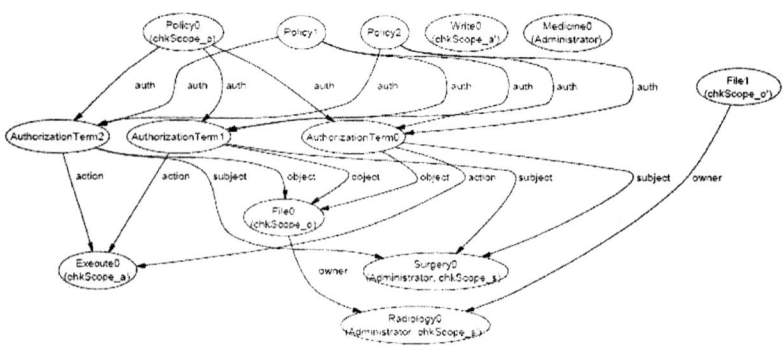

Fig. 3. Counterexample graph

In this example, we make the assumption that if we have two arbitrary sets of authorization terms and we do the scoping restriction based on the first authorization term, the result of the scoping must not equal to the authorization terms of the second set. Then we test our predicate based on this assumption by command check. Obviously, the analyzer could not find the counterexample. We can specify the number of testing objects that we want Alloy to generate for us by adding the parameter for after command run, check. The Alloy code for the predicate Scope and the corresponding assert command is shown below.

```
pred Scope (p: Policy, s: Subject, o: Object, a: Action)
{
    p.auth.subject = s
    p.auth.object = o
    p.auth.action = a
}
run Scope
// After scoping, the remaining authorization terms must satisfy
// the scope condition
assert chkScope
{
    all s, s': Subject, o, o': Object, a, a': Action, p: Policy|
    ((s != s') && (o != o') && (a != a') &&
    Scope(p, s, o, a)) =>
    ((p.auth.subject -> p.auth.object -> p.auth.action) !=
    (s' -> o' -> a'))
}
check chkScope
```

Example 4. To do the addition of two policies, we create the predicate called PolicyUnion. This predicate will accept three policies as input parameters, then it will union the first two policies together and store the result in the third parameter.

For instance, we would like to create the new access control policy from our existing policy. This new policy allows the access from both Radiology department and Surgery department. After the composition, we will verify our model to ensure that the result of composition must be the combination of the set of authorization terms from Radiology departments policy and the set of authorization terms from Surgery departments policy. To satisfy these requirements, our model and the verification command in Alloy will be as below.

```
    pred PolicyUnion (p1, p2, p3: Policy)
        {
p3.auth = p1.auth + p2.auth
    }
    run PolicyUnion
    assert chkPolicyUnion
    {
        all p1, p2: Policy| some p3: Policy|
        (Scope(p1, Radiology, Object, Action) &&
        Scope(p2, Surgery, Object, Action)) &&
        PolicyUnion(p1, p2, p3) =>
        ((Radiology in p3.auth.subject) &&
        (Surgery in p3.auth.subject) && (p3.auth != none))
    }
    check chkPolicyUnion
```

Example 5. To do the conjunction of policies, we create the predicate called Policy-Intersection. This predicate will accept three policies as input parameters, then it will intersect the first two policies together and store the result in the third parameter.

For example, we would like to create a new access control policy which allows only the administrators of the Radiology department to access the resource. The integrated policy is created from the intersection between policy of the Radiology department and the policy of the administrator. To verify the correctness of the model, we create the test that the result policy's authorization term is restricted to the Radiology department and the staff must be the administrator. The Alloy code to support the requirement is as follows.

```
    pred PolicyConjunction (p1, p2, p3: Policy)
    {
    p3.auth = p1.auth & p2.auth
    }
    run PolicyConjunction
    assert chkPolicyConj
    {
        all p1, p2: Policy| some p3: Policy|
        (Scope(p1, Administrator, Object, Action) &&
        Scope(p2, Radiology, Object, Action)) &&
        PolicyConjunction(p1, p2, p3) =>
```

```
            ((p3.auth.subject in Radiology) &&
            (p3.auth.subject in Administrator) &&
            (p3.auth != none))
        }
        check chkPolicyConj
```

Example 6. To do the subtraction of policies, we create the predicate called Policy-Subtraction. This predicate will accept three policies as input parameters, then it will subtract policy p2 from p1 and store the result in the third parameter (policy p3).

To demonstrate the idea, suppose we want to create a new policy which allows only the staff from Radiology department who is not the administrator to access the resource. To achieve this goal, we subtract the members who are the administrator of the Radiology department policy from the policy of the Radiology department itself. To verify the correctness of the integrated policy, we check if the result from subtraction is the set which members are from Radiology set but not from Administrator set. The Alloy code for this example will be as below.

```
        pred PolicySubtraction (p1, p2, p3: Policy)
        {
            p3.auth = p1.auth - p2.auth
        }
        run PolicySubtraction
        assert chkPolicySubtraction
        {
            all p1, p2: Policy| some p3: Policy|
            (Scope(p1, Radiology, Object, Action) &&
            Scope(p2, Administrator, Object, Action)) &&
            PolicySubtraction(p1, p2, p3) =>
            ((p3.auth.subject in Radiology) &&
            (p3.auth.subject not in (Administrator)) &&
            (p3.auth != none))
        }
        check chkPolicySubtraction
```

Example 7. In this example, we will show how to combine the different kinds of policy expressions together. Each department is responsible for granting access to data under their authority domains, where domains are specified by scoping restrictions. The statements made by the departments are then unioned, meaning the hospital considers an access as authorized if any of the department policies so states.

For privacy regulations, the hospital will not allow any access (even if authorized by the departments) to *lab_tests* data unless there is patient consent for that, stated by policy $P_{consents}$. In terms of the algebra, the hospital policy can be represented as

$$[(P_{rad} + P_{surg} + P_{med}) - (P_{rad} + P_{surg} + P_{med})^\wedge(\text{object} = lab\_tests)] + [P_{consents} \& (P_{rad} + P_{surg} + P_{med})^\wedge(\text{object} = lab\_tests)]$$

In this case, we can view $P_{consents}$ as a policy which is closed by a set of rules (the permissions assigned by patient). In Alloy, we defined $P_{consents}$ as a special kind of signature which inherit from the Policy signature and closed by the attached fact. To check the correctness of the model, we claim that there is no staff from the Medicine department that can access *lab_tests* data. The full Alloy model for the hospital policy can be shown as below

```
sig Subject {}
sig Radiology, Surgery, Medicine extends Subject {}
sig Administrator in Subject {}
sig Object
{
        owner: Subject
}
sig File, Form, LabTests extends Object {}
sig Action {}
sig ReadOnly, Write, Execute extends Action {}
sig AuthorizationTerm
{
    subject: Subject,
    object: Object,
    action: Action
}
sig Policy
{
    auth: set AuthorizationTerm
}
sig Consent extends Policy
{
}
{
// Allow only Radiology and Surgery Staff to access lab tests data
    auth.subject = Radiology + Surgery
    auth.object = LabTests
}
fact PolicyGroundRules
{
    Subject = Radiology + Surgery + Medicine + Administrator
    Object = File + Form
    Action = ReadOnly + Write + Execute
    Radiology & Administrator != none
    Surgery & Administrator != none
    Medicine & Administrator != none
    Radiology != none
    Surgery != none
    Medicine != none
    Administrator != none
}
```

```
pred Scope (p: Policy, s: Subject, o: Object, a: Action)
{
    p.auth.subject = s
    p.auth.object = o
    p.auth.action = a
}
// Policy Union
pred PolicyUnion (p1, p2, p3: Policy)
{
    p3.auth = p1.auth + p2.auth
}
pred HospitalPolicy (p1, p2, p3, p4: Policy)
{
    p4 = (p1 - p2) + (p3 & p2)
}
run HospitalPolicy
assert chkHospitalPolicy
{
    all Prad, Psurg, Pmed, Pradsurg, p1, p2: Policy,
    Pconsent: Consent|
    no p4: Policy|
    (Scope(Prad, Radiology, Object, Action) &&
    Scope(Psurg, Surgery, Object, Action) &&
    Scope(Pmed, Medicine, Object, Action)) &&
    PolicyUnion(Prad, Psurg, Pradsurg) &&
    PolicyUnion(Pradsurg, Pmed, p1) &&
    Scope(p2, p1.auth.subject, LabTests, p1.auth.action) &&
    HospitalPolicy(p1, p2, Pconsent, p4) =>
    ((Medicine->LabTests->Action in
    p4.auth.subject->p4.auth.object->p4.auth.action) &&
    (p4.auth != none))
}
check chkHospitalPolicy
```

6 Conclusion and Future Work

In this paper we have shown how the different policy composition operations can be represented in Alloy. Specifying the policies in Alloy allows for formal analysis most of which can be performed automatically using the Alloy Analyzer. A lot of work remains to be done. We assumed that policies can be defined using the set of authorization terms. Towards this end, we need to find the method to automatically transform the component policies to the set of authorization terms. Similar to the problem of software testing, we need a methodology to generate the good test cases that can help us to detect the flaws, if any, in our model.

References

1. Christophe Bidan and Valerie Issarny. Dealing with multi-policy security in large open distributed systems. In *ESORICS*, pages 51–66, 1998.
2. Piero Bonatti, Sabrina De Capitani di Vimercati, and Pierangela Samarati. An algebra for composing access control policies. *ACM Transactions on Information and System Security (TISSEC)*, 5(1):1–35, February 2002.
3. Hilary H. Hosmer. The multipolicy paradigm for trusted systems. In *NSPW '92-93: Proceedings on the 1992-1993 workshop on New security paradigms*, pages 19–32, New York, NY, USA, 1993. ACM Press.
4. Daniel Jackson. Automating first-order relational logic. In *SIGSOFT '00/FSE-8: Proceedings of the 8th ACM SIGSOFT international symposium on Foundations of software engineering*, pages 130–139, New York, NY, USA, 2000. ACM Press.
5. Daniel Jackson. *Micromodels of Software: Lightweight Modelling and Analysis with Alloy.* At http://sdg.lcs.mit.edu/alloy/referencemanual.pdf, 2002.
6. Daniel Jackson. *Alloy 3.0 reference manual.* At http://alloy.mit.edu/reference-manual.pdf, 2004.
7. Sushil Jajodia, Pierangela Samarati, Maria Luisa Sapino, and V. S. Subrahmanian. Flexible support for multiple access control policies. *ACM Trans. Database Syst.*, 26(2):214–260, 2001.
8. Andreas Schaad and Jonathan D. Moffett. A lightweight approach to specification and analysis of role-based access control extensions. In *SACMAT '02: Proceedings of the seventh ACM symposium on Access control models and technologies*, pages 13–22, New York, NY, USA, 2002. ACM Press.
9. Franois Siewe, Antonio Cau, and Hussein Zedan. A compositional framework for access control policies enforcement. In *FMSE '03: Proceedings of the 2003 ACM workshop on Formal methods in security engineering*, pages 32–42, New York, NY, USA, 2003. ACM Press.
10. John Zao, Hoetech Wee, Jonathan Chu, and Daniel Jackson. *RBAC Schema Verification Using Lightweight Formal Model and Constraint Analysis.* At http://alloy.mit.edu/contributions/RBAC.pdf, 2002.

Linking Theories of Concurrency by Retraction

He Jifeng

International Institute of Software Technology United Nations University, Macau

Abstract. Theories of concurrency can be distinguished by the set of processes that they model, and by their choice of pre-ordering relation used to compare processes to prove their correctness. A link between two theories is a function L, which maps the processes of the source theory onto those of the target theory. Its image defines exactly the set of processes of the target theory. The ordering relation of the target theory is obtained by applying the link L to one or both operands of the source theory ordering. We will use the normal transition rules of a structured operational semantics to define a series of linking functions: W for weak simulation, R for refusals, T for traces refinement, D for divergences, etc. We then show that each function is a retraction, in the sense that it is monotonic, decreasing and idempotent. Finally we show their composition is a retraction.

Software Engineering Track Chair's Message

Gopal Gupta

University of Texas at Dallas, USA

Abstract. The Software Engineering track received 63 papers from which 7 papers were selected after an intensive reviewing and selection process. Many good papers could not be selected due to lack of space in the program. The selected papers cover a diverse range of topics within software engineering: from software reliability prediction to middle-ware for component management to runtime validation and code generation. The paper by Roychoudhury, Negi and Mitra analyzes programs loops for estimating program execution time. They use constraint propagation techniques to detect infeasible paths followed by timing analysis that employ memoization techniques. The paper by Sengupta and Cleaveland presents the operational semantics of timed message sequence charts to help detect errors and inconsistencies in specifications. Tripathi and Mall present a method for making predictions about reliability of software during the software development process itself when the failure data from the field cannot be available. The paper by Wang presents a logic programming framework for integrating architecture description languages (ADLs) which allows tools developed for one ADL to be used even though the architectural specification is written in another ADL. In a similar vain, the paper by Stevenson, Fu and Dong presents a framework for automated and validated realization of software architecture designs. The paper by Bhattarcharjee and Shyamsundar presents a method for validated code generation for activity diagrams which are useful in model driven design of software. Finally, the paper by Mousavi et al presents techniques that exploit symmetry for tackling the state-space explosion problem that arises in model checking.

Integrating Architecture Description Languages: A Semantics-Based Approach*

Qian Wang

Applied Logic, Programming-Languages and Systems (ALPS) Laboratory,
Department of Computer Science,
University of Texas at Dallas, USA

Abstract. Numerous architectural description languages(ADLs) have been developed in the last decade. However, none of the ADLs and their toolsets are expressive enough to cover all the requirements that may be specified while developing a software system. An ADL based approach will be more useful and powerful if ADLs can share architectural descriptions and if their analysis tools can be integrated. In this paper, we propose a semantics-based approach to integrating ADLs. A general, abstract executable form is developed for representing architectural information. A uniform query language is also defined that can be used to retrieve architectural information from this abstract form. There are at least three benefits of our framework. First, software designer and analysis tools can use a uniform query language to retrieve architectural information from architectural descriptions written in different ADLs. Second, interpreters and toolsets for ADLs can be developed extremely quickly. Thus, as an ADL rapidly evolves, its implementation infrastructure can be developed at the same pace. Third, an architecture description written in one ADL can be readily translated into another ADL.

1 Introduction

For successfully developing any complex software system, one of the critical tasks is to clearly describe the *architecture* of the software system. At the architectural level of design [4, 5], a software system is typically described as a composition of high-level, interacting components. The choice of an appropriate architecture can lead to a software product that satisfies its requirements and that can be easily modified as new requirements arise, while an inappropriate architecture can lead to cost over-runs and possibly project failure.

Over the last ten years considerable research has been done in the field of software architecture. As a result, numerous architectural description languages(ADLs) have been developed; these include Aesop, Wright, ACME, C2, Rapide, etc. [11]. However, research on ADLs is still primarily an academic endeavor. One of main reason is that each ADL just provides a specific set of capabilities for architectural design and analysis. None of the ADLs (and their

---

* The authors partially supported by grants from the National Science Foundation, Department of Education, and the Environment Protection Agency.

affiliated toolset) are expressive enough to cover *all* the requirements that may be specified while developing a software system. For example, Aesop has a graphical editor [2, 11] that can be specialized with visualizations appropriate to different style. Wright [1, 11] uses a variant of CSP to formalize the behavior of each components and connectors and provides capabilities for statically checking the consistency and completeness of the design. Rapide [9, 11] describes an architecture as a composition of components. Component behavior is specified in terms of the way outgoing events are produced in response to incoming events. Rapide provides tools for analyzing the result of simulations. Ideally, a software designer would like to have as many capabilities as possible available to him/her in the ADL he/she is using. However, given the current situation, the designer will have to use multiple ADLs. Clearly, it will make ADLs more useful and powerful if we can the share architectural description, and integrate the tools that have been developed for various ADLs.

In the paper, we propose a denotational semantics based framework to integrate ADLs. Essentially, the denotational semantics of the ADL notation is written in Horn logic. If the semantics is executable, the denotation of a document written in that notation is also executable and can be used to capture the semantics of architecture information implied in that document. There are at least three benefits for our framework. The first is that software designer and analysis tools can use query language to retrieve architectural descriptions written in different ADLs. The integration becomes more flexible. At the same they can use the desirable format to output query result. We separate the architectural description language and query language. Second, interpreters and toolsets for ADLs can be developed extremely quickly. Thus, as an ADL rapidly evolves, its implementation infrastructure can be developed at the same pace. Third, an architecture description written in one ADL can be readily translated into another ADL due to the use of Horn clause logic for coding their semantics.

The article is organized as follows. Section 2 describes the framework of integration ADLs. Section 3 concentrates on how to write an interpreter for ADLs based on denotational semantics. Section 4 explains the implementation details of our system. Section 5 shows two simple query examples. Finally we draw a conclusion.

2 Retrieving Software Architectural Information Based on Semantic Approach

2.1 ADLs Integration Framework

When you want to integrate multiple languages, a number of approaches can be selected to cope with problems of language heterogeneity. But the common approach can't deal with integration of ADLs. There is a detailed discussion on this issue in ACME paper [3, 6]. In our framework, the whole process is divided into two phases. First we need to extract the architecture information implied in ADL document. In order to integrate more ADLs, we need to obtain more detailed information from documents. Therefore we transfer architectural information into small pieces of information. A whole ADL document can be converted into many small pieces of information. Each small piece of information is a record in a database. We write an interpreter for each ADL to build architectural information database. This kind of interpreter for ADL is easy to implement based on denotational semantics. Such an approach has been applied in lots of applications. In this approach, to transfer one notation Ls to Lt, the denotational semantics of Ls is given in terms of the language constructs of Lt. Given a document coded in Ls, its denotation under this semantics is the document coded in Lt. The executable semantics acts as a translator. Here we can consider that each ADL is Ls and the internal database notation is Lt. Defining the internal fatabase stucture is a challenge. If the information cannot transfer small enough, then database cannot accept all ADLs semantics. If the information become too small, it will effect performance of process. Another point need mention is that the structure of database is different with intermediate ADL language, such as ACME. Because it need not keep ADL syntax and structure according to compatible with other ADLs. It just records architectural information.

In the second phase, software designer and analysis tools can use uniform query language to retrieve architectural information. It is good to use uniform query language to retrieve information. There are two advantages. First is software designer and analysis tools can ignore the format of ADL. Designer and tools just retrieve information from the internal database and not directly from different ADLs. If a newly developed ADL transfers information into internal database, designer and tools also can retrieve information. Second is designer and tools can use declarative query language. The declarative query language is easy to learn and use. The same approach is used to valuate the semantics of query language. Because we can also give denotational semantics for notation of query language. We don't try to translate one ADL into another ADL. We transfer architecture information from database format into certain format which is agreeable to the software designer or analysis tools. Also we transfer the architectural information which is retrieved by query language not whole information in database. Therefore this framework provides more flexibility. For example, Aesop and Wright, ACME developed by CMU, have lots of common conceptions. Therefore it is easy to compare lots of architectural information. Although there are many commonalities, Aesop can not express information about connector behavior. Therefore it is hard to translate CSP part of Wright into Aesop. In our framework, we can ignore to compare or translate this part.

2.2 Denotational Semantics

The denotional semantics-based language [13, 14, 15] consists of three components: syntax, semantic algebra and semantic valuation function. Language syntax is specified as a context free grammar. Semantic algebra is the basic domains along with associated operations. The real meaning of a program is expressed in the terms of these basic domains. Semantic valuation functions are mappings from syntactic structures to corresponding semantic values in the semantic algebra. The implementation of the interpreter exactly follows the theory of denotational semantics.

2.3 Using Horn Logic to Implement Language Interpreter

Traditional method expresses syntax of denotational definitions in the BNF format. The semantic algebras and valuation function are described in lamda-calculus. However a disadvantage of this approach is that while the semantic algebra and the valuation functions can be easily made executable, syntax checking and generation of parse tree cannot. A parser has to be written to do syntax checking and generate parse trees. The two phases constitute an interpreter for the language being defined. An interpreter for a language can be thought of as a specification of its operational semantics, however, using traditional notation it has to be obtained in a complex way.

In our framework we use logic programming (Prolog) to describe all three components. Thus, given a formal language, both its syntax and semantics can be directly specified in logic programming. With logic programming, the syntax of the specification can be specified by Definite Clause Grammars (DCG) [15]. DCG provides some nice methods such as argument passing to obtain a parser to handle context free grammars. Given a grammar written as a DCG, the Prolog interpreter interprets this DCG specification as a logic program which serves as a parser for this grammar.

Semantic specification can be implemented by appropriate valuation predicates, which essentially map the syntax structure (parse trees) of specification to its semantic value. The valuation predicates, defined recursively based on the syntax structure of formal language, not only specify the semantics of the application, but also form an executable application, that can be executed using a logic programming system.

Therefore, logic programming and denotational semantics make it easy to implement an interpreter of a language [7]. All we need to do is to specify the syntactic and semantic specification, and then execute them using logic programming system.

2.4 Semantics-Based Format Translation

Horn logical semantics also provides a formal basis for language translation. Essentially, the meaning of semantics of the language Ls can be given in terms of the constructs of the language Lt. This meaning consists of both syntax and semantic specifications. If these syntax and semantics specifications are executable, then the specification itself acts as a translation system, providing a provably correct translator. The task of specifying the filter from Ls to Lt consists of specifying the DCG for Ls and Lt and the appropriate valuation predicates which essentially map parse tree patterns of Ls to parse tree patterns of Lt. Let Ps(Ss,Ts) to be the top level predicates for the DCG of Ls that take a sentence Ss of Ls, parse it and produces the parse tree Ts for it. Let Pt(St,Tt) be the top level predicate for the DCG of Lt that takes a sentence St of Lt, parse it and produces the parse tree Tt for it. Let Mst(Ts,Tt) be the top level valuation predicate that relates parse trees of Ls and Lt. Then the relation

Translate(Ss,St):-Ps(Ss,Ts),Mst(Ts,Tt),Pt(St,Tt).

Declaratively specifies the equivalence of the source and target sentence under the semantics mapping given. The translate predicate can be used for obtaining St given Ss(and vice versa).

In our Framework, we need not directly translate one ADL to another ADL. We introduce an intermediate structure – internal database. For any ADL, we first transfer architecture information into internal database. Then the user uses query language to retrieve information from internal database. Finally, we transfer the result information into certain ADL format. The predicate of Query(Qc) means there is a query Q and the output format is Lt. The task of query Qc consists of specifying the DCG for Lq and Lt, retrieving information and the appropriate valuation predicates which essentially map result to parse tree patterns of Lt. Let Pq(Qt,Tq) be the top level predicates for the DCG of query language with a sentence Qq of Lq, parse it and produce the parse tree Tq. Let Retrieve(Tq,Ri) be the top level predicate for retrieving information from internal database and produce the result information Ri. Let Mit(Ri,Tt) be the top level valuation predicate that map result information from internal database to Lt. Let Pt(Rt,Tt) be the top level predicate for the DCG of Lt that takes a sentence Rt of Lt, parse it and produces the parse tree Tt for it. The top level query predicate changes to the following form:

Query(Qq,Rt):-Pq(Qq,Tq),Retrieve(Tq,Ri),Mit(Ri,Tt),Pt(Rt,Tt).

3 Introduce Internal Database and Definition of Query Language

In order to explain more detail about internal database structure, we first introduce a very simple example. This example describes a simple client/server structure [6]. In this structure, ADL defines two components, client and sever. They are connected by one connector, rpc. You can find the complete example in ACME [3] paper.

The internal database is used to record architectural information which is described by ADLs. We create the structure of database considered two points. The first is that information must be stored in small pieces of information in order to integrate more ADLs. The second is to keep the semantics first-order. It is not simply because we are interested in using horn logic programming, but also because higher order logic quickly becomes intractable and inefficient. Therefore, we represent ADL document as a set of relations. Different architectural information has different relation name. For example, a whole system is described by relation system. A relation system has three arguments. The first argument denotes the identifier of system or system name. It is a list of name. We use the first argument to identify the elements in database. The second argument indicates type of system. The last argument is used to point to a system body.

Each system body has a unique identifier which is created by system. The system body is described by a relation called systemBody. There are three arguments. The first is identifier of system body. The second is type of body. The third is used to store which elements are contained in the system body. In this example, we can see there are four elements in the system body. They are client, server, rpc and attachment. In order to make the element name unique, we combine the upper level id and element itself to form a unique identifier for elements. Additional benefit is that we can find the relationship between elements using elements name.

Here is part of the internal database for simple client server example.

    acmeADL(acmeADL9, [none_import_define], [[simple_cs]]).
    system([simple_cs], [none_type_appoint], systemBody8).
    systemBody(systemBody8, [none_type_appoint], [[simple_cs, client],
    [simple_cs, server], [simple_cs, rpc], [simple_cs, attachment5]]).
    %define component
    component([simple_cs, client], [none_type_appoint], componentBody2).
    component([simple_cs, server], [none_type_appoint], componentBody3).
    componentBody(componentBody2, [none_type_appoint],
    [[simple_cs, client, 'send-request'], [simple_cs, client, 'request-rate'],
    [simple_cs, client, 'source-code']]).
    componentBody(componentBody3, [none_type_appoint],
    [[simple_cs, server, 'receive-request'], [simple_cs, server, idempotence],
    [simple_cs, server, 'max-concurrent-clients'],
    [simple_cs, server, 'source-code']]).

3.1 Definition of Query Language

We present a query language for ADL, called ADL-QL. ADL-QL requires the following two features. First ADL-QL is declarative. Query users can just express what information is to be obtained. They need not express how to retrieve information. It is easy to use and learn the ADL-QL. Second, query is based on zero or partial knowledge. It is unrealistic to assume the user has complete knowledge about the content and structure of software architecture.

ADL Query language can do the following two tasks. First it can query architectural information from internal database. Second, it can format the query result according to user requirement.

There are two types of architecture information retrieved by the query language. The first is basic information about software architecture. For example, what components are included in current system? What properties the components have? The second is the structure information of software system. For example, the two components are connected or not, the relationship between two components and so on.

The semantics of ADL can be expressed in Horn logic, using the approach described above. An ADL-QL is like this:

    SELECT ArchitectureExpression
    FROM ADL_DOCUMENT
    WHERE WhereClauseExpression
    CONSTRUCT OutputFormat
    USING NameSpace

where SELECT clause indicates what type architectural information is to be retrieved. At present there are eleven predefined types of information. They are system information, component information, connector information, role information, port information, property information, attachment information, path information, contain information, substitution information and connect information. The FROM clause denotes the internal database sources to be queried. The WHERE clause indicates the constraints that the result architectural information need to satisfy. The CONSTRUCT clause defines what format is applied for result information. Currently, we just support ACME and ADML format. ADML [12] is an XML representation for ACME by the Microelectronics and Computer Technology Corporation(MCC). Finally, the USING clause declares the name space that will be used.

ADL-QL queries are also converted to Horn Logic queries, using the same method as before. A syntax specification for ADL-QL as a DCG is developed. The denotational semantics of ADL-QL as a mapping from parse trees to logic programming facts and queries is also specified. Given an ADL-QL query, its denotation can be viewed as a query coded in logic programming. The logic programming coded query can be executed on top of logic programming coded database obtained denotationlly from the database.

4 Implement Integration Framework

4.1 An Interpreter for ADLs to Build Internal Database

In order to build an internal database, we need to write an interpreter for each ADL. As described in section 2, there are three components in the implementation of an interpreter for an ADL. First task is to build a parse tree. The parsing procedure is the first step in implementation of a language interpreter based on denotational semantics approach. The goal of the parsing procedure is to make explicit the hierarchical structure of the input by identifying which parts should be grouped together. The syntactic specification must tell us what hierarchical structure each source code has. Second is to define the semantic algebra. Here the semantic algebra consists of a store domain-internal database and operations used for creating internal database. Third is to define valuate predicate to map from syntactic structures and a global state to a domains that are used to store architectural information.

Build Parse Tree. The syntax of DCG allows context free grammars to be easily expressed in Prolog. The grammar specification automatically acts as a parser after adding one argument to store parser tree. Given the grammar of ADL, the DCG parser builds parse trees for input file. Each node of the parse tree forms the root of a sub tree corresponding to the ADL syntax for that portion of the specification. When transforming BNF grammar into DCG grammar, sometimes we need to make simple changes to the original syntax to remove left-recursion. The following examples illustrate some rules from ACME and their corresponding DCG rules.

For example, ACME system Declaration BNF Grammar rule:

SystemDeclaration ::= <SYSTEM> <IDENTIFIER>
(":" lookup_SystemTypeByName ("," lookup_SystemTypeByName)*)?
("=" SystemBody (";")? | ";")

Change to

SystemDeclaration ::= <SYSTEM> <IDENTIFIER>
   lookup_SystemTypeByName_option "=" SystemBody (";") ?
SystemDeclaration ::= <SYSTEM> <IDENTIFIER>
   lookup_SystemTypeByName_option ";"

DCG Rules:

systemDeclaration(systemArch(ID,TypeList,Body)) ->
   ['System'],id(ID),lookup_systemTypeByName_list_option(TypeList),
   ['='],systemBody(Body),semicolon.
systemDeclaration(systemArch(ID,TypeList)) ->
   ['System'],id(ID),
   lookup_systemTypeByName_list_option(TypeList),[';'].

The above BNF grammar rule states that a system declaration of ACME consists of the key word "SYSTEM" followed by an identifier, and then followed by an one or more type name list which denote types of the current system, and finally followed by a more detail information about system body or terminating with semicolon. We first make little changes to the BNF grammar. Then it is easy to rewrite rules with DCG.

Define Semantic Algebra. In our approach, the semantic algebra consists of two basic domains. One is global store domain, realized as an association list of the form [(Id,Value),] with operations for initialization, accessing, updating the store. The second is internal database domain which is used to store architectural information. It consists of system, component, connector and so on. We also define relative accessing and updating operation for database domain. Logic program can support global data structures through their database facility. It is easy to model the database as a collection of dynamic facts manipulated using assert and retract.

Mapping Semantics. After obtaining the parse tree, we need define a set of valuation predicates. The result of program is obtained by using the semantic mapping function in logic programming to transfer the syntactic tree of ADL to a set of Prolog relation facts. The general structure of evaluation predicate at least consists of four arguments. The first argument is used to express the subtree of parse tree. The second argument is used to return an identifier of current evaluation element. The third is used to express the current global memory. The fourth argument is used to refer to the new global memory after computing the valuation predicate.

The following example illustrates fragments of rules used to map system declaration into a relation of system which store in the global database. The rules essentially compute parse tree to generate the Prolog fact database.

   systemDeclaration_eval(systemArch(ID,TypeList,Body),SystemID,
      Store,NS) :- name_space_push(ID,Store,NS1),
      lookup_systemTypeByName_list_option_eval(TypeList,NameList,
      NS1,NS2),
      systemBody_eval(Body,BodyID,NS2,NS3),name_space_pop(NS3,NS4),
      create_systemDecl(ID,NameList,BodyID,SystemID,NS4,NS).
   systemDeclaration_eval(systemArch(ID,TypeList),SystemID,Store,NS):-

name_space_push(ID,Store,NS1),
lookup_systemTypeByName_list_option_eval(TypeList,NameList,
NS1,NS2),
name_space_pop(NS2,NS3),
create_systemDecl(ID,NameList,[],SystemID,NS3,NS).

In the first evaluation predicate, the value of systemArch(ID,TypeList,Body) denotes a parse tree. It consists of three parts. The first part is identifier of system. The second part is a list of type name. The third part contains the detailed information of system body. We use two evaluation predicates to obtain the list of type name and a unique identifier for system body. Then create a new Prolog facts system(ID,TypeList,BodyID). Here we also use two other predicates:name_space_push and name_space_pop. In order to keep the identifier of elements unique, we need to remember the upper level element identifier. The lower elements identifier consists of an upper level identifier and identifier of itself. For example, one system element called "A" contains one component element called "B". Then the identifier of that component will be [A,B]. Therefore the predicate of name_space_push is to push a new identifier into a global variable called "NameSpace" and name_space_pop is used to remove the end identifier from "NameSpace". The second evaluation predicate has similar semantics except no detailed information about system body.

4.2 An Interpreter for Query Language and Format Result Information

We can use the same approach to deal with query language to retrieve architectural information from internal database. If the query language is simple and has a fix pattern, then we can convert query language to Horn Logic queries. But here the query language is little complex. Therefore it is hard to be converted to horn logic query. We need to write an interpreter for the query language. The procedure is similar to the above description. First we need to write DCG grammar to parse the query language according to the gramma of the query language in BNF. For example, the top level DCG grammar looks as following:

adlQuery(query(Expr,From,Where,Format,NameSpace))->
['SELECT'],architectureExpression(Expr),
['FROM'],adl_document(From),
['WHERE'],whereClauseExpression(Where),
['CONSTRUCT'],outputFormat(Format),
['USING'],name_space(NameSpace).

Then we write a set of evaluation predicates to retrieve architectural information from database. The evaluation predicate first searches all elements which satisfy with architectural expression from database. Then interpreter will compute where clause to erase some elements which can not make where clause true. Finally we format the result information according to construct clause requirement. Here is the top level predicate of evaluation for query language.

adlQuery_eval(query(Expr,From,Where,Format,NameSpace),NS):-
initialize_store(Store),name_space_eval(NameSpace,Store,NS1),
adl_document_eval(From,NS1,NS2),

architectureExpression_eval(Expr, NS2,NS3),
select_whereClauseExpression(Where,NS3,NS4),
outputFormat_eval(Format, NS4,NS).

5 Two Simple Examples of Query Language

Example 1: retrieve component information from internal database
    SELECT component(?ComponentName)
    FROM system(simple_cs) WHERE (?ComponentName = client).
    CONSTRUCT ADML
Show all information of a component "client" from "simple_cs" ADL using ADML format output. The Result is the following:

<AcmeComponentDeclaration id = 'client'>
  <AcmeComponentDescription>
    <AcmePort id = 'send-request'>
    </AcmePort>
    <AcmeProperties>
    <AcmeProperty id = 'request-rate' type = 'float'>17.0
    </AcmeProperty>
    ... ...
</AcmeComponentDeclaration>

Example 2: What elements are contained in an architecture element.
contain(A,B) means an architectural element "A" contains architectural elements "B".
SELECT contain(server, ?List)
FROM system (simple_cs)
WHERE true CONSTRUCT ACME
Show all elements contain in component "server".

    Port send-request;
    Properties {idempotence:boolean = true;}
    Properties {max-concurrent-clients:integer = 1;}
    Properties {source-code:external-file = 'Code-Lib/server.c' }

6 Related Work

Similar work is done by ACME [3, 6] which is an interchange ADL developed by CMU. ACME provides a simple structural framework for representing architectures, together with a liberal annotation mechanism. ACME does not impose any semantic interpretation of an architectural description, but simply provides a syntactic structure on which to hang semantic descriptions, which can then be interpreted by tools.
    An architectural design is shared among several ADLS by first translating the design into an ACME representation. This representation can be read by other ADLs that understand ACME, or it can be manipulated by tools that operate on ACME directly. The main benefit of ACME is that it defines an intermediate language. Due to open semantic framework, ACME can represent more general architecture information compared to previous ADLs. But ACME has a big problem that it only integrate compatible ADLs. Therefore it is hard to integrate new developing ADL.

Comparing our method with ACME, there are three differences:

1. ACME defines an interchange ADL. We define a intermediate structure-internal architectural database. Because our data structure need not to be compatible with other ADL syntax. Therefore it can be used to represent more ADLs.
2. ACME tries to translate the whole ADL file between two or more ADLs. We just transfer the result information of query. It is easy to implement subset language translation.
3. We use uniform query language to retrieve architectural information. There are two different tasks. ADL is used to represent structure of software system. Query language is used to retrieve these information. We use two different languages to describe different tasks.

Another similar work in this area includes research work on developing an XML syntax for ADL(xADL). This work is done by University of California at Irvine. They developed an ADL-neutral interchange format called Extensible Architecture Description Language(xADL) [8]. xADL is designed as a shared language for representing a variety of possible ADLs. xADL can be customized to different style ADL. In the case study of their work, they customized xADL to C2 [10] style. They have adopted XML as key technology for enabling architecture centric tool integration in the ArchStudio 2.0 IDE which is used to support the development of C2 style software.

7 Conclusions

In this paper, we propose a new integration framework to integrate different kinds of ADLs. Under this framework we can integrate more ADLs than intermediate ADL approach. Software designer and analysis tools can use uniform query language to retrieve architectural information from architectural descriptions written in different ADLs. We do not try to write a whole translator among different ADLs. We just transfer subset of ADL.

Second, interpreters and toolsets for ADLs can be developed extremely quickly. Thus, as an ADL rapidly evolves, its implementation infrastructure can be developed at the same pace. Third, an architecture description written in one ADL can be readily translated into another ADL due to the use of Horn clause logic for coding their semantics.

Then we present a denotational semantics method to implement this framework. We demonstrate our approach by developing the Horn logical denotational semantics for ACME, ADML and query language. Interpreters and toolsets for ADLs can be developed extremely quickly. Thus, as an ADL rapidly evolves, its implementation infrastructure can be developed at the same pace.

References

1. R. Allen and D. Garlan. A formal basis for architectural connection. ACM Transactions on Software Engineering and Methodology, July 1997.
2. D. Garlan, R. Allen, and J. Ockerbloom. Exploiting Style in Architectural Design Environments. In Proceedings of SIGSOFT'94: The Second ACM SIGSOFT Symposium on the Foundation of Software Engineering, pages 179-185. ACM Press, December 1994.

3. D. Garlan, R. T. Monroe and D. Wile. Acme: An Architecture Description Interchange Language. In Proceedings of CASCON'97, pages 169-183, Ontario, Canada, November, 1997.
4. D. Garlan and D. Perry. "Introduction to the special issue on Software Architecture". IEEE Transactions on Software Engineering, 21(4), April 1995.
5. D. Garlan and M. Shaw. "An Introduction to Software Architecture". In V. Ambriola and G. Tortora, editors, Advances in Software Engineering and Knowledge Engineering. World Scientific Publishing Company, 1993.
6. D. Garlan and Z. Wang. A Case Study in Software Architecture Interchange. In Proceedings of Coordination'99, Springer Verlag, 1999.
7. G. Gupta. Horn logic denotations and their applications. In The Logic Programming Paradigm: A 25 year perspective. Springer-Verlag, 1999:127-160.
8. R. Khare, M. Guntersdorfer, P. Oreizy, N. Medvidovic, R. N. Taylor. xADL: Enabling Architecture-Centric Tool Integration With XML. In Proceedings of the 34th Hawaii Conference on System Sciences, Mani, Hawaii, January 2001
9. D. C Luckham, L. M. Augustin, J. J. Kenney, J. Veera, D. Bryan, and W. Mann. Specification and analysis of system architecture using Rapide. IEEE Transactions on Software Engineering, Special Issue on Software Architecture, 21(4):336-355, April 1995.
10. N. Medvidovic, P. Oreizy, Robbins, J.E., and R. N. Taylor. Using object-oriented typing to support architectural design in the C2 style. SIGSOFT'96. pp24-32. San Francisco, CA, October 1996.
11. N. Medvidovic and R. N. Taylor. Architecture description languages. In Software Engineering - ESEC/FSE'97, volume 1301 of Lecture Notes in Computer Science, Zurich, Switzerland, September 1997, Springer. Also published as Software Engineering Notes, Vol 22, No 6, November 1997.
12. Open Group Technology Report. "Architecture Description Markup Language (ADML)", available online at http://xml.coverpages.org/adml.html, June 2000
13. D. Schmidt. Denotational Semantics: a Methodology for Language Development. W.C. Brown Publishers, 1986.
14. D. Schmidt. Programming language semantics. In CRC Handbook of Computer Science, Allen Tucker, ed., CRC Press, Boca Raton, FL, 1996. Summary version, CM Computing Surveys 28-1 (1996) 265-267.
15. L. Sterling & S. Shapiro. The Art of Prolog. MIT Press, 1994.

Automated Runtime Validation of Software Architecture Design

Zhijiang Dong[1], Yujian Fu[1], Yue Fu[2], and Xudong He[1]

[1] School of Computer Science, Florida International University,
{zdong01, yfu002, hex}@cs.fiu.edu
[2] Technical center, Dogain securities Co., Ltd.
fuy@ydzq.com.cn

Abstract. The benefits of architecture description languages (ADLs) cannot be fully captured without a automated and validated realization of software architecture designs. In addition to the automated realization of software architecture designs, we validate the realization process by exploring the runtime verification technique and aspect-oriented programming. More specifically, system properties are not only verified against design models, but also verified during execution of the generated implementation of software architecture designs. All these can be done in an automated way. In this paper, we show that our methodology of automated realization of software architecture designs and validation of the implementation is viable through a case study.

1 Introduction

Software architecture plays a critical role in software development processes since it helps us further understand systems through the construction of high-level system structures and it becomes the corner stone for subsequent software development activities. Therefore, lots of work have been done in software engineering community to validate and verify architectures against system requirements or specifications.

However, a complete and correct software architecture at design level does not ensure the correctness of its implementation because the transformation from a model to its implementation is error-prone, and "while architectural analysis in existing ADLs may reveal important architectural properties, those properties are not guaranteed to hold in the implementations" [1]. In order to attack this problem, on the one hand, the transformation had better to be done automatically with tool support, which can prevent man-made errors. Although automatic programming from a formal specification is in general impossible [3], generating the implementation from design models automatically is viable since architectural design provides enough details. Currently, some architecture description languages (ADLs) support the implementation of architectural designs in a number of ways [24, 19], but none of them can enforce communication integrity [20, 18] in the implementation, which is necessary to enable architectural reasoning about an implementation [1]. On the other hand, properties held in

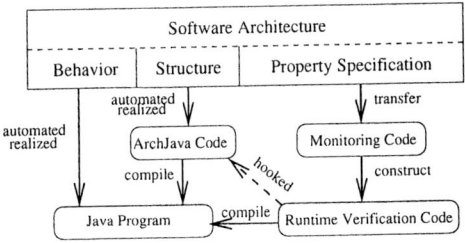

Fig. 1. Framework of Our Approach

architectures should be guaranteed to hold in implementations. This means, the transformation not only ensures the functionality correctness of implementations, but also guarantees the correctness of implementations with regard to architectural properties. Unfortunately, none of current ADLs tools can achieve this goal.

In this paper, we propose an approach to achieve above goals, i.e. not only implements software architectures automatically, but also verifies if an architectural properties are satisfied at the implementation, and applies the approach to a case – station-to-station protocol – to show its feasibility and practicability. As Fig. 1 indicates, the structure and the behavior of software architectures are realized in Java and ArchJava [1] respectively by supported tools. These codes, called functionality code, simulate the execution of architectures. The property specifications that describe important behavioral properties are implemented as aspects of components or connectors. The aspects containing runtime verification code are weaved into functionality code through hooks (joinpoints) provided by aspect-oriented programming. To our best knowledge, we are the first to integrate automated realization, runtime verification and aspect-oriented programming seamlessly for software architectures, which brings some benefits that cannot be achieved by using individual technique: verifying architecture design models at implementation level, presenting counter examples for property violation, validating automated realization process, providing potentiality to detect exceptions and steer model execution at runtime, and most importantly these work can be done automatically.

2 Preliminaries

In our work, SAM (**S**oftware **A**rchitecture **M**odel) [15] is chosen as the architectural description language because unlike other ADLs, SAM not only provides means to define structure and behavior of software architectures, but also provides means to specify behavioral properties for components and connectors that should hold in architectures.

SAM is an architectural description model based on Petri nets [21], which are well-suited for modeling distributed systems. SAM [15] has dual formalisms underlying – Petri nets and Temporal logic. Petri nets are used to describe behavioral models of components and connectors while temporal logic is used to specify system properties of components and connectors.

SAM architecture model is hierarchically defined as follows. A set of compositions $C = \{C_1, C_2, ..., C_k\}$ represents different design levels or subsystems. A set of component C_{m_i} and connectors C_{n_i} are specified within each composition C_i as well as a set of composition constraints C_{s_i}, e.g. $C_i = \{C_{m_i}, C_{n_i}, C_{s_i}\}$. In addition, each component or connector is composed of two elements, a behavioral model and a property specification, e.g. $C_{ij} = (S_{ij}, B_{ij})$. Each behavioral model is described by a Petri net, while a property specification by a temporal logical formula. The atomic proposition used in the first order temporal logic formula is the ports of each component or connector. Thus each behavioral model can be connected with its property specification. A component C_{m_i} or a connector C_{n_i} can be refined to a low level composition C_l by a mapping relation h, e.g. $h(C_{m_i})$ or $h(C_{m_i}) = C_l$.

SAM gives the flexibility to choose any variant of Petri nets and temporal logics to specify behavior and constraints according to system characteristics. In our case, Predicate Transition (PrT) net [12] and linear temporal logic (LTL) are chosen.

Predicate Transition (PrT) net [12] is a high level Petri net. A PrT has a net structure: (P,T,F), where P is a set of places represented by circles, T is a set of transitions represented by rectangles and T is disjoint from P, and F is a relation between P and T represented by arcs. Each place is assigned a sort indicating what kind of tokens it can contain. The tokens in a place can be viewed as a multi-set over the sort. A marking of a PrT net is a function that assigns tokens to each place. A label is assigned to each arc to describe types and numbers of tokens that flow along this arc. Each transition has a boolean expression called guard, which specifies the relationship among arcs related with the transition. A transition is enabled if there is an assignment to all variables occurred in arcs related with the transition such that each incoming place contains the set of tokens specified by the label of the arc, and the guard of the transition is satisfied. A enabled transition is fired under an assignment by removing tokens from incoming places and add tokens to outgoing places.

3 Methodology

Fig. 2 shows the framework of our approach. The core part is the SAM parser, which is responsible for the automatic generation of functionality code and runtime verification code. Runtime verification code is weaved into functionality code through joinpoints provided by aspect-oriented programming. The input of the SAM parser is a XML file, which specifies SAM structures (such as components, connectors, ports and their relationships) and related property specifications. In the XML file, SAM behavior is defined as a reference to a Petri Net Markup Language (PNML) [4] file, which is an XML-based interchange format

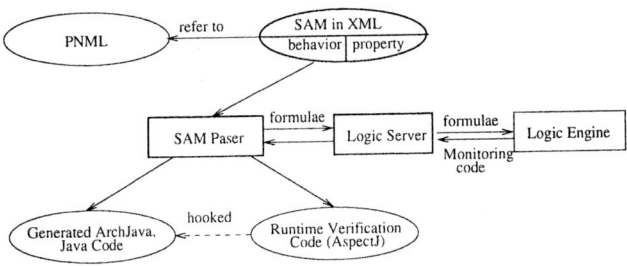

Fig. 2. The Methodology

for Petri nets. The logic engine is responsible to construct a piece of pseudo code called monitoring code for each temporal logic formula. A piece of monitoring code is invoked to check if the corresponding formula is satisfied whenever an interesting event occurs. The logic server is a middleware that translates monitoring code to the target language, here Java. The SAM parser merges all translated monitoring code for properties of a component or a connector into an aspect. All generated aspects are called runtime verification code.

3.1 Automated Generation of Functionality Code

Automated realization of functionality code for SAM models consists of two parts: generating code for structure and behavior respectively. In order to generate code for behavior (PrTs), we predefine a set of classes called templates, which specify structure and dynamic semantics of high level Petri nets. For example, the basic elements of Petri nets such as places, arcs, transitions, guards, inscriptions are defined by individual classes. We also provide dynamic semantics of Petri nets in Java classes *Net* and *Transition*. In other words, we provide a general but maybe not efficient approach to check if a transition is enabled and to fire a transition. In our work, a class is constructed as a child of templates for each net, arc inscription, and guard. The user can provide a more efficient way to check the enableness of a transition and the way to fire it by overloading methods of corresponding classes without any side effects on other transitions. The execution of generated code is non-deterministic, i.e. an enabled transition and a valid assignment is randomly chosen to fire.

It is hard to generate code automatically given a Petri net due to the complexity of sorts, guard conditions of transition and arc labels [17]. Although we cannot achieve this goal for Petri nets in general, we can achieve it if the specifications of Petri nets satisfy the following restrictions:

- The sorts of Petri nets either are Java primitive types such as int, long, and boolean etc., or are defined as a Java classes including its operators, or are a product of already defined sorts.
- The type of variables occurred in the label of an incoming arc of a transition is the same as the token type of the incoming place.
- Only labels of incoming arcs of transitions can introduce variables.

– If a variable is a product type such as int×int and this product type is generated by Petri net code generator, its field is referred in the form of ".field?", where ? is the field sequence number starting at 1. For example, x is a variable of type int×int, then $x.field1$ and $x.field2$ refer to first and second field respectively.

SAM structure is implemented as ArchJava [1] code by the SAM parser. ArchJava is an extension to Java that seamlessly unifies software architecture with implementation, which uses a type system to ensure that the implementation conforms to architectural constraints. In other words, ArchJava is proposed to avoid inconsistency, confusion, and violation of architecture properties when decoupling implementation code from software architecture. To our best knowledge, ArchJava is the best candidate to the target language for the implementation of SAM structure – not only because it provides architecture concepts such as components, ports as first-level entities, but also because it enforces communication integrity. A system has communication integrity of implementation if components only communicate directly with the components they are connected to in the architecture.

In the SAM Parser, it is straightforward to realized components/connectors, compositions, and ports as ArchJava entities such as components, component compositions, and ports respectively. More specifically, an incoming/outgoing port in SAM is realized by a ArchJava port that declares a *provides/requires* method. A SAM component/connector is realized as a ArchJava component class that consists of the declarations of ports, the mapping between ports and places of its behavioral Petri net, reference to its generated behavioral code, and other necessary methods. A SAM composition is realized as a ArchJava component composition that specifies and establishes dynamic connections among sub-components and contains port declarations if necessary. More detailed information about automated generation of functionality code can be found at [11]. Due to the space limit, only generated codes for the component *TrustedAuthority* and the composition *Alice* in Fig. 4 are attached at the appendix.

3.2 Automated Generation of Runtime Verification Code

Runtime verification [16] has been proposed as a lightweight formal method applied during program execution. It can be viewed as a complement to traditional methods of proving design model or programs correct before execution. Aspect-oriented software engineering [22] and aspect-oriented programming [10] were proposed to separate concerns during design and implementation. Aspect-Oriented Programming complements OO programming by allowing the developer to dynamically modify the static OO model to create a system that can grow to meet new requirements. In other words, it allows us to dynamically modify models or implementations to include code required for secondary requirements (in our case, it is runtime verification) without modifying the original code.

The SAM parser generates runtime verification code automatically and weaves it into functionality code seamlessly without side effects on the functionality

```
public aspect Model_Com_AliceMonitorAspect {                          ← pointcut defintion
    pointcut MonitorPoint(): (call(void addMessage(String, Object))
                           || call(void removeMessage(String, Object)));
    after(Model_Com_Alice$C thisObject)
        : target(thisObject) && MonitorPoint() {                        advice
        F_Alice_M1_Exist(thisObject);
        F_Alice_M1_2_M2(thisObject);
        F_Alice_M2_2_M3(thisObject);
    }
}

private boolean Model_Com_Alice$C.F_Alice_M1_2_M2_hasResult = false;
private boolean Model_Com_Alice$C.F_Alice_M1_2_M2_result = false;      helper variables

public void F_Alice_M1_2_M2(Model_Com_Alice$C  thisObject) {
    if (thisObject.F_Alice_M1_2_M2_hasResult)
        return;
    String   info = "Formula  F_Alice_M1_2_M2:\n";
    boolean Pm1_o_A = ( thisObject.isMessageContained("m1_o_A","<Alice,gx>") );
    info += "\tPm1_o_A" + "=" + Pm1_o_A + "\n";
    boolean Pm2_i_A = ( thisObject.isMessageContained("m2_i_A",
                      "<<Bob,B_Public,BobB_Public>,gy,<<gx,gy>,<B_Private,gy,gx>>>") );
    info += "\tPm2_i_A" + "=" + Pm2_i_A + "\n";

    thisObject.F_Alice_M1_2_M2_$pre[0] = thisObject.F_Alice_M1_2_M2_$now[0] ;
    thisObject.F_Alice_M1_2_M2_$pre[1] = thisObject.F_Alice_M1_2_M2_$now[1] ;
    thisObject.F_Alice_M1_2_M2_$now[1] = Pm1_o_A || thisObject.F_Alice_M1_2_M2_$pre[1];
    thisObject.F_Alice_M1_2_M2_$now[0] = thisObject.F_Alice_M1_2_M2_$pre[0] &&
                                        (! Pm2_i_A || thisObject.F_Alice_M1_2_M2_$now[1]);
    if (! thisObject.F_Alice_M1_2_M2_$now[0]) {
        thisObject.F_Alice_M1_2_M2_hasResult = true;
        thisObject.F_Alice_M1_2_M2_result = false;
        info += "Formula F_Alice_M1_2_M2 is violated!\n\n";
        Log.recordPropertyStatus(info);
        return;
    }
    thisObject.F_Alice_M1_2_M2_hasResult = false;
    info += "Cannot judge Formula F_Alice_M1_2_M2 currently!\n\n";
    Log.recordPropertyStatus(info);
}

public void Model_Com_Alice$C.generateSummary() {
    ...
}
```

Fig. 3. Generated Aspect for Composition *Alice*

code. In order to generate monitoring codes for properties (linear temporal formulae), a logic server, Maude [6] in our case, is necessary. Maude, acting as the main algorithm generator in the framework, constructs an efficient dynamic programming algorithm (i.e. monitoring code) from any LTL formula [23]. The generated algorithm can check if the corresponding LTL formula is satisfied over an event trace.

The SAM parser weaves monitoring code into functionality code by integrating them as aspects. In aspect-oriented programming, AspectJ [2] in our case, aspects wrap up *pointcuts*, *advice*, and *inter-type declarations* in a modular unit of crosscutting implementation where *pointcuts* pick out certain join points in the program flow, *advice* brings together a pointcut (to pick out join points) and a body of code (to run at each of those join points), and *Inter-type declarations* are declarations that cut across classes and their hierarchies. In our case, for each component or connector, *pointcuts* specify time spots: whenever a port sends or receives a message; pieces of code brought together by *advice* with *pointcuts* are the generated monitoring code; and *Inter-type declaration* specifies helper variables and methods. Fig. 3, which is a part of generated aspect for composition *Alice* in Fig. 4, clearly shows the way to weave runtime verification code into functionality code through aspects. Currently the SAM parser can handle future time linear temporal formulae as well as past time linear temporal formulae.

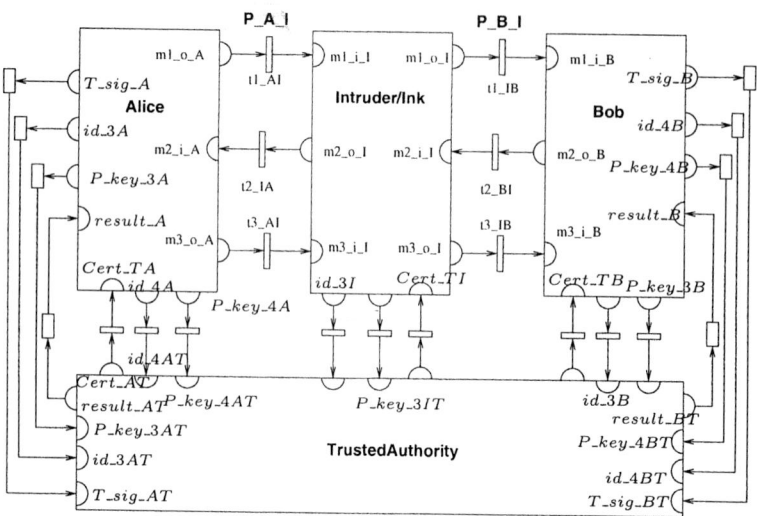

Fig. 4. SAM Architecture of STS with Intruder

By combining runtime verification and automated implementation of software architecture, we can obtain the following benefits:

- The transformation from design models to implementations is generally informal, therefore error-prone. Automated implementation provide a means to prevent man-made errors, and runtime verification can validate transformation indirectly.
- Runtime verification at implementation level is a natural complement to analysis techniques of design level. Not all properties can be verified against a design model either due to the state space explosion problem or due to characteristic of open-systems. In either case, runtime verification can be explored to verify the correctness of design models.
- Runtime verification provides a mechanism to handle exceptions of implementations that are not detected during development or testing.

4 Case Study – Network Security Protocol Under Attack

E-commerce and enterprise systems can be secured in many different ways from simple use of password to digital authentication. State-to-state ENC (STS-ENC) protocol, a version of the authenticated Diffie-Hellman key agreement protocol [7], is to provide desirable security attributes in the network communication. The immunity is achieved by allowing the two parties to authenticate themselves to each other by the use of digital signatures and public-key certificates.

But this is not strong enough to immune from malicious attacks. Public key substitution attacks [5] on the protocol is an attack on a key agreement protocol that mislead one principal to false beliefs. An participant A ends up believing she shares a key with B, and although this is in fact the case, B mistakenly believes the key is instead shared with an entity $I \neq A$. We use $A \hookrightarrow B$ to represent that A sends a message intended for B, but intercepted by intruder I. This attacks can be described in the following message sequence (A for Alice, B for Bob and I for intruder Ink):

1. $M1: A \hookrightarrow B \quad A, \alpha^{rA}$
2. $M1': I \to B \quad I, \alpha^{rA}$
3. $M2: B \hookrightarrow A \quad Cert_B, \alpha^{rB}, E_K(S_B(\alpha^{rB}, \alpha^{rA}))$
4. $M2': I \to A \quad Cert_B, \alpha^{rB}, E_K(S_B(\alpha^{rB}, \alpha^{rA}))$
5. $M3: A \hookrightarrow B \quad Cert_A, E_K(S_A(\alpha^{rA}, \alpha^{rB}))$
6. $M3': I \to B \quad Cert_I, E_K(S_A(\alpha^{rA}, \alpha^{rB}))$

where $Cert_A = (A, P_A, s_T\{A, P_A\})$, is A's certificate containing A's identifying information, A's public key P_A, and a trusted authority T's signature s_T over these information. $S_A(x)$ is A's signature on x using her secret key. $E_K(M)$ is encryption over message M using a symmetric key encryption scheme with key $K = \alpha^{rA \times rB}$, which is the ephemeral Diffie-Hellman shared secret key. rA and rB are the number picked up randomly by A and B respectively. In this message sequence, steps 1, 3, and 5 establish the normal communication between A and B without intruder.

The series of steps indicate an intruder Ink successfully impersonate Alice to communicate with Bob. The communication starts from Alice sending a message $M1$ to Bob, which is intercepted by Ink. Intruder Ink uses P_A as its own public key, to impersonate Alice to get the shared key with Bob. After Ink intercepts message $M1$, he impersonates Alice and sends a modified message $M1'$ with his identifying information to Bob. When Ink receives the message $M2$ from Bob, he sends message $M2'$ to Alice without modification. Thus when Alice sends out the message $M3$, he intercepts and decrypts it with the shared key, and sends the faked message $M3'$ with his certificate to Bob.

4.1 SAM Model of Network Security Protocol Under Attack

The top level of SAM model of STS-ENC protocol under attack scenario is demonstrated in Fig. 4. There are one component *TrustedAuthority*, three compositions *Alice*, *Intruder*, and *Bob* denoted by rectangles, and five connectors in this level. Due to space limit, the mappings from compositions to subcomponents and behavioral specifications are omitted. Because each connector behaves just like a data pipe, we simply explain components functionalities in the following.

The functionalities of component *TrustedAuthority* is either to calculate a certificate given identifying information and a public key, or to check if a certificate is valid or not. The composition *Alice* is responsible for sending message $M1$, receiving message $M2'$, checking the validation of message $M2'$, and sending message $M3$. The composition *Intruder/Ink* intercepts message $M1$, substitutes identifying information, sends message $M1'$, intercepts message $M2$, sends message $M2'$, intercepts message $M3$, substitutes certificate and sends message $M3'$. The composition *Bob* is responsible for receiving message $M1'$, sending message $M2$, receiving message $M3'$, and checking the validation of message $M3'$ according to previous information.

In SAM, components communicate with each other through ports represented as semicircles. An incoming port, represented by a semicircle inside of the component, only receives messages from other components at the same hierarchy, like port $m2\_i\_A$ of composition *Alice* in Fig. 4. Similarly, an outgoing port, represented by a semicircle outside of the component, only sends messages to other components, like port $m2\_o\_I$ of composition *Intruder* in Fig. 4. Therefore, composition *Intruder* can sends a message $M2'$ from the outgoing port $m2\_o\_I$ to the incoming port $m2\_i\_A$ of the composition *Alice* through the connector P_A_I.

4.2 System Properties

In SAM model, we have to make sure that compositions *Alice*, *Ink*, and *Bob* behave as expected from STS-ENC protocol. In other words, composition *Alice* first sends message $M1$, then receives message $M1'$, and finally sends message $M3$. This can be expressed by the following formulae on composition *Alice*:

$$\Diamond(m3\_o\_A(< Cert_B, E_K(S_A(\alpha^{rA}, \alpha^{rB})) >)) \tag{1}$$

$$[*](m2\_i\_A(< Cert_B, \alpha^{rB}, E_K(S_B(\alpha^{rB}, \alpha^{rA})) >) \to$$
$$\langle *\rangle(m1\_o\_A(< A, \alpha^{rA} >))) \tag{2}$$

$$[*](m3\_o\_A(< Cert_B, E_K(S_A(\alpha^{rA}, \alpha^{rB})) >) \to$$
$$\langle *\rangle(m2\_i\_A(< Cert_B, \alpha^{rB}, E_K(S_B(\alpha^{rB}, \alpha^{rA})) >))) \tag{3}$$

The atomic predicate in above formula is in the form $Port(m)$, which is evaluated true if specified port contains the message m. For example, predicate $m1\_o\_A(< A, \alpha^{rA} >)$ is true if the port $m1\_o\_A$ of composition *Alice* has a message $< A, \alpha^{rA} >$. Our work supports future time linear temporal logic and past time linear temporal logic. Formula 1 is a future time LTL formula, while formulae 2 and 3 are past time LTL. In above formulae, $\Diamond$, $[*]$, and $\langle *\rangle$ are future time operator eventually, past time operator SometimeInThePast (sometime in the past), and AlwaysInThePast (always in the past) respectively.

Similarly, we can specify formulae for compositions *Bob* and *Ink* to guarantee the correctness of their behavior. In addition to these formulae, another formula

$$\Diamond(Succ(true)) \tag{4}$$

on composition *Bob* is defined to indicate if STS-ENC protocol can be attacked by the public key substitution attack, where $Succ$ is a outgoing port of a sub component of composition *Bob*. In other words, if formula 4 is satisfied, it means *Alice* thinks she shares a key with *Bob*, but *Bob* thinks he shares a key with third party *Ink*.

4.3 Results

The SAM model of STS-ENC protocol totally has 3 compositions, 16 components, 20 connectors, 312 ports, and 36 high level Petri nets with 290 places, 116 transitions and 331 arcs. It takes about 10 seconds for the SAM parser to generate the implementation of SAM model of STS-ENC protocol on a P4 2.4Ghz machine with 512MB RAM. The generated implementation has 491 files, and it is executable without any modification. Most of them (419) is the implementation of components or connectors behavior (Petri nets). The reason of generating so many files is due to the most important principle for the SAM parser: We have to make the generated code easy to understand and minimize the cost of modification. It takes about 96 seconds for the generated implementation to execute and verify above 10 formulae. The execution of the generated implementation fires transition 114 times, i.e. almost one transition is fired every second. Most of the time is spend on the search of enabled transition and valid assignments to variables. The code can be manually optimized for critical transitions by overriding methods that judge if a transition is enabled.

From the log file generated in the execution of the implementation, the formula 4 is true, which means that the well-known public key substitution attacks on STS-ENC protocol is viable. In other words, *Alice* wants to share a public key with *Bob*. But in fact, *Bob* shares a public key with *Ink*. From the log file, we also can see that the formula 1 holds. However, the evaluations of formulae 2 and 3 are neither true nor false. This seems strange at first since the purpose of runtime verification was to check if formulae are satisfied or not. However this result is correct because these two formulae are past time LTL, which are supposed to be always satisfied. In other words, runtime verification code only reports exception for past time LTL formulae if it is violated, just like code in Fig. 3. Therefore, the unsure results for formulae 2 and 3 indicate that there are no violation detected. This means these formulae hold during the program execution, which assures the behavioral correctness of *Alice*, *Ink*, and *Bob*.

5 Conclusion and Discussion

We have proposed an approach for validating conformance of an architecture model to system properties in an automatic way. The architecture model is automated realized in ArchJava/Java through a SAM parser. This parser not only generates code for structure and behavior of a architecture design model, but also generates runtime verification codes for system properties. The generated functionality code and runtime verification code are executable without any manual modification if SAM specifications follow the restrictions mentioned in section 3.1. By integrating automated realization technique and runtime verification technique on architecture design models, we not only verify the correctness of design models against system properties, but also validate the automated realization process indirectly. To our best knowledge, this is the first work to combine runtime verification, aspect-oriented programming with automated realization of architectural design models.

Currently, most ADLs such as MetaH [25],Unicon [24] and Weaves [13], support semi-automatic code generation from an architecture model. However, none of them can enforce communication integrity [20, 18] in the implementation that is necessary to enable architectural reasoning about an implementation [1].

For the runtime verification part, our work is similar to MaC tool [16]. MaC provides a general framework to verify specified properties against Java program.

It defines two script languages to specify properties and events. However, our work focus on a more specific area – architectural design models, not on any Java program, which makes it possible to hide event definition, event recognize and runtime verification code generation. In other words, our work is more automated. Several other approaches to runtime verification (especially for Java) exist. Java PathExplorer [14] picks up the idea of runtime verification and uses the Maude rewriting logic tool [6] to implement LTL. The Temporal Rover [8, 9] checks time-dependent specifications and handles assertions embedded in comments by source-to-source transformation.

Acknowledgements. This work is supported in part by NSF under grant HRD-0317692 and by NASA under grant NAG 2-1440.

References

[1] J. Aldrich, C. Chambers, and D. Notkin. Archjava: Connecting Software Architecture to Implementation. In *International Conference on Software Engineering, Orlando, FL, USA*, May 2002.

[2] AspectJ Project. http://eclipse.org/aspectj/.

[3] R. Balzer. A 15 year Perspective on Automatic Programming. *IEEE Transactions on Software Engineering*, 11(11):1257–1268, 1985.

[4] J. Billington, S. Christensen, et al. The Petri Net Markup Language: Concepts, Technology, and Tools. In *Proceedings of the 24th International Conference on Applications and Theory of Petri Nets (ICATPN 2003)*, volume 2679 of *Lecture Notes in Computer Science*, pages 483–505. Springer-Verlag, June 2003.

[5] S. Blake-Wilson and A. Menezes. Unknown Key-Share Attacks on the Station-to-Station (STS) Protocol. Technical Report CORR 98-42, University of Waterloo, 1998.

[6] M. Clavel, F. J. Durán, S. Eker, P. Lincoln, N. Martí-Oliet, J. Meseguer, and J. F. Quesada. Maude: Specification and Programming in Rewriting Logic. http://maude.csl.sri.com/papers, March 1999.

[7] W. Diffie, P. C. van Oorschot, and M. J. Wiener. Authentication and Authenticated Key Exchanges. *Designs, Codes and Cryptography*, 2, 1992.

[8] D. Drusinsky. The Temporal Rover and the ATG Rover. In *Proceedings of SPIN: SPIN Model Checking and Software Verification, Stanford, California, USA*, Lecture Notes in Computer Science, pages 323–330, 2000.

[9] D. Drusinsky. Monitoring Temporal Rules Combined with Time Series. In *Proceedings of CAV'03: Computer Aided Verification, Boulder, Colorado, USA*, Lecture Notes in Computer Science, pages 114–118, 2003.

[10] T. Elrad, R. E. Filman, and A. Bader. Aspect-oriented programming: Introduction. *Communnications of the ACM*, 44(10):29–32, 2001.

[11] Y. Fu, Z. Dong, and X. He. A Methodology of Automated Realization of a Software Architecture Design. In *Proceedings of the The Seventeenth International Conference on Software Engineering and Knowledge Engineering (SEKE2005)*, 2005.

[12] H. J. Genrich. Predicate/Transition Nets. *Lecture Notes in Computer Science*, 254, 1987.

[13] M. M. Gorlick and R. R. Razouk. Using Weaves for Software Construction and Analysis. In *Proceedings of the 13th International Conference on Software Engineering (ICSEI3)*, Austin, TX, USA, May 1991.

[14] K. Havelund and G. Rosu. An Overview of the Runtime Verification Tool Java PathExplorer. *Journal of Formal Methods in System Design*, 2004.

[15] X. He. A Framework for Specifying and Verifying Software Architecture Specifications in SAM. volume 45 of *The Computer Journal*, pages 111–128, 2002.

[16] M. Kim, S. Kannan, I. Lee, and O. Sokolsky. Java-MaC: a Run-time Assurance Tool for Java. In *Proceedings of of RV'01: First International Workshop on Runtime Verification, Paris, France*, Electronic Notes in Theoretical Computer Science. Elsevier Science, 2001.

[17] S. W. Lewandowski and X. He. Generating Code for Hierarchical Predicate Transition Net Based Designs. In *Proceedings of the 12th International Conference on Software Engineering & Knowledge Engineering*, pages 15–22, Chicago, U.S.A., July 2000.

[18] D. C. Luckham and J. Vera. An Event Based Architecture Definition Language. *IEEE Transactions on Software Engineering*, 21(9), 1995.

[19] N. Medvidovic, P. Oreizy, et al. Using Object-Oriented Typing to Support Architectural Design in the C2 Style. In *Proceedings of the 4th ACM SIGSOFT Symposium on Foundations of Software Engineering*, pages 24–32, 1996.

[20] M. Moriconi, X. Qian, and R. A. Riemenschneider. Correct Architecture Refinement. *IEEE Transactions on Software Engineering*, 21(5), 1995.

[21] T. Murata. Petri Nets: Properties, Analysis and Applications. *Proceedings of the IEEE*, 77(4):541–580, 1989.

[22] G. Murphy and K. Lieberherr, editors. *Proceedings of the 3rd International Conference on Aspect-oriented Software Development*. ACM Press, 2004.

[23] G. Rosu and K. Havelund. Rewriting-Based Techniques for Runtime Verification. *Journal of Automated Software Engineering*, 2004.

[24] M. Shaw, R. DeLine, D. V. Klein, T. L. Ross, D. M. Young, and G. Zelesnik. Abstractions for Software Architecture and Tools to Support Them. IEEE Transactions on Software Engineering, April 1995.

[25] S. Vestal. MetaH User's Manual, 1998.

Analyzing Loop Paths for Execution Time Estimation

Abhik Roychoudhury, Tulika Mitra, and Hemendra Singh Negi

School of Computing, National University of Singapore
{abhik, tulika, hemendra}@comp.nus.edu.sg

Abstract. Statically estimating the worst case execution time of a program is important for real-time embedded software. This is difficult even in the programming language level due to the inherent difficulty in detecting infeasible paths in a program's control flow graph. In this paper, we study the problem of accurately bounding the execution time of a program loop. This involves infeasible path detection followed by timing analysis. We employ constraint propagation methods to detect infeasible paths spanning across loop iterations. Our timing analysis is exact modulo the infeasible path information provided. Moreover, the analysis is efficient since it relies on memoization techniques to avoid exhaustive enumeration of all paths through a loop. The precision of our timing analysis is demonstrated on different benchmark programs.

1 Introduction

Statically analyzing the *worst-case execution time* (WCET) of a program is important for real-time embedded software. An embedded system contains processor(s) running specific application programs which communicate with an external environment in a timely fashion. These application programs thus have real-time requirements, that is, there are hard deadlines on the execution time of such software. Therefore, it is important to perform static analysis of embedded software to guarantee the satisfiability of all timing constraints. One of the prominent uses of the WCET estimate of a program is in schedulability analysis.

Due to its inherent importance in embedded system design, timing analysis of embedded software has been extensively studied [6, 8, 12, 13, 17, 18, 20]. Usually this involves (a) a programming language level path analysis to find out infeasible paths in the program's control flow graph, and (b) micro-architectural modeling to take into account the effect of performance enhancing architectural features (such as pipeline, cache and branch prediction). In this paper, we only concentrate on path analysis. Program path analysis for WCET estimation involves solving two related problems (a) detecting infeasible paths and (b) using infeasible path information for timing calculation.

Concretely, the contributions of this paper can be summarized as follows.

- We design and implement an infeasible path detection method based on constraint propagation via weakest pre-condition calculation. The infeasible

paths detected by our method can be exploited for WCET analysis as well as other purposes (like reducing test suite sizes, software model checking etc.)
- We provide a programming language level timing analysis algorithm for finding the WCET of a program loop (which is bounded). The algorithm is exact modulo the infeasible path information provided (via our infeasible path detection method). In other words, we can find the longest feasible path through a program loop if the infeasible path information provided is exact. In particular if the detected infeasible path patterns span across at most K loop iterations, we construct a transition system whose nodes denote paths taken in $K-1$ consecutive iterations. This allows us to ensure that no path in the transition system contains any of the infeasible path patterns detected in the first phase; so we can efficiently find the longest path through the program loop. Our technique has been implemented and we show its utility via experimental results on various programs.

We note that different WCET analysis techniques combine the results of path analysis and micro-architectural modeling in different ways. Many of these advocate a *separated* approach (*e.g.* [20]) where the micro-architectural modeling performs a categorization of the program's instructions and this categorization information is fed into path based timing estimation. The WCET analysis technique presented in this paper can also be extended in this fashion; that is, we can augment it to take into account categorization of program instructions based on micro-architectural modeling.

2 Related Work

One of the earliest works on programming language level timing analysis is the *timing schema* approach [18]. It is a bottom-up compositional technique which finds the worst-case execution time of a program fragment without considering the contexts in which it is executed. Another early work by Puschner and Koza [17] studied the conditions for decidability of WCET analysis and provided some rules for WCET analysis.

Techniques to extend the timing schema approach with infeasible path information have been reported in [15]. In this work, the infeasible path patterns are user-provided, that is, the technique only performs path analysis and not infeasible path detection. Lundqvist and Stenstrom [14] provide an instruction level simulation approach for detection and elimination of infeasible paths. Ermedahl and Gustafson [7] present a static analysis method to derive (and exploit) infeasible paths using program semantics. A nice feature of this work is that it also automatically derives minimum and maximum loop bounds in a program. Altenbernd [1] searches for infeasible paths in a control flow graph via branch-and-bound search.

The components of our WCET analysis mechanism are probably most related to the infeasible path detection technique of [3] and the path analysis technique of [10]. The key idea in [10] is to compute the effect of any assignment or a branch on other branch outcomes; if the effect of an assignment a is to force the

outcome of branch b to true, then a path from a to b with the outcome of b being
false is an infeasible path. This is certainly a clever and effective way of detecting
many commonly occurring infeasible path patterns. However, we note that since
our approach is based on constraint propagation, we do not rely on capturing
relationship between individual pairs of branches. In general, the outcome of a
program branch may be correlated to the outcome of *several* previous branches.

We also note that our constraint propagation methods differs substantially
from the propagation method of [3]. This work relies on inferring simple invariant
properties (which hold for all visits to a specific control location) in order to
detect infeasible paths in the control flow graph. The propagation is stopped at
basic block b if the propagated constraint c at basic block b can be be proved to
hold for *all* executions of basic block b. Note that if this condition holds then we
have found an infeasible path: a path from n to b that cannot make the branch
constraint of b false when b is reached. [3] uses some simple sufficient conditions
to check whether a constraint c holds for all visits to basic block n (such as n
containing an assignment statement whose effect constraint implies c).

```
1  sum = 0;
2  for (j=1; j<= limit; j++) {
3      if (j % 2 == 0) {
4                  sum +=j;}
5  }
6  return sum;
```

Fig. 1. Sum of even numbers

To see the difficulties of the approach of [3], let us consider the program in
Figure 1 (taken from [2]) which adds up even numbers. Suppose we want to find
out the infeasible paths ending in the branch at line 3. A backward propagation
of the branch constraint will revisit the branch on line 3 (the previous iterations).
In fact, if we start at the branch on line 3 with the constraint *j is even*, we will
propagate this constraint backwards and visit the branch at line 3 with the
constraint *j is odd*. Note that in this program, the strongest invariant on j that
holds for *all* executions of line 3 is $1 \leq j \leq limit$. From this constraint it is not
possible to infer that line 4 cannot be executed/skipped in consecutive iterations
(which says that both j and $j+1$ cannot be even/odd). Hence the infeasible path
detection technique of [3] will fail to infer this information. In the next section,
we will demonstrate how this information can be inferred in our infeasible path
detection method.

Finally, we note that our infeasible path detection technique is inspired by
the recent progress in abstraction refinement based software model checking of
invariants(*e.g.* see [11]). These works search through an abstract model of the
program to generate a counter-example trace and then show that the given
counter-example trace is an infeasible path in the program's control flow graph.
The proof of infeasibility can be done via a backward (or forward) constraint
propagation *along the counter-example trace*. In our work, we start the propa-

gation from a program branch and backwards propagate the branch constraint to *all* paths leading into the branch. Consequently we need to consider issues like termination/speed-up of propagation. These issues are not so important in checking of counter-examples where the propagation is restricted to one finite (and typically short) counter-example trace.

3 Detecting Infeasible Paths

In this section we concentrate on the problem of *detecting* infeasible paths. First we define the notion of an execution trace.

Definition 1 (Execution Trace). *Given a program P with an initial control location l_{start} and feasible inputs drawn from a (potentially infinite) set I, an execution trace of the program is the sequence of basic blocks traversed by starting from l_{start} with some input $i \in I$.*

In practice, we are always dealing with programs where the length of every execution trace is bounded, i.e., the loops are bounded. Indeed for timing analysis of programs, we cannot work with programs having unbounded loops. Hence we consider programs with bounded execution traces. In the rest of this paper, whenever we refer to an infeasible path, we mean the following.

Definition 2 (Infeasible Path). *Given a program P with feasible inputs drawn from a (potentially infinite) set I, an infeasible path π is a finite sequence of basic blocks which does not appear in any execution trace of P (i.e. π is not contained in the execution trace of P for any input $i \in I$).*

Our approach for infeasible path detection is based on constraint propagation. In general, to detect infeasible paths ending at a given branch b, we need to propagate backwards the constraint of b to all its immediate predecessors (who in turn propagate it to their immediate predecessors and so on). This essentially amounts to weakest pre-condition computation along the various paths coming into b [5]. In other words, let $\varphi_b(\overline{X})$ be the branch constraint for b where $\overline{X}$ denotes the program data variables. Let $stmt_1$ and $stmt_2$ be two statements which may be executed immediately before branch b. We can capture the effect of any program statement as a constraint relating the program variable values before and after the execution of the statement.[1] Let the effect constraint of $stmt_1$ and $stmt_2$ be $\psi_1(\overline{X}, \overline{X}')$ and $\psi_2(\overline{X}, \overline{X}')$ respectively, where $\overline{X}'$ denotes the values of $\overline{X}$ after the statement execution. Then one step of the weakest pre-condition computation (for computing infeasible paths ending at branch b involves computing

$$wp_i(\overline{X}) \stackrel{\text{def}}{=} \forall \overline{X}' \ \psi_i(\overline{X}, \overline{X}') \Rightarrow \varphi_b(\overline{X}') \quad i = 1, 2$$

---

[1] For example, the assignment statement x := x+1 can thus be represented as $x' = x + 1 \wedge \forall y \in \overline{X} - \{x\} \ y' = y$ where the primed variables denote the value of the corresponding program variables after the statement is executed. Effect of branch statements can also be captured as a constraint representing the branch condition.

for the two incoming edges from $stmt_1$ and $stmt_2$ into branch b in the control flow graph.

Clearly such a constraint propagation based approach can detect whether the outcome of a branch b can be deduced from the constraints for several other branches. Termination of the propagation is guaranteed since we only consider bounded loops. However, we still face the practical problem of the constraint propagation amounting to an exhaustive enumeration of paths ending at a branch b. Thus, we need to incorporate mechanisms for speeding up the constraint propagation. In the following, we give our technique for infeasible path detection and illustrate it via an example.

3.1 Technique

We now elaborate our technique for detecting infeasible paths. For simplicity of exposition, let us first consider a single program loop. Let us consider a bounded loop L with k branches inside the loop. Depending on the structure of the control flow within L, the possible number of paths within each iteration can vary from $k + 1$ to 2^k (not all of these paths may be feasible though). To find the infeasible path patterns which (potentially) span across iterations, we first define k propositions $p_1, \ldots, p_k$ corresponding to the conditions in the k branches inside the loop. Let us suppose that the basic blocks which capture control flow within the loop are $B_1, \ldots, B_n$. Then, the infeasible paths detected will be sequences over the alphabet $\{B_1, \ldots, B_n\}$.

Our constraint propagation algorithm proceeds by backwards traversal. Each visit of a basic block B_i is annotated with

- a constraint c_i over the program variables $\overline{X}$.
- a boolean formula b_i over $p_1, \ldots, p_k$.

The constraint propagation terminates if B_i was earlier visited with the same boolean formula b_i, or if c_i is unsatisfiable. If the constraint propagation does not terminate at this visit of B_i, then for each immediate predecessor B_{i_j} of B_i we do the following.

- the constraint c_{i_j} of B_{i_j} is computed by a weakest pre-condition of c_i w.r.t. the statements in B_{i_j}.
- the boolean formula b_{i_j} is the strongest boolean formula over $p_1, \ldots, p_k$ which is implied by c_{i_j}.

Thus, b_{i_j} and c_{i_j} become the annotations of the corresponding visit of B_{i_j}.

We can see that the annotations b_i and c_i for a visit of a basic block B_i serve two different purposes. The boolean formula b_i serves as an approximation of the constraint store c_i. Since the number of distinct boolean formula over a fixed finite set of atomic propositions is bounded, this ensures that the number of visits to any basic block is bounded (thereby ensuring termination).[2] The

---

[2] One can use a canonical representation of boolean functions such as reduced ordered Binary Decision Diagrams to detect whether a basic block was previously visited with the same boolean formula b_i.

check for unsatisfiability of c_i allows us to terminate the detection along certain paths earlier. In other words, we maintain the concrete constraint store c_i to accurately detect infeasible paths. We also maintain b_i, a boolean abstraction of the constraint store c_i, to guarantee termination of constraint propagation.

So far we have outlined the termination condition and each step of the constraint propagation. We have not specified the initial condition. In practice, we run the constraint propagation algorithm $2k$ times, corresponding to the true and false outcomes of the k branches within the loop. This will find out all infeasible paths terminating at any of k branches.

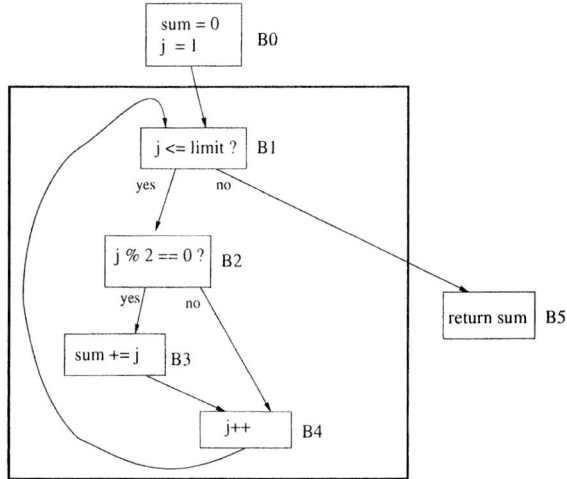

Fig. 2. Control Flow Graph for Example Program in Figure 1

Extensions. In the above, we described a method for detecting infeasible paths within a single loop. However, the constraint propagation mechanism in the method is generic, and can analyze arbitrary nestings and sequences of loops. We will then need to run the constraint propagation for all program branches which are not loop branches. We note that our current implementation performs infeasible path detection for each loop separately. This is not due to a limitation of our infeasible path detection technique; rather this is because of the fact that our WCET analysis method analyzes each program loop separately. So even if we detect infeasible path patterns spanning across different loops, our current WCET analysis cannot exploit such information. In future, we plan to augment our WCET estimation technique to more accurately analyze complex control flow involving sequences and nesting of loops.

3.2 An Example to Show Infeasible Path Detection

We now work out the even number addition example in Figure 1 to detect infeasible paths using our constraint propagation technique. The program in

Figure 1 illustrates a class of infeasible paths which are hard to detect statically using current methods. In particular, these paths:

- span across multiple iterations of a loop
- contain branches whose outcome is different in different iterations (the differing outcomes make it impossible to use strong invariants for all executions of the branch).

The control flow graph of the program fragment in Figure 1 is shown in Figure 2. The loop is shown in a bold box. There is only one branch inside the loop, the branch in basic block B2. Thus, the constraint propagation algorithm will be executed twice corresponding to the yes/no outcomes of this branch. We also define only one proposition corresponding to the condition in the only branch inside our loop. Thus, proposition p_1 is defined as $p_1 \equiv$ j % 2 == 0. Let us now illustrate the constraint propagation for finding infeasible paths which end at a no outcome at basic block B2. Note that during constraint propagation, for each visit of a basic block we maintain a boolean formula (over the branch propositions) and a constraint (computed via weakest pre-condition analysis). So, we start with

$$B2, \neg p_1, \text{ j\%2} \neq 0$$

We now propagate backwards and visit B1. This produces

$$B1, \neg p_1, \text{ j} \leq \text{limit} \wedge \text{j\%2} \neq 0$$

Now, the predecessors of B1 are B0 and B4. Since we are only analyzing the infeasible paths spanning the iterations of a loop (this of course can be relaxed), we only visit B4. This produces

$$B4, p_1, \text{ j}+1 \leq \text{limit} \wedge \text{(j}+1)\%2 \neq 0$$

Note that this involves inferring the truth of p_1 from (j+1) % 2 $\neq$ 0. This inferencing has to be achieved by an external constraint solver. If this cannot be inferred, then we will visit B4 with the boolean formula *true* instead (i.e., the constraint propagation will anyway proceed). The predecessors of B4 are B2 and B3. When we visit B2, the constraint store implies (j+1) % 2 $\neq$ 0 $\wedge$ j % 2 $\neq$ 0. Since this is false, we can infer that the path B2,B4,B1,B2 cannot end with a no outcome. In other words B2,B4,B1,B2,B4 is an infeasible path. Note that termination of the analysis is guaranteed, since each basic block in this example can be visited at most four times (with the boolean formulae *true*, *p1*, $\neg$*p1* and *false*).

4 WCET Analysis

In this section, we present our analysis technique for estimating the WCET of a program loop. We note that if the input program has nested loops or sequences of loops, we perform the analysis for each loop separately and then compose the results. Thus, for nested loops, the inner loop is analyzed first followed by the outer loop.

The inputs to our analyzer are the following.

- The loop bound N. The loop bound is computed using offline techniques like [9].
- The set of feasible paths IP, each member of which denotes the possible execution of one iteration of the loop. From now on, we will refer to a path in the set IP as **ipath** to distinguish it from a path through multiple iterations of the loop. Each ipath is associated with its WCET.
- The set of infeasible ipath sequences through the loop called the **infeasible patterns**. Each infeasible pattern is a finite string over the alphabet IP. Let $K+1$ be the maximum length for any infeasible pattern for the loop. Clearly $1 \leq K \leq N-1$. Typically, $K << N$.

The basic idea of the technique is based on the following observation. Let the maximum length of any infeasible pattern for the loop be $K+1$. Therefore, given a partially constructed ipath sequence, we need to look back *at most K* iterations to enumerate the feasible ipaths in the next loop iteration such that the sequence does not contain any infeasible pattern. Therefore, in order to compute the WCET for the entire loop, we only exhaustively enumerate all the legal ipath sequences of length K. As K is quite small in practice, this exhaustive enumeration is quite fast. Note that if there is no infeasible pattern, then the WCET of the loop is simply $(max_{p \in IP}\ wcet(p)) \times N$.

Next, we find out whether an ipath sequence can follow another ipath sequence. This information is represented by a directed graph, called the **transition graph** $G = (V, E)$. Each node $v \in V$ of this graph represents a legal ipath sequence of length K. An edge $u \to v \in E$ implies that v can follow u. A node v can follow a node u *if and only if* the concatenation of the ipath sequences of u and v does not include any infeasible pattern. Note that the graph can also contain self-edges. Clearly, in the worst case $|V| = |IP|^K$. Each node $v \in V$ is annotated with its WCET, $wcet(v)$, defined as the summation of the WCETs of its K constituent ipaths.

Given the transition graph $G = (V, E)$, we need to find the WCET of the loop. First, let us assume that N is a multiple of K. Then the problem reduces to finding the sequence of N/K nodes (with possibly repeating nodes) of maximum weight through the transition graph G. This problem can be solved through dynamic programming as follows. Let $WCET_v^l$ be the maximum execution time of any sequence of nodes of length l (i.e., a sequence of ipaths of length $l \times K$) ending at node v. We define $WCET_v^l$ recursively as follow. First,

$$WCET_v^1 = wcet(v) \quad \forall v \in V$$

For $l > 1$

$$WCET_v^l = \max_{u \in V,\ u \to v} \left(WCET_u^{l-1} + wcet(v) \right)$$

Therefore, the WCET of the loop is defined as

$$WCET = \max_{v \in V} \left(WCET_v^{N/K} \right)$$

The complexity of this dynamic programming approach is $O(\frac{N}{K} \times |V|^2) = O(\frac{N}{K} \times |IP|^{2K})$. In practice, both $|IP|$ and K are quite small.

If N is not a multiple of K, then we need to take the remainder iterations $N\%K$ into consideration. First, we enumerate all legal sequences of ipaths of length $N\%K$; the number of such sequences is small since $K << N$. Let these sequences be represented by the set S. Then, the WCET of the loop is defined as

$$WCET = \max_{v \in V, s \in S, feasible(v,s)} \left(WCET_v^{N/K} + wcet(s) \right)$$

where $feasible(v,s)$ is true if and only if the concatenation of the ipath sequence corresponding to v and s does not include any infeasible pattern. A fast but conservative approach can simply use the worst possible ipath for the remainder. That is, the WCET of the loop is

$$\max_{v \in V} \left(WCET_v^{N/K} \right) + (max_{p \in IP} \, wcet(p)) \times (N\%K)$$

Note that the algorithm above works only because the state transition graph is defined in such a way that no path in the graph contains any known infeasible sequence of ipaths (*i.e.* a sequence detected as infeasible in the previous phase of infeasible path detection).

5 Experimental Results

We have implemented a prototype analyzer to estimate the worst case execution time of a loop using the technique described in the previous sections. Figure 3 shows the framework of out timing analyzer which combines the infeasible path detection and WCET analysis. The input to our analyzer is the binary executable. For this particular implementation, we use executables compiled by modified gcc for Simplescalar [4], an architectural simulation platform. The analyzer first disassembles the binary, identifies the basic blocks, and constructs the control flow graph (CFG) of the entire program. It then separates out the CFGs corresponding to the loops. The analyzer first estimates the WCET of inner loops and then uses these information to estimate the WCET of outer loops. For each loop, the analyzer enumerates all the ipaths in the loop. Each ipath is associated with the corresponding execution time. In the prototype analyzer, we simply assume the execution time of an ipath is equal to the number of instructions in the ipath.

The core of the analyzer first identifies the infeasible paths using the constraint propagation method. We use the Simplify theorem prover [19] in this phase to check satisfiability of the constraint store in each step of the weakest precondition computation. The infeasible path information is used to eliminate some ipaths from further consideration. Moreover, this information is also used to generate the infeasible ipath patterns. Finally, we generate the transition graph over ipath sequences and use it to compute the WCET.

In our experiments, we have used the benchmarks shown in Table 1. Each of these benchmarks contains only one loop. Three of them: `fresnel`, `sprsin` and

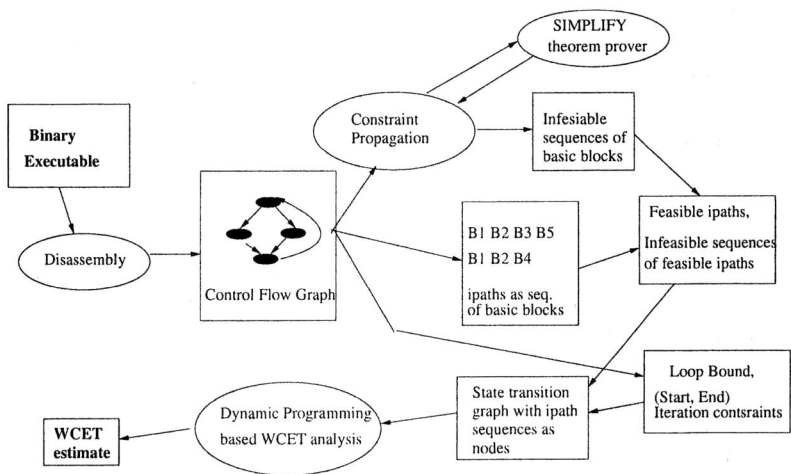

Fig. 3. Design Flow of Timing Analyzer

Table 1. Description of benchmarks used

Benchmark	Description
Wordcount	Counts the number of words in a string of 256 characters
Check_data	Check if the input vector of 100 integers has a negative entry
Fresnel	Computes non-complex Fresnel integrals
Sprsin	Convert 10×10 matrix to row-indexed sparse storage mode
Expint	Computes an exponential integral
SHM	Sequence of variable values repeats in a loop according to Simple Harmonic Motion

Table 2. WCET Estimation Results

Program	# Iterations	Default WCET	Our WCET	Improvement
wordcount	256	9472	8064	14.9%
fresnel	100	5200	5000	3.8%
SHM	100	2200	2002	9%
check_data	100	1900	916	51.8%
sprsin	10	520	476	8.5%
expint	100	185200	6109	96.7%

expint are taken from the book *Numerical Recipes in C* [16]; these benchmarks have been used in other works on program path analysis for estimating WCET (e.g. see [10]). The fresnel program has a loop which takes different ipaths in odd and even numbered iterations. The loop in sprsin avoids the longer ipath when the iteration counter reaches a specific constant value. Expint has the reverse characteristic: the longer ipath in a loop is executed only when the loop iteration counter reaches a specific constant value. The `wordcount` program counts the words in a file by detecting spaces; this is done by a loop which executes different ipaths depending on whether (or not) the next character marks the end of a word. This leads to infeasible path patterns spanning across iterations. The programs SHM and `check_data` also have iteration spanning infeasible path patterns. In particular, since the loop in `check_data` exits when a negative number is encountered, an ipath corresponding to a negative number input can never be followed by any other ipath.

The estimated WCET values for the benchmarks are shown in Table 2. The estimate is given in terms of the number of instructions executed in the loop. The number of iterations for the only loop in each benchmark is shown in the column *# iterations*. *Default WCET* is simply the execution time of the longest ipath multiplied by the number of iterations. In other words, it does not take into account infeasible path information. The column *Our WCET* shows the result of our WCET analysis which takes into account infeasible path information. The column *Improvement* shows the reduction in WCET estimate using our method.

Running Times. On a Pentium IV 2.4 GHz machine, our infeasible path detection phase takes only few seconds for all the benchmarks. The time is primarily spent in the external prover Simplify. We found that the time overheads for using the Simplify prover are tolerable, with each call to Simplify typically taking less than 10 milliseconds. The second phase of our technique (i.e. WCET analysis) takes less than 0.01 second for all the benchmarks.

6 Discussion

Detection of infeasible paths is central for obtaining tight Worst-case Execution Time (WCET) estimates. In this paper, we have developed an infeasible path detection technique based on constraint propagation. We have then exploited these path patterns to develop tight WCET estimates of program loops. Our WCET analysis technique is based on dynamic programming and carefully avoids exhaustive enumeration of feasible path sequences. Experimental results on non-trivial benchmarks show that our technique leads to substantial reduction in WCET estimates.

References

1. P. Altenbernd. On the false path problem in hard real-time programs. In *Euromicro workshop on Real-time Systems*, 1996.
2. T. Ball and J.R. Larus. Programs follow paths. Technical report, Microsoft Research, MSR-TR-99-01, 1999.
3. R. Bodik, R. Gupta, and M. Lou Soffa. Refining data flow information using infeasible paths. In *ESEC/SIGSOFT FSE*, 1997.
4. D. Burger, T. Austin, and S. Bennett. "Evaluating future microprocessors: The simplescalar toolset". Technical Report CS-TR96-1308, University of Wisconsin-Madison, 1996.

5. E.W. Dijkstra. *A Discipline of Programming*. Prentice Hall, 1976.
6. J. Engblom and B. Jonsson. Processor pipelines and their properties for static WCET analysis. In *Intl. Conf. on Embedded Software (EmSoft), LNCS 2491*, 2002.
7. A. Ermedahl and J. Gustafsson. Deriving annotations for tight calculation of execution time. In *EUROPAR*, 1997.
8. C. Ferdinand, F. Martin, and R. Wilhelm. Applying compiler techniques to cache behavior prediction. In *ACM Intl. Workshop on Languages, Compilers and Tools for Real-Time Sys. (LCTRTS)*, 1997.
9. C.A. Healy et al. Supporitng timing analysis by automatic bounding of loop iterations. *Real-Time Systems*, 18(2-3), 2000.
10. C.A. Healy and D.B. Whalley. Automatic detection and exploitation of branch constraints for timing analysis. *IEEE Transactions on Software Engineering*, 28(8), 2002.
11. T.A. Henzinger, R. Jhala, R. Majumder, and G. Sutre. Lazy abstraction. In *POPL*, 2002.
12. X. Li, A. Roychoudhury, and T. Mitra. Modeling out-of-order processors for software timing analysis. In *IEEE Real-time Systems Symposium (RTSS)*, 2004.
13. Y-T. S. Li, S. Malik, and A. Wolfe. Performance estimation of embedded software with instruction cache modeling. *ACM Transactions on Design Automation of Electronic Systems*, 4(3), 1999.
14. T. Lundqvist and P. Stenstrom. Integrating path and timing analysis using instruction-level simulation techniques. In *Intl. Workshop on Languages, Compilers and Tools for Embedded Systems (LCTES)*, 1998.
15. C.Y. Park. Predicting program execution times by analyzing static and dynamic program paths. *Real-time Systems*, 5(1), 1993.
16. W. H. Press, S. A. Teukolsky, W. T. Vetterling, and B. P. Flannery. *Numerical Recipes in C: The Art of Scientific Computing, Second Edition,*. Cambridge University Press, 1988.
17. P. Puschner and Ch. Koza. Calculating the maximum execution time of real-time programs. *Real-time Systems*, 1(2), 1989.
18. A.C. Shaw. Reasoning about time in higher level language software. *IEEE Transactions on Software Engineering*, 1(2), 1989.
19. Simplify. Simplify theorem prover, 1998. http://www.research.compaq.com/SRC/esc/Simplify.html.
20. H. Theiling, C. Ferdinand, and R. Wilhelm. Fast and precise WCET prediction by separated cache and path analysis. *Real Time Systems*, 18(2/3), 2000.

A Technique for Early Software Reliability Prediction

Rakesh Tripathi[1] and Rajib Mall[2]

[1] LRDE Bangalore, KA 560 093, India
tripathir2000@yahoo.com
[2] Department of Computer Science & Engineering,
IIT Kharagpur, WB 721 302, India
rajib@cse.iitkgp.ernet.in

Abstract. In early developmental stages of software, failure data is not available to determine the reliability of software. But developers need reliability prediction for quality assessment and resource planning. We propose a model based on Reliability Block Diagram (RBD) for representing real-world problems and an algorithm for analysis of these models in early phase of software development. We have named this technique Early Reliability Analysis Technique (ERAT). We have performed several simulations on randomly generated software models to compute reliabilities and sensitivity. The simulation result shows that reliabilities are good quality indicator and sensitivity of system reliability to functions reliability can be determined.

1 Introduction

Most software reliability prediction models are failure based growth models [1]. For some models where failure data is not available it is assumed that reliability of component is available [2, 3]. But to get reliability of component, we need prior information on component's failure pattern. In all we can say that, systems quality cannot be assessed until the late stages in the software development process, when failure data becomes available. A problem of this approach is that at the early stage of the software development there is no failure data available, although software reliability predictions are required at the early stage both for customer and developer.

Some software reliability prediction models do provide a reliability estimation without any actual failure data [4]. These methods either model very specific set of problems or makes use of very complicated system model [5].

So, to overcome the problem of system modeling of real-world problems and early-prediction of reliability we propose an algorithm called **Early Reliability Analysis Technique (ERAT)**. ERAT models problem based on **Reliability Block Diagram (RBD)** [6] and **Function Diagram (FD)** [7, 8]. In modeling real-world problems, ERAT makes use of **Operational Profile (OP)** [9] for computation of usage frequency of system operations. System operations are realized by set of system functions. Based on the usage frequency, functions of system are prioritized . ERAT makes use of rank-based **Genetic Algorithms**

(GA) [10] for test suite selection based on functions priority. Functions reliability is computed based on number of test cases testing the function and their error correction capability. Error correction capability is the probability that error will be detected and immediately corrected.

The rest of the paper is organized as follows. In section 2, we review the related work. In section 3, we present the system modeling and test suite selection method. In Section 4 we discuss ERAT algorithm in detail and in section 5 we present experiments and results. Section 6 concludes the paper.

2 Related Work

In most of the reported early reliability prediction methods, it is assumed that component reliability is already available. Also, internal structure of system is rarely considered for the overall system reliability prediction. As a result, predicted reliability is often very inaccurate. In case of multiple scenarios, reliability in situation of failure of some of the least frequently used scenarios are also ignored. This gives an impression that system either fails or works successfully and at no point of time system operations degrade or work less efficiently.

Meng et al. [5] proposed method for early-stage system-level software reliability estimation. This method is based on Petri-nets approach. For large systems Petri-nets approach is not feasible.

Wohrun et al. [11] proposed a method for early reliability estimation based on formal description technique. This technique does not consider multiple scenarios and system degradation. This technique is more appropriate for hardware systems.

Yacoub et al. [2] proposed Scenario Based Reliability Analysis (SBRA). In this, system reliability is estimated based on components reliability. It is assumed that components are existing (including Commercial Off-The-Shelf COTS). Also, algorithm that was used for analysis of system assumes that system will consist of serial and parallel configurations of components.

In all the above techniques, either white box model or black box model is considered. But in none of the work, as far as our knowledge, we found application of both models. Each model has got its own advantage. In our work we have tried to take advantage of both. Black box model is used so that internal details are not required for usage frequency computation. For prediction of reliability, we have used the white box model.

3 System Model

To model system used for the purpose of analysis, we have made following assumptions:

1. Software development process is not from scratch. User profile is available for the system.
2. In case of more than one scenarios of a use-case, always there will be one scenario that will be most frequently used.

3. System fails if use-case fails.
4. System will not fail under failure of scenario(s) of use-case except the most frequently used (MF) scenario. In case of scenario(s) failure, we consider system to be degraded.
5. There is no loop in any of the scenario or use-case.
6. Functions used as start or terminate function of system cannot be reused. Otherwise it will introduce loop i.e. contradiction to #5.
7. Transition probability from one function to other is 1.

In our work, system model(as shown in Figure 1) is composed of following components in bottom-to-top order.

- **Functions:** Correspond to functions, procedures, object in a software. There are two special set of functions called $Start$ and $Terminal$ functions. These functions are unique. In figure 1, A and G are the start and terminal functions respectively.
- **Scenarios:** Correspond to different usage of use-cases. Scenario consist of one each $Start$ and $Terminal$ function and intermediate functions. In figure 1, $ABDG$, $ADFG$ and $ACFG$ represents the scenarios of use-case.
- **Use-cases:** Corresponds to high-level functionality of a software. Use-case consist of one each $Start$ and $Terminal$ function and intermediate functions. Figure 1 shows an use-case.

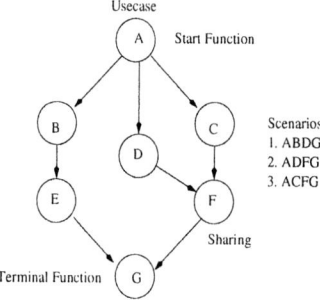

Fig. 1. Block diagram for system model

All the components and models used to represent our real-world problem are described in following subsections.

3.1 Use-Cases

In our work use-cases represent high level functionalities identified during requirement specification. System usage probability provided by Operational Profile are used as use-case usage probability. Usage probability tells frequency of usage of particular use-case by set of user groups. For a system to be operational, all use-cases must be operational.

3.2 Scenarios

Scenarios represent different run-types and operations [4, 12] of an use-case. That means for any use-case there will be one or more scenarios. And these scenario will be sharing some of the functions as we know that in real-life problems, re-usability is very common. For any use-case to be operational, at-least most frequently used scenario must be operational. In other words we have considered parallel configuration among scenarios of a use-case. Also we have assumed that there can be dependence for functions among scenarios.

3.3 Function Diagram

A Function Diagram (FD) [7, 8] is a directed graph. Each node of an FD corresponds to a function of the program. The edges of the graph represent either control dependency or data dependency among the nodes. These dependencies are represented as directed arrows. We do not use different symbols to represent these two types of dependencies since we are considering these two dependencies as same in our work. We have used FD to model our scenarios of use-case.

3.4 Reliability Block Diagram

A Reliability Block Diagram (RBD) is a graphical representation of the components of the system and how they are reliability-wise related [6]. An overall system reliability prediction can be made by looking at the reliabilities of the components that make up the whole system. In order to construct a RBD, the reliability-wise configuration of the components must be determined.

Series Configuration. In a series configuration, a failure of any component results in failure for the entire system. The reliability of a serial system is the probability that unit 1 succeeds and unit 2 succeeds and all of the other units in the system succeed. So, all n units must succeed for the system to succeed. The reliability of the system is then given by

$$\begin{aligned} R_s &= P(X_1 \cap X_2 \cap \ldots \cap X_n) \\ &= P(X_1)P(X_2 \mid X_1)P(X_3 \mid X_1 X_2) \ldots P(X_n \mid X_1 X_2 \ldots X_{n-1}) \end{aligned} \quad (1)$$

Where:
R_s = reliability of the system; R_i = reliability of unit i
X_i = event of unit i being operational; $P(X_i)$ = probability that unit i is operational
If components are considered independent then equation (1) becomes

$$R_s = P(X_1)P(X_2)\ldots P(X_n) = \prod_{i=1}^{n} P(X_i) = \prod_{i=1}^{n} R_i \quad (2)$$

In a series configuration, the component with the smallest reliability has the biggest effect on the system's reliability. As the number of components in series increases, the system's reliability decreases.

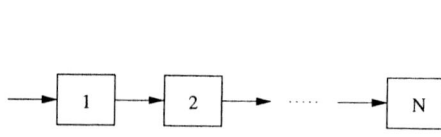

Fig. 2. Block diagram for serial configuration

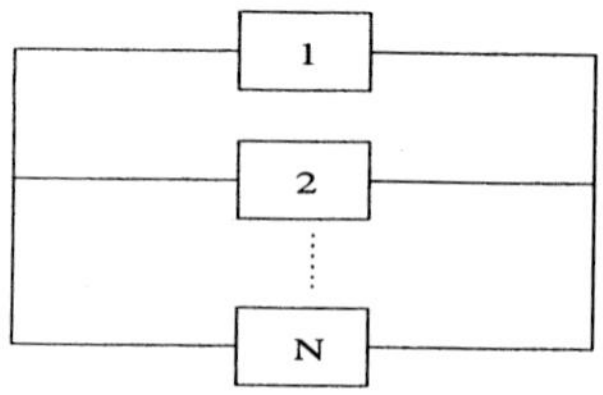

Fig. 3. Block diagram for parallel configuration

Parallel Configuration. In a parallel system, as shown in Figure 3, at least one of the units must succeed for the system to succeed. The probability of failure, or unreliability, for a system with n statistically independent parallel components is the probability that unit 1 fails and unit 2 fails and all of the other units in the system fail. Putting another way, if unit 1 succeeds or unit 2 succeeds or any of the n units succeeds, then the system succeeds. The unreliability of the system is then given by

$$Q_s = P(X_1 \cap X_2 \cap \ldots \cap X_n)$$
$$= P(X_1)P(X_2 \mid X_1)P(X_3 \mid X_1 X_2)\ldots P(X_n \mid X_1 X_2 \ldots X_{n-1}) \quad (3)$$

Where:
Q_s = unreliability of the system; Q_i = unreliability of unit i
X_i = event of failure of unit i ; $P(X_i)$ = probability of failure of unit i
If the components are considered independent then, Equation (3) becomes

$$Q_s = P(X_1)P(X_2)\ldots P(X_n) = \prod_{i=1}^{n} P(X_i) = \prod_{i=1}^{n} Q_i \quad (4)$$

The reliability of the parallel system is then given

$$\begin{aligned} R_s &= 1 - Q_s = (Q_1 \cdot Q_2 \cdot \ldots \cdot Q_n) \\ &= 1 - [(1-R_1)\cdot(1-R_2)\cdot \ldots \cdot (1-R_n)] \\ &= 1 - \prod_{i-1}^{n}(1-R_i) \end{aligned} \quad (5)$$

In a parallel configuration the component with the highest reliability has the biggest effect on the system's reliability, since the most reliable component is the one that will most likely fail last. For a parallel configuration, as the number of components increases, the system's reliability increases.

Complex Configuration. A complex configuration system cannot be broken down into a group of series and parallel systems as shown in Figure 4. This is primarily due to the fact that component C has two paths leading away from it, whereas B and D have only one. Several methods exist for obtaining the reliability of a complex system including

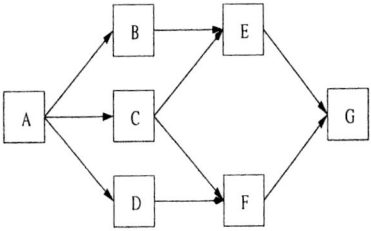

Fig. 4. Block diagram for complex configuration

- The decomposition method
- The event space method
- The path-tracing method

In our work we have used the path-tracing method, as in our reliability model we are available with scenarios in form of paths. In the path-tracing method, every path from a starting point to an ending point is considered. System success involves having at least one path available from one end of the RBD to the other. The reliability of the system is simply the probability of the union of these paths. General equation for union of n paths P_i can be given as

$$\bigcup_{i=1}^{n} P_i = \sum_{i=1}^{n} P_i - \sum_{1 \leq i < j \leq n} (P_i \cap P_j) + \ldots + (-1)^{n-1} \bigcap_{i-1}^{n} P_i. \tag{6}$$

3.5 Test Suite (TS)

Test suite consists of all the test cases that are going to be used for testing software. Generally test suite is selected out of tests pool. For our work we have used Genetic algorithm (GA) for test suite (TS) selection. As GA's are popularly used for optimization, we have used GA for selecting TS to optimize system reliability for assessing the effectiveness of our algorithm.

4 Early Reliability Analysis Technique (ERAT)

In this section we will discuss our reliability estimation technique. We stress that ERAT is more appropriate during the early stages of system development.
    Our proposed algorithm $ERAT$ is presented in the following.

Algorithm: ERAT
Input: $F_i, p_i, p_{ij}, s, slice(U_i), slice(s_{ij}), numTest, slice(T_i)$
Output: System_Reliability , System_Reliability$_{MF}$
    a. Model the system
        Normalize probabilities
        Compute OP for use-cases
        Compute operations run-type probability

b. Compute priority of each function
   $pv(F_i) = \sum_{j=1}^{k} q_j$
   where $q_j = p_j$ if $F_i \in slice(U_j)$ else $q_j = 0$
c. Select test cases that optimizes reliability using GA
   $T_i \in TS$ consists of all test cases in test suite selected using GA
   $Utility(T_i) = \sum_{F_k \in slice(T_i)} pv(F_k)$
d. Find number of test cases testing F_j
   $k_i = \sum x$
   where $x = \begin{cases} 1 & \text{if } F_j \in slice(T_i) \\ 0 & \text{if } F_j \ni slice(T_i) \end{cases}$
e. Compute functions reliability
   $rel(F_i) = 1 - s^{k_i}$
f. Manipulate functions reliability to measure sensitivity
   $rel(F_i) = rel(F_i) * p$
   where p can take values between [0-1] depending upon reliability degradation
g. Compute use-case reliability
   Generate combinations p_i of different paths
   Compute union of different combinations P_i
   Let $slice(P_i)$ contains functions available in P_i without repetition
   $rel(P_i) = \prod_{F_k \in slice(P_i)} rel(F_k)$
   $rel(U_i)$ is addition of terms according to equation 6.
   $rel(U_i) = \prod_{F_k \in slice(P_i)} rel(F_k)$
h. Compute MF scenario reliability
   $rel(MF_i) = rel(s_{ik})$
   where $rel(s_{ik}) = \prod_{F_k \in slice(s_{ij})} rel(F_k)$
i. Compute overall system reliability
   $System\_Reliability = \prod_{i=1}^{N} (1 - ((1 - rel(U_i)) * p_i))$
j. Compute MF system reliability
   $System\_Reliability_{MF} = \prod_{i=1}^{N} rel(U_{MF_i})$

4.1 Test Suite Selection

We have used Pareto Convergence Genetic Algorithm *PCGA* [10] based on Pareto-ranking for test suite selection. PCGA works on the notion of *Pareto optimality* [13], which is based on the concept of *dominance*. We have used the concept of *intra-island rank histogram* [10] in formulating our stopping criterion for selection.

4.2 Functions Reliability Estimation

Functions diagram(FD) are prepared by system analyst to model system for analysis. Functional analyst, with the help of modeling tools provides important details that will be used in later stages of analysis.

In early stages of software development, as failure rates and error correction rate will not be available, we have used fixed error correction rate. Let s be the probability that errors remain undetected in a function, after it has been tested using a single test case. We have taken s to be equal to 0.95. This means we have assumed that each test case has a 5 percent chance of uncovering an error existing in a function.

Let a function F_i be tested by k_i test cases in the test suite TS. Then, the reliability $rel(F_i)$ associated with the function F_i can be defined as follows,

$$rel(F_i) = 1 - s^{k_i}.$$

4.3 Scenario Reliability Estimation

The functionality of any system can be modeled using use-cases [14]. Each use-case typically has multiple scenarios. Each scenario is an alternate path through the use-case.

We compute the slice $slice(s_{ij})$ of the FD corresponding to each scenario s_{ij}. We define a *slice* of an FD due to a scenario as the set of all the functions that influence execution of this scenario.

To compute $slice(s_{ij})$, we transitively traverse along all data and control dependence edges starting from the directed edge corresponding to the input to the scenario s_{ij} and include all functions so traversed in the slice.

Since scenarios of an use-case are considered inter-dependent, we will not compute scenario reliability separately. But for most frequently used scenario (MF), if the probability of usage of scenario j of use-case i is p_{ij}, then its probability of usage will be $max(p_{ij})$. Now let k be the index having value $max(p_{ij})$, then the *reliability* of MF scenario s_{ik} is the product of all $rel(F_i)$, such that $F_i \in slice(s_{ij})$.

$$rel(s_{ik}) = \prod_{F_k \in slice(s_{ij})} rel(F_k)$$

Hence,

$$rel(MF_i) = rel(s_{ik}).$$

4.4 Use-Case Reliability Estimation

Different scenarios of an use-case are connected either in parallel, serial/parallel or complex configuration. But we always considers complex relationship for worst case analysis.

If the functions are connected in series or parallel configuration, we can compute reliability of scenario and subsequently use-case by making use of algorithm given by [2]. As this algorithm considers OR and AND path to be in parallel and series configuration. But as we are more concerned with accurate estimation, we always consider complex configuration. So, we will make use of path tracing method described in equation (6).

In case of MF scenario, use-case reliability will be the probability that most frequently scenario will not fail i.e.,

$$rel(U_{MF_i}) = 1 - fail(MF_i).$$

4.5 System Reliability Estimation

If we consider system consisting of N use cases, then the system reliability $System\_Reliability$ for a selected test suite TS can be computed as follows:

$$System\_Reliability = \prod_{i=1}^{N}(1 - ((1 - rel(U_i)) * p_i))$$

In case of most frequently used scenario, we will have

$$System\_Reliability = \prod_{i=1}^{N} rel(U_{MF_i}).$$

4.6 Sensitivity Computation

We have computed sensitivity of ERAT by modifying reliability of individual functions based on its priority. In ERAT it is important to note that reliability modification should not be done immediately after computation of functions reliability. As this modification will allow test case selection algorithm to select test cases based on the new reliability of functions.

Lets assume F_i be the function and $rel(F_i)$ be its reliability for which we want to modify, then reliability of F_i after 25% degradation will be

$$rel(F_i) = rel(F_i) * 0.75.$$

5 Experiments and Results

In this section we illustrate the working of the algorithm with the help of an example. We have tabulated all the intermediate results obtained. The example consists of randomly generated model of a system representing the real-world problem. We have chosen, $Total\ Functions = 40$, $Total\ Use-cases = 6$, $Number\ of\ test\ cases = 500$ and $Test\ Suite\ size = 400$.

a. System Modeling. Model of the system is generated randomly and satisfies all the assumptions we have made to represent the system. Table 1 shows model with usage probability p_i of an use-case U_i and usage probability p_{ij} of a scenario s_{ij}.

Table 1. System model of working example

$Use-case\ U_i$	$Usage\ Prob.\ p_i$	$Scenarios\ s_{ij}$	$Probability\ p_{ij}$
1	0.3631	1,2,3,4	0.2916,0.0947,0.4795,0.1343
2	0.1319	1,2,3	0.4796,0.3173,0.2030
3	0.1133	1,2	0.2641,0.7359
4	0.2806	1	1.0
5	0.0295	1,2,3,4	0.2232,0.0858,0.5641, 0.1269
6	0.0816	1,2,3,4	0.2413,0.2228,0.2913, 0.2445

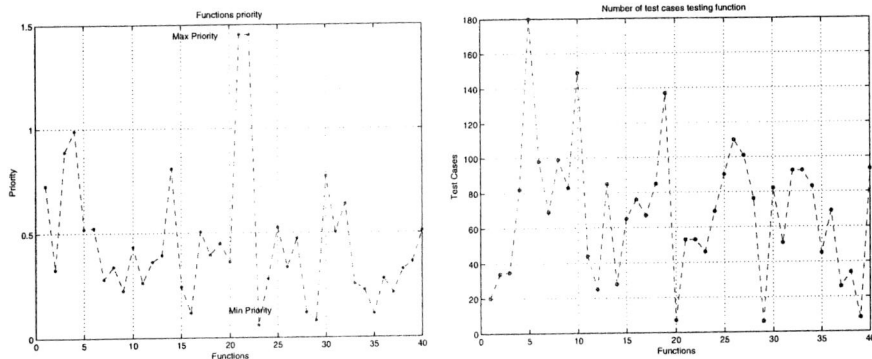

Fig. 5. Graph showing priority of functions

Fig. 6. Graph showing number of test cases testing functions

b. **Functions Probability Computation.** Probability of functions F_i are shown in Figure 5

c. **Test Cases Testing Functions.** Number of test cases, available in TS testing functions F_i are presented in Figure 6.

d. **Functions Reliability Computation.** Reliability of function F_i is shown in Figure 7.

e. **Use-case Reliability Computation.** Reliability of use-cases U_i is presented in Figure 8.

f. **Reliability Range Computation.** Range of reliability, one for the system as a whole and another for most frequently used scenario in a use-case are presented in Table 2.

g. **Sensitivity of ERAT.** Sensitivity of algorithm to functions reliability is presented in Table 3.

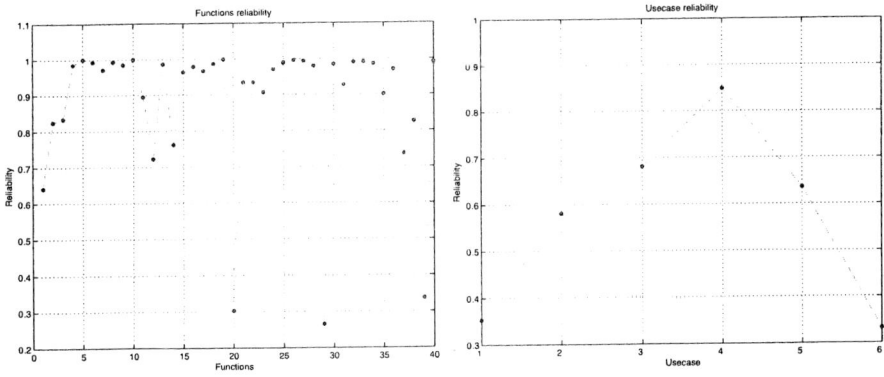

Fig. 7. Graph showing functions reliability

Fig. 8. Graph showing use-case reliability

Table 2. Reliabilities computation for overall system and for MF

Expt#	Test Cases	System Reliability	MF Reliability
1	100	0.4162	0.3312
2	200	0.4885	0.3320
3	300	0.5216	0.3348
4	400	0.6378	0.4342

Table 3. Sensitivity of System reliability to functions reliability

Expt#	Function Type	% Degradation	Sys. Reliability
1	Maximum Reliable	0,25,50,75,100	0.6362,0.6090,0.5819,0.5548,0.5277
2	Minimum Reliable	0,25,50,75,100	0.6362,0.6340,0.6319,0.6297,0.6276

5.1 Analysis of Results

Results in Table 3 shows that any system will be more sensitive to functions having high priority. So, testing efforts for such functions must be maximized. Due to high reliable function failure, degradation in system reliability is close to 17%, whereas low reliable causes just 1.35% degradation.

Results in Table 2 shows that even though system reliability is a good measure, but it is better to rely more on reliability of most frequently used scenarios. Reliability range demonstrates the maximum degradation that can be caused to system reliability in event of failure of other scenarios of use-case.

6 Conclusions and Discussion

In this paper we have proposed an early stage reliability estimation technique (ERAT). Application of reliability estimation during early stages of development is a good measure of initial design. We observed that even if error data is not available for software development efforts, this algorithm will provide reliability estimation.

We observed that system reliability is sensitive to functions reliability. But this sensitivity varies from function to function, as functions with higher usage frequency affects system reliability more as compared to ones with lesser usage. So, just by increasing the number of test cases testing a function does not help much in increasing system reliability. As there is a limit beyond which improvement will be insignificant. Rather than increasing more test cases, we should try to make sure that only those test cases that improve system reliability should be made available in test suite. We have planned to continue efforts in future to extend the capabilities of ERAT.

References

1. Runeson, P., Wohlin, C.: Statistical usage testing for software reliability control. Informatica **19** (1995) 195 – 207
2. Yacoub, S., Cukic, B., Ammar, H.H.: A scenario-based reliability analysis approach for component-based software. IEEE Transactions on Reliability **53** (2004) 465 – 480

3. Kuball, S., Hughes, G., Gilchrist, B.I.: Scenario-based unit testing for reliability. In: IEEE Proceedings Annual Reliability and Maintainability symposium. (2002) 222 – 227
4. M., L.: Handbook of Software Reliability Engineering. McGraw-Hill and New York (1996)
5. Yin, M.L., Hyde, C.L., James, L.E.: A petri-net approach for early-stage system-level software reliability estimation. Proceedings Annual Reliability and Maintainability Symposium (2000) 100 – 105
6. 6, B.: (System analysis reference, reliability, availability and optimization) Provided by Reliasoft.
7. Sarkar, A.: (A novel scheme for regression test suite selection) Master of Technology 2004, Thesis , IIT Kharagur, WB 721302, India.
8. Phien, T.T.: (System analysis and design, chapter 2, systems analysis) Training of computer specialists, trainers and users, Sponsored by UNESCO, Implemented by IIT-NCST-Vietnam 1999-2000.
9. Musa, J.D., Iannino, A., Okumoto, K.: Software Reliability: Measurement, Prediction, Application. McGraw-Hill, New York. (1987)
10. Kumar, R., Rocket, P.: Assessing the convergence of rank-based multi-objective genetic algorithm. In: Proc IEE/IEEE 2nd Int. Conf. on Genetic Algorithms in Engineering Systems:Innovations and Applications, (GALESIA 97) Glasgow, U.K. IEE Conference Publication. (1997) 446
11. Wohlin, C., Runeson, P.: A method proposal for early software reliability estimation. IEEE (1992) 156 – 163
12. Mall, R.: Fundamentals of Software Engineering. Prentice Hall of India (2003)
13. C.M.Fonseca, P.J.Fleming: An overview of evolutionary algorithm in multi-objective optimization. Evolutionary Computation **3** (1995) 1 – 16
14. Jacobson, I., Christerson, M.: Object Oriented Software Engineering: A Use Case Driven Approach. Addison-Wesley, Workingham, England (1992)

Executable Requirements Specifications Using Triggered Message Sequence Charts

Bikram Sengupta[1] and Rance Cleaveland[2]

[1] IBM India Research Laboratory, Block 1, Indian Institute of Technology,
Hauz Khas, New Delhi - 110016
bsengupt@in.ibm.com

[2] Department of Computer Science, SUNY at Stony Brook,
Stony Brook, NY 11794-4400, USA
rance@cs.sunysb.edu

Abstract. Triggered Message Sequence Charts (TMSCs) are a scenario-based visual formalism for early stage requirements specifications of distributed systems. In this paper, we present a formal operational semantics for TMSCs that allow the simulation of TMSC system descriptions, so that errors and inconsistencies in specification may be detected early on. The semantics is defined in terms of Structured Operational Semantics (SOS) rules that guide the step-wise execution of TMSC specifications. We also consider the equivalence of this semantics and the TMSC denotational semantics that has been presented in previous work.

1 Introduction

Triggered Message Sequence Charts (TMSCs) have been proposed in [13] as an extension of the well-known visual formalism of Message Sequence Charts (MSCs) [1, 11]. Like MSCs, TMSCs describe system *scenarios* in terms of exchange of messages and execution of local-actions that a set of processes (or *instances*) may engage in as they execute. Unlike MSCs, however, TMSCs can specify *conditional scenarios*, which represent requirements that constrain system behavior only when certain "triggering behaviors", are observed; and *partial scenarios*, which permit users to leave aspects of system behavior unspecified. The theory is also equipped with a *refinement* ordering (based on the must preorder of [8]) that determines when one specification is a "correct elaboration of" another, by correctly adhering to prescriptive and conditional-scenario constraints and properly "filling in" unspecified behavior in partial scenarios [12].

TMSCs are thus well-suited for early-stage behavioral descriptions, which may be subject to refinement and elaboration as design proceeds. Accordingly, practitioners will find it useful to be able to simulate the behavior of TMSC-based system descriptions. This will allow early detection of inconsistencies and aberrant scenarios, which may otherwise be very expensive to fix once the system has been constructed. However, as evident in the technical development of [13], the formal semantics of TMSCs, which translates TMSC specifications to *acceptance trees* [8], is *declarative* in nature: it provides a precise definition of *what* the acceptance tree should be for a given TMSC specification, without describing *how* it may be constructed step-by-step. Thus this semantics does not allow ready simulation of TMSC specifications.

The goal of this paper is to present an alternative (but equivalent) semantics of TMSCs, which is *operational* in nature. This semantics can serve as the basis for tool-support, and help build executable models of TMSC specifications for early simulation. The rest of the paper is organized as follows: in the next section, we introduce TMSCs and the main ideas behind the acceptance tree semantic model. In Section 3, we explain the operational behavior of single instances in a TMSC; this is then extended to enable simulation of complete, single TMSCs. Section 4 outlines how the ideas may be extended to define the executable behavior of structured TMSC specifications. In Section 5, we discuss the equivalence of the declarative and operational semantics of TMSCs. Section 6 considers tool support. Section 7 presents related work, while Section 8 contains conclusions and directions for future research.

2 Background

Triggered Message Sequence Charts: Graphically, we represent TMSCs as in Fig. 1. There are two new features in the visual syntax of TMSCs when compared to traditional MSCs. The first is the dashed horizontal line running through the instances, which partitions the sequence of events on an instance's axis into two subsequences: the first, located above the line, constitutes the instance's *trigger*, and the second, below the line, constitutes its *action*. This partition, in effect, forms the basis of a *conditional scenario*: for each instance, the execution of the action is conditional on the occurrence of the trigger. In other words, the behavior of the instance is constrained to its action *only* when it has executed its trigger; otherwise, there are no restrictions. The second new feature in a TMSC is the presence/absence of a small bar at the foot of each instance. The presence of such a bar (as in instance I_1 in Fig 1) indicates that the instance cannot proceed beyond this point in the TMSC, while the absence (as in instance I_2) means that the behavior of this instance beyond the TMSC is left unspecified i.e. there are no constraints on its subsequent behavior. Such a scenario is thus *partial*, and may be extended in future.

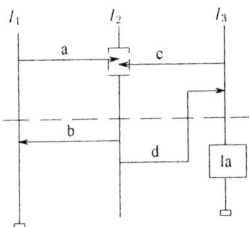

Fig. 1. An Example TMSC

The TMSC in Fig.1 may be read as follows: "If I_1 sends a to I_2, then it should receive b from I_2 and terminate; if I_2 receives a from I_1 and c from I_3, then it should send b to I_1 and d to I_3, and its subsequent behavior is left unspecified; if I_3 sends c to I_2 and receives d from I_2, then it should perform the local-action la and terminate".

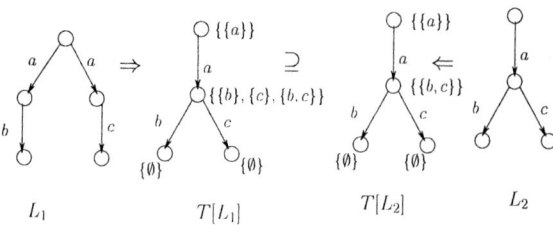

Fig. 2. The *must* preorder: $L_1 \sqsubseteq_{\text{must}} L_2$

Acceptance Trees: Acceptance trees and the must preorder arise in the theory of testing of concurrent processes given in [8]. In this theory, tests, which may also be thought of as processes that are capable of reporting "success", interact with a process under test. When processes and tests are nondeterministic, a process may be capable both of passing and failing a test, depending on how nondeterministic choices are resolved. A process *must pass* a test if, regardless of how such choices are made, the process passes the test. One process refines another with respect to the must preorder if it must pass every test that the less refined process must. We use an alternative characterization of the must preorder that is given in terms of the processes themselves, rather than tests. Specifically, the must pre-order may be characterized in terms of *acceptance sets* (that are a measure of the non-determinism of a process) when the processes are given as Labeled Transitions Systems (LTSs).

Definition 1. *Let* $\mathcal{P} = \langle P, E, \longrightarrow, p_I \rangle$ *be a Labeled Transition System (LTS), where P is a set of states, E a set of events,* $\longrightarrow \subseteq P \times E \times P$ *the transition relation, and* $p_I \in P$ *the start state. Then, for* $p \in P$ *and* $w \in E^*$. *the following may be defined.*

$$L(\mathcal{P}) = \{w \in E^* \mid \exists p' \in P . p_I \xrightarrow{w} p'\} \text{ (Language)}$$
$$S_{\mathcal{P}}(p) = \{a \mid \exists p' \in P . p \xrightarrow{a} p'\} \text{ (Successors)}$$
$$Acc(\mathcal{P}, w) = \{S_{\mathcal{P}}(p') \mid p_I \xrightarrow{w} p'\} \text{ (Acceptance set)}$$

We now define a *saturation operator*, sat, on acceptance sets. Let $\mathcal{A} \subseteq 2^E$; then $sat(\mathcal{A})$ is the least set satisfying:

1. $\mathcal{A} \subseteq sat(\mathcal{A})$.
2. If $A_1, A_2 \in sat(\mathcal{A})$ then $A_1 \cup A_2 \in sat(\mathcal{A})$.
3. If $A_1, A_2 \in sat(\mathcal{A})$ and $A_1 \subseteq A \subseteq A_2$, then $A \in sat(\mathcal{A})$.

The alternative characterization of $\sqsubseteq_{\text{must}}$ can now be given as follows [8].

Theorem 1. *Let* $\mathcal{P}_1 = \langle P_1, E_1, \longrightarrow_1, p_{I_1}\rangle$ *and* $\mathcal{P}_2 = \langle P_2, E_2, \longrightarrow_2, p_{I_2}\rangle$ *be two LTSs, and let* $E = E_1 \cup E_2$. *Then* $\mathcal{P}_1 \sqsubseteq_{\text{must}} \mathcal{P}_2$ *iff for all* $w \in E^*$, $sat(Acc(\mathcal{P}_1, w)) \supseteq sat(Acc(\mathcal{P}_2, w))$.

Intuitively, $\mathcal{P}_2$ refines $\mathcal{P}_1$ if it has "less nondeterminism." This alternative characterization forms the basis for representing processes as *acceptance trees* [8], which map sequences of events to acceptance sets.

Definition 2. *Let $\mathcal{E}$ be a finite set of events. Then an* acceptance tree *T is a function in $\mathcal{E}^* \to 2^{2^{\mathcal{E}}}$ satisfying:*

1. *For any $w \in \mathcal{E}^*$, $sat(T(w)) = T(w)$.*
2. *For any $w, w' \in \mathcal{E}^*$, if $T(w) = \emptyset$ then $T(w \cdot w') = \emptyset$.*
3. *For any $w \in \mathcal{E}^*$, $e \in \mathcal{E}$, $T(w \cdot e) \neq \emptyset$ iff there exists $A \in T(w)$ such that $e \in A$.*

We say that $T_1 \supseteq T_2$ if for all $w \in \mathcal{E}^*$, $T_1(w) \supseteq T_2(w)$.

For any LTS $\mathcal{P}$ there is an immediate way to construct an acceptance tree $T[\mathcal{P}]$: $T[\mathcal{P}](w) = sat(Acc(\mathcal{P}, w))$. It immediately follows that $\mathcal{P}_1 \sqsubseteq_{\text{must}} \mathcal{P}_2$ if and only if $T[\mathcal{P}_1] \supseteq T[\mathcal{P}_2]$. For example, in Fig. 2, $L_1 \sqsubseteq_{\text{must}} L_2$ because $T[L_1] \supseteq T[L_2]$.

3 Executing Single TMSCs

Having introduced TMSCs, let us now consider how they may be executed. The operational behavior of single TMSCs will be described by Plotkin-style [7] Structured Operational Semantics (SOS) rules. A SOS rule of the form R. $\dfrac{l}{p \xrightarrow{a} p'}$ denotes a rule R which describes the operational behavior of a process p that can perform an event a to evolve to p' provided each predicate in the list l is true. Since a TMSC consists of a set of *instances* executing asynchronously, we begin by defining SOS rules to model the operational behavior of individual instances in a TMSC.

Notational Convention. We fix finite sets $\mathbb{I}$, $\mathbb{M}$ and $\mathbb{A}$ as the set of all instances, message types and local action names, respectively. We write $\mathbb{R} = \{\text{in}(I, J, m) \mid I, J \in \mathbb{I}, m \in \mathbb{M}\}$ for the set of all receive events, and similarly define $\mathbb{S} = \{\text{out}(I, J, m) \mid I, J \in \mathbb{I}, m \in \mathbb{M}\}$ as the set of all send events; in each case, I denotes the sender and J the receiver of message m. We use $\mathbb{L} = \{\text{loc}(I, \ell) \mid I \in \mathbb{I}, \ell \in \mathbb{A}\}$ as the set of all local actions. Our semantics also uses events of form $\text{end}(I)$, where $I \in \mathbb{I}$, which instances emit when they terminate, and "potential events" of form $\text{wait}(r)$, where $r \in \mathbb{R}$, to denote that an instance is capable of performing r once the corresponding send event occurs. $\mathbb{T}$ and $\mathbb{W}$ denote the set of all end events and wait events respectively.

An instance in a TMSC M is initially specified by the term $Ins(I, S, t, p, q)$, where I is the name of the instance, S is the set of all events it may possibly perform, t indicates if the instance terminates on performing its action or not (with t = "yes" if the instance terminates, "no" otherwise), and p and q are sequences of events that constitute respectively, the trigger and action of I in M. In addition to the Ins form, I may also be specified by three other instance terms in course of its execution:(i) it may assume the form $Nondet\_ins(I, S)$, when its behavior is completely non-deterministic (e.g. when the trigger has been violated, or I has performed the trigger, followed by the action, and I is not required to terminate subsequently), (ii) it may be of the form $Term\_ins(I)$, after it has terminated, or (iii) it may move to the form $Restr\_ins(\{e\}, I_t)$, (where only event e is enabled, and I_t is an instance term) from the Ins and $Nondet\_ins$ forms, once it has non-deterministically chosen to perform event e, from the set of possible events. As we will see, these instance forms are necessary to capture the evolution of an instance in a conditional/partial scenario.

Table 1. Operational semantics for Instances

I1. $$\frac{p \neq nil, e \in possible\_ev(S, me)}{me : Ins(I, S, t, p, q) \xrightarrow{\tau} Restr\_ins(\{e\}, Ins(I, S, t, p, q))}$$

I2. $$\frac{e = \mathsf{wait}(r), r \in me, p = r \cdot p'}{me : Restr\_ins(\{e\}, Ins(I, S, t, p, q)) \xrightarrow{\tau} Ins(I, S, t, p', q)}$$

I3. $$\frac{e = \mathsf{wait}(r), r \in me, p = r' \cdot p', r' \neq r}{me : Restr\_ins(\{e\}, Ins(I, S, t, p, q)) \xrightarrow{\tau} Nondet\_ins(I, S)}$$

I4. $$\frac{e = \mathsf{wait}(r), r \notin me}{me : Restr\_ins(\{e\}, Ins(I, S, t, p, q)) \xrightarrow{e} Restr\_ins(\{e\}, Ins(I, S, t, p, q))}$$

I5. $$\frac{e \in \mathbb{R} \cup \mathbb{S} \cup \mathbb{L}, p = e \cdot p'}{me : Restr\_ins(\{e\}, Ins(I, S, t, p, q)) \xrightarrow{e} Ins(I, S, t, p', q)}$$

I6. $$\frac{e \in \mathbb{R} \cup \mathbb{S} \cup \mathbb{L}, p = e' \cdot p', e \neq e'}{me : Restr\_ins(\{e\}, Ins(I, S, t, p, q)) \xrightarrow{e} Nondet\_ins(I, S)}$$

I7. $$\frac{e \in \mathbb{T}}{me : Restr\_ins(\{e\}, Ins(I, S, t, p, q)) \xrightarrow{e} Term\_ins(I)}$$

I8. $$\frac{e \in possible\_ev(S, me)}{me : Nondet\_ins(I, S) \xrightarrow{\tau} Restr\_ins(\{e\}, Nondet\_ins(I, S))}$$

3.1 Operational Semantics for an Instance

We will now present SOS rules that govern the operational behavior of an instance in a TMSC. These rules, defined in Tables 1 and 2, assume the existence of a message environment me which represents the set of enabled in events; an instance J may perform an event $\mathsf{in}(I, J, m)$, only if $\mathsf{in}(I, J, m) \in me$. Thus me corresponds to messages that have been sent but not yet received.

In **I1** (Table 1), instance I begins in its initial state $Ins(I, S, t, p, q)$, and as long as its trigger has not been completely satisfied (i.e. $p \neq nil$), I may non-deterministically choose to perform any event in S that is allowed by me; $possible\_ev(S, me)$ returns the set of such events and may be defined as:

$$possible\_ev(S, me) = \{e \mid e \in S \land (e \in \mathbb{S} \cup \mathbb{L} \cup \mathbb{T}$$
$$\lor (e \in \mathbb{R} \land e \in me))\}$$
$$\cup \{\mathsf{wait}(e) \mid (e \in S \cap \mathbb{R}) \land e \notin me\}$$

Thus, an out, loc or end event is always possible. An in event is only possible if it is in me, otherwise the corresponding wait event is possible. For each such possible event

Table 2. Operational semantics for Instances (Cont.)

I9. $$\dfrac{e = \mathsf{wait}(r), r \in me}{me : Restr\_ins(\{e\}, Nondet\_ins(I,S)) \xrightarrow{r} Nondet\_ins(I,S)}$$

I10. $$\dfrac{e = \mathsf{wait}(r), r \notin me}{me : Restr\_ins(\{e\}, Nondet\_ins(I,S)) \xrightarrow{e} Restr\_ins(\{e\}, Nondet\_ins(I,S))}$$

I11. $$\dfrac{e \in \mathbb{R} \cup \mathbb{S} \cup \mathbb{L}}{me : Restr\_ins(\{e\}, Nondet\_ins(I,S)) \xrightarrow{e} Nondet\_ins(I,S)}$$

I12. $$\dfrac{e \in \mathbb{T}}{me : Restr\_ins(\{e\}, Nondet\_ins(I,S)) \xrightarrow{e} Term\_ins(I)}$$

I13. $$\dfrac{(e \in \mathbb{S} \cup \mathbb{L}) \vee (e \in \mathbb{R} \wedge e \in me)}{me : Ins(I,S,t,nil,e.q) \xrightarrow{e} Ins(I,S,t,p,q)}$$

I14. $$\dfrac{e \in \mathbb{R} \wedge e \notin me}{me : Ins(I,S,t,nil,e \cdot q) \xrightarrow{\mathsf{wait}(e)} Ins(I,S,t,nil,e \cdot q)}$$

I15. $$\dfrac{t = yes}{Ins(I,S,t,nil,nil) \xrightarrow{end(I)} Term\_ins(I)}$$

I16. $$\dfrac{t = no}{Ins(I,S,t,nil,nil) \xrightarrow{\tau} Nondet\_ins(I,S)}$$

e, I non-deterministically moves to a restricted mode represented by $Restr\_ins(\{e\},$ $Ins(I,S,t,p,q))$ (**I1**).

If e is a wait(r) event and r subsequently becomes enabled (because the corresponding message has been sent), then there are two possibilities: (i) r is the next event in the trigger, and the instance performs r, and evolves to the mode $Ins(I,S,t,p',q)$, where p' represents the suffix of the trigger that is left to be performed; this is shown in **I2** (ii) r is not the next event in the trigger, in which case performing r violates the trigger, and the instance moves to a totally unconstrained (non-deterministic) mode given by $Nondet\_ins(I,S)$ (**I3**). If e is a wait(r) event and r is currently not allowed, then the instance stays in the same mode as indicated by **I4**. (Note that wait events are only *potential* events, not actual ones, hence, they do not cause a change of state).

If e is an in, out or loc event, and is also the next event in the trigger, then the instance moves to a mode $Ins(I,S,t,p',q)$ (**I5**), where p' represents the suffix of the trigger yet to be performed, as in **I2**. If e is not the next event in the trigger, then performing e causes the instance to move to the (unconstrained) mode $Nondet\_ins(I,S)$ (**I6**). If the end is enabled in the restricted mode, then the instance terminates by performing e, as it moves to the mode $Term\_ins(I)$ from which no transitions are enabled (**I7**).

If I is in the mode $Nondet\_ins(I, S)$, then it may non-deterministically choose to perform any event e that is possible, and move to a restricted mode where e is enabled. This is shown in **I8**. If e is a wait(r) event and r gets enabled, then r is performed, and the instance returns to the non-deterministic state (**I9**, Table 2); however, if r is not allowed, then the instance *waits* in the same mode (**I10**). If e is an in, out or loc event, then it may be immediately performed, and the instance returns to the non-deterministic mode (**I11**). If e is an end event, then the instance terminates on performing e (**I12**).

I13, I14, I15 and **I16** describe the behavior of I once it has satisfied its trigger. If the next event e in the action is enabled, then it is performed (**I13**), else the corresponding wait event is performed (**I14**). Once the action has been completely executed, the parameter t comes into play. If I has to terminate immediately ($t = yes$), then I performs the end(I) event (**I15**), else it moves to the nondeterministic mode (**I16**).

3.2 A Single TMSC M = me:IL

A single TMSC M consists of a set of instance terms IL, having a common message environment me, which represents the set of enabled receive events. Initially me is empty. Table 3 presents the execution behavior of TMSC M in terms of the execution of its instances. In rule **M1**, we first compute the set of instance names that are explicitly mentioned in M, using the function $Ins\_name\_list(IL) = \{Ins\_name(I_t) \mid I_t \in IL\}$, where $Ins\_name(I_t)$ returns the instance name of I_t. We then get $T = \mathbb{I} - Ins\_name\_list(IL)$ as the set of instances which are not explicitly mentioned in the TMSC M. According to the TMSC semantics [13], these instances are assumed to terminate immediately. As rule **M1** shows, IL is annotated with T, to record this set of instances.

As long as an instance term I_t in IL is *unstable* i.e. may perform a τ transition, M is also unstable: if I_t evolves to I'_t on performing τ, M also performs τ and moves to a new state where me remains unchanged, but within IL, I_t is replaced by I'_t (**M2**). The $update\_msc$ function may be written simply as $update\_msc(IL, I_t, I'_t) = (IL - I_t) \cup I'_t$.

Once all the instances have resolved their internal non-determinism and stabilized ($I_t \xrightarrow{\tau}\!\!\!\!\!/\ $ is taken to mean I_t is unable to perform a transition labeled by τ), and an instance term I_p may perform an event e to become I'_p, M may also perform e, as shown in **M3**. In this case, me may get updated (if e is an in or out), and the instance term list IL now contains I'_p in place of I_p. The $update\_env$ function may be written as

$$update\_env(me, e) = me \cup in(J, I, m), \quad \text{if } e = \text{out}(J, I, m)$$
$$= me - in(I, J, m), \quad \text{if } e = \text{in}(I, J, m)$$
$$= me, \quad \text{otherwise}$$

Thus, if e is an out event, the corresponding in event becomes enabled in me, whereas if e is an in event, it is removed from me upon execution. Finally, **M4** indicates that when the system reaches a stable state, any instance not explicitly mentioned in M may terminate immediately; the parameter T is then updated to reflect all remaining instances that are still *active*.

Table 3. Operational semantics for TMSC M = me: IL

M1. $\dfrac{T = \mathbb{I} - Ins\_name\_list(IL)}{me : IL \xrightarrow{\tau} IL_T}$

M2. $\dfrac{I_t \in IL, me : I_t \xrightarrow{\tau} I'_t}{me : IL_T \xrightarrow{\tau} me : update\_msc(IL, I_t, I'_t)_T}$

M3. $\dfrac{\forall I_t \in IL, me : I_t \not\xrightarrow{\tau}, \exists I_p \in IL.me : I_p \xrightarrow{e} I'_p}{me : IL_T \xrightarrow{e} update\_env(me, e) : update\_msc(IL, I_p, I'_p)_T}$

M4. $\dfrac{\forall I_t \in IL, me : I_t \not\xrightarrow{\tau}, J \in T}{me : IL_T \xrightarrow{end(J)} IL_{T-\{J\}}}$

4 TMSC Expressions

Single TMSCs can express single scenarios of systems. In order to provide capabilities for structured system specifications, the TMSC language also includes a suite of operators for assembling sub-specifications. The resulting terms, called *TMSC expressions*, are defined by the following grammar:

$$
\begin{array}{ll}
S ::= M & \text{(single TMSC)} \\
\mid X & \text{(variable)} \\
\mid S_1 \parallel S_2 & \text{(interleaving parallel composition)} \\
\mid S_1 \mp S_2 & \text{(delayed choice)} \\
\mid S_1 \oplus S_2 & \text{(internal choice)} \\
\mid S_1; S_2 & \text{(sequential composition)} \\
\mid S_1 \wedge S_2 & \text{(logical and)} \\
\mid recX.S & \text{(recursive operator)}
\end{array}
$$

$S_1 \parallel S_2$ denotes the "interleaving" parallel composition of expressions S_1 and S_2: it allows the interleaving of events from S_1 and S_2 while the expressions execute independently. $S_1 \mp S_2$ represents the "deterministic choice" between S_1 and S_2: a correct refinement must be able to behave like both S_1 and S_2 until their behaviors differ, at which point a choice is allowed. $S_1 \oplus S_2$ is the nondeterministic choice between S_1 and S_2; a successful refinement can choose either. $S_1; S_2$ denotes the "instance-level" (asynchronous) sequential composition [11]; $S_1 \wedge S_2$ represents logical conjunction, and is primarily used in our framework to weave together individual constraints on system behavior Finally, the recursive operator $recX$ allows us to model infinite behavior of processes, where a new execution cycle starts whenever there is a reference to the variable used in the recursive definition (say X).

4.1 Executing TMSC Expressions

The operational behavior of TMSC expressions may also be defined in terms of SOS rules. Due to space constraints, we are unable to provide the entire semantics here. However, to provide some illustrative examples, we present the semantics of the two choice operators, $\oplus$ and $\mp$. This will also help bring out the difference between these two operators.

$S_1 \oplus S_2$: The SOS rules for the TMSC expression $S_1 \oplus S_2$ are shown in Table 4. The rules simply state that $S_1 \oplus S_2$ may non-deterministically (internally) choose between S_1 (**O1**) or S_2 (**O2**).

Table 4. Operational semantics for $S = S_1 \oplus S_2$

O1. $\dfrac{}{S_1 \oplus S_2 \xrightarrow{\tau} S_1}$ O2. $\dfrac{}{S_1 \oplus S_2 \xrightarrow{\tau} S_2}$

$S_1 \mp S_2$: In $S_1 \mp S_2$, the choice between S_1 and S_2 is delayed till a point is reached where their behaviors differ; at that point, a choice is made. Thus initially, S_1 and S_2 are allowed to resolve their internal non-determinism through sequences of τ transitions, till they both reach a *stable* state (**D1** and **D2** in Table 5); if S_1 and S_2 can then both perform an event a to evolve to S_1' and S_2' respectively, then $S_1 \mp S_2$ can also make an a transition to the state $S_1' \mp S_2'$ (**D5**). The choice between S_1 and S_2 is thus delayed. However, if S_1 (S_2) can make an a transition and S_2 (S_1) cannot, then $S_1 \mp S_2$ may perform an a transition thereby resolving the choice in favor of S_1 (S_2). This is shown in **D3** (and **D4**).

Table 5. Operational semantics for $S = S_1 \mp S_2$

D1. $\dfrac{S_1 \xrightarrow{\tau} S_1'}{S_1 \mp S_2 \xrightarrow{\tau} S_1' \mp S_2}$ D2. $\dfrac{S_2 \xrightarrow{\tau} S_2'}{S_1 \mp S_2 \xrightarrow{\tau} S_1 \mp S_2'}$

D3. $\dfrac{S_1 \xrightarrow{a} S_1', S_2 \not\xrightarrow{a}, S_1 \not\xrightarrow{\tau}, S_2 \not\xrightarrow{\tau}}{S_1 \mp S_2 \xrightarrow{a} S_1'}$ D4. $\dfrac{S_2 \xrightarrow{a} S_2', S_1 \not\xrightarrow{a}, S_1 \not\xrightarrow{\tau}, S_2 \not\xrightarrow{\tau}}{S_1 \mp S_2 \xrightarrow{a} S_2'}$

D5. $\dfrac{S_1 \xrightarrow{a} S_1', S_2 \xrightarrow{a} S_2', S_1 \not\xrightarrow{\tau}, S_2 \not\xrightarrow{\tau}}{S_1 \xrightarrow{a} S_1' \mp S_2'}$

5 Operational vs. Declarative Semantics

The TMSC declarative semantics is given as a set of equations [13] that define what the acceptance tree should be for a given TMSC expression. For a single TMSC M, this computation considers if an execution sequence w satisfies the triggers of the instances, and then either selects the next events from the action sequences (if an instance's trigger is complete), or non-deterministically chooses any enabled event (since there are no constraints on the instance's behavior). Acceptance tree computation for a TMSC expression S then proceeds by induction on the structure of S. For example, $T[S_1 \oplus S_2](w)$ = $sat(T[S_1](w) \cup T[S_2](w))$. The interested reader is referred to [13] for more details.

Although the declarative semantics gives a precise definition of the acceptance tree for a TMSC expression, it does not support ready simulation through the construction of executable models. This motivates the need for the operational semantics we presented in this paper. Given a TMSC expression S, we may apply the SOS rules repeatedly to generate a behavioral model of S in the form of a labeled transition system, from which an acceptance tree may be extracted, as outlined in Section 2. We make a reasonable assumption that variables inside recursive TMSC expressions are *guarded* i.e. preceded by a sub-expression in which no constituent instance may terminate immediately. This ensures that a TMSC expression may not be infinitely unrolled without making any actual progress. The aim is to constrain the TMSC language to those expressions S for which $LTS(S)$ is actually constructible using the TMSC SOS rules.

We will now relate the TMSC operational semantics with the declarative semantics. To distinguish the two semantics, for a TMSC expression S, we will denote by $T^D[S]$, the acceptance tree of S that is derived from the declarative semantics, and by $T^O[S]$, the acceptance tree that is derived from the transition system of S, generated by the operational semantics, i.e. SOS rules. The following theorem captures the equivalence of the two semantics. The result may be proved by induction on the structure of S; for brevity, we do not include the proof details here.

Theorem 2. *Let S be a TMSC expression such that $LTS(S)$ is constructible. Then, for any execution sequence w, $T^D[S](w) = T^O[S](w)$.*

The above theorem implies that the executable models we build using the TMSC SOS rules described in this paper are "correct" i.e. they conform to the original (declarative) TMSC semantics. Note that we may define a refinement notion on TMSC expressions, based on the *must* preorder, in terms of the LTSs obtained through the operational semantics as follows:

Definition 3. *Let S_1 and S_2 be TMSC expressions such that $LTS(S_1)$ and $LTS(S_2)$ are constructible. Then, $S_1 \sqsubseteq_{must} S_2$ iff $T^O[S_1] \supseteq T^O[S_2]$.*

6 Tool Support for TMSCs

The TMSC operational semantics outlined in this paper provides the basis for automated analysis of TMSC expressions through the TRIM tool. TRIM provides a simulator for executing TMSC expressions (according to the SOS rules) and also includes routines for checking refinement ordering between TMSC expressions and for returning diagnostic information when refinement fails to hold. TRIM is built on top of the Concurrency Workbench (CWB-NC) [10] an easy-to-retarget verification tool for finite-state sysems. A brief description of the TRIM architecture and some of the implementation considerations may be found in [4].

7 Related Work

The formal MSC language appears in a recommendation of the ITU [1]. An executable semantics for this language has been defined in [11] in a process algebraic setting, where the system behavior is interpreted in terms of SOS rules. However, basic MSCs in the ITU standard are expressively weak, offering only a visual partial ordering of events. The technical development in [1, 11] does not provide a natural way for expressing conditional/partial behavior and for the step-wise refinement of behavior. TMSCs were motivated by a need to enhance the MSC language along these directions. Accordingly, our operational semantics had to account for aditional considerations that arise from the specification of conditional and partial behavior, as also new structuring constructs (like $\oplus$ and $\wedge$) that TMSCs support. Note that [5], [9] have also proposed MSC extensions that support variations of trigger/action-like behavior as captured by TMSCs.

Several tools have been developed to support the use of scenarios in practice. MESA [3] allows certain properties, such as process divergence to be efficiently checked on MSCs. UBET ([2]) detects potential race conditions and timing violations in an MSC, and also provides automatic test case generation over HMSCs. The *play-in/play-out* approach of [6] is based on LSCs and has been implemented via a tool called the *play engine*. [15] shows how Constraint Logic Programming (CLP) may be used to support symbolic execution of LSC requirements. LTSA-MSC [14] supports synthesis of behavior models from MSC-based specifications and implied-scenario detection.

8 Conclusions

In this paper, we presented an operational semantics of the TMSC language in terms of SOS rules. This semantics complements the denotational TMSC semantics presented in earlier work [13] and provides the basis for simulation and analysis of TMSC-based specifications. We also considered the relation between the operational and denotational semantics of TMSCs, and discussed related work. In future, we intend to study how to generate test cases from TMSC specifications.

References

1. Message sequence charts (MSC). *ITU-TS Recommendation Z.120*, 1996.
2. R. Alur, G. J. Holzmann, and D. Peled. An analyzer for message sequence charts. *Software Concepts and Tools*, 17(2):70–77, 1996.
3. H. Ben-Abdallah and S. Leue. MESA: Support for scenario-based design of concurrent systems. *Proc. of the Fourth International Conference on Tools and Algorithms for the Construction and Analysis of Systems TACAS'98*, LNCS volume 1384:118–135.

4. B.Sengupta and R.Cleaveland. TRIM: A tool for triggered message sequence charts. *Proceedings of 15TH Computer Aided Verification Conference (CAV'03) (tool paper)*, 2003.
5. W. Damm and D. Harel. LSCs: Breathing life into message sequence charts. *Formal Methods in System Design*, 19(1), 2001.
6. D.Harel and R.Marelly. Specifying and executing behavioral requirements: The play-in/play-out approach. *Software and System Modeling (SoSym)*, 2003.
7. G.Plotkin. A structural approach to operational semantics. Technical report, University of Aarhus, Denmark, 1981.
8. M. Hennessy. Algebraic theory of processes. *The MIT Press*, 1988.
9. I. Kruger. Distributed system design with message sequence charts. *PhD Thesis, Technical University of Munich*, 2000.
10. R.Cleaveland and S.Sims. The ncsu concurrency workbench. *Computer Aided Verification (CAV), 1996*, LNCS volume 1102:394–397.
11. M. A. Reniers. Message sequence chart: Syntax and semantics. *PhD Thesis, Eindhoven University of Technology*, 1998.
12. B. Sengupta and R. Cleaveland. Refinement-based requirements modeling using triggered message sequence charts. 11th IEEE Int'l Requirements Engineering Conference, 2003.
13. B. Sengupta and R. Cleaveland. Triggered message sequence charts. *ACM SIGSOFT 2002, 10th Int'l Symposium on the Foundations of Software Engineering (FSE-10)*, pages 167–176.
14. J.Kramer S.Uchitel and J.Magee. Ltsa-msc: Tool support for behaviour model elaboration using implied scenarios. *TACAS'03*.
15. T.Wang, A.Roychoudhury, R.Yap, and S.C.Choudhary. Symbolic execution of behavioral requirements. *PADL 2004*, LNCS vol. 3057.

Efficient Symmetry Reduction for an Actor-Based Model

M.M. Jaghoori[1], M. Sirjani[2], M.R. Mousavi[3], and A. Movaghar[1]

[1] Sharif University of Technology, Tehran, Iran
[2] University of Tehran and IPM, Tehran, Iran
[3] Eindhoven University of Technology, Eindhoven, The Netherlands

Abstract. Symmetry reduction is a promising technique for combatting state space explosion in model checking. The problem of finding the equivalence classes, i.e., the so-called *orbits*, of states under symmetry is a difficult problem known to be as hard as graph isomorphism. In this paper, we show how we can automatically find the orbits in an actor-based model, called Rebeca, without enforcing any restriction on the modeler. The proposed algorithm solves the orbit problem for Rebeca models in polynomial time. As a result, the simple actor-based Rebeca language can be utilized efficiently for modeling and verification of systems, without involving the modeler with the details of the verification technique implemented.

1 Introduction

Model checking is the automatic and algorithmic way for the verification of system correctness. State space explosion is a major obstacle in exploiting model checking in practice. The problem arises when we try to explore all the possible states of a system to see whether a specific property is met or not. To overcome this problem, numerous methods have been proposed in order to avoid the construction of the complete state graph [6]. Among these methods are symbolic verification, partial order reduction, modular (parameterized) model checking, and symmetry reduction [8, 13, 18]. These techniques are sometimes combined to achieve even more compression in the representation of the system under analysis [1, 9, 11].

The symmetry technique is based on the fact that many systems are composed of similar and symmetric parts. These symmetric parts yield a similar behavior and have similar state graphs. The sub-graphs of these parts are usually interchangeable with respect to some permutation on the states. Therefore, it is possible to divide the state graph into symmetric graph quotients. One of these quotient graphs, annotated with the corresponding permutations, is shown to be enough for checking a general class of properties for the whole system [8]. However, for the technique to be useful, we need to find these permutations without constructing the total state space.

In concurrent systems, we can make use of the notion of *processes* running in parallel. Theoretically, a process is responsible for the behavior of some part of the system. We can consider the symmetry among processes and look for the permutations of processes, as suggested in [10]. Compared to permutations on states, permutations on processes are easier to find and maintain. However, checking all possible permutations for finding the ones that reveal the symmetries is not computationally efficient. Therefore, heuristic methods should be utilized for this purpose.

Alternatively, designer's insight may be use to reveal symmetry. Some tools, such as Murphi [13, 14], SMC [17] and SymmSpin [4], use the notion of scalar sets or a similar concept. Scalar sets are fully symmetric indices that are added to the model by the modeler to expose the symmetry of the system, so that the compiler can detect the symmetries automatically. In this paper, an algorithm is presented for finding the symmetry in Rebeca models automatically, with no changes to the syntax of Rebeca.

Rebeca [15] is an actor-based language, which can be used at a high level of abstraction for modeling concurrent systems. Using an object-based approach, and the asynchronous message-passing paradigm, Rebeca provides a basis that naturally fits in modular verification methods. Reactive objects are instantiated from reactive classes as templates. This suggests the idea that there is an inherent symmetry among the reactive objects of the same type (instantiated from the same reactive class).

It is preferred that the modeler is only involved in modeling issues, rather than the details of verification techniques. The interesting characteristic of Rebeca is that the only communication mechanism among the rebecs is through asynchronous message passing. This helps us find the symmetric permutations in polynomial time in the number of processes, without any extra work in modeling. We show that symmetry can be utilized in the presence of dynamic object creation and a special kind of changing topology.

In the rest of this paper, we first provide an overview of the symmetry reduction technique in Section 2. In Section 3, we introduce Rebeca and its semantics. Section 4 shows how symmetry reduction can be applied to Rebeca models and demonstrates the algorithm proposed for automatically detecting the symmetry in a Rebeca model. Section 5 extends our approach to the setting with dynamic creation of rebecs and dynamic topology. In Section 7, we present a brief comparison of our approach with related work. The concluding remarks and future work are presented in Section 8.

2 The Symmetry Reduction Technique

In this section, we explain the symmetry reduction technique [13, 8, 18]. The aim of this technique is to find the parts of the system that yield similar behavior. Intuitively, it is enough to run the model checking algorithm on one of these similar parts.

Consider a system M, consisting of n concurrently executing processes that communicate through shared variables.[1] Let I be the set $[1..n]$ of natural num-

---

[1] In later sections, we will use a restricted form of shared variables to represent asynchronous message passing in Rebeca.

bers. We assume that each process is identified by a unique index from I. The variables in M are also subscripted by an index set, which denotes the processes that access the variable, e.g. the variable $v_{1,3}$ is accessed by processes 1 and 3, and the variable w_2 is a local variable of process 2. Each process is defined as a set of actions, where each action is a conditional assignment of values to some of the variables. A specific action is said to be enabled at some state, if the respective condition evaluates to true. The whole system, called an *indexed transition system or briefly a* program, is viewed as the interleaving of the processes. In other words, each process may have zero or more actions enabled at each particular state, and which move the system to (probably) another state. Figure 2.(a) (taken from [8] with minor changes) shows a simple system composed of n identical processes that start in a non-critical state and try to enter their critical section (by executing action a_i), and then leave the critical section (by executing action b_i). There is a variable associated to each process, which shows whether it is in its critical section or not.

The formal definition of an *indexed transition system* M is given as a 4-tuple $\langle S, A, T, s_0 \rangle$. S denotes the set of *global states*, where a global state is a valuation of all the variables; and s_0 is the *initial state*. The *transition relation* is defined as $T \subseteq S \times A \times S$, where A denotes the set of the *actions* of different processes. The transitions in T represent the behavior of the system; i.e. $(s, a_i, t) \in T$ when the action a from process i is enabled in state s and its execution leads to state t. We may write $s \xrightarrow{a_i} t$ for (s, a_i, t).

A permutation $\pi : I \to I$ is a bijection on the index set I. Recall that I is the set $[1..n]$. We write a permutation as $\pi = (i_1, \ldots, i_n)$, which means $\forall_{1 \leq x \leq n} \pi(x) = i_x$. The set of all permutations on I is denoted by $Sym I$.

The application of a permutation π on a global state s should result in the global state $\pi(s)$, which is defined as follows. For every variable $v_{i_1,\ldots,i_k}$, its value in the state s is given to the variable $v_{\pi(i_1),\ldots,\pi(i_k)}$, in the state $\pi(s)$. If $v_{\pi(i_1),\ldots,\pi(i_k)}$ does not exist, then $\pi(s)$ is undefined and π is said to be *inconsistent*. In addition, the application of π on an action a_i is the action $a_{\pi(i)}$, which must be a valid action in the system; otherwise, π is inconsistent. We say that a consistent permutation π is an *automorphism* of the indexed transition system M, when $\pi(s_0) = s_0$, and π preserves the transition relation, i.e., $s \xrightarrow{a_i} t \in T$ when $\pi(s) \xrightarrow{\pi(a_i)} \pi(t) \in T$.

The *set of automorphisms* of M is denoted by $AutM$ and is a subgroup of $SymI$ [8]. Given any subgroup $G \in AutM$, we can define an equivalence relation on S. The states s and s' are equivalent with respect to G when there is a $\pi \in G$ such that $\pi(s) = s'$. Each equivalence class is called an *orbit*. Intuitively, for model checking M, it is sufficient to construct the state space for the representatives of each orbit.

The system shown in Figure 2.(a) is an example of a symmetric state graph. Representatives of the two orbits of this system are distinguished by an ellipse around them; for example, the states $(C_1, N_2, \ldots, N_n)$[2] and $(N_1, C_2, \ldots, N_n)$

---

[2] Assume that each process i has a variable v_i that can be either C or N; then, by C_i or N_i we mean that v_i has the value C or N, respectively.

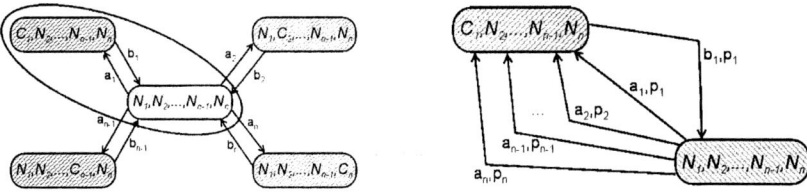

(a) Selecting a Representative From Each Orbit   (b) Annotated Quotient Structure

Fig. 1

are equivalent, because applying the automorphism $(2, 3, \ldots, n, 1)$ on the former produces the latter.

The *annotated quotient structure (AQS)* for M is $\overline{M} = \langle \overline{S}, \overline{T}, s_0 \rangle$, where $\overline{S}$ is the set of the representative states (which contains exactly one state from each orbit) and $\overline{T} \doteq \{\overline{s} \xrightarrow{a_i, \pi} \overline{t} \mid \pi \in G, \overline{s} \in \overline{S} \land \overline{t} \in \overline{S} \land \overline{s} \xrightarrow{a_i} \pi(\overline{t}) \in T\}$. Figure 2.(b) shows the annotated quotient structure of the previous example. Note that in this graph, there is only one edge with action b. Each p_i shows the permutation $(i, i+1, \ldots, n, 1, 2, \ldots, i-1)$, which maps the i'th process to the first one (this notation for permutations is explained earlier in this section).

Emerson, et.al, in [8], show that $\overline{M}$ can be used in the automata theoretic approach to model check M against formulas that respect the symmetry of the system. This approach is extended in [10] for efficient model checking under fairness conditions. Bosnacki in [3] shows how symmetry reduction can be combined with the *nested depth-first search* algorithm. In these methods, it is always assumed that the orbit relation is previously known. However, the problem of finding the equivalence relations (orbits), known as the orbit problem, is in its general form shown to be as hard as graph-isomorphism [8, 5]. In the following sections, we introduce Rebeca as an actor based language and explain how we can automatically compute the equivalence relation without engaging the modeler in the details of the verification method used. The algorithm proposed in the later sections solves the orbit relation for a Rebeca model in polynomial time (with respect to the number of the processes in the system).

3 Rebeca: An-Actor Based Model

The actor model was originally introduced by Hewitt [12] as an agent-based language. It was later developed by Agha [2] into a concurrent object-based model. Rebeca (Reactive objects language) [15] is based on the actor model with an operational semantics.

3.1 Basic Definitions

A Rebeca model is constructed by the parallel composition of a set of *rebecs*, written as $R = \|_{i \in I} r_i$, where I is the index set that is used to identify each rebec. For the sake of simplicity, we ignore the dynamic features of Rebeca in this section, and hence, assume that I is a fixed set for a given model. We relax this assumption in Section 5, where dynamic behavior in Rebeca models is addressed.

The concurrent execution of rebecs is modeled by interleaving, i.e., rebecs are given turns for execution. For model checking a Rebeca model, all fair sequences of execution are considered. An infinite sequence is considered fair when all the rebecs are infinitely often executed or disabled.

The rebecs communicate by sending asynchronous messages. The messages that can be serviced by the rebec r_i are denoted by the set M_i. There is a message server corresponding to each element of M_i. Each rebec has an unbounded queue for storing its incoming messages. In each state, the message at the head of the queue of a rebec specifies which one of its message servers is enabled. Each rebec, in its turn, removes one message from the top of its queue and atomically executes the corresponding message server.

The local state of a rebec r_i is distinguished by the valuation of its local variables and its queue. The global state of the model is obtained by the combination of the local states of all rebecs. For each rebec r_i, an ordered list of known rebecs is introduced, whose indices are collected in K_i. The rebec r_i can only send messages to its known rebecs. Since a rebec can also send messages to itself, we always have $j \in K_j$. The known rebecs of all rebecs are specified statically. As a result, we can derive the *communications graph* of a Rebeca model, from the known rebecs lists. In this directed graph, nodes are rebecs, and there is an edge from r_i to r_j when $j \in K_i$.

The behavior of a Rebeca model is defined as the interleaving of the enabled rebecs in each state. A rebec is enabled, if its message queue is not empty. There is at least a message server 'initial' in each rebec, which is responsible for the initialization tasks, and the corresponding message is assumed to be in the queues of all rebecs in the initial state. The execution of a message server is defined as the atomic sequential execution of its statements. Statements may be either '(nondeterministic) assignments' or 'send' operations. An assignment changes the values of the local state variables. In the case of a nondeterministic assignment, a set of values is used to specify the next value of the variable. A rebec can send messages to its known rebecs. The messages may be accompanied by parameters. The sent messages, together with their parameters are placed (immediately) in (the tail of) the queue of the receiving rebec. The execution of statements may be restricted by some conditions (on the values of the local variables, the sender or the parameters of the message).

3.2 The Formal Semantics of Rebeca

The semantics of a Rebeca model is expressed with an indexed transition system $\langle S, A, T, s_0 \rangle$ (introduced in Section 2). Each state in the system is identified by the values assigned to the local variables of the rebecs, together with the messages (and their parameters and sender) in the queues of the rebecs. Without loss of generality, we assume that all local variables take values from the domain set D. This domain set includes the *undefined* value represented by $\bot$.

It is also necessary to distinguish between the message, sender and parameter queues. Suppose that the message servers of r_j accept at most h_j number of parameters. Therefore, r_j has one message queue, one sender queue, and h_j parameter queues. To make queues easier to represent, we regard each queue as an array of variables. We assume an upper bound x_j on the number of the queue variables of r_j (all queues of r_j have the same upper bound). The domain of the message queue variables is $M_j \cup \bot$, where $\bot$ is re-used to represent an empty queue element. The domain of the sender queue variables is $I \cup \bot$, where I is the set of the indices (identifiers) of rebecs. The domain of parameter queue variables is also D. We write the i'th local, message queue and sender queue variable of rebec r_j as $r_j.v_i$, $r_j.m_i$ and $r_j.s_i$, respectively. The i'th element of the k'th parameter queue is written as $r_j.p_{ki}$.

Assuming that there are w_j local variables in r_j, a local state of r_j can be represented formally as $s_j = (r_j.v_1, \ldots, r_j.v_{w_j}, r_j.m_1, \ldots, r_j.m_{x_j}, r_j.s_1, \ldots, r_j.s_{x_j}, r_j.p_{11}, \ldots, r_j.p_{h_j x_j})$, where $h_j \geq 0$, $x_j \geq 1$ and $w_j \geq 0$. A global state of the system is defined as the combination of the local states of all rebecs: $s = \prod_{i \in I} s_i$. The set S denotes the set of all the global states. In the initial state s_0, $r_i.m_1 =' initial'$ for all rebecs r_i. If the initial message server of r_i accepts i_j parameters, the variables $r_j.p_{11}, r_j.p_{12}, \ldots, r_j.p_{i_j 1}$ are also initialized as specified in the model. All other (local and queue) variables are assigned the value $\bot$.

Since message servers are executed atomically, each message server is equivalent to an action, unless there are nondeterministic assignments, in which case, one action is defined per each nondeterministic choice. The set A denotes the set of all actions resulting from the message servers. Therefore, the transition relation $T \subseteq S \times A \times S$ is defined as follows. There is a transition $s \xrightarrow{a_j} t$ in the system, if the value of $r_j.m_1$ in the state s is equal to the message corresponding to the action a, and the execution of a results in the state t.

In the following, we define different possible types of sub-actions that a transition $s \xrightarrow{a_i} t$ may contain. In the formulas below, the variables on the left hand side of $\leftarrow$ refer to variables in t and the ones on the right hand side refer to their values in s.

1. Message removal: This sub-action includes the removal of the first element of message, sender and parameter queues. By removing the first element, we mean shifting other elements of the queue toward the queue head. This sub-action exists in all actions. It can be written as:

   $\forall_{0 < i < x_j} r_j.m_i \leftarrow r_j.m_{i+1}$, and $r_j.m_{x_j} \leftarrow \bot$, and
   $\forall_{0 < i < x_j} r_j.s_i \leftarrow r_j.s_{i+1}$, and $r_j.s_{x_j} \leftarrow \bot$, and
   $\forall_{0 < i < x_j, 0 < k \leq h_j} r_j.p_{ki} \leftarrow r_j.p_{k(i+1)}$, and $r_j.p_{k(x_j)} \leftarrow \bot$.

2. Assignment: An assignment can be a statement like '$w \leftarrow d$', where w is the i'th local variable in r_j and $d \in D \setminus \bot$. This statement simply means: $r_j.v_i \leftarrow d$. The right hand side of an assignment may also be a more complex expression based on the local variables of r_j. In such cases, the expression can be evaluated with the values of the local variables in state s, and finally

a value like d is obtained. Therefore, for the sake of simplicity, we can assume that the right hand side of an assignment is always an explicit value.

3. Send: The rebec r_j may send a message m to r_k, where $m \in M_k$ and $k \in K_j$. As stated earlier, by K_j, we mean the ordered list of (the indices of) the known rebecs of r_j. The message m is assumed to have h_k parameters, say $n_1, \ldots, n_{h_k}$, where $n_i \in D$, $1 \leq i \leq h_k$. Like an assignment, a parameter may also be represented by an expression, which finally resolves into an explicit value from D. Recall that rebec r_k has h_k parameter queues. Note that n_i may be $\bot$; and for $i < h_k$, if n_i is $\bot$, then n_{i+1} must also be $\bot$. In addition, the number parameters that are not $\bot$ must agree with the number of arguments that the message server corresponding to m accepts. The result of this sub-action is:

If $\exists_{0<y\leq x_k}(r_k.m_y = \bot \wedge \forall_{0<z<y} r_k.m_z \neq \bot)$, then
$r_k.m_y \leftarrow m$, $r_k.s_y \leftarrow j$, $\forall_{1\leq i \leq h_k} r_k.p_{iy} \leftarrow n_i$

Otherwise, x_k must be increased and the transition system of the Rebeca model cannot be constructed.

4 Symmetry in Rebeca

To exploit symmetry in an indexed transition system associated to a Rebeca model, we need to find a permutation group acting on the index set $[1..n]$ of the rebecs. With the permutation group, the state space is partitioned into orbits (equivalence classes). Since the rebecs of the same type (i.e. they are instances of the same reactive-class) exhibit similar behavior, it is reasonable to limit the permutations to those that preserve rebecs types. Theorem 1 helps to derive the symmetry in Rebeca models in a straightforward way. It simplifies the orbit problem by helping to obtain possible permutations prior to the real construction of the state space.

From now on, consider a system $R = \langle S, A, T, s_0 \rangle = ||_{i \in I} r_i$ of a Rebeca model. Here, we redefine the application of a permutation on a global state. Definition 2 is repeated for easier reference.

Definition 1. *The application of a permutation π on a global state s, denoted by $\pi(s)$, is defined as follows:*

1- Variables that are not of 'rebec index' type (i.e., don't get their value from the set I), like $r_j.v_i$, $r_j.m_i$ and $r_j.p_{ki}$: Their values in state s, is assigned to the local or queue variables $r_{\pi(j)}.v_i$, $r_{\pi(j)}.m_i$ and $r_{\pi(j)}.p_{ki}$ in state $\pi(s)$, respectively.
2- Variables that are of 'rebec index' type, like $r_j.v_i$ and $r_j.s_i$ (sender queue): Suppose their value is state s is x. In state $\pi(s)$, the value $\pi(x)$ is assigned to variables $r_{\pi(j)}.v_i$ and $r_{\pi(j)}.s_i$, respectively.

For static Rebeca models, the latter case shrinks only to the case of sender queue variables. However, the more general case applies to dynamic Rebeca models, which is discussed in the next section.

Definition 2. *A permutation π, defined in I, is said to preserve the transition relation when $[s \xrightarrow{a_i} t \in T] \rightarrow [\pi(s) \xrightarrow{a_{\pi(i)}} \pi(t) \in T]$. Such a permutation is called an automorphism of R, if $\pi(s_0) = s_0$.*

Definition 3. *A permutation π is said to preserve rebec types, if for all i,j such that $\pi(i) = j$, the rebecs r_i and r_j are instances of the same reactive-class.*

Definition 4. *If $K_i = (t_1, t_2, \ldots, t_{P_i})$ denotes the ordered list of the indices of the known-rebecs of r_i, where $i \in I$, a permutation π is said to preserve the known-rebec relation iff: $\forall_{i \in I} K_{\pi(i)} = (\pi(t_1), \pi(t_2), \ldots, \pi(t_{P_i}))$.*

Theorem 1. *If a permutation π preserves both rebec types and the known-rebec relation, and $\pi(s_0) = s_0$, then π is an automorphism of R.*

Given an automorphism of a Rebeca model, we can partition the rebecs into equivalence classes. To examine whether $\pi(s_0) = s_0$, the initialization of the system must be checked to ensure that the parameters sent with the *initial* message do not break the symmetry; i.e. equivalent rebecs receive similar values for the normal parameters to *initial*, and symmetric values for rebec parameters.

The obtained equivalence relation on rebecs can be used to derive a symmetry group on the states of the underlying structure. It shows how the simple natural object-based syntax of Rebeca helps us find the symmetry automatically. Next section presents an efficient algorithm that finds the symmetry groups of a given Rebeca model, if there is any.

4.1 Implementation

In this section, we present an algorithm for detecting symmetry in Rebeca models based on Theorem 1 of the previous section. In the following, we demonstrate how symmetry can be detected from normal Rebeca models, i.e., with no change in the syntax of Rebeca.

Theorem 1, implies that checking for equivalence of two rebecs, is reduced to finding a permutation that maps one to the other and preserves the known-rebec relation. The ordering among the known rebecs of each rebec helps us implement a polynomial time algorithm for this purpose. First, we show that checking whether two given rebecs belong to the same equivalence class can be done in linear time. It is performed in the *check* algorithm given below.

```
check (i, j) : boolean;
if (i.type != j.type) return false;
define pi as an empty array of size n;// pi[i] = permutation acting on i
Let pi[i] := j;    // suppose permutation of i is j
Let p1 := K(i);   // the ordered known rebecs of i
Let p2 := K(j);   // the ordered known rebecs of j
while p1 not empty do
    x := removeFirstElementOf (p1);
    y := removeFirstElementOf (p2);
    if (pi[x] is undefined)
      Let pi[i] := j;
```

```
          p1 += K(x);  // add to the end of the list
          p2 += K(y);  // add to the end of the list
        else if(pi[x] != y) // knownrebec relation is not preserved
          return false;
    od
    return true;
end
```

The inputs to *check*, i and j, are the indices of two rebecs. In this algorithm, we try to find a permutation π that maps i to j, and also respects the known-rebec relation. For this purpose, we take a constructive approach. The permutation is represented by an array of size n. The i'th element of this array shows the result of the permutation for rebec i. The algorithm starts with defining $\pi(i) = j$. Then it tries to find the other elements of the permutation. It is expected that i and j are rebecs of the same type. Therefore, they have equal number of known rebecs, which are also of similar types. Since the permutation must respect the known-rebec relation, it must also map the known rebecs of i to the known rebecs of j. It is assumed that $K(i)$ returns the ordered list of the indices of the known rebecs of rebec i. In the algorithm, $p1$ and $p2$ are the lists of rebec indices that must be checked for equivalency. Therefore, $K(i)$ and $K(j)$ are added to $p1$ and $p2$. Then at each step, one element from $p1$ and $p2$ are removed and checked against previous values of π. If π has another value then the algorithm returns false and terminates. If a new pair has been added to π, the indices of their known rebecs are added to $p1$ and $p2$. The algorithm continues until a contradiction is encountered, or there are no other rebecs to be checked. The return value shows whether they belong to the same equivalence class. As we explained in section 3, we can construct a communication graph of a Rebeca model. If this graph is not connected, the permutation of rebecs not connected to i and j, are not important to the equivalence of i and j. This algorithm in the worst case (i and j are equivalent), gives the answer in time linear in the number of rebecs in the system.

For finding the biggest equivalence classes of rebecs, which yields the most reduction in the state space, we first assume that each rebec by itself constitutes an equivalence class. Then at each step, we take representatives of two different equivalence classes, and check their equivalence. If they are equivalent, their corresponding equivalence classes can be combined. In the worst case (which is the case of an asymmetric system), every pair of rebecs of the same type are checked for equivalence. It means $O(n^2)$ times calling of check, which is in turn linear; and in total find is $O(n^3)$ in the number of rebecs in the system.

```
find ()
    classes := empty list;
    for every rebec r in the system add {r} to classes;
    for each m,n classes such that m != n  do
        if check (m.rep, n.rep)  // check representatives of m and n
            replace m and n by the union of (m, n);
    od
end
```

The *find* algorithm computes the equivalence classes of rebecs in a Rebeca model. With these equivalence classes, the algorithms introduced in [17] or [3] can be used to model check Rebeca models while exploiting the symmetry of the models.

5 Dynamic Features in Rebeca

In this section, we deal with the dynamic features of a Rebeca model. Then we show that Theorem 1 applies to dynamic models, too. In a dynamic Rebeca model, rebecs may be created dynamically, i.e., during the execution of other rebecs. We allow the definition of variables of rebec type, which can hold references to rebecs (i.e., the index of the rebec). Due to dynamic creation, I is no longer fixed and (only) changes upon creation of new rebecs. We use $I(s)$ to denote the set of (indices of) rebecs in state s. In addition, rebec references can be passed as parameters to messages. Therefore, the set of rebecs that receive messages from a given rebec includes its known rebecs, plus the rebecs dynamically assigned to the rebec variables. Remember that the known rebec list of a rebec must be determined upon creation, and may not change during the execution.

5.1 Formal Semantics

The behavior of a dynamic Rebeca model $R = \|_{i \in I} r_i$, where I is the (dynamic) set of rebec indices, is defined as an indexed transition system $\langle S, A, T, s_0 \rangle$. The set of states S contains all the global states and s_0 is the initial state. The set of actions, which are indexed by indices from I, is denoted A, and is the set of all transitions. We use the notion $I(s)$ to mean the index set in state s. We may drop the s argument and just write I when s is irrelevant or clear from the context. By a (rebec) reference, we mean an index from the set I. The domain of rebec variables is $I \cup \bot$. Furthermore, like local variables, parameter queue variables can also be divided into two groups of normal parameters, and rebec parameters. The domain of normal parameters is D, and the domain of rebec parameters is I.

The apparent difference here is the introduction of some new sub-actions. Consider a transition $s \xrightarrow{a_j} t$ in a dynamic Rebeca model. In the following, the new sub-actions of a_j are introduced. In addition, the changes to some of the sub-actions with respect to Section 3 are also explained.

1. Assignment: Assignment to local variables of rebec index type is only possible in the form of $w \leftarrow z$ where w is a local variable and z is either a local variable or an argument of the containing message server. Both w and z take values from I, the set of rebec indices. As a result of this assignment, the value of z in state s is assigned to w in state t. Assignment to normal variables does not change compared to static models.

2. Rebec creation: A statement of the form '*new* $rc(kr_1, kr_2, \ldots, kr_m)$: $(p_1, \ldots, p_d)$', where rc is the name of a reactive-class, and kr_u represents an index from the current set I, and shows that u'th known rebec of the newly created rebec must be bound to r_{kr_u}, and p_u shows the u'th parameter to the

initial message. The execution of this sub-action in a_j, results in a new index v being added to I. This index is assigned to the newly created rebec. The effect of this new index is that the global state t, which is defined as $\prod_{i \in I} t_i$, will also include the local state t_v. The local state t_v of rebec r_v is defined in the same way as other rebecs, i.e. based on the variables and (message, sender and parameter) queues of the reactive-class rc. The valuation of the local variables of r_v in t is defined as follows. The message *initial* is placed in $r_v.m_1$, and the parameters $p_1, p_2, \ldots, p_d$ are placed in $r_v.p_{11}, r_v.p_{21}, \ldots, r_v.p_{d1}$, respectively, and $r_v.s_1$ is assigned the value j (the index of its creator or parent). All other (local and queue) variables of r_v are undefined ($\bot$).

3. Send: In dynamic Rebeca models, messages can be sent both to known rebecs, and to local variables of rebec type. Like the case of a static model, the rebec r_j may send a message m to r_k with the parameters $n_1, \ldots, n_{h_k}$, where $m \in M_k$, and either k belongs to K_j or $r_j.v_g$ is a rebec variable and holds the value k. In addition, n_i may be a normal parameter ($n_i \in D$) or a rebec parameter ($n_i \in I$). In the case of a normal parameter, n_i can also be an expression that evaluates to some value from $D \setminus \bot$. However, in the case of a rebec parameter, n_i must be a local variable or an argument of the containing message server, and must be of rebec index type. This send operation, results in the message m being placed in the first empty slot of the queue of the receiving rebec. The result of sending $m(n_1, \ldots, n_{h_k})$ is: (recall that h_k is the number of parameter queues of r_k and for $i < h_k$, if n_i is $\bot$, then n_{i+1} must also be $\bot$):

If $\exists_{0 < y \leq x_k}(r_k.m_y = \bot \land \forall_{0 < z < y} r_k.m_z \neq \bot)$ then $r_k.m_y \leftarrow m, r_k.s_y \leftarrow j$, $\forall_{1 \leq i \leq h_k} r_k.p_{iy} \leftarrow n_i$

Otherwise, x_k must be increased and the transition system of the Rebeca model cannot be constructed.

Passing a rebec reference as a parameter is treated the same as passing normal variables. Note again that the known rebecs of a rebec must be determined upon creation of that rebec.

5.2 Symmetry in Dynamic Rebeca Models

Detecting symmetry in the dynamic Rebeca models is possible in a similar way as in the static ones. Theorem 1 applies to dynamic Rebeca models without any changes. Note that Theorem 1 takes into consideration only the rebecs that are created in the initial state (and the known rebec relation among them). Theorem 2 carries over without any change to the extended setting.

Theorem 2. *If a permutation π preserves both rebec types and the known-rebec relation, and $\pi(s_0) = s_0$, then π is an automorphism of R.*

The interesting point is that since we made no changes to the theorem, the same algorithm is sufficient for detecting the symmetry in dynamic models.

6 Case Study

In this section, we give an example to show how our algorithm works. We use the 'load balancer' example from [7] with some changes. In this example, there are six identical clients that need some service, which is provided by three identical servers. Instead of communicating directly with the servers, the clients send their requests to load-balancers. The responsibility of the load-balancers is to distribute the load evenly among the servers. In our example, the round robin policy is used for load balancing, i.e., each load balancer sends the incoming requests to the servers in a round-robin manner. The servers, however, reply directly to the clients. In a static structure, the servers know all the clients beforehand; but in a dynamic model, the reference of the requesting client is passed to the server. The server uses that reference for sending its reply.

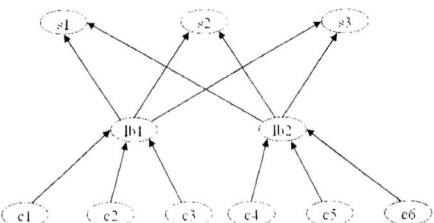

Fig. 2. The Load-Balancer

We first model it using only static features. In this case, the clients must be assigned a distinguishing identifier. This identifier is passed to their initial message server. Furthermore, all the clients are introduced to servers as known rebecs. The clients pass their identifier together with their request message, which is passed on by the load balancer. Thus the server knows to whom it should direct the answer.

The initialization of this system is shown below:

```
main {
    Client c1(lb1):(1),c2(lb1):(2),c3(lb1):(3),c4(lb2):(4),c5(lb2):(5),c6(lb2):(6);
    LoadBalancer lb1(s1,s2,s3):(), lb2(s1,s2,s3):();
    Server s1(c1,c2,c3,c4,c5,c6):(), s2(c1,c2,c3,c4,c5,c6):(),s3(c1,c2,c3,c4,c5,c6):();
}
```

In this model, the load-balancers and servers constitute two orbits. However, clients are not symmetric (each client adds up to one orbit). That is because of the symmetry-breaking identifiers passed to their initial message server. Using dynamic features of Rebeca, we can change the model, so that each load-balancer sends the reference of the sender of a request message to the servers. Therefore, the servers do not need to know the clients in advance. They just forward the reply to the rebec, whose reference is sent by the request.

The initialization of this system is shown below:

```
main {
    Client c1(lb1):(),c2(lb1):(),c3(lb1):(),c4(lb2):(),c5(lb2):(),c6(lb2):();
    LoadBalancer lb1(s1,s2,s3):(), lb2(s1,s2,s3):();
    Server s1():(), s2():(), s3():();
}
```

In the dynamic model, the clients also form one orbit. This shows that using dynamic features, we could model this example more naturally, which helps us find bigger orbits. This encourages the use of this technique in model checking symmetric Rebeca models. Figure 2 shows the static communication graph (defined in Section 3) of the dynamic load-balancer example.

7 Related Work

Symmetry reduction technique has been implemented in many model checking tools such as Murphi [13, 14] and SMC [17] and SPIN [4, 7]. Murphi is the first language (and tool) that provided support for symmetry reduction. If the modeled system is symmetric, the modeler must be aware of it, and use scalar sets properly to expose the symmetry of the system. SMC was developed by Sistla et.al., as a symmetry based model checker for verification of safety and liveness properties. SMC uses a notion of 'modules', which play the same role as scalar sets of Murphi. Other tools, like UPPAAL, SMV and SPIN, use the approach of Murphi for handling symmetry; namely, adding scalar sets to expose the symmetry of the system by the modeler. Using scalar-sets (or modules in SMC) is error prone and sometimes makes modeling a symmetric system more difficult. In our approach, no change to the syntax of Rebeca is made, and therefore the modeler does not need to know about the symmetry of the system. Instead, the symmetry in a Rebeca model is automatically detected, if there is any.

The work of [7] is similar to ours, in the sense that static graphs of channels are used to detect the symmetry automatically from (dynamic) Promela models. The dynamicity in their models is caused by sending the channels around. They do not consider the dynamic creation of processes. In our approach, rebec references (which can be interpreted as their inbox address) can be sent around, and rebecs can also be created dynamically.

8 Conclusions

Rebeca is an object based language for modeling and verification of reactive systems. Since rebecs of the same type show similar behavior, it is easy to find symmetry in Rebeca models. We showed in this paper that if the static communication graph of a Rebeca model is symmetric, then the whole model is symmetric. Furthermore, an algorithm is presented for solving the orbit problem for Rebeca models in polynomial time. The algorithm finds the orbits of rebecs by examining the known-rebec relation that defines the composition of the system. In contrast to most other symmetry-related tools, no new construct needs to be added to the syntax of Rebeca to be used by this algorithm. The same algorithm still works when dynamic features, such as 'the dynamic creation of rebecs' and 'the dynamic changing of topology', are added to the models. As a result, the symmetry reduction technique can be efficiently implemented in current Rebeca model checkers [16], or in the direct model checking of Rebeca.

References

1. P. A. Abdulla, B. Jonsson, M. Kindahl, and D. Peled. A general approach to partial order reductions in symbolic verification. In *Proceedings of CAV'98*, pages 379–390, 1998.
2. G. Agha. The structure and semantics of actor languages. In *Proceedings of the REX Workshop*, pages 1–59, 1990.
3. D. Bosnacki. A light-weight algorithm for model checking with symmetry reduction and weak fairness. In *Proceedings of the SPIN Workshop*, pages 89–103, 2003.
4. D. Bosnacki, D. Dams, and L. Holenderski. Symmetric spin. *Software Tools for Technology Transfer*, 4(1):92–106, 2002.
5. E. M. Clarke, E. A. Emerson, S. Jha, and A. P. Sistla. Symmetry reductions in model checking. In *Proceedings of CAV'98*, pages 147–158, 1998.
6. E. M. Clarke, O. Grumberg, and D. A. Peled. *Model Checking*. MIT Press, 1999.
7. A. Donaldson, A. Miller, and M. Calder. Finding symmetry in models of concurrent systems by static channel diagram analysis. In *Proceedings of AVOCS'04*, pages 161–177, 2005.
8. E. Emerson and A. Sistla. Symmetry and model checking. *Formal Methods in System Design*, 9(1–2):105–131, 1996.
9. E. A. Emerson, S. Jha, and D. Peled. Combining partial order and symmetry reductions. In *Proceedings of TACAS '97*, pages 19–34, 1997.
10. E. A. Emerson and A. P. Sistla. Utilizing symmetry when model checking under fairness assumptions: An automata-theoretic approach. In *Proceedings of CAV'95*, pages 309–324, 1995.
11. E. A. Emerson and T. Wahl. On combining symmetry reduction and symbolic representation for efficient model checking. In *Proceedings of CHARME'03*, pages 216–230, 2003.
12. C. Hewitt. Procedural embedding of knowledge in planner. In Proceedings of IJCAI'71, pages 167–184, 1971.
13. C. Ip and D. Dill. Better verification through symmetry. *Formal methods in system design*, 9(1-2):41–75, 1996.
14. C. N. Ip and D. L. Dill. Verifying systems with replicated components in Murphi. In *Proceedings of CAV'96*, pages 147–158, 1996.
15. M. Sirjani, A. Movaghar, A. Shali, and F. S. de Boer. Modeling and verification of reactive systems using Rebeca. *Fundamamenta Informaticae*, 63(4):385–410, 2004.
16. M. Sirjani, A. Shali, M. M. Jaghoori, H. Iravanchi, and A. Movaghar. A front-end tool for automated abstraction and modular verification of actor-based models. In *Proceedings of ACSD'04*, pages 145–150, 2004.
17. A. P. Sistla, V. Gyuris, and E. A. Emerson. SMC: a symmetry-based model checker for verification of safety and liveness properties. *ACM Transactions on Software Engineering Methodology*, 9(2):133–166, 2000.
18. A. P. Sistla. Employing symmetry reductions in model checking. *Computer Languages, Systems & Structures* 30(3-4):99–137, 2004.

Validated Code Generation for Activity Diagrams

A.K. Bhattacharjee[1] and R.K. Shyamasundar[2]

[1] Reactor Control Division, Bhabha Atomic Research Centre,
Mumbai 400 085
anup@barc.ernet.in
[2] School of Technology and Computer Science,
Tata Institute of Fundamental Research, Mumbai 400 005
shyam@tifr.res.in

Abstract. *Activity Diagram* is an important component of the set of diagrams used in UML. The OMG document on UML 2.0 proposes a Petri net based semantics for Activity Diagrams. While Petri net based approach is useful and interesting, it does not exploit the underlying inherent synchronous concepts of activity diagrams. The latter can be effectively utilized for validated code generation and verification. In this paper, we shall capture activity diagrams in synchronous language framework to arrive at executional models which will be useful in model based design of software. This also enables validated code generation using code generation mechanisms of synchronous language environments such as Esterel and its programming environments. Further, the framework leads to scalable verification methods.

1 Introduction

Activity Diagram is one of the important diagrams in UML. It is used to model sequence of actions to capture the process flow actions and its results. It focuses on the work performed in the implementation of an operation (a method), and the activities in a use case instance or in an object. In UML 2.0, activity diagrams support concurrent control and data flow, loops, conditionals and exception handling. The two basic entities are *Actions* and *Activities*. An *Action* is the fundamental unit of executable functionality and an *activity* provides the coordinated sequencing of subordinate units whose individual elements are actions. This coordination is expressed as a graph of *ActivityNodes* connected by *ActivityEdges*. Since there are actions that invoke activities, that may be nested and possibly form invocation hierarchies invoking other activities (ultimately resolving to individual atomic actions). The OMG document [6] classifies activity diagrams as *Fundamental, Basic, Intermediate, Structured, Complete* in terms of complexity in the process flow. In this paper, we are concerned with the Intermediate Level of Activity Diagrams that include control and data flow and decisions. A simple activity diagram describing the order processing and account is shown in Fig. 1.

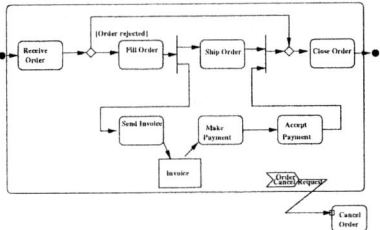

Fig. 1. Simple Activity Diagram

Although the OMG document [6] provides an intuitive semantics of Activity Diagrams, it lacks a formal semantics required for analysis and automatic code generation. Hence, in the recent past there has been a lot of interest in giving a formal semantics to Activity Diagrams.

Most of the works on the semantics of UML activities in general have been based on Petri nets. Two of the significant efforts toward formalization of UML activities are [7] and [8]. Eshuis [7] proposes the semantics at the following two levels : *Requirement Level* and *Implementation Level*. The first level is based on Statechart like semantics and is transformed into a transition system for model checking by NuSMV. The second level is based on STATEMATE semantics of statecharts extended with properties to handle data. It is to be noted that the implementation semantics has not been obtained as a refinement of the requirement level semantics. The semantics also covers activity charts of UML 1.5 but not of activity diagrams of UML 2.0[1]. Storrle [8] envisages a semantics by mapping activities into *procedural Petri nets*, which excludes data type annotations but includes control flow. He has defined mappings to *procedural Petri nets* to prevent multiple calls which otherwise would result in infinite nets.

In this paper, we propose a reactive formalism of Activity Diagrams of UML 2.0 description; for description purpose we use Esterel language. Our approach combines the requirement level and implementation level semantics. Further the notion of procedure call transitions as used in activity diagrams are captured nicely through the ''run module'' construct and one can specify the number of incarnations of the same module when called multiple times. Since it is based on Esterel, that has efficient code generation tools, the transformations can be used to realize a system directly from the model. Thus in our approach, we can not only reason about activity diagrams but also generate validated code automatically.

2 Activity Diagrams: Informal Interpretation

An action is the fundamental unit of executable functionality in an activity [6]. The execution of an action represents some transformation or processing in the

---

[1] It should be pointed out that UML 2.0 is a significantly re-engineered version of UML 1.5, particularly in the context of activity diagrams.

modeled system, which could be a computer system or a process. An action may have sets of incoming and outgoing activity edges that specify control flow and data flow from and to other nodes. An action will not begin execution until all of its input conditions are satisfied. The completion of the execution of an action may enable the execution of a set of successor nodes and actions that take their inputs from the outputs of the action. The sequencing of actions are controlled by control edges and object flow edges within activities, which carry control and object tokens respectively. An action can only begin execution when all incoming control tokens are present and all input pins have object tokens. An action execution represents the run-time behavior of executing an action within a specific activity execution. When the execution of an action is complete, it offers tokens in its outgoing control edges and output pins, where they are accessible to other actions.

3 Synchronous Framework for Activity Diagrams

In this section, we capture activity diagrams in a synchronous framework. Synchronous framework is based on the perfect synchrony hypothesis: *the system reacts instantaneously to events producing outputs along with the input compiling away the control commands.* Synchronous languages are based on this hypothesis and model reactive systems effectively and have a sound and complete semantics. One of the distinct advantages of using synchronous languages for specifying reactive systems is that the description of the system analyzed or validated is very close to implementation. One of the oldest languages in the family of synchronous languages Esterel has good developmental facilities such as efficient code generating compilers, verifiers etc. For these reasons, we have chosen Esterel as the underlying language for description of activity diagrams. A brief characteristics of Esterel is given below.

3.1 Esterel

The basic object of Esterel without value passing, referred to as PURE Esterel, is the signal. Signals are used for communication with the environment as well as for internal communication. The programming unit is the module. A module has an interface that defines its input and output signals and a body that is an executable statement:

```
module M:
    input I1, I2;
    output O1, O2;
    input relations
    statement
end module
```

At execution time, a module is activated by repeatedly giving it an input event consisting of a possibly empty set of input signals assumed to be present and satisfying the input relations. The module reacts by executing its body and outputs the emitted output signals. We assume that the reaction is instantaneous or perfectly synchronous in the sense that the outputs are produced in no time. Hence, all necessary computations are also done in no time. The only statements that consume time are the ones explicitly requested to do so. The reaction is also required to be deterministic: for any state of the program and any input event, there is exactly one possible output event. In perfectly synchronous languages, a *reaction* is also called an *instant*. Instantiation of a module is done through the run statement. For instance, run *exchange [X1/E1, ... Xn/En]* copies the body of the module *exchange* in place of the run command after renaming all occurrences of the signals X1, ... Xn by E1, ... En respectively; in other words, the parameters are *bound by capture*.

Asynchronous tasks are those tasks which do take time; that is, the time between initiation and completion is observable. In the terminology of Esterel, this can be interpreted to mean that there will be at least one instant between initiation and completion. The exec primitive provides the interface between Esterel modules and asynchronous tasks. An asynchronous task is declared by the statement "task task_id (f_par_lst) return signal_nm (type);" where task_id is the name of the task, f_par_lst gives the list of *formal* parameters (reference or value) and the signal returned by the task is given by the signal_nm with its type after the keyword return Instantiation of the task is done through the primitive exec. For example, the above task can be instantiated from an Esterel program as "exec task_id (a_par_lst);".

A typical task declaration appears as "task ROBOT_move (ip, fp) return complete" and the call appears as "exec ROBOT_move (x,y)". The execution of this statement in some process starts task ROBOT_move and awaits for the return signal complete for it to proceed further. In other words, exec requests the environment to start the task and then waits for the return signal.

4 Synchronous Interpretation of Basic Activity Diagrams

The synchronous model for the Activity Diagrams is represented as a collection of transformation rules for each construct of the Activity Diagrams. A basic *ActivityNode* is modeled by an Esterel module named after the node. The invocation of the activity is modeled by instantiating the module using the run module construct.

A basic ActivityNode can invoke an asynchronous task which can handle system specific functions and can be modeled by an Esterel task statement such as exec taskA ()() return ExitA, where taskA is the external process performing the actual action written in the host language. The completion of the task is signaled by emitting the signal ExitA referred as a return signal. A return signal cannot be internally emitted by the program. In our model we ignore the external action for the purpose of simplicity.

Each activity node has the following set of signals associated with it.

– EntryS is the signal emitted when a particular activity node is entered.

- InS is the signal emitted when an action in a particular activity node is being performed.
- ExitS is the signal emitted when a particular activity node is completed.

We also assume that there is a root activity node which contains and controls the sequencing of the activity nodes through the activity edges. In the example shown in Fig. 2, the module simpleActivity performs the task of passing control tokens from the activity sendPayment to the activity receivePayment and is the the root activity. The activities sendPayment, receivePayment and simpleActivity in the above example, can be interpreted through the Esterel fragments shown in the Fig.2.

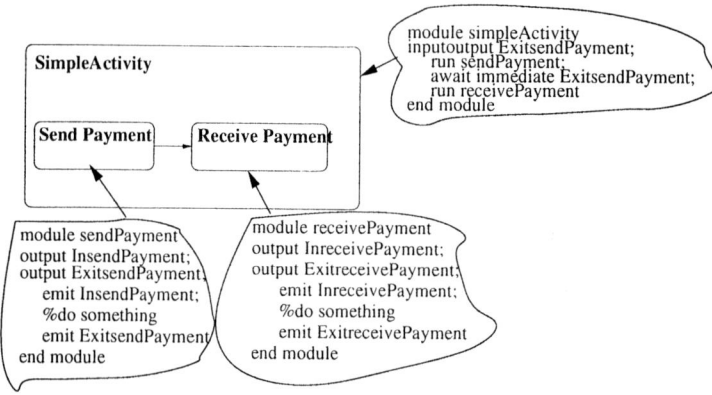

Fig. 2. Simple node

Merge Node: A merge node (cf. Fig. 3) is a control node that brings together multiple alternate flows. It is not used to synchronize concurrent flows but to accept one among alternate flows. It has multiple incoming edges and a single outgoing edge. It can be described as follows

```
module mergeNode
      run A % the module A implements activity A
      ||
      run B % the module B implements activity B
      ||
      await ExitA;
            run C % The module C implements activity C
      ||
      await ExitB
            run C % The module C implements activity C

end module
```

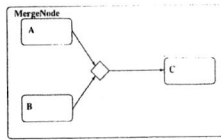
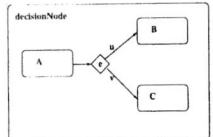

Fig. 3. Merge Node   **Fig. 4.** Decision Node

Here the activities A and B are started concurrently, but whichever activity completes earlier, starts the activity C. If activity A and B completes together, then two instances of C would be running at the same time. This interpretation is in line with the recent OMG document [6].

Decision Node: A decision node (cf. Fig. 4) is a control node that chooses between the outgoing flows. It has one incoming edge and multiple outgoing edges. It can be described by the following Esterel fragment.

```
module decisionNode
var e in
        run A;
        if e = u
            run B; % e is the guard which if  u then run B
        else if e = v
            run C; % e is the guard which if  v then run C
        end
end
end module
```

Here after the activity A completes, the control passes to activity B or C depending on the guard condition e being equal to u or v respectively.

ForkJoin Node: A forkJoin node (cf. Fig. 5) is a control node that splits a flow into multiple concurrent flows. It has one incoming edge and multiple outgoing edges. Tokens arriving at a fork node are duplicated across the outgoing edges. Tokens offered by the incoming edge are all offered to the outgoing edges.

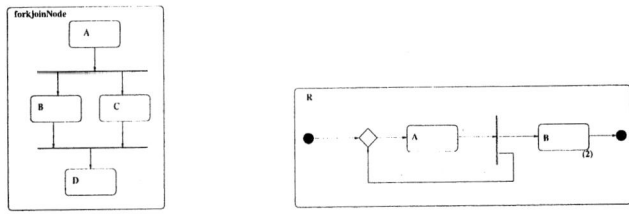

Fig. 5. Fork Join Node   **Fig. 6.** Reentrant Node

The forking and joining of activities can be described by the following Esterel fragment.

```
module forkJoinNode

    run A       % run activity A
    [
        run B   % run activity B
        ||
        run C   % run activity C
    ]
    run D       % run activity D

end module
```

Here after the activity A completes the activities B and C are started concurrently. Once both of B and C are complete, D is started. If concurrent activities are not modeled carefully this may lead to problem. Let us consider the case as shown in the Fig. 6. Here completion of A forks A once again with B. Thus, a possible run of the system is $A \rightarrow AB \rightarrow ABB \rightarrow \cdots$. That is there can be an infinite incarnation of B. This causes problem with verification because of unboundedness of states.

If we need to consider finite number of instances, we can use the parallel construct in Esterel to specify a finite number of concurrent activities. This is an advantage of the model, where one can specify the number of instances of the same activity which could be forked simultaneously. This closely maps to Workflow Management Systems, where one would specify the maximum number of such concurrent instances of an activity. The Esterel model of the activity diagram shown in Fig. 6 is shown below. The module R is the coordinating module for A and B. In this model we assume that there could be at most two instances of activity B as shown by the two modules named B1 and B2 in the code. In Fig.6 the number shown in bracket indicates the maximum possible number of instances of activity B. Here we assume calling external tasks as final activities for ActivityNodes A and B.

```
module A:
output InA;
return ExitA;
task activityA ()(); % external asynchronous task declaration

    exec activityA()() return ExitA % external action
    ||
    abort
        sustain InA; % indicates module A is active
    when ExitA
end module

module B:
return ExitB;
output InB;
task activityB ()();% external asynchronous task declaration

    exec activityB()() return ExitB % external action
    ||
    abort
        sustain InB;
    when ExitB
```

```
end module

module R:
return ExitA,ExitB1,ExitB2;
input InA, InB1,InB2;
task activityA ()();% external asynchronous task
task activityB ()();% external asynchronous task
input start;
signal b1b2, free in
   loop
         await  [start or ExitA];
         present free then [
               abort
                    run A
                    when ExitA
         ]
            end
   end
   ||
   loop
         present [not InB1 ] then % First instance of B
         [
             await ExitA;
             run B1/B[signal ExitB1/ExitB,InB1/InB] % Signal renaming
         ]
         else [ present not InB2 then
                   [              % Second instance of B
                    await ExitA;
                    emit b1b2;
                    run B2/B[signal ExitB2/ExitB,InB2/InB] %Signal renaming
               ]
                   else [
                         await [ExitB1 or ExitB2];
                         emit start
                         ]

               end
             ]
         end present
   end
   ||
   loop
      await start;
      abort
         sustain free % free is on when B1 is active but B2 is dormant
      when b1b2
   end
end
end module
```

Since each run B produces a separate instance of the task associated with the activity B, several simultaneous instances of activity associated with B can exist. In this case one should specify the number of instances of such activities. The model here shows capability of running two identical activities concurrently.

Modeling Exception: Fig. 7, shows the exception in an activity diagram. The node which is aborted due to the exception is called the protected node and the receiving node is the exception handler node. An exception handler is an element that specifies a body to execute in case the specified exception occurs during the execution of the protected node. In Fig. 7, Activity Node

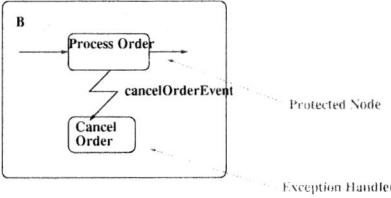

Fig. 7. Exception Node

ProcessOrder is the protected node and CancelOrder is the exception handler and CancelOrderEvent is the exception input. This can be modeled in Esterel as shown below.

```
module B
input cancelOrderEvent, ExitProcessOrder;
   trap T in
       run ProcessOrder
       ||
       abort
           loop
               await cancelOrderEvent; % Watch exception event
               exit T
           end
       when ExitProcessOrder
   handle T  do
       run cancelOrder % Exception Handler
   end
end
```

Here the activity ProcessOrder is preempted and the the activity cancelOrder is executed on raising the exception event cancelOrderEvent.

4.1 Activity with Data and Nesting

In many instances one *ActivityNode* may need to pass a data to another ActivityNode for processing by the *Activity* performed at that ActivityNode. For example if P and Q are two ActivityNodes and P is required send a data X to Q. as shown in Fig.8. This can be modeled using the mechanism shown below. The ExitS signal emitted by the activity node S is used for synchronizing the fact that the data token is available at the end of activity P.

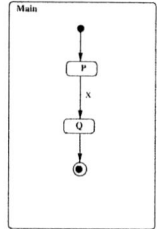
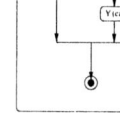
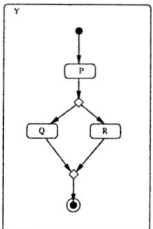

Fig. 8. Object node with data   **Fig. 9.** Activity with Nesting

```
module main
inputoutput X:type % X is the data which is passed between
%                    activities
```

```
    run P(X)
    await immediate exitP
    run Q(X)
end module
module P
output X:type
...
    emit ExitP
end module

module Q
input X:type
task QActivity()(); % declaration of asynchronous task
...
    exec task QActivity(X) return ExitQActivity;
...
end module
```

In our model, Activity Diagrams with nested *call* can be modeled naturally. Let us assume that one activity Y is nested in another activity X as a `call Y` action in the activityNode C of X shown in Fig. 9. This can be modeled by using the *run Y* construct of Esterel. The following Esterel fragment describes the nested call of the Fig.9.

```
    module X              ||module Y
    ...                   ||  ....
              run A       ||          run P;
              ||          ||          if e = u then
              run B;      ||                            run Q
              run Y       ||          else if e = v then
              ...         ||                            run R
              ...         ||          end
    end                   ||end
```

4.2 Communication in Activity Diagrams

The notion of communication between two Activity Diagrams can be nicely modeled in the Communicating Reactive Processes (CRP) [3] framework. The CRP model consists of network $M1||M2||..Mn$ of Esterel modules, each having its own inputs and outputs and its own notion of instants. The network is asynchronous and the nodes communicate though synchronous channels. In this model, each M_i is an Activity Diagram each of which evolve locally with its own input and output and mutually independent notions of time [3]. Signals may be sent or received in activity diagrams through channels and is denoted by the common send and receive nodes. As an implementation model, one can think of an asynchronous layer (task) that handles rendezvous by providing the link between the asynchronous network events and node reactive events. The shared task can be called as channel. Fig. 10, shows a simple example of an activity diagram showning two component activities *PrintServer* and *PrintClient* communicating data (as files) through a channel. The CRP code for the same is shown below.

```
module PrintServer
input channel printq from PrintClient : FILE % CRP channel
......
    receive(printq,file) % send data file to printq
.....
end module
module PrintClient
output channel printq from PrintServer :FILE % CRP channel
...
    send(printq,file)    % receive data file from printq
....
end module
```

The send and receive [1] are communication primitives realizing the communication rendezvous between two locally synchronous programs. The primitive **send** blocks until sending data on the named channel succeeds and the primitive **receive** blocks until a communication succeeds on the named channel and the value assigned to the variable.

5 Simulation and Code Generation

Above we have shown how activity diagrams can be transformed into Esterel model. We are augmenting our previous work [4] to translate them automatically. The Esterel model can be simulated by using the *xes* interface. *Xes* is the simulator freely available along with the Esterel distribution. The simulator can be generated by compiling the Esterel program with the xes library. The simulation gives the user a clear picture of the execution of the activity diagrams and checking conformance to requirement is easy. We are also building simulators directly in the domain of input activity diagrams whereby one can see the simulation graphically.

5.1 Code Generation

There are two orthogonal levels of semantics, both indispensable: the intuitive level, where semantics must be natural and easy to understand, and the formal level, where the semantics is rigorously defined and fully non-ambiguous. Having formal semantics for the languages also makes code generators much easier to develop and verify. The translation process from Activity Diagrams to High Level Language (HLL) code like C is based upon sound proven algorithms that the Esterel code generators directly implement. By providing a formal semantics based on the synchronous paradigm and Esterel, it is easy to build correct code

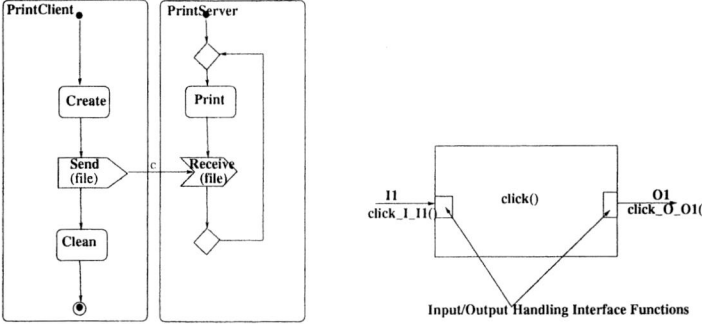

Fig. 10. Activities with communication **Fig. 11.** Activity to Code Mapping

by construction, using Esterel-C/Java code generators. We assume Esterel-C code generator for further discussion.

For actual execution of the code, the generated code must also be linked with some extra layer of code that realizes the interface with the outside world which detects input events, read data and realizes output events and send data. If for example the module `click` should react to an input event, composed for example of one input tokens I1 as shown in Fig. 11. The sequence will include call to one automatically generated input C function `click_I_I1()`. This should be followed by call to the reaction function by executing the C code `click()`, followed by a call to output C function `click_O_O1()`.

The automatic code building process is achieved using the rules described above

1. Model the flow as an activity diagram model
2. Transform the model into the Esterel model following the rules as described above. These can be automated by encoding them in a model transforming algorithm similar to [4,5].
3. Describe interfaces as required by the Esterel modules regarding inputs and outputs.
4. The activities to be performed in the software `exec tasks` are to be encoded in the host language and operating systems.

6 Verification

The above model captures the operational semantics of activity diagrams. However it is not amenable to formal verification using model checking due to presence of asynchronous tasks invoked by the `exec` statements. For the purpose of verification, it is required to do a control abstraction of the Esterel models whereby we only retain the labels where the task is to be created. The derived model is thus converted into a pure Esterel program and one can perform a constructive causality analysis using the Esterel compiler option of *causal*. This

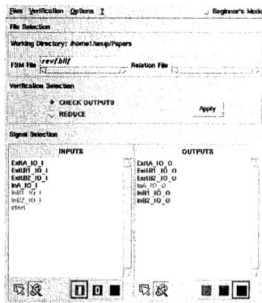 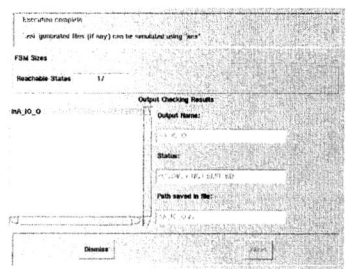

Fig. 12. Verification Screen   **Fig. 13.** Output of Verification

model can then be converted into an automaton in BLIF (Berkley Logical Interchange Format) format, which is accepted by the Esterel model checker *xeve*.

As an example, let us consider the activity diagram given in Fig. 6 with the following very simple safety property: *when both B1 and B2 activities are going on activity A cannot be started.* It is to be noted here that B1 and B2 are two incarnations of the activity B. This is assuming that there is no queuing of input. This could be verified by *xeve*. The screen shots taken from *xeve* are included here in Figs.12,13 for reference.

7   Conclusion and Future Work

We have explored the specification of operational semantics for the Activity Diagrams of UML 2.0 in a synchronous style. The semantics is good for simulation, code generation and verification. Our initial experience shows that verification of Activity Diagrams in this approach can be applied to moderately large examples. Further study is in progress. All the constructs can be expressed uniformly in the constructs of Esterel. In this approach the external action done in the activitynode can be easily modeled as an external task in the Esterel language. The exception handling in Petri Nets as shown in [8] is rather difficult which can be modeled easily in our framework. Presently, we are building a translator which can translate the activity diagrams into Esterel models. We need to test the effectiveness of the Esterel code generators in the context of real-life activity diagrams.

Acknowledgment

The first author wishes to acknowledge the travel grant made by DST, Government of India under the ITPAR proposal for visiting the University of Trento, Italy during which most part of the work was carried out. The first author also wishes to acknowledge the encouragement and institutional support received from Mr. S.D. Dhodapkar, Head, Software Reliability Section, BARC during the work, without which this would not have been possible.

References

1. Rajan Basant and Shyamasundar R.K., *An Implementation of Communicating Reactive Processes* IASTED - PDCN'97, Int. Conf. on Parallel and Distributed Computing and Networks, Singapore, 1997
2. Berry G, Gonthier G., *The Esterel synchronous programming languages: Design, semantics,implementation.*, Science of Computer Programming, 19(2):87-152, 1992
3. Berry G., Ramesh S., Shyamasundar R.K. :*Communicating Reactive Processes*, 20th ACM Symposium on Principles of Programming Languages, 1993
4. Bhattacharjee A.K., Dhodapkar S.D., Seshia S., Shyamasundar R.K. *PERTS: an environment for specification and verification of reactive systems*, Reliability Engineering & Systems Safety Journal, 71(2001), Elsevier, UK, 2001.
5. Seshia S., Shyamasundar R.K., Bhattacharjee A.K., Dhodapkar S.D. *A Translation of Statecharts to Esterel* Lecture Notes in Computer Science, Vol 1698, Springer, 1999
6. OMG: *Unified Modeling Language : Superstructure*, Version 2.0, Revised Final Adopted Specification, October 8, 2004, Source: www.omg.org
7. Eshuis Rik, *Semantics and Verification of Activity Charts*, Ph.D Thesis, University of Twente, 2002
8. Harald Storrle, *Semantics of UML 2.0 Activities*,German Software Engineering Conference, 2005.

Data Mining Track Chair's Message

Mukesh Mohania

IBM India Research Lab., India

Abstract. The unprecedented growth of electronic data and ever increasing user dependence on electronic data in today's world suggests that data should be regarded as one of the most important assets of the users. Within the last few years Data Mining and Knowledge Discovery technology has established itself as a key technology for enterprises that wish to improve the quality of the results obtained from data analysis, decision support, and the automatic extraction of knowledge from data. The Data Mining Track focuses on the logical and physical design of knowledge discovery systems, particularly, on data classification and clustering, association rules, data mining techniques, data analysis and discovery, and data mining applications.

An Approach to Find Embedded Clusters Using Density Based Techniques

S. Roy and D.K. Bhattacharyya

Dept of Computer Science & Information Technology,
Tezpur University, Napaam 784 028, Assam, India
dkb@tezu.ernet.in, swarup@india.com

Abstract. This paper presents an efficient clustering technique which can identify any embedded and nested cluster over any variable density space. The proposed algorithm is basically an enhanced version of DBSCAN [4] and OPTICS [7]. Experimental results are reported to establish that the proposed clustering technique outperforms both DBSCAN and OPTICS in terms of complex cluster detection.

Keywords: Variable density, embedded cluster, core-distance, cluster, core neighborhood, unsupervised.

1 Introduction

Clustering is the process of grouping data into classes or *clusters* so that objects within a cluster have higher similarity, but very dissimilar to objects in other clusters [1]. From a machine learning perspective, clusters correspond to hidden patterns and the search for clusters is a *unsupervised learning*. From a practical perspective, clustering plays an outstanding role in data mining applications such as scientific data exploration, information retrieval and text mining, spatial database applications, Web analysis, CRM, marketing, medical diagnostics, computational biology, and many others.

Cluster analysis has been considered as a difficult problem [2] because of many factors such as effective similarity measures, criterion functions, initial conditions, high dimensionality and different types of attributes, come into play in devising a well tuned clustering technique for a given clustering problem. A clustering algorithm has to be capable to identify any irregular and intrinsic cluster shapes over variable density space with outliers, as can be found in *Figure 1*.

Several good clustering algorithms have been proposed in the past decade ([1],[2]). *DBSCAN* is one of them, which can efficiently detect any clusters of arbitrary or hollow structure in presence of outliers or noise. However, a major deficiency of this algorithm is that it can not detect nested clusters over variable density space. Another major drawback of DBSCAN is that the results produced by DBSCAN are highly dependent on input parameters. Another successful successor of DBSCAN is OPTICS. It is also a density based clustering technique, which can work over variable density space successfully. However with the interactive version of OPTICS, a similar problem is encountered as we found in case of DBSCAN, it requires an additional

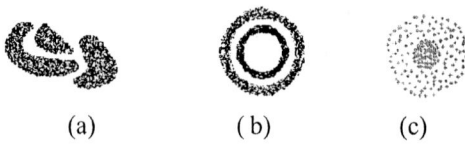

(a)　　　　　　(b)　　　　　(c)

Fig. 1. Irregular shaped clusters

parameters i.e. ε'. Since OPTICS provides an augmented ordering, it requires an additional cost to classify the objects. From our experiments, it has been observed that without a proper tuning of parameters it is very difficult to obtain qualitative clusters with OPTICS (Interactive). This paper presents an enhanced version of DBSCAN and OPTICS, which can detect any embedded cluster structures efficiently along with other constraints as mentioned above.

2　Related Works

Overtime, a number of clustering algorithms have been developed. Some of these are evolutionary, some are enhancements of some previously developed work and some others are revolutionary, introducing new concepts and methods. Major clustering techniques can be broadly classified into *partitional, hierarchical, density based, grid based* and *model based*. In this section, a selective review of some of the major techniques has been reported.

Partitioning methods like *k-means* [9] or *k-modes* [10] are most commonly used clustering algorithms. All the partitioning approaches have a similar clustering quality and vulnerable towards outliers. It cannot detect clusters of concave or non-globular shapes. Moreover, it requires number of clusters i.e. *k* as input parameter. The *Single Link* agglomerative clustering [11] is a suitable method for capturing clusters with non-globular shapes and nested structure, but this approach is very sensitive to noise and cannot handle clusters of varying density. On the other hand, it requires a post processing to achieve natural clusters. Other agglomerative clustering algorithms, e.g., *complete link* and *group average*, are capable of handling noise effectively, but sometimes they have a problem of finding globular clusters. CURE [8] is a bottom-up hierarchical clustering algorithm, which employs a method of choosing a well-formed group of points to identify the distances among clusters, instead of using a centroid-based approach or an all-points approach. In fact, CURE begins by choosing a constant number, *c* of *well scattered* points from a cluster. These points are used to identify the shape and size of the cluster. The next step of the algorithm shrinks the selected points towards the centroid of the cluster using some predetermined fraction. A *k-d* tree is used to store the representative points for the clusters. By definition, clusters are represented minimally, using DNF and minimal bounding rectangles. Here, emphasis is given on finding the clusters, not on the accuracy of the shapes of the clusters. CHAMELEON [5] combines a graph partitioning algorithm with a hierarchical clustering scheme that dynamically creates clusters. The first step of the algorithm partitions the data using a method based on a *k*-nearest neighbor approach to graph partitioning. In the graph, the density of a region is stored as the weight of the connecting edge. The data is divided into a large number of small sub-clusters. The first step uses a multi-level graph partitioning algorithm. The partitioning algorithm used by CHAMELEON produces high quality partitions with a minimum number of edge cuts. The second step uses an agglomerative, or bottom-up hierarchical clustering algorithm to combine the sub-clusters and find the real clusters. CHAMELEON has been found to be very effective in clustering convex shapes, but can not handle outliers. WaveCluster[6] follows a grid-based approach. It maps the data onto a multi-dimensional grid and applies a wavelet transformation to the *feature space* instead of the objects themselves. Initially, it assigns the data to units based on their feature values. The number or size of these units affects the time required for clustering and the quality of the output. Then it identifies the dense areas in the transformed domain by searching for the connected components. If the feature space is examined from a signal processing perspective, then a group of objects in the feature space forms an n-dimensional signal. Rapid change in the distribution of objects, i.e., the borders of clusters, corresponds to the high frequency parts of be used to find areas of low and high frequency, and thus identifies the clusters. Wavelet transformation breaks a signal into its different frequency sub-bands, creating a representation that shows multi-resolutions, and therefore provides for efficient identification of clusters. Areas with low frequency and low amplitude are outside the clusters. With a large number of objects, signal processing techniques can be used to find areas of low and high frequency, and thus identify the clusters. WaveCluster has several significant positive contributions. It is not affected by outliers, and is not sensitive to the order of input. WaveCluster's main advantage, apart from its speedy handling of large datasets, is its ability to find clusters of arbitrary and complex shapes, including concave and nested clusters. However, one disadvantage of it is that the clustering results are highly sensitive to parameters settings. Next, we discuss two popular and efficient density based clustering algorithms, most relevant to our work, in detail.

3 Density Based Approach

The idea behind density-based approach for clustering is that within each cluster the typical density of points is considerably higher than outside of the cluster. Furthermore, the density within areas of noise is lower than the density in any of the clusters. In addition, some other definitions [5] are also associated with density based approach.

- The neighborhood within a radius ε of a given object is called the ε-*neighborhood* of the object.
- If the ε-*neighborhood* of an object contains at least a minimum number, *MinPts*, of objects, then the object is called a *core object*.
- Given a set of objects, D, we say that an object p is *directly density-reachable* from object q if p is within the ε-*neighborhood* of q and q is a *core object*.

- An object p is *density-reachable* from object q with respect to ε and *MinPts* in a set D, if there is a chain of objects $p_1,....p_n, p_1=q$ and $p_n=p$ such that p_{i+1} is directly density reachable from p_i with respect to ε and *MinPts*.
- An object p is *density-connected* to object q w.r.t. ε and *MinPts* in a set of objects, D, if there is an object $o \in D$ such that both p and q are density-reachable from o w.r.t. ε and *MinPts*.
- *Density-based cluster* is a set of *density-connected* objects that is maximal with respect to *density-reachability*. Every object not contained in any cluster is considered to be a *noise*.

3.1 DBSCAN [4]

To find a cluster, DBSCAN starts with an arbitrary point p and retrieves all points density-reachable from p wrt. ε and *MinPts*. If p is a *core point*, this procedure yields a cluster wrt. ε and *MinPts*. If p is a border point, no points are density-reachable from p and DBSCAN visits the next point of the database. DBSCAN is suitable for any large spatial domain with global density. However, in case of variable density space, DBSCAN suffers. Since it uses global parameters, i.e. ε and *MinPts*, DBSCAN may merge two clusters into one cluster, if the densities of those clusters are different and they are "closed" to each other. Let the *distance between two sets of points* S1 and S2 be defined as *dist (S1, S2)* = *min {dist(p,q) | p∈S1, q∈S2}*. Then, two sets of points having at least the density of the thinnest cluster will be separated from each other only if the distance between the two sets is larger than ε. Consequently, a recursive call of DBSCAN may be necessary for the detected clusters with a higher value for *MinPts*.

3.1.1 Analysis of DBSCAN

Usually, the complexity of a neighbourhood query processing is $O(n)$ and with the use of a spatial index such as a R^*-tree, it is $O(log_m n)$, where n is the size of the dataset and m is the number of entries in a page of R^*-tree. Similarly, the complexity of the DBSCAN algorithm becomes $O(nlog_m n)$ if a spatial index is used, otherwise it is $O(n^2)$. The algorithm can handle large amounts of data. DBSCAN is capable to handle noise efficiently and can identify all shapes of clusters; however, it can not identify complex cluster structures over variable density space.

3.2 OPTICS [7]

Another well known density based clustering algorithm is OPTICS (Ordering Points to Identify the Clustering Structure), which can address the issues of variable density cluster successfully. OPTICS creates an augmented ordering of the points in the database according to its densities. In addition to those common definitions used by other density based approaches, it includes the following concepts:

- The *core distance* of an object p is the smallest ε' value that makes p a *core object*. If p is not a *core object*, the core distance of p is undefined.
- The *reachability distance* of an object q w.r.t. another object p is the greater value of the two distance measures, i.e. the *core distance* of p and the Euclidean distance between p and q. If p is not a *core object*; the *reachability distance* between p and q is undefined.

The algorithm creates an ordering of the objects in a database based on *reachability distance*, additionally storing the *core distance* and a suitable *reachability distance* for each object. Two algorithms were proposed in [7] to extract clusters interactively as well as automatically.

3.2.1 Analysis of OPTICS

The OPTICS algorithm does not produce a clustering of a data set explicitly, but it is basically a preprocessing step for other clustering algorithms like DBSCAN. In contrast with the DBSCAN method, OPTICS provide a solution to the global density issue and varying density by giving every point object the augmented cluster-ordering containing information which is equivalent to the density-based clustering that corresponds to a broad range of parameter settings. The visualization technique proposed in [7] paper provides a good representation of the clustering structure, thus it can be used as a tool to get insight into the distribution of a data set. However, some limitations exist in this algorithm. The visualization technique of this algorithm requires proper values in the parameter settings in order to get good results. The experiments have been done to get a range of values that are considered as good values, but the usability of values may not be applicable to all types of data sets.

Our experiments reveal that interactive version of OPTICS can not detect embedded cluster structures even after several parameter settings. Apart from it, it requires $O(nlogn)$ complexity only for ordering the dense units, if a spatial index is used; further, it requires $O(n)$ time to cluster the ordered data sets. So, overall complexity will be at least $O(nlogn)+O(n)$ to extract the clusters.

4 Better Approach to Find Embedded Clusters

4.1 Motivation

Databases like gene expression databases, MR Image database and other real-data sets have the pattern of embedded or nested cluster structures. Moreover, they may have variable density. Since DBSCAN works with global density parameters, it can not detect underlying dense structure of varying density. If a low value for ε is set, it will detect several small clusters, which may not have significance in the real sense. Again, a larger value for ε may lead to ignorance of some useful clusters. So, with a single global parameter setting, DBSCAN is unable to detect the variable density clusters, as can be found in *Figure 2*.

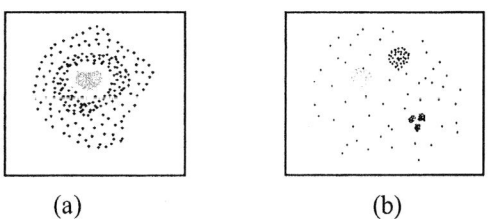

(a)   (b)

Fig. 2. Nested and Varying density clusters

On the other hand, in case of OPTICS, it is capable to detect those irregularly shaped variable density clusters, as shown in *Figure 1(a)*, *1(b)* and *2(b)*; however, it fails to detect those nested clusters, as can be found in *Figure 1(c) & 2(a)*. In case of *Figure 2(a)*, with a low ε' setting, it can detect the interior two clusters with the outer region as noise and if a high value for ε' is set, it gives the similar results as DBSCAN. Moreover, it requires a prior ordering of objects in terms of *reachability distance*, which incurs additional cost. Thus, an algorithm which can detect embedded cluster structures as well as clusters of all shapes, as discussed in *Section 1* in presence of outliers is a current need.

4.2 Our Contribution

We present an integrated clustering approach, where both the density based ordering and clustering based on ordering, are integrated. Our approach can effectively address the previously mentioned clustering challenges. In addition, it can detect embedded or intrinsic clusters. It is basically an extension of those popular density based clustering algorithms, such as DBSCAN and OPTICS. It extends the concept of *core distance* of OPTICS and introduced the concept *core neighborhood* which enables to handle the problem of global density parameter setting, suffered by DBSCAN. It also handles the problems with varying density clusters as well as embedded clusters. Furthermore, like other well known density based approaches, it also gives the number of clusters naturally, in presence of noise.

4.3 Terminology Used

Here, we redefine some of the concepts used in DBSCAN in terms of our requirements. Concept of *core neighbor* is an extension of the concept of *core distance* used in OPTICS.

4.3.1 Definition: (Core Neighbor): A point p is a *core neighbor* of a point q if
  1) *core-distance(q)* <> UNDEFINED, and
  2) p resides within the *core distance* of q.
All the points within the *core distance* of q form the *core neighborhood* of q.

4.3.2 Definition: (Directly Core Density Reachable): A point p is *directly core density-reachable* from a point q w.r.t. *core-distance, MinPts* if
  1) $p \in N_{core\text{-}dist}(q)$;
  2) *core-distance(q)* <> UNDEFINED (core point condition) ; and
  3) Diff(*core-distance(p)*, *core-distance(q)*) $\leq \alpha$, where α is the pre-defined
    tolerance factor.

4.3.3 Definition: (Core Density-reachable): A point p is *Core density reachable* from a point q wrt. *core-distance* and *MinPts* if there is a chain of points $p_1, ..., p_n$, $p_1=q$, $p_n=p$ such that p_{i+1} is directly core density-reachable from p_i.

4.3.4 Definition: (Core Density Connected): A point p is *Core density connected* to a point q wrt. *core-distance* and *MinPts* if there is a point o such that both, p and q are core density-reachable from o.

4.3.5 Definition: (Cluster and Noise): Let *D* be a database of points. A cluster *C* wrt. *core-distance* and *MinPts* is a non-empty subset of *D* satisfying the following conditions:

1) $\forall p, q$: if $p \in C$ and *q* is density-reachable from *p* wrt. *core-distance* and *MinPts*, and diff(*core-distance(p)*, *core-distance(q)*)$\leq \alpha$ then $q \in C$, where α is the pre-defined tolarance factor.
2) $\forall p, q \in C$: p is *Core density-connected* to *q* wrt. *core-distance* and *MinPts*.

An object is *noise* if its *core distance* is greater than global parameter ε.

4.4 Finding Clusters

Intuitively, all the *core neighbors* of a point having *core distance* difference within α, form a uniform dense region. In the *Figure 3* the point *P* is a core object w.r.t. *MinPts*

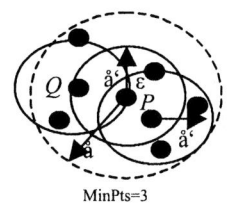

Fig. 3. Cluster expansion

= 3 and *core distance* of *P* is ε'. The ε' must be less than equal to ε (the user defined radius). The points within the *core distance* ε' are the core neighbors of *P*. OPTICS use that *core distance* and *reachability distance* to order the points. On the other hand DBSCAN expands clusters by expanding the points within ε-neighbour-hood. From our observation we find that core distance is very much effective in detecting density variations. Variation in core distance implies a variation in density. Unlike OPTICS additional ordering is not essential to detect clusters.

Cluster can easily be extracted same way as by DBSCAN, with a difference of expanding the ε'-neighbors instead of ε-neighbors. Our approach integrates these two approaches. It expands the *core neighbor* of a *core object* say *P* instead of expanding ε-neighbors. Iteratively the point *Q* is also expanded same way. If the core distance of *P* and *Q* are within a tolerance factor α then both of them are considered as belonging to the same cluster. If *core distance* of a point is greater than ε then it is a noise point. During expansion of *Q*, *P* becomes the *core neighbor* of *Q*. But if *P* is processed earlier than *Q* and it is already assigned a *cluster id*, then *P* is ignored.

5 The Algorithm

The algorithm proceeds as DBSCAN and OPTICS by expanding each *core-object* to get cluster structure. It continues to scan the datasets until all the objects are not processed. Each core object begins to expand all its neighbors of it, with respect to generating distance i.e. *core distance (ε')*.

If the core distances of two objects do not differ by a pre-defined variance factor, say α, we consider them belonging to the same cluster or their density is same.

The main module of the algorithm is illustrated in *Figure 4*. It starts with an initial *core-distance* of an arbitrary object from the data sets. *GetCoreDist* computes the core distance of a unclassified object with respect to *MinPts* and ε. If the *core distance* is undefined i.e. if *core distance* is greater then ε, then the object is marked as noise. Otherwise, it will go for expanding the cluster with its neighbor objects within its *core neighbourhood*. Assign a new *cluster id* to the candidate object and mark all the neighbors of it with the same *id*, if it is not already assigned an *id*. Next, in an iterative

```
EnDBSCAN (SetOfPoints, ε, MinPts) // SetOfPoints is
UNCLASSIFIED

FOR i FROM 1 TO NoOfObjects DO
        Point: = SetOfPoints.get (i);
   IF Point already not UNCLASSIFIED THEN

        CORE_DIST:=GetCoreDist (Point, MinPts, ε);

        IF CORE_DIST=UNDEFINED
                Mark Point as Noise;
        ELSE

        Expand Cluster (Point, CORE_DIST);
        END IF

   END IF
   END FOR
END; // EnDBSCAN
```

Fig. 4. Module EnDBSCAN

manner it expands for each of the objects in the neighborhood. *Figure 5* illustrates the sub module *Expand Cluster*. We consider the *core distance* of the starting object of a new cluster as the initial *core distance*; which is termed here as *previous core distance*. Two objects are in the same cluster if the difference between *previous core distance* and current candidate object's *core distance* is not more than a factor α. Otherwise, the candidate is considered to belonging to a different cluster and ignored that objects i.e. it will not expand that object. The underlying idea behind is that such a situation generally indicates a density variation, and the current candidate object is considered as belonging to a different cluster. Such a decision making may lead to some amount of repetition works on object processing. However, based on observation, it has been found that such a situation usually occurs only in the boundary of two different dense regions and the number of objects to be processed in repetition is also negligibly small. Thus, it can be easily handled by any trivial memory based technique (by storing *core-distance* and *core neighbor* of the rejected object).

5.2 Complexity Analysis

Because of the structural equivalence of the proposed EnDBSCAN to both DBSCAN and OPTICS, it has the same run-time complexity as that of DBSCAN and OPTICS that is, $O(n\log n)$, if a spatial index like R^* tree is used. However, EnDBSCAN requires to carry out some amount of repetition work in the boundary of two dense regions, but the number of points to be processed repeatedly is significantly very less when compared with the total number of points, so it can be neglected.

```
Expand Cluster (Point, Prev_Core)

IF Point already CLASSIFIED
      RETURN;
END IF

CORE_DIST:=GetCoreDist (Point, MinPts, ε);

IF CORE_DIST= =UNDEFINED THEN
   Mark Point as Noise;
    RETURN;
END IF

IF diff(CORE_DIST-Prev_Core) > α
    RETURN;
END IF

Mark the Point as CLASSIFIED;
Neighb:=GetNeighbour(Point,CORE_DIST);


IF Point not assigned ClusterId THEN
     Assign the Point with nextId ();
END IF

Mark all the objects of Neighb (core neighborhood),which
are not already classified ,with Point.ClusterId.

FOR each NewPoint in Neighb DO
       Expand Cluster (NewPoint, Prev_Core);
END FOR

      END;// End Expand Cluster
```

Fig. 5. Cluster Expansion Module

6 Experiments

To carry out an experimental study on the proposed algorithm and to study its performances with its other counterparts, we developed a Java based user interface for easy synthetic data set generation as well as for visualizing the test results. We used a PIV Server with 128 MB RAM and the language used for coding is *Java 1.3* in *Windows Xp*. We used five sets of datasets, i.e. the *CHAMELEON* t7.10k.dat [5] dataset and four other synthetic data sets, as shown in *Figure 6* & *7* respectively. In case of *t7.10k.dat dataset*, it has been observed that all the three algorithms identify the desired clusters correctly. However, this dataset does not contain any nested cluster structure.

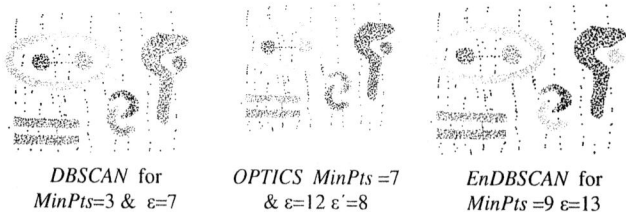

DBSCAN for OPTICS MinPts =7 EnDBSCAN for
MinPts=3 & ε=7 & ε=12 ε'=8 MinPts =9 ε=13

Fig. 6. Results from *t7.10K.dat*

Next we tested the algorithm in light of synthetic datasets (*Figure 7*) and compared the results. It has been observed that our approach outperforms DBSCAN and OPTICS (interactive) in terms of nested cluster identifications. EnDBSCAN has been able to detect variable density clusters as well as nested or embedded cluster structures successfully, whereas the other two counterparts fail, even after multiple parameter settings.

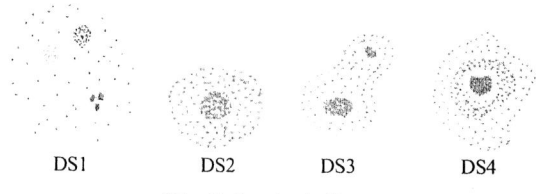

DS1   DS2   DS3   DS4

Fig. 7. Synthetic Data

In case of test dataset *DS1*, both OPTICS (interactive) and EnDBSCAN are found successful (Figure 8) in detecting five natural clusters, where as DBSCAN fails to do so.

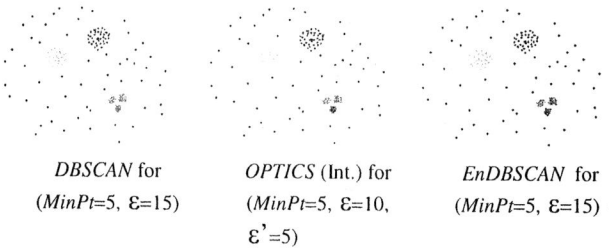

DBSCAN for OPTICS (Int.) for EnDBSCAN for
(MinPt=5, ε=15) (MinPt=5, ε=10, (MinPt=5, ε=15)
 ε'=5)

Fig. 8. Results from DS1

In case of *DS2*, DBSCAN can only detect a single cluster. In case of OPTICS, for a smaller value of ε', it can only detect the interior cluster pattern and rest as noise; otherwise it works same as DBSCAN. On the other hand, EnDBSCAN can successfully detect both the natural clusters.

In case of *DS3* (*Figure 10*), both DBSCAN and OPTICS fail to give the proper results. OPTICS gives two interior clusters and rest as noise. On the other hand, EnDBSCAN can detect all the three natural clusters. However, due to the order

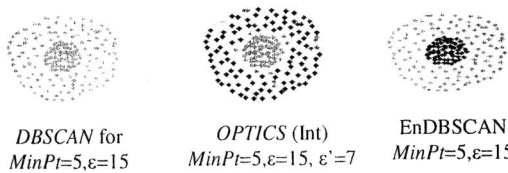

DBSCAN for
MinPt=5,ε=15

OPTICS (Int)
MinPt=5,ε=15, ε'=7

EnDBSCAN
MinPt=5,ε=15

Fig. 9. Results from DS2

dependency nature of DBSCAN, it also results in overlapping of a boundary point between two different dense regions. In such case, generally the boundary point is assigned to that cluster which is scanned first. In case of *DS4* also, similar results found not included due to space limitation).

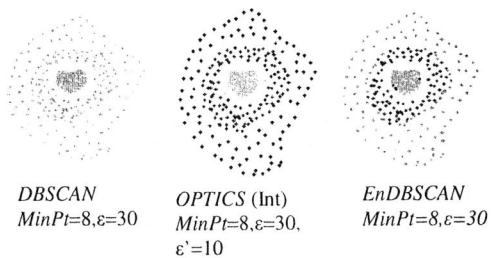

DBSCAN
MinPt=8,ε=30

OPTICS (Int)
MinPt=8,ε=30,
ε'=10

EnDBSCAN
MinPt=8,ε=30

Fig. 10. Results from DS3

Based on our exhaustive experimental study it has been observed that for a tolerance factor i.e. α=2, the clustering results of the proposed algorithm can be found to be more effective. So, rather than considering it as an input parameter, we prefer to consider it as a constant. However, α may need to be tuned based on the distribution of data for different datasets. We reported execution time needed by EnDBSCAN in comparison with other counterparts, in the following figure. We implemented these algorithms without using any spatial indexing techniques. We generate data in such a way that density of data increases with the increase in size of the data.

Data Size	ε	ε'	MinPts	DBSCAN	OPTICS	EnDBSCAN
5000	8	6	3	7	10	15
8000	8	6	6	23	31	38
10000	8	6	7	35	48	56
15000	8	6	15	143	128	132
20000	8	6	20	271	202	226
25000	8	6	22	562	390	408
30000	8	6	25	946	609	654

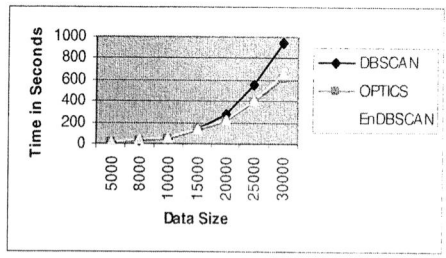

Fig. 11. Scalability Curve

From the graph it can be seen that when the data are sparse DBSCAN performs better than other two. But the scenario reversed when data become dense. In such case our's performs well over DBSCAN. However, from execution time point of view, performance of OPTICS is superior in comparison to EnDBSCAN, though OPTICS can not detect embedded cluster structure.

6.1 Clustering Effectiveness Comparison

A detailed comparative study among the three algorithms (i.e. EnDBSCAN, DBSCAN & OPTICS (Int.) was carried out in light of those real and synthetic datasets (as discussed in the previous *sub-section*). *Table 1* presents the same in terms of six crucial factors. As can be seen from the *column 1* of the table that like DBSCAN, the proposed algorithm also requires less number of input parameters than OPTICS. Similarly, *column 5* depicts that embedded clusters can be detected only by the proposed algorithm. Also, from the complexity point of view, *column 6* clearly shows that the performance of *EnDBSCAN* is similar with *DBSCAN* when a spatial index is used. However, OPTICS requires an additional complexity $O(n)$ (at least) to classify those points after ordering, apart from $O(n \log n)$, when a spatial index is used. The rest other columns establish that in terms of the other quality parameters, the performance of the proposed algorithm is equally good with its other two counterparts.

Table 1. Comparison of EnDBSCAN with DBSCAN and OPTICS (Int)

Algorithms	Input Parameters (1)	Outlier. Handling (2)	Scalability (3)	Varying Density (4)	Embed. Cluster (5)	Complexity (6)
DBSCAN	*MinPts*, å	Yes	Yes	No	No	$O(n \log n)$
OPTICS(Int)	*MinPts*, å, å'	Yes	Yes	Yes	No	$O(n \log n) + O(n)$
EnDBSCAN	*MinPts*, å	Yes	Yes	Yes	Yes	$O(n \log n)$

7 Conclusions

This paper presents an enhanced version of DBSCAN and OPTICS (Int.). The proposed enhanced version can detect any embedded cluster structure over spatial domain successfully. Another significant advantage of EnDBSCAN is that it requires less input parameters as well as less complexity than OPTICS.

References

[1] Han & Kamber, *Data Mining: Concepts & Technques*, Morgan Kaufmann, 2001.
[2] Kotsiantis & Pintelas, *Recent Advances in clustering: A Brief Survey,* www.math.upatras.gr/~esdlab/en/members/ kotsiantis
[3] Jiang, Tang & Zhang, *Cluster Analysis for Gene Expression Data: A Survey.* IEEE Trans. KDE, 2004.
[4] Ester, Kriegel, Sander and Xu. 1996, *A Density-Based Algorithm for Discovering Clusters in Large Spatial Databases with Noise* in KDD96, Portland, pp 226-231.
[5] Karypis, Han & Kumar, *CHAMELEON: A hierarchical clustering algorithm using dynamic modeling.* IEEE Computer, 32(8), pp 68-75, 1999
[6] Sheikholeslami, Chatterjee and Zhang. *Wavecluster:A muti-resolution clustering approach for very large spatial database* in the *SIGMOD'98* Seattle, 1998.
[7] Ankerst, Breuing, Kriegel and Sander. *OPTICS: Ordering points to identify the clustering structure* in the *ACM-SIGMOD'99,* pp 49-60, 1999.
[8] Guha, Rastogi, and Shim, *'CURE: An Efficient Clustering Algorithm for Large Datasets* in the ACM SIGMOD Conf., 1998.
[9] McQueen, 'Some Methods for Classifications and Analysis of Multivariate Observations', in the Sympos. on Math, Statis. and Probabilty', pp 281-197, 1967
[10] Z Huang, 'A Fast Clustering Algorithm to cluster very large categorical datasets in Data Mining', SIGMOD'97.
[11] Kaufman and Rousseeuw.Finding Groups in Data: An Introduction to Cluster Analysis. New York: John Wiley & Sons, 1990.

Using Sub-sequence Information with kNN for Classification of Sequential Data

N. Pradeep Kumar[1,2], M. Venkateswara Rao[1,2], P. Radha Krishna[1], and Raju S. Bapi[2]

[1] Institute for Development and Research in Banking Technology IDRBT,
Castle Hills, Masab Tank, Hyderabad, India-500057
Ph No: 91-40-23534981, Fax No: 91-40-23535157
[2] University of Hyderabad, Gachibowli, Hyderabad, India-500046
{pradeepkumar, prkrishna}@idrbt.ac.in,
mvrao@mtech.idrbt.ac.in, bapics@uohyd.ernet.in

Abstract. With the enormous growth of data, which exhibit sequentiality, it has become important to investigate the impact of embedded sequential information within the data. Sequential data are growing enormously, hence an efficient classification of sequential data is needed. k-Nearest Neighbor (kNN) has been used and proved to be an efficient classification technique for two-class problems. This paper uses sliding window approach to extract sub-sequences of various lengths and classification using kNN. We conducted experiments on DARPA 98 IDS dataset using various distance/similarity measures such as Jaccard similarity, Cosine similarity, Euclidian distance and Binary Weighted Cosine (BWC) measure. Our results demonstrate that sub-sequence information enhances kNN classification accuracy for sequential data, irrespective of the distance/similarity metric used.

Keywords: Sequence mining, k-Nearest Neighbor Classification, Similarity/Distance metric, Intrusion detection.

1 Introduction

Data are very vital for a commercial organization. These data are sequential or non-sequential in nature. Sequence mining helps us in discovering formal relations in sequence data. Sequence pattern mining is the mining of frequently occurring patterns related to time or other sequences [7, 15]. An example of the rule that sequence mining algorithm would discover is -- *"A user who has visited rediff website is likely to visit yahoo website within next five page visits."* Sequence mining plays a vital role in domains such as telecommunication records, protein classification, signal processing and intrusion detection. It is important to note that datasets in these problems need not necessarily have inherent temporality [7, 15].

Studies on sequential pattern mining mostly concentrate on symbolic patterns [1, 10, 17]. As in symbolic patterns, numerical curve patterns usually belong to the scope of trend analysis and prediction in statistical time series analysis. Many other parameters also influence the results of sequential pattern mining. These parameters include duration of time sequence (T), event folding window (w) and time interval between two events (int). If we assign w as the whole duration T, we get time independent frequent patterns. An example of such a rule is " *In 1999, customers who bought PCs also bought digital cameras*". If w is set to be 1, that is, no event sequence folding occurs, then all events are considered to be discrete time events. The rule of the type *"Customers who bought hard disk and then memory chip are likely to buy CD-Writer later on"* is example of such a case. If w were set to be something between 1 and T, events occurring between sliding windows of specified length would be considered. An example rule is *"Sale of PC in the month of April 1999 is maximum"*.

Sequential data are growing at a rapid pace. A pre-defined collection of historical data with their observed nature helps in determining the nature of newly arriving data stream and hence will be useful in classification of the new data stream. In data mining, classification algorithms are popularly used for exploring the relationships among various object features at various conditions. Sequence data sets are similar in nature except that they have an additional temporal dimension [22].

Classification algorithms help in predicting future trends as well as extracting a model of important data classes. Many classification algorithms have been proposed by researchers in machine learning [21], expert systems [20], statistics [8]. Classification algorithms have been successfully applied to the problems, where the dependent variable (class variable) depends on non-sequential independent (explanatory) variables [3]. Typical classification algorithms are Support Vector Machines, Decision Trees, Bayesian Classification, Neural Networks, k-Nearest Neighbor (kNN) and Association Classification. To deal with the sequential information, sequential data are transformed into non-sequential variables. This leads to a loss of sequential information of the data. Although traditional classification is robust and efficient for modeling non-sequential data, they fail to capture sequential information of the dataset.

Intrusion detection is the process of monitoring and analyzing the events occurring in a computer system in order to detect signs of security problems [2]. Computer security can be achieved by maintaining audit data. Cryptographic techniques, authentication means and firewalls have gained importance with the advent of new technologies. With the ever-increasing size of audit data logs, it becomes crucial for network administrators and security analysts to use some efficient Intrusion Detection System (IDS), to reduce the monitoring activity. Data mining techniques are useful in providing important contributions to the field of intrusion detection.

IDSs based on examining sequences of system calls often define normal behavior of an application by sliding a window of fixed size across a sequence of traces of system calls. System call traces are normally produced with programs like *strace* on Linux systems and *truss* on Solaris systems. Several methods have been proposed for storing system calls traces' information and to use these for detecting anomalies in an IDS. Forrest et al. [5, 9] stored normal behavior by sliding a window of fixed size L across sequence of system call traces and recorded which system call followed the system call in position 0 at offsets 1 through L 1. Liao et al. [12] applied kNN classifier with Cosine similarity measure considering frequencies of system calls with sliding window size w =1. A similar work with modified similarity measure using a combination of Cosine as well Jaccard has also been carried out in [18].

The central theme of this paper is to investigate that vital information stored in sub-sequences, plays any role in building a classifier. In this paper, we combine sequence analysis problem with kNN classification algorithm, to design an efficient classifier for sequential data. Sequence analysis can be categorized into two types, depending on the nature of the treatment. Either we can consider the whole sequence as one or sub-sequences of different sizes. Our hypothesis is that sequence or order of information plays a role in sequence classification. We extracted sequence information from sub-sequences and used this information for building various distance/similarity metrics. With the appropriate distance/similarity metric, a new session is classified using kNN classifier. In order to evaluate the efficiency and behavior of the classifier with the encoded vector measures, Receiver Operating Characteristics (ROC) curve is used. Experiments are conducted on DARPA 98 IDS [13] dataset to show the viability of our model.

Like other classification algorithms, kNN classification algorithm does not make a classifier in advance. Hence, it is suitable for classification of data streams. Whenever a new data stream comes, kNN finds the k near neighbors to new data stream from training data set using some distance/similarity metric [4, 6]. kNN is the best choice for making a good classifier, when simplicity and accuracy is important issues [11].

The rest of the paper is organized as follows - Section 2 gives a brief description of the nearest neighbor classification algorithm. In section 3, we briefly discuss about the distance/similarity measures used in the experiments. In section 4, we outline our proposed approach. The Section 5 provides the experimental results on DARPA 98 IDS dataset. Finally, we conclude in section 6.

2 Nearest Neighbor Classification

kNN classifier are based on learning by analogy. *K*NN classification algorithm assumes that all instances correspond to points in an *n*-dimensional space. Nearest neighbors of an instance are described by a distance/similarity measure. When a new sample comes, a kNN classifier searches the training dataset for the k closest sample to the new sample using distance/similarity measure for determining the nature of new sample. These k samples are known as the k nearest neighbors of the new sample. The new sample is assigned the most common class of its k nearest neighbors. Nearest neighbor algorithm can be summarized as follows:

Begin
  Training
    Construct Training sample T from the given dataset D.
  Classification
  Given a new sample s to be classified,
    Let $I_1 \ldots I_k$ denote the k instances from T that are nearest to new sample s
    Return the class from k nearest neighbor samples.
    Returned class is the class of new sample.
End

In the nearest neighbor model, choice of a suitable distance function and the value of the members of nearest neighbors (k) are very crucial. The k represents the complexity of nearest neighbor model. The model is less adaptive with higher k values [7].

3 Distance/Similarity Measures

Distance/similarity measure plays an important role in classifying or grouping observations in homogeneous groups. In other words, a distance/similarity measure establishes the relationship between the rows of the data matrix. Preliminary information for identifying homogeneous groups is provided by the distance/similarity measure. Between any pair of observations x_i and x_j function of the corresponding row vector in the data matrix is given by:

$$D_{ij} = f(x_i, x_j) \text{ where } i,j = 1, 2, 3,\ldots,n$$

For an accurate classifier, it is important to formulate a metric to determine whether an event is deemed normal or anomalous. In this section, we briefly discuss various measures such as Jaccard similarity measure, Cosine similarity measure, Euclidian distance measure and BWC measure. We used sub-sequence information with these different measures in kNN classifier for cross comparison purpose.

3.1 Jaccard Similarity Function

Jaccard similarity function is used for measuring similarity between binary values [19]. It is defined as the degree of commonality between two sets. It is measured as a ratio of number of common attributes of X AND Y to the number of elements possessed by X OR Y. If X and Y are two distinct sets then the similarity between X and Y is:

$$S(X,Y) = \frac{|X \cap Y|}{|X \cup Y|}$$

Consider two sets X =⟨ M, N, P, Q, R, M, S, Q⟩ and Y = ⟨P, M, N, Q, M, P, P⟩. X ∩ Y is given as ⟨M, N, P, Q⟩ and X ∪ Y is ⟨M, N, P, Q, R, S⟩. Thus, the similarity between X and Y is 0.66.

3.2 Cosine Similarity

Cosine similarity is a common vector based similarity measure. Cosine similarity measure is commonly used in text databases [16]. Cosine similarity metric calculates the angle of difference in direction of two vectors, irrespective of their lengths. Cosine similarity between two vectors X and Y is given by:

$$S(X,Y) = \frac{X \bullet Y}{|X \| Y|}$$

Direct application of Cosine similarity measure is not possible across sets. Sets are first converted into n-dimensional vector space. Over these transformed vectors Cosine similarity measure is applied to find the angular similarity. For two sets, X = ⟨M, N, P, Q, R, M, S, Q⟩ and Y = ⟨P, M, N, Q, M, P, P⟩ the equivalent transformed frequency vector is X_v = < 2,1,1,2,1,1> and Y_v = < 2,1,3,1,0,0 >. The Cosine similarity of the transformed vector is 0.745.

3.3 Euclidean Distance

Euclidean distance is a widely used distance measure for vector spaces [16]. For two vectors X and Y in an n-dimensional Euclidean space, it is defined as the square root of the sum of difference of the corresponding dimensions of the vector. Mathematically, it is given as

$$D(X,Y) = \left[\sum_{s=1}^{n}(X_s - Y_s)^2\right]^{1/2}$$

Similar, to the Cosine similarity metric, application of Euclidean measure on sets is not possible. Similar approach as used in Cosine similarity measure to transform sets into vector is applicable here also. For two sets, X = ⟨ M, N, P, Q, R, M, S, Q⟩ and Y = ⟨P, M, N, Q, M, P, P⟩ the equivalent transformed frequency vector is X_v = < 2,1,1,2,1,1> and Y_v = < 2,1,3,1,0,0 >. The Euclidean measure of the transformed vector is 2.64.

3.4 Binary Weighted Cosine (BWC) Metric

Rawat et.al.[18] proposed BWC similarity measure for measuring similarity across sequences of system calls. They showed the effectiveness of the proposed measure on IDS. They applied kNN classification algorithm with BWC metric measure to enhance the capability of the classifier. BWC similarity measure considers both the number of shared elements between two sets as well as frequencies of those elements in traces. The similarity measure between two sequences X and Y is given by

$$S(X, Y) = \frac{X \bullet Y}{|X||Y|} * \frac{|X \cap Y|}{|X \cup Y|}$$

BWC measure is derived from Cosine similarity as well as Jaccard similarity measure. Since the Cosine similarity measure is a contributing component in a BWC similarity measure hence, BWC similarity measure is also a vector based similarity measure. The transformation step is same as carried out in Cosine similarity measure or Euclidean measure for sets. For two sets, X =⟨M, N, P, Q, R, M, S, Q⟩ and Y = ⟨P, M, N, Q, M, P, P⟩ the Cosine similarity is given as 0.745 and Jaccard similarity as 0.66. Hence, the computed BWC similarity measure comes out to be 0.49.

4 Proposed Methodology

This section illustrates the methodology for extracting sequential information from the sets, thus making it applicable to be used by various vector based distance/similarity metrics. We considered sub-sequences of fixed sizes: 1,2,3… This fixed size sub-sequence is called window. This window is slided over the traces of system calls to find the unique sub-sequences of fixed length s over the whole dataset. A frequency count of each sub-sequence is recorded. Consider a sequence, which consists of traces of system calls.

execve open mmap open mmap mmap mmap mmap mmap open mmap exit

execve open mmap open mmap mmap mmap mmap mmap open mmap exit

Sliding window of size 3

Total length of sequence is 12 with the sliding window size w (=3) we will have total sub-sequences of size 3 as 12 –3 + 1= 10. These 10 sub-sequences of size 3 are

execve open mmap   open mmap open   mmap open mmap   open mmap mmap
mmap mmap mmap   mmap mmap mmap   mmap mmap mmap   mmap mmap open
mmap open mmap   open mmap exit

From among these 10 generated sliding window-sized sub-sequences unique sub-sequences with their frequencies are as follows:

execve open mmap	1	*mmap open mmap*	2
open mmap open	1	*mmap mmap open*	1
open mmap mmap	1	*open mmap exit*	1
mmap mmap mmap	3		

With these encoded frequencies for sub-sequences, we can apply any vector based distance/similarity measure, thus incorporating the sequential information with vector space. The traditional classification algorithm – the kNN classification algorithm [4, 7] with suitable distance/similarity metric can be used to build an efficient classifier.

Our proposed methodology consists of two phases namely training and testing phase. Dataset D consists of m sessions. Each session is of variable length. Initially in training phase, all the unique sub-sequences of size s are extracted from the whole dataset. Let n be the number of unique sub-sequences of size w, generated from the dataset D. A matrix C of size m × n is constructed where C_{ij} is given by count of jth unique sub-sequence in the ith session. A distance/similarity metric is constructed by applying distance/similarity measure over the C matrix. The model is trained with the dataset consisting of normal sessions.

In testing phase, whenever a new process P comes to the classifier, it looks for the presence of any new sub-sequence of size s. If a new sub-sequence is found, the new process is marked as abnormal. When there is no new sub-sequence in new process P, calculate the similarity of new process with all the sessions. If similarity between any session in training set and new process is equal to 1, mark it as normal. In other case, pick the k highest values of similarity between new process P and training dataset. From this k maximum values, calculate the average similarity for k-nearest neighbors. If the average similarity value is greater than user defined threshold value (τ) mark the new process P as normal, else mark P as abnormal.

5 Experimental Results

Experiments were conducted using *k*-Nearest Neighbor classifier with Jaccard similarity function, Cosine similarity measure, Euclidean distance and BWC metric.

Each distance/similarity metric was individually experimented with kNN classifier on DARPA 98 IDS dataset.

DARPA 98 IDS dataset consists of TCPDUMP and BSM audit data. The network traffic of an Air Force Local Area Network was simulated to collect TCPDUMP and BSM audit data [13]. The audit logs contain seven weeks of training data and two weeks of testing data. There were 38 types of network-based attacks and several realistic intrusion scenarios conducted in the midst of normal background data. Detailed discussion of DARPA dataset is given at [12]. For experimental purpose, 605 unique processes were used as a training dataset, which were free from all types of attacks. Testing was conducted on 5285 normal processes. In order to test the detection capability of proposed approach, we incorporate 55 intrusive sessions into our test data. For kNN classification experiments, k=5 was considered. With various discussed distance/similarity measures in the above section (Jaccard similarity measure, Cosine similarity measure, Euclidean distance measure and BWC similarity measure) at different sub-sequence lengths (sliding window size) L=1,3,5 experiments were carried out. Here, L=1 means that no sequential information is captured whereas, for L > 1 some amount of order information across elements of the data is preserved.

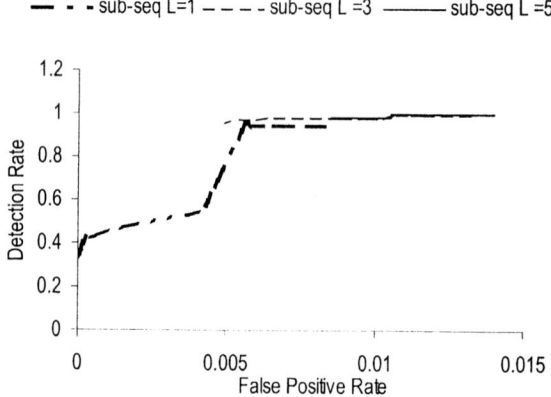

Fig. 1. ROC curve for Jaccard similarity metric using kNN classification for k =5

To analyze the efficiency of classifier, ROC curve is used. The ROC curve is an interesting tool to analyze two-class problems [14]. ROC curve is very useful where situations detection of rarely occurring event is done. ROC curve depicts the relationship between False Positive Rate (FPR) and Detection Rate (DR) at various threshold values. DR is the ratio of the number of intrusive sessions (abnormal) detected correctly to the total number of intrusive sessions. The FPR is defined as the number of normal processes detected as abnormal, divided by the total number of normal processes. ROC curve gives an idea of the trade off between FPR and DR achieved by classifier. An ideal ROC curve would be parallel to FPR axis at DR equal to 1.

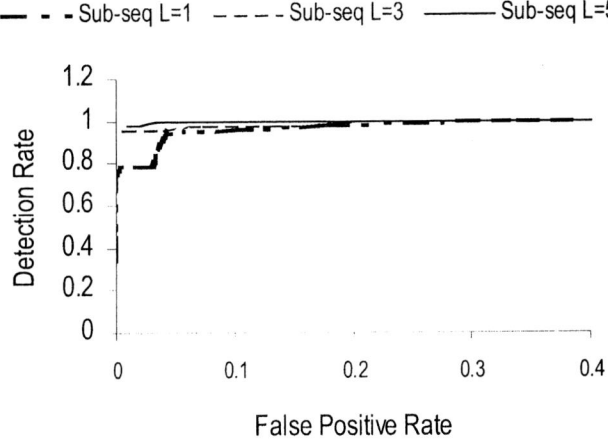

Fig. 2. ROC curve for Cosine similarity metric using kNN classification for k =5

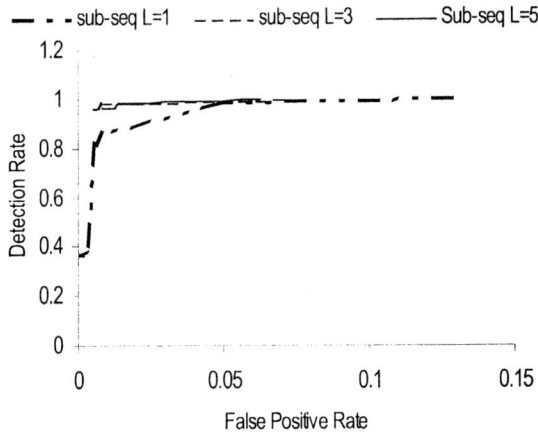

Fig. 3. ROC curve for Euclidian distance metric using kNN classification for k =5

Corresponding ROC curves for Jaccard similarity measure, Cosine similarity measure, Euclidean distance measure and BWC measure are shown in fig 1, 2, 3 and 4 respectively. It can be observed from fig 1,2,3 and 4 that as the sliding window size increases from L =1 to L = 5, high DR (close to ideal value of 1) is observed with all the distance/similarity metrics.

Rate of increase in false positive is less for Jaccard similarity measure (0.005-0.015) as compared to different distance/similarity metrics such as Cosine similarity (0.1-0.4), Euclidian distance (0.05-0.15) and BWC similarity (0.1-0.7). Table 1 depicts the factor (FPR or Threshold value) that was traded off in order to achieve high DR. For example, in the case of Jaccard similarity measure, FPR was traded off for threshold values (highlighted in bold face) in order to achieve high DR.

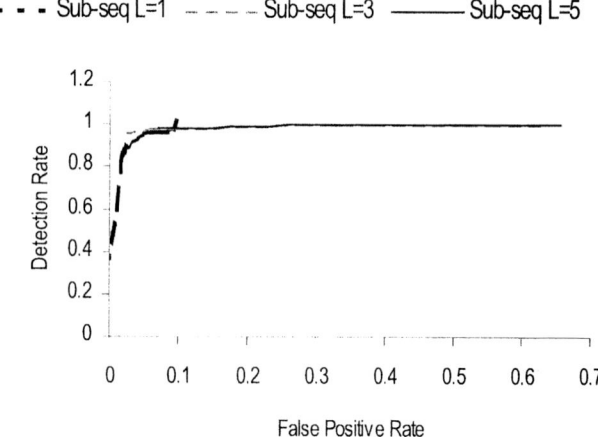

Fig. 4. ROC curve for BWC similarity metric using kNN classification for k =5

Table 1. Results for different distance/similarity metric

	Jaccard similarity measure		Cosine similarity measure		Euclidian distance measure		BWC similarity measure	
	τ	FPR	τ	FPR	τ	FPR	τ	FPR
L =1	0.94	0.0056	0.99	0.29	0.99	0.12	0.89	0.096
L =3	0.95	0.011	0.99	0.12	0.99	0.07	0.7	0.28
L =5	0.89	0.0105	0.75	0.03	0.99	0.06	0.65	0.30

Thus, our results support the hypothesis that classification accuracy of sequential data can be improved by incorporating the order information embedded in sequences. We also performed experiments with different k values for nearest neighbor classifier with all the four measures.

Table 2. False positive rate at maximum attained detection rate for different sub-sequence length for different distance/similarity measure at k =7

	L = 1	L = 3	L =5
Jaccard similarity	0.0058	0.0102	0.0105
Euclidian distance	0.94	0.0047	0.0085
Cosine distance	0.3286	0.1799	0.0387
BWC measure	0.0885	0.0783	0.0787

We present the false positive rate at maximum attained detection rate for different sub-sequence lengths L = 1, 3, 5 with all the distance/similarity measures in table 2 for k =7. It can be observed that, as per the trend, the FPR is increasing with the increasing sub-sequence lengths for all the four measures. We also performed experiments with k =10 and the trend is also found to be consistent (Results are not included here).

6 Conclusion

Using Intrusion Detection as an example domain, we demonstrated in this paper the usefulness of utilizing sub-sequence information for kNN classification of sequential data. We presented results on DARPA 98 IDS dataset wherein we systematically varied the length of the sliding window from 1 to 5 and used various distance /similarity measures such as Jaccard similarity, Cosine similarity, Euclidian distance and BWC similarity measure. As the sub-sequence information is increased, the high DR is achieved with all the four measures. Our results show that if order information is made available, a traditional classifier such as kNN can be adapted for sequence classification problem. We are currently working on design of new similarity measure, for capturing complete sequential information. Although the current paper presented results in the domain of information security, we feel this methodology can be adopted for the domains such as web mining, text mining and bio-informatics.

References

1. Agrawal, R., Faloutsos, C. and Swami, A.: Efficient similarity search in sequence databases. In proceedings of the 4th Int'l Conference on Foundations of Data Organization and Algorithms. Chicago, IL, 1993. pp 69-84.
2. Bace, R.: Intrusion Detection. Macmillan Technical Publishing, 2000.
3. Buckinx, W., Moons, E., Van den Poel, D. and Wets, G: Customer-Adapted Coupon Targeting Using Feature Selection, Expert Systems with Applications 26, No. 4 2004, 509-518.
4. Dasarathy, B.V.: Nearest-Neighbor Classification Techniques, IEEE Computer Society Press, Los Alomitos, CA, 1991.
5. Forrest S, Hofmeyr S A, Somayaji A and Longstaff T.A.: A Sense of self for UNIX process. In Proceedings of the IEEE Symposium on Security and Privacy, pages 120-128, Los Alamitos, CA, 1996. IEEE Comuputer Socity Press.
6. Gludici, P: Applied Data Mining , Statistical methods for business and industry, Wiely publication, 2003.
7. Han, Jiawei., Kamber, Micheline.: Data Mining , Concepts and Techniques, Morgan Kaufmann Publishers, 2001.
8. Hastie, T., Tibshirani, R. and Friedman, J. H.: The Elements of Statistical Learning, Data Mining, Inference, and Prediction, Springer, 2001.
9. Hofmeyr S A, Forrest S, and Somayaji A.: Intrusion Detection Using Sequences of System calls. Journal of Computer Security, 1998, 6:151-180.
10. Keogh, E., Chakrabarti, K., Pazzani, M. and Mehrotra, S.: Locally adaptive dimensionality reduction for indexing large time series databases. In proceedings of ACM SIGMOD Conference on Management of Data. Santa Barbara, CA, 2003. pp 151-162.
11. Khan, M., Ding, Q. and Perrizo, W.: k-Nearest Neighbor Classification on Spatial Data Streams Using P-Trees, In the Proceedings of the 6th Pacific-Asia Conference on Advances in Knowledge Discovery and Data Mining, 2002.
12. Liao, Y., Rao Vemuri, V.: Using Text Categorization Techniques for Intrusion Detection. USENIX Security Symposium 2002: 51-59.
13. MIT Lincoln Laboratory, http://www.ll.mit.edu/IST/ideval/.

14. Marques de sa, J.P: Pattern recognition: concepts, methods and applications, Springer-Verlag 2001.
15. Pujari, A.K.: Data Mining Techniques, Universities Press INDIA, 2001.
16. Qian, G, Sural, S., Gu, Y., Pramanik, S.: Similarity between Euclidean and cosine angle distance for nearest neighbor queries. SAC 2004: 1232-1237
17. Ratanamahatana, C. A. and Keogh. E..: Making Time-series Classification More Accurate Using Learned Constraints. In proceedings of SIAM International Conference on Data Mining (SDM '04), Lake Buena Vista, Florida, 2004. pp. 11-22.
18. Rawat, S. Pujari, A.K., Gulati, V.P.,and Vemuri, V. Rao.: Intrusion Detection using Text Processing Techniques with a Binary-Weighted Cosine Metric. International Journal of Information Security, Springer-Verlag, Submitted 2004.
19. Sams String Metrics, http://www.dcs.shef.ac.uk/~sam/stringmetrics.html
20. Sholom M. Weiss and Casimir A. Kulikowski: Computer Systems That Learn: Classification and Prediction Methods from Statistics, Neural Nets, Machine Learning, and Expert Systems (Machine Learning Series), Morgan Kaufmann Publishers Inc. San Francisco, CA, USA , 1991.
21. Tom M. Mitchell.: Machine learning, Mc Graw Hill 1997.
22. Wang, Jason T.L.; Zaki, Mohammed J.; Toivonen, Hannu T.T.; Shasha, Dennis: Data mining in bioinformatics, Springer-Verlag 2005

Distance-Based Outliers in Sequences

Girish Keshav Palshikar

Tata Research Development and Design Centre (TRDDC),
54B Hadapsar Industrial Estate Pune 411013, India
GK.Palshikar@tcs.com

Abstract. Automatically finding *interesting*, *novel* or *surprising* patterns in time series data is useful in several applications, such as fault diagnosis and fraud detection. In this paper, we extend the notion of distance-based outliers to time series data and propose two algorithms to detect both global and local outliers in time series data. We illustrate these algorithms on some real datasets.

Keywords: Novelty detection, Outlier detection, Time series, Sequence mining.

1 Introduction

Analyzing a sequence of values is an important task in many practical applications. For example, the sequence of observed values of the parameters of a chemical process is analyzed to understand output quality and for process diagnosis. Telemetry data sent by a system onboard a satellite is analyzed to evaluate the system's health. The trades performed by a trader in a stock exchange can be analyzed to understand his/her financial performance in the market.

In such applications, the sequence to be analyzed consists of an ordered list of records (points). If each record consists of a single field then the sequence is *univariate*; otherwise it is *multivariate*. The ordering of records within a sequence is often based on a timestamp, in which case the sequence can be considered as a time series. An important question during the analysis of the sequence is: how do we identify *interesting*, *novel* or *anomalous* subsequences in the sequence? Note that identifying such subsequences is different from identifying single outlier points. We now need to define the meaning of terms such as interesting or anomalous. In the simplest case, extreme (high or low) values occurring in the sequence can be found out using standard statistical techniques for outlier detection in a time-series. However, in practice, we are often interested in more complex kinds of interesting or anomalous regions in the sequence. For example, (1) contiguous subsequences; or (2) noncontiguous subsequence (list of points not necessarily contiguous) etc. In this paper, we focus on the problem of automatically identifying contiguous subsequences of a given sequence, which are interesting or anomalous in a well-defined sense.

2 Related Work

Basic statistical techniques for outlier detection, including in time series data, are discussed in [1]. The notion of distance-based outliers in (non time series) datasets was proposed in [4]. A related notion was proposed in [6]. This paper extends the approach in [4] to time series data. Several other techniques for *novelty detection* have been proposed [2], [7], [3], [5] for identifying *interesting* subsequences in a time series. See also H. Geirsson et al [http://hraun.vedur.is/ja/skyrslur/contgps/ node8.html].

3 Distance-Based Outliers Detection in Sequences

3.1 Outlier Subsequence

An *n-sequence* (or *a sequence of length n*) is an ordered finite sequence $s = <s_0, s_1, ..., s_{n-1}>$ of $n \geq 1$ elements. Elements of a multivariate (or multidimensional) sequence are tuples (or vectors). An *m*-sequence $<x_0, x_1, ..., x_{m-1}>$ is a (*contiguous*) *subsequence* of another sequence $s = <s_0, s_1, ..., s_{n-1}>$ if $x_0 = s_i, x_1 = s_{i+1}, ..., x_{m-1} = s_{i+m-1}$, for some $0 \leq i \leq n - m$ i.e., a subsequence is a contiguous part of the original sequence; e.g., $<2, 8, 5>$ is a subsequence of sequence $<8,7,2,8,5,4,4>$. We consider the problem of detection of interesting or anomalous subsequences in a given single sequence. For this, we adapt the notion of a distance-based outlier in a set of points, proposed in [4], to distance-based outlier subsequence of a given sequence.

Let $\mathbf{d}(\mathbf{x}_i, \mathbf{x}_j)$ denote the function to compute the distance between two elements $\mathbf{x}_i$ and $\mathbf{x}_j$ of a sequence; e.g., $\mathbf{d}$ could be Euclidean, Mahanttan or general Minkowski distance. There are several ways in which the distance $d(\alpha, \beta)$ between two *m*-sequences $\alpha = <\mathbf{x}_0, \mathbf{x}_1, ..., \mathbf{x}_{m-1}>$ and $\beta = <\mathbf{y}_0, \mathbf{y}_1, ..., \mathbf{y}_{m-1}>$ can be computed. For example, the *Minkowski distance* is defined as

$$d(\alpha, \beta) = \sqrt[p]{\mathbf{d}^p(\mathbf{x}_0, \mathbf{y}_0) + \mathbf{d}^p(\mathbf{x}_1, \mathbf{y}_1) + ... + \mathbf{d}^p(\mathbf{x}_{m-1}, \mathbf{y}_{m-1})}$$

For example, for $\alpha = <7, 2, 3>$, $\beta = <3, 0, 5>$, $\mathbf{d}(\mathbf{x}_2, \mathbf{y}_2) = \mathbf{d}(2, 0) = 2$, whereas $d(\alpha, \beta) = [(7 - 3)^2 + (2 - 0)^2 + (3 - 5)^2]^{1/2} = 4.9$. When each $\mathbf{x}_i$ and $\mathbf{y}_i$ is either 0 or 1, $p = 1$ and when $\mathbf{d}(\mathbf{x}, \mathbf{y}) = XOR(\mathbf{x}, \mathbf{y})$, the above distance d reduces to usual Hamming distance between two Boolean *m*-sequences.

3.2 Algorithm 1

We now adapt Knorr's notion of distance-based outliers in a set of points to distance-based outlier *m*-subsequences of a given sequence. Let $s = <s_0, s_1, ..., s_{n-1}>$ be a given *n*-sequence. Let $m \geq 1$ be a given integer. Let $\Omega(s, m)$ denote the set of all possible *m*-subsequences of s; e.g., $\Omega(<8,7,2,8,5,4,4>,4) = \{<8,7,2,8>, <7,2,8,5>, <2,8,5,4>, <8,5,4,4>\}$. Clearly, $\Omega(s, m) = n - m + 1$. Knorr [4] proposed a distance-based definition of an outlier in a given set S of points: a point $x \in S$ is an outlier if at least $p\%$ points in S are at a distance $> D$ from x, where p and D are user specified positive real numbers. We propose a simple generalization of this definition to adapt it for outlier subsequences of a given sequence.

Definition 1. Let $s = <s_0, s_1, ..., s_{n-1}>$ be a given *n*-sequence. Let m be a given integer such that $0 \leq m \leq n-1$. Let $0 \leq p \leq 1$ and $D \geq 0$ be two given real numbers. An

m-subsequence $a = <x_0, x_1, ..., x_{m-1}>$ of s is a (p, m, D)-*outlier* in s if at least $p\%$ of the m-subsequences in $\Omega(s, m)$ are at a distance $> D$ from a.

Consider a 19-sequence $s = <2, 5, 6, 2, 3, 1, 2, 9, 9, 9, 1, 2, 2, 1, 3, 1, 0, 2, 1>$. For $m = 3$, $\Omega(s, m)$ contains $19 - 3 + 1 = 17$ 3-subsequences. Suppose $D = 10.0$ and $p = 60\%$. For the 3-subsequence $<2, 3, 1>$ starting at 4th position, there is only 1 subsequence in $\Omega(s, m)$ at a distance > 10.0 (using Euclidean distance); thus the fraction of 3-subsequences at a distance > 10.0 from this subsequence is $1/17 = 5.9\%$. Since $5.9 < 60.0$, this 3-subsequence is not an outlier. For the subsequence $<9, 9, 9>$, there are 11 subsequences (i.e., $11/17 = 64.7\%$) which are at a distance > 10.0 from it. Thus this 3-subsequence is an outlier, for the given values of p and D.

Knorr [4] contains an algorithm to find a set of distance-based outliers from a given set of points. We present below a simple generalization of the core of Knorr's algorithm to detect outlier m-subsequences of a given sequence.

```
// Modified Knorr's algorithm for distance-based outlier m-
// subsequences; m ≥ 1. 0 ≤ p ≤ 1 = fraction of m-subsequences
// at distance > D from an outlier; D = a distance value
algorithm knorr_seq
input sequence s of n elements;
input m, p, D;
M := n - m + 1; // no. of m-subsequences of s
for (i = 0; i <= (n - m); ) {
    for (j = 0, count = 0; j <= n - m; j++) {
        d := d(<s_i,s_{i+1},...,s_{i+m-1}>, <s_j,s_{j+1},...,s_{j+m-1}>);
        if ( d > D ) then count++; end if;
    } // end for
    if ( count/total > p ) then {
        printf("Outlier sub-sequence from %d to %d\n",i,i+m-1);
        i = i + m;
    } else i++; end if;
} // end for
```

Essentially, the algorithm compares every candidate m-subsequence $a = <s_i, s_{i+1}, ..., s_{i+m-1}>$ with every other m-subsequence $b = <s_j, s_{j+1}, ..., s_{j+m-1}>$, incrementing *count* if $d(a, b) > D$. Thus, for every candidate m-subsequence of the given sequence, the algorithm counts the number of m-subsequence that are at a distance $> D$ from it. If this number exceeds the specified limit, that m-subsequence is declared as an outlier. The user has to provide values for the parameters p, D and m. Our implementation offers a choice of various distance measures to the user (e.g., Manhattan, Euclidean, etc.). Clearly, the complexity of the algorithm is $O(n^2)$ where n = size of the given sequence. For correctness, we state the following without proof:

Proposition 2. Every m-subsequence declared as an outlier by the algorithm knorr_seq satisfies Definition 1. Conversely, every m-subsequence that satisfies Definition 1 is declared as an outlier by the algorithm, provided no subsequence overlapping with it has already been declared an outlier.

This algorithm will not generate overlapping outlier subsequences, due to the jump in the value of i (statement $i = i + m$) after an outlier sub-sequence is found. Fig. 1

shows the daily quantity of a commodity traded on a stock exchange for 52 days. The above algorithm, called with $m = 4$, $p = 0.40$ (40%), $D = 150000.0$ and using Euclidean distance, reports the following two 4-subsequences as outliers: 43 ... 46 and 47 ... 50. This is reasonable, since the volume is drastically different in these periods compared to the other days.

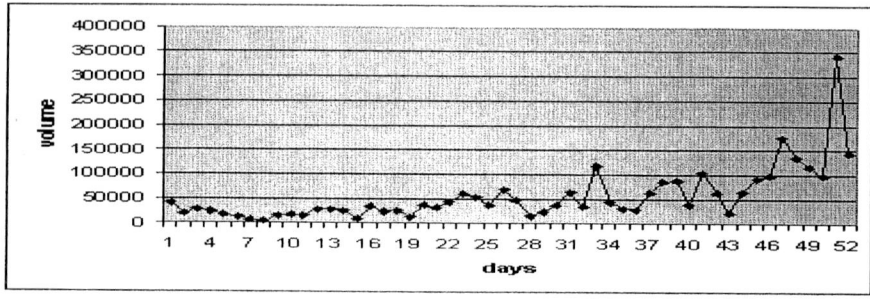

Fig. 1. Daily trading volume for a period of 52 days

3.2 Algorithm 2

Consider the time series in Fig. 2. The subsequence from 100 to 124, consisting of two cycles that are much shorter than their neighbours, is naturally an *interesting*. However, it is difficult to find it as an outlier using the above algorithm, since the values in this region occur as part of many other cycles. This is an example of a *local outlier*, which is an outlier only in relation to a few of its immediate (left and right) neighbouring subsequences. In contrast, Definition 1 considered the entire sequence and hence the resulting outliers can be called *global outliers*.

Definition 3. Let s be a given sequence. Let $\alpha = <s_i, s_{i+1}, ..., s_j>$ be a given subsequence of s. Let $0 \leq m \leq n-1$, $k \geq 1$ be given integers. The set $\Psi_L(m, k, \alpha)$ of k *left neighbours* of α contains the following k m-subsequences $\{<s_{i-m-k+1},...,s_{i-1}>,...,<s_{i-m}, s_{i-k}>\}$. The set $\Psi_R(m, k, \alpha)$ of k *right neighbours* of α contains the following k m-subsequences $\{<s_{j+1},...,s_{j+m}>,...,<s_{j+k}, s_{j+k+m}>\}$. We define the *set of neighbours* of α as $\Psi(m, k, \alpha) = \Psi_L(m, k, \alpha) \cup \Psi_R(m, k, \alpha)$.

For $s = <3,5,4,6,8,9,5,5,4,6,3,5,6,2,5>$, $\alpha = <5,5,4>$, $m = 3$, $k = 4$, the set of 4 left neighbours of α is $\Psi_L(3, 4, \alpha) = \{<6,8,9>, <4,6,8>, <5,4,6>, <3,5,4>\}$; the set of 4 right neighbours of α is $\Psi_R(3, 4, \alpha) = \{<6,3,5>, <3,5,6>, <5,6,2>, <6,2,5>\}$.

Definition 4. Let s be a given sequence. Let $0 \leq m \leq n-1$, $k \geq 1$ be given integers. Let $0 \leq p \leq 1$ and $D \geq 0$ be two given real numbers. An m-subsequence a of s is a (p, m, D, k)-*left-local-outlier* (or, simply *left outlier*) in s if at least $p\%$ of the m-subsequences in $\Psi_L(m, k, a)$ are at a distance $> D$ from a. Right outlier and *local outlier* are defined similarly using $\Psi_R(m, k, a)$ and $\Psi(m, k, a)$.

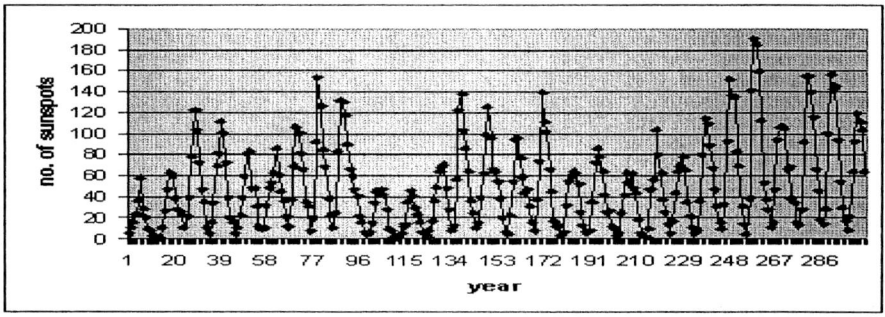

Fig. 2. Average number of sunspots per year

We now modify the algorithm to detect left local outliers in a given sequence; algorithms to detect right outliers and local outliers are similar. The algorithm counts how many of the k left neighbours of a particular candidate m-subsequence a are at a distance $> D$ from it. If this number is $> M$, where M is given by the user, then it declares a as a left outlier. Our implementation offers a choice of various distance measures to the user (e.g., Manhattan, Euclidean etc.). The complexity of the algorithm is $O(k*n)$ where n = size of the given sequence and k = the no. of neighbours to be checked on the left side. For correctness, we state the following without proof:

Proposition 5. Every m-subsequence declared as a left outlier by the algorithm knorr_seq2 satisfies Definition 4. Conversely, every m-subsequence that satisfies Definition 4 is declared as a left outlier by the algorithm, provided no subsequence overlapping with it has already been declared a left outlier.

```
algorithm knorr_seq2
input   sequence s of n elements;
input   m, k, M, D;
for (i = 0; i <= (ps->N - m); ) {
   for (j=i-m-k+1,count=0; j >= 0 && j+m-1 < i; j++) {
         d := d(<sᵢ,sᵢ₊₁,...,sᵢ₊ₘ₋₁>, <sⱼ,sⱼ₊₁,...,sⱼ₊ₘ₋₁>);
         if ( d > D ) then count++; endif;
   } // end for
   if ( count > M ) then {
         printf("Left outlier: start=%d end=%d\n",i,i+m-1);
         i = i + m;
   } else
         i++;
} // end for
```

We have also extended the approach to detect inliers, such as those in Fig. 2.

4 Conclusions and Further Work

We proposed an extension of the distance-based outlier detection approach of [4] to detect interesting subsequences of a given sequence. The essential idea is that interesting subsequences can be modeled as *outliers* in the distance-based framework. We presented two algorithms to detect both global and local outliers in a given time-series data. An implementation provides a choice of several variants of these algorithms, along with different types of distance (or similarity) measures. We demonstrated the use of these algorithms to detect some interesting subsequences in some example datasets. The first limitation of this approach is that the user has to provide values for 3-4 parameters, which requires some experimentation. We are looking at the use of machine-learning algorithms for automatically learning values for these parameters, from a given set of already known interesting subsequences. Also, the quadratic complexity makes the algorithms too slow for large time series datasets. We are looking at the use of some well known index structures to improve the efficiency. Though, in principle, our techniques should work well even with multidimensional time series, we need to validate this on real-life time series. We are conducting several experiments to compare our results with those reported by other well-known algorithms for novelty detection in time series.

Acknowledgements

I would like to thank Prof. Mathai Joseph for his support and colleagues in TRDDC for useful discussions and help. Sincere thanks to Dr. Manasee Palshikar for providing the foundation for all my research work.

References

1. V. Barnett, T. Lewis, *Outliers in Statistical Data*, John Wiley and Sons, 1994.
2. D. Dasgupta, S. Forrest, "Novelty Detection in Time Series Data using Ideas from Immunology", Proc. 5th Conf. Intelligent Systems, 1996.
3. E. Keogh, S. Lonardi, B. Chiu, "Finding Surprising Patterns in a Time Series Database in Linear Time and Space", Proc. 8th ACM Int. Conf. Knowledge Discovery and Data Mining, ACM Press, pp. 550 – 556, 2002.
4. E. M. Knorr, R. T. Ng, "Algorithms for Mining Distance-based Outliers in Large Datasets", Proc. VLDB Conf., 1998, pp. 392 – 403.
5. J. Ma, S. Perkins, "Online Novelty Detection on Temporal Sequences", Proc. Int. Conf. Know. Discovery Data Mining, Springer-Verlag, pp. 275 – 295, 2003.
6. S. Ramaswamy, R. Rastogi, K. Shim, "Efficient Algorithms for Mining Outliers from Large Datasets", Proc. SIGMOD2000, ACM Press, pp. 162-172, 2000.
7. C. Shahabi, X. Tian, W. Zhao, "TSA-Tree: A Wavelet based Approach to Improve the Efficiency of Multilevel Surprise and Trend Queries", Proc. 12th Int. Conf. Scientific Statistical Database Management, pp. 55 – 68, 2000.

Capturing Market Intelligence from Customer Feedback E-mails Using Self-enhancing Boltzmann Machine-Based Network of Knowledge Maps

N. Pradeep Kumar and Tapati Bandopadhyay

Faculty Member, ICFAI Business School, Gurgaon-122016, Haryana, India
{pkgarg, tapati}@ibsdel.org

Abstract. With the proliferation of the Web, capture of market intelligence data has become more difficult in reality from the system's point of view, as data sources on the web are voluminous, heterogeneous in terms of structures and semantics, and some part of it may be irrelevant to a specific organizations' marketing decision making context, which is the primary premises of market intelligence (MI) systems. To address these requirements of MI, we are proposing a method for creating an MI network using customer feedback messages and e-mails as inputs. We have proposed the use of knowledge map (KM) method for representing textual and unstructured resources as a network using KMs and clustering and then incrementally enhance itself as the new customer e-mails keep coming. At last, we have proposed a self-enhancing network using Bolzmann Machines concept where the new messages are treated as new hypotheses, and they get absorbed into the MI network based on their similarity values.

1 Introduction

1.1 Market Intelligence

Market Intelligence is a specific functional form of Business Intelligence or BI. A definition [10] on Business Intelligence says that it is a systematic and ethical program for gathering, analyzing, and managing external information that can affect a company's plans, decisions, and operations. It is also defined as the result of "acquisition, interpretation, collation, assessment, and exploitation of information" [5] in the business domain. According to the report of Nucleus, a market research firm on IT, in their research about Top 10 IT predictions for 2005, [10] on BI has emerged as the first among the maximum sought-after solutions. Amongst various Business Intelligence elements, Market Intelligence is one of the most significantly and practically applied concept or tool. Gathering market intelligence (MI) is one of the critical operational tactics for the marketing-strategic success of an enterprise. A study found that the world produces between 635,000 and 2.12 million terabytes of unique information per year, most of which has been stored in computer hard drives or servers [5]. Among these huge, heterogonous and unstructured data domain, one of the crucial and valuable source of Market Intelligence for any company is the on-line customer feedback system. Gathering customer feedback online through e-mails or form-based interfaces is one of the most common activities that companies are engaged in doing on the net, because it gives the customer the flexibility to communicate in an asynchronous domain (which is not the case with the telephone calls) and also gives them a platform to communicate in writing which is a more convenient way as perceived by people for putting the problems or thoughts in a more structured fashion.

This customer feedback information – either in the form of e-mails or some structured textual form-based inputs, is a precious source of MI for any organization. In this paper, we are thereby proposing a method for collecting market intelligence from customer e-mails using Knowledge Maps as the Knowledge extraction and description mechanism, and incorporating a self-enhancing MI network. In contrast with traditional knowledge portal methods where document-level technologies are quite popular, our design uses the Knowledge Map method for extraction and collection of Market Intelligence data, based on the concept developed and presented by the author [3]. Consequently, we present the process of extracting market intelligence using knowledge maps, which is generated by an information synthesis process and can provide semantic services through various application interfaces and analytical or filter or enterprise-data search engines.

1.2 Collecting Market Intelligence: Sources and Tools

Generally, MI research and system development efforts have focused on storage and data mining technologies. Data warehousing and on-line analytical processing (OLAP) have typically been used to solve data extraction, transformation, data cleaning, storage, and mining issues. Previous efforts have used document-based technologies and supported document-level functions such as full text search, document classification, and so on. Business practitioners have developed automated tools to support better understanding and processing of information. In recent years, business intelligence tools have become important for analysis of information on the Web [4]. Researchers have also developed advanced analysis and visualization techniques to summarize and present vast amount of information. It is [4] found that the global interest in intelligence technology has increased significantly during the years of early twenty-first century. Automated search capability in many tools has been shown to lead to information overload.[5] Despite recent Improvements in analysis capability [4], there is still a long way to go to assist qualitative analysis effectively. Most tools that claim to do analysis simply provide different views of collection of information {e.g. comparison between different products or companies). Various [9] display formats were identified for handling multi-dimensional data e.g. hierarchical displays- an effective information access tool for browsing, network displays, scatter displays.. Regarding document visualization, it primarily concerns the task of getting insight into information obtained from one or more documents. Most processes of document visualization involve three stages i.e. document analysis, algorithms, and visualization. Web content mining treats a web document as a vector of weights of key terms [1]. He et al. [6] proposed an unsupervised clustering method that was shown to identify relevant topics effectively. The clustering method employed a graph-partitioning method based on a normalized cut criterion. This method we are using in this paper to extract intelligence from customer e-mails for creating an MI network using Knowledge maps.

1.3 MI Network Creation with Customer E-mails as Inputs

Aside from the document level operations, an effective Market Intelligence collection system should combine extraction technology with semantics, and should generate a network structure to store knowledge. In this section, we present these requirements of an effective market intelligence collection system using customer feedback e-mails as inputs. Towards this end, we first introduce the concept of Bolzmann machine as an effective self-enhancing network to dynamically and incrementally capture MI from e-mail inputs. Then we explain the process of creating high-dimensional KMs(Knowledge Maps) from an existing e-mail repository, using similarity-based clustering and graph partitioning methods, at say Time T_0 when an organization starts building it's MI network. The high-dimensional KM network is then decomposed into 2-D network using MDS or Multi-Dimensional Scaling. This network then accepts periodic incremental inputs from new e-mails from customers and gets self-enhanced by the Bolzmann machine concept application.

1.4 Bolzmann Machine

Bolzmann machines are variations on the basic concepts of Hopfield Networks, [11] which was initially proposed in the field of artificial intelligence, as a theory of memory supporting distributed representations (memory as a pattern of activations across a set of processing elements), distributed and asynchronous control, content-addressable memory and fault-tolerance. Pairs of units in a Hopfield network are connected by symmetric weights and the units update their states asynchronously by looking at their local connections to the other units. The Hopfield network works well as content-addressable memories. They can also be used for constraint-satisfaction problems where each unit can be thought as a 'hypothesis'. [11] Then the network can try to reach a state of equilibrium by adjusting weights as follow:

1. Place positive weights on connections between pair of units representing compatible or mutually supporting hypotheses
2. Place negative weights on connections between pairs of units representing incompatible or in-conflict hypotheses.

By definition, Hopfield networks settle on a number of local minimum, which is workable in case of content-addressable memory, but for hypotheses-based situations, a global equilibrium is to be reached. Towards this end, the concepts of Hopfield networks were combined with that of simulated annealing- another AI algorithm for searching and constraint satisfaction, and this effort produced the idea of Bolzmann machines.

This concept can be exploited very effectively in case of creating and arranging an organizational memory. The paper focuses primarily on the knowledge extraction aspect to build an organizational memory, initially from start-up, and then incrementally. For starting up, we propose the creation of a knowledge map network where every node can represent a hypothesis. During the initial build-up phase, the hypotheses are tested on-build-process and are located as nodes in the knowledge map network. This way the first organizational memory gets built up. Once it gets production released, the incremental building starts with the Bolzmann machine concepts.

2 Creation of Initial MI Network Using Knowledge Map

In this paper, we are taking the form-based text inputs and e-mail messages from customers as the primary knowledge resources to build up an MI network. Treating them as unstructured documents, we can use co-occurrence analysis to find the similarities and then consequently the dissimilarities between the messages/ text contents. Message bodies which are very similar in terms of their contents i.e. many of the identified key-terms (i.e. Terms excluding the general terms like pro-nouns, prepositions, conjunctions etc.)are same, can be clubbed up together to form a cluster. Dissimilar message/ text bodies can be created as other clusters. These clusters can then form a network using hierarchical and partitional clustering method to form a graph with the nodes as representative knowledge maps for a particular group of emails with high-similarity in their message body/text.

Co-occurrence analysis can convert data indices and weights obtained from inputs of parameters and various data sources(i.e.the email/text message bodies in the context of this paper) into a matrix that shows the similarity between every pair of such sources.[6,7].

When measured between two e-mail message bodies, say E_i and E_j,

$$\text{Sim}_{ij} = \alpha \{ A_{ij} / |A|_2 \} + \beta S_{ij} / |S|_2 + (1 - \alpha - \beta) C_{ij} / |C|_2 \qquad (1)$$

$0 < \alpha, \beta$ (parameters) < 1, $0 <= \alpha + \beta <= 1$,
where A, S, and C are matrices for A_{ij}, S_{ij}, and C_{ij} respectively. Values for A_{ij} will be 1 if E_i has a direct link/ reference/ hyperlink to E_j, else 0. S is the asymmetric similarity score E_i and E_j, and is calculated as follows:

$$S_{ij} = \text{sim}(E_i, E_j) = [[\sum_{k=1}^{P} d_{ki} d_{kj}] / [\sum_{k=1}^{n} d^2_{di}]] \qquad (2)$$

where n is total number of terms in E_i, m is total number of terms in E_j, p is total number of terms that appear in both E_i and E_j, d_{ij} = (Number of occurrence of term j in E_i) X log$((N/d_{fj})Xw_j)$X(Termtype factor); d_{fj} is number of Email message-bodies containing term j; w_j is number of words in term j; Termtype factor = 1 + ((10-2 X type$_j$ / 10), where type$_j$ = min 1 if term j appears in subject, 2 if it appears in body, 3 if it appears in 'note' etc.) and C_{ij} is number of Es pointing to both E_i and E_j (co-citation/ cross-referencing matrix).

Once we get the similarity and dissimilarity matrices for the initial build-up phase using an existing repository of e-mails as the knowledge resources, we create a graph and then partition it to form a network of nodes where the nodes are the representative clusters of a group of emails having high similarity scores among them. Partitioning of a graph, say G, can be done in various ways, for example, by using similarity measures as below: [11,12].

Normalized Cut (x) ={cut between (A, B)/ assoc(A, V)}+{cut between (A, B)/ assoc (B,V)} $\qquad (3)$

where, Cut between $(A,B) = \sum_{i \in A, j \in B} Sim_{ij}$, Sim_{ij} is similarity between nodes i and j of the graph. Assoc(A,V) and assoc(B,V) shows how on average nodes within a group are connected to each other. A cut on a graph $G = (V, E)$ is defined as removal of a set of edges such that the graph is split into disconnected sub-graphs. [2,3].

Once the high-dimensional network is created, it can be reduced to a 2-D form using Multi-Dimensional Scaling or MDS. Multidimensional scaling (MDS) algorithms consist of a family of techniques that portray a data structure in a spatial fashion, where the coordinates of data points x_{ia} are calculated by a dimensionality reduction procedure. The distances (d_{ij}) are calculated as follows:

$$d_{ij} = [\sum \{x_{ia} - x_{ja}\}^p]^{1/p} \quad (p >= 1), x_{ia} <> x_{ja} \quad (4)$$

where, p is the Minkowski exponent and may take any value not less than 1. r is the coordinate of point on dimension a, and j is an r-element row vector from the ith row of the matrix containing all *n* points on all r dimensions. The MDS procedure constructs a geometric representation of the data (such as a similarity matrix), usually in a Euclidean space of low dimensionality (i.e. *p = 2)*. MDS has been applied in many different domains[8] It can be implemented using the following steps. First, Similarity matrix is to be converted into a dissimilarity matrix by subtracting each element by the maximum value in the original matrix. This matrix can be called as dissimilarity matrix D. Then matrix B with elements b_{ij} which is a scalar product is to be calculated as follows:

$$b_{ij} = -1/2 \, [\, d_{ij}^2 - 1/n \sum_{k=1}^{n} d_{ik}^2 - 1/n \sum_{k=1}^{n} d_{kj}^2 + 1/n^2 \sum_{g=1}^{n} \sum_{h=1}^{n} d_{gh}^2 \,] \quad (5)$$

where d_{ij} is an element in D, n= number of nodes in the data-source graph.

After calculating B, singular value decomposition is performed using the formula as below:

$$B = U \times V \times U', \quad X = U \times V^{1/2} \quad (6)$$

where, U has eigenvectors in its columns and V has eigenvectors on its diagonal B can then be expressed as $B = X \times X'$.

The first two column vectors of X thus calculated now can be used to obtain the two-dimensional coordinates of points.

Using this process along with MDS, suppose we get a network built up as shown below in Figure 1 based on the similarity and dissimilarity scores among the existing customer-e-mail repository.

Once the initial build-up phase is over and the initial MI network is created from an existing repository of e-mail messages, it should be incrementally self-enhancing with periodic incremental inputs from the e-mail repositories. This is where we propose the use of Bolzmann Machines. Suppose n number of customer messages is to be fed onto the initial MI network as shown in Figure 1. Now, each e-mail message is treated as a new hypothesis (as explained in previous section on Bolzmann Machines). All the nodes (clusters) of the existing network are also treated as hypotheses but they are already tested hypotheses which have been included and used for building up the initial network. Each new hypothesis is tested with all the existing

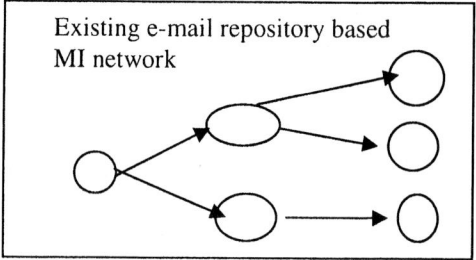

Fig. 1. Initial MI Network using Knowledge Maps with Existing e-mail Repository

hypotheses or nodes. The network places similarity scores as weights on connections between pair of hypotheses which are compatible or mutually supporting. The incompatible ones get 0 similarity score, so there is no connection or edge between them.

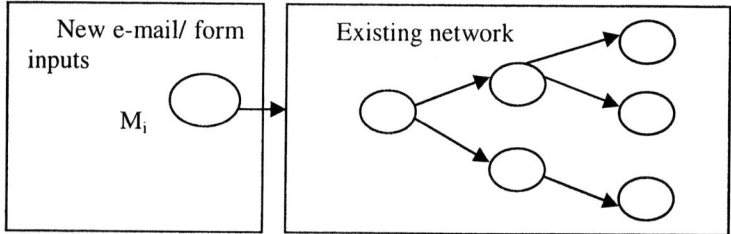

Fig. 2. An Existing Network w.r.t. a New Message

These steps are explained as shown in figure 3 below. Suppose a new e-mail M_i has come to be fed into the MI network

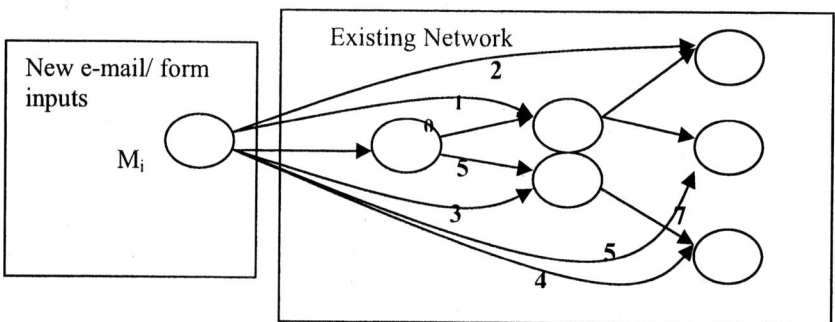

Fig. 3. Similarity and Dissimilarity Value assignment in An Existing Network w.r.t. a New Message

For Mi, it's similarity score with all the existing nodes will be calculated. Say the scores are as shown in Figure 4.

If for M_i, the maximum positive value (similarity score) over it's edges with the existing nodes m, say, with existing node j is W_{ij}, then

- If W_{ij} is more than a given threshold value, M_i will be included in node j.
- If W_{ij} is less than the given threshold value, M_i will be represented as a new node creating another cluster in the network.

Using these principles, If the similarity threshold is given as +8, then M_i will be included in the node for which the edge has the maximum value i.e. =10 and the value is higher than the threshold value.

If the similarity threshold value is given as +12, then the maximum value of edges between new node M_i and existing nodes 1 to j = +10, is lower than the threshold value. So, M_i will create a new node and a new cluster will be created centering on M_i. It will be positioned in the graph using the principles of graph partitioning as mentioned previously, and the resulting network may take the shape as shown below in Figure 4:

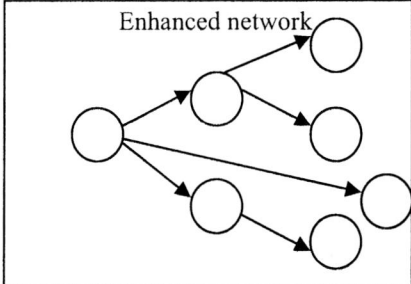

Fig. 4. Enhanced Network in case of similarity threshold value greater than the maximum value of edges

This process will be repeated with all the n new input messages. The weights can be dynamically adjusted as all the n messages are input and tested. Ultimately at the end of one incremental phase with n email messages, the network will have the new hypotheses included in the MI network.

3 Conclusion

The process of creating a market intelligence network as a form of MI repository in an organization, as explained in this paper, is simple and easily implemented. Further extensions may include exploring various other knowledge map creation mechanisms including the GA approaches and extrapolating the Knowledge maps into the analytical systems required for analyzing and visualizing the Market intelligence data. It can also be extend to incorporate various other MI inputs or resources other than customer e-mails, to create a more comprehensive MI network for an organization.

References

1. Bowman. C.M, Danzig. P.B., Manber. U.(1994); Schwartz, F'. Scalable Internet resource discovery: Research problems and approaches. *Communication of the ACM. Vol* 8 . pp 98-107.
2. Chen. H.; Chung, Y.; Ramsey. M.; and Yang. C.(1998) A smart itsy bitsy spider for the Web. *Journal of the American Society far Information Science. 49.* 7, 604-618.
3. Chen, H.; Fan. H.; Chau. M.; and Zeng, D.(2001) Meta Spider: Meta searching and categorization on the Web. *Journal of the American Society for Information Science and Technology. 52,* 13, 1134-1147.
4. Fuld, L.M.: Singh. A.: Rothwell. K.; and Kim, J.(2003) *Intelligence Software Report™ 2003: Leveraging the Web.* Cambridge. MA: Fuld & Company.
5. Futures-Group Ostriches & Eagles. The Futures Group Articles, Washington, DC, (1997) (available at www.futuresgroup.com).
6. He. X.; Ding. C; Zha. H.; and Simon, H. (2001) Automatic topic identification using Webpage clustering. In X. Wu. N. Cercone, TY. Lin, J- Gehrke. C. Clifton. R. Kotagiri. N. Zhong. and X. Hu (eds,). *Proceedings of the 2001 IEEE International Conference on Data Mining.* Los Alamitos. CA: IEEE Computer Society Press. 2(X)I. pp, 195-202.
7. He, Y, and Hui. S.C. (2002) Mining a Web citation database for author co-citation analysis. *Information Processing and Management. 38.* 4. 491-508.
8. Kealy, W.A.(2000) Knowledge maps and their use in computer-based collaborative learning. *Journal of Educational Computing Research, 25.* 4. 325-349.
9. Lin, X.(1997) Map displays for information retrieval. *Journal of the American Society for Information Science. 4H.* 1, 40-54.
10. Nucleus Report on Top 10 IT Spending for 2005: Survey of CIOs in MNCs:Survey Report March 2005 by Nucleus Research, http://www.nucleus.com/surveys/2005.
11. Rich E., Knight K.(2001), *Artificial Intelligence*, Tata McGrawHill Publishing Company Ltd, N. Delhi.
12. Shi. J., and Malik. J.(2000) Normalized cuts and image segmentation. *IEEE Transactions on Pattern Analysis and Machine Intelligence. 22.* S (2(X)0), 8S8-905.

Algorithm for Fuzzy Clustering of Mixed Data with Numeric and Categorical Attributes

Amir Ahmad[1] and Lipika Dey[2]

[1] Solid State Physics Laboratory,
Timarpur, Delhi 110054, India
amirahmad01@rediffmail.com
[2] Department of Mathematics,
I.I.T., Hauz Khas, New Delhi 110016, India
lipika@maths.iitd.ernet.in

Abstract. In many applications numeric as well as categorical features describe the data objects. A variety of algorithms have been proposed for clustering if fuzzy partitions and descriptive cluster prototypes are desired. However, most of these methods are designed for data sets with variables measured in the same scale type (only categorical, or only numeric). We have developed probabilistic distance measure to compute significance of attributes for numeric data, and distance between two categorical values. We used this distance measure with the cluster center definition proposed by Yasser El-Sonbaty and M. A. Ismail [26] to propose Fuzzy-c mean type clustering algorithm for mixed attributes data. The results of the application of the new algorithm show that new technique is quite encouraging.

1 Introduction

Clustering involves partitioning a set of data points into non overlapping groups, or clusters of points where points in a cluster are "more similar" to one another than to points in other clusters. Clustering is one of the principal techniques in the field of data mining [1], data compression [2], information retrieval [3], web mining [4] and many others. In the real world, a majority of the data is described by a combination of numeric and categorical data. K-means algorithm [5] is one of the most popular clustering algorithms used in scientific and industrial applications because of its simplicity and efficiency. While K-means gives satisfactory results for numeric attributes it is not appropriate for data set with categorical attributes since it is not possible to find mean of categorical values. Although the standard hierarchical clustering methods ([6], [7], [8]) can handle data with numeric and categorical attributes they are not very useful for large data set because of its high computational cost. Similarity Based Agglomerative Clustering (SBAC) algorithm [9] based on Goodall similarity measure [10] works well with mixed numeric and categorical features but has high computational cost. Conceptual clustering algorithms developed in machine learning, cluster with categorical values. Conceptual clustering systems ([11], [12]) use conditional probability estimates as a means for defining the relation between groups or clusters. System like COBWEB [11] and its derivatives (e.g., COBWEB/3 [13]; ECOWEB [14]; ITERATE [15]) use the *Category Utility* (CU) measure [16]. AUTOCLUSTER [17] imposes a clusterical finite mixture distribution model on the data and uses a Bayesian method to drive the most probable cluster distribution for the data given prior information (PI). For problems in data mining, which often involves many concepts and very large object spaces, the concept-based search can become a potential handicap for conceptual clustering algorithms to deal with extremely large dataset. Huang [18] proposed an algorithm based on *K*-mean algorithm philosophy to cluster mixed data.

Fuzzy c-means (FCM) proposed by Dunn [19] and extended by Bezdek [20] is one of the most well known methodologies in clustering analysis. Basically FCM is dependent of the measure of the distance between samples. For pure numeric data sets, FCM uses the common Euclidean distance, which take equal importance of each feature. This assumption seriously affects the performance of FCM since in most real data sets, features are not equally important. In [21] the authors stated that the Euclidean distance can give good results when all clusters are spheroids with same size are when clusters are well separated. Krishnapuram and Kim [22] have proposed Mahalanobis distance as the metric in FCM. Recently a gradient descent learning technique [23] has been proposed to compute feature-weights that can improve the performance of FCM clustering. But this improvement is at the price of feature-weight learning which has $O(cn^2)$ time complexity where c is constant and n is number of data objects.

Based on the philosophy of FCM Huang and Ng [24] developed fuzzy *K*-mode algorithm for categorical data with binary distance measure and hard centroid. Recently a fuzzy clustering algorithm has been developed [25] with fuzzy centroid that shows improvement over fuzzy *K*-mode algorithm. Yaser El-Sonbaty and M. A. Ismail [26] developed an algorithm for Fuzzy clustering for symbolic data(Fuzzy symbolic c-means algorithm). They proposed a concept of cluster center for mixed data in their work. For categorical data the center computed using their method are the same as kim et al. [25] fuzzy centroid concept. In their paper Yaser El-Sonbaty and M. A. Ismail [26] presented a framework for fuzzy clustering for mixed data. They suggested that weight associated with the features are calculated heuristically or using some optimization routines.

Amir and Lipika [27] have proposed a *K*-mean type clustering algorithm for dataset having numerical and categorical attributes, that compute distance between two categorical attribute values for the categorical attributes and significance of attributes for the numeric attributes We have extended this algorithm for fuzzy framework. This paper has following organization. Section 2 reviews the fuzzy c-mean clustering algorithm. Section 3 shows how to compute distance between two categorical attributes values and significance of attributes for numeric attributes. Section 4 addresses the problem of computing center for categorical attributes and the distance between data object and center (which will be called *modified center*). Section 5 describes the proposed algorithm. We present the experimental results in section 6. Section 7 summarizes our contribution and describes directions for future work.

2 Fuzzy c- Mean Clustering Algorithm

Fuzzy c-means (FCM) proposed by Dunn [19] and extended by Bezdek [20] is one of the most well known methodologies in clustering analysis. We can describe FCM as follows for data set having n data objects, s attributes, K clusters, Fuzzy partition matrix $U = (u_{ij})_{nxK}$. FCM partitions a set of n-dimensional vectors $X = \{X_1, X_2, ..., X_n\}$ into K clusters where $X_i = \{x_{i1},...,x_{im}\}$ represents the ith sample for i=1,...,n. FCM aims to determine cluster centers v_j (j =1,2,..., K) where $v_j=\{v_{j1}, v_{j2},...,v_{js}\}$ and the fuzzy partition matrix U by minimizing the objective function J defined as follows:

$$J = \sum_{j=1}^{K} \sum_{i=1}^{n} (u_{ij})^m d_{ij} \quad \text{(m is used defined real number, m} \neq 1,) \quad (2.1)$$

subject to $\sum_{j=1}^{K} u_{ij} = 1, \quad i = 1,2,...,n$

For numeric data v_j is computer in following manner.

$$v_{jp} = \sum_{i=1}^{n} (u_{ij})^m X_{ip} / \sum_{i=1}^{n} (u_{ij})^m \quad \text{(for numeric data)}$$

where d_{ij} is the distance from sample X_i to cluster center v_j(Normally Euclidean distance is used for numeric data). The computation of d_{ij} is different for numeric data and categorical data.

$$u_{ij} = 1 / (\sum_{k=1}^{K} (d_{ij}/d_{kj})^{1/(m-1)}) \quad (2.2)$$

The steps for FCM based algorithm are following

Step 1- Choose a threshold value ε. Initialize the fuzzy partition matrix U by generating nxK random numbers in the interval [0,1].
do
Step 2- Compute v_j (1<=j<=K) cluster center.
Step 3- Compute all d_{ij} and then all u_{ij}. Thus update the fuzzy partition matrix U by the new computed u_{ij} using (2.2).
Step 4- Compute the objective function J by using (2.1).

While(the difference between two adjacent computed values of objective function J is more than the given than the given threshold ε).

3 Distance Between Two Categorical Values ($\delta(x,y)$)

Huang and Ng [24] developed fuzzy K-mode algorithm for categorical data with binary distance measure. Kim et al. [25] developed fuzzy clustering algorithm with fuzzy centroid for categorical data. They also used binary distance measure. They took the value equal to $\delta(x,y)=1$ for $x \neq y$. and $\delta(x,y)=0$ for x=y. In our proposed algorithm $\delta(x,y)$ is not to be either 0 or 1 rather it depends upon the distribution of data objects in different clusters. Since distribution of data objects in different clusters changes until clusters stabilize, $\delta(x,y)$ changes values between iteration.

Amir and Lipika [27] proposed new distance measure between pair of categorical values for same attribute for K- mean type algorithm for the mixed data. We have extended that approach for FCM. Amir and Lipika [27] suggested that the distance between two categorical attribute values can be computed in following way.

Let us assume that x and y are two categorical values of ath attribute which is categorical attribute.

$$\delta(x,y) = (1/K)(\sum_{c=1}^{K} |(N_{a,x,c} - N_{a,y,c})/ N_c|)$$

$N_{a,x,c}$ is the number of data objects in Dataset that have the value x for the ath attribute and the data object belongs to cluster c.

N_c is the number of data objects in Dataset that belong to cluster c.

$(1/K)$ term is introduced to make $\delta(x,y)$ between 0 and 1. $\delta(x,y)$ can take any value between 0 and 1.

Some of the properties of $\delta(x,y)$
1- $0 <= \delta(x,y) <= 1$
2- $\delta(x,y) = \delta(y,x)$
3- $\delta(x,x) = 0$

Table 3.1. Dataset

Data Object	Attribute value for 1st attribue	Membership For cluster C	Membership For cluster C'
1	α	0.3	0.7
2	α	0.6	0.4
3	β	0.4	0.6
4	α	0.2	0.8
5	β	0.3	0.7
6	β	0.9	0.1

For FCM type algorithm where membership of data objects is fuzzy we can compute $N_{a,x,c}$, which we will call association of value x for the ath attribute with cluster c, in following way

$$N_{a,x,c} = \sum_{i=1}^{n} 1(x=a)(u_{ij})^m \quad (j^{th} \text{ cluster is c })$$

where $1(x=a) = 1$ for data objects having a^{th} attribute value = x
$= 0$ for data objects having a^{th} attribute value $\neq$ x

N_c is computed in following manner.

$$N_c = \sum_{i=1}^{n} (u_{ij})^m \quad (\text{ where } j^{th} \text{ cluster is c})$$

For data set given in Table 3.1, computation of $N_{a,x,c}$ is shown for attribute value α belonging to attribute 1 and cluster C,
$$N_{1,\alpha,C} = (0.3)^m + (0.6)^m + (0.2)^m.$$

3.1 Significance of Attributes for the Numeric Attributes

Another potentially useful concept is significance of the numeric attributes, which is important not only for the numeric datasets but also for the mixed datasets. Numeric attributes contribute differently for the cluster decision so we need to know the significance of attributes. To compute the significance of numeric attribute, we discretize the numeric attribute. Suppose we have S intervals each of the intervals can be taken as one categorical attribute value. We compute $\delta(x,y)$ for every pair of values. Intuitively if $\delta(x,y)$ value is high for most of the pairs the attribute will be significant. The average value of $\delta(x,y)$ for all pairs will be taken as significance of the attribute. For the categorical attributes we do not need computation of significance of the attribute because it is included in the distance between two categorical values.

4 Modified Center and the Distance from the Modified Center

The problem with Fuzzy c-means algorithm for categorical data set is that we cannot find the mean of categorical values. For categorical attributes the mean is replaced by the mode. Since we are taking only one attribute value as a representation of cluster for that categorical attribute. There will be information loss. In our proposed algorithm we have used the cluster center concept proposed by Yasser El-Sonbaty and M. A. Ismail [26]. We define center C for given cluster c for a^{th} categorical attribute as

$$1/N_c \{(N_{a,\ Aa,1,c}A_{a,1}), (N_{a,\ Aa,2,\ c}A_{a,2}), \ldots, (N_{a,\ Aa,h,c}A_{a,h})\} \quad (4.1)$$

$A_{a,p}$ is the pth attribute value of ath atrribute

$N_{a,Aa,p,c}$ is association of value $A_{a,p}$ for the ath attribute with cluster c
h is the number of distinct attribute values in a^{th} attribute

where $N_c = \sum_{i=1}^{n} (u_{ij})^m$ (where j^{th} cluster is c)

method to compute $N_{a,Aa,p,c}$ is described in section 3.

For data set with one-dimensional categorical data, the distance between data objects with attribute value X and center C for given cluster c (Eq. (4.1)) can be defined as

$$\Omega(X, C) = (1/N_c)((N_{a,Aa,1,c}\delta(X,A_{a,1}) + (N_{a,\ Aa,2,c}\delta(X,A_{a,2})+\ldots+ ((N_{a,\ Aa,h,c}\delta(X,A_{a,h})) \quad (4.2)$$

$\delta(x,y)$ is computed by the method as suggested in section 3.

For the numeric data the mean is computed in following way. Assume we have n objects $X_1, X_2, \ldots, X_n$ belonging to cluster center center j with degree of membership $u_{1j}, u_{2j}, \ldots u_{nj}$.

For p^{th} attribute which is numeric cluster center for cluster j is calculated in following manner,

$$C_{jp} = \sum_{i=1}^{n} (u_{ij})^m X_{ip} / \sum_{i=1}^{n} (u_{ij})^m \quad (4.3)$$

For mixed data set with s attributes (s_r numeric attributes, s_c categorical attributes, $s = s_r + s_c$) We define the distance between D_i data object and C_j the cluster center as

$$(d_{ij})^2 = \sum_{t=1}^{s_r} (w_t (D_{it}^r - C_{jt}^r))^2 + \sum_{t=1}^{s_c} (\Omega (D_{it}^c, C_{jt}^c))^2 \quad (4.4)$$

D_{it}^r are values of the numeric attributes. Whereas D_{it}^c are values of the categorical attributes for data object D_j. Here $C_j = (C_{j1}, C_{j2},...,C_{js})$ is the representative vector for cluster j. C_{jt}^r represents mean of numeric attribute t and cluster j. C_{jt}^c is modified center for j^{th} cluster as defined above for t^{th} categorical attribute. For the numeric attribute we have Euclidean distance measure with w_t term, which defines the significance of attribute of tth attribute(feature weight). For the categorical attributes we use the distance measure defined in Eq. 4.2. For numeric distance we take normalized distance to keep every numeric attribute on same scale (between 0 and 1). The distance between any two-attribute values will be between zero and one. It will be true for every attribute whether it is numeric attribute or categorical attribute.

5 Our Proposed Algorithm

Our proposed algorithm Fuzzy_clustering has following steps.

Fuzzy_Clustering()
Choose a threshold value ε. Initialize the fuzzy partition matrix U by generating nxK random numbers in the interval [0,1].
  Do

For every categorical attribute
Compute distance δ(p,q) between every pairs of categorical values p and q using distribution of data objects in different clusters.

For every numeric attribute
Compute significance of attribute using distribution of data objects in different clusters.
Compute v_j (1<=j<=K) modified cluster center.
Compute all d_{ij} using eq. 4.2 and then all u_{ij}. Thus update the fuzzy partition matrix U by the new computed u_{ij}.
Compute the objective function J by using (2.1).

While (the difference between two adjacent computed values of objective function J is greater than the given than the given threshold ε).

5.1 Complexity of the Algorithm

The proposed algorithm has following steps for each iteration,

(a) Computation of the distance between two categorical attributes values- This step needs reading of two columns (attribute column, class column) s times where s is the number of attributes. This will take sn steps where n is the number of data objects. Computation of the distance between two categorical attributes values after reading will at most take $S^2 Ks$ steps where S is the maximum number of distinct attribute values, K is number of classes hence the total steps will be $O(sn + S^2 Ks)$.

(b) Computation of distance between data object and *modified center*

    (i) For the numeric attributes it will take s_r steps where s_r is the number of numeric attributes.

    (ii) For the categorical values it will take at most $s_c S$ steps where s_c is the number of categorical attributes and S is the maximum number of distinct attribute values.

(c) Step b is to be repeated K times since we are computing distance for K *modified centers*.

(d) Steps b and c will be repeated for n data objects.

Total number of steps will be $nK(s_r + s_c S)$ for steps b, c and d.

For each iteration computation will take $O(sn + S^2 Ks + nKs_r + nKs_c S)$. If there are p iterations, computational cost of this algorithm is $O(p(sn + S^2 Ks + nKs_r + nKs_c S))$ which is linear with respect to number of data objects.

6 Experiments

In this paper we proposed concepts of new distance measure between data point and *modified center* for mixed data. We used normalization scheme presented in [28] for numeric attributes. For i^{th} attribute and j^{th} pattern normalized value of x_{ij} is k_{ij}

    where $k_{ij} = (x_{ij} - x_{i,min}) / (x_{i,max} - x_{i,min})$

($x_{i,min}$, $x_{i,max}$ are minimum and maximum values of ith attribute respectively)

We used equal width discretization (interval = Range of the attribute values of A_i / Number of distinct intervals of attribute A_i (S)) for the converting numeric data into categorical data to compute significance of the numeric attributes. We have taken the value of $S=5$ unless specified otherwise. We used algorithm proposed in section 5 to cluster four data sets Iris (numeric), Soybean (categorical), DNA (categorical) and Cleveland heart disease (mixed data) to see the effectiveness of our proposed algorithm. These data were taken from UCI repository (http://www.sgi.com/tech/mlc/db). Value of m is taken as 1.8 for all experiments for our proposed algorithm. We compared our results with different algorithms (mostly Fuzzy c-mean type algorithms) that are used for different types of datasets (pure numeric dataset, pure categorical dataset, mixed dataset).

6.1 Iris Dataset

It has 150 data objects defined by 4 numeric attributes. These data objects are equally distributed in 3 classes (Iris Setosa, Iris Versicolour and Iris Virginica) with Iris Versicolour, Iris Virginica classes are having some overlap. For the numeric data set our distance function will become $(d_{ij})^2 = \sum_{t=1}^{S_r} (w_t(d_{it}^r - C_{jt}^r))^2$. This is similar to Euclidean distance cost function for FCM. The only difference is inclusion of weight function w_t in our proposed cost function. It is quite logical because every attribute contribute differently towards the cluster assignment. We carried out clustering 100 times and average clustering results are shown in table 6.1. Clustering results suggest significantly improved results with our proposed algorithm as compared to FCM. This suggests the importance of inclusion of significance of attributes in cost function. It also shows the slight improvement over WFCM [23] in which feature weight learning has $O(cn^2)$ time complexity. In our proposed algorithm Feature-weight changes in every iteration, We computed the average feature weight in last iteration of 100 runs. Comparative results with other algorithms are presented in table 6.1.

Table 6.1. Clustering results for Iris data

Algorithm	Feature - Weight	Error rate
FCM	1, 1, 1, 1	15/150
WFCM[23]	0.0001, 0.0002, 1.0, 0.164	8/150
Our proposed algorithm	0.629, 0.597, 0.856, 0.804	6/150

6.2 Soybean Dataset

It is pure categorical data. It contains 47 data points on disease in soybean. Each data point has 35 categorical attributes and is classified as one of the following four diseases: Diaporthe Stem Canker, Charcoal Rot, Rhizoctonia Root Rot and Phytophthora Rot. Phytophthora Rot has 17 data, and rest three other disease have 10 data each. Clustering results of various algorithms are given in table 6.2. Each algorithm was run 100 times. Clustering results in table 6.2 shows the performance of our algorithm is better than K-mode [29], Fuzzy K-mode [24] (m= 1.1) and Fuzzy clustering with fuzzy centroids [25] (m= 1.8) algorithms.

Table 6.2. Clustering results for Soybean data set

Algorithm	Number of time we get correct classification
K-mode [29]	12/100
Fuzzy K-mode [24]	15/100
Fuzzy clustering with fuzzy centroids [25]	87/100
Our proposed algorithm	92/100

6.2.1 Classification of Boundary Data

One of the most difficult problems in clustering is the classification of boundary data objects. To investigate the clustering of the boundary data objects by the last two algorithms considered above, we examined four boundary data (in most of the runs K-mode algorithm and Fuzzy K-mode algorithm fail to cluster the data points correctly) obtained from the clustering results of the Soybean data set. In table 6.3 the distance between the data and centroid are listed. We may observe (we have highlighted the distance between the data objects and the nearest cluster center and the second nearest cluster center) that although both algorithms cluster boundary data objects correctly, with our proposed distance measure we can classify data objects in different cluster more easily. That improves clustering results.

Table 6.3. Distance between boundary data objects and cluster center

Algorithm	Data (D_i)	Distances between data object and Cluster center				Allotted Cluster
		Distance from 1st cluster center	Distance from 2nd cluster center	Distance from 3rd cluster center	Distance from 4rt cluster center	
Fuzzy clustering with fuzzy centroids [25]	D_3	**6.86**	12.94	**11.43**	11.43	1
	D_{23}	10.70	15.27	**8.32**	**8.36**	3
	D_{25}	9.99	14.34	**7.64**	**7.67**	3
	D_{29}	11.31	15.25	**10.13**	**10.17**	3
Our proposed Algorithm	D_3	**1.14**	4.89	**4.26**	4.53	1
	D_{23}	4.64	5.85	**1.03**	**3.58**	3
	D_{25}	4.40	5.68	**1.03**	**3.36**	3
	D_{29}	4.38	5.64	**2.05**	**4.21**	3

6.3 DNA Dataset

It is pure categorical data. It has 3186 data objects, which is defined by 60 DNA sequence elements (A, C, G, T). These data objects are devided into three categories, intron(767), exon(765) and none(1654). Each algorithm was run for 100 times. With K-mode and Fuzzy K-mode we could not find any reasonable clustering. Performance of our proposed algorithm was better than Fuzzy clustering with fuzzy centroids [25] algorithm(table- 6.4).

6.4 Heart Disease Dataset

This data generated, at the Cleveland Clinic, contains a mixture of categorical and numeric features. This data set consists of 303 patients instances defined by 13 features. Five of these are numeric valued features, and eight are categorical-valued features. It has two classes, normal (164) and heart patient (139). Li et al. [9] presented a Similarity Based Agglomerative Clustering (SBAC) algorithm for mixed data. They used heart disease data to show the effectiveness of their algorithm. Comparison with other algorithm ECOWEB [14] is also shown in their paper. They used static method (Expected range of the attribute values of A_i / Expected number of distinct intervals of attribute A_i (n)) and n=8 to compute the interval for ECOWEB. We took those published results for comparison. We used equal width discretization to compute significance of attributes for numeric attributes. Average number of distinct attributes values(for categorical attributes) is taken as number of intervals, which is ≈3 for heart disease data set. We executed our clustering algorithm 100 times. Table 6.5 shows the clustering results obtained by using Similarity Based Agglomerative Clustering (SBAC) [9], ECOWEB [14], Huang's Algorithm [18] and proposed algorithm. Comparative study reveals that the clustering result obtained by our proposed algorithm is comparable with the results obtain with computationally costly SBAC and ECOWEB and much better than Huang's Algorithm.

Table 6.4. Clustering results for DNA dataset

Algorithm	Number of data objects correctly classification (%)
K-mode [29]	36.3
Fuzzy K-mode [24]	38.4
Fuzzy clustering with fuzzy centroids [25]	61.5
Our proposed algorithm	74.7

Table 6.5. Clustering results for heart dataset

Algorithm	Number of data objects correctly classification (%)
SBAC [9]	75.2
ECOWEB [14]	73.9
Huang's Algorithm [18]	58.3
Our proposed algorithm	74.6

7 Conclusion

A fuzzy c-mean type clustering algorithm has been developed to cluster mixed data with numeric and categorical data. This clustering algorithm also works well for pure numeric or pure categorical data. We have proposed a probabilistic distance measure to compute the distance between two categorical values that will depend on distribution of data objects in different clusters. Using this concept we can compute feature weight for the numeric attributes in linear time. Comparative study with other clustering algorithms (mostly Fuzzy c-mean type algorithms) illustrates the effectiveness of this approach.

References

1. Fayyad, U. M, Piatesky-Shapiro, G., Smyth, P., Uthurusamy R.:Advances in Knowledge Discovery and Data Mining. AAA1 press, 1996.
2. Gersho and Gray Vector Quantization and Signal Compression. KAP, 1992.
3. 3. Can, F., Ozkarahan,E.:A Dynamic Cluster Maintenance System for Information Retrieval. In Proceedings of the Tenth Annual International ACM SIGIR Conference, (1987), pp. 123-131.
4. Arotaritei, D., Mitra, S. : Web mining: a survey in the fuzzy frame work. Fuzzy Sets and Systems, Volume 148, Issue 1,(2004), Pages 5-19.
5. MacQuuen, J. B.:Some Methods for Classification and Analysis of Multivariate Observation, In Proceedings of the 5th Berkley Symposium on Mathematical Statistics and Probability, (1967), pp 281-297.
6. Gower., J. C.:A General Coefficient of Similarity and Some of its Properties BioMetrics, 27, (1971), pp. 857-874.
7. Jain, A.K., Dubes, R. C.: Algorithms for Clustering Data. Prentice Hall, Englewood Cliff, New Jersey, 1988.
8. Everitt, B.:Cluster Analysis. Heinemann Educational Books Ltd, 1974.
9. Li, C., Biswas, G.: Unsupervised Learning with Mixed Numeric and Nominal Data. IEEE Transactions on Knowledge and Data Engineering, vol. 14, no. 4, (2002), pp. 673-690.
10. Goodall, D. W.: A New similarity Index Based on Probability. Biometric, Vol. 22, (1966), pp.882-907.
11. Fisher, D. H.:Knowledge Acquisition Via Incremental Conceptual Clustering. Machine Learning, **2**(2)(1987) pp. 139-172.
12. Lebowitz, M.: Experiments with Incremental Concept Formation, Machine Learning 2(2), (1987), pp.103-138.
13. McKusick, K., Thomson, K.: COBWEB/3: A portable Implementation. Technical Report FIA-90-6-18-2. NASA Ames Research Center. 1990.
14. Y. Reich and S. J. Fenves, The Formation and Use of Abstract Concepts in Design. Concept formation: Knowledge and Experience in Unsupervised Learning, D.H. Fisher, M. J. Pazzani, and P. Langley, (Editors)(1991) pp. 323-352, Los Altos, Calif: Morgan Kaufmann.
15. Biswas, G., Weingberg J., Fisher, D. H.: ITERAE: A Conceptual Clustering Algorithm for Data Mining. IEEE Trans. Systems, Man, and Cybernetics, vol. 28C (1998) pp.219-230.
16. Gluck, M., Corter, J.: Information, Uncertainty, and the Utility of Categories. Proc. Seventh Ann. Conf. Cognitive Soc., (1985) pp. 283-287.
17. Cheesman, P., Stutz, J.: Baysian Classification (AUTO-CLASS): Theory and Results. Advances in Knowledge Discovery and Data Mining .1995.
18. Huang, Z.: Clustering Large Data sets with Mixed Numeric and Categorical Values, In Proceedings of The First Pacific-Asia Conference on Knowledge Discovery and Data Mining. Singapore. World Scientific, 1997.
19. Dunn, J. C.: Some recent investigations of a new fuzzy algorithm and its application to pattern classification problems. J. Cybernetics 4(1974) 1-15.
20. Bezdek, J. C.:Pattern recognition with fuzzy Objective Function algorithms, Plenum, New York, 1981.
21. Zhao, S. Y.: Calculus and Clustering. China Renming University Press, 1987.
22. Krishnapuram, R., Kim, J.: A note on the Gustafsno-Kessel and adaptive fuzzy clustering. IEEE Trans. Fuzzy Syst., 7, (1999) pp. 453-461.

23. Wang, X., Wang Y., Wang L.: Improving fuzzy c-means clustering based on feature-weight learning, Pattern Recognition Letters 25 (2004) pp.1123–1132.
24. Huang, Z.,. Ng, M. K : A fuzzy k-modes algorithm for clustering categorical data. IEEE Trans. Fuzzy Systems, 7(4). 1999.
25. Kim Dae-Won, Lee, K. H., Lee, D.:Fuzzy Clustering of categorical data using fuzzy centroids, Pattern recognition Letters, 25(2004) pp.1263-1271.
26. Sonbaty ,Yaseer Ei, M. A Ismail,: Fuzzy Clustering for Symbolic data. IEEE Transaction on Fuzzy Systems, Vol. 6, No. 2. 1998.
27. Ahmad, A., Dey, L.:A K-means Clustering Algorithm for Mixed Numeric and Categorical Data Set Using Dynamic Distance Measure, Proc. of Fifth International Conference on Advances in Pattern recognition, ICAPR2003, 2003.
28. Witten H. I., Frank, E.:Data Mining Practical Machine Learning Tools and Techniques with Java Implementation. San Fransisco, CA: Morgon Kaufmann Publishers. 2000.
29. Huang, Z.:Extensions to the K-modes algorithm for clustering large data sets with categorical values, Data Min. Knowl. Dis. 2(3),1998.

Dissemination of Multidimensional Data Using Broadcast Clusters

Ilias Michalarias[1,2] and Hans-J. Lenz[1]

[1] Institute of Production, Information Systems and Operations Research,
Free University Berlin, Garystr. 21, 14195 Berlin, Germany
{ilmich, hjlenz}@wiwiss.fu-berlin.de
[2] Berlin-Brandenburg Graduate School in Distributed Information Systems

Abstract. The multidimensional modeling of data is steadily gaining popularity, finding adoption not only for business but for scientific applications as well. Data Warehousing is the most prominent example of multidimensional data usage. In parallel, wireless networks, with their rapid growth, already play a fundamental role in facilitating time critical decision-making. Nevertheless, their inherent shortcomings, but also those of the mobile devices operating within their proximity, introduce additional complexity. Access time and energy consumption become, among others, factors that should be taken into consideration. This paper deals with the efficient dissemination of multidimensional data into wireless networks. In this context, a new family of scheduling algorithms, which simultaneously exploits various characteristics both of OLAP data and wireless networks, is introduced. These algorithms clearly outperform existing proposals, on all counts: average access time, energy consumption and network utilization.

1 Introduction

Modeling of data in a multidimensional way came up as an idea, due to the inappropriate nature of the relational model, when vast volumes of data must be first summarized, in order to answer pertinent queries. Such queries are typically used, to enhance decision-making in major enterprises. Data Warehousing and OLAP applications, being a major research area in the last decade, constitute an indispensable part of what is described as business intelligence. The significance of having good and actual information is nowadays more than ever, a key factor for the success of every commercial corporation.

Meanwhile, the mobile and wireless industry has already surpassed its infancy, having matured to a point, where wide-scale adoption is not unrealistic. Demand for mobile technology is growing at a tremendous rate. Organizations are deploying mobile applications because substantial business benefits can be safely assumed. Vendors of mobile devices constantly produce devices with enhanced features, while wireless networks already provide access to data from almost anywhere. This progress poses new challenges for existing applications, since the former are frequently influenced by inherent characteristics of mobility.

In this paper, an effort to bring together two different technologies is sustained, with the goal to enhance $mOLAP$ (mobile-OLAP). Some interesting contradictions arise. On the one hand, OLAP applications usually require intense computations and powerful machines, while on the other hand, in the wireless world, despite the prodigious improvement and enhancement of networks and devices, there is by no means abundance of necessary resources. Devices like PDAs cannot compete with desktop computers, as far as computational power or storage capacity is concerned. Therefore different strategies should be employed, in regard to efficient dissemination of multidimensional data in mobile clients.

It shall become more obvious in following sections of this paper that there exists a trade-off problem when trying to build such systems: there is a trade-off between actual system resources, such as network utilization, overall access time for each request and client energy consumption. Simultaneous optimizing all of these measures is not a trivial issue. We focus on the design of scheduling algorithms, which extend their functionality beyond the classical scheduling paradigm, taking into consideration many system parameters that are crucial for the system efficiency. A traditional scheduler, dealing with incoming requests for any kind of data, primarily concerns about minimizing the average access time. When dealing with mOLAP queries, it will be shown that this is neither rational nor optimal. In this context, we introduce a new family of scheduling algorithms, under the name *FCLOS (Force Clustering OLAP Schedulers)*, which by exploiting various characteristics both of multidimensional data and wireless technologies, outperformed existing proposals, exhibiting in average a 40% reduction of access time, a 15% reduction of energy consumption and a 35% reduction of the total amount of transmitted data.

The remainder of the paper is structured as follows: In Section 2, we describe some fundamental mOLAP architectures and present how some properties of multidimensional data, can be exploited in wireless networks by using broadcasting. In Section 3, we give a short description of existing scheduling algorithms. In Section 4, we introduce our new family of scheduling algorithms under the name *FCLOS* and in Section 5 we present our experimental simulation results. In Section 6, we conclude our results and present topics for future work.

2 Background

2.1 mOLAP Architectures

One could think of two fundamental architectures, where mOLAP functionality is provided. Let us describe these briefly without, for the time being, going into thorough details. Naturally we do not cite the case where a mobile client merely uses a web browser to query OLAP data. A fundamental requirement for mOLAP is offline operation functionality, which cannot be provided in this case. We assume that clients store incoming data locally, not only to allow offline operations, but also to accelerate subsequent queries. The first architecture consists of a central server facility, which typically resides in an application server, and several mobile clients. This is shown in Fig.1a. Mobile clients pose queries to one or more data cubes. We assume that the server is able to respond to any incoming query referring to a data cube, either by having already stored all possible sub-cubes, or by retrieving them from the backend data warehouse, when necessary. In other words, there is no direct connection from the client to the data warehouse. The server is responsible for answering all incoming queries. No communication between clients is assumed. We assume that there is a single broadcast channel that is monitored by all clients and that the channel is fully dedicated to the data broadcast (i.e., the data server can use the entire bandwidth), and of course a uplink channel for posing requests. Clients continuously monitor the downlink channel after making a request, to check for requested data.

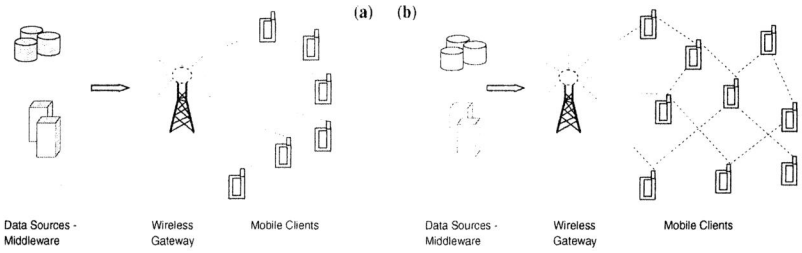

Fig. 1. Two fundamental mOLAP architectures

A second architecture extends the previous one, by enabling clients to directly communicate with each other, in order to minimize connections with the central server. This is quite rational, since this would not only be more efficient, in terms of access time, but it could also be favorable in economical terms, as many wireless networks are volume based. This architecture is depicted in Fig.1b. In this paper we tackle with issues arising in the first architecture, since the majority of existing systems use this infrastructure based scenario (WLAN, GSM, UMTS). Moreover, research regarding the second one, is part of ongoing work of our group.

2.2 Data Modeling

Multidimensional modeling is based on the notion of the data cube. The cube operator produces a data cube, which is the union of all possible *Group-By* operators applied on a fact table [1, 2]. The notion of the data cube lattice (*DCL*) came up from the research area that focuses on designing efficient algorithms for the computation of the complete data cube. It is a directed graph that depicts the relationships between all 2^N sub-cubes in a given N-dimensional space. In Fig.2 a 3-dimensional space is depicted. The three dimensional attributes are *Product, Time* and *Store*. Each of every 8 possible sub-cubes is represented in the lattice by one node.

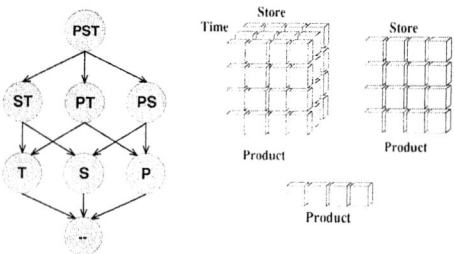

Fig. 2. A Data Cube Lattice for a 3-dimensional Space and some visualized views

A fundamental distinctive of OLAP queries is that it is often possible to reuse the results of queries to answer other queries. This property, which stems from the semantics of the multidimensional model, is called subsumption. The arcs in the data cube lattice represent exactly this relationship. Generally, a sub-cube can be derived by another sub-cube, when there is a path in the *DCL* that connects the nodes that represent these sub-cubes. For example, one can derive the sub-cube *PS (Product, Store)* in the *DCL* from the *PST (Product, Store, Time)* sub-cube, plainly by aggregating over the dimension *Time*.

This derivation is permissible for distributive (inductive) aggregation functions such as sum, min, max or count, but not allowed for algebraic functions such as average or covariance [3, 4] and not for holistic functions like median. For algebraic functions additional information is required so as to derive sub-cubes. For example if avg is used, then the number of tuples (count) is additionally required. In the context of mOLAP, we typically assume that the sum function is used, but that is plausibly not restrictive.

2.3 Broadcasting – Multicasting

Broadcasting is the process in which one node participating in a network sends a packet to all other nodes in the network. In wireless networks, broadcasting gains additional significance, since it is one of the most common operations on the wireless link. Broadcasting can be used for server detection, name resolution, and name reservation, among others.

In general, there are two modes of data dissemination in wireless networks, the push model and the pull model. Using push, data items are sent out to the clients, without explicit requests, whereas using pull data items come in response to explicit requests. Pull can be used either for unicast or for broadcast and is also referred as on-demand broadcast. The transmission of data is initiated by client request and not based on profiles or subscriptions [5]. It has been long argued that push is more beneficial than pull since it provides tremendous scalability. Nevertheless, mOLAP assumes a pull model.

In the context of mOLAP, broadcasting or multicasting can prove very beneficial, since they can, in conjunction with cube subsumption property, improve the system performance. In the architectures described in the previous section, there is a wireless gateway, which acts as the connection point bridging the wired and wireless world. The gateway can use broadcasting to answer queries posed by several clients and thus reduce consumption of system resources. Instead of establishing two separate connections with two clients, that have requested sub-cubes, which are connected in the *DCL*, the gateway broadcasts the bigger sub-cube and both clients are being served. One could think of this procedure as a multicast, since we assume that the mobile clients that are not interested in the transmitted sub-cube simply deny the incoming packets.

Typically as far as the packet content is concerned, the sub-cubes can be represented as a binary number, consisting of so many digits as the number of dimensional attributes N. When a dimensional attribute is contained in the sub-cube, the corresponding digit is 1, else 0. This is just one way, with which a mobile client can interpret the metadata of the transmitted data, but naturally many others exist. For security reasons different representations could be applied.

Obviously, the central server must be able to make intelligent decisions, about the sequence with which incoming queries are answered. A naive approach would be to adopt a point-to-point model, where no scheduler and no queue are necessary. The available bandwidth is divided into as many channels as the incoming requests. Each query is immediately served, without spending time in a queue. No scheduler is required. Naturally such systems exhibit poor performance.

3 Related Work

In the context of mOLAP, Hand-OLAP, [6], is a proposed system for delivering OLAP functionality to mobile clients. In this approach, issues of compression and summarization of data have a leading role. The main purpose of this system is to allow a handheld device to request a bulk of information coming from an OLAP server distributed on a wired network, and store the received (compressed) data locally, in order to query the received information off-line. Cube View, [7], is an academic prototype system, which provides a generic approach, towards the visualization of OLAP data, both on desktop systems and mobile devices. The focus is on the efficient presentation of data, using non-traditional visualization techniques. In the research field of scheduling, in [8] it was pointed out for the first time, that traditional FCFS (First In First Out) scheduling provides a poor average wait time for a broadcast environment, when the access distribution for data items was non-uniform. Several algorithms aimed at providing improved performance. Other algorithms studied can be found in [8, 9]. The $R \times W$ algorithm was introduced in [10]. It provides fine performance across all of these criteria and can be tuned to trade off average and worst-case waiting time. This algorithm does not use estimates of the access probabilities of items, but rather, makes scheduling decisions based on the current queue state, allowing it to easily adapt to changes in the intensity and distribution of the workload. All of them are generic approaches, and generally inappropriate for multidimensional data.

STOBS-a (Summary Tables On-Demand Broadcast scheduler) is the inaugural approach explicitly dealing with dissemination of multidimensional information, where scheduling decisions take into consideration additional parameters such as energy consumption [11]. *STOBS-a* exploits the derivation semantics among OLAP summary tables. *STOBS-a* maximizes the aggregated data sharing between mobile users and reduces the broadcast length. An optimizer is used to control the tradeoff between experienced access time and the energy consumption overhead.

STOBS-a consists of two components. The first component is a prioritizing function based on the popular queue metric $R \times W/S$ [10], where R is the number of requests for a specific sub-cube, W is a factor computed by the time a request has already waited in the queue and S is the size of the sub-cube. The idea is quite straightforward. Initially the $R \times W/S$ metric is computed for each element of the queue and then the sub-cube tr with the maximum metric value is selected for transmission:

$$\forall j \in Queue \quad K_j = \frac{R_j \times W_j}{S_j}, \quad tr := arg\ max(K_j) \qquad (1)$$

The second component controls the degree of flexibility when trying to derive subsumptions. This is done by the a optimizer. *BCL* is the group or cluster of requests that are going to be served by the broadcast. D_j and D_i stand for the dimensionalities of sub-cubes j and i respectively.

$$\forall i \in Queue : i \neq j,\ if\ i\ derivable\ from\ j\ and\ D_j - D_i \leq a\ add\ i\ to\ BCL \qquad (2)$$

For example, use *DCL* of Fig.2, and let $a = 1$, then sub-cube *ST* can be clustered with *PST* whereas *S* cannot. Note, that if $a>2$ then *S* could be clustered with *PST*. *STOBS-a* undisputedly exhibits a superior performance than a point-to-point model [11]. The a-optimizer provides a fairly satisfying flexibility. Despite that, the algorithm does not at all take into account the nature of the transmitted data, which is in this case OLAP summary tables, at least at the first step, namely the prioritizing function. Typically cube querying consists of drill downs or roll ups. This is essentially ignored since only the size of the sub-cube is used in the prioritizing function. However, the size does not offer any particular metadata information. In addition to that, the two components (prioritizing and optimizing) are completely independent. The clustering of requests succeeds, only after the sub-cube to be transmitted has been already selected. As a result, clustering is rather loose. This is justified by the fact, that smaller in size sub-cubes have generally priority. When smaller sub-cubes are selected from the first component to be transmitted, the possibility of making clusters becomes smaller. In the following section we will describe a new proposal, which adopts a more aggressive behavior, as far as the grouping of queries is concerned. We will directly compare our proposal with *STOBS-a*, since there is currently no other proposal, which outperforms it.

4 FCLOS

FCLOS (Force Clustering OLAP Scheduler) is a new family of scheduling algorithms, towards efficient dissemination of multidimensional data into wireless networks. *FCLOS* actively exploits both the metadata of multidimensional sub-cubes and the broadcasting operation of the physical layer in wireless networks, in order to reduce query access time, energy consumption and total number of bytes transmitted through the network.

A prioritizing function and an optimizer are also used, like in the case of *STOBS-a*, but in a totally different way. In *FCLOS* we make use of a new metric *SM (Sub-cube Metric)*:

$$SM = R \times W \times D \tag{3}$$

where R and W have the same meaning described in [11], in order to weigh all the elements of the queue. D represents the dimensionality of a sub-cube. Since the dimensionality of a sub-cube is generally proportional to its size, *SM* distinguishes itself from other metrics in the fact that the dimensionality (or the size) is now a positive prioritizing factor. Dissimilarly, bigger in size sub-cubes now obtain higher priority. Then for each element j (sub-cube) in the queue, its *SM* is computed:

$$\forall j \in Queue \quad SM_j = R_j \times W_j \times D_j \tag{4}$$

Then, still without having decided which sub-cube is going to be actually transmitted, in other words without considering *SM* at all, every possible clustering *BCL (Broadcast Cluster)* is detected. A broadcast cluster consists of one parent and its children. The *parent node* in a broadcast cluster is the sub-cube, from which all other sub-cubes comprising the *BCL* can be derived, according to the criteria of Eq. (2). Obviously, for this detection we also use a similar optimizer, which essentially works exactly as the optimizer in *STOBS-a*. With this, we control the degree of flexibility, when trying to detect broadcast clusters. After having identified all possible *BCLs* we employ a new metric under the name *BW (Broadcast Weight)*. *BW* practically represents the weight not of one specific element in the queue, but the one of a potential broadcast cluster. If k represents a sub-cube belonging to an identified *BCL* then the *BW* of that specific *BCL* is defined as:

$$BW = \sum_{k \in BCL} SM_k \tag{5}$$

Our algorithm computes for each identified BCL_n, its respective BW_n:

$$\forall BCL \quad BW_n = \sum_{k \in BCL_n} SM_k \tag{6}$$

Eventually, what is actually transmitted is the parent node of the cluster BCL_{tr}, namely the cluster with the maximum *BW*. Reasonably all clients that have requested sub-cubes which belong to BCL_{tr} are served.

$$transmit\ parent\ node\ of\ BCL_{tr}\ :\quad BW_{tr} = max(BW_n) \tag{7}$$

Since we formally presented the algorithm, let us now explain the intuition behind *FCLOS*. The fundamental difference with existing approaches resides in the fact that the size of a sub-cube is a positive factor when prioritizing requests. Cube querying has the property, that new queries have high probability to be related with previous ones. In other words, slicing, dicing and drilling occur more often. *FCLOS* exploits this property. This will become clear with a simple example. Let us suppose that client A has requested the sub-cube S and client B sub-cube *PST*, according to Fig.2. For reasons of explanation, let us further assume that no other request exists in the queue. In *STOBS-a*, initially the sub-cube S will be transmitted, since its size is smaller than the size of *PST*, and after that *PST* will be transmitted. In *FCLOS* what is going to be initially transmitted is the sub-cube *PST*, and then there is apparently no need to transmit S, because client A has already got the necessary data to compute S.

By introducing our new metric BW and by separately detecting all possible clusters, *FCLOS* does not broadcast whenever this is possible but rather enforces it. This results in a better exploitation of the broadcasting feature, since quite expectedly the number of members of the served BCL_{tr} is now higher in average.

Results for new queries have now, higher probability that they already exist in client side, partly due to previous scheduling decisions taken by *FCLOS*. Naturally, we assume that clients that receive supersets of what was actually requested, store locally the additional data, and do not discard them, a fundamental idea behind the notion of mOLAP. The algorithm is summarized below:

Algorithm FCLOS

1: Compute SM for every Queue element (sub-cube)
2: Find all possible Clusters ($BCLs$), based on the optimizer a
3: Compute BW_k for every identified Cluster BCL_k
4: Transmit the parent node of the Cluster BCL_{tr}, whose BW_{tr} is maximum

---

5 Experimental Results

In order to analyse the performance of the algorithms, we implemented a simulation testbench, fully parameterized by all factors concerning mobile OLAP querying. We compared the *FCLOS* algorithms with the *STOBS-a* algorithms, in terms of average access time, energy consumption and network utilization.

Our simulation testbench consists of one server, which maintains the scheduler as well as the multidimensional data. Mobile clients query a specifically dimensional query space and pose a specific number of requests. When the answer is received, the client poses a new request. We use three measures to evaluate the algorithms:

- *Average Query Access Time:* The time that a request spends waiting in the server queue, incremented by the time the client is receiving data in his downlink channel being in an active mode incremented by the time spent for the aggregation, if one should be necessary.
- *Average Energy Consumption Overhead:* The energy a client consumes by waiting in a doze mode till the first packet that is directed to him appears in

the downlink channel, incremented by the energy spent listening the downlink channel and being in an active mode, incremented by the energy consumed for a possible aggregation.
- *Total Amount of Bytes sent:* Total amount of data disseminated by the server into the wireless network.

The multidimensional space is simulated as described in [12]. Summary tables are assumed to exist. Given a binary number bin as described in section 2.2, a sub-cube is allocated a size of:

$$size(sc) = min\{bin^2, Product\ of\ sizes\ of\ children(sc)\ in\ the\ lattice\} \quad (8)$$

This method guarantees diversity in the sub-cube sizes. We use Zipfian for the query distribution, where sub-cubes are sorted according to their sizes. Naturally sub-cubes with smaller sizes are more likely to be requested. We simulate the aggregation process as a plain scanning of the summary table, using the device CPU and memory bus. Energy consumption is captured using the $energy = power \times time$ equation. A typical wireless card from Socket [13], as well as common PDA specifications, has been used. All details are shown in Table 1. Default simulation parameters were applied, when comparing *FCLOS* with *STOBS-a*. Next, we evaluate the performance of *FCLOS*, using several values, regarding to cube dimensionality and query skewness.

Table 1. Simulation parameters

Simulation Parameter	Default	Range
Wireless Network	WLAN	-
Wireless Card Power supply	3,3 Volt	-
Wireless Card Idle/Receive Mode Consumption	20/170 mA	-
Device CPU	312 MHz	-
Device Memory Bus	64 bits	-
Cube Dimensionality	7	4-10
Mobile Clients	50	0-150
Requests posed by each client	30	10-50
Query Distribution	Zipf($\theta = 0,5$)	$\theta = 0,3$-$0,9$
Network Bandwidth	11Mbs	1-11Mbs

In the beginning, we compare the average access time experienced by a mobile client for a query. Fig.3 shows the results. The impact by increasing the number of mobile clients is not so strong for both of the algorithms, even if *FCLOS* proves to be more stable. By increasing the value of the a-optimizer, the superiority of *FCLOS* becomes clearer. For example if $a=2$, we have a 15% average reduction, whereas when $a=6$ the average reduction reaches to as high as 50%.

After that, we compare the average energy consumption overhead caused by a given query. Let it here be denoted, that the overhead produced by the aggregations in the mobile device is essentially negligible, though included in these

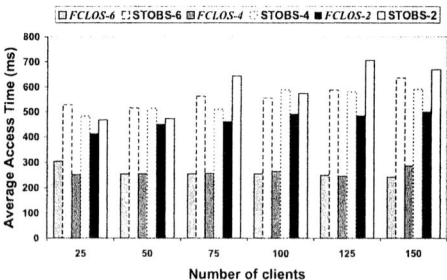

Fig. 3. *STOBS-a* vs *FCLOS* in terms of Average Access Time

results. The major overhead is produced when the client being in active mode receives data. Fig.4 shows the details. Even though the optimization is now not so impressive, as in the case of access time, *FCLOS* still exhibits better performance, proving that is actually feasible to simultaneously reduce access time and energy consumption. Again increasing the value of the a optimizer, positively influences *FCLOS*. When $a=2$, similar energy overheads, were observed. However, when $a=6$ the reduction reaches 25%.

Finally, we compare the two algorithm families in regard to the total amount of bytes transmitted in the network. This can be a very important factor, when volume based networks are used. Again *FCLOS* exhibits an average 40% reduction in actual transmitted data for higher values of a, as depicted in Fig.5. Let it be noted though, that when $a=2$, *FCLOS* exhibit essentially similar behaviors. By having such a little degree of flexibility, the benefits of *FCLOS* in terms of transmitted data are practically eliminated. The transmitted cluster serves not so many members as required, for the characteristics of *FCLOS* to be exploited.

The boost of the performance of *FCLOS*, with higher values for the a-optimizer comes rather unsurprisingly. By adopting a more aggressive strategy in terms of clustering of requests, *FCLOS* makes in average bigger clusters and subsequently the number of total bytes sent as well as the average access time (since the queue time is also reduced), are clearly reduced.

We also run simulations with several dimensions and degrees of query skewness. In Fig.6 and Fig.7 we present the percentage of reduction gain achieved over

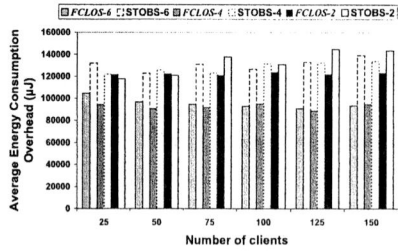

Fig. 4. *STOBS-a* vs *FCLOS* in terms of Average Energy Consumption

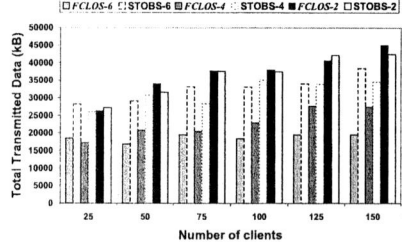

Fig. 5. *STOBS-a* vs *FCLOS* in terms of Total Transmitted Data to the Network

$STOBS$-a. The argument "-$FULL$" means that a is equal to the dimensionality, while the argument "-$/2$" means that a has the half value of the dimensionality. We include all three aforementioned measurements. Negative percentages indicate superiority of $FCLOS$, while positive superiority of $STOBS$-a.

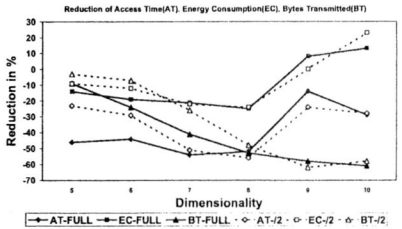
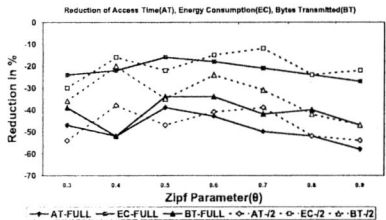

Fig. 6. Reduction achieved with different dimensionalities

Fig. 7. Reduction achieved for different query distributions

As far as dimensionality is concerned, $FCLOS$ exhibits poorer performance only in energy consumption overhead, when the dimensionality gets very big. This is quite rational, since the created clusters become very big in this case, and clients that have requested sub-cubes with small dimensionalities, spend a lot of time receiving data in the downlink channel, and thus consume energy. But even in this case, $FCLOS$ performs better in terms of average access time and total amount of bytes transmitted. We also tested the impact of the wireless bandwidth on the two algorithms. The results show no particular divergence in fractional figures.

6 Conclusions and Future Work

This paper deals with efficient dissemination of multidimensional data into wireless networks. We underlined the importance of multidimensional data, since ever growing volumes of data are being accumulated in traditional relational databases. It's major contribution is the introduction of a new family of scheduling algorithms for multidimensional data, under the name $FCLOS$, which clearly outperforms existing ones on all counts according to experimental objectives: average access time, energy consumption and network utilization, particularly when high scale clustering is used. We showed that inherent characteristics of OLAP data and wireless networks can be combined to accelerate query answering. We also reemphasized the potential benefits gained by using the subsumption property of sub-cubes, especially in wireless networks.

Future work will try to further investigate the role of the a-optimizer in the performance of $FCLOS$ algorithms, with the aim to gain additional energy gain. Our intuition suggests that a more dynamical definition could be beneficial. Simulation of more dynamic scenarios, concerning the number of mobile clients, request rate and query distributions may also prove helpful, to further optimize scheduling decisions.

Furthermore, future work will try to investigate scenarios, which appear in architectures shown in Fig.1b. Additional parameters to the problem of selecting which node will answer an incoming query must be taken into consideration, when comparing our approach with traditional querying. For example, routing is only one part of the selection criteria, but by no means the only one. Additional factors as node load, energy level, and data availability should be considered.

References

1. Jim Gray et all: Data Cube:A Relational Aggregation Operator Generalizing Group-By, Cross-Tab, and Sub-Totals. Data Mining and Data Discovery 1, Kluwer Academic Publishers 29–53
2. Gyssens, M., Lakshamanan: Multidimensional Data Model and Query Language for Infometrics. In the proccedings of the 23rd. VLDB Conference, Athens. (1997) 106–115
3. Lenz, H.J., Shoshani, A.: Summarizability in OLAP and statistical databases. In SSDBM IX, Washington. (1997)
4. Lenz, H.J., Thalheim, B.: OLAP Databases and Aggregation Functions. In the Procceedings of the 13th. International Conference on Scientific and Statistical Database Management, Virginia USA,IEEE Computer Society. (2001) 91–100.
5. Franklin, M., Zdonik, S.:A framework for scalable dissemination based systems. In the Procceedings of ACM OOPSLA Conf. (1997)94–105.
6. Cuzzocrea, A., Furfaro, F., Saccam, D.:Hand-OLAP: a System for Delivering OLAP Services on Handheld Devices. ISADS 2003,Pisa, Italy. (2003) 213–224
7. Maniatis, A., Vassiliadis, P., Skiadopoulos, S., Vassiliou, Y., Mavrogonatos, G., Michalarias, I.: A Presentation Model and Non- Traditional Visualization for OLAP. International Journal of Data Warehousing & Mining (2005) 1–36
8. Dykeman, H.D., Ammar, M., Wong, J.W.: Scheduling algorithms for videotex systems under broadcast delivery. In the Procceedings of the IEEE Int. Conf. Commun., Toronto, Canada. (1986) 1847–1851
9. Wong, J.W.: Broadcast delivery. In the Procceedings of the IEEE, vol. 76. (1988) 1566–1577
10. Aksoy D., Franklin, M.: RxW: A scheduling approach for largescale on-demand data broadcast. IEEE/ACMTransactions on Networking 7. (1999) 846–860
11. Sharaf, M., Chrysanthis, P.: On-Demand Data Broadcasting for Mobile Decision Making. Mobile Networks and Applications 9,Kluwer Academic Publishers. (2004) 703–714
12. Kalnis, P., Mamoulis, N., Papadias, D.: View selection using randomized search. Data & Knowledge Engineering 42(1). (2002) 89–111.
13. www.socket.com

Multidimensional Frequent Pattern Mining Using Association Rule Based Constraints

S. Vijayalakshmi[1] and S. Suresh Raja[2]

[1] Lecturer, Department of Computer Science & Engineering,
Thiagarajar College of Engineering, Madurai-625015
sv_la@yahoo.com
[2] Lecturer, Department of Computer Applications,
K.L.N.College of Engineering, Madurai-625020
csrsuresh07@yahoo.co.in

Abstract. Knowledge about multi-dimensional frequent patterns is interesting and useful. The classic frequent pattern mining algorithms based on a uniform minimum support, such as Apriori and FP-growth, either miss interesting patterns of low support or suffer from the bottleneck of itemset generation. Other frequent pattern mining algorithms, such as Adaptive Apriori, though taking various supports, focus mining at a single abstraction level. Furthermore, as an Apriori-based algorithm, the efficiency of Adaptive Apriori suffers from the multiple database scans. In this paper, we extend FP-growth to attack the problem of multidimensional frequent pattern mining. The algorithm Ada-FP, which stands for Adaptive FP-growth. The efficiency of the Ada-FP is guaranteed by the high scalability of FP-growth. To increase the effectiveness, the Ada-FP pushes various support constraints into the mining process. We show that the Ada-FP is more flexible at capturing desired knowledge than previous Algorithm.

1 Introduction

The explosive growth of many business, government and scientific databases has far outpaced our ability to interpret and digest this data. We are drowning in information yet starving for knowledge. Data mining therefore appears as a useful tool to address the need for sifting useful information such as hidden patterns from databases. Frequent pattern mining is one of the active research themes in data mining. In this paper, we expand the horizon of frequent pattern mining by analyzing an efficient algorithm for mining multidimensional frequent patterns with flexible support constrains.

1.1 Problem Definition

Multidimensional frequent pattern mining is a very promising research topic and plays an invaluable role in real life applications. In this section, we review related concepts and give the definition of multi-dimensional frequent pattern mining.

1.2 Data Mining

Briefly stated, data mining refers to extracting or ``mining" knowledge from large amounts of data. Data mining can be performed on a variety of data stores, including relational databases, transactional databases and data warehouses. A comprehensive data mining system usually provides multiple mining functions. Association is one of the key features that can be found in such systems.

1.3 Association Mining

Association mining searches for interesting relationship among items in a given database and displays it in a rule form, i.e. A $\Rightarrow$ B. With the massive amounts of data continuously being collected and stored in databases, many industries are becoming interested in mining associations among data. Market basket analysis is a typical example among the various applications of association mining.

Example 1.3.1

Suppose, as a manager of an AllElectronics branch, you would like to learn more about the buying habits of your customers. Specifically, you may wonder ``Which groups or sets of items are customers likely to purchase on a given trip to the store?". To answer your question, association mining can be performed on the retail data of customer transactions at your store. The knowledge that customers who purchase IBM Laptop also tend to buy HP Epson Color Printer at the same time is represented in the association rule below.

IBM Laptop $\Rightarrow$ HP Epson Color Printer
[support = 2%, confidence = 60%]

Support and confidence are two measures of rule interestingness. In the above association rule, the support of 2% means that 2% of all the transactions under analysis show that IBM Laptop and HP Epson Color Printer are purchased together. The confidence of 60% means that 60% of the customers who purchase IBM Laptop also buy HP Epson Color Printer. In a nutshell, support represents the percentage of data samples that the given rule satisfies and confidence assesses the degree of certainty of the detected association. Support and confidence are usually set by users or domain experts.

1.4 Multi-dimensional Frequent Pattern Mining

Real transaction databases usually contain both item information and dimension information. Moreover, taxonomies about items likely exist. In this paper, we explore the problem of multi-dimensional frequent pattern mining. We give the Example of multi- dimensional frequent pattern mining as below.

Table 1.4.1. About an AllElectronics database illustration our points

Store Location	Trans- ID	List of Item Ids
BC	001	(TV,Color TV,Sony Color TV); (Computer,Laptop,IBM Laptop); (Printer,Color Printer,HP Epson Color Printer)
ON	001	(Printer, Color Printer, HP Epson Color Printer)
BC	002	(TV,Color TV,Sony Color TV); (Computer, Laptop, IBM Laptop)
ON	002	(Computer,Laptop,IBM Laptop)
BC	003	(TV, Color TV, Sony Color TV); (Computer, Laptop,IBM Laptop)

1.5 Motivation

In this paper multi-dimensional frequent pattern mining, is motivated by the four limitations of existing algorithms.

First, the classic frequent pattern mining algorithms (i.e. Apriori, FP- growth) have been focusing on mining knowledge at single concept levels, i.e., either primitive or rather high concept level. However, it is often desirable to discover knowledge at multiple concept levels. Second, in real life applications, multiple dimensions, such as store locations, may be associated with transactions. Incorporating dimension information into the mining process can produce patterns with more detailed knowledge. Third, to our knowledge, previous proposed algorithms for multi-level frequent pattern mining all adopt an Apriori-like method. It is well known that the Apriori method relies on iterative pattern generation and multiple database scans. Hence the efficiency of the Apriori method might suffer in situations of generating long patterns. Recently, a novel algorithm, FP-growth, is proposed to mine frequent patterns. FP-growth is proved to achieve a better system performance than traditional frequent pattern mining algorithms.

2 Frequent Pattern Mining

The process of discovering the complete set of frequent patterns is also called frequent pattern mining" for short. We give its definition as below.

Definition (frequent pattern mining)
Let $t = \{i_1, i_2, \ldots i_m\}$ be a set of items. Let D be a set of transactions, where each transaction T is a set of items such that $t \Rightarrow T$. Patterns are essentially a set of items and are also referred to as itemsets. In our later discussion, we may use the two terms – "itemsets" and "patterns" alternatively. An itemset that contains k items is a k-itemset. The occurrence of an itemset is the number of transactions that contain the itemset. This is also known as the frequency or support count of the itemset. The task of frequent pattern mining is to generate all patterns (or itemsets) whose occurrences (or support) are greater than or equal to the user-specified minimum support. Researchers have been seeking for efficient solutions to the problem of frequent pattern mining since 1993.

3 Algorithm

This paper Discuss an efficient and effective algorithm for multidimensional frequent pattern mining. In this section, we present the algorithm – **Ada-FP** step by step. We illustrate **Ada-FP** algorithm using an example. There are three critical challenges in designing an efficient multi-dimensional frequent pattern mining algorithm. We list them as below. Our solutions are given as well. **Ada-FP** algorithm is an extension of the FP-growth algorithm. The nitty-gritty features of the FP-growth algorithm, i.e. FP-tree, FP-tree-based pattern fragment, partition-based divide and conquer method, are well preserved. when dimension information are need to be taken into account, there rises the problem of how to amend the existing frequent pattern mining algorithms (FP-growth) to tackle the dimension information. In our Latest **Ada-FP** algorithm, we treat dimension information the same as item information. When reading the transaction database, the dimension is counted as well. A dimension (or dimension-set) is regarded as frequent if its occurrence satisfies the specified threshold. the idea of flexible support constraint. To avoid the problem caused by uniform support threshold, we introduce the concept of mining with various support constraints.

Step 1. Find frequent 1-items and frequent 1-dimensions

In this step, we scan the transaction database D once. During this database scan, we collect the count for each dimension and item. In the meanwhile, we compare their counts with the corresponding two types of thresholds – passage threshold and printing thresholds. For each individual dimension, we compare its count with the dimension passage threshold and the dimension printing threshold. Eliminate dimensions whose support do not even pass the corresponding support threshold. For each individual item, we first detect the abstraction level the item resides in; we then check whether it is a normal item or an exceptional item. If it is an normal item, we compare the item support with the corresponding passage threshold and printing threshold; otherwise, we shall narrow the possibility further and label this item as either a very common one or a very rare one, we then compare the item support with the corresponding passage support and printing support. Under all circumstances, the item will not be printed as a frequent 1- item unless its support passes the corresponding item printing threshold. Also be aware that all items whose support pass the corresponding item passage threshold are possible to appear in the frequent 2 or even longer patterns. The items whose support do not pass the corresponding passage threshold die in the comparison.

Step 2. Construct an FP-tree for the given transaction database

The **Ada-FP** adopts the same prefix-tree structure as the one taken by FP-growth. The structure of FP-tree is defined below. It consists of one **root** labeled as " *null*" , a set of **item prefix subtrees** as the children of the root, and a **frequent item header table**.

- Each node in the item prefix subtree consists of three fields: name, count, and node-link. Name registers which item (or dimension) this node represents. Count registers the number of transactions represented by the portion of the path reaching this node. Node-link links to the next node in the FP-tree carrying the same item-name (or dimension-name). Node-link is *null* if there is none.
- Each entry in the frequent item header table consists of two fields, (1) name and (2) head of node link. Name represents the item name or the dimension name. Head of node link points to the first node in the FP-tree carrying the item-name (or dimension name). The procedure of constructing an FP-tree is described as below. It is a two-step process.
- Create the root of an FP-tree, T, and label it as " null" . For each transaction *Trans* in DB do the following.

Multidimensional Frequent Pattern Mining Using Association Rule Based Constraints 589

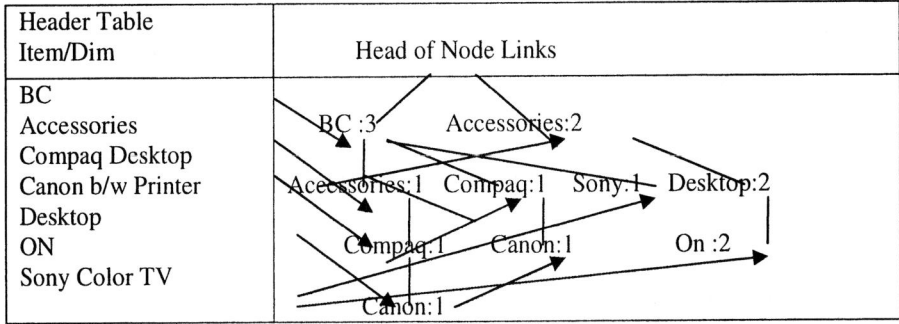

Step 3. Recursively mine FP-tree to generate multi-dimensional frequent patterns
In step 1 and step 2, we gather the counts for each individual item and dimension; we compress the complete information about the transaction database in the FP-tree. They are realized at the cost of two database scans. From now on, we start the pattern generation process by recursively visiting the FP-tree. Note no more costly database operations will be involved.

The essential of the **Ada-FP** is the FP-growth operation. The critical parts are the pushing of various support constraints. We describe the Latest Ada-FP algorithm for pattern generation as below.

The input are: (1) the FP-tree that we construct in step 2, (2) length k-level passage thresholds (k $\geq$2), (3) length k-level printing thresholds (k $\geq$2), (4) item passage thresold for special items, (5) item printing thresold for special items.
Call Ada-FP-growth(FP-tree,null)
Procedure Ada-FP-growth(Tree,α)
{
  if(Tree contains a single path P)then{
   for(each combination-denoted as β of the nodes in the path P) do{
generate pattern $\beta \cup$ α with support-minimum support of nodes in β :
if (pattern $\beta \cup \alpha$ contains special items) then{
  if (pattern $\beta \cup \alpha$'s support is larger than or equal to special item's passage threshold) then {
  if(pattern $\beta \cup \alpha$'s support is larger than or equal to special item's printing threshold) then{
add $\beta \cup \alpha$ to L:
add $\beta \cup \alpha$ to C:
}
}
else{
len=the length of pattern $\beta \cup \alpha$:
if(pattern $\beta \cup \alpha$'s support is larger than or equal to length-len passage threshold) then {
  if(pattern $\beta \cup \alpha$'s support is larger than or equal to length-len printing threshold)then

```
        add β∪α to L;
        add β∪α to C;
    }  }
  }
}
else for (each $a_i$ in the header of Tree)do{
    generate pattern β =$a_i$ ∪α with support = $a_i$ support;
    construct β's conditional pattern base and then β's conditional FP-tree $Tree_p$:
    }
    if($Tree_p \neq \phi$ )then
    call Ada-FP-growth($Tree_p$,β)
        }
```

In the above, we give the pseudo-code of the **Ada-FP-growth**. Starting from the least frequent item/dimension, we generate conditional pattern base and accordingly construct conditional FP-tree for each member of the header table. Conditional pattern base for an item i (or a dimension d) consists of the items/dimensions that co-occur with the item I (or a dimension d). In the same manner, we explore the conditional FP-tree using Ada- FP-growth.

4 Discussion

Briefly speaking, the **Ada-FP** algorithm is a three-step process. In the first step, we scans database once to get the count of every single item and every single dimension. The frequent 1-items or frequent 1-dimensions are those whose counts pass their corresponding printing threshold. In the second step, we scan database again to construct an FP-tree. Notice items or dimensions can appear in the FP-tree as long as their counts pass their corresponding passage threshold. Thus a frequent pattern which includes the whole taxonomy information about an item is also interesting to the user. Finally, we recursively mine the FP-tree (and conditional FP-tree) to generate all frequent patterns. Frequent patterns can appear in one of the three forms: items in the frequent patterns span the entire concept hierarchy.

5 Conclusions

The goal of this paper is to propose an efficient and effective way for Multidimensional frequent pattern mining. Constraint based multidimensional frequent pattern mining is a very interesting and useful tool. It can be used to facilitate decision making and boost business sales. The Difficulties to attack this problem originate from two aspects. On one hand, in real life transaction database, items as well as dimensions may exist at the same time. Moreover, items are likely to appear with hierarchical information encoded. General frequent pattern mining algorithms focus on mining at single level. Besides, only strong associations between items will be discovered.

References

1) R. Agarwal, C. Aggarwal, and V. V. V. Prasad. A tree projection algorithm for generation of frequent itemsets. In Journal of Parallel and Distributed Computing (Special Issue on High Performance Data Mining), (to appear), 2000.
2) R. Agrawal and R. Srikant. Fast algorithms for mining association rules. Proc. 1994 Int. Conf. Very Large Data Bases (VLDB'94), pages 487-499, Santiago, Chile, September 1994.
3) R. J. Bayardo, R. Agrawal, and D.Gunopulos. Constraint-based rule mining on large, dense data sets. Proc. 1999 Int. Conf. Data Engineering (ICDE'99), Sydney, Australia, April 1999.
4) S. Brin, R. Motwani, and C. Silverstein. Beyond market basket:Generalizing association rules to correlations. Proc. 1997 ACM-SIGMOD Int. Conf. on Management of Data (SIGMOD'97), pages 265-276, Tucson, AZ, May 1997.
5) J. Han and Y. Fu. Discovery of multiple-level association rules from large databases. Proc. 1995 Int. Conf. Very Large Datab Bases (VLDB'95)
6) J. Han and M. Kamber. Data Mining: Concepts and Techniques. Morgan Kaufmann Publishers, August 2000.
7) M. Kamber, J. Han and J. Y. Chiang. Metarule-guided mining of multi- dimensional association rules using data cubes. Proc. 3 rd Int. Conf. Knowledge Discovery and Data Mining (KDD'97),
8) W. Lee, S. J. Stolfo, K. W. Mok. Mining audit data to build intrusion detection models. Proc. 1998 Int. Conf. Knowledge Discovery and Data Mining (KDD'98),
9) M. Klemettinen, H. Mannila, P. Ronkainen, H. Toivonen, and A. I. Verkamo. Finding interesting rules from large sets of discovered association rules. Proc. 3 rd Int. Conf. Information and Knowledge Management (CIKM'94), pages 401-408, Gaithersburg, MD, November 1994.
10) R. Ng, L. V. S. Lakshmanan, J. Han and A. Pang. Exploratory mining and pruning optimizations of constrained association rules. Proc. 1998 ACM-SIGMOD Int. Conf. on Management of Data (SIGMOD'98), pages 13-24, Seattle, WA, June 1998. J. Han and M. Kamber. Data Mining: Concepts and Techniques. Morgan Kaufmann Publishers, August 2000.

A Classification Based Approach for Root Unknown Phylogenetic Networks Under Constrained Recombination

M.A.H. Zahid, Ankush Mittal, and R.C. Joshi

Department of Electronics and Computer Engineering,
Indian Institute of Technology Roorkee, Uttaranchal, India 247667
{zaheddec, ankumfec, joshfec}@iitr.ernet.in

Abstract. Phylogenetic networks are the generalization of the tree models used to represent evolutionary relationship between the species. Tree models of evolutionary process are not adequate to represent the evolutionary events such as, hybridization, lateral/ horizontal gene transfer and genetic recombination. A well-formulated problem in phylogenetic networks, due to recombination, is to derive a set of input sequences on a network with minimum number of recombinations. No efficient algorithm exists for this problem as it is known to be NP-hard. Efficient solutions exist for the constrained recombination networks, where the nodes on each recombination cycles are disjoint. These solutions are based on the assumption that the ancestral sequence is known in advance. On the other hand, the more biologically realistic case is that where the ancestor sequence is not known in advance. In this paper we propose an efficient classification based method for deriving a phylogenetic network under constrained recombination without knowing the ancestral sequence.

1 Introduction

The phylogenetic tree construction methods fail to find true relationship between the species, because of the evolutionary events such as, horizontal gene transfer, hybridization, homoplasy and genetic recombination. The network representation of the evolutionary relationship provides a better understanding of the evolutionary process and the non-tree like events [1, 2]. Detection of recombination plays an important role in locating the origin of the gene influencing the genetic disease. A case study on HIV, carried at the center for computational and experimental genomics, Department of Biological Sciences, University of Southern California has shown that the most frequent recombination event make it difficult to design a drug for HIV. Recombination in HIV is recognized as an important mechanism by which the viruses escape the attack against the drug [3].

Since long time, the consequences of the recombination are ignored, and phylogenies were constructed by neglecting the recombination events. Schierup and Hein in [2, 6] and Posada [7] have shown the effect of neglecting the recombination while constructing the phylogeny. When recombination occurs, different parts of the genetic sequence represent different histories violating the conventional assumption of a sequence representing single underlying history. Despite this fact, there is significant lacuna of the methods robust for recombination. A good amount of work has been done for non tree like evolutionary events other than recombination; for an exhaustive survey refer [8, 9].

Wang et al. [4] has shown the problem of finding a perfect phylogenetic network, network with minimum number of recombination nodes, is NP-hard and has given an algorithm for a restricted problem, called node disjoint network, with $O(n^4)$ computing time. The restriction is that in a merge path of a recombination node, there is no node that is in the merged path of a different recombination node. In other words, no node is shared by two or more recombination cycles, also called as "gall". The phylogenetic network, in which every recombination cycle is a gall, is also called a "gall tree". The network construction methods in [4, 5] construct the phylogenetic network with the assumption that the ancestral sequence is known in advance. On the other hand, biologically more realistic case is one in which the ancestral sequence is not known in advance. Gusfield [12] proposed an algorithm similar to [5, 11] for unknown root and used the concepts of split graphs and conflict graphs to construct the phylogenetic network. The algorithm given in [12] computes the root unknown gall tree in $O(nm + n^3)$ time, where n is number of nodes and m is number of sites on each nodes. In this paper we proposed a classification technique, based on biological constraints, for the classification of the nodes in the network. Theses classified nodes are used to construct the phylogenetic network for unknown ancestor sequence. The nodes are classified into mutation, recombination and null classes. The proposed method takes $O(n \log n + mn^2)$ computing time for classifying all the nodes.

The paper is organized as follows. Section 2 deals with the formal definitions and assumptions related to phylogenetic networks. Section 3 deals with the combinatorial background and conditions for the detection of the recombination. The algorithm for classifying the nodes with an example is given in section 4.

2 Preliminaries

This section deals with the basic terminology and assumptions made for the development of algorithm. We follow the terminology from [5] and [11].

Formally, a phylogenetic network is a directed acyclic graph, but underlying undirected graph can have cycles. Each node in the phylogenetic network N has indegree 0, 1 or 2. The nodes with indegree 0 are called independent node as the ancestor to these nodes is unknown, the nodes with indegree 1 are called tree nodes and the nodes with indegree 2 are called recombination nodes. A tree node is the result of mutation and the recombination node is the due the recombination of genetic material of two parent species of the node. Each node in the network N is assigned a binary sequence of length m. The tree or mutation nodes have a single site or character change from 0 to 1, when compared with the parent nodes. The sequence of recombination node is the parts of its two ancestor's sequences.

If a node u is reachable from a node v via a directed path, then v is an ancestor of u, and u is the descendent of the node v. Each node in the phylogenetic network is represented with a binary number of some specified length m. In the perfect phylogeny the transformation of states from 0 to 1, occurs at most ones for each site or the column in the binary sequence. The nodes on perfect phylogenetic networks are organized in such a way that there is unique node having state 1 in site $i, i \in m$, every other node having 1 at site i is the descendents of this unique node. The transformation from 0 to 1 is possible in case of recombination, where the crossovers can change the state from 0 to 1. A phylogenetic network with recombination is said to be perfect if it has minimum number of recombination nodes and follows all the restrictions mentioned above.

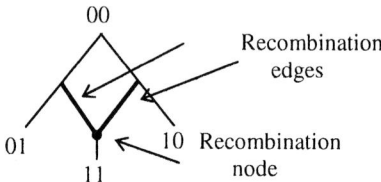

Fig. 1. Phylogenetic network for binary sequences

A set of binary sequences represents a phylogenetic network N, if and only if each sequence labels exactly one leaf of the network N. A phylogenetic network on a set of three binary sequences is shown in Fig. 1. The biological interpretation of a phylogenetic network N, for M binary sequences is that the network represents the possible history of the M sequences under the following assumptions. (1) The change in one site, from 0 to 1, is permitted only once (called mutation). (2) Two sequences are permitted to recombine as a result of recombination event. (3) Each site in the sequence represents a SNP (single nucleotide polymorphism), a site where two of the four possible nucleotides appear in the population with the frequency above some threshold [10].

Given a set of species n species with binary sequences of length m, a phylogenetic network with $O(nm)$ recombination nodes exist. Recombination is a rare event in the evolutionary process. Therefore a phylogenetic network with minimum number of recombination nodes is informative.

3 Conditions for the Classification of Nodes

In this section we formulate the necessary and sufficient condition for the classification of nodes, which has biological significance. We use the similarity and dissimilarly between the sequences as the major tool for the classification of the nodes into mutation, recombination and null classes.

Lemma 1 is crucial for the detection of the recombination cycles in the given binary sequences. It states that the similarity and dissimilarity between the sequences, which shares a common parent, should be computed after the removing the parent's characteristics are removed from each of the child, to avoid the misleading similarity between the species.

Lemma 1. *Let S and S' be the sequences of the children of node v. if S' is not the result of the mutation or recombination in S then the similarity between S and S' is due to common ancestry.*

Proof. Let S' is not a child of the S, then S' is not reachable from S, therefore all the sites or character of S' are different from the characters of the node S or vise versa. Let S and S' are children of node v, then according to the assumption made in section 2 both S and S' are reachable from node v, and show the similarity by at least one character (of site) with the parent node v. Both the nodes S and S' show the similarity with their parent node by at least one character not with each other. Hence this proves that the distinct nodes will show similarity due to common ancestry. □

Lemma 2 gives a method of finding child node and parent node when the compared nodes show some similarity.

Lemma 2. If a node v' is the result of mutation from its parent v then $v < v'$, when the sequences are considered as the binary numbers.

Proof. We prove this by mathematical induction on the length m of the binary sequences. In the first step consider a parent v, with sequence S, contains all 0's in its sequence. According to the definition of the mutation only one site can change the state from 0 to 1 and rest of the sequence remains same. If a mutation occurs at site i of v leading to at least on of the sites of the sequence, S', of the node v' is set to 1 and the rest of the sequence will remain same as the parent sequence. Thus making S less than S', $S<S'$. Now consider the case where the node v has $m-2$ number of 1s in sequence S. A mutation leads to $m-1$ number of ones in S' making $S<S'$. Now we prove it for a generalized case of $m-1$ number of 1s. If a node v, with sequence S having $m-1$ number of 1s mutates to result in new child node v' with sequence S' having m number of ones, which is the highest value binary number for a given length m. therefore $v < v'$ when mutation is reason for speciation. □

Lemma 3 plays an important role in the detection of the recombination nodes. It proves that if a node is the result of recombination then it should be greater than at least one of the parents.

Lemma 3. Let v be a recombination node with sequence S. if P' and P'' are two parent nodes of v, with sequences S' and S'' respectively, then any of the following should hold.
 (a) $S'>S$ and $S''>S$
 (b) $S'>S$ and $S''<S$
 (c) $S'<S$ and $S''>S$

Proof. To prove this it is enough to prove it for the binary sequences of length 2. Let three binary sequences, which give a recombination node v are 00, 01, 10, 11. These sequences can be placed in only three different ways to represent the recombination as shown in Fig.2. The other possibilities are ruled out due to the assumption that back mutation is not permitted.

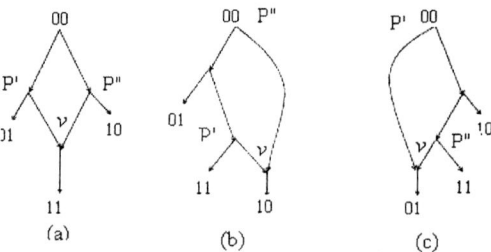

Fig. 2. Three cases for lemma 3

Case (a): Here the two mutations from root node lead to the species 01 and 10. The node v with sequence 11 is the result of recombination of 01 and 10. Clear v is greater than its two parents.

Case (b): In this case the sequence 01 muted from root and the sequence 11 is mutated from 01. The recombination node v is the result of recombination between root and P'. It satisfies the case (b) stating, $S'>S$ and $S''<S$.

Case (C): In this case the sequence 10 muted from root and the sequence 11 is mutated from 10. The recombination node v is the result of recombination between root and P''. It satisfies the case (c) stating, $S'<S$ and $S''>S$. □

Theorem 4 uses the lemma 2 and 3 for the detection of the recombination nodes. It helps in finding the parents of the recombination nodes when any one of the parent is greater than the child.

Theorem 4. Let M be the given sequence matrix representing the node disjoint network. A species or sequence is said to the result of recombination if it holds any of the following conditions.

(a) If two species have, $0<similarity<=100\%$ and $dissimilarity > (100/m) \%$, where m is the length of the sequence, one sequence represent parent and another sequence represent the child, which is the result of recombination.
(b) The similarity between the two parent of a recombination node is always 0.

Proof. Case (a): Suppose that at some node x, mutation occurred at site i, representing the change at site i from 0 to 1 and rest of the sequence remain same. If we calculate its similarity and dissimilarity corresponding to the value 1 at each site, the similarity will be 100% and dissimilarity will be $100/m \%$ exactly. This indicates that only one site has modified its value from 0 to 1. By the assumptions we made for phylogenetic network, there is no provision for back mutation, that is transformation from 1 to 0 or mutation of more than one site at the same instance of time is also ruled out. This restricts the dissimilarity to be exactly $100/m \%$ for mutation. But in case of recombination the restrictions of the mutation are ruled out due to the fact that the resulting sequence may carry a part of the sequence from one parent and rest will be imitated from the other parent (in single crossover). This fact indicates that the similarity can be $0<similarity<=100\%$ and $dissimilarity > (100/m) \%$. Hence the condition (a) is proved.

Case (b): We prove this by contradiction. Suppose the recombination node v has two parents with the sequences S' and S'', show some similarity with each other. From the assumptions made in section 2 and lemma 1, the similarity between the species is due to two reasons (1) common parent, (2) child parent relationship with a single mutation and (3) due to recombination. If S' and S'' shows some similarity then any of the above relation holds. The relation 1 is avoided by removing the parent characteristics while computing the similarity between the children. We are focusing on a constrained recombination problem, where two recombination nodes are disjoint, avoid the relation 3. If S' and S'' shares child parent relationship with mutation then the result of recombination will be a sequence N, similar to child or parent instead of the new sequence, $N \in (S', S'')$. Hence it's proved that the parents of the recombination node are dissimilar to each other. □

Theorem 5 gives a strong basis for the detecting the node disjoint network in the given input data. Any data satisfying the conditions given in theorem 5 will have a gall tree. Otherwise, the data does not represent the gall tree structure.

Theorem 5. If C, C', and C" are child list of sequences S, S', and S" then the following conditions should hold for the gall trees.
  (a) If $C \cap C' \neq \phi$ and $|C \cap C'| = 1$.
  (b) If the number of recombinations node in any of the parents is greater than 1, and $C \cap C' \neq \phi$ then $C \cap C'' = \phi$ or $S'' \cup C'' \subseteq C$ and $C' \cap C'' = \phi$ or $S'' \cup C'' \subseteq C'$.

Proof. Case (a): This is proved by contradiction. Let $|C \cap C'| > 1$, represents that the node S and S' are involved in more than one recombination with each other. The path from root node to the recombination node always has two alternatives, each from one of its parents. If there are more than two recombination nodes for the single pair of parents S and S', then there are two paths for each recombination nodes which involves the same set of parents S and S'. In other words the parent nodes are shared by two recombination cycles. But according to the definition of node disjoint network, the nodes on the path to one recombination node should not be shared with other recombination node path Hence this rejects our hypothesis and proves the condition.

Case (b): The proof is similar as in case (a). Let $C \cap C' \neq \phi$ and the number of recombination nodes in C are two. If $C \cap C' = x$ and $C \cap C'' = y$, then there exist a path from root node to the recombination cycle of node x and node y, which passes through the node C. This violates the node disjoint rule of phylogenetic networks. Let child list C'' and the node S'' itself is a subset of the child list of node S. If the similarity and dissimilarity between the children of S is computed after removing the S's characteristics from each node then the recombination node will not show S in its parent list, according to lemma 1. This parent relationship with the recombination node is due to the common ancestor of all the nodes in the recombination cycle. So when there is common ancestor for the parents of a recombination node then the parent of all the nodes in that cycle is also added as the parent to the recombination node. □

4 Phylogenetic Network Reconstruction Algorithm

In this section we develop a formal algorithm for the phylogenetic network reconstruction with constrained recombination and prove that this algorithm results in minimum number of recombinations in the resulting network. We conclude the section with an example for the algorithm.

4.1 The *Node_Class* Algorithm

The algorithm *Node_Class* classifies the nodes and make the child and parent list of each node given in the data matrix based on similarity and dissimilarity. We assume that all the sequences represent a unique leaf node in the network, and back mutation is not permitted.

The algorithm accepts a $n \times m$ binary matrix as input, where each row represents a node in the phylogenetic network. A similarity and dissimilarity matrix is generated based on the input matrix and is computed corresponding to the value 1 at the sites. The distance (similarity and dissimilarity) between the siblings is measured after removing the parent's characteristics from the children. The parent node is considered as the root to all the nodes in the child list and the parent list represents the parent nodes of the current node. If data does not represent node disjoint network the algorithm terminates by reporting an error message. The algorithm is as follows.

Data structures:
$d \leftarrow$ *is an input matrix of size $n \times m$, where n is number of species and m is length of sequences.*
$sim\_dis_{ij} \leftarrow$ *is the similarity and dissimilarity matrix corresponding to 1's in the sequences.*
Node is a record with three variables: Label, Count (number of parents), and Type(class).
$Child_i \leftarrow$ *An array of child nodes labels for each node.*
$Parent_i \leftarrow$ *An array of parent nodes labels for each node.*
INPUT: - *binary matrix of $n \times m$ size.*
OUTPUT: - *child list for each node.*

ALGORITHM: *Node_Class (d)*
   Sort the matrix by considering each row as binary number.
   for each row in the input binary matrix **do**
      Label $\leftarrow$ *row_value*;
      Count $\leftarrow 0$;
      Type $\leftarrow$ *Null*;
   for each sorted node $1 \le i \le n$ **do**
      $Child_i \leftarrow Null$;
      $Parent_i \leftarrow Null$;
   for each node $1 \le j \le n$ **do**
      if $sim\_dis_{ij} \leftarrow Null$ **then**
         Compute *Similarity* and *dissimilarity* between *i* and *j*;
         Modify sim_dis matrix;
     endif;

if $Node_i.Type = Null\,/\,mutation$ **then**
   if $Similarity = 100\%$ and $Dissimilarity = 100/m\,\%$ **then**
     $Node_j.Count \leftarrow Node_j.Count + 1;$
    $Parent_j \leftarrow Parent_j \cup Node_i;$
   else if $Node_j.Count \leq 2$ **then**
     $Noide_j.Type = recombination;$
     $Child_i \leftarrow Child_i \cup Node_j;$
  endif;
  else
     $Noide_j.Type = mutation;$
     $Child_i \leftarrow Child_i \cup Node_j;$
  endif;
  if $Similarity < 100\%$ and $Dissimilarity \geq 100/n\,\%$ **then**
     $Node_j.Count \leftarrow Node_j.Count + 1;$
    $Parent_j \leftarrow Parent_j \cup Node_i;$
    $Noide_j.Type = recombination;$
    $Child_i \leftarrow Child_i \cup Node_j;$
 endfor;
 for each $x, 1 \leq x \leq |Child_i|$, and $Node_x \in Child_i$ **do**
  Compare $Node_i$ with other element of $Child_i$ after removing parents characteristics;
    Modify sim_dis matrix;
  endfor;
endfor;
Test_Nodedis (*child, Node*)
return;
endAlgorithm;

The function *Test_Nodedis*, takes Child and Node record list as input and based on theorem 5 verifies whether node disjoint network exist in the given data or not. The function is as follows.

Function: *Test_Nodedis* (*Child, Node*)
for each node $1 \leq i \leq n$ **do**
 if number of recombination nodes > 1 or $Node_i.Count > 2$ **then**
   for each node $1 \leq j \leq n$, where $j \neq i$ **do**
    if $|Child_i \cap Child_j| > 1$ **then**

```
        exit "node disjoint recombination cycle does not exist";
      else
        for each node $1 \leq k \leq n$, where $k \neq i, j$ do
          test ← $Node_k \cup Child_k$;
          if $Child_i \cap Child_k \neq \phi$ or $Test \not\subset Child_i$ and
             $Child_j \cap Child_k \neq \phi$ or $Test \not\subset Child_j$ then
            exit "node disjoint recombination cycle does not exist";
          else
            Compute the similarity and dissimilarity matrix, d, after removing the
            parent's characteristics from each child;
            Node_Class( d )
        endif;
      endfor;
    endif;
  endfor;
  return "node disjoint recombination cycle exist";
endFunction;
```

4.2 An Example

The input matrix for the algorithm is shown in Fig. 3(a), which consists of seven leaf nodes with their binary sequences. As the first step in the algorithm we sort the nodes considering each row represents a node and is a binary number. The sorted matrix is shown in Fig. 3(b).

```
A 0 0 0 1 0         A 0 0 0 1 0
B 1 0 0 1 0         C 0 0 1 0 0
C 0 0 1 0 0         G 0 0 1 0 1
D 1 0 1 0 0         E 0 1 1 0 0
E 0 1 1 0 0         F 0 1 1 0 1
F 0 1 1 0 1         B 1 0 0 1 0
G 0 0 1 0 1         D 1 0 1 0 0
      (a)                 (b)
```

Fig. 3. (a) Input binary matrix with labels. (b) Sorted input binary matrix on rows.

After processing each node the values assigned to each variable or properties of the node records is shown in Table 1. The Type values for nodes A and C are 'Null' because they are mutated from the root node, not from any given nodes. The nodes D and F are the result of the recombination and have two parents. All the other nodes are the result of mutation from their respective parents.

The similarly-dissimilarity matrix computed during the detection of the recombination nodes is shown in Fig. 4.

Table 2 shows the child list of each node. The nodes D and F don't have any child so their list carries *Null* entry. On the other hand the nodes D and F are in the child list

A Classification Based Approach for Root Unknown Phylogenetic Networks 601

Table 1. Values of each property of node record after the processing input matrix shown in Fig. 3(a)

Node Label	Type	Count
A	Null	0
B	Mutation	1
C	Null	0
D	Recombination	2
E	Mutation	1
F	Recombination	3
G	Mutation	1

	A	B	C	D	E	F	G
A	1.0	1.1	0.2	0.3	0.3	0.4	0.3
B	1.1	2.0	0.3	1.2	0.4	0.5	0.4
C	0.2	0.3	1.0	1.1	1.1	1.2	1.1
D	0.3	1.2	1.1	2.0	0.2	0.3	0.2
E	0.3	0.4	1.1	0.2	2.0	1.1	0.2
F	0.4	0.5	1.2	0.3	1.1	3.0	1.1
G	0.3	0.4	1.1	0.2	0.2	1.1	2.0

Fig. 4. Similarity and dissimilarity matrix for the input data shown in Fig. 3 (a)

of (B, C) and (E, G) nodes respectively, making D and F, recombination nodes. Table 3 gives the list of parent nodes for each node. This list is computed based on the node disjoint conditions proved in theorem 5. The child list for the node C have two recombination nodes, D and F, and the child F has count value 3 indicating three parents. But it satisfies second condition in theorem 5, therefore the count is reduced by 1 and its super ancestor is removed from its parent list.

Table 2. Child list for the input matrix shown in Fig. 3(a)

Node Label	Child List
A	B
B	D
C	D,E,F,G
D	Null
E	F
F	Null
G	F

Table 3. Parent list for the input matrix shown in Fig. 3(a)

Node Label	Child List
A	Null
B	A
C	Null
D	B,C
E	C
F	E,G
G	C

Given the child and parent list for each of the node in the input data, it is easy to construct the phylogenetic network for it. The procedure starts with scanning the child list table. For each node in the child list a cross verification is performed with the parent list. If both validate each other, then nodes are added and connected accordingly in the child parent relationship. Otherwise, an additional node is created which has the same sequence as conflicting node, called the coalescent node, and child and parent tables are modified. Each internal node is attached with a new node representing the leaf node in the node disjoint network, except the coalescent nodes. The sequence for the new node is same as its parent. The final network for the input data given in Fig. 3(a) is shown in Fig. 5.

Now we prove that the algorithm results in a node disjoint network, if one exists, with the minimum number of node disjoint recombination cycles in it.

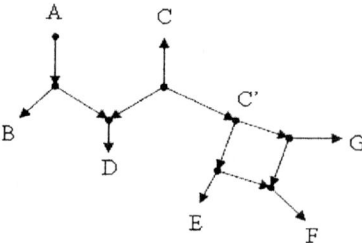

Fig. 5. Node disjoint network for the input shown in Fig. 3(a)

Theorem 6. *If the for the input matrix M there are k recombination nodes then any node disjoint network that minimizes the recombination will have exactly k recombinations.*

Proof. Let T be a node disjoint network for the input binary matrix M. If there is a node disjoint cycle Q in T that contains only the mutation nodes, then the sequence labeling of the nodes on Q can be derived from the perfect phylogeny. The root of the node disjoint cycle Q is the sequence labeling the coalescent node of Q. Replacing Q with perfect phylogeny will result in a node disjoint network with one recombination less than the network T. Hence in any node disjoint network using the minimum number of recombinations must have exactly one recombination node for each node disjoint cycle. Therefore the minimum number of node disjoint cycles in a node disjoint network is exactly the number of nodes with recombination type or class. □

4.3 Correctness and Time Complexity

The results in section 3 and 4 give the proof of correctness of the classification method. When the input data does not display a node disjoint network structure, the algorithm reports an error message and terminates. The phylogenetic network computed by the algorithm will have minimum number of recombinations.

The algorithm computes a node disjoint network, if one exists, in $O(n\log n + n^2 m)$ time, where n is number of nodes, and m is the length of the each binary number. The algorithm sorts the n rows, considering each row as a binary number, using quick sort, which takes $O(n\log n)$ time. In the next step the algorithm computes the similarity and dissimilarity between each of the node with respect to the sites with the value 1. The second step takes $O(n^2 m)$ time. On the basis of the similarity and dissimilarity measure the type of each node is decided and the child list is modified. This child list can be further used to construct the node disjoint network.

5 Conclusions

In this paper we proposed a classification based approach for the construction of phylogenetic network with constrained recombination for unknown root or ancestor. The construction of perfect phylogenetic network is proved to be NP-hard by Wang et al. [4]. Wang et al. [4] gave a polynomial time algorithm for a restricted problem called node disjoint network with known root, in which a node cannot be a part of two recombination paths in the network. It has both algorithmic and biological significance. The method in [4] computes the gall tree or node disjoint network in $O(n^4)$ time. Guesfield et al. [5, 11] proved that the [4] does not give the necessary and sufficient conditions for the gall tree construction and gave a sufficient combinatorial basis for network construction with known root. A similar method as [5, 11] is given by Guesfield et al. [12] for the construction of the node disjoint network for unknown root. The method [12] takes $O(nm + n^3)$ time for constructing a network for unknown root.

The proposed algorithm computes the root unknown network in $O(n \log n + n^2 m)$ time and established the necessary and sufficient condition for the root unknown networks. Unlike the other algorithms, we followed a row-based search to detect the recombination nodes. Other algorithms search the columns for the detection of recombination. The number of columns in a sequence may be far greater than the rows, which increases the complexity of the previous algorithms.

References

1. Posada, D., Crandall, K.: Intraspecific gene genealogies: trees grafting into networks, Trends in Ecology and Evolution. 16 (2001) 37–45.
2. Schierup, M. H., Hein, J.: Consequences of recombination on traditional phylogenetic analysis. Genetics. 156(2000) 879-891.
3. Savai, P., Abulleef, H., Chun, L. L., Skvortsov, D.: Phylogenetic analysis, MS. Project, University of southern California, 2002.
4. Wang, L., Zhang, K., Zhang, L.: Perfect phylogenetic networks with recombination. Journal of Computational Biology. 8 (2001) 69-78.
5. Guesfield, D., Satish, E., Langley, C.: Optimal efficient reconstruction of phylogenetic network with constrained recombination. Journal of Computer and System science. 70 (2005) 381-398.
6. Schierup, M. H., Hein, J.: Recombination and the molecular clock. Mol. Biol. Evol. 17(2000) 1578–1579.
7. Posada, D., Crandall, K.: The effect of recombination on the accuracy of phylogeny estimation. Journal of Molecular Evolution. 54(2002) 396-402.
8. Linder C.R., Moret, B.M.E. L. Nakhleh, and T. warnow, Reconstructing networks part II: computational aspects. A tutorial presented at the ninth pacific symposium on Biocomputing (PSB), 2004.
9. Zahid, M. A. H., Mittal, A., Joshi, R. C.: Use of phylogenetic networks and its reconstruction algorithms. Journal of Bioinformatics India, ISSN 0972-7655. 4(2004) 47-58.
10. Chakravarthi, A., It's raining SNP's hallelujah? Nature Genetics. 19 (1998) 216-866.
11. Guesfield, D., Satish, E., Langley, C.: The fine structure of galls in phylogenetic networks. INFORMS J. on computing, special issue on Computational Biology. 16(2004) 459-469.
12. Gusfield, D.: Optimal, Efficient Reconstruction of Root-Unknown Phylogenetic Networks with Constrained and Structured Recombination, J. Computer and Systems Sciences, Special issue on Computational Biology, 70 (2005) p. 381-398.

Author Index

Agarwal, Rahul   172
Ahmad, Amir   561
Ahn, JinHo   166
Apte, Varsha   154
Arumugam, Mahesh   69

Bandopadhyay, Tapati   553
Bapi, Raju S.   536
Bardhan, Debabrata   105
Barman, Siddharth   117
Bhargava, Anjali   314
Bhargava, Bharat   314
Bhattacharjee, A.K.   508
Bhattacharjee, Subhasis   93
Bhattacharyya, D.K.   523
Bisht, Mahender   172
Biswas, Pradipta   308
Bruhadeshwar, Bezawada   377

Cao, Yukun   278
Chandra, Punit   203
Chandrapal, Paritosh   192
Chen, Huajun   243
Chung, Yon Dohn   143
Cleaveland, Rance   482
Cokuslu, Deniz   56

Dagdeviren, Orhan   56
Dai, Xiaoling   297
Das, Nabanita   93
Das, Sandip   105
Dey, Lipika   561
Dong, Zhijiang   446

Erciyes, Kayhan   56

Flocchini, Paola   132
Fu, Yue   446
Fu, Yujian   446

Gorantla, M.C.   357
Goswami, Diganta   27
Grundy, John   297
Gupta, Gopal   433

Han, Dongsoo   217
Han, Kyeong-Eun   21
He, Xudong   446
Hong, Manpyo   348
Hou, Jia   15
Hwang, Chong-Sun   3

Inoue, Michihiro   82
Iyengar, S.S.   1

Jaghoori, M.M.   494
Janakiram, D.   235
Jiang, Tao   348
Jifeng, He   432
Joo, Kil Hong   255, 321
Joshi, R.C.   592

Kim, Seong-Whan   404, 410
Kim, SungSuk   3
Kim, Young-Chon   21
Kim, Young-Chul   21
Kim, Wonil   348
Kshemkalyani, Ajay D.   203
Kulkarni, Sandeep S.   69, 377
Kumar, Atul   314
Kumar, N. Pradeep   290, 536, 553
Kumar, Padam   192

Lee, Jaeho   255
Lee, Ji Yeon   143
Lee, Junghee   217
Lee, Moon Ho   15
Lee, SooJung   321
Lenz, Hans-J.   573
Lhee, Kyungsuk   348
Li, Yunfeng   278
Liao, Xiaofeng   278
Lobiyal, D.K.   39

Madria, Sanjay K.   242, 314
Maheshwari, S.N.   172
Mall, Rajib   470
Maluk Mohamed, M.A.   235
Michalarias, Ilias   573
Mitra, Tulika   458

Mittal, Ankush 592
Mohania, Mukesh 522
Mousavi, M.R. 494
Movaghar, A. 494
Mukherjee, Nandini 229
Mukhopadhyay, Debajyoti 308
Mukhopadhyay, Debapriyay 334
Murugan, K. 62

Nagaprabhanjan, B. 154
Nandi, Sukumar 397
Nayak, Amiya 132
Negi, Atul 389
Negi, Hemendra Singh 458

Onozato, Yoshikuni 82

Padhy, Smruti 27
Palshikar, Girish Keshav 547
Patro, Ranjeet Kumar 184
Paul, B. 50
Peng, Li-Mei 21
Prasad, Sanjiva 172
Prasanna, S. 364

Radha, V. 290
Radha, Krishna P. 536
Rahman, M.S. 267
Ramakrishna, S. 290
Raman, C.V. 389
Rao, S.V. 50
Ray, Indrajit 333
Ray, Indrakshi 420
Reddy, Suresh 397
Roy, Rajat Shuvro 267
Roy, S. 523
Roy, Sarbani 229
Roy, Sasanka 105

Roy, Suman 334
Roychoudhury, Abhik 458
Ruhil, Anand Praksh 39

Santosh Kumar, S. 235
Saxena, Ashutosh 357
Schulz, Arno 132
Sen, Arunabha 2
Sen, Jaydip 125
Sengupta, Bikram 482
Sengupta, Indranil 125
Seol, Jae-Min 404
Shanmugavel, S. 62
Shukla, K.K. 117
Shyamasundar, R.K. 508
Singh, Anshuman 117
Sirjani, M. 494
Stojmenovic, Ivan 39
Sung, Hyun-Seong 410
Suresh Raja, S. 585

Thejaswi, Chandrashekhar P.S. 184
Toahchoodee, Manachai 420
Tripathi, Rakesh 470

Venkateswara Rao, M. 536
Venkateswara Reddy, M. 235
Vetriselvi, V. 364
Vijay Srinivas, A. 235
Vijayalakshmi, S. 585

Wang, Qian 434

Yang, Sun Ok 3
Yoo, Kyoung-Min 21
Yoshiura, Noriaki 82

Zahid, M.A.H. 592

Lecture Notes in Computer Science

For information about Vols. 1–3745

please contact your bookseller or Springer

Vol. 3860: D. Pointcheval (Ed.), Topics in Cryptology – CT-RSA 2006. XI, 365 pages. 2006.

Vol. 3850: R. Freund, G. Păun, G. Rozenberg, A. Salomaa (Eds.), Membrane Computing. IX, 371 pages. 2006.

Vol. 3838: A. Middeldorp, V. van Oostrom, F. van Raamsdonk, R. de Vrijer (Eds.), Processes, Terms and Cycles: Steps on the Road to Infinity. XVIII, 639 pages. 2005.

Vol. 3837: K. Cho, P. Jacquet (Eds.), Technologies for Advanced Heterogeneous Networks. IX, 307 pages. 2005.

Vol. 3835: G. Sutcliffe, A. Voronkov (Eds.), Logic for Programming, Artificial Intelligence, and Reasoning. XIV, 744 pages. 2005. (Sublibrary LNAI).

Vol. 3833: K.-J. Li, C. Vangenot (Eds.), Web and Wireless Geographical Information Systems. XI, 309 pages. 2005.

Vol. 3829: P. Pettersson, W. Yi (Eds.), Formal Modeling and Analysis of Timed Systems. IX, 305 pages. 2005.

Vol. 3828: X. Deng, Y. Ye (Eds.), Internet and Network Economics. XVII, 1106 pages. 2005.

Vol. 3827: X. Deng, D. Du (Eds.), Algorithms and Computation. XX, 1190 pages. 2005.

Vol. 3826: B. Benatallah, F. Casati, P. Traverso (Eds.), Service-Oriented Computing - ICSOC 2005. XVIII, 597 pages. 2005.

Vol. 3824: L.T. Yang, M. Amamiya, Z. Liu, M. Guo, F.J. Rammig (Eds.), Embedded and Ubiquitous Computing – EUC 2005. XXIII, 1204 pages. 2005.

Vol. 3823: T. Enokido, L. Yan, B. Xiao, D. Kim, Y. Dai, L.T. Yang (Eds.), Embedded and Ubiquitous Computing – EUC 2005 Workshops. XXXII, 1317 pages. 2005.

Vol. 3822: D. Feng, D. Lin, M. Yung (Eds.), Information Security and Cryptology. XII, 420 pages. 2005.

Vol. 3821: R. Ramanujam, S. Sen (Eds.), FSTTCS 2005: Foundations of Software Technology and Theoretical Computer Science. XIV, 566 pages. 2005.

Vol. 3820: L.T. Yang, X. Zhou, W. Zhao, Z. Wu, Y. Zhu, M. Lin (Eds.), Embedded Software and Systems. XXVIII, 779 pages. 2005.

Vol. 3819: P. Van Hentenryck (Ed.), Practical Aspects of Declarative Languages. X, 231 pages. 2006.

Vol. 3818: S. Grumbach, L. Sui, V. Vianu (Eds.), Advances in Computer Science – ASIAN 2005. XIII, 294 pages. 2005.

Vol. 3816: G. Chakraborty (Ed.), Distributed Computing and Internet Technology. XXI, 606 pages. 2005.

Vol. 3815: E.A. Fox, E.J. Neuhold, P. Premsmit, V. Wuwongse (Eds.), Digital Libraries: Implementing Strategies and Sharing Experiences. XVII, 529 pages. 2005.

Vol. 3814: M. Maybury, O. Stock, W. Wahlster (Eds.), Intelligent Technologies for Interactive Entertainment. XV, 342 pages. 2005. (Sublibrary LNAI).

Vol. 3813: R. Molva, G. Tsudik, D. Westhoff (Eds.), Security and Privacy in Ad-hoc and Sensor Networks. VIII, 219 pages. 2005.

Vol. 3810: Y.G. Desmedt, H. Wang, Y. Mu, Y. Li (Eds.), Cryptology and Network Security. XI, 349 pages. 2005.

Vol. 3809: S. Zhang, R. Jarvis (Eds.), AI 2005: Advances in Artificial Intelligence. XXVII, 1344 pages. 2005. (Sublibrary LNAI).

Vol. 3808: C. Bento, A. Cardoso, G. Dias (Eds.), Progress in Artificial Intelligence. XVIII, 704 pages. 2005. (Sublibrary LNAI).

Vol. 3807: M. Dean, Y. Guo, W. Jun, R. Kaschek, S. Krishnaswamy, Z. Pan, Q.Z. Sheng (Eds.), Web Information Systems Engineering – WISE 2005 Workshops. XV, 275 pages. 2005.

Vol. 3806: A.H. H. Ngu, M. Kitsuregawa, E.J. Neuhold, J.-Y. Chung, Q.Z. Sheng (Eds.), Web Information Systems Engineering – WISE 2005. XXI, 771 pages. 2005.

Vol. 3805: G. Subsol (Ed.), Virtual Storytelling. XII, 289 pages. 2005.

Vol. 3804: G. Bebis, R. Boyle, D. Koracin, B. Parvin (Eds.), Advances in Visual Computing. XX, 755 pages. 2005.

Vol. 3803: S. Jajodia, C. Mazumdar (Eds.), Information Systems Security. XI, 342 pages. 2005.

Vol. 3802: Y. Hao, J. Liu, Y.-P. Wang, Y.-m. Cheung, H. Yin, L. Jiao, J. Ma, Y.-C. Jiao (Eds.), Computational Intelligence and Security, Part II. XLII, 1166 pages. 2005. (Sublibrary LNAI).

Vol. 3801: Y. Hao, J. Liu, Y.-P. Wang, Y.-m. Cheung, H. Yin, L. Jiao, J. Ma, Y.-C. Jiao (Eds.), Computational Intelligence and Security, Part I. XLI, 1122 pages. 2005. (Sublibrary LNAI).

Vol. 3799: M. A. Rodríguez, I.F. Cruz, S. Levashkin, M.J. Egenhofer (Eds.), GeoSpatial Semantics. X, 259 pages. 2005.

Vol. 3798: A. Dearle, S. Eisenbach (Eds.), Component Deployment. X, 197 pages. 2005.

Vol. 3797: S. Maitra, C. E. V. Madhavan, R. Venkatesan (Eds.), Progress in Cryptology - INDOCRYPT 2005. XIV, 417 pages. 2005.

Vol. 3796: N.P. Smart (Ed.), Cryptography and Coding. XI, 461 pages. 2005.

Vol. 3795: H. Zhuge, G.C. Fox (Eds.), Grid and Cooperative Computing - GCC 2005. XXI, 1203 pages. 2005.

Vol. 3794: X. Jia, J. Wu, Y. He (Eds.), Mobile Ad-hoc and Sensor Networks. XX, 1136 pages. 2005.

Vol. 3793: T. Conte, N. Navarro, W.-m.W. Hwu, M. Valero, T. Ungerer (Eds.), High Performance Embedded Architectures and Compilers. XIII, 317 pages. 2005.

Vol. 3792: I. Richardson, P. Abrahamsson, R. Messnarz (Eds.), Software Process Improvement. VIII, 215 pages. 2005.

Vol. 3791: A. Adi, S. Stoutenburg, S. Tabet (Eds.), Rules and Rule Markup Languages for the Semantic Web. X, 225 pages. 2005.

Vol. 3790: G. Alonso (Ed.), Middleware 2005. XIII, 443 pages. 2005.

Vol. 3789: A. Gelbukh, Á. de Albornoz, H. Terashima-Marín (Eds.), MICAI 2005: Advances in Artificial Intelligence. XXVI, 1198 pages. 2005. (Sublibrary LNAI).

Vol. 3788: B. Roy (Ed.), Advances in Cryptology - ASIACRYPT 2005. XIV, 703 pages. 2005.

Vol. 3785: K.-K. Lau, R. Banach (Eds.), Formal Methods and Software Engineering. XIV, 496 pages. 2005.

Vol. 3784: J. Tao, T. Tan, R.W. Picard (Eds.), Affective Computing and Intelligent Interaction. XIX, 1008 pages. 2005.

Vol. 3783: S. Qing, W. Mao, J. Lopez, G. Wang (Eds.), Information and Communications Security. XIV, 492 pages. 2005.

Vol. 3781: S.Z. Li, Z. Sun, T. Tan, S. Pankanti, G. Chollet, D. Zhang (Eds.), Advances in Biometric Person Authentication. XI, 250 pages. 2005.

Vol. 3780: K. Yi (Ed.), Programming Languages and Systems. XI, 435 pages. 2005.

Vol. 3779: H. Jin, D. Reed, W. Jiang (Eds.), Network and Parallel Computing. XV, 513 pages. 2005.

Vol. 3778: C. Atkinson, C. Bunse, H.-G. Gross, C. Peper (Eds.), Component-Based Software Development for Embedded Systems. VIII, 345 pages. 2005.

Vol. 3777: O.B. Lupanov, O.M. Kasim-Zade, A.V. Chaskin, K. Steinhöfel (Eds.), Stochastic Algorithms: Foundations and Applications. VIII, 239 pages. 2005.

Vol. 3776: S.K. Pal, S. Bandyopadhyay, S. Biswas (Eds.), Pattern Recognition and Machine Intelligence. XXIV, 808 pages. 2005.

Vol. 3775: J. Schönwälder, J. Serrat (Eds.), Ambient Networks. XIII, 281 pages. 2005.

Vol. 3774: G. Bierman, C. Koch (Eds.), Database Programming Languages. X, 295 pages. 2005.

Vol. 3773: A. Sanfeliu, M.L. Cortés (Eds.), Progress in Pattern Recognition, Image Analysis and Applications. XX, 1094 pages. 2005.

Vol. 3772: M. Consens, G. Navarro (Eds.), String Processing and Information Retrieval. XIV, 406 pages. 2005.

Vol. 3771: J.M.T. Romijn, G.P. Smith, J. van de Pol (Eds.), Integrated Formal Methods. XI, 407 pages. 2005.

Vol. 3770: J. Akoka, S.W. Liddle, I.-Y. Song, M. Bertolotto, I. Comyn-Wattiau, W.-J. van den Heuvel, M. Kolp, J. Trujillo, C. Kop, H.C. Mayr (Eds.), Perspectives in Conceptual Modeling. XXII, 476 pages. 2005.

Vol. 3769: D.A. Bader, M. Parashar, V. Sridhar, V.K. Prasanna (Eds.), High Performance Computing – HiPC 2005. XXVIII, 550 pages. 2005.

Vol. 3768: Y.-S. Ho, H.J. Kim (Eds.), Advances in Multimedia Information Processing - PCM 2005, Part II. XXVIII, 1088 pages. 2005.

Vol. 3767: Y.-S. Ho, H.J. Kim (Eds.), Advances in Multimedia Information Processing - PCM 2005, Part I. XXVIII, 1022 pages. 2005.

Vol. 3766: N. Sebe, M.S. Lew, T.S. Huang (Eds.), Computer Vision in Human-Computer Interaction. X, 231 pages. 2005.

Vol. 3765: Y. Liu, T. Jiang, C. Zhang (Eds.), Computer Vision for Biomedical Image Applications. X, 563 pages. 2005.

Vol. 3764: S. Tixeuil, T. Herman (Eds.), Self-Stabilizing Systems. VIII, 229 pages. 2005.

Vol. 3762: R. Meersman, Z. Tari, P. Herrero (Eds.), On the Move to Meaningful Internet Systems 2005: OTM 2005 Workshops. XXXI, 1228 pages. 2005.

Vol. 3761: R. Meersman, Z. Tari (Eds.), On the Move to Meaningful Internet Systems 2005: CoopIS, DOA, and ODBASE, Part II. XXVII, 653 pages. 2005.

Vol. 3760: R. Meersman, Z. Tari (Eds.), On the Move to Meaningful Internet Systems 2005: CoopIS, DOA, and ODBASE, Part I. XXVII, 921 pages. 2005.

Vol. 3759: G. Chen, Y. Pan, M. Guo, J. Lu (Eds.), Parallel and Distributed Processing and Applications - ISPA 2005 Workshops. XIII, 669 pages. 2005.

Vol. 3758: Y. Pan, D.-x. Chen, M. Guo, J. Cao, J.J. Dongarra (Eds.), Parallel and Distributed Processing and Applications. XXIII, 1162 pages. 2005.

Vol. 3757: A. Rangarajan, B. Vemuri, A.L. Yuille (Eds.), Energy Minimization Methods in Computer Vision and Pattern Recognition. XII, 666 pages. 2005.

Vol. 3756: J. Cao, W. Nejdl, M. Xu (Eds.), Advanced Parallel Processing Technologies. XIV, 526 pages. 2005.

Vol. 3754: J. Dalmau Royo, G. Hasegawa (Eds.), Management of Multimedia Networks and Services. XII, 384 pages. 2005.

Vol. 3753: O.F. Olsen, L.M.J. Florack, A. Kuijper (Eds.), Deep Structure, Singularities, and Computer Vision. X, 259 pages. 2005.

Vol. 3752: N. Paragios, O. Faugeras, T. Chan, C. Schnörr (Eds.), Variational, Geometric, and Level Set Methods in Computer Vision. XI, 369 pages. 2005.

Vol. 3751: T. Magedanz, E.R.M. Madeira, P. Dini (Eds.), Operations and Management in IP-Based Networks. X, 213 pages. 2005.

Vol. 3750: J.S. Duncan, G. Gerig (Eds.), Medical Image Computing and Computer-Assisted Intervention – MICCAI 2005, Part II. XL, 1018 pages. 2005.

Vol. 3749: J.S. Duncan, G. Gerig (Eds.), Medical Image Computing and Computer-Assisted Intervention – MICCAI 2005, Part I. XXXIX, 942 pages. 2005.

Vol. 3748: A. Hartman, D. Kreische (Eds.), Model Driven Architecture – Foundations and Applications. IX, 349 pages. 2005.

Vol. 3747: C.A. Maziero, J.G. Silva, A.M.S. Andrade, F.M.d. Assis Silva (Eds.), Dependable Computing. XV, 267 pages. 2005.

Vol. 3746: P. Bozanis, E.N. Houstis (Eds.), Advances in Informatics. XIX, 879 pages. 2005.